McGRAW-HILL SERIES IN EDUCATION

HAROLD BENJAMIN, *Consulting Editor*

INTRODUCTION TO
AMERICAN PUBLIC EDUCATION

McGraw-Hill Series in Education

HAROLD BENJAMIN, *Consulting Editor*

The Stars and Stripes forever! American public education forever! (*Courtesy of Public Schools, Bakersfield, Calif.*)

INTRODUCTION TO
American Public Education

CHRIS A. De YOUNG

Head, Department of Education and Psychology
Professor of Education and Former Dean of the University
Illinois State Normal University, Normal, Illinois

THIRD EDITION

McGRAW-HILL BOOK COMPANY, INC.

New York   Toronto   London

1955

II

To My Wife

MARION EDNA DE YOUNG

PREFACE

This book is designed as an introduction to American public education, which is interpreted to include schools, colleges, universities, and all other forms of education conducted for the public and supported in whole or in part by the public. For example, the educational program for the veterans of wars is not open to all youth, yet it is one form of publicly financed education. This volume provides an overview of all education in which the American public invests its time or money or both. Private and parochial schools and colleges, also called "independent institutions," constitute an indispensable part of the American educational system. Naturally the public schools, which are for all the children of all the people and which are supported by public funds, constitute the backbone of American public education. Education, however, is broader than mere schooling. Because of the wide reach of American public education, the volume presents basic features rather than minute details. It aims at orienting the prospective teacher or the layman without confusing him with a bewildering mass of minutiae.

This book, which may serve as a handy reference for teachers, principals, supervisors, superintendents, and laymen, is intended primarily for education courses for prospective teachers. It is organized on the basis of teaching-learning units which are components of five major aspects of American public education:

1. Organization and administration of public education
2. Areas of public education
3. Personnel in public education
4. Provisions for educational materials and environment
5. Interpretation of education

1. The organization of the book is flexible, permitting a variety of approaches. The student may start with the broad overview of American public education, provided through Unit I, National Program of Education. Or he may begin with his recent experience in a local school system and then progress outward to the larger areas: the township, county, state, and nation. In that case Unit IV, Local School Districts, is used for the initial approach.

2. The prospective teacher may then study the internal structure and program of American public education on all levels, despite the fact that he may teach in a specific area, such as the secondary school. Lifelong learning starts with birth, advances through the pre-elementary stages of the nursery school and kindergarten, and continues through elementary,

secondary, and higher education. It includes also education for out-of-school youth. The capstone of adult education makes real the cherished goal of continuous learning for modern Americans.

3. The next group of units deals with the personnel involved in American public education. The reader adds to his growing knowledge of the pupils. He analyzes some problems of the classroom teacher and learns of the challenge of the teaching profession. He discovers the diversity of educational work as he studies school personnel other than classroom teachers, such as deans, visiting nurses, attendance officers, county and state school officials, business managers, clerks, and principals.

4. The personnel cannot function effectively without materials and equipment with which to work; hence the next section is devoted to provisions for educational materials and environment. The curriculum today, as broad as life itself, is reinforced by cocurricular activities. The success of curricular and cocurricular activities is conditioned by educational supplies and equipment and by other aspects of the educational environment, such as school sites and buildings. These facilities are made available through educational leadership and financial support.

5. The concluding section, which also may be used as an initial problem approach or collaterally with each unit, deals with an interpretation of education. Here the student is given the opportunity to analyze many of the educational issues, to evaluate the trends, and to synthesize his information and thinking into clearer concepts of the functions of American public education.

CHRIS A. DE YOUNG

SUGGESTIONS FOR USING THIS BOOK

The author makes the following suggestions for the use of this material, which has been subjected to experimental tryouts in typical college classes:

1. This volume may serve as the basal textbook but not as the only source of information. The best way to orient students in education is to expose them to extensive reading of many references and to significant experiences with a wide variety of materials. To this end, each unit contains a descriptive bibliography and aids, with specific chapter or page references to books, and a list of current pertinent periodicals and publications, which may be consulted for up-to-date material. The *Annals, Education Digest, History of Education Journal, Education News, Educator's Dispatch, Teacher's Letter, Educational Summary, Encyclopedia of Educational Research, Dictionary of Education, Dictionary of Psychology, Educational Index,* and *Readers' Guide to Periodical Literature* contain leads to valuable source materials for each unit. Helpful biographical information on American educators is found in such references as *Who's Who in American Education* and *Leaders in Education.* Listings of numerous schools and colleges are available in such works as *American Educational Directory, Educational Directory, American Junior Colleges, American Universities and Colleges, A Handbook of Private Schools,* etc. Students and teachers should be encouraged to survey the ideas and contributions of many authors. *Time, Newsweek, Reader's Digest* and other lay magazines, as well as daily newspapers, contain many current data and ideas on education.

2. The descriptive bibliography and aids also include audio-visual aids. Most of the places where these multisensory aids can be purchased or rented are indicated. Two text-films and filmstrips, *Design of American Education* and *School and Community,* have been prepared by McGraw-Hill Book Company, Inc., specifically for this textbook. Many illustrations and diagrams in the book help students to visualize the contents. Educational programs on radio and television can also be helpful.

3. American public education is not mere formal instruction; hence its study should not be a static recitation procedure or a rehash of factual matter. Modern curriculum guides list suggested activities as well as subject matter. These activities help to ensure learning since they encourage the reader to study pupils, schools, and the community as well as books. Therefore, each unit contains suggested activities in order that the course may function in the lives of the prospective teachers now and later. Individual differences among students may be met by their selecting from

these suggested activities individual or committee projects. Each prospective teacher need not perform all these activities, nor should all students necessarily do the same ones. For instance, it may prove difficult for an entire class to visit a nursery school. A representative or committee from the class may make the actual observations and report to the group.

4. The previews constitute a tool for correlating and organizing the materials in this volume. The preview for each of the five major groups of units is a factor that binds together the various related parts. Thus the Preview for Organization and Administration of Public Education relates the four components—national, state, county, and local systems. Furthermore, the preview facing the first page of each of the 17 units is an organic part of the presentation. The running description of the content that is to follow and the organized outline give the student and the teacher a general frame for the picture of the unit. The instructor may find it helpful to place on the blackboard the points in the skeletal outline, or a modification thereof, as pegs on which to hang the crucial ideas of the unit.

5. Several of the units contain handy historical calendars which present in chronological order some of the notable educational events, paralleled with outstanding high lights in the political, social, and economic world. The calendars are not designed as memorizer exercises, although some dates are well worth remembering. Rather, the calendars serve as a handy chart or time line of the evolution and development of specific areas in American public education.

6. Because of the wide variation in educational practice between and within states, the content of each unit is general, although it is frequently punctuated with specific illustrations. The state in which the text is used has its own educational background and peculiarities. Therefore, the instructor may wish to supplement this volume with concrete data and specific problems for a particular state.

The alert teacher, with the cooperation of the students, will discover many additional ways in which this book can orient students in education and develop a critical understanding of the teaching profession.

CHRIS A. DE YOUNG

CONTENTS

EDITOR'S INTRODUCTION

Primitive man probably first measured the length of his journeys by grunts of weariness and described the size of his fish by exclamations of pride and wonder. Later, his desire for greater precision drove him to further gestures of comparison. He swung an arm from east to west until he had counted off the number of elapsed suns in a journey. He showed the bigness of the fish he had caught by distance between outstretched hands or better yet by head and tail notches on his fishing pole. Thus he came at length to refer many matters of distance and weight to generally agreed-upon, relatively unchanging units like millimeters and light-years, grams and tons.

National programs of education are still commonly measured by the grunt system. They are so big in scope and so small in detail, so simple in purpose and so complex in procedure, so far from a single observer and so close to all observers that they are hard to evaluate by more precise methods. Perhaps the conscious and systematic changing of a people's ways is a process so fraught with possibilities of tragic consequence that men shrink from the task of judging its worth. Certainly students of comparative education have not yet adopted a workable system of appraising culture changes in simple terms of the new needs, wants, problems, and goals which have produced these changes.

Because of a tendency in the United States to confuse the terms "national" and "federal," it should be emphasized that all the educational agencies of this country—federal, state, and local; public and private; school and nonschool—constitute the national system of education. The fact that even educators sometimes think of a national system of education in the United States as meaning a federal system indicates how hard it is to see the country's total pattern of education.

The educators are often more naïve than the laymen in this regard. Professional as well as national pride holds them on the grunt level of evaluation. They exclaim over the details of their professional machinery and then go on turning its cranks and greasing its cogwheels with unquestioning fidelity.

It is therefore particularly important that a broad view of the country's total system of education should be achieved by those whose daily work is with the details of the system. Prospective teachers need to acquire this over-all view early in their professional preparation. This is a technical necessity. A young teacher may enter the profession without knowing whether the additive method of subtraction is superior to the take-away method and still be able promptly to reach a high level of technical skill, but one who begins teaching with no adequate means of looking critically at all the methods, materials, personnel, and agencies of education can only imitate technical skills. The greatest technical fault in any profession is to use a method or device without knowing why it is used. It is an especially grievous and dangerous fault in that profession which calls for all the studied craft and inspired artistry, all the precise knowledge and controlled action, all the shrewd planning and glowing faith which a nation can devote to an activity that holds and foreshadows all its future.

The prospective teacher needs early to acquire this broad view; the experienced teacher must cultivate it both early and late. The present book is designed for both these teachers. In its first and second editions it has demonstrated the soundness of its arrangement and approach. Its wide acceptance by the profession indicates its effectiveness in helping teachers and students of education to appraise their country's educational efforts on a level higher than that of prideful grunt or dramatic swing of the arms.

This book was first published at the beginning of a new era in world education. It was an era in which the prestige and influence of the American school system were to be rapidly and colorfully extended.

In its earlier editions, this book played an important role in that extension of knowledge concerning American education. It was used from 1942 onward in universities and colleges to help prepare a new generation of American schoolteachers, young men and women whose destiny it was to live in a world very different in educational challenges and problems from the world of 1932, 1922, or 1912. It was employed on a large scale by the armed forces. It has served its country in occupied areas overseas. It has traveled as ambassador of American education to many lands.

Few authors of educational works have been so precisely and preeminently qualified for their tasks as has Dean De Young for the original writing and successive revisions of this book. He began the preparation of the volume with wide experience in and comprehensive knowledge of schools and teaching in the United States. He has used this experience and scholarship for many years in the education of American teachers. He has had a most distinguished record as consultant to national systems of education in Europe and Asia. His background fits him uniquely for presenting the total picture of American education both to Americans and to that growing number of persons in other countries who want to know about American education.

HAROLD BENJAMIN

Seoul, Korea
January, 1955

Part I

ORGANIZATION AND ADMINISTRATION
OF PUBLIC EDUCATION

Preview of Part I

ORGANIZATION AND ADMINISTRATION
OF PUBLIC EDUCATION

American public education is presented in five main sections, the first of which is Organization and Administration. The first and highest unit in the hierarchy of organizations is the national, which is vitally related to the state, county, and local educational systems (see Fig. 1–1).

Although the Constitution does not mention education or schools, the federal government has a direct and indirect interest in public education. The chief educational agency of the United States is the Office of Education, with its Commissioner of Education, in the Department of Health, Education, and Welfare, a Cabinet post created in 1953. The United States Office of Education has expanded its staff greatly to meet new needs and demands. Many national activities are connected with those of other countries, especially in UNESCO (Unit I).

The adoption of the Tenth Amendment to the Constitution of the United States made education primarily a state function. Although the state may delegate some of its authority to the local or intermediate districts, the state commissioner of education serves as the chief centralizing agent for public education within the state (Unit II).

The postwar period has witnessed a marked trend toward larger school units. Some school units are as large as a township or county. These may be intermediate units between the state and local districts (Unit III).

American public education has its local application in the public-school district, which is usually administered by an elected board of education and an appointed superintendent of schools. The local school district is a striking example of grass-roots democracy. School administration in a dynamic democracy calls for a high order of educational statesmanship. Organization and administration should be the servants and not the masters of education (Unit IV).

Part I

ORGANIZATION AND ADMINISTRATION
OF PUBLIC EDUCATION

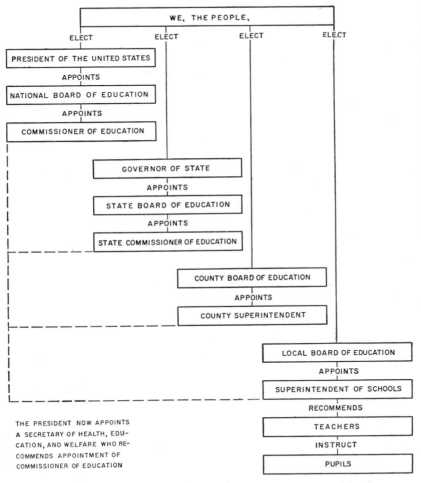

FIG. 1-1. Proposed organization—national, state, county, and local.

NATIONAL PROGRAM OF EDUCATION

The Constitution of the United States does not contain the word "schools" or the word "education." Despite this omission, the federal government, starting with the Northwest Ordinance in 1787, has evinced directly and indirectly its interest in a national program for improving education.

The centralizing agency is the United States Office of Education in the Department of Health, Education, and Welfare. Its main function is to promote education. The Office is headed by the Commissioner of Education.

Federal education is conducted in special jurisdictions, such as the District of Columbia, and many dependencies. Other national efforts in education include schools for special groups, such as the American Indians, and cooperation with federal departments and national organizations. International activities in education are increasing.

A national system of education is slowly evolving. Many proposals have been advanced for its improvement.

OUTLINE OF CONTENTS

Introduction
  Education and American democracy
  Need for federal participation in education
  Federal control undesirable and unnecessary
Development of Federal Activities in Education
  Historical calendar
  Basic federal legislation
  Education for national defense
  Federal grants—nonvocational
  Grants for vocational education
  Other federal provisions for education
United States Office of Education
  Evolution of Office
  Appropriations for federal Office
  Activities of Office of Education
  Organization of federal Office
United States Commissioner of Education
  History of commissionership
  Duties of commissioner
Other Federal Activities in Education
  Education in special federal jurisdictions
  Education of special groups
  Departmental programs of education
  Role of United States in international education
An Evolving National System of Education
  Principles and proposals for improvement of national system
  Conclusion.

NATIONAL PROGRAM OF EDUCATION

James Truslow Adams in describing the growth of America wrote:

But there has been also the American dream, that dream of a land in which life should be better and richer and fuller for every man, with opportunity for each according to his ability or achievement. . . . If we are to make the dream come true we must all work together, no longer to build bigger, but to build better. There is a time for quantity and a time for quality. There is a time when quantity may become a menace and the law of diminishing returns begins to operate, but not so with quality. By working together . . . I mean a genuine individual search and striving for the abiding values of life.[1]

The abiding values in the American dream can be attained through individual and collective striving for perfection. A potent instrument for improving the quality of personal and group living is American public education, which embraces the national program of education, state organizations, large units within the state, and local districts—all dedicated to the promotion of American democracy. As stated by Samuel Miller Brownell:

I assume the office of Commissioner of Education fully conscious of the fact that education is a *State* responsibility which the States have wisely delegated in large part to the *local* communities. I am also very much aware that there is a *national* concern about this education because the effectiveness of America's greatest national resource—its young people—is dependent upon the amount, the kind, and the quality of education they receive from whatever source.

Education and American Democracy. Education is indispensable to democracy, and democracy is a necessity for education. Both are essential to freedom. President Eisenhower has said:

What value dollars, or acclaim, or position in a world where justice, opportunity, and freedom are lost to us by force, by subversion, or by our own neglect?
A chief bulwark of our heritage against any such decay has been, and is, and will be the American school system—from the one-room red-brick building at a country crossroads to the largest of our universities.

The dynamic relationship between democracy and education is attested to by the National Council of Chief State School Officers and the American Association of School Administrators, respectively:

The American system of free and universal elementary and secondary education is unique in world history and a distinguishing characteristic of our society.

---

[1] James Truslow Adams, *The Epic of America*, pp. 411–412, Little, Brown, 1932.

This system is the greatest safeguard of the freedom of the people. It is one of the best guarantees of their social and economic well-being.[2]

The public school is the most democratic institution in American life. It is our nearest approach to a classless society, for all the children of all the people have as near equality of opportunity as native endowment and home environments allow.[3]

To improve education and democracy is a constant challenge to local, county, state, and national officials.

Need for Federal Participation in Education. Federal participation is necessary in order to implement these basic principles of education, *viz.,* equality of educational opportunity and first-rate free education. Federal attention may well be brought to bear upon many pressing related problems, such as the shortage of teachers and buildings, the Americanization of immigrants, the relatively high percentage of illiteracy compared with some other nations, the coordination of all educational work in the various federal departments, and cooperation with other nations in world-wide educational endeavor.

Cooperation between state school systems under aggressive federal leadership will help solve many problems. Since it has been characteristic of Americans to migrate from the state where they were born and educated, what is done in the field of education by the individual states concerns the nation as a whole. Federal headquarters for education are thus necessary even though the administration of the public schools is a responsibility of the states. National interest in education, however, should not be accompanied by federal control.

Federal Control Undesirable and Unnecessary. Much discussion these days relates to federal control, particularly of education. The experience of other countries emphasizes the desirability of decentralization in education in the United States. The totalitarian and communistic nations have disastrously demonstrated the propulsive power of education in shaping or misshaping the thoughts and deeds of men. A noncentralized administration of the schools will help to safeguard freedom of speech and thought.

Past experience with programs of vocational education supported in whole or part by federal funds has led school administrators to be critical and suspicious of regimentation from Washington, D.C. But local schools and state educational systems, like ships caught in a rising tide and driven by prevailing winds, have drifted farther and farther into the dangerous waters of federal domination.

Legislation positively should forbid and prevent federal control of

2 National Council of Chief State School Officers, *Our System of Education,* p. 5, 1951.

3 American Association of School Administrators, *The American School Superintendency,* p. 13, National Education Association, 1953.

education. Federal control of education is not only undesirable—it is unnecessary, as shown by the fact that during the earlier years of the nation's history grants of money and land were made to the states in support of education without any semblance of regulation on the part of the national government.

DEVELOPMENT OF FEDERAL ACTIVITIES IN EDUCATION

Historical Calendar—Federal Activities in Education and Contemporaneous Events

The following historical calendar contains significant events in the evolution of federal interest in education and also contemporaneous national happenings of political, economic, and social importance. The educational events listed are notable milestones on the highway leading toward a national plan of education; the general contemporaneous history marks other varied lanes of national progress. Although the educational calendar does not chronicle all the significant events, it does designate certain outstanding dates in the development of a national program of public education during more than one hundred and fifty years. Several of these events have implications for state, county, and local administration of public education. Most of the events listed in the right column of the calendar are not related directly to the educational achievements. The former merely link the latter to some significant event that occurred at approximately the same time in American political, economic, or social history.

The events listed in the calendar, and others, are described under (1) basic federal legislation, (2) education for national defense, (3) federal grants—nonvocational, (4) grants for vocational education, (5) other federal provisions for education.

Basic Federal Legislation

Northwest Ordinance and Education. Between the official ending of the Revolutionary War in 1783 and the establishment of the Union in 1789, the Congress of the Confederation was faced with many problems, one of which was the westward movement into the new territory ceded by the states to the central government. Congress adopted in 1785 a system of rectangular surveys for its new territory, by which the land was divided into townships, 6 miles square, to be further subdivided into 36 sections, 1 mile square. This ordinance of 1785, reaffirmed two years later, ended with the significant words: "There shall be reserved the lot number sixteen of every township for the maintenance of public schools within the said township." Thus the foundation was laid for a future land and school policy.

Historical Calendar

FEDERAL ACTIVITIES IN EDUCATION	CONTEMPORANEOUS EVENTS
1787—"Schools and the means of education shall be forever encouraged" (Northwest Ordinance)	1787—Northwest Ordinance adopted by Continental Congress for territory northwest of Ohio
1788—"To promote the general welfare" (United States Constitution)	1788—Ratification of the Constitution of the United States
1791—Education reserved to states (Tenth Amendment)	1791—Bank of United States established
1802—School for army officers established at West Point	1800—District of Columbia established
1802—First saline land grants made	1801—Thomas Jefferson inaugurated President of United States
1803—Section 16 given for education in Ohio	1803—Louisiana purchased from France
1818—Five per cent fund distributed (first money grant to states)	1818—Pensions granted Revolutionary soldiers
1841—Internal improvement grants made by Congress to the states	1841—Brook Farm experiment started by Transcendentalists
1845—School for naval training started at Annapolis	1845—Texas and Florida admitted to Union
1862—First Morrill Act passed (land-grant colleges)	1862—Robert E. Lee made commander of Confederate army
1865—Freedman's Bureau created	1865—President Lincoln assassinated
1867—Department of Education created	1867—Alaska purchased from Russia
1887—Hatch Act passed (agricultural experiment farms)	1887—Interstate Commerce Commission created
1908—Forest Reserve returns started by Congress	1908—Conference of governors called to discuss conservation
1914—Smith-Lever Act passed (agriculture extension)	1914—Federal Reserve Banks established
1917—Smith-Hughes Act passed (vocational education)	1917—War with Germany declared by the United States
1920—Nonmetallic royalties paid to states	1920—Woman suffrage ratified (Amendment XIX)
1931—Report of National Advisory Committee on Education published	1931—White House Conference Report on Child Health and Protection published
1933—Emergency education grants started	1933—"Lame Duck" amendment adopted (Amendment XX)
1936—George-Deen Act passed (vocational education)	1936—Tennessee Valley Administration Act declared constitutional

Historical Calendar—(*Continued*)

FEDERAL ACTIVITIES IN EDUCATION (*Continued*)	CONTEMPORANEOUS EVENTS (*Continued*)
1939—Office of Education transferred from Department of Interior to Federal Security Agency	1939—Ruling by Supreme Court that federal and state governments may tax salaries of each other's employees
1941—Funds appropriated by Congress for schools, recreation centers, sanitary facilities, and hospitals in defense areas	1941—War against Axis powers declared by the United States as it officially enters the Second World War
1944—G.I. bill for veterans education passed by Congress	1944—Task of organizing to preserve peace begun at Dumbarton Oaks
1945—UNESCO organized by 44 nations meeting in London	1945—Membership of United States in United Nations approved
1946—Membership of United States in UNESCO approved by Congress	1946—World disarmament resolution adopted by United Nations
1947—National School Lunch Act passed to provide federal funds on permanent basis	1947—Army, navy, and air forces combined through adoption of National Security Act
1948—Mundt law for permanent global program in education adopted by Congress	1948—Bill adopted by Congress to admit over 200,000 displaced persons in two years
1949—National Citizens Commission for Public Schools created by laymen	1949—Global program of technical assistance for underdeveloped countries approved by United Nations
1950—Midcentury White House Conference on Children and Youth called by President Truman	1950—Seventeenth decennial census recorded for the United States as 150,697,361
1952—Second G.I. bill for veterans' education passed by Congress	1952—Dwight D. Eisenhower elected President of the United States
1953—U.S. Office of Education made part of Department of Health, Education, and Welfare, with Secretary in the President's Cabinet	1953—Korean truce arranged between United Nations forces and those of Communist China
1954—Segregation in the public schools ruled illegal by the U.S. Supreme Court	1954—Tenth Inter-American Conference held in Caracas, Venezuela
1954—National Advisory Committee for Education authorized by Congress for appointment by Secretary of Health, Education, and Welfare	1954—New Internal Revenue Code, including numerous changes, adopted by Congress
1955—White House Conference on problems of school housing, finance, personnel, and organization called by President Eisenhower	1955—St. Lawrence River Seaway project launched in cooperation with Canada

In the year 1787 the famous "Ordinance for the Government of the territory of the United States northwest of the River Ohio" postulated that the following important principle should be applied to states to be carved from the territory: "Religion, morality, and knowledge being necessary to good government and the happiness of mankind, schools and the means of education shall be forever encouraged." Although it is customary to consider this statement in the Northwest Ordinance as a philanthropic gesture on the part of Congress, the bald facts are that mercenary motives actuated the proposal. The Continental Congress, which needed money urgently, wanted to sell land rather than aid education; Manasseh Cutler, who "lobbied" for the inclusion of this statement, was interested primarily in reselling the land to speculators rather than in building schoolhouses for children. Ten days after the adoption of this oft-quoted proposal for the encouragement of education, Congress sold 1,500,000 acres of land along the Ohio to the "Ohio Company of Associates" through Manasseh Cutler, who was the nation's first real-estate promoter. The ordinance authorizing the sale contained this provision for education:

> The lot No. 16 in each township, or fractional part of a township, to be given perpetually for the purposes contained in the said (1785) Ordinance. . . . Not more than two complete townships to be given perpetually for the purpose of a university. . . .

Thus, in addition to the two townships given in each state for university purposes, section 16 in every township or one thirty-sixth of the entire Northwest Territory was legally set aside for the maintenance of public schools. The first actual application of this land-grant policy for education was not made until the admission of the state of Ohio in 1803.

Constitutional Provisions for Education. In the meantime the members of the Constitutional Convention had drafted their document and the required nine states had ratified it, so that in 1789 the Constitution of the United States went into effect. This great document, which Gladstone said "was the most wonderful work ever struck off at a given time by the brain and purpose of man," is silent upon the subject of education. The Constitution contains neither the word "education" nor "schools."

Why was education omitted from this famous document? Several answers to the question might be proposed. The framers of the Constitution were undoubtedly afraid of a centralized control, for they had just fought a war for freedom from external domination. The prevailing view was that of state rights. Furthermore, education in those days was the function of the church, the home, and private agencies. The majority of the signers of the Constitution were themselves products of the old aristocratic doctrine that education was for those who could afford to pay for it, and they probably had very little or no sympathy with the idea of schooling for all. Cubberley adds this reason for the omission:

Even the theory of education, aside from that relating to instruction in Latin secondary schools and colleges, had not been thought out and formulated at the time the Federal Constitution was framed. Pestalozzi had not yet done his great work in Switzerland, or written out his ideas as to the educational process. Herbart was a small child at the time, and Froebel a mere infant in arms. The work which the French Revolutionary theorists and enthusiasts did for education in France was as yet undone.[4]

Then, too, at the time, there were weightier problems than education. The wilderness had to be wrested from the Indians, and a new economic and political order had to be established. Minor problems gave way to the larger aims of national unity, in the face of at least one threatened disruption of the Convention. Aside from the question put by Charles Pinckney of South Carolina, which dealt mainly with the founding of a national university, there was little discussion of education in the Constitutional Convention.

Despite the fact that education is not mentioned in the United States Constitution, indirect justification for a national program of instruction may be found in several of its provisions, as indicated later. The general welfare clauses, in the preamble and in the section on taxation, are the closest approach to an authorization. The preamble reads:

We the people of the United States, in order to form a more perfect Union, establish justice, insure domestic tranquility, provide for the common defence, promote the general welfare, and secure the blessings of liberty to ourselves and our posterity, do ordain and establish this Constitution for the United States of America.

Certainly the promotion of "the general welfare" entails the federal obligation to advance public education.

That the central government is not to control education is evident from the Tenth Amendment to the Constitution. The First to the Tenth Amendments enacted by the first Congress and declared in force December 15, 1791, were prompted by the fact that the Constitution contained no code of fundamental civil rights and no statement that the states retained the powers not expressly conferred on the national government. The Tenth Amendment by implication definitely left the subject of education to the individual states: "The powers not delegated to the United States by the Constitution, nor prohibited by it to the states, are reserved to the states respectively, or to the people." The implied pro-

[4] E. P. Cubberley, *State School Administration*, p. 10, Houghton Mifflin, 1927.

hibition against the establishment of a centralized system has markedly influenced the direction and scope of federal participation in education.

EDUCATION FOR NATIONAL DEFENSE

From the days of the earliest settlements through the modern age of atomic energy and supersonic speeds, the people of the United States have been interested in defense. During and after the Second World War, the preparation for defense assumed a distinct educational emphasis. General Dwight D. Eisenhower, later President of the United States, said upon his inauguration as President of Columbia University:

> If this were a land where the military profession is a weapon of tyranny or aggression—its members an elite caste dedicated to its own perpetuation—a life-long soldier could hardly assume my present role. But in our nation the army is the servant of the people, designed and trained exclusively to protect our way of life. Duty in its ranks is an exercise of citizenship. Hence, among us, the soldier who becomes an educator or the teacher who becomes a soldier enters no foreign field but finds himself instead engaged in a new phase of his fundamental life purpose—the protection and perpetuation of basic human freedoms.

This educational accent has continued under the Reorganization Act of 1947, which unified the services under a Secretary of Defense, to whom the Secretaries of the Army, Navy, and Air Force are all responsible. Some of the various educational activities of these three departments are tersely mentioned here.

Army Training. The first educational institution authorized by the federal government was the United States Military Academy at West Point, New York, a site of great strategic importance during the Revolutionary War. It was established by the Congressional Act signed by President Jefferson in 1802. Supported entirely by the federal government, and conducted under the auspices of the Department of War, this collegiate institution provides theoretical and practical training for prospective officers in the regular army. The entrance requirements and standards are very high. Upon completion of the 4-year course, the men are given commissions as army officers. In order that the government may have some return on its investment, the cadets pledge that they will continue in service for a period of at least 8 years from the time of entering West Point. Many graduates have won distinction in civil life as engineers. In addition to the United States Military Academy, two groups of army schools have developed: the general service schools, including the Command and General Staff School, the Army Industrial College, and the Army War College; and the special service schools, such as the Army Dental School and the School of Aviation Medicine.

The Army's education program extends from the first grade up through the university. Many thousands of soldiers have learned to read and write and have received the Army's fourth- and fifth-grade certificates. Others have earned the eighth-grade certificate. On the high-school level thousands, by passing successfully the General Educational Development Tests, have acquired a high-school diploma or equivalency certificate

FIG. 1-2. Cadets during a "bandbox" review in central area at the United States Military Academy, West Point, New York. The Academy celebrated its sesquicentennial in 1952. (*Official United States Army photograph.*)

from their home state. In higher education, some American universities have gone overseas to provide courses for soldiers abroad.

Navy Training. Congress decided in 1845 that an institution was needed to accomplish for the navy what West Point was doing for the army, so a naval training school was established at Annapolis, Maryland, the site of the first Federal Constitutional Convention. In 1850 this school became known as the United States Naval Academy. Under the auspices of the Bureau of Navy Personnel, it is supported entirely by federal funds. As at West Point, the course is usually 4 years in length, and the graduates are commissioned as ensigns. Postgraduate work and special training fields also have been added.

The Naval ROTC program is conducted in colleges and universities throughout the country. Its mission is to provide a permanent system of training and instruction in essential naval subjects at civilian educational institutions and to provide a source from which qualified officers may be obtained for the Navy and Marine Corps and the Naval Reserve and Marine Corps Reserve. Competitive examinations for appointment to the Regular (Holloway Plan) NROTC Program are conducted an-

Fig. 1-3. Air view of the United States Naval Academy at Annapolis, Maryland. (*Official United States Navy photograph.*)

nually. Contract NROTC students are selected locally by the professor of naval science at the college or university.

The Navy, Marine Corps, and the Merchant Marine have, from their earliest history, been joined by an inseparable relationship. The Merchant Marine or "commercial" marine, which consists of the vessels carrying on the water-borne trade of the nation, sprang up in wartime when the great need for transporting American goods all over the world developed a parallel need for officers. The Merchant Marine Academy, located at Kings Point, Long Island, New York, was authorized by Congress to confer a bachelor of science degree beginning with the class of 1950. The graduates are commissioned reserve ensigns, USNR, as well as ensigns in the United States Maritime Service. Like the students at the Naval Academy, "their campus is the seven seas."

Air Force Training. In 1947, for the first time in the history of the United States, a separate department was created for the air force. The educational program of the air force, formerly a part of the army and navy, now is independent in a new age of rocket-fired, jet-propelled, push-button planes. The Air University provides advanced professional work in constituent schools from the time of commissioning to retirement.

The primary training of the Air Force Command is divided into three training air forces—one for flying training, another for instruction in the technical skills, and a third for training of aircrew personnel. Air Training Command, the largest command in the Air Force, accounts for approximately one-third of Air Force personnel with its more than a quarter million students and instructors who are stationed at numerous bases located in virtually all regions of the United States. A government-financed Air Force Academy, along the lines of the United States Military and Naval Academies, opened its doors in temporary quarters in 1955, prior to settling at Colorado Springs.

Women's Services. Women receive training through the Women's Army Corps (WAC), the Air Force (WAF), the Navy (WAVES), the Marine Corps (Women Marines), Coast Guard (SPARS), Nurse Corps of the Army (ANC), Air Force (AFNC), and Navy (NCUSN), or the Women's Medical Specialist Corps of the Army (AWMSC) and Air Force (AFWMSC). Women in the Navy also serve in the Medical Service Corps (MSCUSN).

Others. Many other phases of military education have evolved under the aegis of the federal government. There are, for example, the Naval War College at Newport, Rhode Island; the Submarine School at New London, Connecticut; the Heavier-than-air Training School at Pensacola, Florida; and the Lighter-than-air Training School at Lakehurst, New Jersey. The government furnishes officers to serve at land-grant colleges; it cooperates with the Reserve Officers' Training Corps (ROTC); and it trains men for the Marine Reserve Corps and for numerous other military and semimilitary duties. These have many valuable implications for civilian programs of today and for the participation of the federal government in various civilian and defense activities of tomorrow.

High-ranking officers of the army, air force, and navy, as well as members of the foreign service and Department of State, study the problems of national defense in a college organized under the authority of the Joint Chiefs of Staff and located at the Army War College in Washington, D.C. This institution promotes close integration between the armed services and the Department of State. It is in harmony with the recommendation of the Hoover Commission on the Reorganization of the Executive Branch of Government that "the education of officers should be more definitely aimed at instilling a greater sense of mutual interdependence," and that a military education board be established to give special attention to policies for the joint training of military personnel.

Related to defense education are the fellowship programs established by the Atomic Energy Commission to promote scholarly achievement in the field of atomic energy. Numerous other educational and defense efforts are being financed completely or partly by the federal government.

FEDERAL GRANTS—NONVOCATIONAL

Land Grants for Education. With the admission of the seventeenth state, Ohio, to the Union in 1803, the federal government actually inaugurated its epoch-making practice of giving land for general educational purposes. In the enabling act for the admission of Ohio, Congress gave the sixteenth section of land, 1 mile square, in each township "to the inhabitants thereof" for schools. With certain exceptions and variations, this practice was continued with each new state admitted. With the admission of California in 1850, the gift consisted of two sections, 16 and 36. Three states—Utah, Arizona, and New Mexico—received four sections by the addition of those numbered 2 and 32. The total of these land grants to schools, including Alaska, has been estimated at 90,000,000 acres, or almost 150,000 square miles. The extent of this area is not usually appreciated. It is larger than the combined territory of the three adjacent states of Ohio, Indiana, and Illinois. The funds derived from the sale and lease of these original "school lands" form the major part of the permanent school funds of several states. Although some of the funds were poorly managed, these gifts of the federal government to education have been extremely significant.

Besides these lands, many other federal land grants have been made, both conditional and unconditional, including the saline lands, the swamplands, and the internal improvement grants. There have been donations to seminaries of learning, normal schools, universities, and other types of educational institutions, including especially the land-grant colleges of agriculture and mechanic arts, as established by the First Morrill Act and expanded by subsequent enactments.

Money Grants for Education. The federal government has also aided the public schools by money grants at different times. The first of these subventions followed the admission of Ohio, when 5 per cent of the sales of all public lands in the states was turned back to them. Some of this money was spent for schools. About half the commonwealths receiving the small fund from the so-called "surplus revenue" act of 1836 used it for schools. Other money grants, which in part or whole have gone to schools, have included the Direct War Tax Refund of 1891, which was devoted to education in three states; the Forest Reserve Income Act of 1908, according to which 25 per cent of the money received from each forest reserve goes to the schools or the roads of the county containing the reserve; and the Mineral Royalty Act of 1920, by which the federal government returns to each state a proportion of the royalties on the production of nonmetallic mineral deposits on public lands. One reason why California has developed such a superior system of junior colleges is that all its proceeds from the Mineral Royalty Act go to institutions of that special type. A few states have benefited from the Taylor Grazing Act. All states have received other specialized funds, such as help in inventorying school buildings and in providing some construction and operating costs in federally affected areas.

Among the nonvocational money grants has been that for school lunches. This grant, which began in the depression era of the 1930's, was put on a permanent basis in 1947. The enactment in 1944 of Public Laws 346 and 16—the historic "G.I. Bill of Rights"—was followed in 1951 and 1952 by Public Laws 16 (revised) and 550 respectively for disabled and other veterans of recent military service. These laws have provided perhaps the largest expenditure of federal funds ever made for any educational purpose.

GRANTS FOR VOCATIONAL EDUCATION

Land-grant Colleges and Universities.[5] The United States has always been very aggressive in promoting vocational education through both land and money grants. By the First Morrill Act in 1862 each state received 30,000 acres for each senator and representative then in Congress. All proceeds from the sale of these lands were to be invested at 5 per cent and the proceeds in each state to be used for "the endowment, maintenance, and support of at least one college where the leading object shall be, without excluding other scientific and classical studies and including military tactics, to teach such branches of learning as are related to agriculture and the mechanic arts." These colleges, 69 in number, have been very influential in the fields of agriculture, engineering, and home economics. The original act has been supplemented by other grants in the Second Morrill Act, the Nelson Amendment, and the Bankhead-Jones Act of 1935.[6]

Agricultural Experiment Stations. Further federal impetus was given vocational education through the Hatch Act of 1887, which appropriated $15,000 annually to each state and territory having an agricultural college. The purpose expressed in the law was "to promote scientific investigation respecting the principles and applications of agriculture science." Thus the agricultural experiment stations were established. The Adams

[5] Additional information on these colleges and universities is found in Unit VIII.

[6] For current data on these and other grants, see the periodic reports, *Federal Government Funds for Education*, GPO.

Act subsequently increased these appropriations, as did the Purnell and Bankhead-Jones Acts.

Agricultural Extension Services. Although the United States govern· ment had established agricultural colleges and experimental stations, it felt that the vocational work was still incomplete because the results were not reaching the consumers—the farmers and the housewives. So Congress passed in 1914 what is known as the Smith-Lever or Agricultural Extension Act. The proceeds from this annual grant are used for conferences, meetings, institutes, classes, traveling demonstrators, and county agents—a man to work among the farmers and a woman to help the housewives, especially in the rural communities. In the Smith-Lever Act was applied for the first time the practice, now under severe criticism, of "matching" federal and state aid. Additional grants for agricultural extension have been provided through such acts as the Capper-Ketcham, Clark-McNary, Bankhead-Jones, Norris-Doxey, and Bankhead-Flanagan Acts, and through direct appropriations.

Smith-Hughes Act for Vocational Education in Secondary Schools. The movement for federal aid to vocational education at the secondary school level did not develop until the twentieth century.

During the years between 1900 and 1910 a number of organizations, notably the National Association of Manufacturers, the National Metal Trades Association, certain agricultural organizations, and the National Education Association, began to advocate extended facilities for vocational education in the public schools. The American Federation of Labor, always a strong friend of public education, urged that vocational training be provided under public auspices. The various individuals and groups interested in this problem met in 1906 and established the National Society for the Promotion of Industrial Education. . . . In 1914 Congress by resolution authorized the appointment of a Commission on National Aid to Vocational Education.[7]

In 1917 President Woodrow Wilson signed the Smith-Hughes Act, which provided annual federal funds for distribution to the states for vocational education in public schools of less than college grade. These appropriations, again on the matching basis, were for teachers and supervisors of agriculture, home economics, trade and industrial subjects; for teacher training in these subjects; and for studies in vocational education. Supplemental legislation extended the benefits to some of the dependencies of the United States. The George-Reed Act (1929), increasing the appropriations, was followed by the George-Ellzey Act (1934), and the George-Deen Act (1936).

George-Deen Act and Aid in Distributive Occupations. This act, which became effective in 1937, provided "for the further development of voca-

---

[7] John D. Russell *et al., Vocational Education,* p. 16, Advisory Committee on Education, GPO, 1938.

tional education in the several states and territories," and more than doubled the amount of money previously available for vocational education. Prior to this, only four fields were given federal support: agriculture, trades and industries, home economics, and the training of teachers in these subjects. This act recognized as worthy of federal aid a new field of vocational training, the distributive occupations, such as selling; it gave a somewhat indirect recognition to another field, the public service occupations, such as the position of school janitors. It broke the precedent in the financing of vocational education which required that federal funds be matched dollar for dollar by state and local funds.

Vocational Rehabilitation. After some experimentation, the federal government adopted in 1920 the Vocational Rehabilitation Act, which appropriated money to the states for the training of handicapped persons so that they may, whenever possible, be placed in self-supporting, remunerative employment. This service and that for vocational education have been extended to some of the dependencies through the George-Reed and George-Ellzey Acts.

Other legislation dealing with vocational rehabilitation is the Social Security Act of 1935. The Federal Office of Education and the Social Security Board cooperate in occupational research and in the formulation of state plans for physically handicapped persons who have become permanently disabled through accident or disease or who have been born with serious physical defects. The program is carried out by the casework technique rather than by the public schools; nevertheless it is a public educational service. Most significant are the provisions of the federal rehabilitation acts for war veterans popularly known as Public Law 16. Thousands of veterans, including paraplegics, have been rehabilitated. Through vocational rehabilitation, millions of handicapped persons have been helped to a life of usefulness and independence.

Vocational Guidance and Placement. In its general evaluation of the federally aided programs of vocational education, the Advisory Committee stated that the services of guidance and placement had not received adequate emphasis. The George-Barden amendment has helped to remedy the situation. Under this act, federal funds were made available for the first time for counseling youth, training vocational counselors, and conducting allied activities, including research in guidance and placement. The Veterans Administration has rendered vocational services "beyond the call of duty."

Vocational Education and National Defense. Prior to the official entry of the United States into the Second World War, the federal government launched its defense training, which developed into a huge war program. Congress in 1938 established the Civil Aeronautics Authority, which in the following year inaugurated a pilot training program. In 1940 the first appropriations were made by the federal government for summer training programs in schools and colleges for workers essential in national defense. In the same year the United States Office of Education was allotted several million dollars for a program under which state boards of vocational education and local school officials offered vocational training facilities through the National Youth Administration (NYA), now defunct. The Second World War—and the Korean conflict, in a lesser degree—caused the nation as a whole to overaccent vocational education, which still represents the most important special field of federal activity in education.

OTHER FEDERAL PROVISIONS FOR EDUCATION

Numerous other significant and interesting subventions and activities have become a part of federal legislation on behalf of education. Some of the agencies created thereby are no longer in existence, as is the case of the Freedman's Bureau, through which the government undertook some work independently of the states. The Freedman's Bureau aided schools in the South for Negro children, spending more than $5,000,000 in 4 years. It helped to establish in Virginia the Hampton Normal Institute, a pattern for Negro education.

Annual Appropriations to Privately Controlled Institutions. The federal government has given financial support to some institutions not under its control. It donated land to Tuskegee Institute and now makes annual appropriations to the following three institutions, which are privately controlled but supervised by the federal Department of Health, Education, and Welfare:

1. The American Printing House for the Blind was incorporated by the legislature of Kentucky in 1858. This institution, which is located in Louisville, Kentucky, prints books and makes apparatus for the instruction of the blind of the United States.

2. The Columbia Institution for the Deaf, located in the District of Columbia, was incorporated by Congress in 1857. It is controlled by a board of ten directors, two of whom are Congressmen. This Institution consists of Gallaudet College; Kendall School, a primary and grammar department; a teacher-education division; and a research department.

3. Howard University, located in the District of Columbia, was incorporated by Congress in 1867. Originally planned for the education of Negro youth for the ministry, it now includes nearly all branches of higher education.

Making annual appropriations to privately controlled institutions, however, is not routine with Congress.

The G.I. Bill of Rights. As previously indicated, the greatest single venture of federal government in education has been the schooling of veterans of the Second World War and of other veterans. The United States is spending billions of dollars on education for G.I. Joes and Jills who interrupted or postponed their studies to help win the Second World War or to defend democracy against communism.

Concerning the first bill, former Chancellor Robert M. Hutchins of the University of Chicago wrote:

> The G.I. Bill of Rights is a historic enactment because it makes it possible for the veteran to go to college even if his parents have no money. It thus removes, for a large class of our citizens, the greatest, the most unjust, and the most unwise limitation on higher education.

The G.I. bills have enabled millions of young men and women to attend high schools, colleges, universities, specialized schools, and adult-education classes throughout the land. Several hundred also have studied abroad under their provisions. The quantitative and qualitative impact upon American education of the federal G.I. scholarships cannot be estimated.

Additional Federal Activities in Education. Several temporary subventions were granted during the depression era of the 1930's. These included the Civilian Conservation Corps, National Youth Administration, Works Progress Administration, Public Works Administration, and other agencies.

Although most federal activities in education are conducted by regular agencies of the national government, several special committees and conferences are created periodically to consider problems in education and related areas. For example, White House conferences are held at intervals of approximately ten years to study the welfare of children. These conferences are described in detail in Unit X. Several advisory committees have been authorized by Congress to study the relationship of the federal government to education.

The main channel through which have flowed the various appropriations made by Congress for the development of a national program of education is the United States Office of Education, in the Department of Health, Education, and Welfare.

UNITED STATES OFFICE OF EDUCATION

EVOLUTION OF OFFICE

The "common-school revival," championed by Horace Mann in the 1840's in Massachusetts, caused people all through the then settled portions of the United States to think in terms of schools. Other educational statesmen came forward, notably Henry Barnard, who led the movement for a national agency for education. The dire effects of the Civil War in the sixties and the reunion of the states gave rise to a new interest in national education. In 1866 a proposal of the National Association of State and City School Superintendents (now the American Association of School Administrators) for a federal bureau of education was presented to Congress by James A. Garfield. The "Department of Education" bill was finally approved March 2, 1867.

The Basic Law. The original act as adopted during the presidency of Andrew Johnson is as follows:

> BE IT ENACTED *by the Senate and the House of Representatives of the United States of America, in Congress Assembled,* That there shall be established at the city of Washington, a department of education, for the purpose of collecting such statistics and facts as shall show the condition and progress of education in the several states and territories, and of diffusing such information respecting the organization and management of schools and school systems and methods of teaching as shall aid the people of the United States in the establishment and maintenance of efficient school systems, and otherwise PROMOTE THE CAUSE OF EDUCATION throughout the country.
>
> 39th Congress, 2nd Session
Approved by President Andrew Johnson
March 2, 1867

Thus was the legal foundation laid.

Subsequent Changes. Two years later, owing primarily to opposition by some of the states, the department was made an "Office of Education" in the Department of Interior. The title, changed in 1870 to "Bureau of Education," was restored in 1929, and is now officially the "Office of Education." The duties and activities of the Office have accumulated like a rolling snowball until now the Office is a huge national clearinghouse for education.

On July 1, 1939, in connection with the general governmental reorganization plans, the United States Office of Education was transferred from the Department of the Interior to the Federal Security Agency. In 1953 the Office of Education became a part of the newly created Department of Health, Education, and Welfare, with a secretary in the President's Cabinet. This marks an important milestone in the history of federal education.

APPROPRIATIONS FOR FEDERAL OFFICE

A significant change in the federal Office has been the growth in appropriations. The funds are of two general types: (1) regular expenditures for administration of the Office of Education itself, and (2) grants-in-aid for distribution to the states through the Office.

Appropriations for Administration. The administration of the national headquarters at Washington requires an outlay for personnel, equipment, necessary travel, printing, and other items. From a meager appropriation in 1867 of about $50,000, the annual expenditures have gradually increased to several million dollars. The amount used for actual administration expenses for the federal Office is only a small percentage of the total amount appropriated for federal activities in education.

Grants-in-aid to the States. The federal Office is a channel through which flow the annual grants-in-aid to be distributed to the states, territories, and outlying possessions for educational purposes. These funds are more than a hundred times larger than those for the direct use of the United States Office of Education. The money is primarily for land-grant colleges, vocational education, vocational rehabilitation, and defense education.

ACTIVITIES OF OFFICE OF EDUCATION

The three main duties enumerated in the basic law creating the commissionership are (1) collecting statistics and facts, (2) diffusing information about schools, and (3) otherwise promoting the cause of education.

Collection of Statistics and Facts. The collection of educational data and facts, in a country as far-flung and as full of school districts as the United States, is extremely onerous. The publication of these data is naturally delayed, often as much as 2 years. The preparation of the *Annual Reports* and *Biennial Surveys* is treated later under Duties of Commissioner. The collecting, sifting, and organizing of the data constitute a colossal task.

Diffusion of Information. Commissioner Samuel M. Brownell has said, "The U.S. Office of Education is not an operating agency. Our main task is to gather facts and interpret them for the people." The Office diffuses information in several ways, through its many publications, exhibits, conferences called by the Commissioner, letters answering inquiries, addresses by staff members, radio and television broadcasts, surplus-property information center, and exchange of books, radio scripts, and transcriptions. The printed publications are available free or at a nominal cost from the Superintendent of Documents, Government Printing Office, Washington, D.C.; others, such as mimeographed circulars, are obtainable from the Office of Education. The value of these publications, particularly the monthly periodical *School Life,* is not adequately appreciated by laymen and educators.

Promoting the Cause of Education. The third major duty of the office —"and otherwise promote the cause of education throughout the country"—is an obligation as broad as the country itself. Besides being the national bookkeeper of American education and the official dispenser of information, the Office promotes vocational education, vocational rehabilitation, and other phases of education; conducts investigations; makes research studies and loans theses on important school problems; and maintains a national information center and a library on all phases of American education. Upon request the Office also conducts educational surveys. It administers funds appropriated by Congress for special activities, such as land-grant colleges, vocational education, and vocational rehabilitation.

In recent years, the Office of Education has developed numerous other projects. It has given financial assistance to several states to undertake a study of school-building facilities. Through its exchange program of stu-

Fig. 1-4. Headquarters of the United States Office of Education, located in the Department of Health, Education, and Welfare. (*Courtesy of U.S. Commissioner of Education.*)

dents and teachers it actively promotes international education. The Office also sponsors the Future Farmers of America, a national organization of boys who are studying vocational agriculture in rural high schools.

According to *School Life,* the "clientele" of the Office of Education consists of the following major groups:

State school systems
Local school districts
Schools, colleges, and universities
Public libraries
Foreign students and educators
Radio and television stations
State parent-teacher associations
Local parent-teacher associations

Educational associations
Labor groups
Social-civic organizations
Business and professional clubs
Patriotic societies
Farmers' associations
Service clubs
Other organizations

To these might be added thousands of individuals at home and abroad who rely upon the publications and services of the Office.

ORGANIZATION OF FEDERAL OFFICE

Naturally activities so numerous, for an audience so varied, demand a large staff of workers. These are organized in various groups under the general leadership of the United States Commissioner of Education. Committees also cut across divisional lines, as the Inter-divisional Committee on the Educational Implications of Atomic Energy.

Office Staff. The regular full-time staff of the Office has increased from five workers in 1867 to several hundred. Many additional helpers are needed, since some important fields are undeveloped or placed on a temporary basis. The United States Commissioner of Education has been seriously handicapped by lack of an adequate permanent staff.

UNITED STATES COMMISSIONER OF EDUCATION

HISTORY OF COMMISSIONERSHIP

In 1838 Henry Barnard came to Washington, D.C., in search of reliable facts on the schools of the nation; he found none. For 30 years he led the movement for a federal fact-finding agency, which culminated in the Congressional Act, already quoted, creating the Federal Department of Education in 1867. It was indeed fitting that Henry Barnard was selected as the first United States Commissioner of Education. The first principal of the New Britain Normal School, the first state superintendent of schools for Rhode Island, and a former state superintendent for Connecticut, he brought to this new national office a rich experience in public education. He pioneered in this field from 1867 to 1870.

List of Commissioners. Thirteen men have held the office of United States Commissioner of Education, a title that has not changed. Their names and the years in office are indicated in the accompanying table.

Commissioner	Appointed by President	Years in office	Tenure in office, years
Henry Barnard	Andrew Johnson	1867–1870	3
John Eaton	Ulysses S. Grant	1870–1886	16
N. H. R. Dawson	Grover Cleveland	1886–1889	3
William T. Harris	Benjamin Harrison	1889–1906	17
Elmer E. Brown	Theodore Roosevelt	1906–1911	5
Philander P. Claxton	William H. Taft	1911–1921	10
John J. Tigert	Warren G. Harding	1921–1928	7
William J. Cooper	Herbert Hoover	1929–1933	4½
George F. Zook	Franklin D. Roosevelt	1933–1934	1
John W. Studebaker	Franklin D. Roosevelt	1934–1949	15
Earl J. McGrath	Harry S Truman	1949–1953	4
Lee M. Thurston	Dwight D. Eisenhower	1953–1953	¼
Samuel M. Brownell	Dwight D. Eisenhower	1953–	

Terms of Office. The commissioner, appointed with the consent of the Senate by the President of the United States, upon the recommendation of the Secretary of Health, Education, and Welfare, serves an indefinite term. Sometimes a change in Presidents is followed by the appointment of a new commissioner, although only 13 men have served under 18

FIG. 1-5. Henry Barnard, the first United States Commissioner of Education and author of about 75 volumes and reports, including the monumental work, the *American Journal of Education* in 32 bound volumes. His most widely quoted statement is this: "The common school should be as common as the light and the air because its blessings are open to all and enjoyed by all." (*Steel engraving courtesy of U.S. Commissioner of Education.*)

Presidents. The terms have ranged from 17 years to less than 3 months, Commissioner Thurston having died in office shortly after his appointment.

DUTIES OF COMMISSIONER

Main Duties. The duties of the commissioner, as originally prescribed by law, are "to collect such statistics and facts as shall show the condition and progress of education in the several states and territories"; to diffuse such "information respecting the organization and management of schools and school systems and methods of teaching as shall aid the people in the maintenance of efficient school systems and otherwise promote the cause of education"; and also "to present annually to Congress a report embodying the result of his investigation and labors, together with a statement of such facts and recommendations, as will, in his judgment, subserve the purpose for which the department is established."

Preparation of Annual Reports and Biennial Surveys. A significant duty of the commissioner is the last one listed, *viz.,* that of taking soundings to determine the progress of the educational ship of state. The annual reports and biennial surveys are replete with information and, as standard works of educational reference, are distributed in large numbers to libraries and professional workers. These reports contain many interesting side lights on educational history.

After 1917 the *Report of the Commissioner of Education* was changed to the *Biennial Survey of Education;* the *Annual Report* became a concise summary of the activities of the Office of Education and of educational conditions in general.

Other Activities. In addition to the original duties already mentioned as belonging to the commissioner and the Office of Education, many others have accumulated over the years. Among these may be listed voluntary cooperation with numerous educational agencies, as in the promotion of American Education Week and the Commission on Life Adjustment Education; special tasks assigned by the President of the United States, as the request for the federal Office to act in an advisory educational capacity; duties imposed by Congressional enactments, as by the George-Barden Act; and the surveillance of film service and radio, assigned to the Office by one of the presidential reorganization plans. The Office has also been called upon to extend and expand its services in the territories and dependencies of the United States and in many countries overseas.

OTHER FEDERAL ACTIVITIES IN EDUCATION

EDUCATION IN SPECIAL FEDERAL JURISDICTIONS

The national government assists in promoting education in the special school district of Washington, D.C., the territories, the outlying possessions, the Trust Territory, the federal reservations, and other countries through the United States Point Four program, Foreign Operations Administration, and United Nations Technical Assistance Program. The importance of education in such widespread and strategic areas is obvious. Because of the unique needs of these disparate groups, their educational problems are difficult but challenging.

Among the interesting educational systems in these overseas areas are those in the Ex-Japanese Mandated Islands, now called the Trust Territory, and transferred in 1947 to the United States by the United Nations Security Council. They comprise the Marshall, Caroline, Palau, and Marianas Islands (with the exception of Guam). The United States has done more than conduct experiments in atomic energy on its atolls of Bikini and Eniwetok; it has unleashed in the whole Trust Territory the power of educational energy that transforms rather than destroys. The chain reaction from this significant educational experiment may spread from atolls to islands and mainlands.

Fig. 1-6. Capitol Page Boy School. Class in English grammar and composition on the third floor of the Library of Congress just east of the United States Capitol. This photograph was made at 7 A.M.—pages must go to school early to serve congressmen later in the day. (*Courtesy of Washington Star.*)

Owing to the excellent and inexpensive reports available on the educational systems in these various federal jurisdictions, and owing to the limitations imposed by the nature of an introductory volume in education, descriptions are not presented here.

EDUCATION OF SPECIAL GROUPS

Education of the Indians. In a social-science class in a Michigan high school, students were asked to write an essay entitled, "Who Is a True American?" A member of the class, a young full-blooded Ottawa Indian, wrote just two words, "I am." The Indians were the first Americans. In an early report of a United States Commissioner of Education, the whites are referred to as "Anglo-Americans." For a long time the issue was Indian education vs. Indian destruction. In 1870 the commissioner stated that up to that time $8,000,000 had been spent for educating Indians and at least $500,000,000 for killing them.

The early missions are credited with starting schools for Indians. The first federal appropriation for this purpose was made in the early 1800's.

FIG. 1-7. Balboa High School and Canal Zone Junior College. (*Courtesy of Superintendent of Schools, Canal Zone Government.*)

Private funds also went to Indian education. The origin of Dartmouth College can be traced to Moore's Indian School for the education of Indians.

By the Act of June 2, 1924, every American Indian now born in the United States is a citizen of this country. Approximately one-third of a million Indians live in the United States. It is significant that the Indians, although less than one-half of 1 per cent of the total population, are increasing—they are not a dying race. They usually live in concentrated areas and exhibit strong ethnic characteristics. The largest tribal groups are the Navaho, Sioux, and Chippewa. The largest Indian settlements are located in Oklahoma, Arizona, New Mexico, and South Dakota. Some Indian reservations cannot support all their inhabitants. The problems of Indian welfare and education, as in the case of Negroes, are more acute in some states than in others.

The administration of Indian education in the United States is under the Office of Indian Affairs. The children attend different types of schools: government-reservation and nonreservation boarding schools, government day schools, state public schools, and mission and private schools. The majority go to the public schools; the federal government pays their tuition if they are not residents of the school district. In addition to federal appropriations for Indian service, large sums are expended from Indian tribal funds for education. Many schools are community centers for adults as well as children. Certainly the Indian—the first American and the first of America's forgotten men—is entitled to the best in education, but he generally does not get the best. He often lives in "that cultural void between two civilizations." [8]

Negro Education. Negroes constitute almost one-tenth of the population of the United States. The education of this large group is of major concern to the nation, as well as to the Southern states where the majority of Negroes reside.

An important feature of the Second Morrill Act in 1890 was the recognition by Congress of separate land-grant colleges for "white and colored students." A year earlier the federal government voted its first grant to Howard University, a privately controlled institution for Negroes which today enrolls several thousand students in its many graduate and undergraduate schools. Founded immediately after the Civil War, this institution was named after its first president, General Howard of the Freedman's Bureau.

The Office of Education has conducted several surveys of Negro education, including colleges and universities, secondary education, and vocational education and guidance. It reactivated the National Advisory Committee on Education of Negroes. Although their schooling is primarily a responsibility of the states, the federal government can, through equalization funds and other means, supplement these efforts on behalf of one-tenth of the nation's population.

The United States Supreme Court in its historic decision of 1954 held that racial segregation in the public schools violates the United States Constitution. At that time 17 states and the District of Columbia maintained public-school segregation by specific law, and 4 more states permitted it. For many years these states had justified their policy as giving "equal but separate" facilities to Negro and white children. The Supreme Court ruled that, even if facilities are equal, intangible factors prevent "separate" from being "equal."

[8] Erna Gunther, "The Education of American Indians," *Pi Lambda Theta Journal,* May, 1948, pp. 195–200.

To separate [Negro children] from others of similar age and qualifications solely because of their race generates a feeling of inferiority as to their status in the community that may affect their hearts and minds in a way unlikely ever to be undone. . . . We conclude that in the field of public education the doctrine of "separate but equal" has no place. Separate educational facilities are inherently unequal.

In this unanimous decision of the highest tribunal of the land are involved many complex problems: *when* should public schools be ordered to abolish segregation, *who* should enforce the terms, *how* can educational integration be applied, and *what* can be done to help house and finance programs for nonsegregated pupils? Obviously no uniform pattern for educational integration can or should be applied. Furthermore, evolutionary processes will be employed in implementing a concept that is revolutionary to many people. As indicated by *Time* magazine, "the Supreme Court's decision was another vital chapter in one of the greatest success stories the world has ever known: the American Negro's 90-year rise from slavery."

Other Ethnic Groups. Mexicans comprise about 1 per cent of the population of the United States. Some communities in the southwestern part of the United States are predominantly Mexican.

Large numbers of white people in the United States are foreign born, but, aside from Americanization classes, not much has been done on a national scale for their education. Numerous racial groups of children and adults, including displaced persons, many of whom have difficulty with the English language and the American way of life, have not been given the special care and education necessary for their role as citizens in a democracy.

Other Special Groups. The education of children of federal employees residing on government reservations, in dependencies, and at foreign stations is a unique problem facing the national government. Children in these areas are assured of free public schooling only if the federal government makes special provision therefor. During the Second World War, Congress provided financial aid to schools overburdened with war-caused enrollments. Since then the Lanham Act also provided school-district assistance where it was needed because of reactivation or establishment of defense activities. Partial support is given to some schools at naval stations. Government buildings and cars sometimes lend indirect assistance to schools on reservations. The Tennessee Valley Authority maintains public schools and other educational facilities for children and adults. Where there is a concentration of children of federal employees abroad, as in the countries of Germany and Japan, special schools have been established under federal auspices. Federal personnel in foreign lands, however, often face the necessity of enrolling their children in private or foreign schools, or of sending them back to the United States for their education. It has been recommended that Congress establish a permanent policy by which all children of federal employees residing on a federal reservation or at a foreign station will be assured the right of free education.

Equality of educational opportunity means that each child should be educated in terms of his needs, interests, abilities, and limitations. Special attention is needed by several million children—blind and partially blind, deaf and hard of hearing, crippled, defective in speech, delicate, mentally gifted, mentally retarded, socially maladjusted, and otherwise handicapped.[9] The federal government aids atypical children and adults through general grants such as that for vocational rehabilitation and by specific projects such as the American Printing House for the Blind in Louisville, Kentucky, and the Columbia Institute for the Deaf in Washington, D.C.

DEPARTMENTAL PROGRAMS OF EDUCATION

Federal programs of education are conducted also by (1) the executive departments, each under a secretary in the President's cabinet, and (2) other departments, such as the Federal Security Agency.

Executive Departments and Their Programs of Education. Several educational and semieducational agencies and services are sponsored by the major executive departments of the United States. Chief of these, of course, is the Department of Health, Education, and Welfare with its United States Office of Education, previously mentioned. Illustrative of other educational programs sponsored by executive departments are the military academies in the Department of Defense, prison education in the Department of Justice, and the school for postal inspectors in the Post Office Department. Directly under the President of the United States are several agencies that have direct educational significance, as, for example, the Bureau of the Budget, which prepares estimates for educational expenditures.

Other Federal Departments and Their Programs of Education. Every branch of the federal government conducts several educational activities either directly or indirectly, either in cooperation with the Office of Education or independently. Only a few of these agencies and their activities can be catalogued here. Congress has its committees on education in both the House and Senate. The Supreme Court renders its interpretations in the form of decisions affecting education, as in the Dartmouth College Case, the McCollum and Zorach decisions on public schools and religious instruction, the opinions on segregation in schools and colleges, and the interpretations on loyalty legislation affecting educators. Independent

---

[9] See Unit X for a more complete discussion of exceptional children.

federal establishments that furnish educational service include the Library of Congress and its Copyright Office, the Government Printing Office, the Pan-American Union, the Smithsonian Institution, the National Museum, the National Gallery of Art, the National Academy of Sciences, the Commission of Fine Arts, the Atomic Energy Commission,

FIG. 1-8. Main reading room, Library of Congress, Washington, D.C. This is one of the educational institutions supported by the United States government. Founded in 1800, the Library of Congress moved into these quarters in 1897. A newer annex adjoins this building. The library maintains a National Union Catalog for recording every book of research value in library collections of the United States.

and the National Science Foundation. Much educational research is conducted in the nation's capital and sponsored by the Congress of the United States.

The number of federal activities is ample evidence that the government of the United States is seeking "to promote the general welfare" of its citizens through public education.

ROLE OF UNITED STATES IN INTERNATIONAL EDUCATION

The general welfare of citizens in the United States and other countries includes the well-being and education of all peoples in a global, atomic, supersonic age. The United States government, as a member of the United Nations, and especially the American teachers, are intensely interested in education throughout the world. The total teacher of today and tomorrow needs to be a cosmopolitan—a world citizen who is at home both in his own country and abroad—in an age of interdependence. This interest of American educators in international education is twofold: (1) in sharing with other countries the democratic way of life as taught and lived in these United States, and (2) in learning from other democratic countries, most of which are much older than the United States, how to prolong and enrich education. Educational reciprocity is the goal.

Efforts at International Cooperation in Education. The Office of Education in the United States—a "human melting pot"—has long maintained a special department for comparative education, which later became the Division of International Educational Relations. Through the Pan-American Union, the United States has for years cooperated in educational and cultural activities with the American republics. In 1941 the Office of Inter-American Affairs was created by the United States to stimulate and coordinate certain inter-American activities, including education. In 1944 a joint Canada–United States Committee on Education was appointed. At Endicott, New York, in 1946, the United States was host to the First World Conference on Education attended by delegates from 30 nations. Illustrative of the many world-minded commissions and committees in the United States are the Committee on Internationl Education of the American Association for Colleges of Teacher Education, and the Commission on International Education of Phi Delta Kappa. The teachers of the United States are active in the World Confederation of Organizations of the Teaching Profession, and in the International Council on Education for Teaching organized at Oxford, England, in 1953. Many American educators have served as consultants in Germany, Austria, Japan, Korea, and other lands. Thousands have participated in teacher-exchange programs. Among the postwar federal laws for educational exchange have been the Fulbright Act of 1946, the more permanent Smith-Mundt Act of 1948, the Point Four enabling legislation of 1950, and the joint resolution providing for participation in UNESCO.

UNESCO. Official and striking evidence that educational isolationism is dying both here and abroad is found in the organization and program of UNESCO—the United Nations Educational, Scientific, and Cultural Organization, founded in 1945. UNESCO is one of the specialized agencies provided in the charter of the United Nations and affiliated with the Economic and Social Council. Its broad purpose is "to contribute to peace and security by promoting collaboration among the nations through education, science, and culture."

As indicated in the Preamble to the UNESCO Constitution, "Since wars begin in the minds of men, it is in the minds of men that the defenses of peace must be constructed." Alexander Meiklejohn said of the organization:

> It is an agency of study and of teaching rather than of external action. UNESCO will have none of the responsibilities or powers of the Security Council, of the Economic and Social Council, of the World Food Administration, or of the International Labor Office. And yet it is concerned with them all. It is essential to them all. In a fundamental sense, it is prior to them all. Its aim is the development of that international intelligence upon which the success of any United Nations activity depends.

The historical roots of UNESCO lie deep in history; its genesis is in the medieval community of scholars. According to *International Conciliation,* the "menace of psychopathic nationalism and advanced military technology" are the immediate factors which brought it into existence. The beginnings of this international organization are sketched briefly here.

The definite origin of UNESCO can be traced to the Conference of Allied Ministers of Education in 1942. The United States was not present but sent observers for the meeting the next year. In 1944 the United States Government sent to London a delegation for educational and cultural reconstruction. An American delegate, the late Grayson Kefauver, remained in London to maintain liaison with the Conference of Allied Ministers of Education.

In the meantime, the San Francisco Conference, which adopted the Constitution of the United Nations, passed a resolution favoring the idea of an international organization for education, science, and culture. The Conference of Allied Ministers of Education modified their plans, which served as the basis for discussion at a United Nations meeting in London in November, 1945. Forty-four governments were represented at this Conference and seven international organizations sent observers. The United States delegation, headed by Archibald MacLeish, cooperated with the other nations in preparing a new draft constitution and establishing a preparatory commission. The first meeting of the General Conference of UNESCO was held in Paris in November, 1946.

Official approval by the United States came in July, 1946, when both houses of Congress passed a joint resolution providing for membership and participation by the United States in UNESCO, and authorizing an appropriation therefor. In signing the joint resolution President Harry S Truman said:

> UNESCO will summon to service in the cause of peace the forces of education, science, learning, and the creative arts and the agencies of the film, the radio, and the printed word through which knowledge and ideas are diffused among

mankind. The government of the United States will work with and through UNESCO to the end that the minds of all people may be freed from ignorance, prejudice, suspicion, and fear and that men may be educated for justice, liberty, and peace. If peace is to endure, education must establish the moral unity of mankind.

United States National Commission for UNESCO. The United States Congress, in officially approving its active membership, established a National Commission for UNESCO in 1946. This commission of 100 educational leaders is entrusted with the responsibility of formulating policies for the United States as a member of the group. Thus the government and its citizenry are cooperating on an international scale to help education win the inexorable race with disaster.

Archibald MacLeish, an American delegate to the first session of UNESCO in Paris, said:

History may be about to teach us that the Parliament of Mankind can only be attained through the Republic of Letters. If that is the lesson we are to be taught, then the United Nations Educational, Scientific, and Cultural Organization will be more important to the international evolution of our time than any other part of the United Nations. For it is precisely the function of UNESCO to realize the ancient dream of the Republic of Letters.

UNESCO aims to help end educational isolationism and promote intellectual interdependence. In a highly scientific age which splits atoms, it helps unite peoples of the world. An ancient Chinese proverb says, "The journey of a thousand miles begins with but a single step." The organization of UNESCO may prove to be the single step in education's long journey to lasting peace.

AN EVOLVING NATIONAL SYSTEM OF EDUCATION

A democracy is not static; it either advances or dies. Certainly education in a democracy strives to advance; thus a national system of education is slowly evolving in America.

Henry W. Holmes, former dean of the Harvard Graduate School, wrote in answer to his own question, "What do you mean by a *national* system of education?":

I do not mean a system run from Washington. The bogey of federal control has been raised for years to head off federal aid to schools. . . . It means a system that can do a national job. A national job in education is compatible with immense variation in local patterns; such variation is, indeed, a necessary element in making American education national. . . . The first business of a national system of education is to carry the whole youthful population of the country to the point of its entrance into adult life—and to do so in such wise that every boy and girl is ready for a job or for further education leading toward a job, ready for citizenship in a democracy, and equipped with wholesome personal resources for the "pursuit of happiness." [10]

From the highest educational official in the land down to the youngest member of a student council in an elementary school, there is the desire to perfect American education. This striving toward perfection is furthered collectively by many nongovernmental groups. These organizations, through their nation-wide membership and numerous activities, assist especially in formulating policies, in implementing goals, and in evaluating programs.

PRINCIPLES AND PROPOSALS FOR IMPROVEMENT OF NATIONAL SYSTEM

Basic Policies and Proposals. The Problems and Policies Committee and the Educational Policies Commission created a joint committee to study federal and state relations in education, which has enumerated five basic policies and principles to guide the future developments of the federal program in education:

1. The federal government in its relations to education should recognize that this is a service of primary importance, which makes its greatest contribution in the general welfare as a well-organized, integrated enterprise designed to develop well-balanced citizens for democracy, rather than as a means of advancing unrelated aims or special interests.

2. The decentralized pattern of public educational organization developed in the United States during a period of more than a century and a half, involving basic control and administration of education by the states and localities, is sound policy and should be continued.

3. The nation as a whole, as well as the states and localities, has a stake in education, and the federal government should continue to exercise, within properly defined limits, educational functions demanded by changing national conditions and needs.

4. In its relations to education in the states, the federal government should limit its action to two broad functions: financial assistance and leadership of a stimulating but noncoercive character.

5. The federal government should limit such direct control and administration of education as it exercises in certain special enterprises. Examples are the academies at West Point and Annapolis.[11]

Specific Proposals. This joint commission made two specific recommendations for implementing the policies mentioned: (1) creating a national educational commission or board, composed of 12 to 15 outstanding citizens, to provide a catalytic agent for education; and (2) establishing an

[10] Henry W. Holmes, "The Nation Challenges the Schools," *The Atlantic,* January, 1940, p. 24.

[11] Educational Policies Commission, and Problems and Policies Commission, *Federal State Relations in Education,* p. 7, National Education Association, 1945.

adequate federal educational agency as an independent office of the federal government, since the existing Office of Education is inadequate. The first of these proposals was implemented partially in 1954 through a congressional bill authorizing the appointment of a nine-person National Advisory Committee on Education to "recommend studies of national concern in the field of education."

Other suggestions by various groups and individuals for improving the national system of education in the United States include (3) establishing a separate department of education, with a Secretary of Education in the President's Cabinet; (4) coordinating federal activities in education through a federal council on education, consisting of one representative from each of the several executive departments; (5) coordinating federal-state programs through a national council on public education, composed of the several state superintendents, under the chairmanship of a secretary or commissioner of education; (6) coordinating governmental and non-governmental educational agencies through a national conference on education; (7) creating a federal fund for aiding general education and equalizing educational opportunity and burden through the United States; (8) providing federal funds or loans for specific purposes, such as school buildings; (9) increasing the grant to the United States Office of Education; (10) providing federal scholarships and fellowships; (11) granting subsidies for a national theater; and (12) founding a national university at Washington, D.C., similar to the Australian National University at Canberra.[12]

Dozens of other recommendations affecting national education have been proposed by various groups and commissions, such as the Hoover Commission on Organization of the Executive Branch of Government. In its quest for the best the nation will ever seek improvement in education.

CONCLUSION

The present decentralized system of American public education does not and should not exclude the possibility of an improved federal program of leadership and cooperation. The Advisory Committee on Education, instructed to examine the general relationship of the federal government to education, states:

Education is in a large sense an individual matter. But individuals compose neighborhoods and communities, communities compose states, and in the United States, the states compose the nation. As are the neighborhoods, so will be the states and nation.

Since the formation of the Union, Americans have been citizens both of the states and of the nation. Most Americans now feel that their federal govern-

12 Some of these proposals are considered further in Unit XVII.

ment is their agent as much as is their state government. Our sense of national citizenship has developed rapidly in recent years. For better or for worse, it is becoming more and more evident that all citizens face a common responsibility and that they share a common destiny.[13]

From this common destiny a national school system is slowly evolving. It is not a new concept. Certainly it was in the minds of the statesmen who wrote the Declaration of Independence. It is today in the minds and hearts of educational statesmen who are perfecting an unwritten Declaration of Educational Interdependence. This growing knowledge and feeling of educational interdependence between state systems of education, and between them and the national government, are the bases for helping boys and girls, men and women, to live a fuller life, as envisioned in the great American dream.

SUGGESTED ACTIVITIES

1. Investigate the requirements for obtaining an overseas assignment in education—Fulbright, Smith-Mundt, etc.

2. Study the contributions of United States education to the Point Four and allied programs.

3. Examine the report of a recent meeting of UNESCO. Evaluate its work.

4. Review the ways in which the federal government encouraged schools in the early days.

5. Explain why the words "schools" and "education" were omitted from the United States Constitution.

6. Discuss the implications for education in the Tenth Amendment to the United States Constitution.

7. Give a brief history of the federal Office of Education.

8. Draw a diagram showing the internal organization of the Office of Education.

9. List the duties of the federal Commissioner of Education.

10. Examine an *Annual Report of the United States Commissioner of Education*.

11. Prepare a brief history of the life and work of an early United States Commissioner of Education.

12. Discuss the types of aid granted to school districts by the federal government during and since the Second World War.

13. Debate the issue: "Resolved that there should be a Secretary of Education in the cabinet of the President of the United States."

14. List the geographical areas, other than the 48 states, where the federal Office of Education assists in promoting education.

15. Describe the major features of the educational system in one of the United States dependencies.

16. Report on how the public schools in Washington, D.C., are conducted.

17. Prepare an exhibit of the different types of literature issued under the auspices of the federal Office of Education.

18. Read several articles in a recent issue of *School Life*.

19. Review the activities of the federal government in vocational education.

20. Describe one of the newer federal activities in education of special interest to you.

[13] Advisory Committee on Education, *Report of the Committee*, p. 35, GPO, 1938.

DESCRIPTIVE BIBLIOGRAPHY AND AIDS

BOOKS

ALLEN, HOLLIS P.: *Federal Government and Education,* Chap. X, McGraw-Hill, 1950.
  The U.S. Office of Education as evaluated by the task force of the Hoover Commission.

AMERICAN ASSOCIATION OF SCHOOL ADMINISTRATORS: *Education for American Citizenship,* Chap. III, National Education Association, 1954.
  The ideals Americans live by.

———: *Staff Relations in School Administration,* Chap. I, National Education Association, 1955.
  Administration as a way of working with people.

———: *The American School Superintendency,* Chap. XIII, National Education Association, 1952.
  Democratic principles that underlie the American system of education.

AXT, RICHARD G.: *The Federal Government and Financing Higher Education,* Chap. XI, Columbia University Press, 1952.
  National defense and the future of federal policy toward higher education.

BRAMMELL, ROY P.: *Your Schools and Mine,* pp. 114–126, Ronald, 1952.
  The federal government and education.

DRAKE, WILLIAM E.: *The American School in Transition,* Chap. II, Prentice-Hall, 1955.
  The struggle for independence in education.

EBY, FREDERICK: *The Development of Modern Education,* Chap. XXI, Prentice-Hall, 1952.
  Building of the American school system.

EDUCATIONAL POLICIES COMMISSION, *Public Education and the Future of America,* National Education Association, 1955, 104 pp.
  The story of public education in the United States.

INTERDEPARTMENTAL COMMITTEE ON CHILDREN AND YOUTH: *Programs of the Federal Government Affecting Children and Youth,* Chap. I, GPO, 1951.
  Development of federal programs affecting children and youth.

KNIGHT, EDGAR W.: *Readings in Educational Administration,* Chap. VI, Holt, 1953.
  Selected and edited original sources dealing with federal relations to education.

MOEHLMAN, ARTHUR B.: *School Administration,* Part V, Houghton Mifflin, 1951.
  The federal government and education.

SANFORD, CHARLES W., HAROLD C. HAND, and WILLARD B. SPALDING: *The Schools and National Security,* Chap. VIII, McGraw-Hill, 1951.
  Education as an essential bulwark of the nation.

CURRENT PERTINENT PERIODICALS AND PUBLICATIONS

American Quarterly
Annual reports of U.S. State Department
Biennial Survey of Education
Educational publications of U.S. Government Printing Office
Education Digest
Education Index
Education News
Educator's Dispatch
NEA Journal
Negro Educational Review
Reader's Guide to Periodical Literature
Reports of U.S. Office of Education and Department of Health, Education, and Welfare
School Life
Surveys, national, educational
Teacher's Letter
UNESCO educational reports
Yearbook of the United Nations
Yearbooks of educational organizations

Audio-visual Aids [14]

CHILDREN AT MIDCENTURY   Filmstrip, 30 min., 35 mm.
Dramatizes educational problems confronting American children today. Prepared by *Life* at the request of the Midcentury White House Conference on Children and Youth. Clifton Fadiman, narrator. Available from the National Citizens Commission for the Public Schools, New York 36.

DESIGN OF AMERICAN EDUCATION   16 min., sound
A text-film tailor-made for this book. Portrays nation-wide activities in education. An overview of Units I–IV—national, state, county, and local organization of education. Accents the major characteristics of the American educational system. Pretest and follow-up filmstrip also available from McGraw-Hill, New York 36.

DOES IT PAY TO BE IGNORANT   Radio script, 5 min.
Prepared by experienced script writers for American Education Week. Available from the National Education Association, Washington, D.C.

EDUCATION   Slidefilm, color
One in a series entitled "The Nature of Democracy." A discussional slidefilm on education, available from the Jam Handy Organization, Detroit, Mich.

FOUNDING OF THE AMERICAN PUBLIC SCHOOL SYSTEM   Microfilms, 35 mm., silent
Several hundred selections of source material in a scholarly survey of the establishment and growth of American education to the close of the Civil War. Textbook, *Founding of the American Public School System*, written by Paul Monroe and published by Macmillan, is available for use with the films. Especially helpful here are Chaps. VIII and IX. Microfilm published by University Films, Ann Arbor, Mich. Several sets deposited by the Carnegie Foundation in some of the larger and more important public and university libraries.

REPORT CARD   Transcription, 1 hour
A transcription on records of a CBS broadcast by the same title. Covers a broad survey of education in the United States, indicating the need for linking the classroom with life's realistic needs. Permissions restricted to off-the-air use. Available from the U.S. Office of Education, Washington, D.C., without charge.

TOWARD BETTER SCHOOLS FOR ALL CHILDREN   Filmstrip, 55 frames, 35 mm.
Shows that the difficulties of the public schools are increasing, that the costs of school supplies have advanced more rapidly than revenue, and that federal aid is needed. Available with lecture guide from the National Education Association, Washington, D.C.

[14] In this unit and subsequent ones are found lists of audio-visual aids, including films, filmstrips, slides, radio scripts, and recordings. They may be rented usually from several distributors, but only one is indicated here. A printed or mimeographed syllabus in pamphlet form accompanies some audio-visual aids as an outline for study. Unless otherwise indicated, the films are black and white and 16 mm.

STATE SYSTEMS OF EDUCATION

The adoption of the Tenth Amendment to the national Constitution made education primarily a state function. Although this power may be delegated in part to lower units, the state serves as the chief centralizing agency for public education. Including the territories and dependencies, the United States has a large variety of individual state school systems.

With a few exceptions, all states have a central board of education. Its duties vary with the state constitution and statutes. This agency is usually supplemented by other educational and semieducational boards.

The chief school officer in each state is the superintendent or commissioner of education. His manifold duties and close relationships with others present him with opportunities for varied and vital leadership.

The state department of education, under the superintendent, consists of a well-organized staff of professional and nonprofessional workers.

In cooperation with laymen and educators, the state board of education, the superintendent, and his staff seek to develop a state program of education.

OUTLINE OF CONTENTS

Introduction
    Education primarily a state function
    Evolution of state education
    Role of state education
    State organization and administration
State Boards of Education
    Evolution of state boards of education
    Selection of boards of education
    Qualifications of state board members
    Duties of state boards
    Other state educational boards
State Superintendents and Commissioners
    Evolution of state superintendencies
    Selection of chief educational officer
    Qualifications and term of office
    Duties of state superintendents
    Superintendent's relationships with others
State Departments of Education
    Evolution of state departments
    Organization of state departments
    State staff personnel
State Programs of Education
    Elements in state-wide programs
    State surveys of education
    Cooperative state-wide long-term planning

STATE SYSTEMS OF EDUCATION

In a letter to General Breckenridge in 1821, Thomas Jefferson said of the schools which he envisioned for the state of Virginia: "Let us keep our eye steadily on the whole system." Jefferson saw the need for a system of public education in Virginia so organized and coordinated that the elementary schools and the institutions of higher learning could "go hand in hand forever." This challenge has been met in part by the various states through the establishment of state-wide educational systems.

Education Primarily a State Function.[1] According to the Tenth Amendment to the Constitution, ratified in 1791: "The powers not delegated to the United States by the constitution, nor prohibited by it to the states, are reserved to the states respectively, or to the people." By implication, therefore, education, one of the unmentioned powers thus reserved, is a state function. Judge-made laws in the form of numerous court decisions bear out this inference. It must be recalled that many states existed before the national government came into being and that, when the states formed a federated union, they surrendered but a portion of their sovereign rights to the central government.

More evidence that education is a function of the individual states is found in the provisions of the so-called G.I. bills, in which Congress specified that only the individual states can decide what schools, colleges, or employers are qualified to train veterans receiving money from the federal government.

Early and recent history, physical and human geography, political science, and practical prudence postulate that the state must be the most powerful factor in implementing American public education. Of course the federal government may "promote the general welfare" and may contract with the states. It may, indeed, establish and support schools or offer contributions in aid of such education; but its legal status seems to be that of an outside or private party contracting with the state, for it may not levy upon state property for the support of such schools, nor may it attempt to guide the state-approved machinery in their administration. The federal government has, however, enforced certain stipulations regarding the use of the land which it gave to the states and has exercised control over vocational agriculture and home economics instruction through the granting of land and funds. These functions it has acquired gradually with the cooperation of the states. Collectively the state systems are the educational lifeblood of America.

[1] National Council of Chief State School Officers, *Our System of Education,* p. 17, 1951.

Since education is a responsibility of the various commonwealths, its control is said to be decentralized. Obviously the absence of a strong centralizing agency does not promote uniformity among the states, and certainly not within the states. Although the power to enact laws may be centered in the state government, the administration of such laws may be decentralized in that they are enforced by scores of county and local superintendents and boards of education. Dissimilarity, the most striking characteristic of the state school systems, naturally produces marked inequalities.

Evolution of State Education. Even earlier than the national Constitution, the principles of public education had developed in some Eastern states.

Early in the seventeenth century educational legislation was already formulated in Connecticut and Massachusetts. Before the end of the century Pennsylvania, New Jersey, and Maryland had established the beginnings of state systems of education. . . . The history of the beginnings of American education in all the states shows that local cooperative effort paved the way, laying the foundation which made state legislation necessary.[2]

The first provisional constitution of Pennsylvania in 1776 contained this item, which may be of interest today to teachers who complain about low salaries: "A school or schools shall be established in each county by the legislature for the correct instruction of youth, with such salaries paid to the master by the public as may enable them to instruct youth at low prices, and all useful learning should be duly encouraged and promoted in one or more universities." Although most early state constitutions were as silent on education as was the national Constitution, some of them did provide expressly for the education of the "poor." For example, the Pennsylvania constitution of 1790 stated: "The legislature shall, as soon as conveniently may be, provide for the establishment of schools throughout the state in such manner that the poor may be taught gratis." A school system free to paupers gradually developed into a public school free to all.

Most states have general constitutional provisions for the establishing of schools. A typical statement is Article XII from the constitution of Rhode Island, part of which reads: "The diffusion of knowledge, as well as of virtue, among the people, being essential to the preservation of their rights and liberties, it shall be the duty of the general assembly to promote public schools, and to adopt all means which they may deem necessary and proper to secure to the people the advantages and opportunities

2 S. T. Dutton and D. Snedden, *The Administration of Public Education in the United States,* p. 56, Macmillan, 1908.

of education." Some state constitutions contain very specific sections on education; usually, however, under a general mandate, the legislature, reinforced by the courts, determines the organization and administration of the schools.

Role of State Education. From his long experience F. P. Graves, former New York State Commissioner of Education, concluded that the state administrative agency should render the educational opportunities of the state more effective by holding the local communities up to a high standard of attainment and by encouraging them to rise above this level through new achievements:

> Of the two varieties of service—compulsion and stimulation—the latter is far the more lasting and valuable. The state department of education should seek to be a counselor rather than a bureaucrat, and its main efforts should be devoted to constructive service and professional leadership. It is a happy development of the twentieth century to place the emphasis in state control upon functional rather than structural achievement.[3]

As to the function of the state in education, the National Council of Chief State School Officers recommends that the state coordinate all education within its borders; determine the extent and quality of the foundation program; establish minimum standards; prepare a plan of financial support; develop, evaluate, and adapt plans; cooperate in a system of uniform records and reports; provide consultative services; administer programs made available by the federal government; promote equality of educational opportunity for all; utilize local, state, and national resources; and help plan, produce, and approve educational materials.[4] In order that the state program may function, the work must be organized properly.

State Organization and Administration. No state has undertaken to administer and supervise public education directly through constitutional provisions or legislative action; instead, each one has delegated at least some of these responsibilities to state or institutional boards. Although a state board of education is general, the powers and duties of these boards differ markedly. One central agency or several boards may be in charge of public schools and other educational institutions, as explained later.

The usual pattern consists of (1) the state board of education, which is the policy-making body, (2) the state superintendent of public instruction, who is the chief executive of the board, and (3) the state department of

---

[3] F. P. Graves, *The Administration of American Education*, pp. 557–558, Macmillan, 1932.

[4] National Council of Chief State School Officers, *op. cit.*, pp. 17–19.

education with its staff members, who carry out the policies of the board of education under the immediate direction of the superintendent. Together these three forces are responsible for developing a state program of education.

STATE BOARDS OF EDUCATION

In order to develop a broad program of education, the state had to create an agency through which it could act. Just as a local community has a board of education to determine policies to be carried out by its chief executive officer, as discussed in Unit IV, so too the state has a central body to plan for education.

But for more than a century and a half after the Massachusetts law of 1647, by which public schools were first required in all communities, this state agency, now considered so essential, was not anywhere established because of the fear that autocracy would result from such a centralization of authority and power. It was only in the course of time that the evolution of permanent "literary" funds, state taxation for education, and a body of school law made a definite organization necessary.[5]

As a result, either state boards of education or state school officials, or both, came into being.

Evolution of State Boards of Education

Of the beginnings of state boards of education, F. P. Graves wrote:

Looking first to the state school board, we find that the earliest foundation was that of the Board of Regents for New York in 1784. To this body was granted supervision over collegiate and academic education throughout the state, and the institutions incorporated under its control have ever since been jointly known as the University of the State of New York. There was no other state board organized until 1825, when North Carolina created a body known as the President and Directors of the Literary (or permanent school) Fund. Other boards were then started in various states for special purposes, but not until Massachusetts established its State Board of Education in 1837 were many powers and duties assigned to any of them.[6]

The bill for establishing this important board in Massachusetts was written by James G. Carter, a staunch friend of better schools, and was officially signed by Horace Mann, who was then president of the senate. The act called for a board of ten members, consisting of the governor and the lieutenant governor as ex officio members, and eight additional persons to be appointed by the governor with the consent of the council. Upon the official announcement of the membership of the board, Horace Mann, one of the appointees, who sensed its importance in Massachusetts

---

[5] Graves, *op. cit.,* p. 535.
[6] *Ibid.,* pp. 535–536.

and its potential influence throughout the land, wrote in his diary under the date of May 27, 1837:

This I believe to be like a spring, almost imperceptible, flowing from the highest table land, between oceans, which is destined to deepen and widen as it descends, diffusing fertility and beauty in its course; and nations shall dwell upon its banks. It is the first great movement toward an organized system of common education, which shall at once be thorough and universal. Every civi-

Fɪɢ. 2-1. Horace Mann. He was one of the educators honored in a series of commemorative stamps. He earned this honor by spearheading the "common-school revival." (*From daguerreotype owned by E. I. F. Williams and used as frontispiece in his Horace Mann, Educational Statesman, Macmillan, 1937.*)

lized state is as imperfectly organized, without a minister or secretary of instruction, as it would be without ministers or secretaries of State, Finance, War or the Navy.[7]

This board was empowered to appoint a secretary and to fix a reasonable salary, not to exceed $1000 a year, which was increased in 1838 to $1500. Although he did not seek the office, Horace Mann was appointed the first secretary. On the day he communicated his acceptance, he wrote in his journal: "Henceforth so long as I hold this office I devote myself to the supremest welfare of mankind upon earth. An inconceivably great labor is undertaken. With the highest degree of prosperity, results will mani-

[7] Mary Peabody Mann, *Life of Horace Mann* (centennial edition), p. 72, National Education Association, 1937.

fest themselves but slowly. The harvest is far from the seedtime." [8] From the perspective of a hundred and more years, it is easy to see that the pioneering efforts of the inspired and indefatigable Horace Mann as secretary of the state board in Massachusetts rightfully earned him the title, "father of public-school education." [9] Other leaders, such as Henry Barnard, DeWitt Clinton, Thaddeus Stevens, Caleb Mills, and John Swett, also helped to develop American public education through their harmonious and productive relationships with state agencies.

Today all but three states—Illinois, North Dakota, and Wisconsin—have made legal provisions for the equivalent of a state board of education, usually designated as such, although variations in nomenclature exist.

States with and without a State Board of Education. W. G. Reeder distinguishes two types of state boards of education: "(1) those special boards which have control and supervision over limited and separate phases of education; and (2) those state boards which possess at least some control and supervision over the elementary- and secondary-school systems of the state." [10] Every commonwealth in the United States has the first type, dealing with special aspects of education. For example, the federal government required some type of state board before it would grant aid for vocational education. Some states have special boards which deal with a limited area of education, such as a selected phase of higher education, the state teachers colleges (Illinois).

The second type, with some control and supervision of elementary- and secondary-school systems, is organized in nearly all the commonwealths. Some of these states have had such a board for years, whereas a few are of very recent origin.

Why a State Board of Education? For the same reasons that the county and local school systems need a board of education, the state as a whole should maintain such a group. This board, as the chief educational authority, helps to develop policies and programs for the state department of education.[11] The type of board determines in a measure the nature of its long-term and short-term planning.

SELECTION OF BOARDS OF EDUCATION

The major modes of determining membership on the state boards of education are by (1) ex officio status, (2) election, and (3) appointment.

[8] *Ibid.,* pp. 80–81.

[9] Further information on Horace Mann is found in Louise Hall Tharp's *Until Victory, Horace Mann and Mary Peabody,* Little, Brown, 1953, 367 pp.

[10] W. G. Reeder, *The State Board and State Department of Education,* p. 5, Ohio Education Association, 1939.

[11] National Council of Chief State School Officers, *op. cit.,* p. 20.

Ex Officio Members. These persons hold other state offices and because of that status are automatically members of the board of education. The state superintendent usually holds such membership. In one-third of the states the governor, by virtue of his high office, serves as a member of one

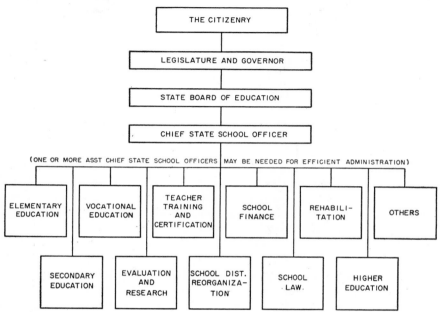

Fig. 2-2. Proposed organization for implementing state responsibility for education. A model state department of education organized on a sound administrative basis is a workable organization whose authority stems from the people, through the legislature and governor, to a single state board of education. A consensus of educational authorities is that the chief state school officer should be chosen by the board to act as its executive officer. He, in turn, should choose, with the approval of the board, the directors of the various divisions. These administrators would be directly responsible to the chief state school officer, while he in turn would answer to the state board of education, which would report directly to the governor and the legislature. Coordinated administration from kindergarten through higher education is the goal. (*From Responsibility of the States in Education—The Fourth R, p. 8, Chamber of Commerce of the United States,* 1947.)

or more governing boards in education, including the state board. Florida has its entire board membership ex officio. The trend over the past fifty years has been away from boards wholly or chiefly ex officio.

Elected Boards. In some states boards are elected. For example, in Texas members are chosen by popular vote—one for each United States Congressional district. Utah was the first state in which local school-board members, assembled in convention, selected the state-board members.

Appointed Boards. Usually all or the majority of the central board of education are appointed. All are appointed in New York by the legislature; in Wyoming, by the state superintendent of public instruction with the approval of the governor.

Recommended Procedures. The Problems and Policies Committee and the Educational Policies Commission recommend "the appointment by the governor or election by popular vote of a state board of education of outstanding citizens of broad vision to replace the ineffective ex officio state boards which exist in some states." Election is recommended by the National Council of Chief State School Officers. In the model organization recommended by the United States Chamber of Commerce, "authority stems from the people through the legislature and governor to a single board of education" (Fig. 2-2).

QUALIFICATIONS OF STATE BOARD MEMBERS

The question of professional qualifications of board members is a controversial one. There are those who insist that the board be composed entirely of laymen. A few states require that some of the members be educators. Most states omit any specific reference to professional qualifications as a prerequisite to board membership.

A qualifying clause in a few states where members are appointed is that "different parts of the state shall be represented." In Wyoming "not more than four members of such board shall be from one political party." That state adds the important general qualifications, which should be applied everywhere, that the members "shall be appointed solely because of their character and fitness. All members of the board shall be persons of mature years, known for integrity, culture, public spirit, business ability, and interest in public education." The National Council of Chief State School Officers recommends that "the non-partisan lay state board be composed of 7 to 12 able citizens, broadly representative of the general public and unselfishly interested in public education." [12] The legal qualifications for members of the state board of education take on significance only as public-spirited citizens demand the best.

DUTIES OF STATE BOARDS

A state may have many boards for specific educational purposes. In most instances, however, the major educational responsibilities are assigned to one central agency which is usually the general state board of education. Originally its chief task was the distribution of state "literary" funds and kindred duties. Today this board is invested with greatly enlarged powers, including the general oversight of the entire state public-school system. Like the school board in the local district, it is usually the

[12] *Ibid.*

policy-forming body, "determining state educational policies within the statutory framework provided by the legislature." [13] Its major task in some states is the appointment of a state superintendent who serves as the chief executive officer of the board. Like city boards, it also makes appointments recommended by the superintendent and approves budgets prepared by him.

OTHER STATE EDUCATIONAL BOARDS

Many commonwealths assign to bodies other than the state board of education the various aspects of the educational program. Among the several hundred state educational boards are: the textbook commission, which selects textbooks to be used in schools throughout the state; the board of trustees or regents, which manages the state university; the teachers college board, which presides over the affairs of the state teachers colleges; the board or boards of control, which have charge of one or more institutions of higher learning; the board for vocational rehabilitation, which collaborates with the federal board in reestablishing in industry persons injured or otherwise handicapped; the board for vocational education, which works with the federal government especially in promoting Smith-Hughes activities; the board of examiners, which prepares and conducts examinations for teachers seeking to be certified; the retirement or pension board, which collects the receipts and controls the distributions for teachers' pensions; and the board of charities and corrections, which takes charge of and provides for the proper training of feeble-minded, deaf, blind, crippled, and other handicapped persons.

In recent years one notes a tendency toward reducing the number of ancillary state boards and centralizing the control of educational affairs in the hands of a single state board of education, which has general supervision of all the schools. This may be supplemented by another board, which has charge of the institutions of higher learning in the state. One also detects a trend toward making the state superintendent the coordinator of all educational activities in the commonwealth.

STATE SUPERINTENDENTS AND COMMISSIONERS

In several instances the president or secretary of the state board of education is the chief educational executive of the state. The evolution of this central office often antedated that of the state board of education.

EVOLUTION OF STATE SUPERINTENDENCIES

Historically and professionally, instruction preceded administration. In the earliest schools there were only pupils and teachers—no administrators. Then slowly evolved the procession and profession of educa-

[13] *Ibid.*

tional administration. The establishment of city superintendencies was preceded by the creation of a chief state official for education.

New York was the first state (1812) to have a state school officer, but the first continuous office of the kind was established in Michigan in 1829. The example of the Massachusetts State Board of Education in engaging Horace Mann as its secretary in 1837 exerted a great deal of influence.[14]

Even before the Civil War each state employed a chief school officer, designated by various titles. In 1913 Delaware reestablished the office after abandoning it for a quarter of a century. Since then all states have had the office as a separate and continuous one.[15]

The most common designation is "state superintendent of public instruction." The term "commissioner of education" is also widely used, especially in the Eastern states. Wyoming has both a state superintendent of public instruction and a commissioner of education. The former is elected and is entrusted with the general supervision of the public schools; the latter is appointed by the state board of education and is charged with executing the educational policies of the state board of education under the general supervision of the superintendent.

Nomenclature and practices differ decidedly between states. For example, in California the chief official is designated the "superintendent of public instruction and director of education," whereas in Illinois these two offices are separated. The superintendent of public instruction, an elected person, heads the state school system, and another official, the director of education and registration, an appointee of the governor, directs the registration of barbers, beauty parlor operators, and others. A title in harmony with the concept of public *education* rather than mere *schooling* is that used by Louisiana, *viz.*, "state superintendent of public education." In line with the trend toward cooperation among educational agencies—public, private, and parochial—the term "state superintendent (commissioner) of education" seems the best. The name, however, is not so significant as the manner in which the official is selected and his qualifications for the all-important task of providing strong educational leadership in the state.

SELECTION OF CHIEF EDUCATIONAL OFFICER

Three practices in the selection of the chief state school official are (1) popular election, (2) appointment by the governor, and (3) appointment by the state board of education.

Popular Election. It is unfortunate that in the majority of states the chief school officer is elected by popular vote. In a recent caucus, one

14 W. A. Cook, *Federal and State Administration*, p. 142, Crowell, 1927.
15 Reeder, *op. cit.*, p. 16.

political party selected its candidate for state superintendent on the basis of geography, since the political leaders wanted their candidates for the various offices to be distributed throughout the state. Many a state superintendent in office has to spend his energy, during the latter part of each term, building political fences for reelection. He is likely to think more of the next election than of the next generation.

Appointment by Governor. This method of selecting the chief state school official is employed in a few states. Opinion may be divided as to whether the state board of education should be elected by popular vote or appointed by the governor, but the preponderance of expert opinion is against the appointment of the state superintendent by the governor.

Appointment by State Board of Education. The third method is the best—appointment, but by the state board of education. Appointment by the state board has its disadvantages, of course; no system will work perfectly because of the human element involved. It is better, however, that the important office of state superintendent of public instruction should depend on selection by a few interested competent persons on an official board of education rather than on party election by a large populace. Upon this board devolves the responsibility of choosing the best qualified man or woman as state superintendent or commissioner.

QUALIFICATIONS AND TERM OF OFFICE

The qualifications and term of office of the chief educational official, like those of other officeholders, are usually stipulated specifically in the laws, although in a few cases, where the board of education appoints the state superintendent, the board is given some latitude.

Qualifications. An example from the school laws of Maryland indicates the general tenor of the requirements for the state superintendent:

He shall be an experienced and competent educator; a graduate of a standard college, have not less than two years of specific academic and professional graduate preparation in a standard university, and not less than seven years' experience in teaching and administration.

Most legal definitions of qualifications are general, and rightly so; however, they should be specific enough to provide a pattern by which the electors, or the group or person selecting the superintendent, may be guided in the quest for the most competent person. Usually a master's degree is the minimum academic preparation.

Term of Office, Tenure, and Salary. The median legal term of office for the superintendent or commissioner is between 3 and 4 years. The specified term may be as short as 1 year, and as long as 6 years, and in a few states tenure is indefinite in the sense that the incumbent serves as long as his work is satisfactory to the appointing agency. The length of time in office averages about 5 or 6 years, with a resultant high degree of turnover. This is due partly to the political manner in which the superintendent is elected or selected, and occasionally to the legal stipulation that an incumbent is inelegible to reelection after serving a few years. Tenure is longer when the superintendent is appointed by the state board than when he is elected or appointed gubernatorially. Sound educational administration suggests that the term of office be many years, subject to the best judgment of the state board, in order to ensure continuity in policy and staff personnel. Furthermore, the salary must be commensurate with the importance and labors of the office. Many cities pay their local superintendents more than the state gives its chief educational official. Naturally this does not draw the best talent into the state office.

Duties of State Superintendents

Most duties of the state superintendents fall into a few main categories: statistical—compiling data on the schools of the state; advisory and judicial—giving advice to school boards and county superintendents, and interpreting the laws; supervisory—promoting means for improving the schools and instruction; administrative—distributing state monies and certificating teachers; integrative—attending meetings of various state boards and coalescing the various educational elements in the state; and special—such as filling vacancies in county superintendencies.

Superintendent's Relationships with Others

A state superintendent may be talented, well educated, and industrious and yet not be a success in office because of his inability to work and get along with others. He needs to be able and willing to confer with officials from other states, to integrate the disparate efforts of the numerous educational workers within the state, and to cooperate with his subordinates.

Nation-wide Relationships. No state can exist by itself economically, nor can it do so educationally. The state superintendent therefore seeks to learn from other departments of education and to pool his interests and achievements with others. To this end he affiliates himself with other state superintendents and commissioners in their national organization, the National Council of Chief State School Officers. Occasionally he and other officials may be called by the United States Commissioner of Education into conference on nation-wide problems, as shown in Unit I. As indicated in Fig. 1-1, which prefaces Part I of this volume, the state superintendent is connected with the United States Office of Education, to which he sends statistics and other data and from which he receives federal grants for vocational education and other assistance.

State-wide Relationships. The state superintendent also has important working relationships within the state he serves. First of all comes his relationship to the state board of education, if such a board exists. Usually the superintendent serves as secretary or president, or at least as an ex officio member. He may also belong to other state boards, which have numerous educational and semieducational duties. Here, serving as a coordinator, he tries to integrate the work of all the boards. He comes into close contact with many other state officials in the health, highway, safety, buildings, legal, and other departments, and with the officers of the state education association.

County and Local Relationships. Naturally the state superintendent, in the hierarchic form of organization, can demand that certain duties be fulfilled by subordinates. In a sense the county superintendent of schools is a member of the state department, representing it in dealing with the local boards of his county. Many a state commissioner calls an annual conference of all county superintendents and local school directors to promote better relationships and to improve the schools. Naturally the state superintendent will have to depend largely on his headquarters staff to represent him in many of these vital relationships.

STATE DEPARTMENTS OF EDUCATION

EVOLUTION OF STATE DEPARTMENTS

In the days when Gideon Hawley was the state superintendent of schools in New York, and Horace Mann the secretary of the state board of education in Massachusetts, each was the state department of education. But, as the concept of the state's function in education broadened, no single official, even in a small commonwealth, could handle all the work; gradually there was an increase in staff personnel. As late as 1890, however, the median number of staff members was only two. After 1917 came a rapid growth in department personnel owing to three major causes: the new duties devolving upon the department as a result of the passage of the Smith-Hughes vocational education law; the startling revelations from physical, mental, and literacy tests administered during the First World War; and the growing appreciation of the need for a strong state program of education to meet present-day needs. Today every state provides its chief school officer with an organization and staff, usually known as the state department of education. This department is not to be confused with the state board of education. For example, Wisconsin has no state board of education, but has a department of education under the direction of the commissioner of education. A state department can operate without a state board, but not vice versa.

ORGANIZATION OF STATE DEPARTMENTS

At the head of this department is the state superintendent or commissioner of education. Next in line are the first assistant state superintendent or associate commissioner, the other assistants, supervisors, and staff members.

FIG. 2-3. California State Education Building, Sacramento. This building, housing all the headquarters offices, was erected exclusively for the state department of education. (*Courtesy of State Superintendent of Public Instruction, California.*)

Examples of Internal Organization. The state department suggested in Fig. 2-2 may be taken as one example of a functional organization. Portrayed are the divisions of the state department, stemming from the citizenry, the legislature and governor, and the state board of education, and operating under the guidance of the chief state school officer.

Many state departments have been reorganized to meet the challenges of modern developments. For example, California consolidated its Department of Education by creating five new divisions as follows: department administration; public-school organization, administration, and finance; instruction; teacher education; and state special schools and services. The other divisions of libraries (state library) and of schoolhouse planning had been previously created by special law.

Housing of Department. The department of education is usually located in the state capital and housed in the capitol building. With the increasing complexity of their work and the numerous additions to their staff, most departments are cramped in small quarters designed many years ago. In large states a separate building houses the state superintendent, his assistants, and other members of the staff. New York, the first to have a state superintendent of schools, in the person of Gideon Hawley, was also the first to erect a building for education. "Central schoolhouses," such as those in Sacramento, Harrisburg, and Albany, are needed in other states.

STATE STAFF PERSONNEL

Function of the State Staff. The staff members of the department of education are not mere machine operators; they are educational servants. Their functions may be classified under three major headings: (1) regulatory, (2) operational, and (3) leadership.[16] In order to perform these duties state departments have generalists and specialists.

Personnel and Activities. The staff of the state department may be divided into two main types according to professional training:

> These may be roughly designated as the professional and the nonprofessional groups, although such a discrimination is somewhat arbitrary and at times inconsistent. Generally speaking, the former group would include all officers whose activities are related to the executive, administrative, supervisory and research phases of education; and the latter, all clerks, stenographers, draftsmen, messengers, and similar employees.[17]

These groups are usually assigned specific tasks in terms of qualifications and experience.

The personnel of the department should be employed by the state board of education upon nomination by the chief state school officer. All appointments should be made on the basis of merit and fitness for the work. The state department should be adequately staffed to provide all needed services.

Each year the federal Office of Education, through the Superintendent of Documents, publishes a list of all the principal state school officers.[18] More than one hundred different services are reflected in their official designation.

In all areas of service the three main functions of state departments are implemented with appropriate activities:

> *Regulatory.* This broad function involves three types of activities: development of standards, rules, and regulation; examination and inspection to determine compliance; and instigation, where necessary, of compliance procedures.

[16] Fred F. Beach, *The Functions of State Departments of Education*, p. 3, GPO, 1950.
[17] Graves, *op. cit.*, p. 552.
[18] *Educational Directory: State and County School Officers*, Part I, GPO, published annually.

Operational. Among the direct operational activities of these departments in some states are the supervision of: teachers colleges, trade schools, schools for handicapped, adult education classes, and other miscellaneous programs.

Leadership. Creative leadership, the key to the door of the state department, stimulates: long-range planning and professional leadership, highly competent consultative and advisory services, leadership in research, coordination of the educational programs of the state, and maintenance of a vigorous public relations for the state educational program.[19]

Many groups, including the Hoover Commission on Organization of the Executive Branch of the Government, have favored special grants for the administration of state departments of education. Unless the state departments are given more financial assistance than they have received in the past, they cannot do their part in developing broad programs of education.

STATE PROGRAMS OF EDUCATION

Units III and IV emphasize the important role played by the educational subdivisions within the state. However, in a hierarchic form of organization, authority flows from the head or source. Upon the individual state, therefore, rests the grave responsibility of developing a program of instruction for all its people. Supreme Court decisions reinforce constitutional and legislative provisions for establishing state programs of education.

Each commonwealth is faced with the direct responsibility of organizing and promoting a functional state-wide system of public education which should extend from kindergarten through college and adult life. In the development of this program, certain principles or procedures ought to be adopted as a tentative guide. In line with these principles, under the direction of the state department, all the people and agencies of the state participate in developing the plans.

ELEMENTS IN STATE-WIDE PROGRAMS

Many basic ingredients make up a state program of education. A few of these are presented here with illustrative material.

Development of Educational Goals. Many leaders have relied too heavily upon educational machinery and have not given sufficient thought to educational policies. These policies or philosophies should underlie all education. Several states have worked out basic goals, as for example, the Goals of Education, developed by the Michigan Public Education Study Commission.

Construction of a Foundation Program. The translation of the educational goals into daily practice necessitates a state foundation program.

[19] American Association of School Administrators, *The American School Superintendency*, pp. 341–342, National Education Association, 1952.

Such a plan, often known as the state's minimum program, consists of a careful formulation of minimal essentials for local communities, and a raising of such requirements from time to time as resources and conditions permit.

The Council of State Governments listed the following six essentials for the sound administration and operation of state school systems:

1. Provision for systematically obtaining and studying the facts as a basis for policy decisions.

2. A state policy-making agency for education through which the will of the people may be voiced and the interests of the state protected.

3. Local administrative units of sufficient size to promote effective local control and to provide appropriate educational opportunities at a reasonable cost.

4. Provisions calculated to assure high-quality professional leadership for both state and local agencies.

5. Conditions conducive to maintaining well-qualified staffs of teachers for all phases of elementary and secondary education.

6. A system of financing that will provide sufficient funds and distribute them in such a way as to assure adequate educational opportunities for all and to encourage both sound administration and a high degree of local initiative.[20]

The evidence in the council's report seems to indicate that several states have fallen short in nearly all these essentials, and that all states are falling short to some extent in at least one. Items 3 and 5 are often Achilles' heels.

Reorganization of Local Administration.[21] The effective working of a foundation program often calls for the reorganization of administrative areas, as indicated in Unit III. Helpful principles and procedures are found in the report of the National Commission on School District Reorganization.[22]

State Financial Support. A problem basic to both the realignment of administrative units and the development of a stable state-wide program of education is that of financial support, considered in detail in Unit XVI. The National Survey of School Finance, in an appraisal of state-aid systems, found that not a single state had attained a desirable status with respect to the financing of public education. Nowhere, however, is the entire burden of school support left to the local school districts; the relative amount of the total cost borne by the state treasury varies from less than 6 to over 90 per cent. Delaware adopted in 1921 the policy of paying for the entire state-approved cost of all public schools. The general plan of paying for the foundation program with funds derived from state-wide

20 Council of State Goverments, *The Forty-eight State School Systems*, p. 7, 1947.
21 For additional information on minimal standards for schools, see Unit III.
22 National Commission on School District Reorganization, *Your School District*, National Education Association, Department of Rural Education, 1948, 286 pp.

sources was followed by North Carolina (1931), West Virginia (1933), and numerous other states.

A marked trend in the financing of education in recent years has been the establishment of a fund for equalizing the educational opportunities and burden within the state. These funds, discussed in Unit XVI, are based on the important principle of collecting the school money where it is and distributing it where the pupils are. The establishing of an equalization fund which is scientifically sound and administratively feasible demands a searching survey of the educational needs, a careful estimate of the costs, and an accurate analysis of the ability of the state to support education and other activities.

STATE SURVEYS OF EDUCATION

Many revised educational programs have originated in a state survey which calls specific attention to the basic need for complete reorganization of the archaic district systems as the initial step toward developing better schools. Helpful check lists and handbooks for a self-survey plan for school systems have been prepared. All phases of state-wide education should be subjected to close analysis in order to determine both the *status in quo* and the distance to be traveled in order to reach minimum standards. The state department of education may well help schoolmen and laymen to conduct resurveys and develop continuous self-surveys. The governors of the various commonwealths, assembled in the Council of State Governments, agreed that "education of the youth of the land is one of the fundamental duties of government, and . . . the provision of adequate and efficient machinery for that purpose is one of the principal costs of government." It therefore launched a series of studies of education—the first ever to be conducted by an agency of all the states in the Union. Utilization of the survey data and recommendations is important. Most reports, prepared by dint of much effort and expense, collect annual layers of dust upon obscure shelves. Occasionally the results are interpreted in public meetings and discussions throughout the state. The acid test of a satisfactory survey is its implementation through an improved program of education for all.

COOPERATIVE STATE-WIDE LONG-TERM PLANNING

In developing these programs, many agencies other than the state school officials exercise a tremendous power. The educational associations through their committees, the presidents of institutions of higher learning, the county superintendents, the association of school-board members, the parent-teacher association, the women's and businessmen's groups— these and many others help to prepare the way. For example, many agencies interested in public education are represented in the Florida Citizens Committee on Education and the Mississippi Citizens Council on Education.

Unfortunately there is a large amount of duplication and lost motion in an eccentric program. More scientific and concentric methods are needed if state systems are to be rescued from the doldrums of short-lived planning. All states must have a long-term planning commission to plot the course for education and other social services for years to come. Several states, beginning with Kansas in 1933, have established a legislative commission that drafts model laws and recommends changes to the legislatures. Education laws in the various states should have a greater degree of uniformity.

A state program for the continuous development of education, like any worth-while reform, calls for four basic steps: education, agitation, legislation, and dedication. Education of school people and laymen as to the need for progress requires months and years devoted to local, state-wide, and national programs of study and analysis. Agitation for change should not precede educating the public and the legislature but should either follow or accompany it. Legislation is not the final goal, for it does not guarantee successful educational results. Dedication to the perennial problems of school improvement will pave the way for state-wide and national progress in education.

SUGGESTED ACTIVITIES

1. Discuss the implications for education in the Tenth Amendment to the United States Constitution.

2. Prepare an interesting biography of Horace Mann, the first secretary of the Massachusetts State Board of Education. Similar reports may be made about Henry Barnard, Thaddeus Stevens, Caleb Mills, John Swett, and John D. Pierce.

3. Review the lives and works of persons who helped develop education in your state.

4. Collect statistics for your state, such as the total number of school districts and elementary and secondary teachers.

5. Consult the latest catalogues of your state-supported institutions of higher learning for information as to their functions and control.

6. Draw an organization diagram of your state, showing the educational boards and the relationships that exist between them.

7. Find out the following in regard to your state superintendent of education: term of office, qualifications, salary, and duties.

8. Debate the issue: "Resolved that the office of state superintendent should be appointive rather than elective."

9. Examine the last annual report of your state superintendent of public instruction.

10. Visit a state department of education and make a diagram of its organization.

11. Secure a member of the state department of education as a special speaker for the class or a group of classes.

12. Make an exhibit of recent educational publications issued by the state office.

13. Discuss the desirability of state adoption of textbooks for all schools.

14. Define what is meant by a foundation or minimum program for a state.

DESCRIPTIVE BIBLIOGRAPHY AND AIDS

BOOKS

ALLEN, H. K., and RICHARD G. AXT: *State Public Finance and State Institutions of Higher Education in the United States,* Chap. VIII, Columbia University Press, 1952.

> Conclusions of the Commission on Financing Higher Education.

AMERICAN ASSOCIATION OF SCHOOL ADMINISTRATORS: *The American School Superintendency,* Chap. XIII, National Education Association, 1952.

> Educational leadership at the state level.

BEACH, FRED F.: *The Functions of State Departments of Education,* GPO, 1950, 70 pp.

> An inventory of the services provided by the 48 state departments of education.

EDUCATIONAL POLICIES COMMISSION: *Education for All American Youth: A Further Look,* Chap. V, National Education Association, 1952.

> Description of how the hypothetical state of Columbia assures the adequate education of all its youth.

GRIEDER, CALVIN, and WILLIAM EVERETT ROSENTENGEL: *Public School Administration,* Chap. II, Ronald, 1954.

> The state's role in school administration.

MOEHLMAN, ARTHUR B.: *School Administration,* Part IV, Houghton Mifflin, 1951.

> Several chapters dealing with the state education authority.

MORPHET, EDGAR L., and ERICK L. LINDMAN: *Public School Finance Programs of the Forty-eight States,* Chaps. IV, V, GPO, 1950.

> State school provisions and analysis of state finance practices.

THARP, LOUISE HALL: *Until Victory, Horace Mann and Mary Peabody,* Chap. XIV, Little, Brown, 1953.

> "Let the next generation be my client." —Lawyer Horace Mann.

WILL, ROBERT F.: *The State Department of Education Report,* Chap. I, U.S. Department of Health, Education, and Welfare, 1953.

> Origins and changing concepts of the state departments of education reports.

CURRENT PERTINENT PERIODICALS AND PUBLICATIONS

Annual reports of state departments of education

Educational Directory, Principal State and County School Officers, Part I.

Publications of National Council of Chief State School Officers

Publications of state education associations

Publications of state superintendent

State Directory of Schools

State School Laws

State U. Newsletter

Surveys, educational

Yearbooks, state, educational

AUDIO-VISUAL AIDS

Collection of State Educational Publications

> The students and instructor can assemble an interesting and useful exhibit of various publications issued by the state department of education and the state educational association.

DESIGN OF AMERICAN EDUCATION   16 min., sound

> A text-film tailor-made for this book by McGraw-Hill. Shows the major activities of a state board of education, the state superintendent, and the state department of education. An overview of Units I–IV—the national, state, county, and local

organization for education. Pretest and follow-up filmstrip are available from the publishers.

HORACE MANN   19 min., sound
Depicts important events in the life of this educational statesman. Produced by Encyclopaedia Britannica under the direction of a Horace Mann scholar, Dr. E. I. F. Williams.

WISCONSIN MAKES ITS LAWS   30 min., sound, color
A complete photographic and sound record of how one of the 48 states makes its laws. Develops the need, passage, and test of Bill 108A—an imaginary bill to educate people to prevent forest fires. Available from University of Wisconsin, Madison, Wis.

COUNTY AND INTERMEDIATE SCHOOL UNITS

The state educational system embraces county, township, town, and local school districts. Several of these are units interposed between the state and local districts as intermediate agencies in public-school organization and administration. The intermediate unit, through leadership and service, helps children by assisting local districts and state departments.

The 3000 counties in the United States function directly and indirectly in education, although historically they are political rather than school units. The county-unit states vary in the degree of county-wide educational administration. Usually authority is vested in a county board of education and a county superintendent of schools who is elected or appointed. The best practice is appointment of a well-qualified man or woman by the board of education. In most counties the superintendent or commissioner is assisted by a staff of educators. One of the main duties of the staff is to improve rural education and thereby community living.

The usual unit of administration in the New England states is the town, which may embrace both rural and urban districts. The township high school and complete township districts are found in several states.

A local district may be a part of or identical with a large unit, such as the county, township, town, or community district.

Thousands of undersized and underprivileged school districts still struggle for existence in rural areas. But consolidation is a twentieth-century password. The second half of this century may see the number of school districts halved. Cooperation, consolidation, and coordination can enhance education for all.

OUTLINE OF CONTENTS

Introduction
   State, county, and local units
   Intermediate units
   Classification of states by types of units
County School Units
   County organization
   County superintendent of schools
   Rural education
Township and Town Units
   Township school districts
   Town school districts
Reorganization of School Administrative Areas
   Cooperation between units
   Consolidation of areas
   Coordination of administrative units

UNIT III

COUNTY AND INTERMEDIATE SCHOOL UNITS

A county superintendent in a Midwestern state described thus his varied activities in campaigning for election to office:

I was elected to the office of county superintendent of schools, with the landslide. I drove 14,000 miles in the campaign from June 1 to November 8; called on 3000 farm families and took their names and addresses; called on over 3000 city homes; gave away 17,000 personal cards and wrote cards to 2000 families. This cost me over $1200, and I won by 1650 votes. I gave an official white cane to each person in the county receiving a blind pension. After the election, I had enough people call on me trying to sell life insurance and other things to take all of my salary for the next four years if I had bought from them. For any of my fellow teachers contemplating becoming a county superintendent I submit this information.

This frank statement reveals one of the many angles in the administration of county education systems.

State, County, and Local Units. The state educational organization may include smaller administrative units, such as the county, township, town, and local school districts. Sometimes the local unit is the county, as in Maryland; or the township, as in Indiana; or a combination of types, as in Kentucky where the local districts may be "subdistricts."

Intermediate Units. In West Virginia, as indicated in Fig. 3-1, the county is the local unit. In Iowa the county is interposed between the local school district and the state. In

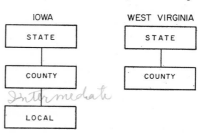

Fig. 3-1. Counties as intermediate and local units.

nearly every state an intermediate unit comes between the county and the local district. The most common area between the local and county districts is the township. A township likewise may be either an intermediate unit or the local district. Where the county or township is the local unit of school organization and administration, the area and population in the district are larger than in the typically small local school district treated in Unit IV.

On the functions and powers of the intermediate unit, the authors of *The American School Superintendency* state:

The intermediate unit exercises quite different powers from those vested in local school districts. For example, the local districts that make up the intermediate unit operate their own schools; the intermediate unit does not operate them. It does not provide the direct avenues for local initiative and local control that the basic districts provide. Instead, the intermediate unit sustains local initiative and control in the basic units by providing types of assistance needed by them to function more effectively. It does not duplicate the functions of basic units but supplements them as the intermediary between the state department of education and the local unit.[1]

According to Frank W. Cyr, professor of education at Teachers College, Columbia University, the intermediate superintendent has five major functions: adaptation, consultation, coordination, shared services, and administrative procedures.[2]

Julian E. Butterworth, former professor of rural education at Cornell University, listed the following essentials of an intermediate unit:

1. A board of education to represent the people of the intermediate district in the determination of policy for the district.

2. A superintendent fully competent to act as leader of the constituent districts and as executive officer of the board.

3. A sufficiently clear definition of functions in the state law so that the intermediate district may confidently exercise progressive leadership without fear of interfering with local boards.

4. Sufficient financial resources available to the intermediate district board to carry out its function.[3]

The intermediate unit is an important administrative and educational concept and reality in rural education. The future may see a marked development of these units to bridge the gap between local autonomy and state centralization.[4] Thus some weaknesses of consolidation will be overcome, and many benefits that accrue from a larger unit will be gained.

Classification of States by Types of Units. The types of organizations distinguished on the basis of their size and their identity with civil units are as follows, with the number of states indicated in parentheses: local district (26), town or township (9), county (12), and state (1). Figure 3-2 reveals the prevailing type of school district in each state, the one state unit being Delaware. Obviously some states have combinations of types.

[1] American Association of School Administrators, *The American School Superintendency,* p. 362, National Education Association, 1952.

[2] Frank W. Cyr, "Developing a Basic Concept of the Intermediate Superintendency," *School Executive,* November, 1953, p. 71.

[3] Adapted from Julian E. Butterworth, "Essentials of the Intermediate District," *Nation's Schools,* May, 1948, pp. 24–26.

[4] National Society for the Study of Education, *Education in Rural Communities,* p. 167, University of Chicago Press, 1952.

The total number of school districts in the United States is approximately 60,000.

The state educational organization is presented in Unit II, and the local district system in Unit IV. Between these are found the county

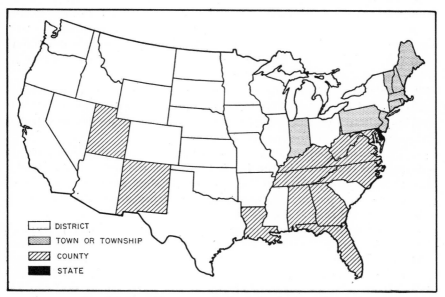

Fig. 3-2. Prevailing type of school district in each state.

and smaller school districts including the township and the town, which are all described here.

COUNTY SCHOOL UNITS

County Organization

The United States has more than 3000 counties. These vary in size from New York County, New York, with 22 square miles, to San Bernardino County, California, with 20,175; and in population from Armstrong County, South Dakota, with about 50 people, to Cook County, Illinois, with about 5,000,000.

The county is the unit for all or some school administrative functions in most states. The degree to which counties are organized for school administrative purposes correlates rather closely with the percentage of the total school revenue derived from county sources. A comparison of legislation in regard to county control of schools places the states in three groups: (1) those which in no way utilize the county as a unit of local school control; (2) those which make the town, township, or district the principal unit of control but delegate some powers to the county organization; (3) those which make the county the principal unit of control.[5]

1. The New England states use the town unit; they do not have a county board of education or county superintendent of schools. Delaware, with its three counties, is in reality a state unit, controlling its districts from the office of the state superintendent of instruction. Nevada, owing to its sparsity of population, employs deputy state superintendents who perform the work usually assigned to county superintendents in other states.

2. Most states delegate some educational activities to a county administration. For example, in Illinois, the county superintendent of schools and his assistants visit periodically the rural schools. State monies channel through the office of the county school officer.

3. The third group of states, 12 in all, is known as those with strong county units. Included in the list is Louisiana, the only state in which the schools are organized on the basis of parishes, somewhat similar to counties. In the parishes, as in the strong county units, much power is lodged with the central boards of education.

County Boards. In a few counties an over-all board of directors employs a county executive, similar to a city manager, who works with the school administrators. In most states, including those with so-called "weak" county units, usually some type of county board is in control of education. Michigan is an example of one of the states where the civil administrative board for the county, *viz.,* the board of supervisors, looks after the schools as well as the roads, the county jail, and other agencies. Thus education is only one function of the supervisors rather than their unique responsibility, as is the case with a strong county board of education. The latter is elected or appointed for the sole purpose of administering the schools, just like a single-purpose board of education in a city. Boards in strong county units have enlarged powers and duties akin to those described later for a district board of education.

County Superintendent of Schools

Evolution of County Superintendency. The development of the chief county school office has been described thus by Cubberley:

As education began to evolve into a state interest in our country, the need for developing some subordinate form of state control became evident. . . . Hence a county school officer, known as a county superintendent of education, a county school superintendent, or a county superintendent of public instruction, was gradually provided for, sometimes by amendment of or during a revision

[5] Shirley Cooper and Charles O. Fitzwater, *County School Administration,* Chap. VI, Harper, 1954.

of the constitution of the state, and sometimes by statute laws. Sometimes, too, the office was gradually evolved out of some other county office, such as auditor, or treasurer, or probate judge. In Iowa and in some of the Southern states the office evolved out of the presidency or executive officer of the county board of education, an organization which in some states preceded the county superintendency. In New York and Michigan too, the township superintendency preceded the county superintendency. The office of county superintendent of schools began about 1835, and by about 1870 was common in most of the older states. In the newer states to the west the office was frequently created in the territorial period.[6]

At first, since his tasks were clerical and statistical and required little or no professional training, the county superintendent was chosen like any other county official. Although his duties have now elevated him to the highest educational rank in the county, this important office is still a "political job" in most states.

Election or Appointment. In the majority of the states that maintain a county educational office, the county superintendent is still elected by the people at popular elections. Usually he is chosen for a 2-year term and is subject to reelection, but in one or two states he is ineligible after 4 years in office. Tenure of office is longer in states using the appointive system. The position of county superintendent is one of importance, but as long as he is elected rather than appointed, and is rewarded with a small salary, the office cannot attract the best talent in the profession.

Qualifications of County Superintendent. Most states require teaching experience and a supervisory or teaching certificate. Some add that he must be engaged in educational work and be of good character. Where the county superintendent competes for election, the *sine qua non* seems to be a master's degree in political strategy, as evidenced by the letter at the beginning of this unit. Despite the handicap of an election campaign, usually on a party ticket, many an elected county superintendent meets the necessary professional qualifications surprisingly well. His minimum professional education should be a master's degree or its equivalent; his experiential background should include teaching, especially on the elementary level; and his personal qualifications should be those innate in the successful school administrator.[7]

His Powers and Duties. The important role of the county superintendent in all the schools of the county, particularly the rural ones, is sometimes underestimated by beginning teachers and by the general public. His office is usually the channel through which flows much of the school money—the economic lifeblood of the educational system. He is often the certificating agent of the state; without his sanction no one is legally qualified to teach. As a legal representative of the state he inter-

[6] E. P. Cubberley, *Public School Administration*, pp. 45–46, Houghton Mifflin, 1929.
[7] In Unit XII the qualifications of county superintendents are considered further.

prets the school laws. He is the technical adviser to the local boards of education. He is frequently the umpire in contests between the rural schoolteacher and the board of education. He is the keyman in the movement toward larger educational units, for with his advice and consent many small districts may be absorbed into or consolidated with larger school administrative areas. He is the "kingpin" in the supervisory and

Fig. 3-3. County bookmobile. This library on wheels which brings free books and magazines to the people of Lucas County, Ohio, is especially welcomed by those in wheel chairs. (*Courtesy of National Foundation for Infantile Paralysis.*)

school accrediting program in many states. He is the direct representative of the state department of education in his county. The duties of the county superintendent vary widely from state to state. In San Diego County (California) his activities are threefold: curricular, special services, and business. In a strong county unit state where there is a county board of education, as in West Virginia, the county superintendent is the chief executive officer of the board.

County Educational Staff. The county superintendents in large areas are aided by several professional and clerical assistants, but in many small counties there is only one educational worker, *viz.*, the superintendent. Almost one-half of the county superintendents in the United

States do not have clerical help. As a result, a high-salaried man may be spending most of his time doing clerical work. Obviously this is false economy, from which the child in school suffers. In counties of medium size the usual staff consists of a deputy superintendent, attendance officer, field supervisor, clerk, and a stenographer. Most counties need a curriculum director to assist in enriching the traditional course of study. Also urgently needed are county librarians, school building consultants, *et al.*

RURAL EDUCATION

The most important duty of the county superintendent and his staff is to help rural people educationally, socially, and economically, for on their development, happiness, and prosperity the welfare of the nation depends in a large measure. Such factors as the relative number of children, the migration of population, income of farmers, farm taxes, farm homes and conveniences, decentralization of industry, and the occupational changes and expectations of rural people are of vital import to making satisfactory educational facilities available to them.

What Is Rural Education? Howard A. Dawson, director of Rural Services, National Education Association, answers thus:

> It is that part of education that serves people who live in rural environment— farmers and their village neighbors who are closely related to agriculture, the extractive occupations, and local allied industries. It is education as it is found in most small communities. It is also the education of rural children and youth even when they are transported to town or city schools.[8]

Over 40 per cent of the children in the United States live in rural areas. The quantitative and qualitative significance of their *education*—broader and deeper than mere *schooling*—is obvious, as corroborated by the yearbook, *Education in Rural Communities,* published by the National Society for the Study of Education, and in the Charter of Education for Rural Children, adopted by a White House Conference.

A Program of Education for Rural Children. The Charter of Education for Rural Children must be implemented by an appropriate program of dynamic education. Despite the recent trend toward larger units of administration, there will always be thousands of small schools. As stated by Howard A. Dawson, "Rural schools are a fundamental and indispensable means of building and maintaining in America the most glorious rural life anywhere in the world." Unfortunately many country schools have serious limitations. The teachers in rural schools generally have less academic preparation and receive lower salaries than do those in cities. The pupils lack in quality and quantity many services provided

---

[8] Howard A. Dawson, "Crucial Issues in Rural Education," *National Education Association Journal,* October, 1953, p. 441.

for their city cousins. However, the opportunities for personalized, whole-some, close-to-nature education are unlimited in rural areas. Also, in an atomic age, accompanied by decentralization of industries, more city pupils are moving closer to their country cousins and are becoming eager consumers of the real fruits of rural education.

Most rural pupils, in the words of the charter, need such special aids as "health services, educational and vocational guidance, library facilities, recreational activities, school lunches, and pupil transportation services." The County and Rural Area Superintendents Association, a division of the National Education Association, and other groups and individuals are striving to enrich and enlarge the rural services. This program raises the pertinent question of the role of the township school districts, which are smaller than the county ones.

TOWNSHIP AND TOWN UNITS

TOWNSHIP SCHOOL DISTRICTS

Organization. Civil townships, which number about 20,000 in the United States, are smaller than the county and usually larger than the towns. Advantages which the county has over the old district system in the matter of economical school administration apply also but in a lesser degree to the township area. The township school unit, as found in Indiana, New Jersey, Pennsylvania, and parts of some other states, contains more taxable wealth and more school children than the small districts.

In most states the original survey of the area within a county divided the land into townships, usually 6 miles square. The "Old Deluder" Act of 1647 ordered every township with 50 householders to appoint a teacher. Later Indiana, one of the first states to adopt this system, provided in its constitution of 1851 that each organized township should constitute a school district. At an even earlier date the township was the school district in Pennsylvania for all except city and large village schools. Many other states adopted or modified the township system for education.

A so-called township high-school district may overlap several smaller elementary-school administrative units. Since pupils of secondary-school age can travel distances better than younger children and since a smaller number of youth goes to high school than to the lower grades, the former lends itself more readily to larger unit organization than does the elementary school. Under the township system, many cities, incorporated villages, and some consolidated schools are set apart as independent school districts. When the electors of an entire township vote to centralize all their administrative functions into one unit with one board of education, as may be done in Michigan, for example, a complete township district may be created. Illinois has many township high schools. In Indiana each civil township is usually a school district.

Administration. The township district, either of the complete or partial type, is usually governed by a township board of education consisting

Fig. 3-4. Township high school and students in Illinois. This school is located at Skokie, Cook County—the most heavily populated county in the United States.

of three or more members, each of whom is elected by the voters of the entire township. The powers of the township boards vary somewhat among the states. Usually these groups have the powers and duties listed for boards of education in Unit IV, whereas the township school principal or superintendent fulfills those duties belonging to the local superintendent of schools. Both the township and town school administrators assume on a small scale some duties of a typical county superintendent.

TOWN SCHOOL DISTRICTS

Organization. The town is a New England institution, although similar subdivisions are found in New Jersey. The New England town often has natural geographic boundaries and commonly embraces a compact community center. It includes all the area within the civil unit and may cover a small city, suburban communities, villages, and rural areas. These are often designated as supervisory unions or districts.

Administration. The unit of school administration, as well as of school revenue, in New England is subject to one board of education and one administrator:

> The educational affairs of each town are managed as a unit by one town school committee, elected by the people of the whole town, and all of the schools of the town—city, village, and rural—are under its control. . . . A superintendent in Massachusetts thus presides over a small and compact school system, either a city school system or a small county system in type.[9]

For example, in Massachusetts several towns may be combined under the direction of a town school committee and a union superintendent of schools. In a town district the latter may also be entitled town and field supervisor, district superintendent, or supervising principal. The town system has produced some degree of centralization and has reduced the number of small districts which formerly prevailed. Frequently, however, the town district represents neither a natural community nor a sufficient area for either economical administration or enriched curriculums.

REORGANIZATION OF SCHOOL ADMINISTRATIVE AREAS

Public education is the direct responsibility of almost 60,000 school districts in the United States. This unnecessarily large number of administrative units may be reduced through elimination and consolidation. The eliminating of schools with few pupils and the combining of small districts, however, should be a part of a state-wide program for reform. It must constantly be borne in mind that this reorganization involves not merely land but also people, particularly children. A child-centered administrative unit in a school-centered community places the welfare of the pupil and society above administration. In consolidation, education is not to be subordinated to economy. The reconstruction of small units is necessary for a richer program of education and for the equalization of educational opportunity and financial burden.

Of course, reorganization or consolidation may create new problems for old and new districts. If the close relation of the schools to the nat-

---

[9] Cubberley, *op. cit.*, pp. 56–57.

ural community and to the people is sacrificed in the name of efficiency, then something that money cannot buy will be destroyed. Structural remodeling will not perform miracles; too many educators and laymen cherish false hopes as to what it will accomplish. Furthermore the larger school unit alone cannot solve the problem of reorganizing districts. In large cities like New York and Chicago better education might result from smaller administrative areas. Although the immediate danger is remote, the creation of larger school units may be carried so far that centralization produces more evils than decentralization.

Some specific ways of effecting changes in school administrative units are (1) voluntary cooperation between school districts, (2) legal consolidation of areas closely juxtaposed, and (3) state-wide coordination of school districts through a higher agency, *viz.*, the state department of education in each of the 48 states. The latter step should be a part of a broader movement for reorganizing all governmental units within a state. State planning commissions may well join hands in a national organization in which ideas and experiences are pooled.

COOPERATION BETWEEN UNITS

People are likely to postpone working for larger school units until legal consolidation can be effected, but active, voluntary cooperation between districts will produce immediate benefits. Even where actual consolidation may be remote or impossible, boards of education can join in common tasks without changing district boundary lines.

In St. Louis County, Missouri, several school systems cooperatively sponsor projects of mutual interest. In some counties two or more districts together employ a music teacher or a school superintendent. Another example of cooperation is the union of separate districts in collective school transportation. Another instance is the joint buying of books and supplies on a county-wide basis. This may be extended to a state-wide basis. As early as 1924, Virginia established a state purchasing office, although even today most of its counties do not have an adequate system of centralized purchasing in order to benefit by this act. In New York State a board of cooperative school services may be established by the board members of a supervisory district, with the approval of the Commissioner of Education. This board can carry out a program of shared educational services in the schools and provide instruction in approved special subjects. Furthermore, the boards of cooperative school services in any number of contiguous supervisory districts may cooperate in providing educational services. Although actual mergers have been few, adjacent counties are working jointly in many fields. Numberless educational improvements are being consummated daily throughout the United States by dint of voluntary cooperation.

CONSOLIDATION OF AREAS

The combining of two districts in Massachusetts in 1838 was the beginning of legal consolidation of school areas. Although more than one hundred years have elapsed since that consolidation, progress in this direction was very slow until the mid-century mark. Since then the tempo has been accelerated, although 60,000 separate and independent school districts still exist. Nevertheless, despite the unpleasant connotation of the words "consolidation" and "reorganization" and despite some rural resistance to larger administrative units, the "little red schoolhouse" is disappearing. Hundreds of one-room schools are advertised for sale in local newspapers; many have become family homes.

Constructive consolidation is necessary and inevitable. Reorganization laws in general have the benediction of courts. The letter of the law is reinforced by the spirit of improved service. Substantial savings, greater efficiency, and better opportunities for children and adults will result and have resulted from the adoption of larger units.

A consolidated school may come from combining attendance units within a single school district. That is, the Jefferson and Washington grade schools in a certain city may be united by the local school board. A consolidated district may result from the union of two or more administrative districts. Two types of consolidated districts are here considered briefly, *viz.,* (1) community schools and (2) regional schools.

Community Schools. These schools may be effected through voluntary cooperation or through legal consolidation. Evaluation of community school practices indicates that most of them fall into four qualitative levels of operation:

1. The first level includes efforts to make the school itself into an ideal democratic community.

2. At the second level teachers and administrators make serious efforts to relate what is learned verbally in school to what goes on in the community.

3. A third level is that of bringing objects and people from the community into the school building, and of taking children into the community.

4. A fourth level is the practice of students, teachers, administrators and lay people together attacking community problems in an effort to improve the quality of their common living.[10]

Sound structural reorganization of school districts can help promote the development of high-level community schools in which educational, social, and economic considerations predominate; arbitrary or academic concepts of size, numbers, and financial ability are contributing but distinctly recessive and secondary factors.

[10] Edward G. Olsen (ed.), *The Modern Community School,* pp. 201–203, Appleton-Century-Crofts, 1953.

Several years ago the rural school survey of New York State brought out the fact that the county is not a community in the real sense, since its boundaries bear no direct relation to church and grange centers, lines of travel, transportation, or to commercial centers. Therefore the county in many cases is too large an administrative unit for an institution so intimate to the life of the community as is the school. Practical experience in that state has shown the need for a unit smaller than the county, as proved by the creation of supervisory districts. The creation of community school units avoids the stranding of small local districts, takes full advantage of neighborhood interest and initiative, and facilitates

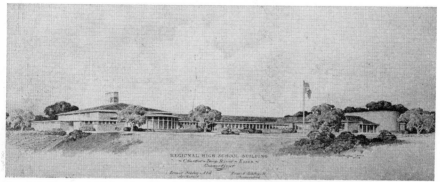

Fig. 3-5. Regional high school in Connecticut. This school serves the towns of Chester, Deep River, and Essex. (*Courtesy of Sibley and Sibley, West Hartford, Conn.*)

the eventual establishment of a larger unit, since community units can be merged as attendance areas within a more extensive system if desirable.

Regional Schools. New York State through its Board of Regents has made progress in the establishment of regional schools—large-area schools for post-high-school education of youth. The first regional high school in New England was opened at Falls Village in the town of Canaan, Connecticut. Called the Housatonic Valley Regional High School, it serves several towns. In many educational ventures the county can be a component part of a regional entity.

County government has been called our greatest national extravagance. But many county units of civil and school administration are under pressure for reorganization as a result of several factors, such as the redistribution of population and wealth, the new and larger social groupings, and the increased mobility of goods and persons. It has been said that county seats were organized originally to meet pioneer conditions so that a person traveling by horse and buggy could reach the county seat in one day from any part of the county. When measured in miles, the distance is unchanged today, but, when measured in minutes, it has lessened markedly. Modern means of transportation make communication between counties comparatively simple.

Transportation of Pupils. In a consideration of consolidation and the state minimum program of education for all children, one cannot ignore the important factor of the availability of education. The democratic principle of equal educational opportunity demands the daily transpor-

FIG. 3-6. Pupils entering school bus. These Minnesota children are part of the throng, millions strong, that travels daily to and from school. (*Courtesy of School Management.*)

tation of pupils to school. Some states have dormitories for secondary-school students. At present many rural youth are denied high-school education because they cannot reach the school.

The transporting of children is not a new educational undertaking. Beginning in a Massachusetts district in 1840, it continued without legal authorization until 1869 when Massachusetts passed the nation's first permissive transportation law for the conveyance of pupils to and from public schools. By 1920 pupils were being carried to and from school in all the states, with or without specific legal sanction. Today the provision of transportation facilities for school children is generally mandatory under certain conditions. Several millions of pupils are transported daily at public expense. Although school busses are the usual means of conveyance, the "old gray mare" and the railroads still serve in some communities, especially during the winter months. The problem of transportation is not of equal importance in all the states, and within states wide variations exist in the proportion of pupils carried by bus. Great differences also exist in safety measures. The National Conference on School Transportation has prepared a code of standards for the selection and training of school-bus drivers.

The transportation of pupils is more than a local problem. Many state treasuries provide financial assistance in defraying the cost of pupil travel as a means toward equalizing educational opportunity and burden. Several state departments lend technical assistance in the mapping of school-bus routes. Because of the close relationship between the transportation of pupils and the consolidation of districts, each state should make continuous analyses of both matters.

COORDINATION OF ADMINISTRATIVE UNITS

Coordination is a general term that covers the integrating activities of legal or extralegal groups, such as a state department or accrediting association, in bringing together small components. These efforts require not only voluntary cooperation and legal consolidation of schools but also a higher authority to appraise existing practices, recommend minimal standards, and integrate the disparate units. Despite practical obstacles, the work of coordinating the various school administrative units within and between states must progress. Upon this task the well-wishers of education everywhere, and especially the state and national authorities, must focus their attention. The maintenance of the individuality of a local school district is important, but even more vital is uniformity in the minimal essentials of sound school organization and administration. This topic is also considered in Unit II.

A program for the reorganization of school units should contain immediate and long-term plans involving three basic elements: (1) the educational plan, which contains a general statement of the philosophy involved and also definite educational specifications for the reorganized units; (2) the spending plan, which involves translating the educational criteria into proposed expenditures; and (3) the financing plan, which proposes means for meeting the cost of the educational program. The last two aspects are treated in Unit XVI. The emphasis here is on the educational program.

Educational Emphasis in Reorganization. The educational plan should form the basis for the whole program of realignment.

Adequate administrative units are . . . merely the means by which an excellent educational program can be initiated and maintained. In the last analysis, the quality of the personnel determines whether or not the administrative unit and the school are worth the effort and money invested.[11]

[11] National Society for the Study of Education, *op. cit.,* p. 192.

A monetary definition has the advantage of objectiveness, but it fails to define the component elements of the educational program sufficiently for the purposes of constructing an administrative unit. In other words, the content as well as the cost of the educational program must be accurately ascertained. The educational characteristics of effective districts are described further in the report of the National Commission on School District Reorganization [12] and in Fitzwater's *Selected Characteristics of Reorganized School Districts.*[13] For example, larger districts attract better trained teachers and have more kindergartens. The locality in which the child receives his education cannot be ignored in the reforms in school organization and administration.

Past, Present, and Future Tenses in Rural Education. Julian E. Butterworth, who spent 33 years in the department of rural education at Cornell University, listed the following achievements in this area of learning: realization nationally that education for rural people must approximate in scope and quality that of the cities; a national and local understanding of the lacks and resources in rural community life; improvement in programs for special educational services; better personnel and enriched curricular programs; and an increase in state aid for rural education.[14]

At present much experimentation is in progress. For example, in Kentucky the Fund for the Advancement of Education made possible the rural-school-improvement project, whereby teachers in small country schools receive competent supervision on the job and scholarships for summer study and travel. The University of Michigan is offering an expanded program of radio and television broadcasts for county schools. Administrators are applying the "federation concept" whereby educational functions are assigned to that level of school administration—federal, state, county, intermediate, or local—which can best perform the specific responsibilities.

Two urgent problems are still unsolved. The rural school should serve its community better, and a new type of county superintendency is needed in most states. According to Butterworth, "the task of developing an adequate education in rural areas is only well begun."

Some of the firmest strongholds of democracy are found in the smaller school systems described here and in the next unit—local school districts. Many of these will continue their identity as separate administrative or attendance or intermediate units.

[12] National Commission on School District Reorganization, *Your School District,* Chap. V, National Education Association, 1948.

[13] C. O. Fitzwater, *Selected Characteristics of Reorganized School Districts,* GPO, 1953, 50 pp.

[14] Julian E. Butterworth, "Rural Education—Past Achievements and Present Problems," *National Education Association Journal,* November, 1952, pp. 520–521.

SUGGESTED ACTIVITIES

1. What is meant by an "intermediate unit" in school administration?

2. Visit the office of a county superintendent of schools in order to learn the nature of his work. A member of the class may be delegated to do this, or the entire class may make the visit if the county office is near by. Ask the county superintendent of schools to address the class on his duties.

3. Examine school laws to learn the exact qualifications and duties of a county or township superintendent of schools.

4. Conduct a debate on the question: "Resolved that the county superintendent of schools should be appointed rather than elected."

5. Examine in the school laws of your state the legal relationships between the local and county school officials and between the latter and the state school officials.

6. Examine the organization of a county that has a strong county board of education.

7. If the county has a course of study, evaluate it.

8. Discuss the role of county institutes as conducted in most states.

9. Procure or prepare a school map of a county. Study its geography and locate the school districts.

10. Visit a rural school, and interview the teacher in order to learn some of the advantages and disadvantages of small schools.

11. Prepare a debate on the topic: "Resolved that all elementary school districts with an enrollment of less than 10 pupils should be abolished or consolidated."

12. Prepare an exhibit of educational materials, bulletins, etc., issued by the county superintendent's office.

DESCRIPTIVE BIBLIOGRAPHY AND AIDS

BOOKS

AMERICAN ASSOCIATION OF SCHOOL ADMINISTRATORS: *The American School Superintendency,* Chaps. XII, XIV, National Education Association, 1952.

Leadership in rural and intermediate school districts.

BRIGHAM, WILLIAM B.: *The Story of McLean County and Its Schools,* published by the author, 1951.

The schools in McLean County, Illinois, as described by a former county superintendent.

BUTTERWORTH, JULIAN E., and HOWARD A. DAWSON: *The Modern Rural School,* Chap. I, McGraw-Hill, 1952.

Rural education yesterday and tomorrow.

COOPER, SHIRLEY, and CHARLES O. FITZWATER: *County School Administration,* Chaps. V, VI, Harper, 1953.

The county superintendent of schools and the county unit.

EDUCATIONAL POLICIES COMMISSION: *Education for All American Youth—A Further Look,* Chaps. IV, V, VI, National Education Association, 1952.

Farmville community school—characteristics, curriculum, and organization.

FITZWATER, CHARLES O.: *Educational Changes in Reorganized School Districts,* GPO, 1953, 53 pp.

The test of reorganization—what happens to pupils.

———: *Selected Characteristics of Reorganized School Districts,* GPO, 1953, 49 pp.

Characteristics such as size, physiographic features, property.

NATIONAL SOCIETY FOR THE STUDY OF EDUCATION: *Education in Rural Communities,* Chap. III, University of Chicago Press, 1952.

Potentialities of education in rural communities.

STUART, JESSE: *The Thread That Runs So True,* Scribner, 1951, 293 pp.
Story of a teacher and former county superintendent in the Kentucky mountain areas.

CURRENT PERTINENT PERIODICALS AND PUBLICATIONS

Annual reports of counties
Bulletins of counties
Bus Facts
County
County and City Data Book
County Herald
Educational Directory, Part I,
   Principal County and State
   School Officers

Novels:
   Giants in the Earth
   The Grapes of Wrath
   Marginal Land
   Tobacco Road
   Winter Wheat
Proceedings of educational organizations
Rural Sociology
School surveys of counties
Yearbooks of educational organizations

AUDIO-VISUAL AIDS

BOARD OF EDUCATION   23 min., sound
Produced by the U.S. Army, this film shows how residents of a rural community organize to obtain a modern consolidated school and improved educational facilities. Available from Government Films Department, World Films, 1445 Park Avenue, New York.

CENTRALIZED SCHOOL   Filmstrip, 54 frames
Presents the educational activities and program of a modern consolidated school. Accents the important role of the school in the community. Available from American Council on Education, Washington, D.C.

COMMUNITY RESOURCES IN TEACHING   20 min., sound
Shows how the school and the community can be knit closer by inviting lay persons into the school as resource persons, and bringing the students into the community to utilize its resources. Available from Iowa State University, Iowa City, Iowa.

COUNTY AND COMMUNITY RECREATION IN ACTION   29 min., sound
Presents case histories of the growth and organization of community recreation programs in three northern counties. Available from Indiana University, Bloomington, Ind.

DESIGN OF AMERICAN EDUCATION   16 min., sound
A text-film tailor-made by McGraw-Hill for this book. Depicts the role of the county board of education and county superintendent. An overview and review of Units I–IV—national, state, county, and local organization of education. Shows consolidation of school districts, transportation of pupils, and raising of educational standards. Pretest and follow-up filmstrip also available from the producers.

ONE-TEACHER SCHOOL   Filmstrip, 57 frames
Depicts the well-conducted one-teacher school as the hub of inspiration and activity for a rural community. Available from American Council on Education, Washington, D.C.

OUR COMMUNITY   12 min., sound
Through the everyday life of a ten-year-old boy are illustrated the many industries and services of an American community. Illustrates interdependence. Available from Encyclopaedia Britannica Films, Wilmette, Ill.

RURAL HIGH SCHOOL   18 min., sound

In a large rural high school the students explain, in reply to a letter from foreign students, their school and home life in the United States. Available from Government Films Department, World Films, 1445 Park Avenue, New York.

SCHOOLS IN CENTERVILLE   20 min., sound

Shows how rural education can be geared to the real problems of learning to live in a community. Seventh-grade classes are seen at work in a model school in Virginia. Produced by the Department of Rural Education of the National Education Association. Available from National Education Association, Washington, D.C.

SCHOOLS MARCH ON   18 min., sound

A picture of rural-school consolidation in Woodford County, Ill. A citizens' educational council, board of education, parents, and others cooperate in this program. Produced by the March of Time. Available from McGraw-Hill, New York 36.

LOCAL SCHOOL DISTRICTS

The organization and administration of education had their origin in the district system in early American life. The autonomous school district is essentially an American innovation.

There are numerous types of local school organization, such as attendance and administrative units. School districts vary in size from one-pupil districts to New York City with more than a million pupils.

The administration of the school district is usually vested in an elected board of education and its administrators. The relation of the board of education to the other agencies in the community should be vital and dynamic.

The chief executive of the local board of education is the superintendent of schools, who is the educational expert. His strategic position demands a high degree of statesmanship.

Democratic school administration calls for the development of policies by all professional and lay workers, and for the execution of these policies in an atmosphere of democratic living.

OUTLINE OF CONTENTS

Introduction
    Local school districts
    Legal status of districts
Types of Local Schools
    Attendance and administrative units
    Local districts of various sizes
    Other types of districts and schools
Local Board of Education
    Evolution of school boards
    Electorate and school boards
    Size, tenure, and selection of boards of education
    Qualifications of board members
    Functions and powers of boards of education
    Board organization and procedure
    Relationships of boards of education
Local Superintendent of Schools
    Types of internal control
    Evolution of school superintendency
    Legal status of city superintendent
    Qualifications of superintendent
    Functions of superintendent of schools
    Superintendent's relationships with others
    Four-dimensional growth for superintendents
    Democratic administration of education

LOCAL SCHOOL DISTRICTS

In the seventeenth century a royal governor of Virginia, Sir William Berkeley, scolded colonial citizens with these startling words: "I thank God there are no free schools nor printing [in Virginia], and I hope we shall not have them these hundred years." Within a few years of his death there were printing presses in Virginia, and not long after many localities had free school systems. The local school unit marked the genesis of American public education.

Local School Districts. Parallel with the growth of the principle of education as a state function, there developed in the United States a pattern of distinctly local operation or home rule.

The controls of education have grown out of the beliefs, the aspirations, and the plans of the American people. And because faith in education has been so much a part of the American dream, the people have kept close to education and have kept education close to themselves in both the expressed and implied belief that education represents the very roots of American democracy.[1]

So home rule has become the predominant pattern in American education.

The United States has more than 100,000 independent units of government, each with the power to spend money and to perform services for the citizenry. These units range in size from the federal government with millions of employees down to the smallest type of school district with one teacher and one pupil. Of these legal units about 60,000 are school districts of various types. The map in Unit III reveals the organizational pattern for all states in the Union.

In the broad sense the local school district is the smallest administrative unit in all these states. The so-called district system is the educational organization that embraces a very small geographical area, as in the district states.

The local school district is usually administered by a board of education, averaging five members, and a superintendent of schools, with his staff. In small districts with but one teacher, the administration of the local school affairs may be handled by four persons, *viz.*, the teacher and three members of the school board. The number of school board members totals nearly 225,000, with an average of about one board member for every four teachers. In a few states the board members almost outnumber the teachers.

The autonomous school district, organized as a separate unit, is essen-

[1] American Association of School Administrators, *The American School Superintendency,* p. 103, National Education Association, 1952.

tially an American innovation. Although England once had and Canada still has some similar administration, it is chiefly in the United States that the district system, with its local board of education, provides the legal form of school control.

Legal Status of Districts. The Tenth Amendment to the Constitution definitely implies that education is a function of the state and not of the federal government. Usually the states delegate the major responsibilities to the local educational subdivision, which in area may be as small as a rural school district of 5 square miles in Illinois or as large as a county

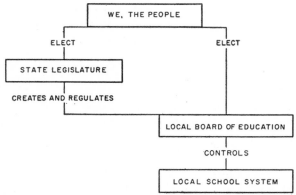

FIG. 4-1. Legal status of local school district. Certain duties may be assigned to an intermediate unit.

unit of 2000 square miles in Utah. Legally, then, subject to the laws passed by the state legislature, the control of the school system resides in the board of education elected by the people in the district (see Fig. 4-1). The board is both a local and a state instrument.

According to school laws, the board of education is the legal authority representing the state. It is an artificial body created by a general or specific law to maintain a system of public education in a certain territory. A state attorney general says: "A school board is a body politic and corporate. It is purely a creature of the statute. Its power may be enlarged, diminished, modified, or revoked by the legislature." Although there are limitations, the board has broad legal powers, such as the right to buy and sell property, erect buildings, and enter into contracts. It is a quasi corporation, subject to numerous laws.

In this overview of American public education, it is pertinent to emphasize the extreme importance of school law. Many students and teachers do not realize that their daily acts within the school are markedly affected by school laws, many of which have been extant for a long time.

Even teachers in service, administrators, and board members reveal an appalling dearth of knowledge as to school laws. This information is readily found in federal and state constitutions, state statutes, and case law or judicial opinion.[2] Copies of the state laws, as revised periodically, can be obtained from the state superintendent of public instruction or from the state capitol. The National Education Association makes periodic studies of legislation throughout the United States. The *Annual Yearbook of School Law* contains a topical summary of decisions of the higher courts in cases involving school law. Through such decisions the higher courts of the various states and the Supreme Court of the United States have established many common-law principles of exceeding importance. In the exercise of its duty the court cannot do otherwise than revert to first principles: the consideration of the purpose for which the schools were established as indicated in the law or in antecedent custom.

TYPES OF LOCAL SCHOOLS

ATTENDANCE AND ADMINISTRATIVE UNITS

The legislature creates or makes possible the establishment of school districts of various types. It is desirable to distinguish between units for attendance and those for the administration of education. An attendance unit, usually established by the local board, is defined as the area served by a single school, such as a Horace Mann School in a city system. An administrative unit, usually the legal district, embraces all the area under a single system of control and may include one, two, or over a hundred attendance areas.

LOCAL DISTRICTS OF VARIOUS SIZES

Local administrative units are of many sizes. The National Education Association has frequently used the following classification in its studies of school systems:

Under 2,500 population	From 10,000 to 30,000
From 2,500 to 5,000	From 30,000 to 100,000
From 5,000 to 10,000	Over 100,000 population

According to the federal census tabulations, all areas under 2500 population are rural. County and intermediate school districts are considered in Unit III. Divisions are here classified roughly as: (1) rural, (2) village, (3) city, and (4) suburban.

[2] Madaline Kinter Remmlein, *School Law*, pp. 1–4, McGraw-Hill, 1950. Consult also the materials of the National Organization on Legal Problems of Education, organized in 1954.

Fig. 4-2. Traditional rural elementary-school building still in use. Many rural-school buildings, with outside pump and toilet facilities, are substandard in several respects.

Fig. 4-3. Modern rural school near Ithaca, Nebraska. (*Courtesy of Clark and Enersen, Architects.*)

Rural Districts. The smallest district, the one-teacher school, is sometimes one-pupil as well. The one-teacher schools of America, usually one-room also, are disappearing rapidly in favor of the more modern and consolidated schools.

A typical one-teacher district is organized as in Fig. 4-4. Some rural elementary schools have two or more teachers, and most rural high schools have at least three teachers.

Village Districts. A village school usually has more than one teacher and may have one or more buildings. The organization and administration of village, community, and small city schools is por-trayed in Fig. 4-5. Here the board selects an ad-

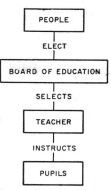

Fig. 4-4. Organization of one-teacher district.

ministrator, who is usually known as the superintendent or supervising principal. He may be assisted by a principal or "head teacher" in each building.

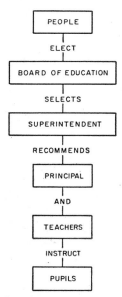

Fig. 4-5. Organization of village school district.

City School Districts. This type, because of its compactness and its aggressive educational leaders, is usually the most progressive of the district organizations. The population varies from the small city of 2500 to the New York City school district, which has more than 1,000,000 pupils in its elementary and secondary schools.

An illustration of a medium-sized school system is that of Santa Monica, California, a city of approximately 75,000 people. Figure 4-6 reveals that the people, as the electorate, choose the members of the board of education, who in turn select the superintendent of schools, their chief executive officer. Under his direction the schools of that city are administered through a three-department organization: business, including such activities as the preparation of budgets and contracts; professional, with such duties as supervision and research; and instructional, embracing teaching and learning on all levels from elementary schools through the junior college, plus the special services of adult and technical education.

Suburban Districts. A rapidly growing type of school district, which may combine some of the characteristics of a rural, village, and/or city system, is that found in the outskirts of crowded cities. Suburban or near-urban schools have increased markedly in the past decade.

Probably the most severe inequalities to children because of outmoded school districts are to be found in the areas near urban centers where the districts that were designed to meet the needs of an agricultural society still prevail, and

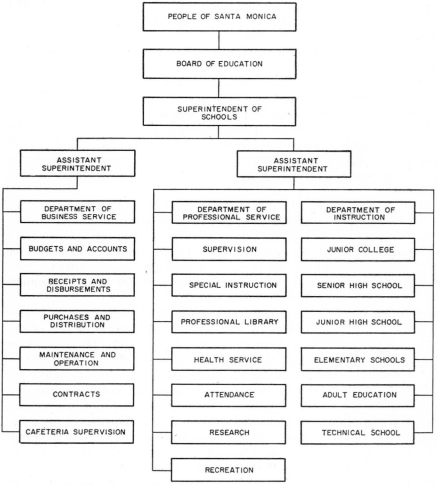

Fɪɢ. 4-6. Organization of unified school district, including the city of Santa Monica, California.

cannot cope with the suburban problem—the "growing edge" of the nearby city in rural school districts. The problem springs from such developments as large trailer camps or low-cost housing subdivisions mushrooming in an otherwise rural area.[3]

[3] Michael S. Kies, "School Redistricting," *School Executive*, June, 1952, p. 11.

Other factors stimulating the growth of these districts are: improved roads, increase in autos, high cost of city living and taxes, inadequate play and garden space in overcrowded cities, and the developing of business establishments away from the limited-car-parking areas and high-tax centers. Since 1945, the dawn of the atomic age, the psychology of fear has augmented the hegira of people and business from cities. In his address to the United Nations President Eisenhower stated frankly: "Atomic bombs today are more than 25 times as powerful as the weapons with which the atomic age dawned, while hydrogen weapons are in the range of millions of tons of TNT equivalent."

Some established suburban schools are the most outstanding in the nation, while others, new-fledged, are afflicted with special problems including population pressures, penurious public purses, and lagging legislation. According to a survey made by Benjamin Fine of the *New York Times,* a bright spot in the picture is the unusual interest of citizens in the public-school program.

OTHER TYPES OF DISTRICTS AND SCHOOLS

Special Charter School Districts. Some schools have a special charter granted directly to the local district by the state. Although the majority of these districts were established in the early history of the state's educational development, some of them operate under a special charter or special laws because of the size of the district. In Illinois, for example, Chicago and Peoria are subject to special laws because cities with a population exceeding 100,000 are exceptions to the general school laws. An instance of a special charter school district is quoted from the *School Laws* of Colorado: "The city and county of Denver shall alone always constitute one school district, to be known as District No. 1, but its conduct, affairs and business shall be in the hands of a board of education consisting of such numbers, elected in such manner as the general school laws of the state shall provide." The multiplication of especially chartered districts is likely to complicate school administration within the state; hence there is a trend toward bringing all existing school districts under the general school laws.

Other Classifications of School Systems. According to the educational level of the offerings, the two basic classifications are elementary- and high-school districts, to which have been added the junior-college and municipal-university areas. In addition, there are many districts classified on a geographical or civil basis, some of which are described in Unit III. Among the special types are town, township, county, parish, consolidated, community, and non-high-school. Some states designate districts by sizes, as first or second class. A wide variation in nomenclature of districts is found between states and within states.

The general impression that every square foot of soil in the United States is a part of an organized school district is not valid. Several states have portions unorganized for educational purposes. The school laws usually guarantee free schooling to all pupils residing in such areas.

Laboratory Schools. Many laboratory or experimental schools, on the elementary and secondary levels, are in reality public in that they are practice or training schools for state institutions like teachers colleges. Generally no tuition is required and the pupils are admitted as to a public school, although the limitation of facilities and the experimental nature of the work may restrict the enrollment. The American Association of Colleges for Teacher Education has been active in improving the laboratory schools. Numerous laboratory schools are affiliated with or are parts of nonstate or independent institutions. Experimental schools have stimulated profound changes in educational practice throughout the United States and abroad.

Parochial and Private Interest in Public Education. The earliest schools and colleges in America were parochial and private. Educational advance in the early years of the United States was due primarily to the interest and support of the church, just as today in foreign countries such as India much financial and educational impetus is given to schools from missionary funds and zeal. Today many children do not go to a public school, since it is not compulsory to attend a public institution. The Oregon anti-private-school law, which sought to compel all pupils to attend public schools, was held unconstitutional by the Supreme Court in 1925. In the parochial field, the Roman Catholic Church maintains the largest number of elementary and secondary schools.[4] The parochial schools have been, are, and will be educational and spiritual bulwarks in a nation that practices freedom of religion—one of the basic four freedoms. The private school affects public education:

> Supported for the most part by a clientele which is alert and ready to venture into new pathways if they promise to lead to desired results, the private school, while it must retain a semblance of conformity for the sake of peace, is none the less free to slough off many of the out-worn barnacles, and to venture more or less extensively into new and more promising ways. The private school yields more readily to initiative, is less hampered by the momentum of a standardized routine, and is more likely to receive the effective cooperation of its constituent group. In other words, because of its relative freedom, the private school can be, and often is, the trail-blazer for the public school, in matters of curriculum, method, and organization.[5]

In addition to billions of dollars given to private schools by individuals, many millions have been donated to public schools and colleges. Furthermore, numerous educational foundations and boards have given millions indirectly to public education by furnishing funds for research, experiments, and stimulation of education within the nation, states, and local communities.[6]

Private and parochial interest in education calls for close coordination with the public schools. Only by the cooperation of parochial, private, and public schools can education present a united front against the common foes, ignorance and superstition. The benefits of joint efforts are

Fig. 4-7. Our Lady of Monadnock Academy, East Jaffrey, New Hampshire. One of the numerous parochial schools in the United States. (*Courtesy of Rev. John A. McSweeney.*)

exemplified in the school laws of Michigan, which provide for a check on school census and attendance by the local board of education through the requirement that private, denominational, and parochial schools must furnish city superintendents with a list of pupils. Thus all educational institutions in the local district join in the effort to build up pupil attendance in all schools.

LOCAL BOARD OF EDUCATION

Nearly every school district in the United States is governed by a group of laymen designated under several names, such as the selectmen, the board of education, the school board, the board of trustees, the school

[4] Annual statistics on parochial and private schools are available in such publications as Sargent's *Handbook of Private Schools,* and *Statistics of Nonpublic Elementary and Secondary Schools,* GPO.

[5] R. A. Schwegler, "The Place of the Private School in the Scheme of Public Education," *The Independent School and Barstow,* Barstow School, Kansas City, Missouri, March 17, 1937, 15 pp.

[6] *Educational Directory: Educational Associations and Directories,* Part IV, GPO, published annually.

committee, the township board of education, or the county board of education. These board members, who today number almost 225,000, are the direct representatives of the people in the school district.

EVOLUTION OF SCHOOL BOARDS

Historically the board of education developed in the following manner:

> At first the planning for the school on the local level was done by all the interested persons in the community. But as communities grew in size, with the attending complexity of school problems, it was not feasible to continue this direct control of schools. Out of this situation grew the practice of appointing temporary committees to whom was delegated the responsibility of performing some important task. . . . Then as the volume of school business further increased, these temporary committees were replaced by permanent committees charged with the entire responsibility of operating the school. Through this process there gradually developed the pattern of selecting boards of education, accountable to the people, who were given the responsibility for organizing and supervising free schools.[7]

The autonomous school district, organized separately under an elected board of education, is essentially an American institution.

ELECTORATE AND SCHOOL BOARDS

Today a notion prevails that in the administration of American public education, as in other public undertakings, all control is far removed from the electorate. Basically the genesis of control resides in the people. "We, the people" elect representatives who, as a board of education, take the place of the unwieldy larger group, the electorate. The board of education is indeed a personalized mechanism of democratic government, yet the electorate has manifested in the past a gross ignorance and a careless neglect of its duties in the conduct of American public education. This attitude of *laissez faire* is revealed in the usually small number of voters who cast their ballots in the election of a school board. Other indexes of popular apathy are the sparseness of attendance at public hearings on educational matters, and the failure of the citizen to be present at board meetings periodically as a part of his civic duties or to attend parent-teacher meetings, or to visit the schools in action. The average citizen seldom checks either on the investment he has made in the public schools or on the persons whom he helped to elect to board membership. The board of education is a kind of unicameral legislature elected and neglected by the public. Yet the schools need the public as much as the public needs the schools.

People must be interested in the schools if they are genuinely con-

[7] American Association of School Administrators, *loc. cit.*

cerned about their children and the future of America. The public in general, and parents in particular, should select for the local board of education the best human resources of the community.

SIZE, TENURE, AND SELECTION OF BOARDS OF EDUCATION

There has been no uniformity in the number of persons on a board of education, or in their term of office. The trend in recent years has been toward boards composed of not more than nine elected members. The publication *School Boards in Action* contains the following recommendations as to size of boards:

A school board should be of such size that (*a*) no one school election would change the majority of its members; (*b*) frequent meetings could be called without involving too many people; (*c*) there would be enough members to represent the different points of view in the community; and (*d*) there would be enough members so that close friends could not deliberate action.[8]

The three-member board found so often in rural and small-town districts does not meet all these criteria.

Methods of nominating board members vary greatly. They may be nominated by petition, primary election, individual announcements, citizens' committees, mass meetings, or school-district meetings. The members are usually elected, although they may be appointed by the mayor and council, by county commissioners, by city managers, or by self-perpetuating boards.

Terms of office for school-board members cover the median length of 7 years. Terms of office may vary even within the board. Authorities in educational administration recommend the election of board members at large rather than by wards, and on a nonpartisan basis.

In Wisconsin, many school districts have two boards of education, one in charge of the regular public schools and the other of the vocational schools. The latter board consists of five members: the superintendent of schools, two employers, and two employees. George S. Counts, in his pioneer study of the social composition of city boards of education, found a heavy preponderance of business and professional men to the exclusion of the middle classes, the lesser occupations of life, and labor. In recent years many occupations have been represented. More housewives have been elected. Collectively, the members of the board of education should have a variety of vocational experiences representative of the community. Quantitatively, school boards must be kept small; qualitatively, men and women on boards of education must be the best obtainable in the community.

[8] American Association of School Administrators, *School Boards in Action*, p. 41, National Education Association, 1946.

Qualifications of Board Members

The magnitude of education as expressed by its annual expenditure of several billion dollars emphasizes the need for a very careful selection of board members. Among the qualifications usually specified by law are that the candidate shall be over twenty-one years of age, a legal voter, and a resident in the school district. Besides these legal stipulations, however, a member of a board of education should possess many other desirable qualities. He should:

1. Be interested in schools
2. Have children in school
3. Have a forward-looking attitude toward schools
4. Understand the financial status of the district
5. Be able to discuss school affairs in an intelligent manner
6. Have some formal schooling
7. Possess ability in dealing with private and public affairs
8. Be a taxpayer
9. Be a person of good moral qualities who has the respect of the community
10. Have community pride
11. Be willing and able to give energy and time to the office he holds
12. Be a cooperative individual—not a rubber stamp or a headstrong person who seeks to run the school singlehanded

Of greatest benefit is intelligent cooperation among the members of the board and between the board and the community.

Unfortunately board members do not always promote the best welfare of the school: "Hardened politicians, not content with the devastation inflicted on city governments, realize that the schools, employing many people and handling millions of dollars, are tempting objects for despoliation." [9] The school system should be made an uninteresting and unattractive field to political spoilsmen. It is "bad politics for even a corrupt spoils administration to use the schools, and good politics to stay out." By and large, however, the schools are governed honestly, largely because the majority of board members take seriously their responsibilities and duties.

Distinguished service awards, honorary degrees, and other forms of recognition are given annually by state educational associations, colleges, and other groups to members of boards of education who have rendered notable service to education in the local community, state, and nation. These tributes are challenges to men and women everywhere to serve their community as members of boards of education.

---

[9] Chris A. De Young, *Budgetary Practices in Public School Administration*, p. 101, Northwestern University, 1932.

FUNCTIONS AND POWERS OF BOARDS OF EDUCATION

The board of education is an effective policy-forming and appraisal-making group; its chief task is to select a competent superintendent of schools who will serve as its administrative officer. The board is generally granted broad powers by the state legislature and is invested with much discretionary power in matters of details.

Edward M. Tuttle, executive secretary of the National School Boards Association, in discussing the functions of boards wrote:

School boards have a far greater responsibility than merely to conduct the "housekeeping" of the district—adopt a budget, levy taxes, pay bills, employ personnel, select school sites, okay architects' plans, issue school bonds, call for bids, etc. It is equally the board's responsibility to study and understand what the schools of the community are supposed to accomplish, how well the schools are succeeding, and what improvements and advances are to be desired. School business outweighs every other kind of business in that its products are human beings.[10]

Too many boards of education limit their attention to school buildings to be used during school hours by school children on school days during the school months. The modern board of public education places all its facilities at the disposal of all members of the community for education at all hours of the day during the entire year. It is a board of *public education* rather than a *school* board.

BOARD ORGANIZATION AND PROCEDURE

Most boards of education are organized with a president who presides at the meetings, and a secretary or clerk who may serve as the treasurer. Business is conducted usually in open meetings held in the school once a month, except in large city systems where the board may convene more frequently.

Much business is transacted through committees. Among the typical standing committees are finance, building and grounds, school management, teachers, and public relations. In recent years, however, the tendency is away from standing committees. If the board meets as a committee of the whole, each member will be more thoroughly informed on all school affairs and able to render more intelligent service. As a general rule there should be no standing committees, since too frequently committee action predetermines board action. If there are committees, certainly the superintendent of schools should serve on all of them as an ex officio member in order to integrate the policies and actions of the board.

[10] Edward M. Tuttle, "The Unique Functions of School Boards," *School Executive,* March, 1952, p. 22.

RELATIONSHIPS OF BOARDS OF EDUCATION

The board of education plays a unique role in American life. Its work impinges on so many areas of public interest that it becomes interdependent with many groups. As the elected representatives of the people, the board members must be able to keep in contact with their constituents or at least to gauge their pulse. The importance of such connections is manifested in the increasing prevalence of committees on public rela-

Fig. 4-8. Board of education and administrators. Reading from left to right, these persons are the superintendent of schools, president of the board, secretary, board member, principal of the junior-senior high school, board member, and treasurer. (*Courtesy of Public Schools, Walsenburg, Colo.*)

tions. Many boards encourage laymen, teachers, and students to attend their sessions, except when personnel matters make a closed session desirable. Some broadcast or televise part of their meetings. Public relations in American public education are further detailed in Unit XVI.

Among the vital relationships maintained by the local school board with other organizations and officials are those with the city government, with other school boards, in area, state, and national affiliations, such as the National School Boards Association, and with the superintendent of schools, whose work is treated in the last part of this unit.

Fiscal Independence and Dependence. The tendency has been to divide school districts into two categories on the basis of their fiscal relationship to the city government:

1. *Fiscal independence.* Those school districts, in which the board of education generally has authority to raise and expend funds without the consent of the municipal government, are financially independent.

2. *Fiscal dependence.* Conversely, those school districts which are a department of some civil agency, such as a city, and hence must depend on it for budget approval and revision, are said to be fiscally dependent.

It is impossible to draw a clear line of demarcation between these two groups, since there is a gradual shading off from one extreme of positive independence to the other of irrevocable dependence. Authorities in political science usually favor the dependent boards, whereas educational writers in the main agree that the school district should be fiscally independent.[11]

School Board Organizations. An unobtrusive but significant development is the banding together of school boards in the common cause of education. In many states the board members have joined formal organizations, by counties, by groups of counties, or by the entire state. The state associations are linked in the National School Boards Association—a group that is emerging as a potent force in American public education. Many board members have profited by attending the annual conventions of the American Association of School Administrators, which is composed primarily of superintendents of schools.

LOCAL SUPERINTENDENT OF SCHOOLS

TYPES OF INTERNAL CONTROL

The internal administration of city schools is (1) unit, (2) dual, or (3) multiple in operation. These are the three main ways in which responsibility is delegated by the board of education.

In the unit type of control, the board of education places the responsibility for the administration of the schools upon the executive officer, the superintendent of schools, who, in large cities, may delegate details to the assistant superintendent, to a business manager, or to others subordinate to him. In the dual and multiple types, responsibility is shared by two or more coordinate officers, such as an attorney and business manager, each answerable directly to the board of education. Modern educational practice favors the unit type of internal control, with the superintendent of schools as the chief administrative officer.

EVOLUTION OF SCHOOL SUPERINTENDENCY

The superintendency of schools evolved in a peculiar manner. The principal was a schoolman, whereas a local person, usually a layman, was elected superintendent to look after the business affairs of the school.

[11] This is one of the issues discussed in greater detail in Unit XVII.

Frequently the principal was paid more than the superintendent. The superintendent was often the president of the board of education, a practice that continued for years at Beloit, Wisconsin. In most districts today the superintendent serves in a unit-control system.

The history of the city superintendency is an interesting story:

> Before 1837 there were no city school superintendents. That year Buffalo, New York, and Louisville, Kentucky, each established the position of superintendent of schools. Other cities followed their example, but up to 1870 there were school superintendents in only 29 of the 226 cities having a population of 8000 or more. . . . After 1870 when cities began to increase in size the educational problems became so numerous and complex that boards of education could no longer exercise direct supervision over the schools. For some years, however, many boards of education continued to exercise some executive functions, but year by year greater and greater responsibility has been placed in the hands of the superintendent of schools until today his responsibilities and duties are such as make the school superintendency a most important public administrative position.[12]

This office today has developed to a high level of educational statesmanship.

LEGAL STATUS OF CITY SUPERINTENDENT

Unfortunately all superintendents do not have a definite legal status. In many districts, provisions dealing with detailed duties for the superintendent are often covered by the "rules and regulations" adopted by the local boards of education. The legal status of superintendents should include provision for long-term contracts. Unfortunately, the average city superintendent stays in one position only 6 years. This tends to make administration not a profession but a procession.

QUALIFICATIONS OF SUPERINTENDENT

A superintendent of schools qualifies for his position through his non-professional academic preparation, his professional education, his experience in teaching, and his personal attributes. The trend is toward the master's degree as a minimum academic requirement for a superintendency. The North Central Association of Colleges and Secondary Schools adopted the following rule in regard to the high schools: "The superintendent or the principal directly in charge of the supervision and administration of the high school shall hold a master's degree from a college belonging to the North Central Association, or the equivalent; and shall have had a minimum of two years of experience in teaching or administration." The academic standards are increasingly being broadened and raised for superintendents, both of high schools and of elementary schools.

[12] W. S. Deffenbaugh, *Know Your Board of Education*, p. 2, GPO, 1939.

The superintendent of schools should be well versed in the field of professional education if he is to be the educational expert. To meet these numerous demands, the superintendent must possess a breadth of information based on broad nonprofessional background, thorough courses, seminars, and field work in education and school administration, and continuous study on the job.

The following general qualifications of a personal nature are desirable: unblemished character, sound physical and mental health, good speaking voice, endless patience and tact, and sound judgment. A successful school executive should rate high in unselfish motivation, scholarly ability, industry, ability to get along with people, and executive capacity. A board of education expects a superintendent to have leadership, see inherent possibilities in others, assign duties intelligently, delegate authority, know the professional literature of the past and present, have a philosophy of education, beware of popular fads and notions in regard to education, and be an independent thinker.

FUNCTIONS OF SUPERINTENDENT OF SCHOOLS

In its yearbook, *The American School Superintendency,* the American Association of School Administrators discusses eight functions of every superintendent:

Planning and *evaluation* overlies the entire complex. *Organization* establishes the framework. *Personnel, business and buildings,* and auxiliary services establish the necessary operating conditions for the educative process. *Information and advice* provide a two-way sharing of knowledge and ideas with the public and the school staff as to the planning and operation of the plan. *Coordination* binds all together so that the manpower and materials of the entire school system may be focused on the major function of *instruction.*[13]

Of the operational functions, instruction is paramount. The over-all duty of the superintendent is to serve as the chief executive officer of the board, since he is the educational expert. According to *Recent Social Trends,* the most notable recognition of the principle of expert and permanent non-political service has been in the rapid rise of the city manager and the school superintendent in American cities—a tribute to the interest in and demands for a different type of administrative personnel. With this growth in importance, questions may well be raised as to the relationships of the educational expert to his fellow workers.

SUPERINTENDENT'S RELATIONSHIPS WITH OTHERS

The superintendent, especially in a large school system with its cumbrous complexity, cannot discharge singlehanded all the duties just enu-

[13] American Association of School Administrators, *The American School Superintendency,* p. 80.

merated. Therefore, the actual performance of many of these acts must be delegated to others, although the superintendent is held responsible and must keep a sharp-eyed perspective of the whole system. He is not a soloist but the professional coordinator of all personnel.

Relationship with Board of Education. Despite the numerous dissimilarities between education and business, the relationship between the superintendent of schools and the board is somewhat like that between the executive officer and the board of directors of any private corporation. The stockholders of a private corporation usually elect a board of directors to control the enterprise. These directors adopt certain policies, the execution of which is placed in the hands of the chief executive officer, who also may be called upon to recommend policies that should be adopted. Likewise, the public elects a board of education, which has control over the school system. This board concentrates on the adoption of policies and the appraisal of practices. The board therefore selects as its professional officer a competent superintendent of schools who makes recommendations on all matters including the selection of subordinates. Among his responsibilities to the board are: providing information as a basis for planning; orienting new members; helping the board understand the schools; furnishing facts about the schools; developing awareness of community attitudes; helping the board to make effective decisions; and pointing the way toward democratic ideals in education.[14]

With Local Administrative Personnel. The large school systems employ administrative officers other than the superintendent. Their number and type depend upon the size and nature of the system. Among these administrative or semiadministrative officers are assistant superintendents of schools, business managers, secretaries of the board, principals, department heads, supervisors, and others, whose duties are considered more completely in Unit XII. The superintendent coordinates the work of all departments.

With Teaching Personnel. Since the administrator must work closely with the teaching staff mentioned in Unit XI, he must develop the philosophy and techniques of group dynamics—working cooperatively and effectively with others. His code of professional ethics ought to include the practice of engaging and promoting teachers on their merit, keeping inviolate their confidential communications, giving them a share in democratic organization, and not criticizing them in the presence of other teachers, patrons, or pupils.

With Pupils. The superintendent in a small system has the advantage of close contact with the pupils; he may even teach some of them in the classroom. In the large schools this is not possible, but the relationship,

14 *Ibid.,* pp. 116–126.

fare and comfort. It means elected representative committees to confer with the superintendents on matters of tenure, salary, sick leave, and the like. . . .

Since democracy is dependent on consent and on public information and understanding, advisory committees for administrators are indispensable—a committee of all types of employees. . . .

Similarly, an ever-growing number of superintendents have developed citizens advisory committees either to assist on a special project or to serve as a continuing advisory group.[16]

The old diagrams in books on administration and supervision had arrows going down from the superintendent to the teacher; the modern plans reveal arrows to and from the teachers and the administrators, or show relationships in group planning. The modern superintendent recognizes the contributions of teachers, principals, pupils, and others in the school. He gives full credit to the teaching staff and does not use their efforts for his self-glorification. He pays more than lip service to the ideal of democratic administration. He works with and through teachers, not above them. He gives an opportunity for teachers to preside at meetings, to share cooperatively through a planning and evaluating council, and to organize experiences around the needs, interests, and abilities of students. More and more the administrator uses less and less authority in his work. He deliberately cultivates courteousness in manner. He uses fewer commands and more questions; he avoids the imperative mood and practices the use of the interrogative. He tries to stimulate rather than dictate, knowing that dictatorship is alien to educational administration in a dynamic democracy.

Conclusion—Democratic Organization and Administration Are Essential. At the conclusion of Part I, embracing Units I through IV, it is pertinent to emphasize the function of democratic organization and administration.

Public education is the cooperative effort of society to provide learning for its people. Schools must be organized in order to be administered, and they should be organized and administered so as to facilitate the education of all the people. Sometimes school structure and its management are stumbling blocks in the path as the children seek to progress along life's educational highway. An administrative unit may be so formed geographically that its boundary lines prevent a boy or girl from receiving adequate instruction. A school may be so conducted that it does not provide a real challenge for the student to continue his studies.

Administration should be the slave and not the master of education. Schools are not organized and conducted in order to provide a board member, a superintendent, or a teacher with a job; schools are dedicated,

16 American Association of School Administrators, *The American School Superintendency,* pp. 14–15.

in all their functions, to the supreme and worthy purposes of education. In its early, restricted scope, schooling was for children, but modern education is now so broad and extensive that it embraces learning for all. In order to be genuinely democratic, American public education should include the five levels described in Part II: pre-elementary, elementary, secondary, higher education, and education for out-of-school youth and adults.

SUGGESTED ACTIVITIES

1. Visit a local school system. Study its organization and administration.

2. Draw a diagram showing how a local public-school system is organized.

3. Draw a map of a city. Locate on it all the school buildings, public, private, and parochial.

4. Study the relationship between the local school officials and the city officials.

5. Find out when school board elections are held in your district and what the election procedures are.

6. Attend an annual school district meeting or election.

7. Examine the school laws of your state to determine the qualifications and duties of the local board of education and the superintendent of schools.

8. Interview a board member to ascertain his personal interest in board membership and his qualifications for it.

9. Conduct a panel discussion on the subject of qualifications for members of boards of education.

10. Debate the topic: "Resolved that more women should serve as members of the board of education."

11. Bring to class newspaper clippings containing the minutes or actions of a board of education.

12. Visit a parochial or private school. Study its organization.

13. Arrange for a superintendent to talk to the class about school administration.

14. Visit the office of a local superintendent of schools and report the findings.

15. Visit a business department of a large school system. Report your findings.

16. Debate the statement: "Resolved that all public-school teachers should be appointed by the board of education upon the recommendation of the superintendent of schools."

17. Prepare an exhibit of educational materials from a local school system.

18. Examine annual reports of school boards and superintendents.

19. Give examples of democratic and undemocratic procedures in schools.

20. Discuss the main functions of educational organization and administration in a democracy.

21. Draw a diagram showing your recommendations for the organization of national, state, county, and local school systems.

DESCRIPTIVE BIBLIOGRAPHY AND AIDS

BOOKS

AMERICAN ASSOCIATION OF SCHOOL ADMINISTRATORS: *The American School Superintendency*, Chaps. III, V, National Education Association, 1952.
> The story of the superintendency and the school board.

———: *American School Curriculum*, Chap. IX, National Education Association, 1953.
> Home and community influence upon education.

———: *Education for American Citizenship,* Chap. IV, National Education Association, 1954.

    Mobilizing school and community in citizenship programs.

BRAMMELL, P. ROY: *Your Schools and Mine,* Chap. XIII, Ronald, 1952.

    School and community relationships.

BREESE, GERALD, and DOROTHY WHITMAN: *An Approach to Urban Planning,* Chap. I, Princeton University Press, 1953.

    Urban areas and the need for planning.

EDUCATIONAL POLICIES COMMISSION: *Education for All American Youth—A Further Look,* Chaps. VII, VIII, National Education Association, 1952.

    Schools for youth in the fictitious community of American City.

GINZBERG, ELI, and DOUGLAS W. BRAY: *The Uneducated,* Chap. XI, Columbia University Press, 1953.

    The role of the school and community in teaching the uneducated.

GRIEDER, CALVIN, and WILLIAM EVERETT ROSENTENGEL: *Public School Administration,* Chap. I, Ronald, 1954.

    The administration of local schools.

MILLER, VAN, and WILLARD B. SPALDING: *The Public Administration of American Schools,* Chap. II, World, 1952.

    General characteristics of local school districts.

MOEHLMAN, ARTHUR B.: *School Administration: Its Development, Principles, and Function in the United States,* Chap. XI, Houghton Mifflin, 1951.

    The local board of education.

OLSON, EDWARD G.: *The Modern Community School,* Chap. VII, Appleton-Century-Crofts, 1953.

    Developing a community school.

PITTENGER, BENJAMIN FLOYD: *Local Public School Administration,* Chaps. V, VI, Mc-Graw-Hill, 1951.

    The local board of education and the superintendent.

POSTON, RICHARD WAVERLY: *Democracy Is You,* Chap. XI, Harper, 1953.

    The role of democracy in education in the community.

REEVES, CHARLES EVERAND, *School Boards: Their Status, Functions, and Activities,* Chap. XIV, Prentice-Hall, 1954.

    Relationships of the board of education to superintendent and other school personnel.

REMMLEIN, MADALINE KINTER: *School Law,* Appendix B, McGraw-Hill, 1950.

    How to find school law.

CURRENT PERTINENT PERIODICALS AND PUBLICATIONS

Administrator's Notebook
American School Board Journal
Annual reports of school districts
Better Schools (Cincinnati)
Chicago Schools Journal
Citizens and Their Schools
Educational Directory, City School Officers, Part II
Journal of Educational Sociology
Local school journals
National Municipal Review

Nation's Schools
Newsletters of local schools
Review of Educational Research
School Administrator
School board journals
School Executive
School Management
School and Society
School surveys
Yearbook of School Law
Yearbooks of educational organizations

AUDIO-VISUAL AIDS

ACTION FOR YOUR PUBLIC SCHOOLS   20 min., sound

Excerpts from speeches made at an annual dinner by Roy E. Larsen, James B. Conant, former president of Harvard, and General Omar Bradley. Produced by the National Citizens Commission for the Public Schools.

BOARD OF EDUCATION   20 min., sound

The story of school-district reorganization in a rural community. Produced by the National Citizens Commission for the Public Schools.

DESIGN OF AMERICAN EDUCATION   16 min., sound

A text-film tailor-made by McGraw-Hill for this book. A preview and overview of Units I–IV—national, state, county, and local educational organization and administration. Devotes a section to local school districts. Pretest and follow-up filmstrip are also available from the publishers.

EAST AURORA IN REVIEW   40 min., sound, color

Depicts six areas where the school helps children—fundamental skills, health and safety, home and community, vocational choice, wise use of leisure time, and character-building—centered around a letter of the superintendent explaining the philosophy of the school. Produced by a local school system in Illinois.

Exhibit of Materials from Local School Systems

The students and the instructor can assemble an interesting and useful exhibit of pictures, newspaper clippings, reports, budgets, and literature issued by local schools.

SCHOOL BOARDS IN ACTION   28 min., sound, color

Depicts the work of the board of education and the superintendent of schools. Presents problems such as: selection and preparation of board members, selection of instructional materials, teachers' salaries, school bonding, and others. Produced by the W. K. Kellogg Foundation and Agra Films, Athens, Ga. Available from the National School Boards Association, 450 East Ohio Street, Chicago.

THE SCHOOL AND COMMUNITY   14 min., sound, b&w or color

A text-film custom-made for this book; can be used with this and other parts of the text. Pictures the old-style school surrounded by a wall, which disappears as school and community work together. Follow-up filmstrip shows sequences from the movie and poses questions which can serve as a basis for discussion of the relationship of school and community.

Part II

AREAS OF PUBLIC EDUCATION

Preview of Part II

AREAS OF PUBLIC EDUCATION

American public education spans the lifetime of the individual: it enrolls him at birth and graduates him at death. As indicated in the educational ladder in Fig. 5-1 on the next page, the four major sequential levels of lifelong learning are (1) pre-elementary, (2) elementary, (3) secondary, and (4) higher education; related to these is (5) education for out-of-school youth and adults.

The first, the pre-elementary period, includes prenatal and postnatal care as well as the early nurture and education of the child. The principal agencies for providing care and education at this early level are the home, the nursery school, and the kindergarten. This period reaches up to the elementary-school age of approximately six years (Unit V).

Elementary education lays the firm foundation for all-round growth of the child through developing in him basic skills, habits, attitudes, and knowledges. The elementary schools in the United States enroll almost one sixth of all Americans on the mainland, and are the main instruments for equipping persons with a common general education (Unit VI).

Secondary education is broadened and lengthened to include all the curricular and cocurricular activities of the preadolescent, adolescent, and postadolescent youth. Theoretically it spans the period covering the junior high school, the senior school, and the junior college. It adds to the general education of youth and often provides some degree of specialization. Eight out of ten youth of high-school age are in school (Unit VII).

Higher education includes both undergraduate and postgraduate study. College and university undergraduate life with its crowded activities may be a prelude to intensive postgraduate work, but more often it is the terminus of formal schooling. However, college enrollments are increasing (Unit VIII).

Education for out-of-school youth affords to an ever-increasing number of young Americans the opportunity for intellectual and social growth. Adult education, the final stage in lifelong learning, can yield satisfying fruits through a rich and varied program of activities (Unit IX).

Part II

AREAS OF PUBLIC EDUCATION

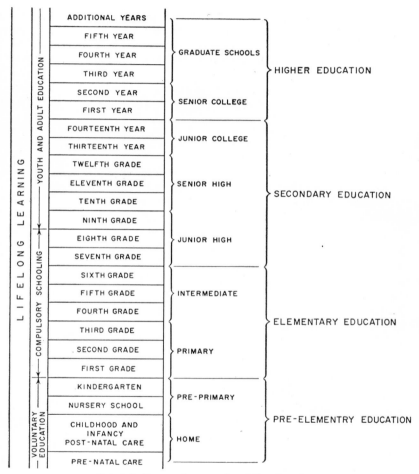

FIG. 5-1. Proposed areas of public education.

PRE-ELEMENTARY EDUCATION

Pre-elementary education extends from the birth of the child to his entrance at the age of six or seven years into the first grade or year of the elementary school.

The movement for early childhood education outside the home commenced historically with the fearless and sympathetic Froebel, who originated the kindergarten. The three major areas encompassed in this broad field are (1) early home care and training for all children, (2) nursery-school education for some pupils, and (3) kindergarten education for some.

Parental education, prenatal and postnatal care, and early infancy training in the home lay the foundation for later childhood. The significance of this early home training cannot be overestimated.

Some children attend one or both of the organized institutions for pre-elementary education, the first of which is the nursery school. Various types of nursery schools are found in the United States.

The second, the kindergarten, continues the education of the home and other agencies. It usually enrolls children at the age of four or five years during the "readiness period." It serves as a transition from pre-elementary to elementary schooling.

OUTLINE OF CONTENTS

Introduction
    Importance of early childhood
Development of Pre-elementary Education
    Historical calendar
    Pioneer work in pre-elementary education
Home Care and Training
    Parental and family-life education
    Early childhood education in the home
Nursery Education
    Scope of nursery education
    Aims of nursery school
    Program and procedures
    Current practices
    Future of nursery schools
Kindergarten Education
    Scope of kindergarten education
    Aims of kindergarten
    Program and procedures
    Current practices
    Future of kindergartens

PRE-ELEMENTARY EDUCATION

After one of his lectures, Francis Wayland Parker, the educator, was interrogated as follows by a woman in his audience:

"How early can I begin the education of my child?"

"When will your child be born?" Parker asked.

"Born?" she gasped. "Why, he is already five years old!"

"My goodness, woman," he cried, "don't stand here talking to me—hurry home; you have lost the best five years."

FIG. 5-2. "Here I come! Soon I'll walk to school!" (*Courtesy of Public Schools, Chicago, Ill.*)

Importance of Early Childhood. Authorities on child life stress the extreme importance of the earliest years in the development of the individual, since it is during this formative period that the foundation is built for future growth. But a child's life really begins at fertilization.

We often think of birth as the beginning of life. But the newborn infant is the product of many weeks of development and in order to understand his achievements and his potentialities we must familiarize ourselves with the events in his life history prior to birth.[1]

The child is not stationary and fixed but is moving through a growth period, itself imbedded in the larger period that extends from conception to maturity. In turn, this is a part of even a greater period that includes the whole life cycle from birth to death. In growth the organism changes from a single cell to an adult with a complex bodily structure and very involved behavior. . . .

The important issues of our times have their effects upon child life. The deep undercurrents of fear intensified by an atomic age, the growing uncertainties of work, the difficulty of meeting basic family needs, the panorama of mixed cultural ideas passing as if in review before our eyes—all these, sometimes subtly but rather surely, affect the well-being of children.[2]

The findings of children's laboratories and nursery schools suggest that the first half-dozen years of a child's life may be more important for educational purposes than all the other years, since many habits that underlie successful living are formed then. This belief is accented by the Educational Policies Commission:

The growth process during the first six years is foundational and tends to set the pattern of future health and adjustment. Healthy, well-adjusted persons are the product of an orderly process of growth. . . . The play and work of the child during these early years can include all the basic elements of good social life: companionship, sharing, and good will.[3]

The basic philosophy toward life itself often has its roots in infancy and early childhood. Therefore, continuous close cooperation between the home and school is necessary, especially during what may be called the preschool or pre-elementary period of a child's life.

Pre-elementary education covers the whole period from the child's birth until his entrance into elementary school at the age of six or seven years. The term "pre-elementary" seems more appropriate than "pre-school," since the nursery school and the kindergarten are part of the school system in many cities. Furthermore, pre-elementary concerns the

[1] Leigh Peck, *Child Psychology*, p. 3, Heath, 1953.

[2] National Society for the Study of Education, *Early Childhood Education*, Part II, pp. 13, 71, University of Chicago Press, 1947.

[3] Educational Policies Commission, *Educational Services for Young Children*, pp. 6–8, National Education Association, 1945.

child not only from two to six years old but from birth to entrance into the elementary school.

The values that parents and educators may expect from the education of children under six are suggested in the following list:

(1) Early recognition of children's physical needs and physical defects; (2) development of good health habits such as cleanliness, eating, safety, and rest; (3) increasing ability of children to play and work co-operatively; (4) increasing ability of children to understand and to appreciate each other; (5) development of children's understanding of their physical environment; (6) growth in children's ability to express themselves through language, art, music, and rhythms; (7) widening of children's experiences and the acquisition of knowledge regarding home and community living; (8) development of good habits of work and care of materials; (9) improvement of physical skills; (10) improvement of family life through the teachers' work with parents; (11) improvement of society through the development of well-adjusted citizens; and (12) special services to children with handicaps or unusual needs.[4]

DEVELOPMENT OF PRE-ELEMENTARY EDUCATION

HISTORICAL CALENDAR—PRE-ELEMENTARY EDUCATION AND CONTEMPORANEOUS EVENTS

This calendar contains several significant developments in pre-elementary education and some contemporaneous events of political, social, and economic importance.

PIONEER WORK IN PRE-ELEMENTARY EDUCATION

During the early nineteenth century many efforts were made to protect small children from neglect and overwork. In France Rousseau emphasized nature as a guide in the early education of young children, as pictured in *Émile*. Reverend Jean F. Oberlin instituted schools for very young children, which later developed into the *écoles maternelles* (mother schools). Among the English philanthropists and leaders were Robert Owen, who started the infant school movement, Samuel Wilderspin, James P. Greaves, and Rev. Charles Mayo. In Germany the leader in pre-elementary education was Froebel.

Pioneer Work of Froebel. The year 1837 was rich in important events in education. In America, Horace Mann was beginning his work as secretary of the state board of Massachusetts and Mary Lyon was opening her school for women which was to develop into Mt. Holyoke College; in Blankenburg, Germany, Friedrich Froebel was starting the first kindergarten called *Kleinkinderbeschaftigungsanstalt.*

[4] Faith Smitter, *A Study of Early Childhood Education in California,* p. 2, California State Department of Education, 1949.

Historical Calendar

PRE-ELEMENTARY EDUCATION	CONTEMPORANEOUS EVENTS
1837—First kindergarten started by Froebel (Blankenburg, Germany)	1837—Great commercial panic prevailed in the United States
1856—First kindergarten founded in America (Watertown, Wisconsin)	1857—Dred Scott decision rendered by Supreme Court
1860—First English-speaking kindergarten opened in America (Boston)	1860—South Carolina ordinance for secession from Union adopted
1868—First kindergarten training school started (Boston)	1868—Southern states readmitted to Congress
1873—First kindergarten that endured established as part of public-school system (St. Louis)	1873—Financial panic swept through the country
1877—First church that included kindergarten in parish work (Trinity Church, Toledo)	1877—Phonograph machine invented by Thomas Edison
1880—Kindergarten departments organized in normal schools (Oshkosh, Wisconsin)	1880—Immigration treaty with China adopted
1884—Kindergarten department added to the National Education Association	1885—Grover Cleveland inaugurated President for first term
1892—The International Kindergarten Union formed (now Association for Childhood Education)	1892—Bering Sea dispute with Canada referred to arbitration
1893—First settlement house that included kindergartens in its program organized (Northwestern University, Chicago)	1893—Columbian Exposition opened at Chicago
1897—Association of Day Nurseries of New York City organized	1897—William McKinley inaugurated President
1897—National Congress of Mothers called (Washington, D.C.)	1898—Spanish-American War fought
1908—National Congress of Mothers and Parent-teacher Associations joined (now National Congress of Parents and Teachers)	1909—North Pole discovered by Robert Peary
1912—Federal Children's Bureau established in United States	1912—New Mexico and Arizona admitted as 47th and 48th states
1913—Division of Kindergarten Education created in United States Office of Education	1913—Parcel post system established by United States Post Office

Historical Calendar—(*Continued*)

Pre-Elementary Education—(*Continued*)	Contemporaneous Events—(*Continued*)
1919—First nursery school established in America	1919—League of Nations proposal rejected by Senate
1921—Sheppard-Towner Maternity and Infant Act adopted by Congress	1921—Washington Arms Conference held
1933—Nursery kindergartens started by Federal Emergency Relief Act	1933—Prohibition Amendment repealed (Amendment XXI)
1936—Legislation implemented by Congress for maternal, child-health, and child-welfare services (Social Security Act)	1936—Joint resolution for peace and security signed by Pan-American Peace Conference at Buenos Aires
1940—White House Conference on Children in a Democracy held	1940—Total population of United States recorded as 131,669,275
1945—Idea of extending school services downward through years four and three endorsed by Educational Policies Commission	1945—Atomic bombs first dropped by the United States on Hiroshima and Nagasaki, Japan
1948—Sixty million dollars voted by Congress for international children's emergency fund of United Nations	1948—Seven billion dollars voted by Congress for military and economic aid to European countries and China
1950—Mid-century White House Conference on Children and Youth called by President Truman	1950—Minimum wage floor of 75 cents per hour made effective in the United States
1955—Birth of more than four million babies estimated for year	1955—Hearings on desegregation in public schools continued by Supreme Court

Not until 1840 was the school solely for pre-elementary children called by its significant name *Kindergarten* (children's garden). The kindergarten was Froebel's crowning contribution to educational thought and practice. He did not plan kindergartens just for the children of the poor, but for all classes. Froebel had a diversity of educational experience as a teacher in a preparatory school, as a tutor of three boys upon whom he practiced some of Rousseau's ideas, and as a friend living with a group of students at Pestalozzi's unique school at Yverdon where he was a devoted follower but intellectual critic of Pestalozzi.

His book, *The Education of Man,* is the account of his school for boys at Keilhau. This publication was followed by his *Autobiography* and *Mother Play and Nursery Songs.* His heart was broken when in 1851 the arbitrary Prussian Edict closed his kindergartens. He said quietly, "Such opposition throws us back on our principles." He then commenced to plan for the transference of his kindergarten work to America, where, he said, "A new life is freely unfolding itself and a new education of man will find a footing."

FIG. 5-3. Grand march in the free kindergarten established by the Society for Ethical Culture in 1879 in New York City. (*Reproduced from School Management.*)

Early Kindergartens in America. The history of the early kindergarten in America is tersely presented in the following paragraph:

The first kindergarten in America was opened in the home of Mrs. Carl Schurz in 1855 at Watertown, Wisconsin. In Boston in 1860, Elizabeth Peabody and her sister, Mrs. Horace Mann, established the work in a house on Pinckney Street. Also in Boston, but about 1868, Madam Kriege and her daughter, from Germany, opened what is believed to be the first training school having both afternoon and evening classes. The first state normal school kindergarten was at Oshkosh, Wisconsin, in 1880. An intimate friend of Miss Peabody, Emma Marwedel, moved to California and helped to establish a kindergarten in Los Angeles; Kate Douglas Wiggin, a student of hers, established the work in San Francisco; her friend, Sarah B. Cooper, became later the first president of the International Kindergarten Union, which later became the Association for Childhood Education. But it was in 1873 at St. Louis, under Supt. Wm. T. Harris, afterward United States Commissioner of Education, that Susan Blow succeeded in opening the first permanent kindergarten under the auspices of the public school.[5]

The growth of the kindergarten may be divided roughly into four periods. (1) The pioneer stage, which had Boston as its center, stressed a few of the most important of Froebel's teachings. (2) The philanthropic era, which began in Florence, Massachusetts, valued the kindergarten largely as a reformatory or redemptive influence. (3) The strictly educational or national stage, which started in St. Louis, Missouri, accented scientific study of the principles underlying kindergarten education. (4) The fourth period, which started from Chicago and spread over the nation, is the maternal or parental era. Like the third stage, it is still extant. It aims at making the kindergarten a link between the home and the school, and at strengthening the foundations of family life. The kindergarten took on an international aspect when the United Nations kindergarten was organized at Lake Success, New York, in 1947.

In connection with the second or philanthropic period, the first church to include the kindergarten in its parish work was the Trinity Church of Toledo, and the first social settlement in slum areas to establish a kindergarten was that of Northwestern University in Chicago. The third stage is an important one, and the credit for its launching goes to Susan E. Blow. Interested in Froebel's philosophy, she had attended training schools for kindergarten teachers in Germany and in New York City, where a young woman taught by Froebel's widow in Germany had started what became a training school for kindergartners. With the cooperation of her superintendent of schools, William T. Harris, Miss Blow opened in St. Louis in 1873 the first public-school kindergarten. About ten years later the school kindergarten movement had won so many adherents that the National Education Association added a kindergarten department. By 1900 many large city schools and several universities and normal schools had set up kindergarten departments. About 1910 the methods of the late Madame Maria Montessori of Italy gained many adherents in this country. Madame Montessori placed great emphasis upon sense training through special teaching materials and upon the freedom of the child. Others who have greatly influenced the American kindergarten through experimental schools are G. Stanley Hall, John Kraus, Maria Kraus-Bolte, Samuel Chester Parker, John Dewey, William H. Kilpatrick, Anne Moore, Alice Temple, Nina Vandewalker, Laura Zirbes, Patty Smith Hill, Elizabeth Harrison, and Edna Dean Baker.

[5] Sybil Shedd, "Kindergarten Centennial," *Texas Outlook*, October, 1937, p. 48. In connection with the work of Elizabeth Peabody and Mrs. Horace Mann, see the interesting biography by Louise Hall Tharp, *Until Victory: Horace Mann and Mary Peabody*, Little, Brown, 1953, 367 pp.

The federal government, through its Children's Bureau, established in the Department of Labor under Grace Abbott in 1912, and its Kindergarten Division organized a year later in the Office of Education, has given much impetus to the kindergarten movement. It gave substantial aid through the establishment of nursery schools as part of the federal emergency education program.

Beginnings of Parental Education. With the evolution of the kindergarten there gradually developed an interest on the part of parents, particularly mothers, in a study of early childhood. Meetings were started for this purpose. In 1894 a mothers' conference was called by a kindergarten teacher in Chicago. Three years later the National Congress of Mothers was organized in Washington, D.C., by a group interested in little children, the home, the school, and the community. In 1900 a formal charter was granted to this organization, which is now called the National Congress of Parents and Teachers. The parent-teacher associations are local, county, state, national, and international in scope. Their major objective is child welfare.

A powerful agent in the development of child health, parental education, and maternal care has been the federal Children's Bureau, already mentioned, which administered what was officially known as the Maternity and Infancy Act of 1921. This law for several years provided federal grants of money to each state accepting the terms of the act and making financial and administrative arrangements for it. It has been supplanted by the Social Security Act of 1936 which, in addition to care for crippled children, provides for maternal care, child health, and child welfare services.

Origin and Development of Nursery Education. The genesis of nursery education goes back to the beginning of families, and in some countries parents are still solely responsible for teaching their young children. Gradually, however, this responsibility is being delegated to established schools. In the United States the nursery school is of rather recent origin. Although this delegated task of nursery education is rather new in the educational system of the United States, it has long received attention in other countries.

The founding of nursery schools in the United States illustrates the fact that sometimes the first is last. Although in the chronology of the child's life the nursery school precedes the kindergarten, yet historically the development of the nursery school came last. The major growth of the nursery movement in this country has taken place in the last few decades.

The kindergarten and the nursery school have a common origin in the early infant school, which appears to have been philanthropic in purpose. As early as 1897 the Association of Day Nurseries of New York City was organized. Although the first public nursery school was started in 1919, the United States had less than three hundred nursery schools up to the advent of the federal nursery-school program in 1933, and most of these schools were under private or semiprivate control. The family-life education program of the now defunct WPA, which included nursery schools, parent education, and homemaking, greatly stimulated the development of pre-elementary education during the depression era of the early 1930's.

Many institutions of higher learning have also been active in the education of the pre-elementary school child. The kindergarten-primary department of Teachers College, Columbia University, opened a nursery school in 1921. The Merrill-Palmer School of Homemaking in Detroit established the first nursery school to be used as a laboratory for the education of young girls. The first land-grant college to inaugurate a nursery school in connection with its home economics department was Iowa State College in 1924. The next year Cornell and Ohio State Universities started similar schools. Probably the first nursery school for the use of high-school students in homemaking was in Highland Park, Michigan. The accumulated influence of all these efforts has markedly affected pre-elementary education in (1) the home, (2) the nursery school, and (3) the kindergarten.

HOME CARE AND TRAINING

The modern home has been referred to ironically as a place for boys and girls to park when they have no other place to go. Although this may be partly true, nevertheless most homes are more than mere houses.

The home is the child's first school. It is there that he learns to talk, to walk, to play, to work, and to perform other basic habits. No teacher can afford to underestimate the power of the home, for it is a physical, mental, social, emotional, and spiritual center for the child.

PARENTAL AND FAMILY-LIFE EDUCATION [6]

The child's first teachers are his parents; hence they should have definite knowledge of and guidance in their responsibilities and duties. Parental education is child- and parent-centered. With this dual and immediate objective of better and happier children and also parents is coupled the ultimate aim of a better civilization. Parental information may be offered to young people long before they marry and have children, while they are still in high school, college, or continuation school. Usually, however, it is given to adults who are already parents, and it may embrace prenatal and postnatal care as well as child study.

The story is told of a visiting nurse who called on an expectant mother in a slum district to help her. "So you're tryin' to tell me how to raise my

---

[6] This topic is discussed further in Unit IX.

children," the mother shouted, "me what's buried seven of 'em!" Efforts are being bent toward changing such an attitude. Some parent-teacher associations sponsor the project of enrolling expectant mothers in classes that meet with the school nurse or doctor. Many city, county, and state health departments distribute free literature on the care of mothers and babies. Uncle Sam's best seller is a publication of the Government Printing Office entitled *Infant Care.*

Among the organizations which today promote the study of children and family life are the National Council of Parent Education, the National Congress of Parents and Teachers, the Child Study Association of America, the American Association of University Women, and the American Home Economics Association. Parent education has also become a part of the regular work of departments in some states. As early as 1926 California created its Bureau of Child Study and Parent Education, using a special grant of money from the Laura Spelman Rockefeller Foundation. Many universities, as well as state departments of education, have received financial aid for child study from similar foundations.

Colleges and Family-life Education. Many colleges are performing significant services in the fields of preparental and postparental guidance. Vassar College, for example, in 1926 inaugurated an Institute of Euthenics —the improvement of the race through environment. Its initial objective was to offer to Vassar alumnae who were mothers the results of scientific research in learning, human behavior, child development, and the techniques of homemaking. The study of pre-elementary children has been advanced by numerous child institutes, such as the one established at Teachers College, Columbia University, in 1924 under the name Institute for Child Welfare Research. At the Iowa Child Welfare Research Station the plans definitely made for school-parent activities and parental education include conferences during registration, teacher and school contacts, contacts with other staff members, and provisions for the study of child development. Beginning with the enrollment of mothers during pregnancy, the Harvard Center for Research in Child Health and Development has followed for several years the growth and development of several hundred boys and girls from birth. The Yale Clinic of Child Development and numerous others have been instrumental in stimulating and organizing a number of important studies and experiments particularly relating to the problems of infants and young children. Monographs published by the Society for Research in Child Development of the National Research Council contain many interesting and helpful scientific studies of child development.

Local Schools, and Parental and Family-life Education. Of the various formal agencies promoting parental education, the local school—public or independent—offers the greatest possibilities for development. These established institutions give instruction to future parents—both boys and girls—in home economics; conduct classes for adults who are expectant parents; hold baby clinics; provide guided observation in play groups; and organize family centers for consultation. They may become the nucleus of the parental education program in the community, with the cooperation of all agencies interested in child welfare, especially the home.

EARLY CHILDHOOD EDUCATION IN THE HOME

Modern society treasures children, the present and future tense of the greatest national resource. Prenatal and postnatal care enhance the worth of these treasures by giving children a good start in life. The foundations for the future are laid in the home, which is the citadel of early childhood.

Role of the Home. Pestalozzi was intensely interested in education in the home. His last formal speech, given when he was more than eighty years old, was entitled, "The Simplest Methods Whereby to Educate a Child at Home from the Cradle to the Sixth Year." The chief objectives of the training and education of the child, up to the time he enters upon the period of group living away from parents, are those found in a good home. The Children's Charter pledges for every child a home and that love and security which a home provides; and for that child who must receive foster care, the nearest substitute for his own home.

Robert J. Havighurst, chairman of the Committee on Human Development at the University of Chicago, lists for infancy and early childhood several vital developmental tasks, most of which are "home work" for the child and parents.[7]

In the early family life of the child, the home is preeminently the educational and social center: it is both the school, with the parents as teachers, and a social laboratory of human relationships. Consequently the home should be a well-designed and appropriately furnished place for living and learning. In a world of change, the child should find the home a haven of hope, a place made increasingly secure by local, state, and national efforts in child and maternal welfare.

NURSERY EDUCATION

SCOPE OF NURSERY EDUCATION

The educational system in the United States was not planned from the bottom up. It is like a long and strong ladder which lacks several rungs at the bottom. To supply these missing rungs, the nursery school and

[7] Robert J. Havighurst, *Human Development and Education*, pp. 9–17, Longmans, 1953. See Unit XIII in this volume for the listing of these and other developmental tasks.

kindergarten are being established. Most adults have never attended either nursery school or kindergarten, since the development of these institutions is of relatively recent date.

The term "nursery" carries many connotations, according to Arnold Gesell:

> It variously suggests the children's room at home, a residential institution for children without a home, a day home for babies with one or both parents working, and more recently the appellation "nursery school" has come to suggest a place where mothers with and mothers without limousines may leave a child of preschool age.[8]

The day nursery and the nursery school are the most common forms of organized education for very early childhood.

> A school for very young children (eighteen months to four years of age) is commonly called a nursery school. This is not to be confused with the day nursery, a much older institution, which is a social welfare agency established to give day care to the child of the working mother.
>
> As its name implies, the nursery school has characteristics of both the nursery and the school. Because the children are so young, many responsibilities, such as feeding, usually associated with the home nursery have to be assumed by the teacher in the nursery school. Nevertheless, the nursery school is more than a home nursery, for its teachers are trained in the field of early childhood education and its procedures are consciously planned in terms of the child's total development.[9]

The nursery school in a sense is a downward extension of the kindergarten so that children at an earlier age may benefit by their removal from home environment for part of the day and by association with others of their own age.

General Types. Obviously no two nursery schools are alike. Some of the types listed in *Educational Services for Young Children* are:

> 1. *The nursery school within an elementary school.* This arrangement suggests itself, from the experience of the kindergarten, as the most advisable arrangement. . . .
>
> 2. *The nursery school and secondary school.* Boys and girls of junior-high-school age are much interested in the care and development of very young children. . . . Similar advantages are afforded the senior-high-school homemaking and social studies classes. . . .
>
> 3. *The nursery school as a part of a new administrative unit of early childhood education.* Many educators would group the nursery-kindergarten-primary grades together as a single administrative unit. These grades include children from three through eight years of age. . . .

[8] Arnold Gesell, *The Preschool Child,* p. 38, Houghton Mifflin, 1923.

[9] *Encyclopedia of Modern Education,* p. 550, Philosophical Library, 1943.

4. *The separate nursery school.* No matter how effective a pattern of articulation of the nursery school and kindergarten with the other units is worked out, there will frequently be separate nursery schools both privately and publicly operated.[10]

Unfortunately some private nursery schools are "fly-by-night" agencies, here today and gone tomorrow. Others are day-care centers and cannot properly be called schools. Within these types are many duplications and variations. For example, one may be an open-air school, and another may be for crippled children, as that at Rainbow Hospital in Cleveland, Ohio. Another variable is the length of the school day. Most of them are full-day, although several operate on a half-day schedule.

Another Classification. According to their main source of financial support, nursery schools, as well as kindergartens, may be classified as: public (local, state, and federal), parochial, and private. The number of nursery schools that are a part of the local public-school system and supported entirely by the local board of education is very small. When there seemingly is not enough public-school money available to educate the primary pupils properly, obviously the preprimary children will not be given much consideration. Fiscal facts—the dearth of public funds and the increase in personal wealth—enhance the role of the independent nursery school, both private and parochial.

Aims of Nursery School

Philosophy of Nursery Education. The three main foci in the educational philosophy of nursery education are indicated as follows by the National Association for Nursery Education:

The very keystone of democracy, respect for individuality, is also the keystone of a good nursery program. The curriculum has as its basis the needs and interests of the children in the group. At very few educational levels are the needs of individuals and the ways of meeting them as well synchronized as they are in the good nursery school.

Since a democratic culture must of necessity be made up of thinking individuals, a second responsibility of our education is to stimulate independent, fearless, creative thinking. The well-planned nursery school offers a myriad of opportunities for investigation, experimentation, problem solving, imaginativeness, and creativeness—activities which require children to develop their intellectual powers.

Another characteristic of the democratic group is its emphasis on cooperative effort in making decisions and solving problems. Here again nursery education can and does lay the groundwork of social attitudes which makes this cooperative effort possible.[11]

[10] Educational Policies Commission, *op. cit.,* pp. 21–26.

[11] Gertrude E. Chittenden, Margaret Nesbit, and Betsy Williams, *Essentials of Nursery Education,* pp. 7–8, National Association for Nursery Education, 1948.

This preschool philosophy is shared by both the nursery schools and the kindergartens, although with different points of emphasis. The objectives of the nursery school are somewhat contingent upon the type of follow-up institutions, either the kindergarten, or the first grade, whose objectives are in turn modified by the child's previous experience.

Major Outcomes of Nursery School. Primarily the goals are derived from the growth needs—physical, mental, social, and emotional—of chil-

FIG. 5-4. Young artists washing their hands after painting. (*Courtesy of Bureau of Research Service, University of Illinois.*)

dren from two to four. The nursery school helps the modern home meet these needs by providing the child with regular association with children in an environment suited to the child and especially equipped for him and under guidance of skilled persons trained to promote his best development.[12]

PROGRAM AND PROCEDURES

The Curriculum. The curriculum of the nursery school, if one can technically call it such, is broad in scope, for it is planned to meet all the needs of growing youngsters from two to four years of age.

Authorities agree that it is necessary to look upon the pupil as a learner from birth and to realize that the habits of learning are more important than the actual material learned. The learning activities are of two gen-

12 *Our Cooperative Nursery School*, p. 9, Silver Spring, Md., 1949.

eral types: routine and free. These activities are usually organized into a flexible schedule.

Program of Activities. The planning of a nursery-school program depends a great deal upon the length of the daily session. Some schedules cover only 2 to 4 hours, whereas some all-day nurseries are planned on a 10-hour day basis. The activities usually cover the hours from 8:30 A.M. to 3:00 or 3:30 P.M., or longer if necessary, for children of working mothers. The following is an illustrative list of everyday activities that provide the requisite learning experiences:

1. *Health supervision.* Each day before the child comes in contact with the other children, it is important that a registered nurse or some other competent person examine the child to see that skin, throat, eyes, and nose show no symptoms of infectious disease. . . .

2. *Health practices.* Various procedures carried out in the course of the daily care of the children, such as toileting, or the serving of food, fish-liver oil, and water, present certain health risks. Such routines must be considered from the point of view of health protection and be utilized to establish desirable health practices.

3. *Eating.* The hot dinner and midmorning and midafternoon "snack" should be served at regular hours at small, low tables, with chairs of correct height for the different ages. The three- and four-year-olds should have opportunities to serve themselves. . . .

4. *Sleep and rest.* Young children need frequent periods for rest and relaxation. They should have a 10- to 15-minute rest period immediately before the noon meal. Frequently, there are some children in the group who need additional rest periods. . . .

5. *Toileting and washing.* It will be necessary for the teacher to observe the children's natural intervals and arrange for toileting on an individual basis. It is possible, however, that regular toileting periods will have to be arranged for small groups of children.

6. *Work-play period indoors.* Children need an opportunity to reproduce familiar adult activities through dramatic play, to manipulate materials such as clay, paints, crayons, peg boards, blocks, wood, hammer, and nails. They also need to look at books and pictures and to respond to music. There should be times when they may tell one another or discuss together what happens at their homes, and during their work and play periods at school. . . .

7. *Work-play period outdoors.* Children should have daily opportunity for outdoor activities. . . .[13]

This shows that the nursery school gives consideration to the child's play, work, food, and sleep.

In some schools, the age groups are separated. Most groups have full day sessions. The schedules are adjusted by the teacher to meet the needs

[13] National Society for the Study of Education, *American Education in the Postwar Period*, Part I, pp. 24–26, University of Chicago Press, 1945.

of each age level. Naturally a good nursery school takes into account the home conditions under which the child lives. It does not exist as an isolated unit but is an integral part of the community, supplementing other agencies supported by the people.

Nursery-school Staff. The superior nursery school has a balanced, competent staff of teachers and also of specialists in parent education and family life, mental hygiene, nursing, medicine, nutrition, and cooking. Small nursery schools often pool their resources in order to obtain all the needed talent for working with young children. It is essential that all staff workers understand and like little children and their parents. Teachers and other personnel workers are discussed in Units XI and XII.

CURRENT PRACTICES IN NURSERY-SCHOOL EDUCATION

By way of recapitulation, some of the many interesting and significant practices current in nursery schools are mentioned briefly. The *status in quo,* however, may not necessarily represent the best ideas and highest ideals.

The terminology employed in early childhood education is being revised. For example, "child-and-mother school" or "family-life school" may replace "nursery school." "Preschool" or "prekindergarten" as applied to nursery school is being discarded, since the terms suggest modification of a program designed for older children. The entire period of growth from two to eight years of age is being considered as a unit for guidance and instruction.

The scope of the nursery school is being broadened. Now it is not merely a safe place to leave a child; rather, it is an educational center for all-round growth. Emphasis is placed upon emotional as well as mental, physical, and social adjustments.

The clientele is changing and enlarging. The nursery school is no longer either a luxury for a few favored children of well-to-do families or a pauper's home. The middle economic group is beginning to reap the benefit of preschool service. Children in new housing projects and in rural areas are being included. A marked trend is the provision of nursery-school education for exceptional children. Many handicapped boys and girls profit even more from early training than do normal youngsters.

More attention is being devoted to nursery-school readiness. Among the main factors considered in determining a child's readiness for group experiences are his age and general maturity; his ability to give and take, to form attachments to other adults besides his mother, and to exchange affection and interests with his peers; and his desire to come to nursery school.[14] Pre-nursery-school parties are often used as an orientation device.

Physical facilities of the modern nursery school include an exposure with plenty of light; ground-floor quarters that are attractive, clean, and safe; space for playing, working, eating, sleeping, bathing, and cooking; radiant heat to

[14] Lili E. Peller, "Nursery School Readiness," *Childhood Education,* September, 1946, pp. 28–33.

warm the cold floors; equipment suited to the child's size and maturity; and direct exits to a covered veranda and enclosed shaded playground. The buildings are being made as attractive as better homes.

Research and observation play an important part in the program. Nursery school is thus becoming a clearinghouse for improved homemaking policies and practices. College and high-school home economics departments are establishing nursery schools as observation and practice centers, for example at Vassar Col-

Fig. 5-5. Three degrees of openness in a school house. This *hogar infantil* in Balbuena, Mexico City, has enclosed rooms with folding doors, a covered veranda, and an open play space. (*Courtesy of Esther Born and Architectural Record. Jose Villagren, Garcia and Enrique de La Mara, Architects.*)

lege and in the high school in Highland Park, Michigan. Thus the unit trains preschool children, adolescents, and adults for participation in wholesome family living. The staffs are producers, consumers, and interpreters of research in child growth and other areas of early childhood education.

Modern programs of early childhood education include guidance for both parents and for prospective fathers and mothers, so that they are playing a greater role in assisting the nursery staff. Thus the gains effected by the children in both school and home are consolidated.

Parent and family-life education has become a part of the regular work of many state departments of education. Some states have established a Council of Parental Education to assist the state departments in developing programs of parent education and nursery schools. A position, Consultant in Family-life Education, was established in the United States Office of Education in order to assist the states in developing programs of education for home and family life to reach both sexes and all age groups.

The increase in the number of babies and parents has increased the need for "baby sitters." Some high schools and public health units give courses or lessons for girls who take baby sitting seriously.

The nursery schools are reexamining their function in the community. Demonstration centers for community programs in home and family-life education have been established in several centers in the United States.

Child accounting systems, which take into consideration the whole child, are being improved. This includes a continuing census of the number of potential nursery-school children. Cumulative recording and evaluating are increasing.

More and more states are providing some form of financial aid for nursery schools, or are authorizing permissive taxation at the local level. Various other laws are being enacted to aid the nursery school and the young child. Adoption laws are being bettered. For example, many state adoption laws now require a trial period in the home of the prospective parents before the adoption is made final.

State departments of education are providing more guidance for and supervision over nursery schools, including higher standards of certification for teachers. Their personnel is being enlarged and improved. Some nurseries have specialized workers such as recreation directors, dietitians, parent-education specialists, home counselors, and other social case workers. Welfare services, such as those performed by visiting housekeepers, are helping to improve conditions in the home. These "traveling mothers" render many services for children. The health program includes the regular services of a physician and daily inspection by a qualified person.

FUTURE OF NURSERY SCHOOLS

Quantitatively the future for nursery schools is bright. According to *Time,* in 1975 the United States will need to set a "fifth plate" for every four now on the table. The large increase in the number of children— over four million a year—has stimulated the demand for more nursery schools.

The nursery school today occupies a marginal position just outside the public-school system, somewhat similar to that held for many years by the kindergarten. When kindergarten education becomes a universal or compulsory part of the school system, the nursery school may then enter on a mandatory-on-petition basis and eventually take its place as the beginning unit in the American public-school system. As the Educational Policies Commission states:

The nursery school now is the new child in the family of public education. If it is wanted and accepted, it will win a place for itself and enhance the value of other members. At first it may seem a stranger, but after it has made its contribution felt, we in public education will gradually realize that our family circle was incomplete until it arrived.[15]

[15] Educational Policies Commission, *op. cit.,* pp. 27–28.

Thus the future of the work lies in coordinating the nursery schools with the next higher educational units, especially the kindergarten.

KINDERGARTEN EDUCATION

SCOPE OF KINDERGARTEN EDUCATION

Kindergarten education usually covers the period of schooling just before the child enters the first grade, whether he has had nursery-school experience or not. The entrance age is generally set at four or five years, although some subkindergartens admit younger children. Several recent studies of eye growth and reading readiness reveal that a child six years old chronologically may not always be ready for reading experience and that he can more profitably spend some time in the preprimary or kindergarten group. Naturally the kindergarten differs somewhat from the nursery school.

Nursery School and Kindergarten. The nursery school may be compared, rather than contrasted, with the kindergarten. Compared with kindergarten, the nursery school admits younger children, generally from two to four years; operates usually on a full-day schedule; keeps a closer touch with the home because the child is younger; provides more opportunities for parental education; stresses more the physical care and development of the child; gives more attention to eating, sleeping, and kindred habits; gives more guidance to children in learning independence in self-control, personal care, respect for property rights, etc.; shows the child how to do a thing with a minimum of telling or explaining; utilizes less appeal to group opinion; has equipment and supplies on a smaller scale; has fewer children per teacher; and does not enroll so many children as the kindergarten. The differences, however, are primarily those of degree. As the child goes from the nursery school to the kindergarten, the scope of his learning experiences widens.

The separate problems of the nursery school and the kindergarten are joined in the common responsibility of providing continuous, broadening, and deepening experiences for the children. Among the numerous means of correlation between the nursery school and the kindergarten are: accurate record keeping of the child's progress, the planning of teacher-education programs so that prospective nursery and kindergarten teachers see their work as one, the elimination of excess emphasis upon organization units, and the development of a comprehensive philosophy of education that carries through from nursery school to adult education.

Kindergarten and Home. Since for many children the first contact with an actual school situation comes in the kindergarten, a constant, vital relationship should exist between the kindergarten and the home. This relationship may be promoted by various means. Some kindergarten teachers send daily reports to the parents on items such as food difficulties, the amount of sleep or play, or emotional disturbances. The mothers may also inform the teachers about the daily home life and antecedents of the children. In many communities, a home visitation plan releases

Fig. 5-6. Two small children start school via the kindergarten. (*Courtesy of Public Schools, Bloomington, Ill.*)

each kindergarten teacher one afternoon a week to call upon parents. A home visit by the teacher and a school visit by the mother provide direct means of solving jointly many perplexing problems.

Types of Kindergarten. Kindergartens may also be classified by type according to the general categories mentioned for nurseries, *viz.,* research, teacher education, home economics, social service, behavior problems, cooperative, summer school, nursery and kindergarten combined, private, federally supported, and public-school kindergarten. The two most common forms of affiliation are with private interests and the public school. According to methodology of teaching, kindergartens are sometimes named as Froebelian, Montessorian, conservative, middle-of-the-road, or progressive. Whatever the label, the prevailing type of kindergarten is that which seeks to educate the whole child from four to six years through supplementing the home, the nursery school, and other educational agencies.

Enrollments. Although most kindergartens are found in cities of 2500 population and over, the increase in consolidated elementary schools is bringing the advantages of the kindergarten to many rural communities. Although kindergartens are theoretically for children from four to six, the ages actually range from two to seven years. Owing to the increased birth rate, the kindergarten enrolls many more pupils than formerly. Still, only about 50 per cent of the five-year-olds and 70 per cent of the six-year-olds are in school. Millions of children miss the advantages of kindergarten because many communities do not provide this opportunity. Much pioneering still remains to be done if the purposes and program of the kindergarten are to be widely accepted.

AIMS OF KINDERGARTEN

For those who have not attended a nursery school, the kindergarten is an extension of home life; for others, it is a continuation of the work begun in the home and the nursery school. The general aim of the kindergarten, which is unhampered by requirements in subject matter and skills, is to give the child abundant opportunity for enriched experiences.

The National Education Association has summarized the main goals of the kindergarten as those of promoting: (1) children's health, (2) their safety, (3) the ability to work alone despite the presence of others, (4) the techniques of working with others in groups, (5) broad opportunities for contacts with other children and adults, (6) a wide variety of experiences that will reveal their interests and aptitudes, and (7) readiness in reading, writing, and number work they will do in the first grade.[16] The general principle is that of assisting children from the age of four to six years in their developmental tasks—present and future. These aims take shape and substance through a full program of carefully planned activities, based upon sound physiological and psychological principles.

PROGRAM AND PROCEDURES

Principles Underlying the Modern Kindergarten Program. The kindergarten program is extremely flexible—it has no required subjects. The

[16] Adapted from Research Division, *The Value of the Kindergarten*, National Education Association, 1952, 13 pp.

key principle is learning by doing. As the late Catherine Mackenzie has stated:

Today's kindergartens are geared more to scientific research and less to metaphysics than those of a half century ago. The symbolism of the circle and the cube served its purpose and has gone into kindergarten limbo along with the small play materials and their prescribed use, the weaving of intricate patterns, and sewing of fine seams.

FIG. 5-7. What time is it? The significance of numbers is included in the kindergarten's program of general readiness. (*Courtesy of Public Schools, Chicago, Ill.*)

Nowadays the program is much more flexible, the play materials big and more varied and used freely. But learning by doing is still the underlying idea. Kindergarten children do things, make things, go on trips, hear stories, sing. This was Froebel's challenge to the concept of learning by precept and from books. And the kindergarten is still working at it.[17]

In planning the curriculum attention is given primarily to promoting physical, mental, social, and emotional growth.[18]

The psychological and physiological principle that colors most of the

[17] Catherine Mackenzie, "Parent and Child," *The New York Times,* Jan. 5, 1947, p. 32.
[18] Clarice Dechent Wills and Willis H. Stegeman, *Living in the Kindergarten,* pp. 42–56, Follett, 1950.

activities in the kindergarten is that of readiness.[19] As early as 1915 John Dewey said, "Maturity is the result of slow growth of powers. Ripening takes time: it cannot be hurried without harm." The kindergarten therefore withholds certain formal training, such as instruction in actual reading, but it provides rich experiences that will help prepare the child for the elementary grades. These experiences include enriching the child's speaking vocabulary; training in speech through careful enunciation and pronunciation; creating interest in books through storytelling and looking at books; developing left-to-right eye movement through reading a story told in pictures; stimulating arithmetic readiness through counting objects and seeing numbers on calendars; and facilitating development in writing through drawing, cutting, and other forms of eye and hand coordination, including printing one's own name.[20] The readiness goal and others are implemented through a flexible schedule of activities.

Schedule of Activities. Most kindergartens have a morning and an afternoon group. The following is an illustrative morning program from the Bakersfield (California) kindergarten:

Morning Session

9:00– 9:20	Opening. Flag salute.
	Greeting song. Roll call. Conversation.
9:20– 9:45	Work period.
9:45– 9:55	Evaluation.
9:55–10:00	Clean up.
10:00–10:20	Play period.
10:20–10:25	Rest.
10:25–10:40	Rhythms.
10:40–10:55	Story time.
10:55–11:05	Songs.
11:05–11:10	Dismissal.

As this schedule indicates, the kindergarten provides a carefully selected, educative environment replete with sensory impressions and with materials stimulating to the self-activity of the young child.

With due respect to Froebel as a great pioneer, the tendency for many years was to cling too tenaciously to his principles. Today in many kindergartens little of the traditional is left, owing to discoveries of oculists and nerve specialists. For example, these scientists have urged less use of minute materials which call into play the small undeveloped muscles of

[19] Gertrude Hildreth, *Readiness for School Beginners,* Chap. III, World, 1950.
[20] John O. Goodman, *Nursery-Kindergarten Education,* pp. 5–7, University of Wyoming, 1949.

the eye and hand, and greater use of large materials to exercise the muscles of the arms, back, and abdomen. Swings, sleds, carts, large blocks, ropes, and similar equipment are symbols of the new kindergarten.

Fig. 5-8. Kindergarten pupils at work and play indoors, Whitehall, Michigan. (*Courtesy of Hedrich-Blessing Studio and Warren S. Holmes Company, Architects.*)

CURRENT PRACTICES

Current kindergarten practices supplementing those reported previously for nursery schools include the following:

Unfortunately the size of the typical kindergarten is increasing, as a result of shortage of funds and superabundance of children. The traditional provision of two or four semesters is supplemented by three-semester programs in several schools.

A public-relations program for the kindergarten, including a brochure for parents, has been developed in many schools.

A trend is to integrate the kindergarten as part of a continuous program in early childhood education. The kindergarten is losing its status as an isolated part of the school system and is being incorporated as part of a primary unit embracing the nursery school and kindergarten, plus the lower two or three grades. There is more intervisitation between nursery-school, kindergarten, and first-grade teachers.

The transition from kindergarten to first grade is facilitated through the emphasis upon reading readiness. The modern kindergarten, while not "teaching reading," provides indirect preparation for reading. It is copiously stocked with books suitable for children of the kindergarten age. But all six-year-olds are no longer assumed to be *ipso facto* ready to read.

Fɪɢ. 5-9. Small deaf children learning at the Jacksonville Institute for the Pre-school Deaf, Jacksonville, Illinois. They read lip movements, feel throat vibrations, and "hear" human voices at an early age. (*Courtesy of Illinois Welfare Bulletin.*)

More attention is being given to developmental tasks which are set by the maturing of the child, his creative self-motivation, and the demands of society.

Many subjects such as fine arts and science are filtering down into the kindergarten. Almost every topic under the sun is discussed. Much emphasis is centered upon creative self-expression.

Many multisensory aids, such as phonograph records and films, help the child to understand the wondrous world of material things. They also assist the teacher in interpreting to parents and public the role of the kindergarten. Radio and television are being used increasingly, especially in parental education. A "kindergarten of the air" was first established in Perth, Australia, and later another in Toronto, Canada. The latter, designed especially for rural areas, includes in its program health talks, songs, stories, suggestions for handwork, and radio-side games.

As with the nursery school, more kindergartens are being established for exceptional children. Greater attention is now given to psychiatric and psychological treatment of emotionally disturbed children.

Early childhood evaluation is more comprehensive and functional than in yesteryears. Parents help supplement the anecdotal records of developmental processes; these are collected and interpreted by teachers and other members of the kindergarten staff. Mental and achievement tests form ancillary aids in guidance.

Parochial- and private-school kindergartens continue to play an important role in early childhood education and research.

Most teachers colleges and universities offer courses in teacher education for kindergartners. Contrary to traditional practice, the modern kindergarten teacher is often one of the most highly educated instructors in the system. The teaching is often the best in the school. No body of teachers more closely reconciles theory and practice than do the kindergartners.

The majority of the state legislatures have considered early childhood education of sufficient importance to enact legislation providing specifically for the establishment and maintenance of kindergartens as a part of the public-school system.

FUTURE OF KINDERGARTENS

Much research is helping to improve practices. A sample is *The Responsiveness of Kindergarten Children to the Behavior of Their Fellows*, conducted by the Society for Research in Child Development of the National Research Council. Gesell Institute of Child Development is one of several devoted to clinical and guidance services and research in early childhood education.

The future presages a steady growth in the number of kindergartens and in their enrollments. The increase of pupils in the elementary schools diminishes the rooms and finances available to house and support more kindergartens. More state departments will add to their staffs specialists in the supervision and guidance of local programs for early childhood education. All states in time will permit the local school board to establish kindergartens by special election, petition, or decision of the board, and will grant aid for their support. Permissive legislation will be replaced by the compulsory establishment of kindergartens on a voluntary attendance basis. In view of the fact that waves of retrenchment often cause public-school authorities to abandon kindergartens, the interest of the young children must be safeguarded against such reverses through adequate legislation. The gradual acceptance of the kindergarten as a legitimate and permanent part of the public-school system is inevitable. It will continue its vestibule function and open doors to wider horizons. Qualitatively the work of the kindergarten will rise with the uplift in standards for the physical facilities, for the educational program, and for the education of teachers.

SUGGESTED ACTIVITIES

1. Discuss the statement: "The home is the child's first school."
2. What can one learn about children from "baby sitting"?
3. Study the child welfare provisions of the Social Security Act.
4. Enumerate some activities of the federal Children's Bureau.
5. Study the program of a national organization especially interested in the pre-elementary child, such as the Child Study Association of America.
6. Attend a child study meeting and observe the type of program.
7. Write up a case study of some child under six years of age.
8. Discuss the relationships between home-economics education and the pre-elementary child.
9. Prepare a detailed program for parental education.
10. Discuss the selection and use of toys in the home.
11. Outline the progress of nursery schools.
12. Visit a nursery school and observe the children, equipment, and activities.
13. Study the history of the kindergarten in the United States.
14. Prepare a brief biography of Froebel, "the father of the kindergarten," G. Stanley Hall, Susan Blow, or any other pioneer in pre-elementary education.
15. Visit a kindergarten and observe the children, equipment, and activities.
16. Discuss the necessary qualifications for teachers in pre-elementary schools.
17. Debate the issue: "Resolved that the nursery school and the kindergarten should be a part of the public-school system."

DESCRIPTIVE BIBLIOGRAPHY AND AIDS

BOOKS

FOREST, ILSE: *Child Development*, Chap. V, McGraw-Hill, 1954.
    The growth levels at school entrance.
FOSTER, JOSEPHINE, and NEITH E. HEADLEY: *Education in the Kindergarten*, Chap. III, American Book, 1948.
    The role of the kindergarten teacher.
HILDRETH, GERTRUDE: *Readiness for School Beginners*, Chap. III, World, 1950.
    General readiness for children as a goal in pre-elementary education.
HOSTLER, PHYLLIS: *The Child's World*, Chap. IX, Roy Publishers, 1953.
    "The hand that rocks the cradle"—the mother's influence in early education.
JERSILD, ARTHUR T.: *Child Psychology*, Chap. XV, Prentice-Hall, 1954.
    Children's make-believe, dreams, and other imaginative acts.
LEONARD, EDITH M., DOROTHY D. VANDEMAN, LILIAN E. MILES: *Counseling with Parents in Early Childhood Education*, Chap. I, Macmillan, 1954.
    Home and teachers sharing responsibility for the child.
RUDOLPH, MARGUERITA: *Living and Learning in Nursery Schools*, Chap. I, Harper, 1954.
    The role of nursery education.
SHEEHY, EMMA DICKSON: *The Fives and Sixes Go to School,* Chap. IV, Holt, 1954.
    Building schools for young children.
STRANG, RUTH: *An Introduction to Child Study*, Part III, Macmillan, 1951.
    The preschool period—years three, four, and five.

WILLS, CLARICE DECHENT, and WILLIS H. STEGEMAN: *Living in the Kindergarten,* Chap. IV, Follett, 1950.

The characteristics of a good kindergarten.

WOLFF, WERNER: *The Personality of the Preschool Child,* Chap. V, Grune and Stratton, 1949.

The preschool child as an individual.

CURRENT PERTINENT PERIODICALS AND PUBLICATIONS

American Childhood
The Child
Child Development
Child Development Abstracts and Bibliography
Childhood Education
Child Study
Children's Activities
Journal of Genetic Psychology
Journal of Pediatrics

Kindergarten-Primary Magazine
National Parent-Teacher
Parents' Magazine
Parent-Teacher bulletins of state organizations
Proceedings of educational organizations
Progressive Education
School and Home
Yearbooks of educational organizations

AUDIO-VISUAL AIDS

DESIGN OF AMERICAN EDUCATION   16 min., sound

This motion picture, produced by McGraw-Hill for this textbook, is primarily designed for Units I–IV. However, it starts out with Jimmy Appleby going to the kindergarten and ends with Jimmy and his wife, years later, taking their daughter to the kindergarten.

DING-DONG SCHOOL   Radio and television programs

This program, which originated over Chicago's WNBQ, is aimed at preschool children, from three to five years. A nursery school of the air, it is built on active participation. "Miss Frances" is Dr. Frances R. Horwich, chairman of the Department of Education of Roosevelt College, Chicago.

THE FRUSTRATING FOURS AND THE FASCINATING FIVES   22 min., sound, color

A documentation of typical behavior at four and five years. Shows a modern nursery school in operation, takes up problems of discipline, and indicates what can be expected of a child at four or five. Available from McGraw-Hill, New York 36.

HEREDITY AND PRENATAL DEVELOPMENT   21 min., sound

This film, for Elizabeth Hurlock's *Child Development,* published by McGraw-Hill, is one of a series which helps students and teachers to understand better the physiological background of pupils in early childhood education. A related film for studying pre-elementary children is *Principles of Development.*

GROWTH OF INFANT BEHAVIOR   Two reels, sound

An inclusive, introductory view of the clinical and research activities of the Yale Clinic of Child Development. Dr. Arnold Gesell's systematic photographic records at advancing stages of the children's development are a noteworthy exposition of scientific methods. Available from Encyclopaedia Britannica Films, Wilmette, Ill.

PREFACE TO LIFE   29 min., sound

A picture of the critical years in a child's life. Begins with a newborn baby; and follows a series of episodes in his early life. Available from the Mental Health Authority in each state.

THE FIRST DAY AT SCHOOL
                                                                10-inch record
A recording of a musical dramatization of the first day at school for children. Dinah Shore sings several charming songs.

THE TERRIBLE TWOS AND THE TRUSTING THREES   20 min., sound, b&w or color
Shows the never-ceasing activity of two-year-olds in a nursery-school playyard. At three the orbit is expanded and many new activities are added. Available from McGraw-Hill, New York 36.

ELEMENTARY EDUCATION

Pre-elementary work ought to be closely articulated with the elementary school. The latter includes grades 1 through 6 in theory, but 1 through 8 in practice. Elementary-school enrollments have been increasing rapidly, with a resultant need for additional teachers. A slight decline, however, is expected by the end of the decade.

Early education in colonial America was influenced by European practices. The dame and pauper schools, however, slowly evolved into the modern elementary schools, through the efforts of pioneer thinkers and workers.

The basic purpose of the elementary school is the all-round development of the child from six to twelve years, with particular emphasis on equipping him with basic skills, knowledges, attitudes, and appreciations. General education is its main function.

Elementary schools throughout the country represent diversified patterns and variegated programs. The traditional divisions are primary, intermediate, and upper grade or junior high school.

The programs of the various elementary schools are determined in a measure by their objectives and organization. The teaching and learning procedures are as diversified as the curriculums, varying from ultraconservative to ultraprogressive. The elementary school has an assured future in American democracy.

OUTLINE OF CONTENTS

ELEMENTARY EDUCATION

Articulation with Pre-elementary Education. The modern elementary school is closely joined to pre-elementary work, particularly for children who enter the first grade with some school experience either in the nur-

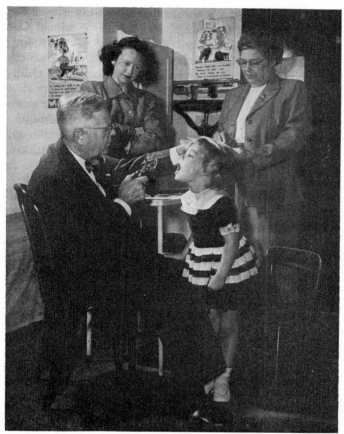

Fig. 6-1. Parents are encouraged to accompany and observe pupils during physical examinations. Many schools sponsor summer roundups for children entering elementary school. (*Courtesy of Arthur Clarke Studios and Public Schools, Richmond, Va.*)

sery school or kindergarten or both. Although an increasing number of pupils have this orientation, the first school contact for most children comes in the first grade. Those beginners who have not had the benefit of preschooling ought to visit the first grade several times before they are actually enrolled. Going from a home with a few members into a classroom with 25 or more pupils is a difficult adjustment for many children. Every effort should therefore be expended to make possible an easy entrance into the elementary school.

The experiences in the nursery school and kindergarten should be vitally related to the first year of the primary school. The so-called "primary unit," an organization embracing kindergarten through grade 2 or 3, has provided a setting in which beginning elementary-school experiences are adjusted so as to remove or to markedly reduce failure.

Whatever the organization, a child's first school experience ought to be preceded by a physical examination. In 1925 the National Congress of Parents and Teachers inaugurated the summer roundup for physical examinations of all children entering school in the fall. This clinic, held in the summer, gives particular attention to the preschool child in order that physical defects may be discovered and corrected if possible before he enters the first grade. Many schools follow the summer examinations with a recheck in the fall. These clinics should be continuous. Periodic health examinations are necessary safeguards in all grades and at all ages, for it obviously is better to prevent illness than to seek to restore lost health. The ultimate objective of the summer roundups is an annual health inventory from childhood through adulthood.

Scope of Elementary Education. Elementary education is difficult to define because of the extreme variety of practices in its organization, administration, and curriculums. In terms of children's ages, it is the educational institution for pupils from approximately six to twelve or fourteen years of age. In terms of group living, it is described thus by the Educational Policies Commission in its historic report *Education for All American Children:*

The elementary school has a unique responsibility for improving group life. It is in the elementary school that most children for the first time become actual members of a group. Here they join with their peers in real group interaction. From this very meager beginning, it is the responsibility of the elementary school to guide children to more competent membership in ever-enlarging groups.[1]

In terms of major foci, the lowest grades develop the child as a person and a citizen.[2] In terms of curricular content and skills, the elementary school is the level in which the pupil is concerned with five major acquisitions, the five R's: reading, 'ritin, 'rithmetic, recreation (health), and relationships, including social adaptations, such as cooperation. In terms of grades, elementary education includes theoretically grades 1 through 6; in practice, however, it generally embraces grades 1 through 8.

---

[1] Educational Policies Commission, *Education for All American Children,* p. 147, Nation Education Association, 1948.

[2] James L. Hymes, Jr., "Better Humans, Better Citizens," *The American Elementary School,* p. 369, Harper, 1953.

The common subdivisions of the elementary school are usually grouped as: primary, grades 1 through 3; intermediate, grades 4 through 6; and upper, grades 7 and 8. Naturally there is overlapping between divisions and organization units (see Fig. 6-2). The kindergarten may be included in the primary level, whereas the junior high school is usually considered a part of secondary education.

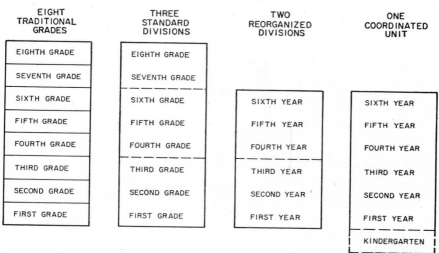

FIG. 6-2. Scope and organization of elementary education. In diagram 1, on the left, elementary education consists of eight compartments called grades, with rigid promotional policies and practices. In diagram 2, the number of divisions is reduced to three: primary, intermediate, and upper grades, with a greater degree of flexibility and articulation. In diagram 3, the seventh and eighth grades are assigned to secondary education, and the two remaining components become the lower and upper elementary school. In diagram 4, division lines disappear and the continuous 6-year unit, with the possible addition of the kindergarten, replaces the traditional grade organization. The seventh and eighth grades may be included in a one-unit organization.

These three major areas are not to be construed as disparate units; rather they are to be recognized as components of an organized whole. Medicine and psychology affirm the continuous rather than periodic growth of children. A child's growth is not measured in annual rings like a tree. In order to eliminate some of the numerous "stop and go signs," several grades may be combined. This is a frequent practice in rural schools where the teachers thus reduce the number of classes. In many city schools also the traditional emphasis on eight disparate grades is being modified. For example, some schools neither promote nor detain pupils at the end of the first grade. The first two or three years of elementary education are considered a primary unit, and not until the end of the third year is the child promoted to the next area. Modern theory suggests "year" for "grade." Some schools obliterate grade lines and organize the 6 or 7 years as a unit, the latter embracing the kindergarten.

Elementary-school Enrollments. A striking phenomenon of American public education is that the number of pupils enrolled in both public and private elementary schools is increasing markedly. Among the basic reasons for the growth are the increased birth rate, the increase in immigration, and the larger percentage of children attending school. During the decade from 1940 to 1950, elementary enrollments dropped to 20,-000,000. Within the 1950-to-1960 period, a new high of 33,000,000 will

Fig. 6-3. A modern elementary-school building—the Franklin Elementary School, Houston, Texas. (*Courtesy of Herbert Volecker, Architect, Houston, Tex.*)

be reached for kindergarten-elementary pupils in public and other schools. This will be followed by a decrease due to fewer babies born to married couples who themselves were the small baby crop in the depression years of the 1930's.

DEVELOPMENT OF ELEMENTARY EDUCATION

Historical Calendar—Elementary Education and Contemporaneous Events

The historical calendar facilitates association of important happenings in elementary education with significant events of a political, social, and economic nature in the United States. The various events listed in the right column of the calendar are not related directly to the educational achievements indicated in the left column. The former merely serve to link the latter to some important event that occurred at approximately the same time in American history. Obviously, as indicated later in the discussion of pioneers in this field, elementary education is of foreign origin.

Historical Calendar

ELEMENTARY EDUCATION	CONTEMPORANEOUS EVENTS
1633—Elementary school established by Dutch (New York)	1634—Maryland settled
1642—Earliest colonial educational law passed (Massachusetts)	1643—New England Confederation formed
1647—"Old Deluder" Act passed (Massachusetts)	1647—Peter Stuyvesant made governor of New Amsterdam
1651—Existence of dame school recorded in New Haven (Connecticut)	1649—First religious toleration law in America passed by Maryland
1834—Free elementary education first adopted by a state (Pennsylvania)	1834—Bancroft's *History of United States,* Vol. I, published
1835—Cousin's *Report on State of Public Instruction in Prussia* published	1835—War begun between Seminole Indians and United States
1837—Stowe's *Report on Elementary Education in Europe* published	1837—Morse system of telegraphy patented
1837—"Common-school revival" started by Horace Mann	1837—Great financial crisis spread over United States
1852—First compulsory law for part-time school attendance passed (Massachusetts)	1852—*Uncle Tom's Cabin* written by Harriet Beecher Stowe
1890—First full-time compulsory school attendance law passed (Connecticut)	1890—Sherman Antitrust Act passed by Congress
1893—Six-six plan of school organization recommended by Committee of Ten	1893—Another financial panic spread throughout United States
1896—Experimental School established at University of Chicago by John Dewey	1896—Gold discovered in Klondike region in Alaska
1918—Compulsory education made effective in all states	1917—United States entered First World War
1948—Basic policy for elementary education presented in *Education for All American Children*	1948—Meeting of ninth Pan-American Child Congress held in Caracas, Venezuela
1953—Report of Mid-century Committee on Outcomes in Elementary Education published by Russell Sage Foundation	1953—First two educational television stations initiated in Houston, Texas, and Los Angeles, California
1955—Elementary-school enrollments increased approximately 6 per cent over previous year	1955—Income tax legislation implemented to give widowed parent additional deduction for child

ESTABLISHMENT OF PUBLIC ELEMENTARY EDUCATION

Early Beginnings of Elementary Education. In colonial America elementary schools were organized much later than the universities. An exception occurred in New York State where under Dutch rule a free tax-supported elementary school was established:

The Dutch West India Company was required by the States General of Holland to maintain a clergyman and a schoolmaster. The schoolmaster's ex-

FIG. 6-4. Elementary school in New York in 1633. In the Dutch period, school was maintained in the city tavern shown above. The Dutch West India Company engaged a schoolmaster for Fort Amsterdam in 1633. (*Courtesy of New York State Teachers Association.*)

penses are entered in early estimates of the company's expenses. The first schoolmaster, Adam Roelansten, arrived in 1633. With his advent a school tax was levied. The schoolmaster was also gravedigger, court bellringer, and precentor.[3]

When New Netherlands became New York, the resultant change in

[3] R. L. Finney, *American Public School,* p. 5, Macmillan, 1921.

policy retarded the development of public elementary education in New York State.

Colonial New England and especially Massachusetts took the first steps toward the permanent establishment of schools for the common people. Some time after the settling of Massachusetts, the law of 1642 was passed. It gave to town officials the "power to take account from time to time of their parents and masters and of their children, especially of their ability to read and understand the principles of religion and the capital laws of the country, and to impose fines on all those who refuse to render such accounts to them when required." [4] This was followed by the "Old Deluder" law of 1647 which required the various towns to establish and maintain schools and even imposed a fine of £5 for failure to do so. Numerous laws were passed in the colonies in regard to free education, but most of them contained the significant word "or." Permissive legislation was the usual type of school regulation. Thus the colonists permitted a system of free public education in theory but in practice supported few free schools.

Dame Schools. According to Cubberley, elementary education in the eighteenth century was entrusted to reading and writing schools. These were followed by dame schools, the first record of which is found in New Haven, Connecticut, in 1651.

The dame school was the characteristic institution of the entire colonial period. It grew out of the responsibility each mother felt to teach her own children to read. Mothers who for any reason wished to be relieved of the responsibility sent their children to a neighbor who taught her own children the rudiments, often busying herself meantime with her housework. Often, too, such a school was conducted by elderly women in straitened circumstances. [5]

These dame schools were primarily for little children; when older pupils came to school in the winter, a man teacher was usually employed. The dame schools were followed by primary schools that became nonsectarian forerunners of the modern elementary system.

Nonsectarian Schools. Public education struggled to become nonsectarian. Throughout the colonial period elementary education had a strong religious tone. Moral and religious truths were emphasized constantly. The school was often made the servant of the church, and numerous religious denominations established their own schools. The pupils were usually taught reading, writing, arithmetic, singing of hymns, prayers, and catechism. Often parochial schools were granted aid from state funds. Gradually the pendulum swung from one extreme to the

[4] William H. Burton, *Introduction to Education*, p. 200, Appleton-Century-Crofts, 1934.

[5] Finney, *op. cit.*, pp. 9–10.

other—from sectarianism to secularism. The first state to adopt a constitutional provision prohibiting sectarian instruction was New Hampshire in 1792. Today it is illegal in most states to teach the Bible or to give sectarian instruction in publicly supported schools.

Elementary Schools Free and Open to All. Elementary education in America encountered many obstacles, including the social beliefs and prejudices that the colonists carried with them from the old country. Prevailing ideas in England, Germany, France, and other countries influenced the new world. The concept of social classes or castes extant in England during the colonial period made education a matter of private rather than state support. Persons of wealth sent their children to privately supported schools or engaged tutors to teach them at home. For those unable to do this, pauper schools were established. But because of the stigma attached to being a pauper, the very schools set up for poor children were often not patronized by them. Many influences and many persons working over a long period of years brought about gradually the establishment of free public schools for all children. Pennsylvania in 1834 adopted a state program of free schools. Other states followed this example until today elementary education is free and available to all.

Elementary Education Compulsory. Another struggle was to make elementary education compulsory. One hundred years ago attendance was generally optional. The histories of the colonies reveal the gradual adoption of the principle of compulsory elementary education, but records are strangely silent as to the degree of its enforcement. One may look to Massachusetts for the contribution of the law and to Connecticut for its administration and methods of enforcement. The first state compulsory school attendance law was adopted in Massachusetts as late as 1852; this legislation for part-time compulsory attendance was followed in 1890 by Connecticut's full-time requirement. Compulsory schooling was bitterly opposed by many people who argued that it deprived the parents of their inalienable rights, it was not necessary in order to secure attendance, it was an uncalled-for assumption of powers by state governments, it was inimical to the spirit of free democratic institutions, and it was an obstacle in the employment of child labor.

The majority of states now demand that every normal child attend the elementary school for at least 8 months annually between the ages of seven and sixteen, or until he has completed the eighth grade. Several states have enacted laws raising the compulsory school age to eighteen years.

Many Foreign Influences on Elementary Education. Compulsory education was one of several ideas that were undoubtedly borrowed from other lands, particularly Prussia. For several years elementary education abroad was studied intensively for suggestions that could be adopted by or adapted to the American primary school. Victor Cousin's *Report on the State of Public Instruction in Prussia,* which appeared first in French and about 1835 in English, was widely read in America. Calvin E. Stowe, the husband of Harriet Beecher Stowe who aroused America with her picture of slavery in *Uncle Tom's Cabin,* exercised a tremendous influence upon American education through the publication of his *Report on Elementary Education in Europe* (1837). This was studied by many state legislators. That same year Horace Mann as secretary of the state board of Massachusetts launched what became known as the "common-school revival." Mann, who in 1843 had visited schools in England, Ireland, Scotland, Germany, Holland, and France, published his carefully prepared observations in his famous *Seventh Annual Report,* which lauded the Prussian educational system and produced his celebrated controversy with the Boston schoolmasters, whom he defeated singlehanded. Henry Barnard in 1854 wrote his *National Education in Europe,* which also left its imprint. For years American education was influenced from abroad through reports on European systems of education, the writings of foreign teachers, and the activities of their pupils in America.

PIONEERS IN ELEMENTARY EDUCATION

Elementary education in the United States has been affected by various educational leaders both here and abroad who struggled valiantly for those reforms that today make the elementary school the most progressive unit of American public education. Among these stalwart thinkers who left their indelible impress are Comenius, Rousseau, Pestalozzi, Herbart, Mann, Barnard, Parker, Dewey, and Kilpatrick.

John Amos Comenius (1592–1670). One of the earliest concepts of general universal education originated in the mind of a Moravian churchman of the seventeenth century, *viz.,* Comenius (or Komensky, if the Bohemian name is used). His program advocated "the teaching to all men of all the subjects of human concern." He severely criticized the schools as "the slaughterhouses of the mind where ten or more years are spent in learning what might be acquired in one." This he said was due to the fact that the mind was fed mostly on words. He, the father of realism in modern education, fought against verbalism and for concreteness. In order to make teaching more concrete he prepared a pictured encyclopedia, *Orbis Pictus,* in which each word is defined and illustrated. This was the first picture book successfully adapted to the teaching of young children. He helped make education less remote, less austere, more sympathetic, and more interesting to children. Because of his early formulation and practical application of sound educational principles, Comenius, though still submerged in obscurity, is one of the leading figures in the history of education abroad and also in America.

He died in the Netherlands—a land very susceptible to his influence; and it was in Dutch New Amsterdam in the new world that the public-school idea thrived early.

Jean Jacques Rousseau (1712–1778). One who helped to explode traditional ideas on the training of young children was the Frenchman Jean Jacques Rousseau. Education, according to Rousseau, should be "according to nature." The learner would then develop the capacity with which he is endowed. Rousseau led the revolt against the extreme insistence upon facts and subject matter and the subordination of the child.[6] He was the progenitor of the child-centered elementary school.

Johann Pestalozzi (1746–1827). Pestalozzi, likewise a true pioneer, was born in Switzerland. In his masterpiece, *Leonard and Gertrude,* he stated that the aim of education was the natural and systematic development of all the powers of the individual. He believed that a child developed in accordance with definite laws and that the aim of education was to assist nature in the observance of these laws. Pestalozzi was unique in that he practiced his theories. His school in Switzerland attracted attention throughout the western world. Americans who had visited this school with its homelike atmosphere suggested for American education many improvements based upon their observations and his work. Pestalozzi himself considered that his recognition of "observation" as the basis of all knowledge was his real contribution to the methodology of elementary education. He emphasized sense perception and "object lessons." Especially through his disciple, Fellenberg, he promoted the idea of associating manual activities and industry with education. Though many of his theories have been proved erroneous and many of his methods became frozen formality, nevertheless his basic ideas, his demonstration teaching, and his experimentation have exerted a tremendous influence upon elementary education both abroad and in America.

Johann Herbart (1776–1841). Among other influential foreign teachers were Froebel, who, as indicated in Unit V, started the kindergarten, and Herbart, who was a German philosopher. The latter studied at Jena and became a pupil of Fichte but later rejected most of Fichte's system and developed his own. His ideas affected both philosophy and education. He taught that character is the main aim of education, which has its real beginning in knowledge and its final end in action. His numerous principles such as those of the "many-sided interests," correlation of subjects, and apperception were introduced into the United States under the leadership of his disciples, notably Charles De Garmo and Charles and Frank McMurray, at Illinois State Normal University, Normal, Illinois. What is now the National Society for the Study of Education was founded at Normal in 1895 as the National Herbart Society. Herbart was one of

6 Stuart G. Noble, *A History of American Education,* p. 198, Rinehart, 1938.

the first educators to give a scientific approach to the study of education. In his methodology, he developed the five formal steps as follows: preparation, presentation, comparison, generalization, and application. This formula is found in detail in older texts on general methods of teaching. These pedagogical steps have had a marked influence on elementary as well as on secondary education. Some of Herbart's ideas are reflected today in the Morrisonian method of unit teaching.

Horace Mann (1796–1859). Known as "the father of the common schools," Horace Mann, during his 12 years as secretary of the state board of education in Massachusetts, started the common-school revival. Armed with no legal authority, but by dint of persuasion, Mann helped to improve the housing of pupils and the professional preparation of teachers. He lengthened the elementary-school term and won an increased measure of popular and financial support for the schools and teachers. In his 12 annual reports, published at the end of each year of his secretaryship, and in his *Common School Journal,* which he started in 1838, Mann covered almost every phase of education. Much of this material is up to date even today. Through his efforts the first normal school was established at Lexington, Massachusetts, in 1839. His indefatigability extended his influence beyond Massachusetts to the nation and, through his friend Sarmiento, to the public schools in Chile and Argentina.[7]

Henry Barnard (1811–1900). Henry Barnard occupied a place similar to that of Horace Mann in Massachusetts by serving as state commissioner of education in Connecticut from 1838 to 1842 and in Rhode Island from 1843 to 1849. After having absorbed Pestalozzi's ideas in Europe, Barnard promoted these ideas in America. His book *Pestalozzi and Pestalozzianism* is one of the outstanding books in English on the subject. Barnard edited the *American Journal of Education,* which treated almost every phase of education here and abroad. He established the first teachers' institute in 1839 and improved the training of elementary teachers. As the first United States Commissioner of Education, Barnard helped to raise the status of education, particularly in elementary schools.[8]

Colonel Francis Parker (1837–1902). Among the American educational pioneers who enriched the elementary curriculum was Francis Parker, who became the leader of the progressive movement. After varied experiences, such as teaching in rural and city schools, fighting in the Civil War, and experimenting with new methods in a normal school in Ohio, he was elected superintendent of schools at Quincy, Massachusetts. There

[7] See Unit II for additional information on Horace Mann. See also Louise Hall Tharp's *Until Victory: Horace Mann and Mary Peabody,* Little, Brown, 1953, 367 pp.
[8] See Unit I for additional information on Henry Barnard.

he became famous as a leader of the Quincy movement, which embodied some of Froebel's principles in making the school less artificial and conventional. Children were taken outdoors for lessons in science and geography, and teachers were given much freedom and expert supervision. His greatest work was that as principal of the Cook County Normal School at Chicago and later as principal of the Chicago Institute, afterward the School of Education of the University of Chicago. Parker was a lover of children, and he had the rare insight to see teaching problems from the standpoint of the child. His enthusiasm and earnestness brought to the Cook County Normal School students from all parts of the country. These teachers whom he trained have gone far in improving the elementary schools of America. Among his writings, which have also had a marked influence, are *Talks to Teachers, Talks to Pedagogues, How to Study Geography,* and *Course in Arithmetic.* His writings, lectures, and teaching prepared the way for John Dewey.

John Dewey (1859–1952). The leading American educational philosopher and molder of the policies of the elementary school was John Dewey. In 1896 Dewey established an experimental school at the University of Chicago where he tried out some of his educational plans. In 1904 he joined the faculty of Teachers College, Columbia University, where he taught and influenced thousands of teachers. His book *School and Society,* published in 1899, affected markedly the function of the school in society. Among his other publications, some of which have been translated into a dozen languages, were: *Interest and Effort, Democracy and Education, How We Think, Quest for Certainty, Experience and Education,* and *Logic: The Theory of Inquiry.* It is said that contributions made by most of his books are in inverse proportion to their size; the small ones, such as *School and Society,* had a greater influence than his huge volume *Quest for Certainty.* He was widely known and honored in both the Orient and the Occident.

The Gary public-school system, which modified its program in 1941, and other innovations in elementary-school organization, such as the Winnetka system, were inspired by John Dewey. His emphasis upon doing and living was basic in the elementary-school program. The following quotation is a brief sample of his philosophy:

If one attempts to formulate the philosophy of education implicit in the practices of the newer education, we may, I think, discover certain common principles amid the variety of progressive schools now existing. To imposition from above is opposed expression and cultivation of individuality; to external discipline is opposed free activity; to learning from texts and teachers, learning through experience; to acquisition of isolated skills and techniques by drill, is opposed acquisition of them as means of attaining ends which make direct vital appeal; to preparation for a more or less remote future is opposed making the most of the opportunities of present life; to static aims and materials is opposed acquaintance with a changing world.[9]

Dewey's philosophy was not so simple that it can be expressed adequately by one quotation or chapter. In America, the John Dewey Society publishes a yearbook on various phases of his pragmatic philosophy and of progressive education. The progressive idealism of John Dewey and his followers has influenced all levels of learning but especially the elementary school.

FIG. 6-5. John Dewey. (*Courtesy of Keystone View Company.*)

William Heard Kilpatrick (1871—). As a professor of education for many years at Teachers College, Columbia University, and since his retirement in 1937, Dr. Kilpatrick has indoctrinated thousands of elementary- and secondary-school teachers who have flocked into his classes, attended his lectures, or read his books. Among his publications are *The Project Method, Foundations of Method,* and *Source Book of Philosophy.* Kilpatrick has stimulated the emphasis upon life activities for school children and has defined learning as living. As an interpreter, he has given impetus to progressive education. Of course, the philosophy of Kilpatrick, like that of any thinker, does not stand alone. Each pioneer

[9] John Dewey, "Experience and Education," *The New York Times,* March 6, 1938, p. 10.

is the recipient of thought processes leading down to his day; he is in a sense the interpreter for his own time and a prophet for the days yet to come.

Other Leaders. Numerous leaders, including traditionalists like William Chandler Bagley and psychologists like Edward L. Thorndike, have made substantial contributions to elementary education. School reforms have been brought about through committee reports, such as that of the Committee of Ten, of which Dr. Charles W. Eliot of Harvard was chairman. This famous group recommended in 1893 that a six-six plan of organization replace the traditional eight-four plan. Among the superintendents of schools who have instituted drastic reforms in elementary education are: W. T. Harris of St. Louis, who led the revolt not only against Pestalozzian formalism by substituting natural science for precise object lessons, but also against rigid gradations of pupils and inflexible promotions; Edward A. Sheldon, who started the Oswego movement for improving elementary curriculums and methods in Oswego, New York; and Carleton Washburne, formerly of Winnetka, Illinois, who, as a disciple of Frederick Burk, introduced the so-called "Winnetka plan" for meeting individual differences in the elementary school.

PURPOSES OF ELEMENTARY EDUCATION

The period of elementary education generally concentrates upon developing in the child a command of the fundamental processes or tools of learning. Elementary education, however, is broader than this. It involves the education of the whole child, physically, mentally, socially, esthetically, and ethically.

IMMEDIATE OBJECTIVES OF ELEMENTARY SCHOOL

Although the various parts of the American public-school system contribute markedly to the general objectives of education,[10] each has its unique role to play in the drama of education. These special functions are the immediate objectives or directives of that particular school unit.

As examples of elementary-school objectives, two sets of purposes are presented.

Education for All American Children. The Educational Policies Commission states that the first requirement for a school is that it rest upon values that are good. The second requirement is that it be efficient in promoting these values.

The controlling values in the United States may best be summed up in the one word "democracy." Three of the enduring values that guide and direct the education of all children in American democracy, and

[10] Unit XIII contains several statements of general objectives and outcomes in education.

respective ways by which they may be implemented in the elementary school, are:

Enduring Values of Democracy	*Ways of Promoting These Values*
1. The democratic ideal calls upon citizens to face their problems with self-reliance and initiative, and to conduct their lives without unnecessary demands upon their fellow members of society. This ideal requires that our young citizens master thoroughly many different kinds of learning.	1. A good elementary school, therefore, will help to develop those basic skills and that sturdy independence and initiative which will enable our citizens to attack the problems that face them and to press forward toward ever-improving solutions.
2. Citizens in a democracy exhibit a concern for the general welfare, a feeling of kinship with others, a respect for the laws and social institutions which protect our rights and the rights of others.	2. A good elementary school, therefore, strives for the discovery and full development of all the humane and constructive talents of each individual.
3. Each member in a democratic society should participate, freely and intelligently, in the process of arriving at important decisions which affect the group of which he is a part.	3. A good elementary school, therefore, emphasizes social responsibility and the cooperative skills necessary to the progressive improvement of social institutions.[11]

The broad values of American society thus seek to determine the general goals of the elementary school.

Report of Mid-century Committee on Outcomes in Elementary Education. This study, sponsored by Russell Sage Foundation, Educational Testing Services, the United States Office of Education, and the Department of Elementary School Principals, produced the following outline of goals, abridged by the author:

1. *Physical development, health, and body care.* This is a broad category as compared with the narrow conception of physiology and hygiene which it has replaced in the elementary school curriculum. Today it involves both health and safety, sportsmanship, and an understanding of growth and maturation. . . .

2. *Individual social and emotional development.* This includes material that is commonly associated with mental health, emotional stability, and growth of personality. Emphasis is on such goals as understanding oneself and evaluating oneself [and other goals]. . . . These goals are not the sole responsibility of the schools but are the result of many learning experiences, both within and outside the schools. . . .

3. *Ethical behavior, standards, values.* This area includes the observance of the moral law and the civil law. This includes the observance of much that gains its

[11] Educational Policies Commission, *op. cit.*, pp. 2–4.

validity from the customs and mores of the culture. It involves sportsmanship, kindliness, helpfulness, and the problems involved in living in a society with other people. It is concerned with the integrity and honesty of people.

4. *Social relations.* This grows out of the two previous goals. It is devoted to the individual as a person in his personal-social relations with others, when he has to consider the needs, interests, motives, convictions, and ideals of others with whom he associates in home, community, and place of work. . . .

5. *Social world.* This considers the child in a somewhat broader social setting than does the preceding objective. Here we set goals for the child in terms of the structure and the institutions of our culture. The behavior of the child is considered in relation to community, state, and nation. Geography in relation to man is in this background. Civics, elementary economics, government, and the traditional American way of life are included. . . .

6. *Physical world* (the natural environment). This goal is centered on an enlarged concept of science, and reference is made to many aspects of the child's environment. Physical science problems, as well as the science that deals with plants and animals, are emphasized. Also stressed are learning to think scientifically and the use of methods of science in solving problems in science and in everyday living. Emphasis is on thinking that associates facts and relates them in various ways to form generalizations. In the atomic age, the substance of this goal assumes increased significance. . . .

7. *Esthetic development.* Emphasis is placed on appreciation and expression. Though the primary emphasis here is on art, music, and the crafts, many types of artistic and creative endeavor are embraced. The moral, the intellectual, and the emotional aspects of esthetic development are all included. . . .

8. *Communication.* This covers the wide variety of means by which man communicates with man. It emphasizes the mechanical and skill aspects of reading, writing, composition, correct usage, spelling, punctuation, speaking, and listening. It includes use of the library and of references of various kinds. It includes group skills, such as conducting and participating in meetings. It stresses the various constructive uses to which communication skills must be put, if mastery is to be of value. . . .

9. *Quantitative relationships.* Here are arithmetic and the elementary aspects of algebra and geometry. Here children are introduced to a great variety of measures by which man describes in quantities the things he finds in this world. This involves the ability to analyze and solve problems on the basis of the particular problem, the information needed to solve it, and how to get the information. Emphasis is placed on giving the child an understanding of how our number system works and why, so that he will have greater competence in using numbers. . . .[12]

This excellent study details further for each of the nine objectives: knowledge and understanding, skill and competence, attitude and interest, action pattern, and determining conditions. Obviously the accepted ultimate and immediate goals of elementary education affect the type of school.

[12] Nolan C. Kearney, *Elementary School Objectives,* Russell Sage, pp. 52–120, 1953.

TYPES OF ELEMENTARY SCHOOLS

It is impossible to group all elementary schools into mutually exclusive categories, for there is bound to be overlapping even within major types. Some schools defy classifications or labels. Among the major types are those classified according to (1) size, as one or two teachers, and location, as rural or village; (2) sources of financial support, as public or private; (3) methodology of instruction, as traditional, middle of the road, or progressive; (4) internal organization, as the platoon type; and (5) special schools, as those for atypical children such as the crippled. A terse description of these illustrative types follows.

SIZE AND LOCATION OF SCHOOLS

The most common form of elementary organization is the small school—the one-teacher or one-room school. Here all six, seven, or eight grades are seated in one room, and a teacher may have as many as 30 classes a day, depending upon the number of pupils, their placement in grades, the curriculum, and the flexibility of administration.

The medium-sized elementary schools are found in the villages and the small cities. Usually one teacher is assigned to each grade or class, and a principal serves as the head of the building or system.

The large schools are located in the larger population centers. Two or more teachers may be assigned to a grade, or a departmental organization may be utilized. The largest elementary-school system is in New York City, which has several hundred elementary schools, the smallest of which is a typical one-teacher school.

SOURCES OF SUPPORT AND CONTROL

The elementary schools may also be grouped according to the main sources of their financial support or control, *viz.*, public, or nonpublic, the latter embracing both parochial and other private schools.

Public Elementary Schools. The elementary schools supported by public taxation are by far in the majority and enroll approximately 90 per cent of all the pupils who attend the elementary grades.[13] These form the backbone of American public education.

Nonpublic Elementary Schools. A few million American pupils attend private elementary schools—both parochial and nonparochial. The word "parochial" originally meant parish or the district committed to one pastor. Parochial schools are those established and supported by some religious sect or denomination. Their curriculums usually include moral and religious instruction and courses in the Bible, church traditions, and

[13] For latest statistics on public- and private-school pupils, see *Biennial Survey of Education,* GPO.

church history. Of the children attending private elementary schools, by far the largest number is enrolled in Catholic parochial schools, the next in Lutheran. Torah Umesorah (Hebrew for "religious law and tradition") is an active organization devoted to the promotion of Jewish all-day schools.

The nonparochial private schools may be differentiated from the parochial in that they are supported primarily by nonchurch funds and that they do not give instruction in religion, particularly in the tenets of any specific denomination. The private schools often carry a very high tuition rate, which may or may not include board and room. Frequently they are endowed, but most of the financial support comes from fees and donations. The most progressive methods are often developed in private schools that are unhampered by the constant criticism of a tax-conscious public.

Of all elementary-school pupils in each state, that proportion which attends private elementary schools varies. The greatest number of private elementary schools is found in the Northeastern and Middle states. The United States Supreme Court, by declaring the Oregon Act of 1922 unconstitutional because it violated the Fourteenth Amendment, definitely established the principle that a state may not, through its police power, prohibit private education.

PHILOSOPHY AND METHODOLOGY

The classification of elementary schools according to the ideology and methodology of the teachers and administrators is difficult, for most schools vary in degree between the two limits of the extremely traditional and the completely progressive. Furthermore, both types of teaching may be found within a particular school.

At one extreme is the vigorous activity school which subordinates subject matter to the many-sided development of the child. Little attention is devoted to subjects as such. Promotions are flexible, and much freedom is accorded to teachers and pupils. These procedures are often referred to as progressive education, a term that is hard to define. The chief protagonists of progressive education have been John Dewey and William Heard Kilpatrick, already mentioned as pioneers in elementary-school work. Even before 1900 Dewey pointed out the shortcomings of the "sitting and listening school." [14] An exponent and friendly critic of progressive movements, Professor Boyd Henry Bode, in his *Progressive Education at the Crossroads*,[15] stated that nothing but chaos can result from exclusive attention to children's individual needs and interests; he urged

[14] John Dewey, *School and Society*, p. 51, University of Chicago Press, 1899.
[15] Boyd Henry Bode, *Progressive Education at the Crossroads*, Newson, 1938, 128 pp.

that schools help pupils to oppose dictatorships and make democracy—
a continuous extension of common interests—the way of life.

Chief critic of progressive education and leading exponent of tradi-
tionalism in teaching was Professor William Chandler Bagley of Teachers
College, Columbia University, who helped organize a group called the
"Essentialists." Their indictment of progressive education is that it has

FIG. 6-6. One of the major academic objectives of the elementary schools is to teach
pupils to read intelligently and critically. (*Courtesy of School Management.*)

made education effeminate, has made children inferior spellers and readers, and has used too many "lollipops" in trying to get pupils to learn.
They would direct more attention to discipline, systematic work, and the
fundamentals or "essentials," such as those found in the traditional subjects in the elementary school.[16] This point of view stresses rather formal
teaching procedures. Most one-teacher schools have been of the traditional type, because the necessity of coaching pupils to pass factual examinations has forced teachers to stress rote memory and the bare acquisition of encyclopedic information.[17]

[16] William Chandler Bagley, "An Essentialist's Platform for the Advancement of
American Education," *Educational Administration and Supervision*, April, 1938, pp.
241–256.

[17] The issue of essentialism and progressivism is discussed further in Unit XVII.

Between these two extremes are scattered the majority of the elementary teachers. Many take the middle of the road, recognizing the importance of basic knowledge and necessary skills and yet giving constant heed to the needs, interests, and abilities of the child as well as those of the adult. Even within the same building one may find teachers whose procedures are traditional, middle-of-the-way, or progressive. A teacher, in the span of several years or even a single year, month, or day may reflect varying degrees of conservative or progressive ideology.

INTERNAL ORGANIZATION OF SCHOOLS

The number of classifications under this heading is endless. Grade, division, and unitary organization are illustrated in Fig. 6-2. Mention is made here of ten selected policies or practices that have important bearing upon the organization of schools, as surveyed in a large number of city systems by the Research Division of the National Education Association and the United States Office of Education:

Neighborhood or Community Lower Elementary School. This unit, planned for kindergarten through the third or fourth grades, enables small children to attend school within a few blocks of home. Every child goes home for lunch. The teachers have released noon-hour periods. Home contacts are more frequent. Less space is necessary for school sites.

Self-contained Classroom Units. This has the single teacher as the base unit for the organization within the school. Often the room has all the facilities so that a child need not leave it during the morning or afternoon session.

Departmentalization. This type of organization is not as popular as in past years, especially for the lower grades. It is usually employed in the upper grades. The subjects are taught by special teachers, the pupils passing from one subject teacher to another. Varying degrees of departmentalism are found.

Ability Grouping. The much debated practice of grouping pupils according to ability is followed in one or more schools in a large number of cities.

Platoon Organization. This type of organization, with its nomenclature borrowed from the military, is not widely used. It permits a high degree of room utilization and enables a home-room teacher to be with her group of pupils for one half of each day. During the remainder of the time the pupils go to special subject rooms, such as art, music, speech, physical education, and library science. Some schools use modified platoon systems.

Elimination of Grade Lines. Classification of pupils into broader school units or divisions, rather than into the traditional grades, is increasing in city-school systems. Wherever grade lines are being eliminated, for the most part in the lower portion of the elementary school, the tendency to extend the plan farther into the pattern of school organization seems quite definite and pronounced. Some cities have ungraded primary units for all pupils.

Ungraded Classes. A device in school organization, particularly for providing special opportunities for exceptional children, is the ungraded room. The great majority of such classes have been maintained for slow-learning pupils, and often they have been known as opportunity rooms. In rare instances gifted children also have been classified in ungraded classrooms for enriched programs of study adapted to their special interests and abilities.

Remedial Classes. Groups classified separately for remedial instruction, particularly in such foundation subjects as reading and arithmetic, are widely but not universally used.

Individualized Instruction. Many plans of individualized instruction have been developed and used in America, especially in elementary schools. Some have attracted nation-wide attention, such as the Dalton and Winnetka plans. Other schools have incorporated the essential elements of individualized instruction in which each pupil more or less independently pursues his own project or works on his own contract for at least part of the day.

Class Periods of Indefinite Length. Several schools have abandoned their traditional fixed periods of so many minutes each, substituting for this fixed schedule a flexible arrangement which, subject to the teacher's control, has periods indefinite in length and variable from day to day.[18]

Elementary schools are organized in many other ways.

OTHER SPECIAL TYPES

Schools for Atypical Children. In the larger cities a marked trend is that of separating by buildings particular types of pupils for special instruction. More frequently special rooms and teachers are set aside for the care of the nontypical pupils. One type of school is for the gifted pupils; another is for the slow learners; others are for those physically handicapped, as the Spalding School for crippled children in Chicago; or for those socially atypical, as the Montefiore School in the same city.[19]

Then, too, there is the part-time or continuation school for employed boys and girls. Special instruction in the elementary subjects is also provided through night-school classes attended by older pupils and adults.

Experimental Schools. Although all schools are in a sense experimental, some are especially designated as experimental or demonstration. These include the large number of elementary schools affiliated with universities and teachers colleges as the training ground for student or cadet teachers. Where practice teaching is done entirely off the campus in affiliated schools, the campus elementary school may become a purely laboratory or experimental school for research, exploration, and demonstration.

The elementary school is noted for its experimental procedures. Sometimes these follow a special plan of teaching or curriculum, such as the Gary plan, the Dalton plan, the McDade plan (Chicago), the Winnetka plan, and the Community School (Glencoe).

[18] Adapted from Research Bulletin, *Trends in City-school Organization,* 1938 *to* 1948, pp. 7–22, National Education Association, February, 1949, and U.S. Office of Education, *Organization and Supervision of Elementary Education in 100 Cities,* pp. 84, GPO, 1949.

[19] See Unit X for more information on elementary schools for atypical children.

Many variations are found in the length of the school year. One is the "all-year school" which offers the complete program throughout the entire calendar year. Some schools follow a modified form by offering a summer term after the regular year. As indicated later, the elementary school is the testing ground for many reforms that later creep up into the secondary schools and colleges.

PROGRAM AND PROCEDURES IN ELEMENTARY EDUCATION

EDUCATIONAL PROGRAM

In the typical elementary school of the past, with its program broken into eight divisions or grades, the pupil had to master the subjects in

FIG. 6-7. Children's creative talents are unleashed at an early age. (*Courtesy of Public Schools, Dearborn, Mich.*)

one grade before he could progress to the next. In many schools today the organizational pattern has been reduced to 6 years, plus the kindergarten. This stretch of years is considered, at least in theory, as one continuous period of growth for the child. Generally, however, for purposes of classification and promotion, certain grades or years are grouped into areas of development.

The programs of the elementary grades, as mentioned earlier, are usually grouped into three levels (1) the primary, (2) the intermediate, and (3) the advanced or presecondary.

Primary Grades. The first three grades are usually called primary. Where the kindergarten is a basic part of the early schooling, the grouping may be kindergarten-primary. Some also add the nursery school. Although in the primary grades the central activity is reading, the child develops other essential abilities, such as writing, spelling, and working with numbers. The child develops not only mentally but also physically, socially, and emotionally. The primary area is the most interesting and significant division of public education.

Intermediate Grades. These are usually the fourth, fifth, and sixth grades. The most important curricular activity is still that of reading, but the emphasis is on extensive and enriched reading rather than its mechanics and on the skillful use of the basic tools acquired in the primary grades. Subjects other than those taught in the primary grades are usually added in the fourth grade. This heavy load of new subjects results in an abrupt transition into the fourth grade and a high percentage of failure. The pupil must be prepared for the transition from grade to grade and from primary unit to the intermediate grades; hence in the lower grades learning materials and activities are by degrees introducing him to such areas as social science and natural science. In the more progressive schools no one subject or field of interest is the particular domain of any grade or year. A pupil, whatever his grade or age, is not withheld from learning materials useful to him at his particular stage of development. As in the primary grades, emphasis in the intermediate years is given to the development of desirable individual and social skills, habits, and attitudes. A quiet but observable trend in elementary education is the gradual but effective merging of the primary and intermediate grades into a unified elementary school.

Advanced Level. This area usually includes grades seven and eight, which in the modern interpretation belong to the period of secondary education. In numerous schools this transfer of the upper grades from elementary to secondary education has been effected only in theory. Many a so-called "junior high school" consists merely of glorified seventh and eighth grades which continue with the traditional curriculum and the old philosophy of the upper grades. Unfortunately, the pupils, particularly in the traditional seventh and eighth grades, are subjected to a recapitulation of material supposedly learned earlier. The place and function of the junior high school are considered in Unit VII.

CURRENT PRACTICES IN ELEMENTARY EDUCATION

A few current practices in elementary education are here presented in abbreviated form.

Organization and Administration. The primary purpose of the pattern of an elementary school is to foster the maximum development of every child. Hence, the trend in organization is toward simplicity and flexibility. A reduction in "stop and go" procedures is effected through a reorganization of administrative units, as, for example, a unified six-year program in place of eight disparate grades. Grade classifications are made more flexible or are eliminated, especially in the primary area. In several cities the primary grades have been withdrawn from platoon organization. A reduction has been made in the number of grades, classes, and subjects, especially in the one-teacher schools.

More schooling is being provided. The school day has been lengthened, at least for those who count time from the moment they board the consolidated-school bus till they return home. The school week has been lengthened in some cities, as Madison, Wisconsin, to include informal activities on Saturdays. Several systems provide summertime supervision for recreational and education programs in an elongated educational year. Southern states have lengthened their seven-year school system by adding a year.

Buildings and Other Facilities. With the great influx of young children, many boards of education cannot provide permanent elementary-school buildings, so hundreds of temporary or semipermanent structures have been erected. Many are portable schoolhouses.

More and more buildings for elementary schools are of the one-story type. They blend more harmoniously with residential building surroundings and are more homelike to the young children. Many are small neighborhood schools.

School buildings and equipment are made more flexible and functional. In many elementary schools a workroom is placed between two classrooms or is a part of the room so that small groups can work on construction activities at any time during the day. Equipment with a high degree of flexibility is installed. Running water and toilet facilities are within or adjacent to classrooms, especially for small children. Libraries are used extensively for enrichment.

Curriculum and Teaching-learning Procedures. The pupil in the elementary school is introduced gradually to the curriculum. A well-graduated program of preprimary experiences is provided in order to facilitate the work of the first year. Reading readiness is emphasized.

The curriculum is becoming more flexible. In connection with time allotments for major fields of learning, some schools set up "weekly percentage range of time" with minimum and maximum ranges of time to be spent each week on each major division.

Curricular materials are being reorganized in different relationships and with different purposes. The correlation or fusion of related materials and activities helps to develop an integrating child. Many teachers organize materials as teaching-learning units.

Many curricular materials are being shifted in the light of studies on maturation. Formal instruction in arithmetic is often withheld until the second or third year, but incidental and planned situations for building number concepts are introduced early. There is a downward extension of several fields, such as social science and natural science, into the lower grades.

New and neglected areas are now emphasized. A foreign language, for example, French, is sometimes taught in the elementary schools. Much more use is made of handicrafts, including pottery, metal, and wood work. Language and the fine arts are used increasingly as means of unleashing the creative efforts of pupils. Print-script writing instead of cursive is used in the lower grades because of its similarity to the printed words. United States history and government are accented. More emphasis is placed on helping children to learn about other

Fig. 6-8. Many current practices are revealed in this picture. The movable desks are grouped in the left corner for committee work, while the teacher assists pupils at their individual desks. Bilateral lighting enters from the corridor on the left and the bank of windows on the right, supplemented by artificial lighting. Citizenship and the American heritage are accented on bulletin board and chalk board. (*Courtesy of American Seating Company and of Public Schools, Yonkers, N.Y.*)

peoples of the world and to develop sympathetic attitudes and understandings toward them.

Learning in the elementary school is a cooperative enterprise. The classroom work is actively and realistically coordinated with other service departments of the school. The home is taken into partnership in many school experiences of the learner. The elementary schools have extended their walls into the community, especially through the "go and see" plan of educational trips.

Pupils and Teachers. Pupils receive much individual attention. But this is being jeopardized by the increased enrollments in the elementary school, and more pupils in a class. Pupil failures are being eliminated, or retardation is being reduced markedly. Teachers, especially in the primary unit, are assigned for a period of 2 or 3 years to the same group of pupils. Provisions for handicapped pupils are being improved and expanded. The mobility of the population causes many changes in class rolls.

The modern elementary school stresses personality development and guidance. It seeks to exalt genuine personality. Several elementary schools have established child-guidance clinics. Cumulative records, including anecdotal reports, contribute to evaluation and functional guidance purposes. Sociometric devices are more widely used.

In connection with the modern accent on democracy, there is increased opportunity for pupils to do socially useful work. Student councils are used increasingly as means of promoting democracy in the administration of elementary schools. A cooperative attack upon elementary-school problems is made by pupils, teachers, school administrators, parents, and community leaders. Several schools are using the cooperative-group plan which is an adaptation of departmentalization but calls for a small number of teachers working as a unit, with almost daily conferences among themselves.

The staff is being enlarged and improved. Many schools have added specialists. More elementary schools have trained librarians and are improving school libraries. The teachers of elementary pupils are becoming better educated, but there still exists a great shortage of well-qualified personnel.

These are but a few of the numerous significant changes that are being effected in the modern elementary school.

A Few Contrasts. Some past and present elementary-school procedures are paralleled in columnar arrangement:

Past	*Present*
Child plunged into first grade	Pupil prepared through preprimary experiences
Traditional subject matter used	Curriculum enriched and broadened
Oral reading emphasized	Oral and silent reading, especially the latter, stressed
Words called in reading	Thought-getting and comprehension sought
One basic reading text used	Several books utilized
Library facilities restricted	Library made the heart of the school
Alphabet used in beginning reading	Sentence or story method employed
Reading largely restricted to copyrighted books	Experience reading from pupil-made stories also used
"Mr. Jones" arithmetic problems assigned	Practical arithmetic based on experience and needs
Short penmanship periods used	Legibility sought in all written work
Geography and history taught in isolation	Social studies and interrelationships stressed continuously
Facts memorized for sake of disciplining the mind	Memorization used as a means of acquiring useful information
Factual materials stressed as the end products	Facts used as a means toward the end of understanding and interpretation

Past	Present
Isolated words spelled orally in "spelling periods"	Spelling made a part of all written sentences
Structural physiology memorized	Functional physiology made to contribute to healthy living
Fine and applied arts permitted	These arts encouraged as emotional and creative outlets
Mass imitation employed	Creative expression cultivated
Teacher hired as "schoolmaster"	Teacher made a director of learning
Discipline imposed by teacher	Growth in pupil responsibility and citizenship cultivated
Formal report card issued with numerical notation	Personal progress report written with emphasis on character traits
Mental development of child made chief objective of elementary school	All-round development of pupil made the supreme goal of education

Elementary education, eager to improve on the past, will undoubtedly continue to be a fruitful field for experimentation and, accordingly, the most progressive area in American public education.

FUTURE OF ELEMENTARY EDUCATION

Bulging enrollments have brought elementary education many growing pains. Matching quantitative increase must come a qualitative growth in which attention will be shifted from mass education to improved personal learning and living. This calls for more time from pupils, parents, and teachers.

The editor of the John Dewey Society yearbook, *The American Elementary School,* writes thus of the future:

The future challenges the present-day worker in elementary education successfully to meet old and new problems which are the products of years of uneven changes in American culture. Among them are clear-headed interpretations of democracy and the social goals they imply; better and more equal educational opportunity for all children; resolution of the old issue of standards; how to plan the curriculum more creatively and cooperatively; and how to strengthen the educational experiences of parents and teachers.

The schools we seek are those in which old problems are solved intelligently and in which teachers work, with a sense of cheerful dedication, to fulfill man's ancient dream of a better world for his children.[20]

Thus emerging elementary education is not a destination but a journey, with learners and teachers always en route to better teaching, learning, and living. In this process the key person is the teacher, but her Achilles' heel is her limited preparation for enlarged tasks. Upon teacher improvement, in the last analysis, depends the betterment of elementary educa-

[20] Harold G. Shane, "The Future Challenges the Present," *The American Elementary School,* p. 395, Harper, 1953.

tion. Higher standards for both preservice and in-service education are necessary. Then, too, the elementary teaching staff may well include more young men who understand boys and work with them in their out-of-class activities.

Elementary education forms the backbone of American public education, and it must shape the sinews of democracy. An unfulfilled objective is that of providing every person, no matter what his age or condition, with the equivalent of an elementary education. This will mean more rigid enforcement of compulsory attendance, more attention to handicapped children, and more evening schools for those youth and adults who lack elementary courses. Furthermore, as educational opportunities increase for youth and adults, the elementary school will cease to be a terminal institution, and will be a vital link in the chain of lifelong learning.

SUGGESTED ACTIVITIES

1. Prepare a brief history of elementary education in your own state.
2. Prepare a brief history of the infant school or the dame school.
3. Trace the historical development of a subject such as reading.
4. Prepare a biography of a pioneer in elementary education.
5. Contrast the methods of teaching and discipline in a typical elementary school of 50 years ago and of today.
6. Draw a picture illustrating the difference between old-time and modern classroom procedure in the elementary school.
7. Arrange a debate on the subject: "Resolved that the traditional school is better than the progressive school."
8. Visit a modern elementary-school building and explain its facilities.
9. Visit several grades in elementary schools. Observe the children and examine the methods of teaching and the program of studies.
10. Observe how holidays, such as Thanksgiving and Christmas, and seasonal activities are employed in teaching in the elementary school.
11. Investigate the place of student councils in the elementary school.
12. Attend a faculty meeting of elementary teachers and study their problems.
13. Examine the laws of your state as to the legal ages for compulsory education, preparation of elementary teachers, etc.
14. Discuss the issue: "Resolved that the seventh and eighth grades belong to secondary rather than elementary education."

DESCRIPTIVE BIBLIOGRAPHY AND AIDS

BOOKS

AMERICAN ASSOCIATION FOR SCHOOL ADMINISTRATORS: *American School Curriculum,* Chap. V, National Education Association, 1953.
     The curriculum in the elementary schools of America.
ASSOCIATION FOR SUPERVISION AND CURRICULUM DEVELOPMENT: *The Three R's in the Elementary School,* Chap. VI, National Education Association, 1952.
     Teaching and learning the three R's as part of the total experience of children.
BAXTER, BERNICE, GERTRUDE M. LEWIS, and GERTRUDE M. GROSS: *The Role of Elementary Education,* Chaps. XIV, XV, XVI, Heath, 1952.
     Life in the primary, intermediate, and upper units of the elementary school.

DRAKE, WILLIAM E.: *The American School in Transition,* Chap. I, Prentice-Hall, 1955.
Foundations of education in colonial America.

EDUCATIONAL POLICIES COMMISSION: *Education for All American Children,* Chaps. I, II,
National Education Association, 1948.
Descriptions of hypothetical elementary schools in Farmville, Oak Hill, American
City, Woodland Park, and Patsburg as observed in 1958.

JOHN DEWEY SOCIETY: *The American Elementary School,* Chap. XVI, Harper, 1953.
The future of elementary education as a challenge to the past.

KEARNEY, NOLAN C.: *Elementary School Objectives,* Part II, Russell Sage, 1953.
A thorough study of recommended goals for the elementary school.

MILLARD, CECIL V., and ALBERT J. HUGGETT: *An Introduction to Elementary Education,*
Part IV, McGraw-Hill, 1953.
Qualifications and opportunities in elementary school teaching.

SHANE, HAROLD G., and E. T. McSWAIN: *Evaluation and the Elementary Curriculum,*
Part I, Holt, 1951.
A guide in clarifying goals and establishing procedures for evaluation.

STEPHENS, ADA DAWSON: *Providing Developmental Experiences for Young Children,*
Chap. I, Teachers College, 1952.
Teachers' understanding of developmental experiences.

CURRENT PERTINENT PERIODICALS AND PUBLICATIONS

Bulletins (elementary education)
California Journal of Elementary Education
Child Life
Childhood Education
Elementary English
Elementary School Journal
Grade Teacher
Instructor
National Elementary Principal
Progressive Education
Scholastic Magazine (teacher's edition)
Yearbooks of educational organizations

AUDIO-VISUAL AIDS

CHILDREN IN THE PRIMARY SCHOOL   Filmstrip, 58 frames
Shows experiences for six-, seven-, and eight-year-olds in the primary school.
Available from Association for Childhood Education International, Washington,
D.C.

EDUCATION FOR ALL AMERICAN CHILDREN   Filmstrip, 52 frames
Illustrates the major conclusions and recommendations of the Educational Policies
Commission book *Education for All American Children.* A summary of the book
is found in *Teach Them All.* Available with literature from the Department of
Elementary School Principals, National Education Association, Washington, D.C.

SKIPPY AND THE THREE R's   28 min., sound, b&w or color
A first-grader learns to read, write, and cipher. A motivating factor in his learning is his zeal for a two-wheel bike. Available from the National Education Association, Washington, D.C.

THE ELEMENTARY SCHOOL   1 hour 10 min., sound, color
Helps teachers and others to develop a better understanding of the elementary
school. Supplements the bulletin, *The Characteristics of a Good Elementary
School.* Divided into three parts: 25, 25, and 20 min. Produced by the Virginia
State Board of Education. Available from Virginia Department of Education, Rich-
mond, Va.

SECONDARY EDUCATION

Secondary education embraces in theory the seventh through the fourteenth years of schooling, from the junior high school through the junior college. Often it is delimited to the intermediate institution—the high school, in which up to 1940 the enrollments doubled nearly every decade. It should be closely articulated with elementary education and with that for post-high-school youth.

The evolution of the secondary school has been marked into three periods named after the characteristic institution: the Latin grammar school, the academy, and the public high school. •A fourth period is here, *viz.,* that of the extended secondary school, which reaches downward to include the junior high school and upward to embrace the junior or community college.

The purposes of secondary education are stated in terms of objectives, issues, and functions. The implementation of these purposes has resulted in various types of secondary schools.

Among these are (1) the junior high school, (2) the senior or the 4-year high school, and (3) the junior college. A fourth category includes combinations of the above, as the 6-year high schools, and special schools, as vocational institutions and technological institutes.

Modern secondary education is teeming with changes; the future will see many more.

OUTLINE OF CONTENTS

Introduction
    Articulation of elementary and secondary education
    Scope of secondary education
    Secondary schools and their enrollments
Development of Secondary Education
    Historical calendar
    Four periods of development
    Leaders in secondary education
Purposes of Secondary Education
    Changing concepts of secondary education
Types of Secondary Schools
    Junior high schools
    Intermediate secondary schools
    Junior colleges, community colleges, and other postsecondary institutions
    Other secondary schools
Practices in Secondary Education
    Organization and administration
    Curriculum and teaching-learning procedures
    Personnel
Future of Secondary Education

SECONDARY EDUCATION

Articulation of Elementary and Secondary Education. Most elementary-school pupils advance to the next level of American public education, *viz.,* the secondary school. If they live in a city that has a junior high school, they start the seventh grade in this new unit; if they are in a typical 8-year elementary system, they enter the high school in the ninth grade. Whatever the system, the transition should be smooth for the pupils as they continue their education; they must not be delayed and discouraged by unnecessary "stop" and "go" signs.

Scope of Secondary Education. The fifty-second yearbook of the National Society for the Study of Education defines thus the scope of secondary education:

It embraces the education of youth between the ages of approximately twelve and twenty; these years are commonly referred to as the period of adolescence. In terms of grade levels, secondary education comprises grades VII through XIV; thus it includes the junior high school, the senior high school, and the junior college.[1]

It embraces every phase of the process by which society seeks to develop socially significant abilities and characteristics in preadolescent, adolescent, and postadolescent individuals. It is broader and longer than what was traditionally encompassed by the 4-year high school. Today secondary education has doubled in length; it covers the seventh through the fourteenth year of schooling, extending downward to include the junior high school and upward to embrace the junior college.

Secondary Schools and Their Enrollments. The growth in the number of secondary schools and their enrollments has been phenomenal. Except for a temporary slump in the 1940's, 3- and 4-year senior high schools and their students have increased steadily. By decades, for a 100-year period, the number of high schools is shown in the accompanying table. Prior to 1900 the rate of increase was greater than during any decade in the twen-

Year	Number of high schools	Year	Number of high schools
1850	11	1910	10,213
1860	44	1920	14,326
1870	160	1930	23,930
1880	800	1940	25,467
1890	2,526	1950	27,873
1900	6,005	1960	29,000 (est.)

[1] National Society for the Study of Education, *Adapting the Secondary Program to the Needs of Youth,* p. 2, University of Chicago Press, 1953.

tieth century. In the decade after the Civil War, which included the favorable court decision in the famous Kalamazoo High School Case, the increase in the number of schools was 500 per cent. The number of high schools has increased and will probably continue to enlarge during the next decade, despite the accelerating elimination of small schools through consolidation and larger units. This trend should not cause educational decadence; quantitative growth must be accompanied by qualitative advancement through enrichment of opportunities for modern youth.

The enrollments in high schools almost doubled every 10 years to the 1940's, when there were over seven million pupils enrolled. During the Second World War a large number of boys and girls, especially the former, left high school or did not enter it, in order to work in industry or serve in the armed forces. Academic credit for military service enabled many veterans to accelerate their high-school graduation. Successful completion of the General Educational Development (GED) Tests reduced or eliminated high-school attendance for many youth. The long period of decreasing birth rates previous to 1940 also produced a slump in enrollments. However, it is estimated that during the 1955-to-1965 decade a new high of more than ten million will be reached.

Nowhere in the world is so large a percentage of youth enrolled in secondary schools as in America. Nearly 75 per cent of the population of high school age is attending school. Indications point to a steady increase to a possible total of 90 per cent.

The future enrollments in secondary education will be determined in a large measure by military, political, economic, social, and educational factors, the latter a challenge to teachers to reduce dropouts and to recruit students. The armed services, industry, business, and the professions have placed a high premium upon having a high-school diploma. Unfortunately many young persons cannot attend high school because of economic factors. The secondary school is not yet effectively free for all who can benefit therefrom.

Another factor influencing enrollment is legislation. For example, in some states the compulsory school age has been extended to eighteen years. Naturally such legislation if enforced will cause the walls of many high schools and junior colleges to bulge with their teeming pupil population, thus helping to produce another era of expansion in secondary education.

DEVELOPMENT OF SECONDARY EDUCATION

HISTORICAL CALENDAR—SECONDARY EDUCATION AND CONTEMPORANEOUS EVENTS

The historical calendar found on the next page contains some significant dates in the evolution of modern secondary education juxtaposed with contemporaneous events.

Historical Calendar

SECONDARY EDUCATION	CONTEMPORANEOUS EVENTS
1635—First Latin grammar school founded (Boston)	1635—First English settlement located in Connecticut
1751—Franklin Academy organized (Philadelphia)	1753—George Washington sent by Virginia to the Ohio region
1821—First English high school started for boys (Boston)	1821—Monroe elected President for second term
1826—First high school organized for girls (Boston)	1825—Erie Canal completed
1856—First coeducational high school established (Chicago)	1857—Dred Scott decision rendered by Supreme Court
1872—Taxation for secondary schools upheld (Kalamazoo)	1871—City of Chicago damaged by great fire
1884—Manual-training high school started (Baltimore)	1885—World's Industrial Exposition held at New Orleans
1893—Recommendations of Committee of Ten published	1893—Columbian Exposition (World's Fair) opened at Chicago
1899—Recommendation of Committee on College Entrance published	1899—First Philippine Commission appointed by the United States
1902—First public junior college founded (Joliet, Illinois)	1902—Panama Canal treaty advocated by President Theodore Roosevelt
1907—G. Stanley Hall's *Adolescence* published	1907—Financial panic spread through United States
1910—First junior high schools started (Berkeley, and Columbus)	1910—Postal savings banks established
1918—Report of Commission on Reorganization of Secondary Education published	1918—Two million American troops engaged overseas in First World War
1933—Reports of National Survey of Secondary Education published	1933—Gold standard abandoned by United States
1941—Eight-year study of Progressive Education Association published	1941—Constitutionality of Wage and Hour Act upheld by Supreme Court
1949—Commission on Life Adjustment Education for Youth appointed	1949—Increase in amount of customs exemption granted by Congress
1950—Revision of Cooperative Study of Secondary School Standards issued	1950—Point Four enabling legislation approved by President Truman
1953—Council for Advancement of Secondary Education formed	1953—Korean truce signed ending war between U.N. and Communists there
1955—Three-year study on economic education launched by Council for Advancement of Secondary Education	1955—Fiscal year for federal government ended with another deficit—22d in 25 years

Four Periods of Development

The history of secondary education is usually chronicled in three rather distinct periods named after the institution characteristic of each era: (1) the Latin grammar school, (2) the tuition academy, and (3) the free public high school. Leonard V. Koos, director of the National Survey of Secondary Education, states that the present century has brought to the American educational scene another period (4) distinguished by the vertically extended or reorganized secondary school.

1. *Latin Grammar School.* In 1935 American education celebrated the three hundredth anniversary of the establishment of the Boston Latin School—the first secondary school in America. British forerunners of the Boston Latin School were the Winchester (1394) and the Westminster (1561) schools. The first step toward organizing the Latin grammar school in America was taken by Bostonians on April 23, 1635, in a town meeting, where it was voted, "that our brother, Philemon Pormont, shal be intreated to become scholemaster for the teaching and nourtering of children with us." In August of the following year 45 inhabitants of Boston subscribed a sum of money to maintain a "free schoolmaster for the youth with us, Mr. Daniel Maud being now also chosen thereunto." Such efforts as these mark the beginnings of secondary education in the colonies, and by 1700 approximately forty grammar schools had been founded in New England. The schools of secondary education were not so common everywhere.

In the Middle and Southern colonies private tutors were engaged and many young boys and girls were sent back to Europe for schooling.

The academy in the South as in other parts of the United States was called a product of the frontier period of national development and the *laissez faire* theory of government. In the Southern States, as elsewhere in this country, the academy generally developed from private or denominational interest and effort just as many colleges developed.[2]

The main purpose of the Latin grammar school was to prepare pupils for college. This major objective was clearly stated in the Massachusetts law of 1647, which decreed that: "when any town shall increase to the number of 100 families or householders, they shall set up a grammar school, the master thereof being able to instruct youth so far as they shall be fitted for the university. . . ." The task of preparing for college is reflected in the Harvard statutes of 1643, which defined entrance requirements for that university as follows:

[2] Edgar W. Knight, *A Documentary History of Education in the South before 1860*, Volume IV, "Private and Denominational Efforts," p. 2, University of North Carolina Press, 1953.

When any scholar is able to understand Tully, or such like classical Latin author *extempore,* and make and speak true Latin in verse and prose, *suo ut qiunt Marte;* and decline perfectly the paradigms of *nouns* and *verbs* in the *Greek* tongue: Let him then and not before be capable of admission into the college.

The Latin grammar schools, especially the earlier ones, offered a limited curriculum. As indicated by its name, the school was primarily restricted to the study of classical languages and literatures. It was very selective in

Fig. 7-1. America's first secondary school, Boston Latin School, founded in 1635. (*Courtesy of New York Herald Tribune.*)

character and sought to establish an aristocracy of educated intellectuals.

Admission to the Latin grammar schools was usually conditioned by the social and economic rank of the applicant. A sort of dual system, patterned on an European plan, prevailed in early American education. In this system an elementary education open to all was distinct from a secondary education closed to all but a chosen few.

Financial support for the Latin grammar school was provided in one or more of the following ways: tuition, donations, taxation, leases, legacies, lotteries, and land grants by civil authorities or private persons. Its control was at first considered the right and duty of the clergy since most of the pupils pursued studies that fitted them for the ministry or professions. Gradually the Latin grammar schools with their emphasis on theology began to lose their popularity. Leadership in the community was no longer with the clergy but rather with the town and commercial execu-

tives. Out of the new economic and social conditions in America arose
the next period of secondary education, *viz.*, that of the tuition academy.

2. *The Tuition Academy.* Benjamin Franklin, who has never been
accorded his just place in American education, was primarily responsible

FIG. 7-2. The first academy, founded by Franklin in 1751. This painting by Charles
Lefferts shows on the left the first secondary school of the academy type, founded by
Benjamin Franklin, former student of the Boston Latin School. The building was
erected in 1740 to house a charity school and meetings held by wandering preachers.
The dormitory at the right was built in 1762, seven years after a confirming charter
was granted, incorporating the charity school, the academy, and the college. The institution first became known as a university in 1779. The University of Pennsylvania
thus traces its corporate growth to the charity school. (*Courtesy of University of Pennsylvania.*)

for the establishment of the first academy. Franklin in his *Autobiography*
thus describes the genesis of the academy:

> The first step I took was to associate in the design a number of active friends,
> of whom the Junto furnished a good part; the next was to write and publish a
> pamphlet, entitled *Proposals Relating to the Education of Youth in Pennsyl-
> vania.*[3]

These proposals contained many practical and progressive suggestions.
According to Carl Van Doren, "in a day of rigid classical schools, Franklin
took his stand with reformers like Milton and Locke and the most advanced contemporary Americans." [4] A board of 24 trustees was formed, of

[3] Benjamin Franklin, *Autobiography*, p. 203, Century, 1901.
[4] Carl Van Doren, *Benjamin Franklin*, p. 192, Viking, 1938.

which Franklin was president from 1749 to 1756. This academy, which absorbed a charitable school erected in 1740 and later became the University of Pennsylvania, opened in a hired house in Philadelphia in 1751. The curriculum was broader than that of the Latin grammar school, although not so extensive as Franklin planned it should be. Since it aimed to prepare for life as well as for the ministry, its students included those not intending to go to college as well as the college bound.

Although a large number of academies were founded between 1750 and 1800, the movement reached its greatest height in the decade from 1840 to 1850, flourishing best in Massachusetts and New York.

The academies differed from the Latin grammar schools in several aspects. Besides expanding the curriculum to include such fields as commerce and science, the academy permitted young women to enter. From the days of Mary Chilton, the first woman to step off the *Mayflower*, to the present, women have played a conspicuous role in American life, yet their education was grossly neglected for many decades.

The academy, supported in the main by tuition and donations, was semipublic in control. In its organization, administration, and program it was more democratic than the Latin grammar school. The person in charge was usually called the headmaster or principal. Several private academies still exist in the United States as military academies or special schools, but most of the older ones have either disappeared or transformed themselves into public high schools.

3. *The Free Public High School.* The third period in the history of the American secondary school covers the rise and growth of the free public high school, inaugurated with the establishment of the English Classical School in Boston in 1821. This school for boys, later called the English High School, was followed by a high school for girls in the same city in 1826. During the next half century various types of high schools were organized. Among these were the first coeducational high school, started in Chicago in 1856, and the first manual training school, founded in Baltimore in 1884. Many factors contributed to the steady development of these schools, particularly in the democratic West.

Kalamazoo High School Case. A legal decision of a supreme court, state or national, may affect markedly the flow of events—political, economic, or social. Two signal decisions that stimulated the growth of educational institutions were handed down in the Dartmouth College Case (1819), and the Kalamazoo High School Case (1872). The former is discussed in Unit VIII; the latter is presented here.

In 1872 in Kalamazoo, Michigan, now the home of a flourishing state college of education, a person objected to supporting the high school by public taxation. A friendly suit was started in which the citizen stated that he was willing to support the elementary school but that he objected to

FIG. 7-3. The first high school, English High School, opened in 1821. This was the first institution to be called a "high school" and was so styled in 1824. (*Courtesy of the First National Bank of Boston.*)

paying for the high school, since it was not a legitimate part of the publicly supported system. The final opinion of the court as to the legality of free high-school instruction was rendered thus:

We content ourselves with the statement that neither in our state policy, in our constitution, nor in our laws, do we find the primary-school districts restricted in the branches of knowledge which their officers may cause to be taught, or in the grade of instruction that may be given, if their voters consent in regular form to bear the expense and raise the taxes for the purpose.[5]

This decision of the Supreme Court of Michigan has become famous in school law because it lent legal sanction to the movement for the establishment of publicly supported high schools. Similar decisions followed in several other states, thus removing any question as to the legality of communities' taxing themselves for the support of public high schools. The Kalamazoo decision thus paved the way for a phenomenal growth in this new institution of democracy. It must be remembered that although other countries have so-called "public high schools" they are not public and free to all in the sense that the American high school is. In America the high school is "the people's school."

4. *The Extended Secondary School.* As previously mentioned, the history of the American secondary school is usually divided into three stages. A fourth period is here in which a new type of institution is slowly evolving, *viz.,* the vertically extended secondary school or the reorganized high school.

Of this new period in the evolution of secondary education, Leonard V. Koos says:

I refer to the extensions of the high school downward to effect junior-high-school reorganization and upward to include junior college years. Many communities, to be sure, have made the extension in one direction only, either downward or upward. However, many other communities have introduced the extensions in both directions and have thereby achieved an 8-year period of secondary education. In the light of the fact that all the earlier types in our succession of secondary schools have been dominantly 4-year institutions, the emergence of an institution covering a period twice as long is a change notable enough to mark a new type.[6]

That the twentieth century marks the beginning of the fourth period is substantiated by the reports of the National Survey of Secondary Education. Two new public institutions have arisen, *viz.,* the *junior* college, which was first established in 1902 in Joliet, Illinois, and the *junior* high school, which was first organized in 1910 in Berkeley, California, and Columbus, Ohio.

Reorganization is modifying the last two years of the elementary school, the four years of high school, and the two years that follow. The United

[5] E. P. Cubberley, *Readings in the History of Education,* p. 589, Houghton Mifflin, 1920.

[6] Leonard V. Koos, "The Rise of the American High School," address presented at the Sixty-ninth Convocation of the University of the State of New York celebrating the 150th anniversary of the establishment of the University, Oct. 13, 1933.

States Office of Education presents biennial statistics on the growth of re-organized high schools. A steady movement is evident toward the re-organization of existing high schools and the establishment of such secondary schools as junior, junior-senior, and senior high schools, and junior colleges.

Fig. 7-4. First public junior college, opened in 1912. This picture of the Joliet Junior College, Joliet, Illinois, shows the entrance to the original building.

The downward extension of secondary education, which commenced with the establishment of the first junior high schools in 1910, was preceded by the upward extension, which began with the organization of the first junior college. Although the earliest public junior college was that at Joliet, Illinois, in 1902, the Decatur Baptist College, which was founded in Texas in 1891 and reorganized as a private junior college in 1898, claims the distinction of being the oldest junior college. Some of the privately controlled junior colleges began as academies or seminaries over a hundred years ago, as is the case of Colby Junior College, which started as the "New London Seminary" in New Hampshire in 1837. The organization of junior colleges is described later in this unit.

LEADERS IN SECONDARY EDUCATION

Three hundred years and more of secondary education in America have produced some three hundred leaders in this field. Only a few can be mentioned here. One of the earliest was the versatile Benjamin Franklin (1706–1790), who replaced the narrow curricular offerings of the Latin

FIG. 7-5. Benjamin Franklin. In 1954 the American Philosophical Society and Yale University launched a 15-year program to bring together all known facts about this man called "one of the three or four greatest Americans." (*Courtesy of the Metropolitan Museum of Art, New York.*)

grammar school with an enriched program in the Franklin Academy. His uncommon common sense helped to make secondary education more practical. Another leader, G. Stanley Hall (1846–1924), through his monumental work *Adolescence,* published in 1907, helped to make secondary education more aware of the psychological needs of youth.

Another pioneer thinker in this field was Charles W. Eliot (1834–1926). Although he is best known for his long and effective service as president of Harvard University, his imprint upon secondary education is indelible. His efforts to raise the entrance requirements for Harvard were reflected in the improved standards in the high schools. His provisions for choice in entrance units allowed greater freedom in secondary curriculums. His work as chairman of the national Committee of Ten (1890) led eventually to the junior-high-school movement. His oral and written emphasis on seeing, hearing, and feeling stimulated the development of vocational education in the secondary schools.

Another university president who directly influenced the secondary schools was William Rainey Harper (1856–1906), who received his Ph.D. degree at the age of nineteen and became president of the University of Chicago at thirty-five. As chairman of a national committee he recommended that the period of elementary education be reduced. His argument that the small ineffective college should drop senior work and become a junior college earned for him the title "father of the junior college."

The University of Chicago added another leader in secondary education in the person of Leonard V. Koos, already mentioned in connection with the extended secondary school and the National Survey of Secondary Education. He has emphasized the role of the reorganized secondary school.

Another personality in secondary education is Thomas H. Briggs, emeritus professor of secondary-school administration at Teachers College, Columbia University. Through his contact with hundreds of secondary-school principals and teachers in his college classes, through his numerous publications, and through his chairmanship of the Committee on Orientation of Secondary Education, he has had tremendous influence on secondary education in America and abroad. In 1953 he was elected chairman of the Council for the Advancement of Secondary Education, Inc., which was formed with representatives of business, labor, and industry, and the National Association of Secondary-school Principals.

To this group of statesmen, college presidents, and university instructors could be added an endless list of secondary-school principals, classroom teachers, and board members who daily display courage, vision, and common sense in striving to make the objectives of secondary education function in a given locale. These collectively have helped to change America—educationally, socially, and economically. Frederick Lewis Allen, in his survey of America from 1900 to 1950 in *The Big Change,* writes thus about the responsibility for the convergence between the ways of living among the rich and the poor:

Another important factor in the change has been the immense spread of education. In 1900 less than one American boy or girl out of ten of high school age was actually in high school; now over four out of five are. This means not only book learning for them; it means a considerable social education in the ways of living of a variety of families of the community.[7]

[7] Frederick Lewis Allen, *The Big Change,* p. 222, Harper, 1952.

Undoubtedly the quantitative growth of the American high school has helped to improve the qualitative aspects of living.

PURPOSES OF SECONDARY EDUCATION

CHANGING CONCEPTS OF SECONDARY EDUCATION

The objectives or directives of secondary education have been numerous and varied. In the days of the Latin grammar school, the main aim was to prepare a select group of boys and a few girls for both college and life activities. Within the last fifty years, however, have come changed concepts of what should be the objectives and who should be the recipients of secondary education. Contrast with modern objectives the statement from the report of the Committee of Ten in 1894 that the high school should be planned for "that small proportion of all the children in the country—a proportion small in number, but very important to the welfare of the nation—who show themselves able to profit by an education prolonged to the eighteenth year, and whose parents are able to support them while they remain so long at school."

Seven Cardinal Principles of Secondary Education. A well-known set of objectives of historical significance is that prepared in 1918 by the Commission on the Reorganization of Secondary Education, which advocated "such reorganization that secondary education may be defined as applying to all pupils of approximately twelve to eighteen years of age." Briefly stated, these seven objectives, usually called the "cardinal principles of education" and applied to elementary as well as secondary education, are:

1. Health
2. Command of fundamental processes
3. Worthy home membership
4. Vocational efficiency
5. Civic participation
6. Worthy use of leisure time
7. Ethical character

These objectives stress life out of school as well as in school. They resemble somewhat the activities listed in 1859 by Herbert Spencer in his essay "What Knowledge Is of Most Worth?" and those presented by Bobbitt in 1924 in his *How to Make a Curriculum*.

Issues and Functions of Secondary Education. A vital force in formulating the objectives and program of secondary education has been the National Association of Secondary-school Principals, a department of the National Education Association. Under the dynamic and intelligent chairmanship of Professor Thomas H. Briggs of Teachers College, Columbia University, the Committee on Orientation in 1933 published statements of "Issues and Functions of Secondary Education." These have been studied in a large number of discussion groups throughout the United States, each state being organized under a coordinator. Issues, as defined by Briggs and the committee, are the questions of fundamental policy that have grown out of conflicting opinions, policies, and practices. They are to be decided primarily by reference to philosophies rather than by fact finding and by experimentation, although the latter are needed to direct judgments.

The Committee on Orientation also prepared a statement of special functions for secondary education in the United States. These particular tasks, which may in varying degree begin in the later elementary school and continue at least till the end of the junior college, are briefly:

1. Integration
2. Satisfaction of needs
3. Revelation of racial heritage
4. Exploration of interests, aptitudes, and capacities
5. Systematization and application of knowledge
6. Establishment and direction of interests
7. Guidance
8. Differentiation and general education
9. Methods of teaching and learning
10. Retention and direction of pupils [8]

These functions, to be modified in the light of developments, represent a perennial challenge to all laymen and educators.

Education for All American Youth. Prior to developing a basic set of principles for elementary education in its volume, *Education for All American Children,* the Educational Policies Commission published *Education for All American Youth,* in which it formulated policies for secondary education. This was supplemented by *A Further Look.* Schools should be dedicated, said the Commission, to the proposition that every youth in these United States—regardless of sex, economic status, geographic location, or race—should experience a broad and balanced education which will:

1. Equip him to enter an occupation suited to his abilities and offering reasonable opportunity for personal growth and social usefulness.
2. Prepare him to assume the full responsibilities of American citizenship.
3. Give him a fair chance to exercise his right to the pursuit of happiness.
4. Stimulate intellectual curiosity, engender satisfaction in intellectual achievement, and cultivate the ability to think rationally.
5. Help him to develop an appreciation of the ethical values which should undergird all life in a democratic society.

The commission further adds that it is the duty of a democratic society to provide opportunities for such education through its numerous schools.

[8] T. H. Briggs, *Secondary Education,* "The Special Functions of Secondary Education," pp. 252–288, Macmillan, 1933; also, Department of Secondary-school Principals, *Bulletin,* National Education Association, January, 1937, pp. 23–263.

THE IMPERATIVE NEEDS OF YOUTH

The Common and Essential Needs that All Youth Have in a Democratic Society

RECOMMENDATION: *Through curriculum planning, the educational program in the secondary school should meet these needs of all youth adequately.*

1 All youth need to develop saleable skills and those understandings and attitudes that make the worker an intelligent and productive participant in economic life. To this end, most youth need supervised work experience as well as education in the skills and knowledge of their occupations.

6 All youth need to understand the methods of science, the influence of science on human life, and the main scientific facts concerning the nature of the world and of man.

2 All youth need to develop and maintain good health and physical fitness.

7 All youth need opportunities to develop their capacities to appreciate beauty in literature, art, music, and nature.

3 All youth need to understand the rights and duties of the citizen of a democratic society, and to be diligent and competent in the performance of their obligations as members of the community and citizens of the state and nation.

8 All youth need to be able to use their leisure time well and to budget it wisely, balancing activities that yield satisfactions to the individual with those that are socially useful.

4 All youth need to understand the significance of the family for the individual and society and the conditions conducive to successful family life.

9 All youth need to develop respect for other persons, to grow in their insight into ethical values and principles, and to be able to live and work co-operatively with others.

5 All youth need to know how to purchase and use goods and services intelligently, understanding both the values received by the consumer and the economic consequences of their acts.

10 All youth need to grow in their ability to think rationally, to express their thoughts clearly, and to read and listen with understanding.

FIG. 7-6. Imperative Needs of Youth. (*Adapted from Planning for American Youth and based on Education for All American Youth by National Association of Secondary-school Principals and Educational Policies Commission respectively.*)

It is the obligation of every youth, as a citizen, to make full use of these opportunities; and it is the responsibility of parents to give encouragement and support to both youth and schools.[9]

Life Adjustment Education for Youth. In 1947 the Commission on Life Adjustment Education for Youth was created. This commission, which consists of representatives from several national organizations, including the United States Office of Education and the National Association of Secondary-school Principals, has stimulated programs that more adequately meet the imperative needs of students now in school. Even more, it has encouraged the types of education required for adolescent youth who drop out of school because their needs are not satisfied. The goals, "Imperative Needs of Youth," are summarized in Fig. 7-6 and are described in detail in various publications, including *Education for All American Youth—A Further Look.* The commission has implemented its goals through a persistent and continued attack on the problems of secondary education.

TYPES OF SECONDARY SCHOOLS

To meet the varied purposes of secondary education and the diverse needs of secondary pupils many types of schools have developed. As indi-

SCHOOL YEAR	4-YEAR (TRADITIONAL)	6-YEAR (EXTENDED DOWN)	6-YEAR (EXTENDED UP)	8-YEAR (FOUR-FOUR)	8-YEAR (THREE-THREE-TWO)
FOURTEENTH					JUNIOR COLLEGE
THIRTEENTH				UPPER SECONDARY SCHOOL	JUNIOR COLLEGE
TWELFTH	HIGH SCHOOL	SIX YEAR HIGH SCHOOL	JUNIOR COLLEGE AND HIGH SCHOOL	UPPER SECONDARY SCHOOL	SENIOR HIGH SCHOOL
ELEVENTH	HIGH SCHOOL	SIX YEAR HIGH SCHOOL	JUNIOR COLLEGE AND HIGH SCHOOL	UPPER SECONDARY SCHOOL	SENIOR HIGH SCHOOL
TENTH	HIGH SCHOOL	SIX YEAR HIGH SCHOOL	JUNIOR COLLEGE AND HIGH SCHOOL	LOWER SECONDARY SCHOOL	SENIOR HIGH SCHOOL
NINTH	HIGH SCHOOL	SIX YEAR HIGH SCHOOL	JUNIOR COLLEGE AND HIGH SCHOOL	LOWER SECONDARY SCHOOL	JUNIOR HIGH SCHOOL
EIGHTH	HIGH SCHOOL	SIX YEAR HIGH SCHOOL	JUNIOR COLLEGE AND HIGH SCHOOL	LOWER SECONDARY SCHOOL	JUNIOR HIGH SCHOOL
SEVENTH					JUNIOR HIGH SCHOOL

Fig. 7-7. Organizational patterns for secondary education.

cated in Fig. 7-7, when secondary education is restricted to 4 years it is traditionally the function of one institution, *viz.,* the high school. In some communities secondary education is extended downward 2 years to em-

[9] Educational Policies Commission, *Education for All American Youth*, p. 21, National Education Association, 1944, and *A Further Look*, p. 32, 1952.

brace the last 2 years of what was elementary education, plus the traditional 4 years of the high-school period, thus creating the undivided or 6-year secondary school. In communities where there is rigid separation of the elementary and secondary schools, the secondary period of learning may reach not downward but upward to include the junior college in connection with the regular high school. Many cities are now reorganizing secondary education into a unified 8-year program or into two divisions—the lower secondary school, covering grades 7, 8, 9, and 10, and the upper secondary school, embracing grades 11, 12, 13, and 14. These seem to be two of the future patterns for secondary education. Currently there is much emphasis upon the 8-year model, divided into three sections, the junior high school (7, 8, and 9), the senior high school (10, 11, and 12), and the junior college (13 and 14). To this classification may be added other groupings by years or special curricular schools, such as vocational.

Junior High Schools

Seventh- and Eighth-grade Schools. In its shortened form the junior high school may consist of two grades, the seventh and eighth. Many so-called "junior high schools," however, are merely glorified seventh and eighth grades minus the philosophy, program, and procedures of the genuine junior high school. The latter is more than a grouping or re-

Fig. 7-8. Easter choir, Roosevelt Junior High School. (*Courtesy of Public Schools, Coffeyville, Kans.*)

grouping of grades, and new names. School-board members and administrators do not produce a junior high school by erecting a new building
with the words "Junior High School" carved in stone over the entrance.
Teachers do not create a junior-high-school curriculum by using pupil
textbooks labeled *Junior High School Mathematics, Junior High School
English,* etc. Even where the seventh and eighth grades are grouped with
the ninth, a real junior high school may not exist. Adding the ninth
grade may be as incongruous as sewing a new piece of cloth onto an old
garment. What is needed is a new pattern and a new institution—a junior
high school in name, function, and curriculum—dominated by the philosophy and purposes of secondary rather than elementary education.

Junior High School. This school, first called "intermediate," was later
christened the "junior high school." Arising out of dissatisfaction with
the established order of things, the junior high school has advanced until
it now forms the lowest rung on the ladder of secondary education. Although its progress was retarded during the First and Second World Wars,
this institution has taken Herculean strides, particularly in the larger
cities. Its usual range embraces the seventh, eighth, and ninth grades, although the last is often omitted. As just indicated, however, the junior
high school is more than a regrouping of grades.

The junior high school is an organization of the seventh, eighth, and ninth
grades into an administrative unit for the purpose of providing instruction and
training suitable to the varied and changing physical, mental, and social natures
and needs of immature, maturing, and mature pupils.[10]

The National Survey of Secondary Education listed nine major features
of the organization of junior high schools:

1. Flexibility in admission and promotion
2. Arrangement of instruction
3. Program of studies
4. Extracurriculum program
5. Educational-vocational guidance
6. Special features for articulation
7. Specially trained teaching staff
8. Supervision of instruction
9. Special housing and equipment

According to nation-wide surveys of actual practices in junior high
schools, there is much room for improvement. Junior-high-school administrators appear to be more influenced by past practice and by financial
expediency than by advanced theory.

INTERMEDIATE SECONDARY SCHOOLS

The middle area of secondary education usually embraces the senior
high school, or the typical 4-year high school, or variations thereof.

Senior High School. This is usually a 3-year high school with grades 10,
11, and 12 linked with a junior-high system for grades 7, 8, and 9. Often

[10] Ralph W. Pringle, *The Junior High School,* p. 68, McGraw-Hill, 1937.

the existing buildings determine what the organization of the high school shall be. In cities with a fluctuating population and changing building facilities, the first-semester students of the tenth grade may be housed in the senior high school one year and in the junior-high building the next.

Although the graduation requirements from the 4-year schools are 16 units, those for the senior high are reduced to 12. Since colleges and accrediting agencies are not vitally concerned with the content of the last year of junior high schools (the ninth grade), wider experimentation and more orientation are possible in a six-three-three organization than in an eight-four plan. The six-three-three system, however, has the disadvantage

Fig. 7-9. Modern school structure—Rich Township High School, Park Forest, Illinois. This high school was built at a cost of $1,600,000. (*Courtesy of Bernard Klein and Public Schools, Park Forest, Ill.*)

of an extra hyphen (indicating a transition) not found in the eight-four plan. With an increase in attendance units the need for articulation is also increased. On the other hand, once the students are in the senior high, its holding power is stronger than that of the 4-year school since the usual ninth-grade "drop-outs" have come during or at the close of the junior-high period. With the increasing growth of the junior high is linked the future of the senior high school.

Four-year High School. The secondary school that includes grades 9, 10, 11, and 12 is the prevailing type of high-school organization in the United States. Under present conditions it will continue to lead in states like Illinois, where many high schools under a separate board of education are divorced from the elementary-school district. This practically prohibits the combination of seventh, eighth, and ninth grades. The high school commencing with the ninth grade is also popular in small rural areas and may be only a 2- or 3-year institution. Although several states still recognize these 2- and 3-year schools, the regional accrediting associations do not put their stamp of approval upon them because of their limitations in equipment, staff, enrollment, curriculums, and social living.

The traditional 4-year school is undergoing significant changes. Especially since the beginning of the present century, marked internal improvement has been effected. Where it is neither desirable nor possible to reorganize the 4-year high school into a new type of secondary school, much is being done to rejuvenate the existing institution. Even though the 4-year unit does not reorganize externally, it can improve internally through curricular modifications and other changes. The comprehensive high school, offering a common core plus a wide variety of experiences for all adolescents, is a unique national contribution.

JUNIOR COLLEGES, COMMUNITY COLLEGES, AND OTHER POSTSECONDARY INSTITUTIONS

Position of the Junior College. Traditionally, a junior college has been defined as an institution of higher education that gives 2 years of work equivalent in prerequisites, scope, and thoroughness to the work done in the first 2 years of college. On the other hand, the conviction is growing that the junior college, as well as the freshman and sophomore years of colleges and universities, belongs to the secondary-school level. California, which ranks first in the number of junior colleges, has made the independent junior college a definite part of its common-school system, and rightly so, since the junior college should not be a separate entity. Whether it belongs to secondary or to higher education may be a debatable issue, but the junior or community college should be integrated with the high schools on one hand and with the higher institutions on the other.

Its Growth. The junior college, a product of the twentieth century, has spread gradually from West to East. Originating in Illinois and Texas, it has had the greatest growth in the western and southwestern parts of the United States. Junior colleges now exist in almost every state. The growth in the number of colleges and their enrollments is revealed in the accompanying tabulation. Data on junior colleges and their enrollments are published in the annual directory of the *Junior College Journal.*

Year	Number of colleges	Enrollment in colleges	Year	Number of colleges	Enrollment in colleges
1922	207	16,121	1942	627	267,406
1927	325	35,630	1946	591	251,290
1930	429	67,627	1950	648	465,315
1934	514	103,592	1954	594	560,732
1938	553	136,623	1958	700	700,000 (est.)

Types of Junior Colleges. The legal control of junior colleges is vested in (1) public bodies, *viz.,* city, township, county, state, and district officials; (2) the church, with Roman Catholic, Methodist, and Baptist in the lead, and other religious organizations such as the Y.M.C.A.; and (3) private corporations independent of church or state, such as Penn Hall Junior College for women located in Chambersburg, Pennsylvania. Approximately one-half are public, but their enrollments far outnumber those in the other two types. The typical junior college is coeducational.

According to the President's Commission on Higher Education the 2-year college is about as widely needed today as the 4-year high school was a few decades ago. Such a college should fit into the community life as the high school has done. "Hence the President's Commission suggests the nomenclature 'community college' to be applied to the institution designed to serve chiefly local community educational needs."

Community colleges in the future may be either publicly or privately controlled and supported, but most of them obviously will be under public auspices. They will be mainly local or regional in scope and should be locally controlled, though they should be carefully planned to fit into a comprehensive state-wide system of higher education. They will derive much of their support from the local community, supplemented by aid from state funds.[11]

These community colleges are destined to increase in number and influence.

Another type of junior college is the specialized one—the technical institute or institute of applied arts and sciences. For example, New York State, after an extensive survey of postwar educational needs, launched a number of postsecondary technical institutes whose regular program provides 2 years of education and training for post-high-school youth or others whose maturity, needs, interests, and abilities justify admission. Some of these schools are designed primarily for general, regional service, but a few postsecondary institutes are for highly specialized occupations, to serve either the upstate area or the whole state.

Origin of Junior Colleges. Originally the junior college was considered a 2-year institution, but today its program may extend over 1, 2, 3, or even 4 years. As to method of establishment, these colleges may be classified on the following bases: (1) adding 2 years to the high school, (2) subtracting 2 years from the college, (3) affiliating with existing colleges and universities, and (4) organizing a separate new institution. Authorizing legislation usually falls into two categories: *general,* such as a state-wide law for the establishment of junior or community colleges, and *specific,* such as a separate charter for an institution. Some states, like New York, have both types of legislation.

Their Functions. The four well-known functions of the junior college are:

(1) *Popularizing higher education,* or offering college opportunities to local high-school graduates and adults who would otherwise be deprived of a college education; (2) *preparatory,* or providing 2 years of standard college work or pro-

[11] President's Commission on Higher Education, *Higher Education for American Democracy,* Volume III, p. 5, Volume I, p. 67, GPO, 1947.

fessional work for entrance to the senior college or professional school; (3) *terminal,* or preparing students in 2 years for a career and for "social" citizenship; and (4) *guidance,* or aiding in shaping the lives of young students and directing them educationally and vocationally.[12]

These functions demand an extensive curriculum for youths and adults.

Their Curriculums. Most curriculums of the various junior colleges may be grouped into (1) basic courses, stressing general education and culture; (2) preparatory courses for advanced study, leading toward the bachelor's degree or beyond; (3) semiprofessional courses, preparing for professional schools such as journalism; and (4) occupational courses, usually terminal in nature and leading directly to employment. These types are described in the next unit, but reference is made briefly here to general and terminal education in secondary and postsecondary institutions.

General Education in Secondary and Postsecondary Education. The basic purpose of secondary education must be accented, especially in a highly specialized and scientific age. This fundamental function is general education, the common denominator that develops a basic and wide range of competencies which one needs as a person and a citizen in a democratic society. The general education one acquires in the elementary school must be supplemented by further "common learnings" in secondary and postsecondary education. The President's Commission on Higher Education in its recommendations for community colleges stated: "If the semiprofessional curriculum is to accomplish its purpose it must not be crowded with vocational and technical courses to the exclusion of general education." The Regents' plan for technical institutes in New York stated: "The institutions will be charged with the multiple task of combining technical training with general education." In the earlier years of secondary education the highest priority should be given to general education, while in postsecondary institutions an adequate balance must be maintained between general education and activities leading to occupational competence.

Terminal Education. The Commission on Junior College Terminal Education, working under the auspices of the American Association of Junior Colleges through a grant from the General Education Board, found that most junior-college students do not continue their education beyond this limit, yet only about a third of the young men and women enrolled are taking courses that are terminal in character. Obviously, junior colleges should devote more attention to the development of terminal education, including not only vocational and semiprofessional training but also general cultural education for social and civic intelligence. Phebe Ward, author of *Terminal Education in the Junior College,*

---

[12] Walter S. Greenleaf, *Junior Colleges,* pp. 22–23, GPO, 1936.

writes, "A half century of development in the junior college movement has resulted in the establishment of the junior college as one of the most important aspects of post-high-school education in the nation." [13]

In this connection, the query is raised: "Should completion of junior-college work be officially recognized?" Some type of formal benediction seems desirable. In India the "intermediate" degree is given to those who successfully complete 2 years of work beyond the high school. Associate in Arts or Associate in Science is the degree usually granted in America. In a program shorter than 2 years a certificate is generally awarded. Since the junior college is at present in a sort of "no man's land" between secondary and higher education, practices in granting degrees and building curriculums are in a state of flux.

Role of Junior College and Postsecondary Institutions. Charles H. Judd once stated that "the particular institution which is likely to produce the most important readjustment in the whole educational system is the junior college." The depression, postdepression, war, and postwar periods have consolidated and strengthened the position of the junior colleges in America. In California they are banded together in sectional associations as well as in a state federation. In many states they form independent associations, as in Oklahoma, or constitute a part of the state teachers association, as in Iowa. The American Association of Junior Colleges, chartered in 1920, has its national headquarters at Washington, D.C. *The Junior College Journal* is its official publication. This association's comprehensive study of the role of the junior colleges, with particular emphasis on terminal education, states: "If junior colleges, instead of trying to imitate the 4-year program, would offer courses close to the interest of the student and suited to his abilities, they would begin to occupy one of the most important places in American education."

For many years the junior college, community colleges, and technical institutes, as the youngest members of the educational family, were on the defensive. Their arrival tended to jeopardize the traditional solidarity of the college; furthermore, the question was raised as to whether these colleges were regular members of the public education group. The legality of taxation for their support was debated as in the earlier case of the high school. In 1930 the Supreme Court of North Carolina held that the city of Asheville had the right to tax itself to maintain a junior college out of funds set aside for the conduct of a public school. The parallel between the Kalamazoo High School Case and the Asheville Case is obvious. In most states the maintenance of public junior colleges has been legalized by specific statute. Recurring unemployment for youth of the post-secondary age and the complexity of modern living have promoted the

[13] Phebe Ward, *American Junior Colleges,* "Development of the Junior College Movement," p. 17, American Council on Education, 1952.

demand for vertical and horizontal extension of educational opportunities. As the concept spreads that secondary education does not end with the high school, there will be a marked increase in junior colleges, community colleges, and technical institutes, which probably will become the "people's colleges."

OTHER SECONDARY SCHOOLS

This general classification includes schools that may extend over all levels of secondary and postsecondary education.

Vocational Schools. The main group is that of the vocational or technical schools so prevalent in large cities and in certain states, notably Wisconsin. Charles H. Judd, who was born in India and who received part of his education in Europe, made the following significant observation as to who may attend these schools:

A unique characteristic of the American social system which has been of importance in determining the development of American education is the freedom of individual choice of occupations. In this country a boy or girl is free, as no child of older civilizations ever has been, to follow his or her personal bent in the choice of an occupation. There are no social barriers to prevent any individual from entering any vocation. The educational system is, accordingly, at liberty to arrange the education of its wards in keeping with their individual abilities and degrees of perseverance.[14]

In several foreign countries the vocational choices of young people are decidedly restricted by the requirement of prolonged compulsory military or national service, by the social limitations such as a caste system, or by the handicap of extreme poverty. In the United States, although the vocational choices of young people may be modified somewhat by factors outside themselves, there is no predestined job that a boy or girl must follow. This situation has tremendous implications for vocational guidance in secondary schools. The years to come will undoubtedly see much more emphasis upon prevocational and vocational education in all secondary schools. Central High School in Cincinnati, for example, offers a common core of general, required subjects, plus three programs: industrial, vocational, and technical.

Other Types. Many other types of special secondary schools might be listed, according to size, as small, medium, or large; pupils, as those for pupils gifted in art or music; sex, as girls, boys, and coeducation; age, as adolescent and adult; organization, as platoon or 6-year school; legal control, as public, private, or parochial; methodology or philosophy, as liberal, middle-of-the-road, or conservative; school time, as part-time, continuation, correspondence, night-school, or summer, camp, or year-round school; and numerous others.

[14] Charles H. Judd, *Recent Social Trends*, pp. 328–329, McGraw-Hill, 1933.

PRACTICES IN SECONDARY EDUCATION

A few of the more salient characteristics of modern secondary education are presented here through brief descriptions of some current practices in (1) organization and administration, (2) curriculum and teaching-learning procedures, and (3) personnel.

Organization and Administration. Modern secondary education postulates its organization and administration upon the concept of an extended educational period of approximately 8 years. Both the junior high schools and the junior colleges are dynamic components within the complete program of secondary-school organization. The traditional organization of secondary education as a short-span high-school institution is giving way to various patterns of structural reorganization, embracing such variations as the three-three and the four-four plans.

Private and parochial high schools are increasing in number. Enrollments in parochial high schools doubled in the past decade. One of every 10 secondary students attends a nonpublic high school.

Although secondary education is the period usually designated as general education, specialized schools are increasing in number and effectiveness. We find, for example, the Apprenticeship and Journeyman School in San Francisco, the High School of Music and Art and the Maritime High School in New York City, the Brooklyn High School of Automotive Trades, and the Miami, Florida, Technical High School. The latter offers a boat-building course, which attracts students from several states. New York State has established a number of regional and state-wide technical institutes.

State programs of secondary education are being promoted and coordinated through state educational agencies, such as the state departments. The establishment of junior colleges and community colleges as "community-wide centers of social and civic education for both adults and youth" calls for more state aid for junior colleges.

Regional associations that accredit secondary schools are stressing qualitative standards as well as revising quantitative measures. An example is the Cooperative Study of Secondary School Standards.

The relationships between secondary schools and institutions of higher learning have been markedly improved through such experiments as the high-school and college agreement of the Michigan Secondary Curriculum Study, and Eight-year Study of the Commission on the Relation of School and College, sponsored by the Progressive Education Association. Releasing secondary schools from the usual course and unit requirements for college entrance has stimulated more effective programs in these schools. The domination of high schools by colleges and universities is decreasing while effective cooperation is increasing.

Curriculum and Teaching-Learning Procedures. The objectives of secondary education, embracing all areas, are being adjusted to the functional needs of students and society, rather than being too heavily oriented to college preparation. The emphasis today is upon giving students opportunities to become and to be intelligent, happy, self-sustaining members of a democracy. These objectives are

being implemented through a virile program of amalgamated curricular and cocurricular activities, such as advocated by the Commission on Life Adjustment
Education for Youth. Consideration of developmental tasks is producing curriculum changes.

Schools have introduced many instructional areas, such as automobile driving,
aviation, atomic-energy, radioisotopes, home economics for boys, income-tax cal-
culations, democratic living, semantics, Hebrew, international relations, radio

Fig. 7-10. Practice in preparing, serving, and eating meals is an important phase of
secondary-school education, especially for girls, although some boys take "home ec"
too. (*Courtesy of Community High School, St. Anne, Ill.*)

and television, work experience, labor relations, baby sitting, mental hygiene,
world literature, economics, social institutions, public education, personal typing,
general shop, etc. In several high schools that have revised their curriculums,
separate courses in the same general field have been fused. For example, history,
economics, civics, geography, sociology, and related subjects are coalesced in the
broad survey of social science. Since high schools are offering survey courses, the
junior colleges are "digging postholes deeper." High-school courses in common
learnings or core curriculums are followed by additional general education,
which digs deeper into some special areas or selects intensive samplings.

The technological aspects of agriculture, industry, defense, commerce, and
allied fields are demanding more and more prevocational, semioccupational, and
vocational work in the secondary schools. Smith-Hughes aid, which restricted

the use of federal funds to courses of "less than college grade," has delayed the development of vocational education in junior colleges and technical institutes. The current need is for a local-state-federal program of financial aid for stimulating more vocational education, including terminal courses, in junior colleges.

The Smith-Hughes and George-Barden acts have promoted much more emphasis upon the work-study plan of education. This type of realistic community education is exemplified in the home experience project, where housewives cooperate with local school authorities in opening their homes to senior and junior homemaking students. As former Commissioner J. W. Studebaker has stated, "We will move on a graduated scale from full-time learning to part-time learning —the degree of time spent in organized education being different at different age levels with different groups of people."

The methodology of extrinsic teaching is giving way to an emphasis upon motivation, which produces intrinsic learning. The development of teaching-learning units has led to the reorganization of traditional courses around personal problems and realistic experiences. Newer instruments are being devised to measure growth and outcomes in junior and senior high schools and junior colleges. They are designed as a part of a broad program of evaluation, which is replacing mere pencil-and-paper tests. State-wide evaluation programs are increasing.

Personnel. The complexity of modern civilization, which necessitates more education, and the recurrent unemployment situation, which postpones the entrance of youth into regular gainful employment, are two of the many forces bringing more youth to the secondary schools in America. The democratic provisions of supplying state aid for transporting rural students and paying all or part of the tuition charges are giving more rural youth the benefits of secondary education. In some cases, dormitories have been provided for youth attending public high schools. Residential boarding schools are increasing. School cafeterias are important adjuncts of modern high schools, especially in consolidated school districts.

A minimum of 14 years of schooling for everyone is in consonance with the need for a higher level of education for all persons in the American democracy. The recipients of secondary education include both youth and adults. Many secondary-school plants are being kept open day and night in the interests of preparing youth and adults "to function efficiently—vocationally, avocationally, and civically."

Large crowds of students graduating from the elementary schools are knocking on the doors of the high school for admittance. Quantitatively there is a huge reservoir of students. Secondary students are urged and motivated to remain in school longer. One-fourth are employed.

There is increased emphasis on guidance and employment for youth along with the follow-up work as outlined by the Occupational Adjustment Study of the National Association of Secondary-school Principals. Much attention is devoted to keeping student personnel records including test scores, anecdotal records, parent or student interviews, photographs, etc.

Special attention to veterans has been given by secondary schools through high schools for veterans, credit for military service and G.E.D. tests, trade schools, apprenticeship programs, and correspondence courses, especially those furnished by the "world's largest secondary school"—the United States Armed Forces Institute (USAFI). The G.I. bills, through federal grants or scholarships, have enabled many veterans to complete their secondary education.

There is a definite trend toward employing only teachers who possess a master's degree or its equivalent. Secondary-school teachers, as the best educated members of the public-school family, are called upon increasingly to participate in and to share democratically in the preparation of policies and programs for the education of youth. Self-evaluation of teachers themselves and of their schools, as promoted through the Cooperative Study of Secondary Schools Standards, is helping to raise the standards of secondary schools.

FUTURE OF SECONDARY EDUCATION

In a forward look, this unit concludes with the statements from two notable bodies: the Educational Policies Commission, and the Harvard Committee.

The former, in its report *Education for All American Youth,* and in its revision *A Further Look,* has called attention to the grave danger that the locally administered high school may join "the Latin grammar school of the seventeenth century and the academy of the nineteenth in the great wastebasket of history." If, however, American educators and laymen accept the challenge, and launch an effective program of educational planning and action, then:

It may be that the future historian will make an entirely different report. He may say that the schools of the nation had anticipated the youth needs of the postwar years; that they were ready to move to meet these needs as they developed; that every state and every large locality had a definite plan for doing so; that the federal government was at last persuaded to supply adequate financial aid to make this service possible; that the teaching profession was prepared to make the necessary changes in curriculum and administration; that the local organization of education was sufficiently flexible to permit the establishment of secondary schools adequate to the tremendous educational job that waited to be done; and that secondary schools of America, under state and local control, were transformed into agencies serving all American youth, right through the period of adjustment to adult life.[15]

Briggs, a long-time recognized leader in secondary education, and his experienced coauthors, Leonard and Justman, argue for a vision of secondary education—an expression of what might be; of what by idealism, hope, and hard work may be brought to realization. The vision postulates that secondary education must be: important, comprehensive, planned, for all youth, and well taught.

[15] Educational Policies Commission, *Education for All American Youth—A Further Look,* p. 10.

There is also a vision of many changes in organization, in administration, and in all auxiliary agencies. But they need not concern us until the general plan is plotted. Then and then only can we know what kinds of schools we shall need, what types of buildings and equipment, what rearrangement and extension

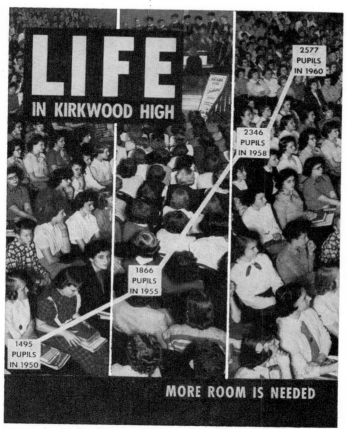

FIG. 7-11. Many schools, like Kirkwood High, may experience an increase in enrollment from 75 to 100 per cent in a decade. Many more rooms and teachers will be needed. (*Courtesy of Life and Public Schools, Kirkwood, Mo.*)

of an outworn academic calendar, and what methods of instruction are suitable.[16]

This is a summarized statement not of what is, but of what might be.

After this period of secondary education, with its emphasis on general education for all and on special preparation for practical life for those

[16] Thomas H. Briggs, J. Paul Leonard, and Joseph Justman, *Secondary Education*, pp. 456–464, Macmillan, 1950.

who will not go beyond secondary education, the schools of higher learning then offer a wide variety of opportunities for continuing institutionalized education. In the next unit in this volume, these opportunities for higher education are presented, and in the unit following, the education of out-of-school youth and adults is treated.

SUGGESTED ACTIVITIES

1. Trace separately or collectively the growth of (*a*) the Latin grammar school, (*b*) the academy, (*c*) the public high school, (*d*) the junior high school, and (*e*) the junior college.

2. Prepare a special report on the Kalamazoo High School Case or the Asheville Case, showing the effects of the court decision.

3. Compare secondary education in America with that in England, France, Germany, or an oriental country.

4. Debate the subject: "Resolved that all should attend high school."

5. Prepare a survey of your own high-school graduating class, including such data as how many went to college, how many are out of school, how many are gainfully employed. Draw conclusions.

6. Make a list of subjects you studied in high school. What changes would you recommend if you were to take the work again?

7. Study the college entrance requirements of your state university. How do these influence the high-school curriculum?

8. Prepare a spot map of your state or county indicating the location and size of the secondary schools.

9. Study the work of agencies that accredit the high schools in your state. List their standards for accrediting high schools.

10. Describe vocational education as found in a secondary school today.

11. Describe the locus, purpose, procedures, and results of a significant experiment in junior college education, for example, at Blackburn or Stephens College.

12. Report on "Private and Parochial Secondary Schools in the United States."

13. Visit a high-school principal's office and interview the administrator regarding the organization and administration of the school.

14. Examine the certification requirements for teachers of secondary schools in your state.

15. List the special qualities and preparation that you think a secondary-school teacher should possess.

16. Discuss the statement that the high school is the "great American experiment." Why should it be so called?

DESCRIPTIVE BIBLIOGRAPHY AND AIDS

Books

AMERICAN ASSOCIATION OF SCHOOL ADMINISTRATORS: *American School Curriculum*, Chap. VI, National Education Association, 1953.
    Curriculum development in secondary schools.

ASSOCIATION FOR SUPERVISION AND CURRICULUM DEVELOPMENT: *Creating a Good Environment for Learning*, Chap. VI, National Education Association, 1954.
    Community services rendered by high-school seniors.

BRIGGS, THOMAS, PAUL G. LEONARD, and JOSEPH JUSTMAN: *Secondary Education,* Chap. XIX, Macmillan, 1950.

   A vision of secondary education.

CHISHOLM, LESLIE L.: *The Work of the Modern High School,* Chap. II, Macmillan, 1953.

   The development of secondary education in America.

CONANT, JAMES BRYANT: *Education and Liberty,* Chap. III, Harvard University Press, 1953.

   A forward look at secondary and collegiate education.

EDUCATIONAL POLICIES COMMISSION: *Education for all American Youth—A Further Look,* National Education Association, 1952.

   An overview of the developing secondary school.

HAVIGHURST, ROBERT J.: *Human Development and Education,* Chap. III, Longmans, 1953.

   Developmental tasks of adolescence and the challenges to curriculum builders.

KNIGHT, EDGAR W.: *A Documentary History of Education in the South before* 1860, Volume IV, Chap. I, University of North Carolina Press, 1953.

   Academies and other private efforts in education in the South.

MACOMBER, FREEMAN GLENN: *Teaching in the Modern Secondary School,* Chaps. II, III, McGraw-Hill, 1952.

   Basic psychological and philosophical considerations in teaching in the secondary school.

NATIONAL SOCIETY FOR THE STUDY OF EDUCATION: *Adapting the Secondary-school Program to the Needs of Youth,* Chap. I, University of Chicago Press, 1953.

   The youth-needs motive in secondary education as discussed by the yearbook chairman, William G. Brink.

NOAR, GERTRUDE: *The Junior High School—Today and Tomorrow,* Chap. I, Prentice-Hall, 1953.

   The functions of the junior high school.

CURRENT PERTINENT PERIODICALS AND PUBLICATIONS

American Junior College Directory

Bulletin of National Association of
   Secondary-school Principals

California Journal of Secondary
   Education

Clearing House

High School Journal

Journal of General Education

Junior College Journal

North Central Association Quarterly

Scholastic

School Activities

School Review

Schools in Action

Secondary Education

Southern Association Quarterly

Student Life

Teachers College Record

Yearbooks of educational organizations

AUDIO-VISUAL AIDS

ADOLESCENCE   5 films, sound

   Helpful in understanding high-school adolescents is this series of 5 motion-picture films developed by McGraw-Hill to correlate with the book *Adolescent Development* by Elizabeth B. Hurlock.

   Age of Turmoil (20 min.) illustrates the behavior during the emotional turmoil of the early teen-ager—unrealistic ideas about the future, destructive criticism of the school and of people, and other acts stirred with emotionalism. Follow-up filmstrip is available for this and the other films in this series.

Meaning of Adolescence (16 min.) is an overview of the emotional, physical, and mental changes which occur between childhood and adulthood. Suggestions are presented for helping adults deal with the problems and help in adjustments.

Meeting the Needs of Adolescents (19 min.) depicts a family that includes a boy of 14 years and a girl of 17 and shows how their physical, mental, social, and spiritual needs are met.

Physical Aspects of Puberty (19 min.) explains the physiological aspects of puberty, chiefly by means of animation. The problems of social adjustment and behavior that accompany the physiological changes are indicated.

Social-sex Attitudes in Adolescence (22 min.) shows how teen-agers meet the problems involved in becoming aware of and adjusted to the opposite sex. A boy and girl are taken through their entire adolescent experiences, culminating in their marriage.

BROADER CONCEPT OF METHODS: PART I

13 min., sound
Also filmstrip, 35 mm., silent

This film, *Developing Pupil Interest*, presents a frank picture of a secondary-school teacher and his class. One part shows the teacher-dominated, lesson-hearing type of recitation. Typical effects of this method upon student attitudes, responses, and learning are revealed. Then the film presents the alternative techniques to achieve broader educational objectives. Pupils are permitted to share in the planning of their work, and are thereby stimulated toward worth-while and meaningful learning experiences. Available from McGraw-Hill, New York 36.

BROADER CONCEPT OF METHODS: PART II

19 min., sound
Also filmstrip, 35 mm., silent

Development of the secondary-school project shown in Part I is continued. Students are shown learning to work together, to organize themselves into functional groups, to make and carry out plans for investigation, to present their findings and recommendations in a final report, and to put into practice some of their recommendations. Shows how the secondary-school teacher can provide tactful guidance in the solution of difficulties encountered by the various groups. Available from McGraw-Hill, New York 36.

FINDING YOUR LIFE WORK

22 min., sound

This is one of a series of "Your Life Work Films." Since one of the basic problems of a secondary-school pupil is that of trying to find his life work, to prepare for it, to enter upon it, and to advance in it, this film shows the important work of guidance. Available from Carl F. Mahnke Productions, Des Moines, Iowa.

HIGH SCHOOL READING TRAINING FILMS

14 films, average 112 feet, sound

Designed for use with ninth-grade students to help improve facility in reading. Comprehension tests and supplementary reading materials available from the University of Iowa.

THE JUNIOR HIGH SCHOOL STORY

30 min., sound, color

Visits to 49 junior high schools. A superior, fast-moving film. Produced by the California State Department of Education and the Junior-high School Administrators. Available from the State Department at Sacramento, Calif., or the National Association of Secondary-school Principals, Washington, D.C.

School-made Films and Kodachrome Slides

Many secondary schools have prepared films or slides of their various activities. Available from individual school systems.

So You're Going to High School   29 min., sound

This film is an over-all picture of the high-school offerings and guidance procedures in the New York City schools. Available free from the New York City Board of Education.

Tale of Two Towns   45 min., sound, b&w or color

Shows how two neighboring communities in Michigan cooperate in a program for the improvement of their community school system. Available from Agrafilms.

HIGHER EDUCATION

Secondary education should be closely articulated with higher education, since an increasing number of high-school graduates attend college. Colleges and universities offer advanced schooling, which is divided on the basis of undergraduate and graduate work. Enrollments in higher education have increased greatly.

The American college was built upon European antecedents.

The major purposes of higher education are intellectual, cultural, practical, and social. Numerous and varied are the types of higher institutions.

Cooperation and experimentation are conspicuous in higher education.

HIGHER EDUCATION

On the entrance gates of Cornell University at Ithaca, New York, is this inscription:

> So enter, that daily thou mayest become
> more learned and thoughtful;
> So depart, that daily thou mayest become
> more useful to thy country and to mankind.

Robert M. Hutchins, former chancellor of the University of Chicago, once said: "College is the greatest place in the world for those who ought to go to college and who go for the right reasons. For those who ought not to go to college or who go for the wrong reasons, college is a waste of time and money." To the question, "Who should go to college?" John Dale Russell, former director of the Division of Higher Education in the United States Office of Education, answers: "All who have the ability and the incentive should go to college, but they should be given guidance so that they may distribute themselves suitably among various lines of occupational preparation." These persons would benefit markedly from closer cooperation between high school and college.

Articulation of Secondary and Higher Education. So wide a gap exists between the completion of high school and the beginning of college that many students who should continue their schooling fail to do so. In answer to the question: "Why do so many superior youth not go to college?" the Commission on Financing Higher Education states:

Reasons for failure to pursue higher education can be put into two broad categories—financial and motivational. Making rough estimates, we may say that, of the superior fourth of our youth, 40 per cent are not sufficiently motivated to go beyond high school, 20 per cent would go if they had financial assistance, and 40 per cent go under present conditions.[1]

Various efforts are being made to bridge the chasm between the high school and college, especially through preventive and corrective guidance. Historically significant was the work of the Commission on the Relation of School and College, sponsored by the Progressive Education Association. But college admission policies and practices still need to be improved markedly, according to various surveys. As a result of his com-

[1] Byron S. Hollinshead, *Who Should Go to College?* pp. 161–162, Columbia University Press, 1952.

prehensive study of the achievements of the junior high school and junior college, Leonard V. Koos considers the six-four-four plan as the best for integrating high school and college. The 4-year junior college, combining grades 11 through 14, tends to eliminate the barrier that traditionally isolates the twelfth from the thirteenth years.

Guidance and structural reorganization of secondary education must be accompanied by financial aid to deserving and needy students. The Commission on Financing Higher Education states: "We believe all present forms of philanthropic scholarship assistance from individuals, organizations, foundations, and corporations should be encouraged and increased and that tax support for scholarships from local, state, and federal sources should also be increased." [2] A combination of guidance, selection, reform in admission policies, and fiscal support were used in the School and College Study of Admissions with Advanced Standing, initiated with the help of the Ford Foundation Fund. Undoubtedly many superior high-school students can complete the regular college course in 3 years, rather than the traditional 4. Furthermore, as demonstrated by such institutions as Columbia University's School of General Studies, many mature persons can gain a bachelor's degree without having been awarded a high-school diploma.

Accrediting Agencies. The hiatus between secondary school and universities is also being reduced by the ceaseless efforts of various accrediting associations. The entire United States is covered by a network of state and regional associations, which have six geographical divisions: New England, Middle States, Southern, North Central, Northwest, and Western. The states in each of these associations are indicated in Fig. 8-1. More than 100 nation-wide organizations, such as the National Council for Accreditation of Teacher Education, and the National Commission on Accrediting, certify institutions in all states. Accreditation practices are in a state of flux. Ultimately may come one association that evaluates elements common to all institutions and other accrediting bodies that appraise particular aspects. The numerous state, sectional, and national organizations at work on the problems of accrediting have shifted in recent years from quantitative to qualitative standards or to a synthesis of both, with emphasis on the total pattern of the secondary school or the institution of higher learning.

Scope of Higher Education. The period of so-called "advanced education" has been measured in various ways. Traditionally it includes 4 years of college or university and from 1 to 3 years of graduate work. Today the scope of secondary education, as indicated in Unit VII, includes at least in theory the work of grades 7 through 14. Therefore the scope of higher education in this newer sense is delimited to the senior-college

2 *Ibid.,* p. 129.

division—that is, the fifteenth and sixteenth years of schooling—plus the graduate work.

Until recently it was assumed that graduate work in education was limited to 3 years of work beyond the bachelor's degree. There is a trend, however, toward additional courses for persons who have completed the doctor's degree. This is true of a few colleges of education and of some

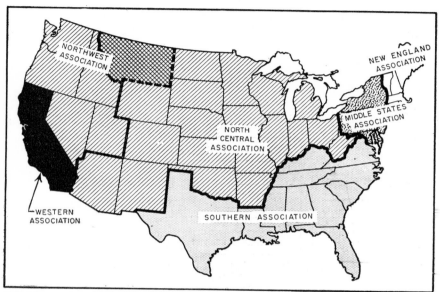

FIG. 8-1. Territory in which each of the six regional associations operates. The North Central Association of Colleges and Secondary Schools embraces the largest number of states. Montana has a double affiliation. The Western Association became an accrediting agency in 1948. It certifies all junior and other colleges and universities in California, and the colleges in Hawaii. It has affiliations with colleges and universities in Arizona. (*Adapted from School Life.*)

professional schools, such as those of medicine and dentistry, which sponsor postdoctoral work. The traditional practice and the modern concept are pictured in Fig. 8-2, which applies specifically to persons working for a degree such as Doctor of Philosophy. The degree of Doctor of Medicine requires at least 3 years of medical school. This period of study is followed by internship.

Public and Private Control. Diversity is the key to freedom in higher education. It permits not only different types of institutions but also diverse sponsorship. The latter is generally public or private. The Commission on Financing Higher Education presents succinctly and convincingly the need for duality in the control of higher education in the United States:

There are weighty reasons why higher education should not follow the example of primary and secondary education which is preponderantly under public control. By its very nature higher education cannot be universal. The vigor of higher education depends upon its being free. Higher education is exploratory in nature. Its inquiries are speculative. These characteristics set it apart from primary and secondary education. Monopoly in control is incompatible with the free market of ideas. . . .

The two systems of control, public and private, are a challenge to each other. Public higher education is aided by the independence of the private institutions.

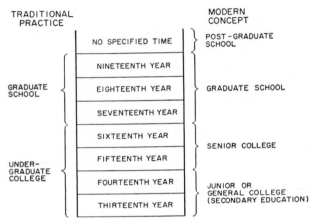

Fig. 8-2. Organization of higher education.

Private colleges and universities are encouraged to broaden their clientele and to maintain their standards by the example of public institutions. Our society would be impoverished by the decline in vigor of either kind.[3]

This unique American duality of structure and support is indeed a heritage to be preserved. Although the number of private institutions of higher education exceeds that of public colleges and universities, the enrollments have been about equally divided.

Enrollments and Colleges. All the colonial colleges were small. In 1800 the 25 colleges had fewer than 100 instructors and 2000 students. Today many of the 1850 institutions have more than that number of instructors and students on a single campus. Except for temporary losses during the First World War, the depression of the 1930's, and the Second World War, the college population has increased steadily.

One contributing cause is the influx of college students from other lands. Although dollar shortages abroad are limiting factors, neverthe-

[3] Commission on Financing Higher Education, *Nature and Needs of Higher Education,* pp. 41–42, Columbia University Press, 1952.

less various positive influences—the efforts of the Institute of International Education, the scholarships provided by military governments in some of the occupied countries, the federal exchange plans, the generosity of American collegiate institutions in providing scholarships, and the unquenchable zeal of foreigners for learning—bring many hungry-minded visitors to the college campuses from the four corners of the earth.

The greatest single factor skyrocketing increases has been the G.I. bills for veterans. Approximately fifty-five times as many people were eligible for training following the Second World War as after the First. Many more qualified after the Korean conflict. Many thousands of veterans have taken advantage of the opportunity to get a college education.

The next decade will undoubtedly witness a continuation of a flood of college students. The President's Commission on Higher Education was, however, too optimistic in its estimates "that in 1960 a minimum of 4,600,000 young people should be enrolled in nonprofit institutions for education beyond the traditional twelfth grade." The popularity of college education in the United States is attested to by the fact that this country has more college students than all the rest of the world.

The United States now has 1850 institutions of higher learning, including approved and nonapproved colleges, universities, and junior colleges. These numerous branches of higher learning grew out of the seed brought from Europe and planted in Massachusetts in 1636.

DEVELOPMENT OF HIGHER EDUCATION

EUROPEAN ANTECEDENTS

Universities, like cathedrals and parliaments, are a product of the Middle Ages. The world's oldest university dates back to A.D. 841, when the Moslems founded Al Azhar ("The Resplendent") in Cairo, Egypt. In the days of ancient Greece and Rome, the source of much wisdom was a man of great knowledge and personal magnetism, such as Plato, at whose feet sat young and old. This personal and informal fellowship in learning was the remote genesis of the modern university, which unfortunately has lost some of the teacher touch in its colossal campuses, big buildings, and scurrying students.

More or less formal institutions of higher education did arise in Athens during the fourth and fifth centuries B.C. These institutions were in the form of separate "schools of philosophy" and "schools of rhetoric" to which modern historians have often applied the misleading term "The University of Athens." . . . The schools of philosophy were the Academy of Plato, the Lyceum of Aristotle, the Stoa of the Stoics, and the Garden of the Epicureans, and the rhetorical schools were best typified by that of Isocrates.[4]

[4] R. Freeman Butts, *The College Charts Its Course*, pp. 20–21, McGraw-Hill, 1939.

These early schools, however, were not university organizations in the modern sense of the term. It was the intellectual activity of the twelfth and thirteenth centuries that gave rise to the university type of organization. When the number of students and professors at a church or cathedral school grew so large that they found it necessary to organize themselves into a guild or *universitas,* for mutual welfare and protection, then a university may be said to have come into existence.[5]

Bologna and Salerno. The oldest university in Europe was Bologna, founded by a guild of students in a city of that name in northern Italy during the twelfth century. The study of law was of prime interest to medieval Italians, and soon Bologna developed a position of leadership in this field. In the course of its history it enrolled such scholars as Dante, Petrarch, and Galvani. In southern Italy the city of Salerno, a health resort, became famous for its lectures and collection of materials in the field of medicine.

Paris. Farther north, in France, arose another of the medieval institutions of higher learning, the University of Paris, which developed from a cathedral school. Naturally this school attracted a large number of students of religion, and Paris was for a long time the most noted university for theology. Although theology was the core, other fields, such as the arts, were stressed. This university with its branches was the "University of Masters," its origin having been the *universitas,* or guild organized by the teachers in Paris.[6] Paris was the greatest of the medieval universities.

Prague. Another interesting old university was that of Prague, founded in 1348, which was attended by students from many nations. One of its earliest graduates was John Huss, famous Protestant martyr. All the early universities had a very loose form of organization, a crude type of democracy. When a group became discontented, they moved to another center, where in turn they established a new college.

Oxford. Thus emigrants from Paris established in the twelfth century the great University of Oxford, 50 miles northwest of London. Modeled after Paris, Oxford stimulated the development of the "college" to the point where it overshadowed the "university" and provided the prototype for the colleges of today.[7] Today Oxford is a federation of 20 or more colleges, such as Exeter, Queen's, and Jesus, each with its own government, but the degrees are granted by the University. Many students from the United States and Canada have won the highly prized Rhodes scholarships to this outstanding university.

[5] *Ibid.,* p. 28.
[6] Nathan Schachner, *The Medieval Universities,* p. 62. Stokes, 1938.
[7] *Ibid.*

Contrasts in Higher Education. The contrasts between these early institutions of higher learning and those of today are striking. The medieval university had no libraries, laboratories, or museums, no endowment or buildings of its own; it could not possibly have met the requirements of modern accrediting associations. The old university was *bâtie en hommes*—built of men. It created the university tradition and laid a firm foundation for higher education in America. The late Edgar W. Knight, an authority in the history of education, states that the American college is a native institution only in the sense that it is a European institution transplanted here in the seventeenth century by the early settlers who brought it from England along with their Bibles and their axes.[8]

The European university today differs markedly from the American in that the European student has in a great measure finished his general education by the time he enters the university, that European higher learning is more restricted than in the United States, and that student life is less highly organized than in America.

Historical Calendar—
Higher Education and Contemporaneous Events

The calendar on the next page shows some notable dates in higher education and contemporaneous events of political, social, and economic significance in the United States. Others are found in Unit IX.

Early American Colleges

Early Colleges in the Americas. Although the first institution of higher learning in the United States was Harvard College, it was not the oldest in the Americas. The University of San Marcos at Lima, Peru, and the University of Mexico at Mexico City both opened their doors in 1553—83 years before Harvard. The University of Mexico is reputed to have used *Recognita summularum,* the first textbook in philosophy written in America. The oldest university once under the American flag was established in Manila in 1611, some forty years after the capture of Manila by the Spaniards. This, the University of Santo Tomás, was a "seminary-college where the religious . . . might read the sciences of arts and theology." [9] It was at Santo Tomás that the Japanese interned hundreds of American prisoners during the Second World War. It is one of at least three institutions in the new world antedating Harvard.

---

[8] Edgar W. Knight, *Twenty Centuries of Education,* p. 284, Ginn, 1940.

[9] J. G. Wingo, "Oldest University under the United States Flag," *Catholic School Journal,* July, 1937, pp. 207–208.

Historical Calendar

HIGHER EDUCATION	CONTEMPORANEOUS EVENTS
1636—Harvard University founded (Cambridge, Massachusetts)	1636—Rhode Island settled by Roger Williams
1693—William and Mary College established (Williamsburg, Virginia)	1693—Salem "witchcraft" imposed on people
1785—First state university chartered (Georgia)	1785—Thomas Jefferson appointed minister to France
1803—First federal land granted for state "seminary of learning" (Ohio)	1803—Ohio admitted to the Union
1819—Dartmouth College Decision rendered by U.S. Supreme Court	1819—First transatlantic steamship piloted across the ocean.
1837—Coeducation started at Oberlin College, founded in 1833	1837—Michigan admitted to the Union
1838—Mt. Holyoke College organized as first woman's college	1838—Longfellow's "Psalm of Life" published
1839—First state normal organized (Lexington, Massachusetts)	1839—Vulcanized rubber patented by Goodyear
1862—Land-grant college act passed by Congress	1861 to 1865—War waged between the states
1868—Hampton Institute organized as 1st Negro school of higher education	1868—Negro citizenship amendment to Constitution ratified (Amendment XIV)
1876—First graduate work begun at Johns Hopkins University.	1876—R. B. Hays nominated as Republican candidate for Presidency
1902—First public junior college established (Joliet, Illinois)	1903—Federal Departments of Commerce and Labor organized
1944—G.I. bill for veterans' education passed by Congress	1944—Germany invaded by Americans
1947-48—Reports issued by President's Commission on Higher Education	1947—Marshall Plan proposed in address delivered at Harvard
1948—First Fulbright Act scholarships opened for China and Burma	1948—Charter for International Trade Organization adopted by U.N.
1949—Southern Regional Education Program launched	1949—Harry S. Truman inaugurated as President
1952—Reports issued by Commission on Financing Higher Education	1952—First successful test of hydrogen bomb in the United States
1953—Commission on Education for Women organized	1953—Eisenhower inaugurated as the 34th President
1955—U.S. Air Force Academy opened for training of officers	1955—Control of both houses in Congress regained by Democrats

First College in the United States. The first college in continental United States was Harvard, founded in 1636 in Newtowne, Massachusetts, which was later renamed Cambridge. The basic motive for its establishment may be gleaned from this inscription on the west gate on its campus:

After God had carried us safe to New England, and wee had builded our houses, provided necessaries for our livelihood, rear'd convenient places for God's worship, and setled the Civil Government: One of the next things we longed for, and looked after was to advance Learning and perpetuate it to Posterity; dreading to leave an illiterate Ministry to the Churches when our present Ministers shall lie in the Dust.

According to the Charter of 1650, the purposes of Harvard were as follows:

The advancement of all good literature, arts and sciences.

The advancement and education of youth in all manner of good literature, arts and sciences.

All other necessary provisions that may conduce to the education of the English and Indian youth of this country in knowledge and godliness.

Considering the times, these purposes were highly significant. On the other hand the late James Truslow Adams candidly wrote:

We make much in our history of the founding of Harvard in 1636, but this remained the only institution above an ordinary school in the colonies for nearly sixty years, and was pitiably unimportant in the training it afforded and the scholarship it produced as compared with the universities in New Spain. In fact nearly two hundred years were to pass before any English institution in America reached the point which the Spanish had attained even before the English had settled at all.[10]

Undoubtedly higher education in colonial America was not of a high caliber.

Other Early Colleges. For many years Harvard was the only voice of higher education in the wilderness of America. Attempts to found a college in Virginia began, before the *Mayflower* sailed to Plymouth, with the grant of land for a university by the Virginia Company, but not until 1693 were the planters able to obtain adequate aid from England for their "place of university." Thus started the College of William and Mary at Williamsburg, Virginia. It had for a time a distinctive building designed by Sir Christopher Wren, who created St. Paul's Cathedral and many other notable buildings in London. This structure has been restored.

In the colonial period of the United States nine colleges were founded. In connection with the last arose the historical Dartmouth College Case.

[10] James Truslow Adams, *The Epic of America*, p. 43, Little, Brown, 1932.

The decision of the Supreme Court threw protection around higher education and stimulated the growth of colleges. All nine colonial colleges with the exception of Benjamin Franklin's Academy were sectarian. By 1800 there were 25 colleges in the United States but their enrollments were small. Not only did the president's house occasionally serve for recitations in these early colleges, but he was often the sole member of the faculty, teaching all subjects. Even in later years the faculties were small. A professor did not fill "a chair," but occupied an entire settee, as in the case of an "intellectual Hercules" at Columbia who taught moral and mental philosophy, English literature, history, political economy, and logic.[11]

Name	Location	Year
Harvard	Cambridge, Massachusetts	1636
William and Mary	Williamsburg, Virginia	1693
Yale	New Haven, Connecticut	1701
Princeton	Princeton, New Jersey	1746
Pennsylvania [Franklin's Academy (1740) and College]	Philadelphia, Pennsylvania	1751
Columbia (King's College)	New York, New York	1754
Brown	Providence, Rhode Island	1764
Rutgers	New Brunswick, New Jersey	1766
Dartmouth	Hanover, New Hampshire	1769

The history of these institutions of higher learning affords interesting reading. Most of them were supported financially by grants of land or money from legislatures, by donations of money or kind, and by miscellaneous means, such as lotteries.

State support was slow to develop. As late as 1860, only 17 of 264 institutions of higher learning were financed by the state. The first state university to be chartered was in Georgia; the first to be opened was in North Carolina, and Ohio was the first commonwealth to receive federal land grants to start a "seminary of learning." Nearly sixty years later the passage of the Morrill Act by Congress inaugurated the development of the so-called "land-grant colleges" for agriculture and mechanical arts. Hampton Institute at Hampton, Virginia, organized in 1868, was the first school of higher education for Negroes. One of its early graduates was Booker T. Washington.

HIGHER EDUCATION FOR WOMEN

In the biography *Madame Curie* is found, by inference, this interesting reflection on the educational restraint upon women in the latter half of the nineteenth century:

[11] Allan Nevins, *The Emergence of Modern America*, pp. 265–266, Macmillan, 1927.

At the moment when Manya [later Madame Curie], dulled by the tiresome journey [from Poland], descended from the train to the smoky platform of the Gare du Nord [in Paris], the familiar grip of servitude was suddenly loosened, her shoulders straightened, her lungs and heart felt at ease. For the first time she was breathing the air of a free country, and in her enthusiasm everything seemed miraculous. . . . Before and above everything else, it was miraculous that these straight wide avenues, inclined in a gentle slope toward the heart of the city, were leading her, Manya Sklodovska, to the wide-open doors of a university. And what a university! The most famous; the one described centuries ago as "an abridgement of the Universe"; the very one of which Luther had said: "It is in Paris that we find the most celebrated and most excellent of schools: it is called the Sorbonne." The adventure was fit for a fairy tale.[12]

Thus Eve Curie describes the enthusiasm of her mother at the prospect of quenching that "thirst for knowledge that was her essential characteristic." Later when the Sorbonne appointed Mme. Curie to carry on the work of her husband in the Faculty of Science in 1906, it "was the first time that a position in French higher education had been given to a woman." It is significant that in England women were not admitted to degrees at Oxford until 1920.

During the nineteenth century higher learning in America gradually ceased to be the prerogative of one sex. Most of the women from coast to coast who today confidently attend college classes are perhaps unaware that their sex was once denied entrance to the portals of higher institutions. Coeducation on the college level began as late as 1837 when four women were accepted in a standard course at Oberlin College, and exposed to the following program:

Life at Oberlin was deeply dyed with piety. The day was begun with private prayers in the individual rooms. Following breakfast a brief religious service for the young ladies was held in the boarding hall. Classes were always begun with prayer—occasionally continued throughout the hour. Of course no meal began without grace. Chapel, or afternoon prayers, at five o'clock was attended by all; one of the professors read from the Bible and a hymn was sung. On Thursdays a religious lecture was added—a kind of weekday sermon. Young people's prayer meetings, generally one for each class, were held on Monday nights. The first coeds, like most students, joined the church; it was something of a disgrace not to belong. On the Sabbath all were required to attend the services, morning and afternoon, in old Colonial Hall or the tent, perhaps to hear the fiery Finney preach a "double-header" on "The Wages of Sin," "Robbing God" or "Your sin will find you out." . . . The college course of a century ago was still truly classical and without "electives." All studied the same subjects. The standard curriculum included classes in Latin and Greek in every year with the first devoted mostly to the ancient languages.[13]

[12] From *Madame Curie: A Biography* by Eve Curie, copyrighted by Doubleday, Doran and Company, Inc., 1937, p. 94.

[13] R. S. Fletcher, "The First Coeds," *The American Scholar*, Winter, 1938, pp. 86, 87.

FIG. 8-3. Contrasts in higher education for women. One of the contrasts is in the wearing apparel. Above are pathfinders of sports for women in a calisthenics class in the early days of Vassar College, Poughkeepsie, New York. Below are the sportswomen of today in an archery class at Barnard College, New York City. The top picture was painted inside the "Calisthenic Hall," and the lower was made out of doors.

Life for women in the early days of higher education and today is a vivid contrast.

Mount Holyoke, the first college for women in America, was established in 1838 by the academy teacher, Mary Lyon, who begged pennies, nickels, and dimes in order to found a "permanent seminary in New England with accommodations, apparatus, etc., somewhat like those for the other sex." Mount Holyoke epitomizes the history of education for women; as a seminary and later as a college, it exemplifies in its evolution

FIG. 8-4. Original Mount Holyoke Seminary, South Hadley, Massachusetts. (*Currier print, made available through the courtesy of Mount Holyoke College.*)

every stage of the general advancement. Mary Emma Woolley, former president of Mount Holyoke, demarcates these three periods in woman's educational progress:

The first, which lasted until after the Civil War, was the period of intellectual stir and questioning, from which women's college education ultimately resulted, and in which the first experiments in coeducation were made at Oberlin and Antioch. Typically, however, it was the heyday of the female seminary which hardly dared or cared to call itself a college and a few women's colleges which often amounted to little more than seminaries.

The second period, from 1865 to the turn of the century, was the era of justification and expansion, when three distinct types of new higher educational facilities for women sprang up rapidly all over the country. (1) It was the time of the founding of Vassar, Smith and Wellesley, the first women's colleges to have heavy endowments and classical curricula much like those of Harvard. (2) It saw, too, the opening of the great universities, such as Michigan, Cornell and Chicago, and (3) the founding of the coordinate colleges for women in connection with such universities as Columbia, Harvard, and Brown.

Finally, in the years since 1900 has come the era of internal improvement. Women's colleges have been much more slowly added. Those already in existence, finally established and confident, have been expanding their campuses, courses and equipment.[14]

Today coeducational institutions and women's colleges have gained for women the right and the opportunity to obtain higher learning comparable with that for men. Not only is general education theirs, but also a wide selection among the professional curriculums. Women outnumber men in the teaching profession; in the medical field they comprise a small percentage of the doctors. What a numerical contrast between almost a million women now in attendance at institutions of higher learning and the three "females" who in 1841 were the first American women to earn a regular bachelor of arts degree by the completion of a program of studies identical to that required of men candidates for the same degree! The granting of several thousand advanced degrees annually to women is a far cry from the days when there appeared in *The Atlantic* a caustic article entitled "Should Women Learn the Alphabet?"

Role of Higher Education in Defense

An important chapter in the history of higher education for women and men in the United States was written during the Second World War.

Training of Women for War. Approximately one-third of a million American women were in the military services during the Second World War. An undetermined but very large number were engaged in work closely related to the war, in business, in industry, and in various volunteer services such as the Red Cross. These experiences have had profound effects upon the position of women as citizens and as students, particularly in higher education. A woman in uniform on a college campus is a long cry from 1837 when coeducation started. The trend toward coeducation has been definitely continued by the war and postwar training programs for women. The G.I. bills for education have been benefiting women as well as men, on an equal basis.

Training Programs of the Armed Services. All the colleges and universities of the land cooperated indirectly and directly in the gigantic struggle to win the Second World War. Thousands of students left the campuses to fight in all parts of the world, hundreds of colleges loaned the services of their best professors to the United States government, and one-third of all the institutions participated directly in war-service training programs. Even the atomic age dates back to a pile of fissionable material on the campus of the University of Chicago. Such procedures

[14] Eunice Fuller Barnard, "Women and Colleges," *The New York Times Magazine,* May 2, 1937, pp. 8, 9, 12.

as accelerating programs, retooling the minds of faculty members, meeting the needs of more mature and motivated students, stimulating research, and equalizing educational opportunities for students to secure higher education are some of the by-products of college war-training programs which will influence higher education for a long time.

Currently many universities participate in defense programs. More than one hundred institutions of higher education are offering off-duty courses for men and women in military bases in the United States. Among the overseas affiliations are: University of California for the Pacific theater, Louisiana State for the Caribbean, and University of Maryland for the European area. Many other college programs are detailed in *Federal Activities in Higher Education after the Second World War.*[15]

HISTORIC LEADERS IN HIGHER EDUCATION

In the long history of higher education in America there have been numerous dynamic leaders. It was John Harvard who donated his name, library, and money as the initial gifts to Harvard College. It was Charles W. Eliot who fought for the elective system in higher education and sponsored five revolutionary advances during the first years of his administration at Harvard: the elevation and amplification of entrance requirements; the enlargement of the curriculum and the development of the elective system; the recognition of graduate study in the liberal arts; the raising of professional training in law, medicine, and engineering to a postgraduate level; and the fostering of greater maturity in student life.[16] Eliot was one of a half-dozen statesmen who emerged as personal forces in American higher education immediately following the Civil War. Others were: Andrew D. White of Cornell, James McCosh of Princeton, Noah Porter of Yale, James B. Angell of Michigan, Daniel Coit Gilman of Johns Hopkins, William Rainey Harper at Chicago, Horace Mann at Antioch, Mark Hopkins at Williams, Mary Lyon at Holyoke, and Herman Schneider, father of cooperative education, at the University of Cincinnati. The catalogue of "who was who" and "who is who" in American higher education makes a ponderous tome.

OBJECTIVES OF HIGHER EDUCATION

WHY ARE YOU GOING TO COLLEGE?

An interesting collection of statements regarding the objectives of higher education results from asking students on different campuses the question, "Why are you going to college?" Their answers include these:

[15] James Earl Russell, *Federal Activities in Higher Education after the Second World War,* Chap. I and Appendix, King's Crown, 1951.

[16] Nevins, *op. cit.,* pp. 268–269.

To continue my education

To carry out a family tradition

To get a degree

To be a better citizen

To render better service to society

To do research or specialize

To earn more money

To explore vocational possibilities

To prepare for a vocation or career

To get semiprofessional education

To complete preprofessional education

To enter a profession

To broaden my outlook

To develop a philosophy of living

To acquire more culture

To get a liberal education

To develop higher ethical standards

To meet people

To get a spouse

To acquire social prestige

To enjoy college social life

To share in extracurricular life

To escape doing other work

To develop avocational interests

Many other sources of student motivation might be listed.

PRESIDENT PUSEY'S PURPOSES

Nathan Pusey, who was inaugurated in 1953 as the twenty-fourth president of Harvard University, the nation's oldest institution of higher learning, believes that the true business of liberal education is greatness:

> It is our task not to produce safe men, in whom our safety can never in any case lie, but to keep alive in young people the courage to dare to seek the truth, to be free, to establish in them a compelling desire to live greatly and magnanimously, and to give them the knowledge and awareness, the faith and the trained facility to get on with the job. Especially the faith, for as someone has said, the whole world now looks to us for a creed to believe and a song to sing.[17]

Thus the Harvard president believes that the purpose of liberal education is not merely to impart knowledge but also to "transform personality by transforming minds."

SUGGESTIONS FROM STATESMAN STEVENSON

Adlai E. Stevenson, a former governor of Illinois and Democratic presidential candidate in 1952, said in 1954, at the bicentennial of Columbia University in New York, that the American people, beset with doubts and difficulties, seek direction.

> And we look, finally, to the free university, whose function is the search for truth and its communication to succeeding generations. Only as that function is performed steadfastly, continuously, and without interference does a university keep faith with a great humanist tradition of which it is a part. . . . Men may be born free; they are not born wise, and it is the duty of the university to make the free wise. The university is the guardian of our heritage, the teacher of our teachers. It is the dwelling place of the free mind.

[17] "Unconquered Frontier," *Time*, Mar. 1, 1954, pp. 62, 64.

It is symbolical that Columbia University, founded as a *King's* college, accented in its bicentennial the advancement of *free men.*

Four Fundamental Facets

According to the Commission on Financing Higher Education, the basic pattern of higher education is made up of four interlocking designs:

Liberal education. The goal of liberal education is quality of mind as much as a body of knowledge. . . . It is vital to a free society.

Professional education. It builds upon knowledge; it applies and uses it in concrete situations. And yet professional education changes and develops as knowledge grows.

Graduate study and research. It is graduate scholarship which above all other parts of higher education seeks constantly to enlarge the horizons of man's knowledge. . . . This is a favorable atmosphere in which to carry on research; it commits the mind to the search for truth above all else.

Public services. Besides contributing new knowledge, colleges and universities have become centers of information and trained ability to which society can bring its problems. In them adults can gain information and skills.[18]

Within these patterns—cultural, practical, intellectual, and social—are discernible many other plans and purposes.

TYPES OF SCHOOLS OF HIGHER LEARNING

President Pusey's predecessor, James Bryant Conant, who left Harvard to become United States high commissioner for Germany, says of higher education in America, "As regards the numbers and diversity of institutions there is nothing faintly resembling it anywhere in the world." [19] Previous mention has been made of the two major types, public and private. But many institutions of higher learning defy classification, either because they cannot be placed in a general category or because their work is of a multiple nature. The types selected for emphasis here are the following: (1) junior colleges, (2) community or technical colleges, (3) general colleges, (4) liberal arts colleges, (5) municipal colleges and universities, (6) universities, (7) land-grant colleges and universities, (8) professional schools, (9) graduate schools, and (10) other institutions of higher learning.

At the outset it may be helpful to differentiate between the terms "college," "university," and "school," as applied to institutions of post-secondary education, although there are no standard definitions:

In general, the first is used to designate the institution with a four-year general course leading to a B.A. or B.S. degree, unless qualified specifically in the case of

[18] Commission on Financing Higher Education, *op. cit.,* pp. 15–25.

[19] James Bryant Conant, *Education and Liberty,* p. 53, Harvard University Press, 1953.

a technical institution, as a "teachers college" or "agricultural college." The second ordinarily is applied to institutions having in addition to an undergraduate nonspecialized college, a general graduate school and special professional schools reaching a graduate level. Not a few institutions lacking these characteristics call themselves universities, and there is no legal restriction upon such use. The term "school" is applied to divisions of a university as the "graduate school," the "school of journalism" and to many special institutions such as "agricultural school," "law school," "normal school," and the like.[20]

Obviously the name of an institution is not a reliable guide to its academic rank or its special function. The inconsistency in nomenclature is often confusing to visitors from other lands.

JUNIOR COLLEGES [21]

It is a moot question whether junior colleges belong to the field of higher secondary education or lower higher education. The independent junior college often forms the upper division of secondary education, whereas the freshman and sophomore years of college may constitute a junior-college division in a school of higher education. The junior division of Louisiana State University affords an example of the latter. The University of Chicago once sought to unify the program of general education by means of a 4-year college program beginning with the junior year of the high school and continuing through the first 2 years of college.

Junior colleges, like most institutions of higher learning, may be classified by: sex admitted, men, women, or both; length of course, 1 to 6 years; function, terminal or preparatory; size of enrollment; age, that is, date of establishment; method of origin, such as high-school elongation or university amputation; and method of control or support, such as public or private.[22] The latter is the most fundamental basis for classification.

COMMUNITY AND TECHNICAL COLLEGES

Shakespeare wrote, "A rose by any other name would smell as sweet." Many colleges do not like to be called "junior," with its diminutive and preparatory connotation. This dislike is a sign that these institutions are growing up and assuming a new role, as indicated in a book title like *The New American College*. The Educational Policies Commission suggests the name "community institutes." The President's Commission on Higher Education, as previously mentioned, uses the nomenclature "community colleges," although private colleges usually draw some of their students from a wide geographical area.

[20] L. M. Wilson and I. L. Kandel, *Introduction to the Study of American Education*, pp. 234–235, Nelson, 1934.

[21] See Unit VII for a more complete consideration of junior colleges.

[22] For a directory of these and other types, see periodic publications of the American Council on Education and of the American Association of Junior Colleges.

Some community colleges may offer a full 4 years of college work, but most of them probably will stop at the end of the fourteenth grade, the sophomore year of the traditional college. . . . Whatever form the community college takes, its purpose is educational service to the entire community, and this purpose requires of it a variety of functions and programs.[23]

The commission recommends that the community college emphasize programs of terminal education planned specifically for the needs of youth who will end their formal education with their junior-college years.

One variety of community college is the technical institute, or institute of applied arts and sciences. Those in New York State are designed "to make preparation for occupational competence the core of education for social living." The technical institutes usually combine general education with specialized training for a single technical and semi-professional occupation or for a cluster of allied tasks. Geographically they are local, regional, state, and interstate in the area served.

Most junior colleges, community colleges, and technical institutes have one or more outlets in a four-faceted program embracing: (1) semiprofessional and professional education, including senior-college preparation, (2) training for trades and technical skills, (3) adult education, and (4) general education.

General Colleges

As indicated previously, one objective of higher learning is to provide general education. For the attainment of this goal, courses replete with basic information are given in many colleges during the first year or two. In some instances a specific organization unit called the general college, consisting usually of 2 years of study, has been established. This type of school does not follow a uniform pattern. The variety in experimental procedure is illustrated in the following brief explanation of the program at Boston University General College:

The program is an attempt to restore collegiate training to meaningful and intelligent unity. The 2-year curriculum of the General College, followed *in toto* by all students, includes material from five broad areas of human interest: science, social science, English and literature, guidance, and history and government. These are taught without reference to the lines of demarcation which normally set off one subject from another. The aim is *fusion* within each of these broad fields, and careful integration among all fields.

In contrast to the subject-matter of conventional approach, the purpose of general education is to equip the student with a wide understanding of the world about him and the social system in which he lives, rather than with a detailed, but more or less isolated, knowledge of certain particular subjects. As a natural corollary, emphasis is placed on the ability to think clearly and logically.

[23] President's Commission on Higher Education, *Higher Education for American Democracy*, Volume I, "Establishing the Goals," p. 67, GPO, 1947.

After 2 years of study in the general-education program, transfer to another college of the university is arranged through our guidance department in co-operation with the registrar of the senior college concerned. This placement of the student in a course of advanced study with junior-class standing, or his place-ment in a job, represents the culmination to an intensive 2-year program.[24]

Many other institutions have organized specific programs for general education.

Liberal Arts Colleges

The liberal arts program is usually offered by two types of institu-tions: the liberal arts college and the division of liberal arts of the large university. Their purposes are those of liberal education, preprofessional preparation, and some specialization. When the college is organized on a 4-year basis, there is usually a gradual shift in emphasis, with the first two years devoted primarily to general education and the last two years directed toward majors or fields of concentration. Although students are permitted some degree of concentration, it is undoubtedly desirable that they dip into each of the three great divisions of the curriculum, *viz.*, the humanities, the natural sciences, and the social sciences, as recommended by H. W. Dodds, former president of Princeton University, who once said, "Never in our history has the need for the liberally educated mind been so grave." The liberal-arts college and divisions in private and state universities constitute a bulwark against too early overspecializa-tion. These institutions, catering to men and/or women, have a greater enrollment than any other type of school for higher learning. Nearly all the 400 and more liberal-arts colleges are privately controlled.

Municipal or Urban Colleges and Universities

Another type of higher institution is the locally financed municipal college or university, which, under the control of a municipal or city board of education, offers a standard degree after four or more years of work. This institution represents secularization in the extension of edu-cation, because, being supported primarily by city taxes and controlled by public authorities, it is in effect a part of the public-school system and a people's university. Dual support is found in Detroit's Wayne Univer-sity, which, controlled by the city board of education, receives some state support. A board of higher education appointed by the mayor of New York governs the largest city college system in the world, *viz.*, the College of the City of New York, embracing four colleges: City (men, with women admitted in some branches), which was the first tuition-free, city-owned college in the United States; Hunter (women); Brooklyn (coeducational); and Queens (coeducational).

[24] Judson Rea Butler, "A General Education Program in Action," *School and Society,* May 3, 1947, pp. 321–326.

These colleges, few in number but great in influence, arose through a wide variety of circumstances: a normal college became a city college; a bequest was given to the city for educational purposes; a financial foundation started another; the public junior college and normal school

FIG. 8-5. One of the city colleges of New York. Hunter College, the largest college for women in the world, is housed in one of the largest educational buildings in the world—a 16-story unit. Many students also attend the Bronx center. (*Courtesy of Hunter College.*)

were extended upward; a favorable vote of the people authorized the establishment of the school; and existing institutions changed their status to city colleges. The latter was the case with Charleston and Louisville, two municipal institutions that reach back over a hundred years. The next decade will undoubtedly see many more city colleges established in connection with the present accent on youth. A factor in promoting stability and improvement in the city colleges is the Association of Urban Universities, founded in 1914.

UNIVERSITIES

Many institutions are "universities" in name only. The Commission on Financing Higher Education defines universities as "large, complex institutions which offer the usual undergraduate curriculum, graduate studies leading to the degree of Ph.D., and a variety of professional curriculums—medicine, law, agriculture, engineering and others." The universities, both public and private, conduct most of the federally sponsored research in higher education. They render many other services, such as extension work and adult education. They enroll approximately half of all the students in higher education. The hundred-odd universities are about evenly divided according to public or independent support. These two types "supplement and complement each other extraordinarily well."

State Universities. These institutions, which are usually a general responsibility of all the citizens of a state, are under one or more publicly controlled boards of higher education, elected by the people or appointed by state officials. Every state of the Union has its university or university system. The state university, as part of American public education, is regarded as a natural and inevitable culmination of the public-school system. Its function is assumed to be that of supplying all the needs of society that fall within the sphere of higher education. Many state universities claim that the whole state is their campus. Several extend their activities beyond the boundaries of the commonwealth and some to other countries, as for example, the program of the University of Illinois in Japan.

Private Universities. The so-called "independent" universities, and colleges too, are a vital part of the American educational system, drawing most of their support directly from private purses, and serving the American citizen at home and abroad. In *Freedom's Faith* a business executive writes:

The preservation of the principle of providing higher education supported altogether by private resources is just as important to our freedom as the preservation of private enterprise in the field of production, and the competition of such institutions with those that are tax-supported is just as important to our way of life as business competition in our market economy.[25]

As indicated previously, the Commission on Financing Higher Education believes that there are weighty reasons why higher education should not follow the example of elementary and secondary education, which is primarily under public control. The private institutions are usually under a board of trustees selected from executives and patrons. The

25 C. B. Randall, *Freedom's Faith*, p. 83, Little, Brown, 1953, and *Atlantic Monthly*.

American eagle of higher education can soar to greater heights if it has two well-balanced wings and a pair of eyes focused on the lofty goals of the American way of life. It can also stand solidly on the twin legs of public and private support.

FIG. 8-6. Cathedral of Learning, University of Pittsburgh, Pittsburgh, Pennsylvania. This etching by Louis Orr is of "the tallest schoolhouse in the world." Pittsburgh University is one of the many private institutions of higher learning. (*Courtesy of University of Pittsburgh.*)

LAND-GRANT COLLEGES AND UNIVERSITIES [26]

Origin and Development. A land-grant college or university is an institution of higher education that has been designated by the state legislature as qualified to receive the benefits of either or both of the Morrill funds. The term "land-grant college" originated from the wording of the First Morrill Act, adopted by the Congress of the United States in

[26] See Unit I for additional material on land-grant colleges and universities.

1862. This act provided on the basis of each senator and representative in Congress for a land grant of 30,000 acres or its equivalent in scrip to the several states for an endowment, the interest from which was to furnish instruction in "agriculture and the mechanic arts, without excluding other scientific and classical studies and including military tactics." This act, sponsored by Justin S. Morrill, who represented Vermont in Congress for 44 years, and signed during the Civil War by Abraham Lincoln, was followed by several related acts.

Appropriation from Bankhead-Jones funds depends on congressional action each year, whereas appropriation of other Morrill funds continues as long as the funds are spent in accordance with the terms of these laws. Annual appropriations are made through the United States Office of Education. The use of this money is confined to salaries and facilities for instruction in seven major fields of study. As recipients of these federal aids, the land-grant colleges are required to make annual reports to the Office of Education. Expenditures by the separate states have increased to such an extent that at present more money is provided by the state than from the federal budget.

Number and Types of Institutions.[27] There are 69 land-grant colleges and universities which may be grouped as follows:

24 separate colleges
28 universities, in which agriculture, engineering, and home economics form a component part of the work
17 institutions of higher education devoted to the education of Negroes

Many are state universities, several are agriculture or technical universities and colleges, and a few are junior colleges and teachers colleges.

Functions, Activities, and Influence. A typical land-grant college consists of three divisions: resident instruction, research, especially by the experiment stations, and the extension service. On-campus instruction is effectively supplemented by the two other services. After the land-grant colleges had been in existence some twenty-five years, arrangements were made to establish experimental stations for agricultural research. At present an agricultural experiment station is found in every state that has a land-grant college. The most widely known activity is the extension service, or off-campus teaching, made possible by the Smith-Lever Act in 1914. This work is conducted by a well-trained personnel consisting of county agricultural agents, country home demonstration workers, boys' and girls' club workers, and other specialists. In many instances these representatives are partly supported from county funds. The land-grant

[27] See the annual report on statistics of land-grant colleges and universities published by the GPO.

colleges are directly concerned with the welfare of a large group of the population, *viz.,* the homemakers and the farmers.

The triangular base of research, campus instruction, and extension education makes the land-grant college a potent force in American higher education. The land-grant movement created many new institutions, such as the universities of Illinois, California, and Minnesota, and the

FIG. 8-7. Michigan State College—one of the land-grant institutions—located at East Lansing, Michigan, takes to wheels for some of its television programs. (*Courtesy of Michigan State College.*)

agricultural colleges in Michigan, Massachusetts, and Texas. It also led to reorganization in numerous existing institutions, for example, the University of Wisconsin. It definitely gave breadth to coeducation. It has been called democracy's college. It represented a liberalizing of the old classical college course, particularly in the emphasis on agriculture and home economics. In line with its own expanded offering, a land-grant college may change its name and shift its emphasis.

The land-grant colleges have had and are having a marked influence on American secondary education, since thousands of Smith-Hughes home economics and agriculture teachers now in the public schools have been educated at these institutions.

All the land-grant colleges and universities require that men students take military training unless excused for reasons of health or age. When the original Morrill Act went into effect, instructors assigned by the War Department taught military tactics. The Student Army Training Corps (SATC), authorized during the First World War, was the forerunner of the Reserve Officers' Training Corps (ROTC), established in 1920 with passage of the National Defense Act. ROTC units are now maintained at all land-grant institutions as well as at many other colleges and universities. Through providing a reserve of competent officer strength in virtually all arms of the service, the land-grant colleges play an important role in the defense program for the United States.

In 1887 a permanent organization of land-grant institutions was effected under the name "Association of American Agricultural Colleges and Experiment Stations," which was changed in 1920 to "Association of Land-grant Colleges and Universities." The Negro land-grant colleges also are banded together in their national organization. These professional associations are promoting a country-wide program for the improvement of these schools. The future presages a continuous growth in attendance for both full-time and part-time students.

PROFESSIONAL SCHOOLS [28]

Former President James B. Conant has stated that "the common denominator among all universities past and present is professional education." An avowed purpose for the establishment of Harvard College in 1636 was the preparation of learned ministers for the church. Since the middle of the eighteenth century professional education has developed gradually in American colleges and universities. In 1765 the University of Pennsylvania started its medical department; Harvard opened the first law school in 1817; and in 1823 Reverend Samuel R. Hall established a private normal school for teachers in Concord, Vermont. These were followed by schools for dentistry, pharmacy, and other professions, but, owing to the competition with the apprenticeship system, the growth of professional and technical schools was slow. Some of the land-grant agricultural colleges were set up as special technical and engineering schools combined. Some states established separate engineering or technical schools, for instance, Purdue University.

GRADUATE SCHOOLS

The system of American education reaches its apex in the graduate or advanced professional school. A technical distinction between a college and a university is that the former offers only undergraduate work while the latter offers both undergraduate and graduate courses. Many colleges, however, have a graduate division, whereas many so-called uni-

[28] Professional schools for teachers are considered in Unit XI.

versities have none. In some universities all the graduate work is centered in the graduate school, although part of the work is offered in the professional schools. Genuine graduate training was not known in the United States until after the Civil War; in 1876 Johns Hopkins became the first school to organize graduate study.[29] Recent years have brought a significant expansion of graduate work. A large percentage of the entire student body of Howard University in Washington, D.C., is composed of students holding one or more degrees. Many in the graduate division of Howard are holders of scholarships awarded by their respective states. The professions are dependent upon specialization and research, and the university of today and tomorrow will continue to give much attention to its graduate program.

Master's Degree. Beyond the baccalaureate is the master's degree which usually requires (1) at least a year of residence beyond the bachelor's degree, (2) completion of a certain number of credits or courses totaling approximately thirty semester hours, (3) examinations, both preliminary and final comprehensives, oral and written, and (4) the completion of some research project, either a thesis, or its equivalent, or added course work. Certain schools and departments stipulate additional requirements or permit substitutes. For the master of education, Harvard and the University of Illinois require 2 years beyond a bachelor's degree. The University of Chicago has established a plan for awarding master's degrees for consumers rather than for producers of research. It recognizes that some students intend to engage later in research activities and that others, although not intending to use experimental and statistical procedures, will need to understand and evaluate the results of research. Hence one is not required to perform research but to understand and interpret it. Some institutions offer an intermediate degree between the master's and doctor's.

Doctor of Philosophy. Numerous doctors' degrees, such as doctor of medicine, doctor of dentistry, and doctor of philosophy, are offered in the graduate and advanced professional schools. The degree usually granted for advanced graduate work in education is that of doctor of philosophy. The usual requirements for this degree are 2 years of residence beyond the master's degree; accumulation of courses and credits amounting approximately to seventy-five or eighty semester hours; written and oral examinations; a dissertation or its equivalent; a reading knowledge of two foreign languages, usually French and German; and other requirements or substitutes, some of which must be met prior to admission to candidacy. From a nation-wide study of Ph.D. programs for the Commission on Teacher Education, Ernest V. Hollis of the

---

[29] Richard J. Storr, *The Beginnings of Graduate Education in America*, p. 159, University of Chicago Press, 1953.

United States Office of Education concludes: "(1) the doctoral programs must be adjusted to the uses to which recipients can put the degree in the scheme of American life today, and (2) the graduate school must function as an integrated organism—rather than an aggregate of competing departments—if it is to be able to fulfill its mission." [30]

Doctor of Education. Another degree, the doctorate of education, is advancing in popularity and significance among educators. The nature of this degree is determined by the character of the institution that confers it. In the main, the Ed.D. differs from the Ph.D. in direction and requirement. Whereas the Ph.D. is primarily a research degree, the Ed.D. is basically a professional award. The former requires foreign languages and accents specialization; the latter demands cognate work and stresses professional competence in teaching or administration. For example, some graduate schools require that the doctor of education candidate show 3 years of successful teaching experience in the field of professional education.

Postdoctoral Work. Teachers College, Columbia University, and a few other institutions have arranged a program and scholarships for persons who desire to study beyond the Ph.D. or Ed.D. degree. These postdoctoral programs are increasing in popularity in all professions. It has been suggested that all graduate degrees be abolished within 10 years after they have been granted, unless the recipient shows tangible evidence of professional growth within that period.

OTHER INSTITUTIONS OF HIGHER LEARNING

Federal Institutions.[31] Another group of institutions consists of federal or semifederal colleges and universities. The United States government has always entertained an interest in higher education, although it has never established a national university. One of the universities already mentioned as being supported by national funds is Howard University, a school primarily for Negro students, located in Washington, D.C. Since many of its students are college graduates, advanced work constitutes a conspicuous phase of the program.

The Military Academy at West Point, New York, established in 1802; the Naval Academy at Annapolis, Maryland, organized in 1845; the Coast Guard Academy at New London, Connecticut, started in 1876; and the Air Academy at Colorado Springs, Colorado, launched in 1955—these and others are in reality schools of higher learning dedicated to national defense. A national institution to educate leaders for public service of a nonmilitary nature at home and abroad has been suggested

---

[30] Ernest V. Hollis, *Toward Improving Ph.D. Programs*, p. 204, American Council on Education, 1945.

[31] See Unit I for a further treatment of federal institutions.

repeatedly. Fortunately numerous colleges and universities are now training young men and women for public service. The major objective of these schools is to elevate public service from the slough of political despond to the worthy calling of social and civic statesmanship.

Summer Schools. A product primarily of the twentieth century is the ubiquitous summer session. These schools are attended largely by teachers who are employed in the public and private schools during the balance of the year. Many city schools grant a bonus to teachers for summer attendance, or other incentives in the form of salary increments. Furthermore, there has been a marked increase in summer-school attendance by graduate students seeking advanced degrees such as the master's and doctor's.

Other Types. Somewhat related to the summer school is higher education in the form of extension and correspondence courses, which are discussed in the next unit. The President's Commission on Higher Education included in its report a classification called proprietary schools—those educational institutions authorized to earn a profit. The most common examples are the private technical schools and business colleges. The number of these colleges increased markedly after the passage of the G.I. bills for veterans' education. A National Committee on Fraudulent Schools and Colleges has been organized to check the growth of spurious institutions of all types.

COOPERATION AND EXPERIMENTATION IN HIGHER EDUCATION

COOPERATIVE COLLEGES

The term "cooperative colleges" is applied to certain higher educational institutions that offer instruction to students with the cooperation of industrial or commercial concerns. A brochure of Northeastern University, Boston, Massachusetts, entitled *Higher Education on the Cooperative Plan,* contains this definition:

Cooperative education in simplest terms may be defined as a complete and thorough college training complemented and balanced by an extended experience in industry under faculty supervision. It aims to consolidate in a single well-integrated educational program the values of classroom study and industrial-commercial experience. The plan provides for the alternation of pairs of students between school and cooperative work.

This plan originated in the College of Engineering of the University of Cincinnati in 1906. At first the labor unions were opposed to the scheme, but later, owing largely to the friendly attitude of the American Federation of Labor, they recognized that the plan would help rather than injure the cause of labor. Since this initial experiment, many institutions have adopted or adapted the cooperative plan, which now enrolls several thousand students. The aid of local businessmen is essential to the success of these plans. For example, the Peoria (Illinois) Manufacturers and Merchants Association cooperates with Bradley University of that city in its study-work plan, which is a 5-year course.

Although the plan is practiced largely by schools and colleges of engineering, cooperative courses may be offered in many fields and may reach several states. For example, Antioch College (Yellow Springs, Ohio), where the first year of the 5-year study-work program is spent on the campus, has numerous cooperative employers located in the majority of the states and in the District of Columbia. The University of Cincinnati, which pioneered in this field, now has numerous cooperative firms. Much of the success of the plan depends upon an official who is known as the coordinator and who confers with employers, students, instructors, and others.

Students are usually paid while on the job, and at the end of the full period of cooperative study they are awarded the baccalaureate. In some colleges the cooperative idea is extended to the graduate level. A modification of this plan is that of internships in teaching, as at Northwestern University, Evanston, Illinois. The major objective of these cooperative plans is to project the student into the practical aspect of the workaday world. Another type of work-study plan is employed in the cooperative or semicooperative living centers such as are found at Syracuse University, where economical housing is provided for women students who spend part of each day working in their houses. Many colleges maintain an industries plan for providing work for deserving students.

COOPERATION AMONG INSTITUTIONS OF HIGHER LEARNING

Cooperation with the Federal Government. The federal government cooperates with institutions of higher learning in many projects, such as giving financial aid to the land-grant colleges, providing tuition and subsistence for veterans' education, furnishing funds and personnel for military units, and aiding in research projects like atomic energy. The atomic age was launched and advanced by the federal government in cooperation with several universities. The Division of Higher Education in the United States Office of Education assists various institutions of higher learning. During and since the Second World War many colleges loaned personnel and facilities to the national government. Many professors serve overseas in the Point Four work. The American Council on Education has a Committee on the Relationship of Higher Education to the Federal Government.

State Programs of Cooperation. In several states, coordination has been effected by legislative enactment creating one board to control all the state higher institutions. For example, the board in charge of the State

University of New York has general direction over a large cluster of state institutions.

Regional Programs in Higher Education. A regional program within a state is exemplified in Southern California where several colleges have established an intercollege graduate program. The most conspicuous example of regionalism in higher educational efforts is found in the South, where several states have banded together to improve educational opportunities and facilities in the related states.

Cooperative Agreements between Colleges. Although coordination among state-controlled institutions is usually effected by legislative enactment, numerous cooperative agreements are entered into voluntarily by schools of higher learning, especially privately controlled colleges and universities. One of the oldest plans of affiliation has been between a state-supported university (North Dakota) and a church-related college (Wesley College), whereby students at either institution could take courses at the other. The Midwest Interlibrary Corporation, consisting of several cooperating colleges and libraries, renders wide research service from its center in Chicago. Many universities are joint sponsors of the nonprofit Oak Ridge Institute of Nuclear Studies, with the nation as the campus. Such joint efforts are supplemented by many experiments in individual institutions.

Experimentation and Research in Higher Education

Unfortunately many colleges and universities are afflicted with an unwarranted faith in the infallibility of their practices. There is, however, a distinct trend toward an experimental approach in higher education. Under the captions (1) organization and administration, (2) curriculum and teaching-learning procedures, and (3) personnel, the epitomes that follow sketch a few of the many interesting and varied experiments in higher education.

Organization and Administration. Under the stimulation of grants from the Fund for the Advancement of Education, several institutions of higher learning are conducting self-surveys.

Several state surveys of higher education have been completed recently.

Accreditation procedures are being reevaluated and modified, looking toward the reduction in the number of accrediting agencies. Qualitative as well as quantitative standards are being developed.

Many colleges have been reorganized internally within the component divisions, and externally in a state pattern.

With the unprecedented demand for higher education, many institutions are expanding. Several have established off-campus branches or centers.

Colleges, returning toward the European pattern of administration, are becoming more democratic in control. Faculty salary committees and faculty councils are on the increase.

Following the accent on technical courses in two world wars and the Korean conflict, many colleges are increasing the required courses in general education. College counseling procedures seek to help the individual student.

Laymen, as members of advisory committees and boards of trustees, are participating in a greater degree in forming policies for colleges. However, studies show that women and rural people have only slight representation on official boards.

FIG. 8-8. Brandeis University, the first Jewish-sponsored nonsectarian university. This young university, named after the late justice of the Supreme Court, is located in an historic setting, including "the Castle" which towers over the 200-acre campus. One of its divisions is a School of Creative Arts. (*Courtesy of Brandeis University.*)

Regional planning continues to play a conspicuous role in the development of higher education.

The United States Office of Education has expanded its services to colleges.

The work of the Commission on Financing Higher Education has directed the nation's thinking toward these problems, especially in the private and parochial institutions. The Council for Financial Aid to Education was organized in 1953 as a corporation to coordinate fund-raising efforts of various independent college associations. Non-tax-supported institutions in various states have joined to raise "free enterprise" money for regular sources of income from large business and industrial enterprises.

With the increased cost of higher education many colleges permit the payment of tuition on the installment basis. The "tuition plan" provides a method by which parents of students in certain approved schools and colleges can pay monthly, while the institution receives its fees in full before the term commences.

Curriculum and Teaching-Learning Procedures. Religion, so important in the early colleges, is being reaccented today in higher education. Public as well as independent institutions are seeking to convey to students the significance of religion in human affairs. The American Association of Colleges for Teacher Education received a grant from the Danforth Foundation to conduct a 5-year study of the role of religion in teacher-educating institutions. A Commission on Christian Higher Education is working on the problem of making religion a vital force in the curricular and extracurricular life of Protestant and Catholic colleges and universities.

The Committee on Institutional Research of the American Council on Education is seeking to develop a balance between "practical" research aimed at solutions for immediate and specific problems, and "basic" research designed to increase human knowledge broadly.

An increasing number of institutions are adding television stations or are participating in television and radio programs. A few have credit courses over the air. The Allied University TV Council assists laboratories for educational ideas in television.

Internship programs are on the increase. The Ford Foundation for the Advancement of Education has provided several internships in teaching.

Countless curricular reforms have been initiated, such as the abolition of course credits, course examinations, compulsory class attendance, and time requirements. Instead, comprehensive examinations are taken when the student is ready for them. Many colleges permit students to omit required courses through passing proficiency examinations.

Several institutions are experimenting with concentrated and intensive study plans, such as dividing the year into five 7-week periods, during each of which only one subject is studied.

Students are encouraged to take interdepartmental majors.

Several colleges are employing professional musicians, artists, dramatists, and other specialists in order to broaden cultural life and liberal education on the campus.

Scores of new courses have been added: courtship, marriage, and sex education; geopolitical interpretations of current affairs; great issues; communications; musical therapy; languages such as Hebrew, Russian, Urdu, and Hindustani; geography, history, and literature of various areas, such as India and Korea.

Among the newer specialities which are dignified with degrees in the undergraduate or graduate fields are: bachelor of science in editing and publishing, doctor of social work, master in public service, and degrees in nuclear physics and electronics.

In order to give selected students a more realistic approach to national affairs, a group of institutions cooperate in providing a "Washington seminar" in the nation's capital.

Cocurricular or extracurricular activities have been expanded markedly to include such activities as forums, intercultural clubs, mock presidential elections, volunteer fire departments, and an extracurricular course in college teaching.

University presses are furnishing leadership in the publication of scholarly studies.

Research remains one of the most important functions of the universities. A few examples of technological and scientific investigations in higher education are the Atomic Energy Commission's sponsored programs, as the Oak Ridge Institute of Nuclear Studies, atomic-energy education, radioisotope units, cosmic-ray cyclotron, aeronautical research, radio and television centers, statistical centers, cancer and polio research, and investigations of the earth's microorganisms as friends and foes of mankind.

FIG. 8-9. The Technological Institute at Northwestern University, Evanston, Illinois. Like Brandeis University, the Technological Institute was also started in the 1940's. The former, starting *de novo*, moved into historic structures in a sylvan setting; the latter erected its new laboratories as part of a century-old institution along the shores of Lake Michigan. (*Courtesy of Northwestern University.*)

Personnel in Higher Education. Since the proper study of mankind is man, institutions of higher learning accent personnel relationships in guidance programs and human relations centers.

Intercultural and intergroup relations are being studied from coast to coast and overseas. Many "white" institutions admit Negroes, and several Negro colleges are open to all.

One striking phenomenon in higher education is the added stress on international and world relationships—a reflection of the position of the United States in world leadership.

Many American universities have arrangements for a year abroad. Overseas summer sessions are numerous.

Fulbright and Smith-Mundt programs have stimulated the exchange of students and professors. With the aid of G.I. bills, hundreds of United States veterans have studied overseas.

Many college campuses are meccas for students and teachers from other lands.

Scores of international educational conferences are being held.

Special student visas are issued by the United States government to students from other lands.

The New York State Board of Regents has given a provisional charter to the Free University in Exile, a corporation formed to organize an educational institution—undergraduate and graduate—for refugees and exiles from certain communist-dominated countries.

Much unpublicized experimentation and many innovations of significance are being conducted in many institutions. As in the making of books, there is no end to experimentation in higher education. It is a symptom of the fact that colleges and universities rely not upon dogmatic but upon flexible purposes which can be adjusted to meet new needs.

FUTURE OF HIGHER EDUCATION

Higher education is on the threshold of many changes—internal and external, quantitative and qualitative.

The further development of junior colleges, community colleges, and technical institutes will affect the traditional senior college, which may be more closely integrated with the graduate years. The future will see many changes in the graduate school, which the late F. P. Keppel, formerly of the Carnegie Corporation, caustically called "the sacred cow in American education, to be worshipped rather than studied, understood, and improved." The colleges of the future will be better coordinated. The many separate schools within a university will be less guilty of encouraging "intellectual parochialism" or "mental myopia."

Surveys of higher education for Negroes, the reports of the President's Commission on Higher Education and the Commission on Financing Higher Education, federal and state supreme court decisions on segregation, and other developments may lead to a revision in this field. More Negroes will seek and gain higher education.

Many millions of Americans will be enrolled in the colleges and universities in the next decade or two. The Commission on Financing Higher Education stated "the conclusion seems justified that perhaps 35 percent of youth might be expected to profit substantially from formal full-time post-high school education of the kind given at present by such institutions." [32]

The Commission adds that many of these students will not go to college because of financial difficulties or lack of motivation. A conservative estimate figures the number of college students in 1972 as approximately twice that in 1952, when it was 2,148,000.

But higher education is more than high numbers. Largeness is not synonymous with greatness. Many institutions are already afflicted with

[32] Hollinshead, *op. cit.*, p. 138.

the dreaded disease of elephantiasis. Portal-to-portal time is being lost in many universities because of the extent of the campuses. A former president of the first college in the United States recommends that:

> We do not expand our four-year colleges either as to number or size.
>
> We do not expand the four-year programs in our universities; rather, we contract them.
>
> We endeavor to transform all the present four-year colleges into institutions with high academic standards. . . .[33]

Conant would make a 2-year college course fashionable and experiment with general education at every level.

From the perspective of his long association with higher education, Dr. Oliver C. Carmichael, in one of his reports of the Carnegie Foundation for the Advancement of Teaching, states: "The great need today is for a restatement of the function of higher education, a redefinition of the college and its purpose, and a reformation of the fundamental goals of the university." Past experience is helpful, but it does not always give point and direction for the future.

One challenge for the future is the proposal of Robert M. Hutchins that an international institution of higher education be developed for intellectual leadership in the world:

> Such an institution would be composed of men who were prepared to conduct a continuous Socratic dialogue on the basic issues of life. . . . They would establish a genuine communion of minds. They would know no limitations of national boundaries, for they could be assembled from all parts of the world. They could therefore at once advance and symbolize that world community, that world republic of learning, without which the world republic of law and justice is impossible.[34]

Of all levels of learning, higher education can best promote the international mind and the parliament of man.

SUGGESTED ACTIVITIES

1. Indicate ways for articulating secondary and higher education.

2. Evaluate the standards of the sectional accrediting association for the state in which you are located.

3. Consult old newspapers, magazines, and books for interesting side lights on the history of American higher education.

4. Write a brief paper on "The History of Higher Education for Women."

5. Write a brief history of "Land-grant Colleges in America."

6. Review the circumstances and effects of the Dartmouth College Case.

7. Prepare a special report on municipal universities.

8. Arrange a panel discussion on the topic "Why Go to College?"

9. Name 10 outstanding college presidents and their institutions.

[33] Conant, *op. cit.*, pp. 57–58.

[34] Robert M. Hutchins, *The Conflict in Education in a Democratic Society*, pp. 107–108, Harper, 1953.

10. Identify 30 prominent colleges in the United States.

11. Prepare a list of all the institutions of higher education in your state.

12. Make a list of the various divisions or schools in your state university.

13. Draw a diagram showing the way in which institutions of higher education are administered in your state.

14. Study the program and requirements of a profession other than teaching, such as medicine, dentistry, or law. Compare or contrast that program with preparation for the teaching profession.

15. Stage a debate on the subject: "Resolved that the federal government of the United States should establish a national university."

16. Prepare a list of national organizations for teachers in institutions of higher learning.

17. Examine masters' and doctors' theses and comment as to the practicality of the research.

18. Describe clearly a significant college experiment in higher education.

DESCRIPTIVE BIBLIOGRAPHY AND AIDS

BOOKS

ARBUCKLE, DUGALD S.: *Student Personnel Services in Higher Education,* Chap. III, McGraw-Hill, 1953.

Selection and admission of students to college.

AXT, RICHARD G.: *The Federal Government and Financing Higher Education,* Chap. X, Columbia University Press, 1952.

Suggestions for a federal scholarship program.

BOGUE, JESSE PARKER: *The Community College,* Chap. II, McGraw-Hill, 1950.

Philosophies of the community college today.

CHAMBERS, M. M. (ed.) : *Universities of the World outside U.S.A.,* American Council on Education, 1950, 924 pp.

A helpful handbook of universities in other lands.

COMMISSION ON FINANCING HIGHER EDUCATION: *Nature and Needs of Higher Education,* Chap. I, Columbia University Press, 1952.

The nature and needs of higher education in the United States.

CONANT, JAMES BRYANT: *Education and Liberty,* Chap. II, Harvard University Press, 1953.

The American college.

CUNNINGHAM, WILLIAM F.: *General Education and the Liberal College,* Chap. II, Herder, 1953.

Educating the whole man in a whole world.

HUTCHINS, ROBERT M.: *The Conflict in Education in a Democratic Society,* Chap. VI, Harper, 1953.

The role of the university in a democracy.

MELAND, BERNARD EUGENE: *Higher Education and the Human Spirit,* Chap. IX, University of Chicago Press, 1953.

Religious sensitivity and discernment in higher education.

MILLETT, JOHN D. (ed.): *An Atlas of Higher Education in the United States,* Columbia University Press, 1952, n.p.

A publication of the Commission on Financing Higher Education, showing maps of each state with the accredited colleges.

PRESIDENT'S COMMISSION ON HIGHER EDUCATION: *Higher Education for American Democracy,* Part I, GPO, 1947.

Establishing the goals for higher education.

RANDALL, CLARENCE B.: *Freedom's Faith,* Chap. V, Little, Brown, 1953.
The businessman and the college professor.
STORR, RICHARD J.: *The Beginnings of Graduate Education in America,* Chap. III, University of Chicago Press, 1953.
German influence on the American university.
TAYLOR, HAROLD: *On Education and Freedom,* Chap. V, Abelard-Schuman, 1954.
The education of women.
TURNGREN, ANNETTE: *Choosing the Right College,* Chap. IX, Harper, 1952.
The role of junior colleges.

CURRENT PERTINENT PERIODICALS AND PUBLICATIONS

Accredited Higher Institutions
American Junior Colleges
American Universities and Colleges
Antioch Notes
College Blue Book
College catalogues
College Placement Directory
College and University
College and University Bulletin
Educational Record
Higher Education
Improving College and University Teaching
Journal of the American Association of University Women
Journal of General Education
Journal of Higher Education
Junior College Journal
Lovejoy's Complete Guide to Colleges and Universities
North Central Association Quarterly
Patterson's American Educational Directory
Quarterly Review of Higher Education among Negroes
Regional Action in Higher Education

School Life
So They Say about Higher Education
State U. Newsletter
Stephens College News Reporter
Teachers College Record
Yearbooks of:
American Association of Collegiate Registrars
American Association of Colleges for Teacher Education
American Association of University Professors
American Association of University Women
American College Public Relations Association
American Council on Education
Association of American Colleges
Association of American Universities
Association for Higher Education
Association of Land-grant Colleges and Universities
Association of Urban Universities
National Association of State Universities

AUDIO-VISUAL AIDS [35]

COLLEGE YOUR CHALLENGE   One reel, sound
A film to challenge high-school youth, especially those of ability, to improve themselves and their opportunities through attending college. Produced by Coronet Films.

LETTERS FROM A STUDENT   Two reels, 20 min., sound
Student life and reconstruction in the universities of Europe and Asia. Prepared under the sponsorship of UNESCO and the World Student Service Fund. Available rental-free from UNESCO, New York.

[35] Numerous colleges and universities offer films describing their campuses and activities.

PRINCETON   29 min., 16 or 35 mm., sound
Does not accent university buildings, but stresses human relations—the story of
a student and his teacher. Available from Princeton University, Princeton, N.J.

Recordings
Available are phonograph recordings of various college songs. For example, the
late Peter Christian Lutkin's "Quaecumque Sunt Vera" is obtainable from Northwestern University, Evanston, Ill.

THE WIDENING CIRCLE   40 min., sound, color
Exemplifies the widening circles caused by dropping a pebble into the water,
through the enlarging influence of land-grant colleges. Produced at East Lansing,
Michigan, for Michigan State College, one of the first of the land-grant colleges.

YOUR COLLEGE   35 min., sound, color
This picture, prepared by Pennsylvania State College, shows the wide variety of
its activities over the state. Available rental-free from Pennsylvania State College.

YOUR HERITAGE IN OLE MISS   27 min., sound, color
Activities at the University of Mississippi, established in 1844. Produced by the
university's department of audio-visual education and a commercial firm.

EDUCATION FOR OUT-OF-SCHOOL YOUTH AND ADULTS

Several million out-of-school youth in America need education, guidance, and employment. Educators are seeking to reduce the number of dropouts by curricular modifications and enrichment in secondary and postsecondary education. Men, and especially women, are coming closer and closer to the Biblical allotment of three score years and ten for life on this planet. The number of adults in need of reeducation increases as the span of life lengthens. Historically, the education of youth and adults in America reaches back to the pilgrimage of the early pioneers.

Among the provisions for educating out-of-school youth are guidance programs, more schooling, more vocational education, part-time and continuation schools, apprenticeships, placement, and follow-up services. During and since the Second World War thousands of American youth received additional education, as well as training, through military programs in colleges and universities and through such off-duty facilities as the United States Armed Forces Institute. Since the war additional thousands of veterans have received full-time or part-time instruction under the G.I. bills. Much is being done in the field of vocational rehabilitation.

Adult education no longer needs justifying arguments. Its diversified program includes literacy instruction, Americanization, opportunity schools, extension services, correspondence schools, chautauqua programs, public forums, town meetings, church nights, clubs, alumni colleges, workers' education, libraries, federal programs, and other activities. Coordination of adult education with other areas of education is necessary. American education starts early, in order to embrace learning for little children, and never ends, so as to include the education of youth and adults.

OUTLINE OF CONTENTS

EDUCATION FOR OUT-OF-SCHOOL YOUTH AND ADULTS

In his humorous account of Mr. Parkhill's efforts as a teacher in the American Night Preparatory School for Adults, L. Q. Ross thus describes the prize pupil, Hyman Kaplan:

Mr. Kaplan was certainly his most energetic and ebullient pupil. He never missed a lesson; he never grew discouraged; the smile of undaunted hope and good will never left his cherubic face. But, unfortunately Mr. Kaplan never seemed to *learn* anything. His spelling remained erratic, his grammar deplorable, his sentence structure fantastic. There was only one word for Mr. Kaplan's idioms—atrocious. As for Mr. Kaplan's speech, if anything it grew more astounding from day to day. Only last week Mr. Kaplan had announced that his wife suffered "from high blood pleasure." And in his drill on adjectives he had given the positive, comparative and superlative forms of "cold" as "cold, colder, below zero." Mr. Parkhill often wondered whether there wasn't something sacrilegious in trying to impose the iron mold of English on so unfettered an intelligence.[1]

Certainly the English language is a difficult one to conquer. Yet in thousands of night schools throughout the country both foreign and native-born youths and adults are grappling with English and other subjects.

Many Youth Out of School. In the no man's land between adulthood and early adolescence lies the area of life generally known as youth. Complementing the current emphasis upon adult education is the growing concern of the nation about the status of its youth, particularly those out of school. Naturally in a land of compulsory elementary education more children are in school than out. Nevertheless, many boys and girls of elementary- and secondary-school age are not found in school. Only about 50 per cent of high-school youth graduate.

Many employed youth feel that they are in "blind alley" or "dead end" jobs. All available statistics on youth and its status compel legislators, educators, prospective teachers, and laymen to think seriously on the plight of out-of-school youth in a land of so-called "equality of opportunity."

The G.I. bills brought many out-of-school youth back to school and college. The ages of World War II service women and men ran from nineteen to sixty, and the educational levels varied from primary to postdoctoral courses. At the peak over a million veterans were in higher education and over a million and a half in all types of educational in-

---

[1] L. Q. Ross, *The Education of Hyman Kaplan*, pp. 163–164, Harcourt, Brace, 1937.

stitutions. Many veterans of the Korean conflict further advanced their education with federal fiscal assistance.

Increase in Adult Population. The United States is no longer a country of young and middle-aged people. Less than 1 per cent of the population dies every year. Both numerically and proportionately, the adult population of this country is increasing. America, historically and humanly, is growing older. As indicated in Fig. 9-1, the span of life has been length-

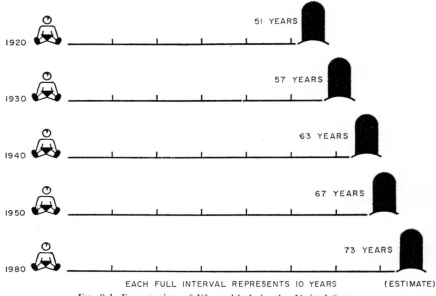

1920   51 YEARS

1930   57 YEARS

1940   63 YEARS

1950   67 YEARS

1980   73 YEARS

EACH FULL INTERVAL REPRESENTS 10 YEARS   (ESTIMATE)

Fig. 9-1. Expectation of life at birth in the United States.

ened. A baby born in 1954 could look forward, as a personification of all babies born that year, to a life expectancy of over sixty-eight years. Body and mind usually do not march side by side toward the chronological milestones and inevitable tombstones. Gerontologists—those interested in the complex problems of old age—accent the need for research with oldsters rather than youngsters. They corroborate their contentions convincingly with these data:

Year	Persons over sixty-five
1900	4,000,000
1940	9,000,000
1950	11,000,000
1980	22,000,000 (estimate)

The percentage of the total population over sixty-five years in the United States will soon reach 10 per cent. Americans will have to live longer in order to die! With more elders, both proportionately and numerically, American public education will increase the emphasis upon the personal aspects of culture, as the ripe reflection of maturity replaces the hurried impulsiveness of youth. Adult education, with its accumulated learnings, is the final step in lifelong learning; it is the fulfillment of the partly attained objectives of earlier education. Through adult education, the declining years when one was expected to go downhill become the period of ascendancy when one reaches the mountaintop of human living.

HISTORICAL CALENDAR—YOUTH-ADULT EDUCATION AND CONTEMPORANEOUS EVENTS

The historical calendar contains significant events in the evolution of education for youth and adults, and also contemporaneous events of social, political, and economic importance. The development of education for these two groups is treated separately later.

Historical Calendar

YOUTH AND ADULT EDUCATION	CONTEMPORANEOUS EVENTS
1620—Shortly after Pilgrims landed, town meetings started	1620—Pilgrims landed in America
1826—First lyceum held in Massachusetts	1927—First railroad built in the United States at Quincy, Mass.
1842—First child labor law passed in Massachusetts	1843—First telegraph line opened in United States from Washington to Baltimore
1852—First compulsory school attendance law passed in Massachusetts	1852—*Uncle Tom's Cabin* by Harriet Beecher Stowe published
1859—Cooper Union opened in New York City with public forums	1858—Famous Lincoln-Douglas debates held in Illinois
1874—The Chautauqua Institution founded by Bishop H. H. Vincent	1873—United States swept by financial panic
1876—University extension movement started	1876—First telephone line built between Boston and Cambridge
1883—The Correspondence University founded at Ithaca, New York	1883—Pendleton Civil Service Act passed by Congress
1899—First juvenile court established in Chicago	1899—Spanish-American war started
1914—Federal legislation passed for agricultural extension work (Smith-Lever)	1914—Panama Canal opened to traffic

Historical Calendar—(*Continued*)

YOUTH AND ADULT EDUCATION— (*Continued*)	CONTEMPORANEOUS EVENTS— (*Continued*)
1924—A community organized for adult education program (Cleveland); 1934 —(Springfield, Mass.)	1924—Flight around world made by three American airplanes under L. H. Smith
1924—Department of Adult Education organized by National Education Association	1924—Federal immigration act passed by Congress
1926—American Association of Adult Education formed	1927—First nonstop airplane flight from New York to Paris made by Lindbergh
1933—Emergency education for youth and adults started by the federal government	1933—Diplomatic relations with Soviet Russia resumed by United States
1935—American Youth Commission organized by American Council on Education	1935—Proposal to join the World Court rejected by United States Senate
1940—Vocational and military training for youths and adults provided through national defense plan	1940—First peacetime selective service —many youth and adults called for military service
1946—USAFI established officially as permanent peacetime organization	1946—Fourth atomic bomb of history exploded by U.S. over Bikini
1946—Negro Adult Education project started by U.S. Office of Education and Carnegie Corporation	1946—Republic of Philippines created after 10-year transitional period
1949—National Training Laboratory in Group Development organized by National Education Association	1949—International Conference on Adult Education held at Elsinore, Denmark
1951—American Association of Adult Education and Department of Adult Education joined in Adult Education Association (AEA)	1951—Loan made by the United States to India for the purchase of grain
1951—Fund for Adult Education established by the Ford Foundation	1951—Amendment XXII, limiting President to two terms, made effective
1952—*Adult Leadership* magazine launched by the AEA	1952—First successful test of hydrogen bomb made in U.S.
1952—Council of National Organization of the AEA formed	1952—Mrs. O. C. Hobby appointed as Federal Security Administrator
1955—First issue of *Senior Citizens* published as official organ of Senior Citizens of America.	1955—Review of UN Charter placed on agenda for UN General Assembly

EDUCATION FOR OUT-OF-SCHOOL YOUTH

Scope and Function of Youth Education

Scope of Youth Education. The military regimentation of youth in totalitarian countries and the national selective service of youth in the United States helped to make adults more "youth-conscious." This is a healthful sign in a country where the grandfather is becoming the leading competitor of the grandson in his efforts to get an education and a start in life. "Youth" is a flexible term as to age. It has often been defined as a quality of spirit rather than a quantity of years.

Each year approximately two millions in America reach the age of employability. Their employment or nonemployment, their education and reeducation, are matters of national concern. It is the obligation of the community to provide a suitable educational program for all youth over sixteen years. The scope of this education includes out-of-school youth as well as those in school.

Objectives in Youth Education. The education of youth in America, as part of a broad program of lifelong learning, has many objectives in common with the education of persons of all ages. These common objectives are detailed in Unit XIII. Youth has, however, specific problems that must be taken into consideration. Society must aid in the solution of these problems, but youth itself must assume certain responsibilities. The objectives in this program of reciprocity are clearly stated in the Declaration of Interdependence published by the American Association of School Administrators in its yearbook, *Youth Education Today.* This declaration states what society is to provide in opportunities and then lists the responsibilities to be met by youth.

Prevention and Reduction of Juvenile Delinquency. One goal of youth education is to prevent and reduce youth delinquency. Teen-age law transgressors are increasing at an alarming rate. Several million boys and girls annually are dealt with by the police; more than a third of a million are brought to the attention of the juvenile courts each year. The increase in the number of children living in the United States naturally would cause more cases of law infractions, but the rate of delinquency is rising five times as fast as the population's increase in the ten- to seventeen-year age group.

On youth delinquency, the *U.S. News & World Report* states:

The problem reaches into every area of society. It is not confined to the slums. It hits well-to-do families as well as poor ones. Children of school age are stealing automobiles, engaging in armed robberies, setting up gangs, performing acts of violence and vandalism, throwing wild parties in which dope, liquor and sex are mixed. They stop at no crime—including murder.[2]

[2] "What Every Parent Should Know," *U.S. News & World Report,* Dec. 11, 1953, p. 35.

Studies, such as *Delinquents in the Making,* by Sheldon and Eleanor Glueck of the Harvard Law School, provide a picture, and a dark one, of some overriding causes of delinquency that arise within and outside of the home. For example, twice as many delinquents come from broken homes as from father-mother homes. Most experts agree that the basic reason for the current wave of youthful misdemeanors is the feeling of insecurity.

The sense of security for youth can be bolstered through the joint efforts of home, school, and community. The best way to deal with juvenile delinquency is to prevent it. A forward-looking community supports a positive program of prevention and plans for the treatment of misdemeanors. The four major agencies entrusted with the responsibility for the treatment are: the police, juvenile court, detention home, and training school. According to a pamphlet prepared by the Special Juvenile Delinquency Project of the U.S. Children's Bureau, each of these four agencies has a different job, but they have certain common needs and purpose:

The greatest single need is probably that for more and better-trained personnel. And the second most important need is for good equipment and adequate physical quarters. The common purpose is to help the child "un-make" the pattern of behavior that brought him into conflict with the law.[3]

The "un-making" of a delinquent is, of course, a complicated and long-term task. Furthermore "the juvenile delinquent today is the adult criminal tomorrow."

The bulletin *Schools Help Prevent Delinquency* [4] contains several excellent suggestions to challenge educators. As more and more emotionally disturbed children come to school, the teacher himself must have a "peace that passeth all understanding." The delinquent or nondelinquent child beholds the conduct of the teacher and silently thinks, "What you are speaks so loudly that I cannot hear what you say."

Development of Youth Education

In a real sense, the pilgrimage of the early pioneers from Europe was the genesis of the youth movement in America. These people came not merely with the short-term view of better living for themselves, but also with the long-span outlook of improved conditions in living and learning for their offspring. Schools and colleges were soon established by law, but early legislators did not make school attendance compulsory or im-

---

[3] Children's Bureau, *Helping Delinquent Children,* GPO, 1953, p. 11.

[4] Research Bulletin, *Schools Help Prevent Delinquency,* pp. 99–113, National Education Association, October, 1953.

prove the lot of those who were out of school. With the passage in 1842 of the first child labor act in the United States, Massachusetts helped to make the young nation legally conscious of its growing youth and their problems. Ten years later, this same state passed the first compulsory school attendance law. In the city of Chicago in 1899 was established the first juvenile court. The creation of a separate court where the youthful delinquents could be heard by a sympathetic judge marked a great step forward. Most early reforms for youth, however, such as child labor laws, compulsory attendance laws, and the creation of juvenile courts were negative or redemptive measures. In recent years, emphasis has shifted to a positive plus a curative approach to the problems.

Major Governmental Agencies Engaged in Youth Education. Nation-wide organizations, both public and private, have made aggressive attacks on the problems of youth. Among the federal agencies directly concerned with youth welfare are the Wage and Hour Division of the Department of Labor, the Cooperative Extension Service of the Department of Agriculture, and the U.S. Department of Health, Education, and Welfare. The latter, including the federal Office of Education, has several significant youth-serving agencies such as the Public Health Service and the Children's Bureau. The main governmental agency interested in youth education during the Second World War and the postwar period has been the National Security Organization, under the Secretary of Defense, with the departments of the army, navy, and air force. In their recruitment, enlistment, and training programs the major aims of national defense have stressed the continuance of education for youth rather than its interruption through military service. Through their off-duty programs, affiliations with schools and colleges, and other activities, the armed forces actively promote education.

Nation-wide Nongovernmental Agencies Interested in Youth Education. A private organization, American Youth Hostels, sponsors the hostel movement in America and abroad. The National Congress of Parents and Teachers, to its slogan "Child Welfare," added the "Welfare of Youth" as a major objective of its program. As previously indicated, the National Education Association, through the American Association of School Administrators, devoted a yearbook to *Youth Education Today,* as did also the National Society for the Study of Education in its *Juvenile Delinquency and the Schools.* The American Library Association is working on reading problems for out-of-school youth and adults. The current problems of youth, especially those out of school, have been studied and analyzed by several organizations. Outstanding in its accomplishments was a nonpartisan, nonsectarian, and nongovernmental agency, the American Youth Commission, created by the American Council on Education in 1935.

PROVISIONS FOR EDUCATING OUT-OF-SCHOOL YOUTH

Supplementing the nation-wide efforts are many state and local programs for youth. Educators, parents, and laymen are awaking to the problem; newspapers, periodicals, and books are focusing a searchlight upon it; and curriculum specialists on all levels are emphasizing youth's need for specific guidance and practical help. Those who need definite assistance may be grouped as rural and urban youth, as native and foreign groups, as boys and girls, or as an employed and unemployed youth. The latter classification includes the unemployable, the unemployed, the misemployed, those employed part-time, and those employed full-time in gainful occupations or professions.

The education of youth in school and college has been treated in preceding units in the volume. Without segregating them into the groups mentioned above, the section that follows is devoted primarily to the education of youth who are not full-time students in schools and colleges.

Guidance Programs. While they are still in school and also after they have been graduated, young people need guidance, which has been defined simply as "seeing through John and then helping John to see himself through." John Dewey once said: "Guidance is not external imposition. It is freeing the life processes for its own most adequate fulfillment." Frank E. Baker, former president of Milwaukee State Teachers College, distinguished three processes in guidance: therapeutic, to cure cases of emotional and mental maladjustment; preventive, to help the individual avoid emotional and mental tensions; and developmental, to help individuals in those forms of self-expression that have distinct value to personality growth. Guidance is usually directive or nondirective in nature.

The Educational Policies Commission in *Education for All American Youth—A Further Look* accents the role of guidance thus:

The keystone of the school program is guidance—personal assistance to individual boys and girls in making their plans and decisions about careers, education, employment, and all sorts of personal problems.

Guidance is no mechanical process, whereby counselors and teachers sort out boys and girls as a grading machine sorts apples. . . . Guidance is rather the high art of helping boys and girls to plan their own actions wisely, in the full light of all the facts that can be mustered about themselves and about the world in which they will work and live.

Guidance is not the work of a few specialists. . . . Guidance is not limited to vocational matters. It includes the whole gamut of youth problems. . . .[5]

Programs usually include mental, physical, social, personal, recreational, educational, and vocational guidance. Since the other phases are treated

[5] Educational Policies Commission, *Education for All American Youth—A Further Look,* p. 49, National Education Association, 1952.

elsewhere, especially in the next unit, vocational guidance is mentioned briefly here.

Obviously secondary schools have a responsibility for follow-up services to those who continue their education elsewhere and especially to those youth who seek employment in the world of work. The task force

Fig. 9-2. Youth hospitalized goes to school *in absentia*. School-to-home telephone instruction, which permits the patient's participation, is on the increase. (*Courtesy of Dick Greene and Executone's Special Education Division.*)

report of the Hoover Commission reflects "the widespread recognition today that proper provision for enabling the student to think and choose for himself in selecting his working career is a necessary part of every good school program."

The National Society for the Study of Education points out these four characteristics of a good guidance program:

1. Every student will be known well by someone on the school staff.
2. Provisions will be made in planning the teacher's "time" and pupil load for individual conferences as well as the group guidance in classes.
3. Secondary school plants will be built or redesigned to include conference offices where teachers and students can meet privately.

4. A premium will be placed on the development of a faculty which is guidance conscious and trained in guidance techniques.[6]

A functioning guidance program will help keep more youth in school.

More Schooling for More Youth. Providing adequate education for all the people is still an unfulfilled challenge in America. Many youngsters are not in school because they had to drop out. Fiscal factors often force students to leave school. Many of them would prefer to remain in school. In some communities the permissible school-leaving age must be raised, and compulsory attendance laws more rigidly enforced. The boy or girl temporarily out of school because of prolonged illness or hospitalization needs more opportunities for schooling *in absentia.*

Varied Educational Program. Some young people are out of school because the institutions do not meet their needs. The program of instruction that may possibly have been appropriate when the pupils were few and selected does not fit at all the needs of the great majority of those now in the secondary schools.

The need still exists today for a common denominator of school experiences—a "core" or "common learnings" program, plus health activities, for all secondary-school youth. As the student advances through school, the amount of time devoted to the core decreases and the work in individual programs of prevocational and vocational work increases. Differentiation is found even within curriculums and courses.

"Off the streets into the school" is a necessary slogan, but all adolescents cannot pursue a traditional full-time course. Many a boy or girl does not need more schooling, but a different type of education with more vocational training, rationed out over a longer period of time and concurrent with employment.

Work Experience. The first of the 10 imperative needs of youth, as described in *Planning for American Youth,* is stated thus: "All youth need to develop salable skills and those understandings and attitudes that make the worker an intelligent and productive participant in economic life. To this end, most youth need supervised work experience as well as education in the skills and knowledge of their occupations." The National Society for the Study of Education, which recommends wider use of work and outdoor experiences, defines them as follows:

Work experience is that experience which students obtain through participating in production of needed goods or services in a normal situation in industry, business, community at large, or school, under the direction of the schools.

The phrase "outdoor experience" requires little definition. . . . The most

6 National Society for the Study of Education, *Adapting the Secondary School Program to the Needs of Youth,* p. 142, University of Chicago, 1953.

significant aspect is that it requires a shift of educational forces from the physical environment of the classroom to the outdoors.[7]

Such experience can help youth understand the world at work—the role of labor, capital, and management. He then becomes a more intelligent and socially sensitized consumer as well as producer.

Vocational Education. Youth needs more exposure to and experience with education that is vocational. It is difficult to distinguish between general, prevocational, and vocational education, for the classification varies in accordance with the individual purposes of the learner. Usually the term "vocational education" is used in the broad sense to indicate all the services provided by the schools or social agencies for increasing the occupational efficiency of present and future workers. Examples are the distributive-education and diversified-occupation programs.

Part-time and Continuation Schools. A combination of work and study is also effected by means of part-time and continuation schools. This type of education is not the prerogative of young men only, for national statistics indicate that of all people gainfully employed, a minority but nevertheless a significant percentage are women. Most states require both boys and girls to attend school at least part time. Some industries and department stores maintain their own schools. The Smith-Hughes law provides that one-third of the money available for trade and industrial education should be spent for part-time or continuation classes, in which anything that contributes to civic or vocational intelligence may be taught.

Adjustments within the regular schools, fewer failures, and less junior employment have affected the programs of the part-time schools which are closing their doors, or establishing pre-employment classes, or forming classes for overage students and unemployed adult workers. Where employment is available for youth, the continuation schools maintain their original function of combining earning and learning. The working conditions of young people must be made more educative and learning in school more practical, for youth is both worker and learner.

Apprenticeships. From Europe came the apprenticeship system whereby a young man left his home to learn a trade under a master. Laws were passed in colonial America making it obligatory for poor parents to apprentice their children. By means of long and involved contracts minors were sold into semislavery. The main advantage of the system was that a youth learned a trade thoroughly over a prolonged period. Naturally modern working conditions and the machine age do not permit this long close contact between the learner of the trade and the

---

[7] *Ibid.*, pp. 183, 185.

master craftsman. The American Federation of Labor in 1909 made the following statement: "If we are to secure industrial supremacy, or even maintain our present standing in the industrial world, we must in some way in our educational system acquire an equivalent of the old apprenticeship system." A new type of apprenticeship, available under the federal-state-local programs, now provides for instruction in related subjects paralleling experiences in the occupations in which youth are employed half of each week. A coordinator is responsible for this part of the apprentices' school program, either as an instructor in these subjects or as a sponsor of apprentices working with teachers of these or other subjects such as chemistry or physics. The Bureau of Apprenticeship, U.S. Department of Labor, and the federal Office of Education, through its vocation division assist local and state apprentice-training programs, which today usually combine job experience with attendance at part-time or continuation schools.

Placement and Follow-up Services. Educators and laymen are seeking to promote the welfare of out-of-school youth, particularly of those between the ages of sixteen and twenty-four who are unemployed as a result of technological advances and economic conditions. The adolescent in school is usually an asset; out of school and out of work he is generally a liability.

Some youth, of course, are unemployable: they are physically, mentally, or otherwise so atypical that they cannot be gainfully occupied. Some of these are at home; others are in penal, health, or charitable institutions that strive to provide a minimum education in terms of needs, interests, and abilities. Others are helped to employment through the federally aided programs of vocational rehabilitation.

Of all the employed youth in the nation, many are misemployed. Many well-educated, superior young men and women have to be content with low-grade occupations, which stunt high-quality abilities. Vice versa, some persons are misemployed because they try temporarily to hold jobs above their abilities by dint of sheer force of will, working long hours and using excessive nervous energy at the expense of health. Obviously, these misfits are soon detected and weeded out. But the greatest human tragedy is that of capable persons burying their talents in "dead-end" jobs. One reason for misemployment is the lack of adequate guidance and satisfactory placement.

For many students, commencement night severs all connections with the school. An increasing number of secondary schools, however, are establishing junior placement bureaus and follow-up services for their ex-students. In the Baltimore plan, the schools assume the full responsibility for vocational guidance, training, and placement in the first job. After that, the employment service carries on. A White House conference recommended that "schools make available to young people, while in school and after they leave school, systematic personal and vocational guidance and organized assistance in job placement, in cooperation with public employment services."

Other Educational Opportunities for Youth. Besides the possibilities of learning already mentioned in this unit and those preceding, numerous other forms exist. Since these educational activities are closely allied or identical with those provided for adults, they are treated in connection with adult education.

ILLUSTRATIVE PRACTICES AND PROPOSALS

To supplement the pertinent examples of education for youth already mentioned in the preceding units on elementary, secondary, and higher education, a few of the many interesting and significant practices in youth education are cited here under the following headings: (1) national, including governmental and nongovernmental, (2) state, (3) regional, and (4) local programs.

National Programs. The United States Congress has been investigating the status, causes, and cures for juvenile delinquency.

Important governmental agencies interested in youth education during the Second World War and in the postwar period have been the military forces—army, navy, and air force—now under the Secretary of Defense. In their recruitment, enlistment, and training programs the major arms of national defense have stressed continuance of education of youth rather than its interruption through military service. Through their training, their off-duty programs, their affiliations with schools and colleges, and their other activities, the armed forces actively promote education for the youth in service.

World-wide in scope is the United States Armed Forces Institute (USAFI). This program, unprecedented in war and peace, was started by the nation's armed services. Established during the Second World War with headquarters at Madison, Wisconsin, this institute provides opportunities for women and men to continue their educational training while in military service. In addition to the correspondence and self-teaching courses offered for credit, there are group-study classes in the United States and overseas. Many service men are enrolled in nearby educational institutions during off-duty hours, taking courses for which the government pays a part of the tuition.

As previously indicated, the Veterans Administration has rendered distinguished service to the discharged veterans. In addition to formal full-time education in schools and colleges, many ex-service men and women receive part-time training.

The American Council on Education has been very active in helping out-of-school youth. Its Committee on Measurement and Guidance prepared the helpful *Guide to the Evaluation of Educational Experiences in the Armed Services,* which has been a handbook for the armed services, schools, and colleges in their accreditation programs. Its American Youth Commission issued many helpful publications based upon national and regional surveys. The Council's Committee on Youth Problems continues the implementation of the findings of the commission through such publications as *Helping Students Find Employment.*

The Educational Policies Commission, appointed by the National Education Association and the American Association of School Administrators, has out lined basic policies in various areas, such as the education of all youth in *Education for All American Youth—A Further Look,* and veterans' education in *A Program for Returning Veterans.*

Countless national voluntary organizations are at work, for example, the Rural Youth of the United States of America, American Youth Hostels, and the Christian Youth Conference. Among other programs are national hookups in radio and television with appropriate syllabuses and guides, new-voter preparation and recognition, a nation-wide attack on the prevention and cure of juvenile delinquency, and National Youth Month in September which is spearheaded by Theatre Owners of America. The National Music League signs up only unknown beginning performers. Plans are evolving slowly for uniting the various efforts into one youth movement, as part of a national-state-local program.

State Programs. The National Council of Chief State School Officers has been active in stimulating and coordinating programs for out-of-school youth. Several states hold annual conferences on youth problems. Michigan, for example, has made surveys of lifework opportunities for youth. The New York legislature established a youth commission. Minnesota legalized a Youth Conservation Commission.

Many states by legislative enactment have raised the age for compulsory school attendance, for permissive school leaving, and for beginning employment, with the result that many more youth remain in school during their teens. At least one has lowered the voting age to eighteen years, thus challenging schools to accent civic education earlier.

Regional. Area vocational schools, technical institutes, and community college programs have been established for youth on interstate and intrastate bases. Illustrative of county efforts are the older-rural-youth programs in Muskingum County, Ohio, and the Saturday classes for secondary-school dropouts in Ventura County, California.

Local. Many cities have organized community youth councils.

Hundreds of local elementary and secondary schools are making intensive studies of dropouts and modifying their programs in the light of these findings.

Many institutions of higher learning, as for example the municipal University of Louisville, have two student bodies: one on the campus and one in the community. The goal of serving all youth is especially characteristic of community colleges and schools.

The Junior Town Meeting League and other agencies are promoting the broadcasting and telecasting of youth discussion programs.

Many school systems offer trade extension classes. Young-farmer classes are popular.

Local public and school libraries are cooperating in an aggressive campaign for youth education by setting up shelves and departments for out-of-school and postsecondary youth. Since the hand that rocks the cradle is becoming younger, many libraries accent parental education in their book lists and discussion groups.

Thousands of secondary schools are following the recommendations of the American Council on Education in regard to the granting of credit and the awarding of high-school diplomas to veterans on the basis of the General Educational Development (GED) Tests. This privilege is being extended to all civilians.

Some Proposals for Youth Education. In a state of the Union message, President Dwight D. Eisenhower recommended the adoption of a constitutional amendment permitting youth to vote at the age of eighteen. The Educational Policies Commission, in its publication *Education for All American Youth—A Further Look,* lists countless suggestions for helping out-of-school youth. In addition to recommending that many receive more education through elimination of dropouts in high school and through the establishment of community institutes, the commission suggested the following in its imaginary state system of youth education:

The members of the state planning groups were quick to see that, even in the best of school systems, all the educational needs of youth could not possibly be met within twelve or fourteen years of school attendance. Some aspects of education must wait upon experience and maturity. . . .

Legal provisions were therefore made for the support of a comprehensive program of free public adult education which would be open to all youth not in full-time attendance at school. The law authorized but did not require districts to admit adults and out-of-school youth to regular classes in community institutes and in the thirteenth and fourteenth grades of secondary schools. It also authorized districts to organize and maintain part-time and evening classes in any subject and to receive financial aid from the state for classes in subjects approved by the state board of education. The board's approvals, we may add, have been broad enough to encompass practically the whole range of interests of adults and older youth—vocational, avocational, civic, cultural, family life, homemaking, and health. . . .

In anticipation of the possible establishment of work camps for youth in public parks and forests and on public conservation and construction projects, the law provides that state and federal aid may be applied to the support of the educational programs in such camps.[8]

The Hoover Commission on Organization of the Executive Branch of the Government also listed many proposals in its task force report. A few recommendations dealing with vocational and trade education are:

Training for employment should be based upon some preliminary estimate of employment opportunities in the field of the individual's preferences and apti-

[8] Educational Policies Commission, *op. cit.* pp. 336–337.

tudes. It must also be predicated upon some fairly uniform terminology and understanding of the trades and skills for which training is to be given. These requirements involve the collaboration of the employer, the worker, the schools, and the employment office. . . . Local apprenticeship and school programs should be developed in close collaboration with the local employment office to avoid wasteful loss of students' time and energy . . .

The matter of federal aid again brings up the proposal of a federal system of scholarships for youth so as to enable each one to work in the occupation where he can be most productive. A somewhat similar proposal was made years ago by President Thomas Jefferson, who, in his plan for education in Virginia, called for "the selection of the youth of genius from among the classes of the poor."

Unleashing Creativity in Youth. America must utilize all human resources through developing the latent talents of relatively young men and women. It must be remembered that: William Cullen Bryant wrote "Thanatopsis" at the age of sixteen; Oliver Wendell Holmes wrote "Old Ironsides" at twenty-one; Jean Simmons was only eighteen when she performed brilliantly with Olivier in "Hamlet"; Daniel Chester French was but twenty-four when he finished his first major statue, the bronze "Minute Man," at Concord; Stephen Foster composed his first music, "The Troga Waltz," at the age of fourteen; George Westinghouse at age nineteen patented a device for replacing derailed cars; and Thomas A. Edison obtained one-third of his 1076 patents between the ages of thirty-three and thirty-six. In his scholarly work *Age and Achievement,* Harvey C. Lehman enumerates many examples of "Young Thinkers and Great Achievement." [9] Countless living examples demonstrate the creative power of young people.

After a down-to-earth survey of millions of teen-agers, members of the staff of the *Ladies' Home Journal* concluded:

Youth is always important because it determines what the future will be; at this time the future of the world is being decided. We are part of an ideological battle than can be won or lost, without a shot being fired or a bomb being dropped; and all nations are fighting for the loyalties and minds of their youth.[10]

Since youth is a state of mind, each one should educate himself to remain young. During the Second World War, over General MacArthur's desk in Manila hung a message, "How to Stay Young," based upon a poem written by the late Samuel Ullman. It read in part as follows:

[9] Harvey C. Lehman, *Age and Achievement,* Chap. XIII, Princeton University Press, 1953.

[10] Maureen Daly and members of the staff of the *Ladies' Home Journal, Profile of Youth,* p. 225, Lippincott, 1951.

Youth is not a time of life—it is a state of mind; it is a temper of the will, a quality of the imagination, a vigor of the emotions, a predominance of courage over timidity, of the appetite for adventure over the love of ease.

Nobody grows old by merely living a number of years; people grow old by deserting their ideals. Years wrinkle the skin, but to give up enthusiasm wrinkles the soul. . . .

You are as young as your faith, as old as your doubt; as young as your self-confidence, as old as your fear; as young as your hope, as old as your despair.

André Gide once wrote, "The wise man is he who constantly wanders afresh." A great truth was expressed by the French poet Alfred de Vigny, who said, "A fine life is a thought conceived in youth and realized in maturity."

ADULT EDUCATION

SCOPE AND FUNCTION OF ADULT EDUCATION

Scope of Adult Education. In its broadest sense, adult education embraces all informal and formal activities which promote more learning and better living for persons of approximately twenty-one years of age and older. In its narrowest sense, it is institutionalized instruction for mature persons who usually are not full-time students. Most summer-school and graduate students in the regular session of the colleges and universities are adults.

In what activities do adults engage as part of this lifelong learning?

The process goes on *through* the media of radio, television, motion pictures, press, and classroom; *for* farmers, parents, business men, workers, and housewives; *in* schools, libraries, museums, settlement houses, and public auditoriums; *with* programs ranging from social dancing to Sanskrit and services ranging from childcare training to old-age counseling. Quantitatively, at least, the American effort is unequaled in any other part of the world. Qualitatively much remains to be done by way of improving both the facilities and the procedures for adult learning.[11]

The list of activities today is a far cry from the early days when the emphasis was concentrated upon literacy and Americanization of foreigners. Adult education is not merely a process of "Simonizing the mind"; it is a meaningful way of improving life.

Its Major Objectives and Functions. Malcolm S. Knowles in his *Informal Adult Education* states that learning should enable adults to produce at least these outcomes:

1. Acquire a mature understanding of themselves.
2. Develop an attitude of acceptance, love, and respect toward others.
3. Develop a dynamic attitude toward life.

[11] Paul H. Sheats, Clarence D. Jayne, and Ralph B. Spence, *Adult Education*, p. 3, Dryden, 1953.

4. React to the causes, not the symptoms, of behavior.
5. Acquire the skills necessary to achieve the potentials of their personalities.
6. Understand the essential values in the capital of human experience.
7. Understand their society and be skillful in directing social change.[12]

Among the important and specific aims in national, state, and local programs are these: to liquidate illiteracy, to Americanize foreigners, to supplement inadequate education, to reeducate people, to promote healthful living, to give parental education, to render vocational and avocational guidance, to raise the level of consumership, to provide workers' education, to provide general education, to lift the cultural level of the nation, to dispel individual and group ignorance, and to supply opportunities for life enrichment, deeper insights, creative thinking, and social action in a democracy.

Implications of Adult Education for a Democracy. Particularly necessary is adult education in America, since a democracy draws more upon the intelligence and character of its citizens than does any other form of government. In an informed democracy it is difficult for a government to enforce censorship and for demagogues to operate successfully. As William H. Kilpatrick pointed out, America needs more, not less adult learning:

> The way to save democracy is to get more people to study our problems and find out what is wrong in order to change it before it is too late. If we don't do that, we will get social catastrophe and dictatorship. If we do that, democracy will solve the problems in some fashion.[13]

Former Commissioner John W. Studebaker once raised the question: "What sort of educational base supports democracy in America?" He answered with the illustration of an inverted pyramid precariously balanced on a small apex of those who have had ample education. Even the adults who constitute the educational apex of the inverted pyramid are constantly in need of reeducation.

Many others need basic training in how to read. Through various educational agencies, the number of illiterates has been reduced. But even though statistics show a high degree of literacy in America, a large percentage of the literate do not know how to read in the modern sense. The late Edward L. Thorndike, in "Why We Behave Like Illiterates," said, "The ignorance of people concerning economics and business is on a level with their ignorance concerning physiology and medicine." Too many adults are economically illiterate.

Can Adults Learn? This is an old question. The usual answer has been, "You can't teach an old dog new tricks." William James and other

---

[12] Malcolm S. Knowles, *Informal Adult Education,* pp. 9–10, Association Press, 1950.
[13] W. H. Kilpatrick, "Implications of Adult Education for a Democracy," *Character and Citizenship,* p. 9, November, 1938.

For age is opportunity no less
Than youth itself, though in another dress,
And as the evening twilight fades away
The sky is filled with stars, invisible by day.

In the starlit eventide of life, with head lifted skyward, the adult marches briskly to his task of continued learning. Old age is challenged by new ideas.

DEVELOPMENT OF ADULT EDUCATION

Early History of Adult Education. Informal adult education is as old as history. Biblical records and other historic documents show numerous efforts in this direction. Formal adult learning may be credited to England, where a Workingmen's College was founded in the middle of the nineteenth century.

In America informal education for adults was promoted through tribal practices among the Indians long before the arrival of the Pilgrims in 1620, when town meetings were started among the white colonists. Thomas Jefferson called the town meeting "the wisest invention ever devised by the wit of man for the perfect exercise of self-government and for its preservation." Formal adult education in this country commenced with such experiments as Cooper Union forums in New York in 1859, Chautauqua in 1874, the work of the social settlements in the eighties, the Lowell Institute in Boston, the lecture courses called "lyceums" in the time of Emerson, and similar undertakings.

One objective of the lyceum, as listed by its founder Josiah Holbrook, was "to increase the advantages and raise the character of existing district schools." Among those who appeared on the programs were Webster, Thoreau, Lowell, Holmes, Hale, Beecher, Phillips, and Emerson. Emerson frequently lectured for $5 and oats for his horse, and he wrote most of his essays for oral delivery from the lyceum platform. The chautauqua program, which followed the lyceum, has run a course similar to it; the parent institution, the Chautauqua Summer School at Chautauqua, New York, is still alive. Other forms of adult education, *viz.*, the university extension and correspondence courses, were organized in the 1870's and 1880's. (For these and other events, see the historical calendar, at the beginning of this unit.)

Organized Movement of Adult Education. Adult education as an organized movement is of recent origin in the United States, its development following the First World War. The first attempt to consolidate adult learning facilities for a community took place in Cleveland in 1924. The term "adult education" did not come into general use until about 1924, when the Carnegie Corporation of New York called the first conference in America. In 1924 the Department of Immigration Education changed its name to the Department of Adult Education, which, as part of the National Education Association, published the *Adult Education Bulletin.* Two years later the interest in this work led to the establishment of a national organization, the American Association of Adult Education, which in 1951 joined with the Department of Adult Education of the NEA in the Adult Education Association of the United States of America. Its journal, *Adult Leadership,* and other projects, some of which have been financed by the Fund for Adult Education, have given impetus to the organized movement of adult education. The National Congress of Parents and Teachers, organized as the National Congress of Mothers in 1897, and the National Council of Parent Education, started in 1926, particularly through their groups of parents banded in child study, have made nation-wide contributions to one phase of adult learning, *viz.,* parental education. The federal Office of Education cooperates closely with national organizations of parents, with public forums, and with other phases of adult learning. In view of the past, it is necessary to establish a broadened concept of American public education which is lifelong learning for all—full-time schooling for all children and most youth, and continuing education for out-of-school youth and adults.

PROVISIONS FOR EDUCATING ADULTS

Literacy Education. For many years part of the adult education program has been directed toward reducing illiteracy. Literacy education aims to provide "classes for adults unable to read and write English with sufficient facility to be able to read a newspaper with understanding and to write an intelligible letter." Nearly three million persons in the United States have had no schooling whatever, and approximately 10 per cent have completed only the first four grades. Although over half the human race is still illiterate, the United States should seek to equal the record of such countries as Denmark, where the illiteracy is only 0.1 per cent. May the time come when American checks and legal documents will not bear the wording: "If you cannot write your name, place a cross and have it witnessed by two persons."

Army Literacy Program. In the Second World War the armed forces conducted very successful programs of literacy training. After rejecting more than 200,000 men of draft age because of illiteracy alone, the armed services eventually inducted twice that number who had never reached the fourth-grade standard of literacy. A large percentage of them was brought up to or beyond that level over a period of 2 or 3 months.

Americanization Program. Formerly this type of adult education was designed to teach the rudiments of the English language and the elements of the United States Constitution to resident alien adults seeking formal admission to American citizenship. The rigid subject matter of earlier years, in which the letter rather than the spirit of the immigration laws dominated the program, has expanded into a functional Americanization program which includes vocational and avocational guidance, civic awareness, and participation in all aspects of democratic processes. Typical of Americanization classes years ago was a lecture by a salesman of American ideals to a group of bewildered "foreigners"; illustrative of the present program is a folk festival in which the people of all nations are given a chance to recreate the cultural values of their homelands. Public policy regarding the Americanization and assimilation of various foreign stocks appears to be changing from one based on the concept of the "melting pot" to one based on the newer idea of cultural pluralism. This type of pluralism is not incompatible with democracy. Under the requirements for citizenship set up by the Immigration and Naturalization Service, a period of 2 to 7 years must elapse from the time an alien takes out the first papers until he receives final citizenship. This period is long enough for interested agencies to provide a broad naturalization program.

In recent years the number of aliens granted citizenship papers has risen sharply. The unsettled world conditions, the arrival of many displaced persons, the overseas friendships established during and since the Second World War, and the ruling that certain federal-state benefactions, like old-age pensions, be paid only to citizens of the United States are causal factors in the increase.

The arrival of many well-educated and cultured newcomers necessitates a revision of the Americanization curriculum with literature on a higher level of difficulty and with more emphasis on oral English and on American institutions, traditions, and practices. Among the by-products of a modern functional Americanization program are more effective cooperation and better understanding between home and school, and between foreign-born parents and their American-born children.

Opportunity Schools and Classes for Adults. Another source of enlightenment is the so-called "night school." The evening classes of universities, particularly in large cities like Chicago and New York, are opportunity schools for thousands of adults who, equipped with brief cases, inquiring minds, and pointed questions, nightly go willingly to school in order to learn and to earn undergraduate or graduate credit. In addition numerous public night schools, usually held in school buildings, have become centers of community light and life. The work offered is academic on the elementary or secondary level, or recreational and cultural. Educational trips to museums and other cultural centers are popular. Consumer education, commercial courses, homemaking, and parental education are some of the practical phases of adult learning. In many cities expenses are defrayed by means of local school taxes, state contributions for part of instructors' salaries, and enrollment fees. In some cities more adults are enrolled in their opportunity schools than there are children in daytime attendance. The Denver, Colorado, opportunity school teaches thousands of adults and youth each year. Many so-called "night schools" are becoming opportunity schools for adults, with evening sessions, Sunday afternoon forums, and day meetings. The New York City school system through its department of adult education offers day courses for adults who cannot attend in the evening. In most cities informal noncredit courses are proving very popular.

Fig. 9-3. The lighted school—a symbol of enlightened adulthood. Many public schools, like this one in Whitehall, Michigan, are lighthouses for all—offering the largest single systematic program of adult education. (*Courtesy of Hedrich-Blessing Studio and Warren S. Holmes, Architects.*)

Adult classes as conducted at present are not drawing a proportionate share of older people. Yet many oldsters, through adult study classes, have gained a new surge of courage and a new joy in living. Older people can be buoyed up so that they talk of their recent accomplishments and current interests rather than of their remote past and alleged or actual physical infirmities. Many grandfathers and grandmothers have learned to ride a hobbyhorse youthfully.

Extension Courses. Extension credit work embraces both extension and correspondence courses. Often the work started with lectures, then came a publications department and finally formal university courses. In line with the statement of the late F. P. Keppel, formerly of the Carnegie Corporation, that it is not the business of society to force people into adult education but to see that facilities for self-education are available, numerous teachers colleges and universities offer extension courses as one of the avenues of adult education. They enable many people to obtain academic, cultural, and professional courses. Several

Fɪɢ. 9-4. Day-school opportunities for achievement by youth and adults. Day and night, night and day, people wend their way to wisdom's light. (*Courtesy of Emily Griffith Opportunity Schools, Denver, Colo.*)

colleges have abandoned correspondence work but continue the off-campus extension credit courses which are taught by college instructors in nearby cities or centers. Many institutions offering these courses are affiliated with the National University Extension Association or the Teachers College Extension Association.

Correspondence Courses. The influence of correspondence schools is widespread. Anne Lindbergh, in *North to the Orient,* made this observation while on the extreme northern tip of the United States, in Barrow, Alaska: "One of the young Eskimo men was hopefully taking a correspondence course in aviation. Poor man, he was waiting at that moment for the *Northland* to bring in his homework for the next year." [16] In some sparsely settled western regions of Canada and the United States children are taught elementary- and high-school rudiments by correspondence courses. The Benton Harbor, Michigan, plan seeks to meet individual needs of high-school students through public-school-administered correspondence courses purchased by the local board of education from nationally known correspondence schools.

Mail-order lessons are a very old form of adult education. Following the formation of the Society to Encourage Studies at Home in 1873, came the so-called Correspondence University of Ithaca, New York, in 1883, then the extension correspondence from the Chautauqua Institution and the extension division of the University of Chicago under William Rainey Harper.[17] Prior to the establishment of college extension divisions, much pioneering work in "selling education" to adults was done by the commercial correspondence schools. The International Correspondence Schools of Scranton, Pennsylvania, developed out of an experiment by Thomas A. Foster, editor of the *Mining Herald* of Shenandoah, Pennsylvania, who began in the eighties to print questions and answers dealing with the problems of safety in the mines.[18]

Today thousands of different home study courses are available to the individual who finds it impractical to attend a resident institution of learning. Of the many correspondence schools only a small proportion are admitted to membership in the National Home Study Council, which was organized in 1926 for accrediting correspondence schools. This council, with headquarters at Washington, D.C., is attempting to eliminate "racketeering" schools and salesmen from the home study field. The United States government through USAFI offers to enlisted men correspondence courses, and through the Federal Trade Commission has adopted trade practice rules for private home study schools in order to foster and promote fair competitive conditions. The importance of correspondence work is reflected in the numerous bills that have been introduced into Congress to establish a national system of supervised correspondence courses.

Chautauquas. The original Chautauqua Institution was started in the 1870's on the shores of the lake of that name in western New York, as a summer training camp for Sunday school teachers in the Methodist Church. Each summer at Chautauqua many adults add to their education while on their vacation. In evaluating the work of the Chautauqua, Dorothy Canfield Fisher wrote:

[16] Anne Lindbergh, *North to the Orient*, p. 109, Harcourt, Brace, 1935.
[17] Lyman Bryson, *Adult Education*, pp. 20–21, American Book, 1936.
[18] *Ibid.*

Chautauqua not only was the first organized Summer School (most of our colleges have since stolen its thunder), it also did pioneer work in correspondence teaching. After two false starts in 1883 a successful course was started whereby summer students could carry on their work by mail in the winter. Those courses were continued for 17 years and when they were dropped in 1900 President Harper, formerly principal at Chautauqua Institution, had taken the new idea to Chicago University. Chautauqua brought out the reading-club idea, at first a part of correspondence courses.[19]

The chautauqua programs of later years with their lectures and money-making schemes helped to keep Americans informed and entertained and saved many a small town from its year-round stagnation. Its place, however, is being taken by the public forum, radio, television, public lectures, and organized educational efforts such as summer schools.

Public Forums. The forum movement originated in Cooper Union in New York in 1859, but not until recent years has it spread widely and rapidly. While John W. Studebaker was superintendent of schools in Des Moines, Iowa, he was instrumental in launching, under the auspices of the American Association of Adult Education and with the financial backing of the Carnegie Corporation, a successful demonstration program in public forums. In 1935 as United States Commissioner of Education he was granted through the Office of Education federal funds for establishing experimental forums in a number of states. Some of these were cooperative forum centers involving three or more communities. The Des Moines experiment showed the value of a multiplicity of small groups in separate neighborhoods. The city school is often the center of the activities. Public-school administrators, boards of education, and citizens' committees are playing a conspicuous role in the development of panel discussions, round tables, and open forums—improved substitutes for the old "cracker barrel discussions."

Town Meeting of the Air. The press and radio help to make Americans "the best informed people of any nation of the earth." America's Town Meeting of the Air, a coast-to-coast broadcast of a forum program, has won great popularity chiefly through the importance and timeliness of its topics and the high caliber of its speakers. It is now linked with several hundred self-organized local town meeting discussion groups in nearly all states of the Union. Town Hall of New York, where the broadcasts usually originate and where nonbroadcast lectures and concerts are also held, has organized an advisory service to assist listeners who wish to study intensively the subjects treated in the broadcasts. These individuals and groups receive advance information on the programs, background material, and supplementary reading lists on issues involved. A thought-provoking broadcast on a crucial issue, followed by simultaneous discussions

[19] Dorothy Canfield Fisher, *Why Stop Learning?* p. 156, Harcourt, Brace, 1927.

by interested groups throughout the nation, is a timely tool in adult learning and in democratic living. The publication of these broadcasts at a nominal price preserves and spreads their usefulness.

Church Nights. Many forums and educational discussions, some of long standing, are conducted variously by individuals, schools, universities, public libraries, citizens' committees, and political, educational, social,

FIG. 9-5. Adult-education class in photography. This is one of the many interest groups or hobbies taught by adults for adults. (*Courtesy of Public Schools, San Francisco, Calif.*)

and religious organizations. An example of the latter is "church night," which consists of a series of evening programs of interest and help to churchgoers and nonchurchgoers. Church nights are intended to meet the whole need from worship, to education, to play, for the whole family.

Adult Clubs. A club has been facetiously defined as an organization that keeps minutes and wastes hours. Despite this criticism, the lecture-instructed club for women and men is an agency for self-improvement.

Women's clubs were pioneers in adult education and still constitute a vital factor. Bryson says that in spite of ridicule and masculine opposition, women's clubs have been educational institutions of real value. He points out also that the historic function of these clubs has been in some degree fulfilled and that younger women are being drawn into associations with specific interests, such as the League of Women Voters, the Business and Professional Women's Club, the Junior League, the American Association of University Women, and an endless chain of other societies for women only.

Men eat, talk, and listen at their luncheon and dinner clubs, which are also infinite in number and variety. Numerous evening study and discussion clubs include both men and women. Social, educational, cultural, recreational, political, religious, racial, and professional groups provide intermittent avenues of adult learning.

Alumni Colleges. "Indeed there is evidence," writes former President Ruthven of the University of Michigan, "that the minds of our alumni not only may cease to grow but often actually may deteriorate." Several colleges, among them Dartmouth, Wilson, and Barnard, hold annual alumni or alumnae college sessions which seek to refresh the minds of their graduates. This refresher college, which usually consists of a series of lectures and tours immediately following or preceding commencement, is increasing in popularity among graduates, especially women. The American Association of University Women, the American Alumni Council, and countless other groups are interested in stimulating the minds of alumni through various phases of adult learning.

Workers' Education. Workers' education in its broad sense applies to everyone. In its unfortunate restricted meaning it tends toward class difference, in meeting the practical, educational, and cultural needs of a special group of adults, *viz.*, industrial workers. Workers' education is not new either in the United States or in Europe. Its early growth in America consisted in the establishment of mechanics' institutes and evening classes which were largely brought about by workers themselves through trade unions and other agencies. A. J. Muste and others have been instrumental in developing labor colleges, which first came into existence about 1900. The International Ladies Garment Workers Union in 1916 started the first educational department among the American trade unions, to which have been added recreational and social activities. The Cafeteria Employees Union in New York City through its educational director has developed a well-rounded educational program for its members. In 1921 the Workers' Educational Bureau of America was established by members of trade unions and teachers to serve as a clearinghouse and as a guide in the development of the activities.

The workers' education movement has developed various forms of instructional organization and techniques. Many types of institutions participate in the program.

Increased college and university participation is the most striking development in workers' education in recent years. In a few cases, at the University of

Michigan for example, institutions of higher learning entered the field to operate programs geared solely to trade union needs. In other cases, workers' education activity exists within the broader framework of an industrial relations center institute. The result has been that college and university programs for workers today are addressed to all levels of the union hierarchy and include on-campus and undergraduate and graduate work, extension classes, seminars and conferences, research and the preparation of materials.[20]

One growing area in workers' education is that of counseling. The tool of guidance has a double cutting edge: it helps the worker to earn more money as a worker and to live more richly as a citizen in a democratic society. Labor education today is one of the most varied and vital aspects of the adult education movement.

Public Library and Adult Learning. As early as 1732 the versatile Benjamin Franklin, through his famous Junto Club, started the first subscription library in the world. The city of Boston initiated the public library movement. A Frenchman, wishing to start an international exchange of books, persuaded the city of Paris to present the city of Boston with 50 volumes. Consequently a Bostonian committee was named to "consider and report what acknowledgment and return should be made to the city of Paris for its gift of books, and to provide a place for the same." This committee, which was acquainted with the publicly used privately supported libraries, contributed to library ideology by giving public support to the public library. A few years later the city of Boston was granted legal authority by the Massachusetts legislature to tax itself for this purpose. Thus started the free public library movement in the United States, which at the turn of the twentieth century was accelerated by the numerous gifts from Andrew Carnegie. Now every state in the Union legalizes public libraries and every city of any size supports one.

A marked contrast exists between the old museum of books and the modern public library. It is the difference between taking a container to the pump several rods away and bringing a public water system into one's own home with water available on tap. The chains that once shackled the books to the reading desks have been broken. Whereas many librarians used to hoard books, they now wish to show how many are off the shelves in actual use. An active reading public eliminates the librarian's dustcloth. The open-shelf system, while costly in losses, is the open-sesame to the wonderland of books. Furthermore, where the library was once a repository for books only, it is now an instructional and information center with files replete with clippings, pictorial aids, phonograph records, and many other multisensory aids; with reference, committee, lecture,

[20] Irvine L. H. Kerrison, *Workers' Education at the University Level*, pp. 16–17, Rutgers University Press, 1951.

radio, and television rooms; and with other facilities, not the least of which is the telephone, which enables a person to use the public library without leaving his home.

Despite good libraries, the United States is not a book-reading nation. Not many adults make constant companions of books, as did the clerk of Oxenford thus described by Chaucer:

> For him was lever have at his beddes heed
> Twenty bokes, clad in blak or reed,
> Of Aristotle and his philosophye,
> Then robes riche, or fithele, or gay sautrye.

The bookmobiles, therefore, constitute a great advance in educational engineering. The library truck and its trained attendant carry a rich cargo to remote parts of the United States. Not only are adults the recipients of these books, but children are given the opportunity to develop good reading habits and tastes which will carry over into maturity.

The Library Service Division, established by Congress in 1936 in the federal Office of Education, lists as one objective that of "furthering library participation in the adult education movement." The American Library Association, which held its first meeting in 1876, has been a tremendous force in adult learning, particularly through its Commission on the Library and Adult Education. The librarians, the books, and the supplementary aids are making people not only literate but also "librarious." A publication of the American Association for Adult Education has predicted that the public library in the future will be the center of the adult education movement and will function as a people's university.

Library of Congress. The public library movement finds its highest fulfillment in the Library of Congress at Washington. It was established in 1800 by an act providing for a library for the two houses, at an initial cost of $5000. Housed in the Capitol, it was burned by the British in 1814 and revived by Thomas Jefferson with his own books as a nucleus. In 1886 Congress decided to dedicate the library to the services of all the people, and a new building was commenced.

Of all the institutions in the United States that have a part in the American dream, the late James Truslow Adams said:

The one which best exemplifies the dream is the greatest library in this land of libraries, the Library of Congress. . . . The Library of Congress has come straight from the heart of democracy, as it has been taken to it, and I here use it as a symbol of what democracy can accomplish on its own behalf. Many have made gifts to it, but it was created by ourselves through Congress, which has steadily and increasingly shown itself generous and understanding toward it. Founded and built by the people, it is for the people. Anyone who has used the great collections of Europe, with their restrictions and red tape and difficulty of access, praises God for American democracy when he enters the stacks of the Library of Congress.[21]

This national institution of public learning is a prototype for other adult educational agencies.

Federal Education for Adults. When the United States government started its program of relief in 1933, one of the first projects undertaken was that of adult education, which enabled several million adults to rise to higher levels. Likewise in the Second World War the army literacy program, previously mentioned, helped a half million men to reach or exceed the fourth-grade level of reading.

The off-duty study programs of the various branches of the Defense Department during and since World War II have been essentially adult-education in character. To meet the needs of both the young and mature training and fighting men and women, many books, magazines, and entire libraries go to campus and to battlefields. The off-duty program is necessarily varied, diffuse, pervasive, and conducted through a wide variety of agencies. It includes such activities as library services; the United States Armed Forces Institute; information and educational service sections; the program of special training for functional illiterates; the part-time and full-time collegiate programs; and numerous related activities.

More firmly established in principle and practice is federal support of numerous permanent projects in adult education. As already indicated, the United States government has supplied millions of dollars annually for rural adult education through the agricultural extension services. Through the Smith-Lever, Smith-Hughes, and George-Barden Acts and through other legislation the federal government has declared its financial support of adult learning. It has assumed the responsibility of helping states to rehabilitate the physically handicapped. The establishment of the United States Employment Agency was a significant step in the placement and advancement of both younger and older persons. Hundreds of adults are enrolled in governmental schools like the part-time graduate school of the Department of Agriculture. Programs of informal adult education are being carried forward aggressively in federal territories, dependencies, and Indian reservations. The future presages increased activity by Uncle Sam, the schoolteacher, in the field of permanent long-time adult education.

Other Forms of Adult Education. It is nearly impossible to catalogue all the agencies engaged in adult education. Informal learning is provided by numerous radio and television programs that are accompanied by men-

---

21 James Truslow Adams, *The Epic of America,* pp. 414–415, Little, Brown, 1932.

tal, physical, and aesthetic "audience participation." This is exemplified in the bodily movements in the setting-up exercises, the mental collaboration in quiz and forum programs, and the instrumental and vocal participation at home by amateur musicians as they actively hear and see productions of symphonic music over radio and television. Malcolm S. Knowles states that informal adult education is a movement so vast and so formless that large numbers of people who are engaged in it do not realize they are working in the field of adult education.

An illustration of other formal adult learning is that of correctional education in prisons and reformatories. Acording to a survey conducted by the Federal Bureau of Prisons, the typical inmate of a federal prison reads from five to ten times as many books a year, preferably nonfiction, as the average citizen. Many states have launched significant education programs in their correctional and eleemosynary institutions.[22] Efforts are being made to meet special group and individual needs in a broad enriched program of nation-wide adult education.

ILLUSTRATIVE PRACTICES AND PROPOSALS

Some Practices in Adult Education. Supplemental to the procedures already described, brief descriptions are here provided of a few illustrative practices in adult education, as found in (1) international, (2) national, including governmental and nongovernmental, (3) state, (4) regional, and (5) local programs.

International Programs. The program of the U.S. Foreign Operations Administration is basically adult education.

The United States National Commission for UNESCO maintains an active Panel on Adult Education. Since over half the human race is still illiterate, one of the most significant movements in adult education is the mass or fundamental education movement launched by UNESCO.

National Programs. A renewed attack against illiteracy among adult Negroes has been made by the United States Office of Education, with the help of such organizations as the American Association of Adult Education, the Carnegie Corporation, the Negro Elks, Phi Beta Sigma, Conference of Negro Land-grant Colleges, and the American Teachers' Association.

In its adult education campaign, the American Legion issued thousands of booklets, written simply, with language keyed to a basic 1000-word vocabulary, and with readability tested through reader surveys.

The American Library Association and other groups have published books for adult beginners, geared to the reading ability and interests of older learners. The Association also spearheads many campaigns such as the great-issues program.

The Metropolitan Museum of Art in New York City expanded on a nation-

[22] For further details on prison education, see the yearbooks of the Committee on Education of the American Prison Association.

wide scale its program to "take the art treasures of the museum into the homes of people everywhere."

The American Medical Society, colleges of medicine, and other organizations and institutions are stimulating and evaluating work in gerontology (the study of the aging process). The medical emphasis is shifting from pediatrics to geriatrics. National conferences on aging are held periodically.

Specialists in adult and post-high-school education have been added to the staffs of organizations such as the National Education Association, which has organized a National Training Laboratory in Group Development.

The Center for the Study of Liberal Education for Adults works with member institutions of the Association of Evening Colleges in experimental liberal-arts discussion groups.

A cooperative and critical reexamination of university extension work has been made.

The U.S. Revenue Division helps adults prepare their income-tax returns.

Federal and state governments through their old-age relief, pensions, or insurance are helping to finance senescence so that fewer old people need to work. Thus they have more leisure for study and hobbies.

Radio and television programs interest oldsters as consumers and producers. An example of the latter is the program "Life Begins at Eighty," where octogenarians form juries that analyze questions sent in by listeners.

A practical form of personalized adult reeducation is furnished by Alcoholics Anonymous through the rehabilitation of alcoholics.

The American Council on Education, through its Commission on the Implications of Armed Services Educational Programs, made descriptive and evaluative studies of adult education as reported in *The Armed Services and Adult Education.*

The education of adults has been complicated by war and postwar displacement of population. This includes the high mobility of population within the United States and the arrival of displaced persons from other lands.

For many years the Immigration and Naturalization Service of the United States government has sent to public schools the names of new arrivals and of applicants for citizenship. These lists have been helpful in recruiting adults for Americanization classes.

The Displaced Persons Commission has developed functional programs for refugees who come here to begin a new life.

The third Sunday in May has been designated by Congress as "I Am an American Day." On this day ceremonies are held for those foreign-born persons who become citizens through naturalization, and also for those native-born who come of age.

State. More and more states are giving legal recognition and financial support to adult education as an integral part of public education. Several state departments have added directors in this field. Iowa publishes an adult-education handbook for public schools. Several states are conducting experiments in adult education, as for example, Michigan.

Many states issue a high-school equivalent certificate to qualified adults. Illustrative is Missouri, which requires that the certificate candidate be at least twenty-one years old, pass a written examination, and meet certain standards in occupational success, social, civic, and cultural development.

Many a state university has adopted the philosophy that all people in the state live on its campus, and hence it extends educational services to everyone, irrespective of his age or location. Many have adult-education departments.

Purdue and Indiana Universities jointly publish *Community Teamwork*—a newsletter for Hoosier adult workers.

FIG. 9-6. Two mature students in the class for foreign-born conducted by the local board of education as part of the adult-education program. (*Courtesy of Public Schools, Jersey City, N.J.*)

Of the many new degrees offered in adult education is that of a Master of Science in Extension Education conferred by Kansas State College.

Iowa State University has established an Institute of Gerontology.

Regional. An interesting and significant regional project in adult education has been the community school at Norris, Tennessee, located four miles from Norris Dam. In Norris, which is one of the few cities in America built from the ground up as a planned community, the school is the center of an educational program serving both children and adults in Norris and the surrounding community.

Bookmobiles play an increasing role in adult education in rural areas. Many mobile libraries carry phonograph records as well as books, pictures, and other learning aids.

Local. Local adult education councils are multiplying rapidly. One of the oldest in the country is the Denver Council, which publishes monthly *Educa-*

tional Opportunities. Community planning and group consultation are increasing.

Many councils have developed programs that are tailor-made for the participants. For example, Bloomington, Illinois, organized a course for expectant mothers. Salt Lake City had an investment course for women only. New York City offered classes for the deaf in the evening high schools. El Paso, Texas, maintained a school-sponsored homemobile which moved from one community to another instructing small groups of women in foods, clothing, and family-life education. The Central Y.M.C.A. in Chicago had a unique adult education class entitled "Visits with Interesting People." Class sessions consisted of visits to the homes of distinguished leaders in business, journalism, religion, education, and labor.

Many colleges have added courses or departments in adult education. More institutions are admitting mature students who have not graduated from high school. Some provide tuition-free courses for anyone over sixty-five years.

Some communities have established community centers for adults, local gerontological societies, adult study camps, and periodic exhibits of the products of leisure-time learning of adults.

Discussion techniques for adults are being studied and improved through greater attention to group dynamics. One discussion technique is the 66 method, by which a large group is divided into committees of not more than six persons and each committee then discusses the problem for approximately 6 minutes. Then the committees elect spokesmen who report ideas back to the group.

Psychologically and economically significant is the growing practice of employing part- or full-time workers who have passed the traditional retirement age.

Illustrative of radio procedures in adult education are the University of Minnesota's credit correspondence courses, the lectures for which are broadcast to the students by radio.

Popular over television are how-to-do-it courses, such as one conducted by a "handy man about the house," who gives directions and demonstrates how to fix things.

The United Nations Council of Philadelphia organized a letter exchange for adults in order to develop "pen pals" for peace. Thus Americans learn of other people and they in turn know more about Americans.

This consideration of practices is concluded with the statement from a long-time worker in adult education, Morse A. Cartwright, who said that one-third of the American people are "attending forums, preparing for jobs in vocational classes, learning handicrafts, folk dancing, reading with a purpose, and otherwise using leisure time for educational purposes."

Some Proposals for Adult Education. Among the many proposals for federal participation in improving adult learning are these:

Several bills before Congress have proposed that special federal grants for library service to rural areas be made through the states.

It has also been proposed that Congress appropriate funds for labor extension education, similar to that conducted by the Agricultural Extension Service for farm families.

In connection with collecting and analyzing decennial census data on illiteracy, it has been suggested that arbitrary levels of academic attainment or schooling, such as completion of the fourth grade, be eliminated. In its place would be substituted adequate criteria of literacy based upon functional requirements of American citizens.

It has also been proposed that a continuous nation-wide program be organized for liquidating illiteracy in the United States.

Additional suggestions for adult education include such state and local features as:

State and local programs should make more extensive use of junior or community colleges for adult education purposes.

Every state and local community should have an adult education council to assist in coordinating and extending the existing programs of adult education. These can form a "common denominator for community educating agencies."

The proposals of the Educational Policies Commission for extending and improving the program of public education include "carrying qualified persons through education beyond 14 years, providing vocational retraining, and other desirable forms of adult education."

Appropriations for public education in all states should include financial aid for adult education as part of lifelong learning.

The great needs in adult education in America are a concise set of objectives for adult education, a more definitely organized program, a better educated corps of teachers for public and nonpublic agencies, adequate financing, and a better coordinated plan of action and evaluation.

Coordination of Adult Education with Other Areas of Education. It is highly possible that adult education will discover new techniques which will gradually seep downward into the schooling of the young. Learning at all preceding stages is subject to the tradition that it is for some future more important than the present, but adult education has the advantage that it scarcely can be diverted to preparation for anything beyond itself.[23] Conversely, according to Kilpatrick, if adult study and learning are an assured part of American public education, then childhood and youth, freed of the burden of learning things needed only in adult life, can give due attention to their own evolving needs.[24]

The various levels of learning are not in conflict or in disjunction. Preelementary education lays the foundation for the arch of lifelong learning, and adult education provides the capstone for the symmetrical structure.

[23] Ruth Kotinsky, *Adult Education and the Social Scene*, p. 39, Appleton-Century-Crofts, 1933.
[24] William H. Kilpatrick, Foreword, in Kotinsky, *op. cit.*

SUGGESTED ACTIVITIES

1. Make a list of youth organizations in your state.

2. Suggest a program for the out-of-school unemployed youth.

3. Visit a part-time school and note the characteristics of the youth enrolled and the program offered.

4. Visit a public library and evaluate its program for out-of-school youth and adults.

5. Arrange a debate on the topic: "Resolved that all males between the ages of twenty-one and thirty should render 1 year of military service to their government of the United States."

6. List great men and women who made contributions to civilization in their youth; make another list for persons over sixty years.

7. Discuss the role of the public school in the education of youth and adults.

8. Describe programs for vocational education and rehabilitation.

9. List some informal means of adult education.

10. List all agencies in your community which are directly or indirectly connected with adult education.

11. Write a brief history of some phase of adult education, such as the labor colleges, the Chautauqua, religious activities, and others.

12. Describe the program of adult education in a foreign country.

13. Visit an extension class conducted by a college or university.

14. Visit an Americanization class and note the teaching procedures used.

15. Indicate how the problem of teaching refugees differs from that of teaching typical immigrants.

16. Make a case study of some adult who is enrolled in a night school.

17. Defend the statement: "An old person can learn new tricks."

18. Report on one of the scientific investigations of the learning ability of adults.

19. Report some of the educational implications of the fact that America as a nation is growing older.

20. List desirable qualfications for a teacher of adults. Do you possess these qualifications?

DESCRIPTIVE BIBLIOGRAPHY AND AIDS

BOOKS

ESSERT, PAUL L.: *Creative Leadership of Adult Education,* Chap. IX, Prentice-Hall, 1951.
Adult education in the world community.

FEDERAL SECURITY AGENCY: *Man and His Years,* Chap. I, Health Publications Institute, 1951.
"Our aging population" as discussed at the first National Conference on Aging.

HILDRETH, GERTRUDE: *Readiness for School Beginners,* Chap. XII, World, 1950.
Readiness for parents of school children.

HYMES, JAMES L.: *Effective Home-School Relations,* Chap. III, Prentice-Hall, 1953.
Parents and schools in today's world.

KERRISON, L. H.: *Workers' Education at the University Level,* Chap. V, Rutgers University Press, 1951.
Trends in college and university workers' education.

KNAPP, ROBERT H.: *Practical Guidance Methods,* Chap. II, McGraw-Hill, 1953.
Helping youth through vocational guidance.

KNOWLES, MALCOLM S.: *Informal Adult Education,* Chap. XI, Association Press, 1950.
Evaluation of programs of adult education.

LANDIS, PAUL H.: *Adolescence and Youth,* Part IV, McGraw-Hill, 1952.
The struggle for economic adulthood.

LEHMAN, HARVEY C.: *Age and Achievement,* Chaps. XIII, XIV, Princeton University Press, 1953.

    Great achievements of younger and older thinkers respectively.

OVERSTREET, H. A.: *The Mature Mind,* Chap. II, Norton, 1949.

    Criteria for maturity.

OVERSTREET, H. A., and BONARO OVERSTREET: *The Mind Alive,* Chap. XVI, Norton, 1954.

    The mind's health in an age of conspiracy, especially communism.

ROSEN, VICTOR: *The Mature Woman: Her Richest Years,* Chap. I, Prentice-Hall, 1953.

    "You don't have to be young to be happy."

SHEATS, PAUL H., CLARENCE D. JAYNE, and RALPH B. SPENCE: *Adult Education: The Community Approach,* Chap. VII, Dryden, 1953.

    The role of the public schools in adult education.

WOODS, JAMES H., and MARGARET W. WAGNER: *Helping Older People Enjoy Life,* Chap. X, Harper, 1953.

    A community center for older people.

CURRENT PERTINENT PERIODICALS AND PUBLICATIONS

Adult Education

Adult Leadership

Aging

Community Teamwork

Focus

Fundamental and Adult Education Bulletin (UNESCO)

Geriatrics

Handbook of Adult Education in the United States

Helps for Teachers of the Foreign Born

Home Study Blue Book and Directory of Private Home Study Schools & Courses

Jewish Parents

Journal of Educational Sociology

Lifetime Living

National Parent-Teacher

Occupational Index

Occupations

Proceedings of various educational organizations

Review of Educational Research

Senior Citizens

Yearbooks of educational organizations

Youth Leaders' Digest

AUDIO-VISUAL AIDS

AN ADVENTURE IN FRIENDSHIP   25 min., sound

    Shows how constructive a force the friendship of an interested and stable adult can be in the life of a deprived boy, as seen by the Big Brother Movement. Available on loan from Big Brothers of America, 1347 Broad Street, Philadelphia 3.

ARE YOU READY FOR SERVICE?   Series of films, sound

    A series designed to orient high-school students in their planning for military service, well in advance of enlistment or induction. The initial group serves as an introduction to the series and consists of three films: *What It's All About, Your Plans,* and *Service and Citizenship,* available from Coronet Films, Chicago 1.

CONDUCTING A MEETING   10 min., sound

    Deals with parliamentary procedure. Available from Young America Films, New York 17.

A PHOTORAMA OF ADULT ACTIVITIES IN DETROIT EVENING SCHOOLS   1000 feet, sound, color

    A glimpse of the activities in more than 100 courses offered in Detroit's evening schools. Illustrative of systematic programs in adult education conducted by public schools. Available from Adult Education Division, Board of Education, Detroit.

RIGHT OR WRONG?   10 min., sound
   Shows how a case of vandalism by teen-age boys becomes a problem for the
various agencies and persons in a community. Available from Coronet Instructional
Films, Chicago 1.

SCHOOL AND COMMUNITY   14 min., sound
   Accents the partnership of school and community in youth and adult education.
Produced by the publishers of this book, McGraw-Hill, New York 36.

V FOR VOLUNTEERS   Two reels, sound
   The story of a volunteer who learns the joys that come from community participation. A by-product is the reopening of a neglected youth center in the community. Dramatizes the need for unpaid workers in welfare and civic work. Available from Association Films, New York 17.

Part III

PERSONNEL IN PUBLIC EDUCATION

Preview of Part III

PERSONNEL IN PUBLIC EDUCATION

The administrative structure of American public education and the various academic levels are avenues through which constantly flow the influence of the educational personnel. The human factor is paramount. Numerically, one in five persons in the United States is actively engaged in education as learner or teacher.

As indicated in Fig. 10-1, the child is the center surrounded by the major forces that influence him—the home, the community, the church, and the school. The latter exists primarily for the pupil. The child grows and develops in at least four dimensions: physical, mental, social, and spiritual. Many children are atypical—they deviate from the norm sufficiently to warrant special consideration and treatment. Modern society treasures the child, be he normal or atypical (Unit X).

Among the persons who exert an abiding influence upon the child is the teacher. The pupil and the teacher are joint partners in learning and teaching. The teacher is not an automaton but a human worker, who should be well educated and professionally alert. Teaching is becoming less of a procession and more of a profession. Standards for selection, as well as preservice and in-service education, are being elevated. Teacher welfare provisions are being improved. The great shortage of well-qualified teachers constitutes a threat to the welfare of the nation (Unit XI).

The classroom teacher, however, is but one of the numerous persons engaged in education in the United States. Special teachers, administrative and supervisory officers, educational personnel from other professions, and other nonteachers contribute to the education of the well-rounded pupil. The opportunities to serve in educational work are numerous and varied. Persons not interested in direct classroom teaching can find many opportunities for other significant service. No economy is so shortsighted as that which dictates the employment of unqualified personnel in education, where human values are paramount (Unit XII).

Part III

PERSONNEL IN PUBLIC EDUCATION

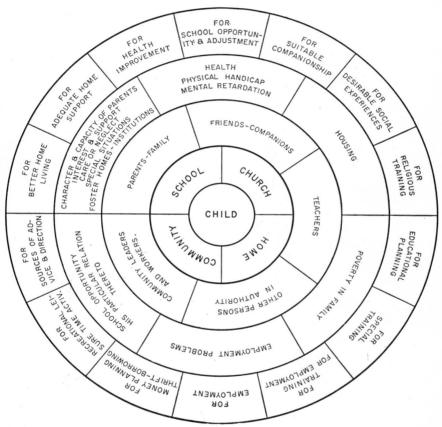

FIG. 10-1. The important factors in child education and welfare. The child is the central figure. The major forces that influence him are indicated in the next ring: the home, the community, the school, and the church. Next in order are shown the persons who exert influence over him—parents, family, friends, companions, teachers, other persons in authority, and community leaders and workers. In the next ring are indicated conditions in himself or his family or elsewhere which affect him, such as health, housing, employment problems, etc. In the outer ring are some of the opportunities the child may need: for school opportunity and adjustment, for religious training, for money planning, for health improvement, for recreational leisure time, for better home living, for adequate home support, etc. (*Courtesy of New York State Department of Education and School Board Journal.*)

PUPILS

The central and constant figure in the ever-changing design of American public education is the individual pupil. Be he typical or atypical, upon him are centered the interests and the efforts of parents and teachers.

All pupils need four-dimensional growth and development—physically, mentally, socially, and spiritually. Good teachers study their pupils as well as their lessons. They learn much from their pupils. They study pupils longitudinally through the accumulating years and horizontally through all areas of human living. Teachers and pupils are partners in teaching, learning, and living.

Atypical or exceptional pupils are found everywhere. They may differ physically, as do the visually handicapped, the crippled, the deaf and hard of hearing, those handicapped in speech, the delicate, and others; mentally, as do the gifted and the slow learners; socially, as do the delinquent; and in other ways, as do those emotionally unstable, those with impaired mental health, those from minority, low-income, and migrant families, and those who are refugees from foreign shores. Within and between these groups are numerous deviations and handicaps to challenge the alert teacher.

OUTLINE OF CONTENTS

Introduction
  White House conferences
  The individual pupil
  Understanding a child
Child Growth and Development
  Physical growth
  Mental development
  Social development
  Spiritual growth
  Other characteristics
Physically Handicapped Pupils
  Visually handicapped
  Crippled pupils
  Deaf and hard of hearing
  Handicapped in speech
  Delicate children
  Others physically atypical
Mentally Exceptional Pupils
  Gifted pupils
  Slow learners
  Mentally maladjusted
Socially Handicapped Pupils
  Social variants as a group
Other Exceptional Pupils

PUPILS

Payson Smith once told the following story about Colonel Francis Parker, who came to Quincy, Massachusetts, at a time when the schools were regimented and the children were stratified:

One day some of the teachers came to him and said, "Colonel Parker, we don't understand what you are trying to do, and we would like you to call us together and explain this new theory of the place of the individual in education." This he agreed to do. After the teachers were assembled in a classroom Colonel Parker came down the aisle from his office in the rear of the building accompanied by a little girl. He placed her in a chair at his side and turning to the teachers he gave this, the shortest and best of all educational addresses, "My fellow teachers, you have asked me to tell you why we are making changes in our schools here in Quincy." Moving from his place at the desk he went over and placed his hand on the shoulder of the little girl and said to them, "Here is your answer," and he left them wondering and thinking.

Under the stress of committee meetings and other professional activities, teachers sometimes forget the child in their midst. Likewise in its business deliberations the local board of education often ignores the child, the central figure in the ever-changing design of American education.

White House Conferences on Children. The United States government and the people recognize the role of children in American democracy through periodic conferences held in Washington, D.C. These nationwide meetings, popularly known as "White House Conferences," were called for the indicated year by the following respective occupant of the White House:

Year of conference	Called by President
1909	Theodore Roosevelt
1919	Woodrow Wilson
1931	Herbert Hoover
1940	Franklin D. Roosevelt
1950	Harry S. Truman
1955	Dwight D. Eisenhower

Although these conferences on children and youth are held at intervals of approximately ten years, a mid-decade meeting, preceded by state workshops, was called for 1955 by President Eisenhower to consider such pressing problems as shortages in facilities and personnel for American schools. The Midcentury Conference adopted, among other resolutions, the "Pledge to Children" which is reproduced in its entirety on the following page.

PLEDGE TO CHILDREN

Midcentury White House Conference on Children and Youth)

our children, who hold within you our most cherished hopes, nbers of the Midcentury White House Conference on Children and ... , relying on your full response, make this pledge:

From your earliest infancy we give you our love, so that you may grow with trust in yourself and in others.

We will recognize your worth as a person and we will help you to strengthen your sense of belonging.

We will respect your right to be yourself and at the same time help you to understand the rights of others, so that you may experience cooperative living.

We will help you to develop initiative and imagination, so that you may have the opportunity freely to create.

We will encourage your curiosity and your pride in workmanship, so that you may have the satisfaction that comes from achievement.

We will provide the conditions for wholesome play that will add to your learning, to your social experience, and to your happiness.

We will illustrate by precept and example the value of integrity and the importance of moral courage.

We will encourage you always to seek the truth.

We will provide you with all opportunities possible to develop your own faith in God.

We will open the way for you to enjoy the arts and to use them for deepening your understanding of life.

We will rid ourselves of prejudice and discrimination, so that together we may achieve a truly democratic society.

We will work to lift the standard of living and to improve our economic practices, so that you may have the material basis for a full life.

We will provide you with rewarding educational opportunities, so that you may develop your talents and contribute to a better world.

We will protect you against exploitation and undue hazards and help you grow in health and strength.

We will work to conserve and improve family life and, as needed, to provide foster care according to your inherent rights.

We will intensify our search for new knowledge in order to guide you more effectively as you develop your potentialities.

As you grow from child to youth to adult, establishing a family life of your own and accepting larger social responsibilities, we will work with you to improve conditions for all children and youth.

Aware that these promises to you cannot be fully met in a world at war, we ask you to join us in a firm dedication to the building of a world society based on freedom, justice and mutual respect.

SO MAY YOU grow in joy, in faith in God and in man, and in those qualities of vision and of the spirit that will sustain us all and give us new hope for the future.

Fig. 10-2.

The Individual Pupil. Joy Elmer Morgan has expressed thus the importance of the child:

Let us set the child in our midst as our greatest wealth and our most challenging responsibility. Let us exalt him above industry, above business, above politics, above all the petty and selfish things that weaken and destroy a people.

Fig. 10-3. Twenty pupils, but each one an individual. (*Courtesy of Library of Congress.*)

Let us know that the race moves forward through its children, and by the grace of Almighty God, setting our faces toward the morning, dedicate ourselves anew to the service and the welfare of childhood.

As every parent thinks and lives in terms of his child, so too the teacher thinks first of the child and second of the subject matter. The White House Conference on Children in a Democracy stated: "The supreme educational and social importance of individual traits should be recognized throughout the educational system."

In his book, *Man, the Unknown,* Dr. Alexis Carrel, the famous scientist, devoted an entire chapter to "The Individual," saying in part:

Human beings are not found anywhere in nature. There are only individuals. . . . Mental, structural, and humoral individualities blend in an unknown manner. . . . Each individual is conscious of being unique. . . . Individual specificity persists during the entire life, although tissues and humors continually change. . . . Modern society ignores the individual. . . . But each one has his own personality. He cannot be treated like a symbol. Children should not be placed at a very early age in schools where they are educated wholesale.[1]

Mass education must be counteracted by emphasis on the individual pupil. Each child not only has a distinctive fingerprint—he has a unique personality. Naturally pupils vary in abilities, attitudes, and accomplishments. The school child may be normal in several ways and exceptional in others, but as a composite he is usually considered typical or atypical.

Understanding a Child. All children must be studied longitudinally over accumulating years and horizontally through all areas of their living. Good teachers study their pupils as well as their lessons; they learn about pupils while teaching them. Among the experimental methods used in child study are: questionnaires and direct questioning, systematic observation, standardized tests, ratings, projective techniques, parallel groups, laboratory techniques, and case histories.[2]

A pupil, like any human being, is a biological organism, consisting of skin, bones, muscles, nerves, glands, organs of special sense, a digestive system, and a circulatory system, working interdependently. Integration in its restricted sense exists within the pupil rather than between bits of subject matter. An integrat*ing* child who adapts himself at all levels of learning and life is the goal rather than an integrat*ed* mass. To this end the teacher should be familiar with the developmental patterns at various levels as revealed in numerous current texts on child growth. Furthermore, the teacher ought to understand lifelong human growth and development.

What is meant by "understanding" a child? The staff of the Division of Child Development and Teacher Personnel, in its report *Helping Teachers Understand Children,* indicated in a general way the kinds of attitude, knowledge, and habits that characterize sympathetic teachers:

1. Teachers who understand children think of their behavior as being caused. They see a youngster's present action as based upon his past experience, as shaped by his present situation, and as influenced by his desires and hopes for the future.

[1] Alexis Carrel, *Man, the Unknown,* pp. 235, 242, 244, 267, 269, 270, Harper, 1935.
[2] Leigh Peck, *Child Psychology,* pp. 87–88, Heath, 1953.

2. A second characteristic for teachers who understand children is that they are able to accept all children emotionally, that they reject no child as hopeless or unworthy.

3. Teachers who understand children invariably recognize that each one is unique.

4. The various sciences concerned with human growth and behavior have demonstrated that young people, during the several phases of their development, face a series of common "developmental tasks."

5. A fifth characteristic of understanding teachers is that they know the more important scientific facts that describe and explain the forces that regulate human growth, development, motivation, learning, and behavior.

6. Finally, the understanding teacher habitually uses scientific methods in making judgments about any particular boy or girl.[3]

Understanding a child is a difficult but challenging and necessary task for the teacher. Individual differences increase as the child progresses through the various stages and areas of growth.

Child Growth and Development

Research with Children. As Arthur T. Jersild of Columbia University has stated, "The proper study of children is children." A long-time observer of the child, Dr. Arnold L. Gesell, formerly of the Yale University Clinic of Child Development, studied youngsters for forty years. His research indicates that "there is a basic ground plan of growth peculiar to the species, and always a variation of the ground plan distinctive for the individual."

In summarizing a half century of learning about children, John E. Anderson, director of the Institute of Child Welfare of the University of Minnesota, states that out of the manifold research has come "a genetic or developmental point of view which sees the child at any age, not as a single moment independent of the past and the future, but as a transition point in a stream of experiences that go back to infancy and will continue on into the future." [4]

Developmental Periods. While no clear-cut line divides the different developmental stages, nevertheless man's major ages can be distinguished as follows, with the approximate years:

1. *Prenatal period.* This extends from conception, when the female ovum is fertilized by the male spermatozoon, to the time of birth, roughly 9 calendar months or 280 days. . . .

---

[3] Commission on Teacher Education, *Helping Teachers Understand Children,* pp. 8–12, American Council on Education, 1945.

[4] John E. Anderson, "A Half Century of Learning about Children," *NEA Journal,* March, 1953, p. 141.

2. *Infancy.* Beginning with birth and extending to the age of ten to fourteen days is infancy.

3. *Babyhood.* This period extends from the age of two weeks to approximately two years.

4. *Childhood.* Strictly speaking, the childhood years include the years from age two to puberty. . . .

5. *Adolescence.* The adolescent years extend from the onset of puberty, between the ages of eleven and thirteen years in the average child, to the age of maturity, twenty-one years. . . . It may be subdivided into three shorter periods, pre, early, and late adolescence.[5]

Postadolescence is the next step in the long road to adulthood, which adds three more stages:

6. *Early adulthood.* This period from mid-twenties up to about 45 is a time people are expected to be productive and independent. . . .

7. *Middle adulthood.* This period from 45 to retirement is in some respects an extension of early adulthood, and in others a transition to the period after retirement.

8. *Later adulthood.* This span of life from 65 to three score years and ten or four score years is often characterized by "goneness," but it can take on positive characteristics of usefulness.[6]

Most normal individuals pass through these major stages.

Phases of Growth. A pupil, typical or atypical, has not one but several ages. He may have simultaneously a chronological age, which is his actual span of life in years; a mental age, which is his ability to perform certain intellectual tasks; an educational age, which usually denotes his academic level of achievement; a physical age, which ranks him among his colleagues in such matters as stature and weight; an emotional age, which may be revealed in his affective behavior; a social age, which depends greatly upon his experiences with people; a vocational age, which may provide much of the drive for completing his studies; and an avocational age, which in an activity like stamp collecting may place a sixth grader high above a college student. Unevenness may exist in these various ages within a pupil, especially if there is poorly synchronized growth among the different systems of the body. Through cumulative continuous growth the individual pupil becomes a well-balanced person in all areas of living.

An excellent description of all-round growth and development is furnished by that great textbook of life, the Bible, in this terse account of the early life of the Great Teacher: "And Jesus increased in wisdom and stature, and in favor with God and man" (Luke 2:52). He increased in

[5] Elizabeth B. Hurlock, *Child Development,* pp. 53–55, McGraw-Hill, 1950.

[6] Lester W. Bartlett, "Pioneering the Later Years," *Adult Leadership,* March, 1954, pp. 9–10.

wisdom (mentally), in stature (physically), in favor with God (spiritually), and man (socially). The teacher and parent should promote this four-dimensional growth for every child.

PHYSICAL GROWTH

Life and growth do not begin at birth, but at the time of conception.

Growing during the prenatal period is very rapid, resulting in the development of an organism capable of a large number of complex activities in the short span of nine months. Birth is, therefore, merely an interruption in the normal development of the individual, caused by a change in environment from that of the mother's body to that of the world outside the mother's body.[7]

Human growth is influenced by many glands: the pituitary, in the center of the head; the thyroid, at the base of the throat; the adrenals, each lying just above the kidneys; and the sex glands. It is also affected by environmental factors of the outside world: food, clothing, shelter, sunlight, air, water, communicable diseases, injuries, regional temperature, cultural climate, and social status.

After birth the general nature of physical development is as follows:

Young children grow very rapidly. Increase in height is accompanied by increase in weight. As children increase in stature their legs become longer in relation to trunk length, and hands and feet show rapid growth. This means change in roles and a shift in the rhythm of development during certain periods of maturation. . . . Certain types of growth are dormant during some periods of maturity and active at others. Throughout all periods, however, normal development is harmonious and characteristically individualistic.[8]

Motor growth is one of the many marked characteristics of the child's development. Sampling studies at the Bellevue Medical Center in New York showed that many American school children are "muscularly deficient." Growth, of course, is not merely a matter of increasing muscles, stature, and weight; it involves many complex rhythms and differentiations. A related factor is intelligence.

MENTAL DEVELOPMENT

One of the most important factors in personality is intelligence.

The child's intelligence, even in a higher degree than that of the adult, is a dynamic, and not a static phenomenon; it cannot be separated from its relationship to the child's emotional world and to his environmental pattern. . . . The child's intelligence is in a *statu nascendi*, a state of development. His intelligence

[7] Hurlock, *op. cit.*, p. 56.
[8] Cecil V. Millard, *Child Growth and Development in the Elementary School Years*, p. 61, Heath, 1951.

cannot be considered from a fixed level but only as a part of the dynamic process related to the search for his self.[9]

Each pupil differs from the other in mental as well as physical characteristics. Some of these differences are discussed later under Mentally Exceptional Pupils. Obviously the mental growth of the pupil is one of the major concerns of the school.

SOCIAL DEVELOPMENT

A child is born into a world teeming with human beings. "His social development begins with his family: the first social relationships the child experiences are those with father, mother, and siblings. Psychoanalysis emphasizes that the child's position to father and mother becomes one of the most determining factors in his later life." [10] Gradually and slowly his social relationships expand, especially when he enters school. The school is a great social arena. Many modern studies on socialization in the classroom agree on two main ideas: that the group climate in the classroom is the most important factor in the child's socialization at school, and that the teacher is the principal agent in establishing this climate.[11] Observation of a pupil's play periods and the preparation of a sociogram are two of many means for measuring social growth.

SPIRITUAL GROWTH

Ethical, moral, and spiritual development is a continuous process:

The child at a very early age begins the behavior sequences which continue through his life. This idea negates the thought that morals and ideals can be developed only when a child is mature enough to rationalize and distinguish between right from wrong. Concepts regarding moral and ethical behavior continue from early childhood throughout life.[12]

Horace Mann in his "Letter to School Children" stressed the importance of moral and religious growth. All-round development of the individual, as indicated in the concluding chapter of Wiggam's *The Marks of an Educated Man,* includes spiritual growth. A weakness of American public education is that it has avoided, neglected, or slighted the spiritual nature of the child.

America, which was founded by God-fearing people, needs to reaccent the spiritual. The Educational Policies Commission states:

[9] Werner Wolff, *The Personality of the Preschool Child,* pp. 194–195, Grune & Stratton, 1949.

[10] *Ibid.,* p. 49.

[11] Arthur W. Foshay and John Hawkes Green, "The Development of Social Processes," *Review of Educational Research,* April, 1953, p. 146.

[12] Millard, *op. cit.,* p. 362.

The development of moral and spiritual values is basic to all other educational objectives. Education uninspired by moral and spiritual values is direction-less. . . . In every aspect of education, the need for guidance in terms of moral and spiritual values is clear. . . . If the individual personality is supreme, each person should be offered the emotional and spiritual experiences which transcend the materialistic aspects of life.[13]

The home, the school, and the church should share in the moral and spiritual development of the young. A comprehensive policy relating religious education to the schools is generally lacking, except in parochial schools and colleges which seek to link mental and spiritual development. Although public education will never return to the extreme emphasis on religious education, especially the narrow sectarian type so prevalent in the early colonial days, it will, in the future, strive to develop a spiritual emphasis in its program for balanced, well-rounded growth in every direction, for both the typical and atypical pupil.

OTHER CHARACTERISTICS

Emotional Behavior. The term "emotion," which comes from the Latin word *emovere,* "to move out," describes a condition of excited feeling.

The child brings with him into the world at least the disposition to some basic emotion. Watson distinguished three, namely, fear, rage, and love. However, recent research has not substantiated a theory assuming any number of basic emotions. While the child at birth seems only to manifest one undifferentiated emotion of general excitement, the emotions differentiate during his growth. . . . The emotional patterns grow further with the child's growth. . . . Emotions are not only a product of learning through experiences from without, but also a product of maturation, i.e., an unfolding of given potentialities.[14]

The child's entire life is colored by emotions, the role of which is much more involved and complex than his physical growth. Emotions are so personal and so internal that they are hard to understand. They markedly influence conduct. Teachers and parents therefore seek to identify not merely the overt types of emotional behavior, but also the indirect symptoms of emotional stress and strain. The Detroit Citizenship Project indicates that emotional adjustment of pupils plays a great part in determining the nature and kind of citizenship qualities they exhibit.

Several of the references previously cited describe the growth and development of the so-called "normal" pupils.[15] The remainder of this unit is devoted to a discussion of exceptional pupils.

13 Educational Policies Commission, *Moral and Spiritual Values in the Public Schools,* pp. 6, 7, 29, National Education Association, 1951.

14 Wolff, *op. cit.,* p. 34.

15 Parents especially are urged to read *These Well-adjusted Children,* by Grace Langdon and Irving W. Stout, John Day, 1951, 245 pp.

PHYSICALLY HANDICAPPED PUPILS

Atypical or exceptional pupils are found everywhere. According to the White House Conference on Child Health and Protection, "The term exceptional children includes both the handicapped and gifted, or children who deviate from the average child to such an extent as to require special treatment or training in order to make the most of their possibilities." Several million children of school age in the United States are handicapped in ways that demand educational facilities in addition to those provided for normal children. The four major groups of exceptional children described in this unit are the physically handicapped, the mentally exceptional, the socially atypical, and miscellaneous types.

Five major types of physically handicapped pupils, plus the mentally maladjusted and an omnibus classification for others, are described here. The percentage of incidence of physical disability, based upon age groups from five to nineteen years, is the figure suggested by Elise H. Martens of the United States Office of Education as a general guide:

Type of physical handicap	Percentage
Visually handicapped	0.2
Crippled	1.0
Deaf and hard of hearing	1.5
Handicapped in speech	1.0–2.0
Delicate children	1.5

Many pupils are handicapped permanently or temporarily in such a way that they do not come under the common classifications. Some have combinations of several disabilities.

Visually Handicapped

Identification of Visually Handicapped. If a person with normal vision were enjoying a television program, and then the pictures were completely eliminated or badly distorted, he would realize the handicap of a blind or partially seeing individual, respectively. The blind recognize their defect, but the partially seeing often fumble in semidarkness without realizing their difficulty. To supplement the detective work of the medical profession, the alert teacher is always on the lookout for any physical disadvantage which the pupils in her classroom may manifest, especially defective vision. Among the symptoms are these: frequent mistakes with words or figures; inability to study without eye discomfort; complaint of headaches; peculiar head positions, as in the case of cross-eye or strabismus; bodily tension; squinting or frowning; stumbling or falling; losing place on the printed page; ability to see objects at a distance more clearly than those at close range; inability to see objects at a distance, such as words on a blackboard; inability to distinguish colors; redness and swelling of the lids; congestion of the vessels of the eyeball; discharge of tears or pus from the eye; and inability to pass a satisfactory test with an eye chart.

The typical screening test for locating those pupils who should be sent to an ophthalmologist for thorough eye examination is the Snellen letter chart or the symbol E chart, the latter being used with young and foreign children who cannot read. This test given both with and without glasses helps to identify cases of lowered visual acuity. The Snellen test, however, does not identify heterophoria, or small amounts of muscular imbalance in the external muscles of the eye. A newer chart, based largely on the research of Dr. Charles F. Shephard, uses Arabic numerals instead of the miscellaneous letters and symbols of the Snellen chart. Furthermore, it takes into account many distinct skills involved in visual recognition, including light perception, resolving power, line perception, and shape perception. It is designed to test meaningful vision rather than mere visual acuity. The test is given at various distances. On the test the average person achieves a score of 1, comparable to 20/20 fraction on the Snellen chart. For identifying some eye troubles the Betts or Eames test is helpful. A skilled oculist can detect and help correct muscular impairment and many other afflictions.

Teachers and other nonmedical examiners perform a genuine service in locating by observation and preliminary examination cases that require special attention. But the teacher, administrator, and parent must remember that in no case should a test made by an examiner other than a specialist be considered final. Any symptoms of defects discovered by the teacher should be reported for further examination, diagnosis, and remedial treatment by an expert. Many schools employ the services of an ophthalmologist, oculist, or doctor who makes examinations or to whom suspicious cases are referred for decision. (While the ophthalomologist or the oculist is an M.D., the optometrist is a nonmedical practitioner who is skilled in measuring vision, and the optician is trained to make and supply glasses and optical instruments.) If these services are not available, the school should advise the parents to obtain the necessary assistance.

Provisions for Visually Handicapped. Medical treatment obviously is the first provision. In a few cases this may even involve a corneal graft from an eye bank. The educational treatment of blind and partially seeing pupils varies according to the degree of visual acuity. The degrees are: the blind, the partially seeing, and those with eye difficulties that can be corrected readily with glasses.[16] The last group is not usually considered visually handicapped. In the other two groups combined each classroom has statistically at least one pupil.

[16] Romaine Mackey, *Education of Visually Handicapped Children*, pp. 5–6, GPO, 1951.

For the blind the tactile method, usually the Braille system of raised dots, is employed to supplement the auditory sense. Six raised dots are six high spots in the mitigation of human blindness. These six colorless dots arranged in two upright rows three high, as on the domino six—embossed in a space a fourth the size of the index fingernail and used under that finger—mean to sightless people the world over the difference between illiteracy and education, frequently the contrast between being parasites and useful, happy people. These magic dots constitute the basic Braille

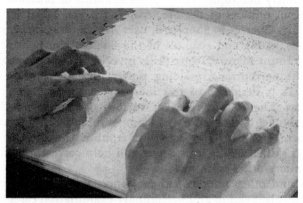

Fig. 10-4. Reading Braille. To many sightless people throughout the world, six raised dots liquidate illiteracy. Under the auspices of UNESCO a World Braille Council is assisting in the promotion of greater use and uniformity throughout the world. Braille is becoming the "light bearer to a world of darkness." The majority of the Braille users read with one hand, using the other chiefly as a guide. (*Courtesy of American Foundation for the Blind.*)

"cell," worked out in 1829 by Louis Braille, a twenty-year-old blind teacher in the Paris Institution for the Young Blind. This "Prometheus of the blind" opened the way for the enlightenment and expression of such brilliant minds as that of Helen Keller and hundreds of others, through silent unassisted reading. In 1952 at the Sorbonne, Paris, in connection with the 100th anniversary of the death of Braille, Helen Keller said that the blind are as indebted to Braille as mankind is to Gutenberg for the invention of the movable type. The blind Braille's vision spanned centuries and continents.

The collection of Braille books for the blind at the Library of Congress numbers many thousands in all the main branches of knowledge. Many libraries, public and state, serve as depositories from which books are sent to readers in all parts of the country without charge, even free of postage. The American Printing House for the Blind at Louisville, Kentucky, which is subsidized by the federal government, produces a great variety of books, textbooks, special supplies, and equipment for the

Fig. 10-5. A blind girl feels and studies a relief map (top). The circular slide rule (center) aids the blind in doing multiplication, division, and in taking roots. Pressed in plastic, a logarithmic C scale is embossed around the outer edge, with large arabic numbers. The pointers are of plastic. The student's left hand "reads" an algebraic problem, while his right hand works it out on a Braille graph (bottom). (*Courtesy of Acme and American Foundation for the Blind.*)

303

blind. For classroom use, a small steel punch (stylus) and a Braille slate enable blind students to take notes. Used increasingly are the Braille typewriters, operated by the touch method, arithmetic slates and cubes, sand tables, handcraft materials, and musical instruments. The Braille classroom is usually treated acoustically. Its standard of lighting is similar to that in the sight-saving room, described later.

Perhaps not more than one-fourth of the blind people in the United States make any practical use of books in Braille, since reading by touch is a slow and fatiguing method. Furthermore, many have lost their sight at an advanced age which makes it difficult for them to learn the art of reading by touch, particularly if manual labor has lessened the sensitivity of the fingers. For these persons a great boon is the "talking book," of which several hundred volumes are circulated annually. The talking book consists of voice transcriptions of written material recorded on large phonograph disks, each of which will play many pages. The electrical talking-book machine is a combination phonograph and radio set contained in a single unit so that it may be carried with ease. The machines and records, made under the auspices of the American Foundation for the Blind, are sold at cost. The talking books service at the Library of Congress began with the distribution of records in October, 1934, and included modern popular fiction, Shakespeare, parts of the Bible, poetry, and patriotic documents. Since then many new and appealing titles have been added. The disks provided by the Library of Congress under federal appropriations are also available at the distributing libraries scattered over the United States. The periodical, *Talking Topics,* contains reviews of talking books.

Another interesting development has been "The Seeing Eye." In 1923 on her estate in Switzerland, Dorothy Harrison Custis, a relative of Martha Washington, began breeding and training German shepherd dogs to patrol the Swiss borders for customs service. Mrs. Custis and others, including geneticist Humphrey, were impressed by the teachability of these sturdy dogs. In an article for *The Saturday Evening Post* in 1928, Mrs. Custis mentioned the fact that German shepherd dogs were guiding German soldiers blinded in the World War. Morris Frank, a young blind man in Nashville, Tennessee, became interested in the project, sent for one of the dogs, and found a pair of shining, intelligent eyes to replace his own darkened ones. Not long after, the Seeing Eye School was started in Nashville, Tennessee, and later was moved to Morristown, New Jersey, where under skilled instructors the dog is taught his lesson, the blind person learns his, including the fundamentals of dog psychology, and then they are taught together. Many a blind student is led to his college classes by his "seeing eye" or "leader" dog—a real instrument in human rehabilitation.

In some states, starting with New York in 1907, blind college students are provided at public expense with persons who read aloud to them the course assignments. The blind usually have a well-developed auditory sense and powers of retention. The American Foundation for the Blind gives annually several scholarships for sightless students. The G.I. bills give many blind veterans financial assistance in their schooling. A blind person and his companion may now travel on most railway and bus lines for the price of only one fare if his financial status does not permit the payment of two fares. Under the Federal Security Act needy blind persons of all ages are eligible for financial aid. The Randolph-Sheppard Act allows blind persons to operate concession stands in federal buildings.

The organized education of the blind in the United States, which commenced in the decade from 1830 to 1840, has reached the point where every state now makes provision for them either in a school within its own boundaries or in a neighboring state. The residential schools for the blind enroll a number of pupils in the low-vision group as well as totally blind children.

Sight-saving classes originated in Europe in 1908. The first two public day-school classes for partially seeing children in the United States were opened in Cleveland, Ohio, and Boston, Massachusetts, in 1913. Now several hundred such classes are well established in the United States, but the program is still far from adequate. A sight-saving class is one for pupils whose eyes do not permit them to do the work of the regular grades, either because their sight will be further impaired by such study or because their vision is too low to assure their progress in school by the usual methods and equipment. Candidates for sight-saving classes are those whose vision ranges from 20/70 to 20/200 by the Snellen chart—the latter representing 90 per cent loss of vision.

The sight-saving classes are located in special rooms. The United States Office of Education makes the following recommendations regarding rooms and equipment:

A standard of 50 foot-candles of light correctly diffused and distributed is recommended for sight-saving classrooms. The ceiling should be white, the walls of light tints, the woodwork of dull finish and light in color. A light-colored, dull-finished floor will also improve the seeing conditions. . . . A pair of buff or light gray translucent shades should be attached at the center of each window, one shade pulling up, the other down. . . . Light gray-green is recommended color for the chalk boards. Bulletin boards should be light in color or covered with light paper. Pictures should be large and have little detail. To eliminate a source of glare, glass should be removed from framed pictures.

Equipment and materials should be selected to help children secure their education with the least amount of eyestrain. All the furniture should be light in color and have dull finish. . . . Most sight-saving classes have typewriters with large type, other mechanical devices such as dictaphones and wire recorders, books in large print, a dictionary in large type, colored outline maps, paper with dull finish and buff color for pupils to use, pencils with soft, thick lead, and chalk which is large and soft.[17]

Often one finds in these classroom model buildings, projection magnifiers, pet animals, radios, and other inert and live materials.

Visiting teachers often supplement the regular classroom work. Interdistrict arrangements make special schooling available for youngsters in small districts, but the majority of partially seeing pupils depend largely on the regular teacher in the usual classroom. Sight-saving instruction has been increased to include pre-elementary children and the parents of children with sight handicaps.

The work of the schools with the visually handicapped is reinforced by that of many other agencies, including such national organizations as the American Foundation for the Blind, the American Printing House for the Blind, and the National Society for the Prevention of Blindness.

CRIPPLED PUPILS

Identification of Crippled. Whatever the defect, all crippled children should be enumerated through the official agencies operating under the laws of the local, state, and federal governments. The classroom teacher can bring cases to the attention of the local school nurse or physician. County and state health authorities are always eager to cooperate in helping those who are afflicted physically. The state and federal rehabilitation services and some phases of the Social Security program are also available for the older persons, many of whom are placed in gainful occupations through cooperative efforts on the part of the schools and all concerned. Many organizations, such as luncheon clubs, seek to locate and help children who are crippled or otherwise handicapped.

In connection with identification, it is necessary to give serious thought to the causes of orthopedic defects. The major causes are poliomyelitis or infantile paralysis, which produces the destruction of nerve tissue with the resultant flaccid type of paralysis; spastic paralysis, which is caused by some defect in the brain center, congenital or acquired at birth; brain injury, which is often caused by accidents; rheumatic fever, childhood's greatest enemy, which is due to infection of the heart valves; tuberculosis, which often involves the bones and joints; and other congenital or acquired deformities, which may come before, at, or after birth. The major cause is poliomyelitis (infantile paralysis). The constant care of and remedial measures for victims of this motor paralysis, which strikes the rich and poor, must be supplemented by efforts at its prevention. Helping the postpoliomyelitic victims is necessary and commendable, but preventive,

[17] *Ibid.,* pp. 8–9.

not just palliative, procedures are imperative. Education of the public as to the nature of the disease, its prevention, and its manner of spread is needed. Environmental sanitation is an important factor. Isolation of the patient, early intelligent treatment in order to prevent permanent paralysis, and adequate medical and surgical care from the outset are of prime consequence.

Provisions for Crippled Pupils. Safety education is a vital part of the school curriculum. The preventive program calls attention to ways in which pupils may be injured when riding on school busses and suggests ways of preventing such accidents.

Transportation of crippled pupils to and from school is provided free in many school systems, either by means of busses, taxis, or other arrangements. In some cities an attendant helps the bus driver and children. In a one-teacher school a crippled pupil may be transported by the teacher, parents, or other adults. In some instances rural children are boarded in near-by cities where special classes are maintained. Recent programs of state aid are recognizing the need for paying transportation and boarding costs of all children who need these services. States also reimburse local school systems over and above the cost of educating a normal child, if special instruction is given.

Although many crippled children need no special educational treatment, there are several thousand who do and for whom no opportunities are provided. Great is the tragedy of isolated bedridden crippled children who do not have a chance to learn. Instruction is usually given in the home, the hospital, or the school, either local or state. In home and hospital teaching the regular classroom instructor or the visiting teacher helps at the bedside or chair of the crippled child. The seriously handicapped often find it difficult to attend school, especially during bad weather.

Formal school for cripples is a twentieth-century development. The first public-school class for crippled children was organized in England in 1899; the second was in Chicago in 1900; and the first state school was established in Massachusetts in 1904.

At school the crippled pupil is helped to forget his handicap. As much as possible he should be placed in an environment filled with wholesome fellowship and given an opportunity to participate in group experiences.[18] Active membership in clubs and organizations is encouraged. There was a time when all the crippled children were excused from physical-education classes; today no child is forgotten during physical-education or recreation periods. Play therapy is accented. If the child is also a cardiac case, he rests on a cot. Under the direction of a doctor, nurse, or physiotherapist the paralytic pupil may take exercises or receive

[18] Karl C. Garrison, *The Psychology of Exceptional Children,* p. 365, Ronald, 1950.

treatment under a health-giving lamp or in the heated swimming pool. Tanks and pools facilitate muscular treatments, since the water reduces the weight of the body and often calls into play dormant or withered muscles. Besides victims of poliomyelitis, the spastics and the pupils with congenital club feet and other deformities resulting from infections and injuries receive warm-water treatment.

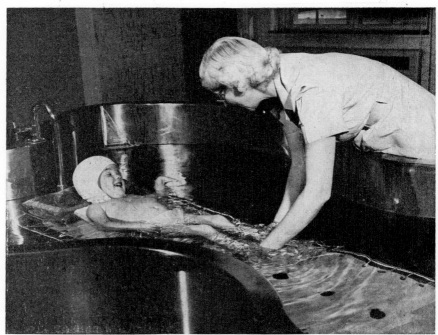

FIG. 10-6. Hubbard tank in use. In this tank, which is equipped with electric agitators and filled with warm water, the skilled physiotherapist gives treatments in postpolio cases. (*Courtesy of Nelson Smith, Doris Robie, and Illinois State Normal University.*)

Most school systems do not have a separate classroom for crippled pupils. Several schools, however, may cooperate to provide a special room for this purpose. This room should be located on the first floor with an approach by ramp in order that the wheel chairs may be rolled in conveniently. Adjustable seats are advisable. All facilities should be at hand so that the child need not leave the room during the day.

Buildings constructed especially for crippled pupils are usually fire resistive and one story high or equipped with elevators or ramps connecting floors. In some, luncheon is served in the regular classroom or in an easily accessible lunchroom. The teachers are specially trained for their work and often are provided with helpers. For pupils who come late or for a few days a week the teacher seeks to adjust the work and to provide adequate individual help. Often the school day is shortened for pupils who tire easily.

Cincinnati has night schools, and Detroit and many other systems hold summer sessions for crippled children. An outstanding school for crippled and other handicapped children is the Spalding School in Chicago. The

FIG. 10-7. Students sketch and paint at "Sunny View" Eastern New York Orthopedic Hospital School. The easels and lapboards are scaled to the needs of the user, and clear floor space accommodates wheel chairs and beds. These physically afflicted artists may recall that the celebrated French painter Renoir, although crippled with arthitis, completed "Misia and the Muses" with a brush attached to his hand with a rubber band. (*Courtesy of American Foundation for Infantile Paralysis.*)

Chicago Board of Education operates it, other elementary schools, and some high-school branches for the benefit of several thousand crippled children ranging in age from twenty-one months (Sunbeam League Nursery School at Spalding) to twenty-one years or high-school graduation. A boarding school for child victims of spastic paralysis has been organized in Chicago. Despite wheel chairs, crutches, and braces many of these children forget their handicaps.

Among the major problems in educating crippled children are transportation, since the children must be carried to and from the school; type of equipment, since many pupils need special desks, cots, and other furniture; curriculum, which may differ from the typical one since the cripple's vocational area is limited and he often needs activities of a special nature; follow-up work, which is usually neglected; and costs, since the instruction of crippled children calls for larger per-pupil expenditures. The extra cost, however, is a profitable investment that reaps dividends for the crippled as he becomes a self-confident, economically efficient member of society. The National Society for Crippled Children and Adults is sponsoring a program of federal aid to match state aid, similar to the present rehabilitation program, in order to secure bedside teaching or transportation of crippled pupils to special schools.

DEAF AND HARD OF HEARING

Identification of Deaf and Hard of Hearing. If one were again enjoying a television program, and this time the sound were eliminated or badly

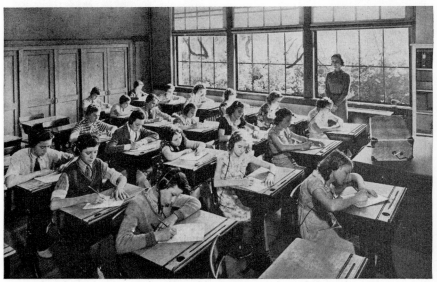

FIG. 10-8. The quickest and surest way to test the hearing of a group of children. By means of a portable audiometer the teacher can test the hearing of as many as 40 pupils at one time. In a few minutes one obtains written records of each pupil's exact degree of loss of hearing—with left and right ears tested separately. (*Courtesy of Audi-vox.*)

distorted, he would realize temporarily the handicap of a deaf or hard-of-hearing person. The acoustically handicapped are grouped into two major classes, distinguished by the type of instruction needed. They are the deaf and the hard-of-hearing. The ratio of the hard-of-hearing to the deaf is 100 to 1.

Naturally there are graduations in hearing loss. For example, in Chicago, which was one of the first cities to provide for the oral instruction of the acoustically handicapped in public day schools, the high-school students are classified in four groups according to their educational needs: the deaf individuals whose handicap dates from birth or infancy, the deafened individuals, the severely hard-of-hearing, and the moderately hard-of-hearing.[19]

Since defective hearing is less detectable than faulty eyesight, identification of the former is neglected more frequently than the latter.

The teacher should suspect a pupil has difficulty in hearing if he observes one or more of the following: failure to respond to calling of a name, cocking of the head to one side, failure to follow directions, looking in a direction other than the source of sound, watching others and following their movements, frequent requests for repetition of a word or phrase, faulty pronunciation of common words, speaking with an unusual sounding voice, inattention, restlessness, aggressiveness, apathy, earache, discharge from the ear and persistent mouth breathing.[20]

It was not until 1935 that New York passed the first state compulsory law for hearing testing, although the first legislation requiring vision testing was passed almost thirty-five years earlier by Connecticut. Deaf or partially hearing pupils may be detected through alert observation or by means of the (1) watch-tick or tuning-fork test, (2) whisper test, (3) audiometer test, or (4) complete otological examination by a competent physician.

The watch-tick, tuning-fork, and whisper tests are generally conceded as unreliable. The easiest and surest way of identifying pupils with impaired hearing in one or both ears is through the use of the audiometer. Four to five hundred children may be examined in a day in groups up to 40 each by means of the audiometer, which consists of a portable phonograph with several attached phones. The children wear these head telephone receiving sets and write on specially prepared ruled paper the numbers spoken by the phonograph in gradually decreasing degrees of intensity. Then may follow a more accurate examination with a vacuum-tube type of individual audiometer, which tests many sound frequencies at controlled intensities. By means of this mechanical aid one can determine in decibels the amount of the hearing loss for many pure tones. Tests with audiometers and other approved scientific devices should be made periodically.

For large school systems or consolidated areas, Josephine B. Timberlake, editor of the *Volta Review*, recommends the establishment of a hearing conservation clinic with an otologist in charge, assisted by a nurse and clerk, and equipped with a soundproof room, modern testing equip-

---

[19] Fred M. Manz and Elberta E. Pruitt, "Phases of Deaf-oral Education," *Chicago Schools Journal*, March–April, 1951, p. 145.

[20] Charles C. Wilson (ed.) *School Health Services*, p. 90, National Education Association and American Medical Association, 1953.

ment, and such instruments for diagnosis and simple treatment as may be needed.

Progressive deafness comes on so gradually and so insidiously that it frequently escapes notice until it is too severe to be corrected. Since nearly all instances of deafness in adults are traceable to the first 10 years

Fig. 10-9. Teacher explains the results of individual hearing test to pupil and parent. In addition to screening tests for groups, it is desirable to give individual pure-tone audiometer tests of the type administered by physicians. The Minnesota Society for Crippled Children and Adults, in cooperation with the University of Minnesota, has a mobile speech clinic in the field to test the hearing and speech of children. (*Courtesy of Minnesota Society for Crippled Children and Adults.*)

of life in the so-called "delicate age," periodic checks and adequate medical care for young children are all-important. Chief among the numerous causes of deafness are diseases and accidents. Among the former are running ears; enlarged and diseased tonsils and adenoids; bad teeth and malnutrition, which make it easy to contract diseases; severe colds, infections, and diseases, some of which are accompanied by dangerous inflammation of the middle ear. Among the accidental causes are automobile collisions, especially those producing a fractured skull; hard boxes on the ears; and things placed in the ear. One of the simplest causes of hearing impairment is hardened impacted wax in the ears. A complicating cause may be the Rh factor in the red blood cells.

After detection the next steps are to induce the pupil and his parents to take advantage of corrective physical treatment. Antibiotics, such as penicillin, and radium therapy have cleared up many infections. Fenestration operations which "open the window of the ear" often let in more sound. Many modern miracles are wrought by medical men. The teacher works less dramatically as he adjusts the details of educational training to the degree of hearing loss.

Provisions for Deaf and Hard of Hearing. The earliest known teacher of the deaf was Pedro Ponce de Leon, a Spanish monk of the Order of St. Benedict, who lived in the sixteenth century. The first real work with the deaf began in America in 1814–1815 when Thomas Hopkins Gallaudet became interested in the "deaf and dumb" child of a neighbor, and as a result went abroad to study the teaching of the deaf. Upon his return in 1816 he started a school at Hartford, Connecticut. In 1857 the Columbia Institution at Washington was incorporated, and 7 years later the National Deaf Mute College, later renamed after Mr. Gallaudet, was opened as the only institution of higher learning for the deaf in the United States. The education or reeducation of deaf and hard-of-hearing children is conducted in private and public institutions, the latter including local schools and state residential institutions. Boston was the first city to educate its deaf when in 1869 it established a school named after Horace Mann, who helped to introduce the oral method from Europe. The first state institution was established in Connecticut in 1817.

In the early history of deaf education, only writing and the so-called "manual" or sign language produced by the hands were used. More modern procedures involve the communication of ideas by means of speech and lip reading, as well as the sense of vibration through tactile experience. Oral methods are generally employed in public schools. The majority of the state schools use the oral and the manual method or manual alphabet. Those skilled in lip or speech reading add to what they hear that which they see in the movement of the speaker's lips and facial expression, and thus they are able to hold effective conversation. Speech or lip reading, however, is not a 100 per cent adjunct to a deafened ear. Many persons must also have a hearing device of some kind.

Children with residual hearing are usually given auricular training by means of mechanical aids, such as the radio ear, an instrument that magnifies the human voice so that the pupils can hear the words of the teacher. Every desk is equipped with a headphone and a rheostat so that each pupil can adjust the intensity to his own need. In addition there are, primarily for adults, the individual mechanical hearing aids, the effective use of which requires persistent practice. With more than a hundred different hearing devices on the market to select from, no hard-of-hearing person should buy one until he is quite sure it suits his type of deafness. A small mechanical hearing aid may bring large returns in social as well as vocational life.

The military forces have developed very effective programs for the rehabilitation of fighting men injured acoustically in service. Deaf and hard-of-hearing persons have the ability to make adjustments to a wide variety of employment situations. In some jobs deafness may even be a valuable asset in that the worker is not disturbed by outside influences and monotonous machine noises. Despite the handicap of being deaf, many persons have risen to renown. It is said that Beethoven never heard a note of his great work, the Ninth Symphony. Helen Keller and others have incontrovertibly demonstrated that the deaf can learn to "hear" and speak.

HANDICAPPED IN SPEECH

Identification of Speech Disabilities. A basic guarantee in American democracy gives to all persons the inalienable right of free speech. This should include those oft-forgotten persons who cannot talk freely because of speech defects. This handicap has been defined as any acoustic variation from an accepted speech standard so extreme as to be conspicuous in the speaker, confusing to the listener, or unpleasant to either or both. Among these defects are: stammering and stuttering, lisping, lalling, cluttering, nasality, thick speech, baby talk, hoarseness, foreign accent, and defects caused by organic difficulties.

Owing to the complex physiological and psychological processes involved in talking, many undesirable personality traits may accompany poor speech. An enfeeblement of the general health or extreme nervous excitement may aggravate the condition of a confirmed stammerer. Because of speech defects a child may not display his normal ability and may thus be rated falsely as low in mentality. Hence teachers should seek to identify pupils with speech difficulties and to understand the major causes of the trouble. The chief causal factors are anatomical handicaps, mental shortcomings, educational backwardness, lack of motivation, diseases, injuries, and environmental handicaps. Examples of these disabilities respectively are cleft palate, low I.Q., defective learning, lack of interest, cerebral palsy, broken nose, and foreign accent. All speech defects can be classified roughly under one or more of four types: phonatory, or voice defects; articulatory, or pronunciation and enunciation defects; linguistic, or language defects; and weaknesses in speech rhythm.[21]

The classroom teacher through her daily contacts with the pupils is the usual avenue for locating speech defectives. Many a teacher with a trained alert ear and a knowledge of the symptoms of major speech irregularities detects pupils who need help. Some schools employ speech

[21] Virgil A. Anderson, *Improving the Child's Speech*, p. 39, Oxford, 1953.

specialists who make periodic surveys of all children. The auditorium teacher in platoon schools, the teacher of reading and English, the foreign-language teacher, the visiting teacher in the home, the nurse or doctor, the speech specialists at clinics conducted by universities—these and others, particularly the parents, can help identify pupils with minor or major speech difficulties.

A simple survey method of locating speech disorders is the oral interview. Many schools employ mechanical testing aids, such as speaking over a public address system or recording the voice on a disk which later can be used in remedial work and for a record of progress.

Provisions for the Handicapped in Speech. Interest in speech correction in America, which stems from the first school to be organized in Europe at Potsdam, Germany, in 1887, was nourished for several years by the American Medical Association. The establishment of classes, clinics, and corrective work in public schools in America is a twentieth-century accomplishment, the first public-school class dating back to that founded in New York City in 1908.

A very common but fallacious observation is that a child will outgrow a speech defect. Fortunately it is true that no group of physically handicapped children can be helped more completely than those having speech defects. Since the causes of defective speech are so varied, the corrective work reaches across many departments of school and living. The treatment may include diaphragmatic breathing and relaxation exercises, speech drills, remedial reading, special work in English, and conversational exercises, in school, in the clinic, and at home. Many social and medical agencies cooperate in supplying the skilled assistance of such personnel as an oral surgeon, a specialist in the eye, ear, nose, or throat, a nurse, a psychiatrist, a dietitian, a social worker, and a vocational-guidance expert. According to many case studies, pupils of antisocial habits have improved their personalities as a result of corrective treatment in speech. To effect such changes, the pupil must be more than a passive participant in the process; he must have the will to improve, plus courage, patience, and perseverance.

Lisping tends to cure itself, but other defects are more deep-seated and complex in origin. These require the attention of the specialists mentioned. In some instances a surgical operation, such as the removal of hypertrophied tonsils, has produced a marked improvement. Orthodontia helps markedly in improving speech through proper alignment of poorly placed or irregular teeth. Miracle drugs often reduce allergies and thus decrease nasality in voice. Listening to his own voice recorded on a phonographic disk or wire aids the pupil in perfecting his pronunciation. The mirror technique for seeing speech is also helpful. Visual and auditory stimulation may be supplemented by motokinesthetic training which stimulates the correct pattern through touch, so successfully used by reading instructors like Stella Center. Since the general health affects the voice, physical examinations and health-building activities play important roles. Ability to relax mentally and physically is a great aid to fluent speech. Role playing and drama work give impetus to speech correction. Habits of independence and self-confidence are also assets. The voice

FIG. 10-10. Teacher and pupil as he views himself while speaking words in lip-reading instruction. (*Courtesy of Public Schools of Cincinnati, Ohio.*)

quality of handicapped and normal children may be made more pleasing and effective by their activities in creative speech classes and choral speaking.

Today speech is an important part of teacher education. The improvement of one's own enunciation and the development of clear articulation devolve upon every classroom teacher. Shakespeare wrote in *Hamlet,* "Speak the speech, I pray you, as I pronounced it to you, trippingly on the tongue: but if you mouth it, as many of your players do, I had as lief the town-crier spoke my lines. . . ." Many teachers without a serious speech defect may have lip laziness so marked and articulation so blurred that the listening pupils whisper, "What did she say?" or "What is the assignment she made?" Attention by the teacher to her own speech will help decidedly to improve the imitated utterances of the pupils.

A neglected means for overcoming hesitancy in speech is the development of a copious vocabulary. A person poverty stricken in words frequently is halting in speech. To this end all teachers should seek to develop in themselves and in their pupils an extensive vocabulary. A dictionary for each pupil is an investment in speech education and communication.

The human values of speech reeducation cannot be overemphasized. People are prone to make allowances for the blind, the deaf, and the crippled in limb, but not for those crippled in speech. A child may actually be punished for reciting. Even though he knows his lesson, a stammering pupil is often a source of merriment to his comrades, a torment to himself, and an object of sympathy to his teacher. The child with defective utterance may take heart from accomplishments of distinguished historic personages like Aesop, Demosthenes, Aristotle, Cato, Virgil, Erasmus, Boyle, Priestley, Lamb, and Charles Darwin. A more modern example is the late King George VI of England, who gave to Lionel Logue, an Austrian speech expert, membership in the Royal Victorian Order as a reward for personal services in teaching him to overcome a stammer. An interesting organization in the United States for youth and adults is the exclusive Kingsley Club, which is restricted to stammerers, many of whom have become ex-stammerers through systematic treatment and exercises.

DELICATE CHILDREN

Identification of Delicate Pupils. This group includes a wide variety of lowered-vitality children who because of weakening conditions are not able to keep pace physically with normal children in their daily school life. Among these are the malnourished, the undervitalized, the nervously unstable, and those suffering from cardiac, tubercular, and other defects. Children differ widely in energy and physical strength. The malnourished child is usually identified by the teacher, nurse, or doctor through observation and the daily health inspection. Although some children are naturally small, underweight is due often to infection, faulty food habits, or incorrect diet. Malnutrition is a matter of diet, either quantitative or qualitative. The child may not be receiving a sufficient quantity of food; therefore he is undernourished and does not do effective schoolwork. This group increased decidedly during the depression, postdepression, and war periods. On the other hand a child may be receiving the proper quantity of food but not the right quality. He may be having an unbalanced diet with overemphasis upon carbohydrates and insufficient emphasis upon other elements, such as iodine, protein, fats, minerals, and water. All these are needed to maintain body balance.

A delicate child may be one who has a nervous disease. The nervous system is important in every period of human development. From the simple reflex activities of the infant to the highly integrated reactions of the adult, physical or mental stresses and strains may cause excessive nervousness. The diagnosis, prognosis, and treatment for nervous diseases should be assigned to an expert, although the teacher can help identify these maladies by a functional knowledge of the anatomy and physiology of the nervous system.

The teacher should refer to doctors suspected cases of heart trouble, anemia, and tuberculosis. The most common signs of heart weakness are shortness of breath, cold extremities, and blue lips. Anemic pupils are often identified by absence of healthy color in face and lips. If a child tires readily, sleeps in class, has a persistent cough, and fails to participate in the normal activities, the teacher should refer him to a doctor for tuberculin and X-ray examinations. Periodic physical examinations often reveal incipient tuberculosis.

Provisions for Delicate Children. Outstanding among the provisions for delicate children is the supplying of adequate individual care within the school. The undervitalized pupil is given a school day and program commensurate with his physical ability. Delicate children who are the victims of too much irregularity in the home routine develop regularity. Those with a digestion span requiring food midmorning and midafternoon benefit from eating food and drinking a half pint of milk once or twice daily during school hours. Many school boards have provisions for supplying needy children with food, cod-liver oil, and other essentials. In 1938 the federal government started a program of providing undernourished school children with free lunches. Ten years later, federal aid for the school lunch program was placed on a permanent basis. In large schools the cafeterias are a boon to pupil health. Even in small and rural schools the children should enjoy at least one warm dish for their noon lunch.

In helping tubercular children medical science has accomplished much through preventoriums, sanitariums, and various treatments. Many special rooms or schools have been established for delicate and potentially tubercular children, both abroad and in America. The first "open-air" school was opened in Charlottenburg, a suburb of Berlin, in 1904. The earliest school of this type in the United States was in Providence, Rhode Island, in 1908. As early as 1838 Horace Mann advocated temperature control, ventilation, and a thermometer in each classroom.

A significant treatment for nervousness, debilitation, and other afflictions is the ample use of rest periods during the school day, when the child relaxes completely on a rug or cot. Large windows let in generous amounts of fresh air and sunshine. It is a common criticism that too much emphasis is placed upon instruction within walls. Even with good ventilation in schools, there should be more open-air work for delicate children, who may be dressed in Eskimo suits in the wintertime, and also for the normal pupils. To this end some buildings are erected in such a way that the entire side of a room can be swung open, or the roof can be used for educational activities. Playground space has also been multiplied in order to provide facilities for exercise in the open air. Glass windows in pivotable sections, glass bricks or blocks, and skylights permit more light and sunshine to enter many classrooms.

The physical care of the undervitalized child should not be discontinued during the summer. Many delicate pupils benefit from a vacation on the farm or in the summer camp. The Tappan school of Ann Arbor maintains a camp 200 miles north to which the children go in school busses. The public schools of Baltimore have a day-camp school which the department of education operates for boys whose attitudes and conduct indicate an extreme need for social adjustment.

More adequate health programs are also needed for students in college, according to the health surveys of college students. The problem of student health is one that extends from the kindergarten through graduate work and adult years. It is significant that many men who in infancy or in youthful years were weaklings became phsyically vigorous and internationally known in later years. Among these men were Voltaire, Rousseau, Isaac Newton, Victor Hugo, Napoleon Bonaparte, and Theodore Roosevelt.

OTHERS PHYSICALLY ATYPICAL

Several other less pronounced types of physical difficulties exist. Many pupils have posture defects and minor foot trouble. Some children receive an unfortunate start in their school career because of excessive underweight or overweight due to glandular disturbances or improper diet. A puny boy may be an object of scorn, and an oversized girl may be so embarrassed by her "avoirdupois" that she suffers from social maladjustments and mental conflicts. A survey conducted by the dental profession, in cooperation with the United States Public Health Service, revealed that nine out of ten American school children had one or more decayed teeth, or teeth in the process of decay.

Education and health are intimately tied together. The education of a child may be facilitated through the correction of a physical defect like muscular imbalance of the eyes; likewise, the health of a child may be improved through health education, as in the case of preventing diseases. Nation-wide programs, such as prepared by the American Association for Health, Physical Education, and Recreation, by the American Medical Association, by the American Public Health Association, by the American

Organization for the Rehabilitation through Training, and by the United States Office of Education will help markedly to prevent and correct physical handicaps among children and adults.

MENTALLY EXCEPTIONAL PUPILS

Mental as well as physical ability varies greatly. A standard classification for grouping pupils according to intelligence quotients (the ratio obtained by dividing the mental age by the chronological age) is as follows:

I.Q.	*Classification*
Above 140	Highly gifted
120–140	Moderately gifted
110–120	Superior
90–110	Normal
80–90	Dull
70–80	Borderline
50–70	Mentally retarded
Below 50	Mentally deficient

The growth and development of normal pupils were considered earlier in this unit. Pupils in the other groups are described here under the captions: (1) gifted pupils, and (2) mentally retarded or slow learners.

GIFTED PUPILS

Identification of Gifted Pupils. The Educational Policies Commission, in its report *Education of the Gifted,* defines the term "giftedness" as meaning high general intellectual ability and certain specialized abilities, such as musical, artistic, and mechanical.[22] This same volume designates as "highly gifted" those whose I.Q.'s are above 137, and as "moderately gifted" those whose I.Q.'s fall between 120 and 137. The former include approximately 1 per cent of the total population, while the latter fall within the top 10 per cent but below the highest 1 per cent.[23] These millions of United States citizens are among the nation's richest resources.

It was once assumed that mentally gifted children were anemic, undersized, bespectacled, unsocial, and eccentric. It was thought that their mental gifts were offset by inferiority along nonintellectual lines—"the inferiority of the superior" cliché. These gifted were supposed to come from the homes of professional and highly successful business people. When the pioneering Lewis M. Terman published his classic work *Genetic Study of Genius* in 1925, "child prodigies were in bad repute because of the prevailing belief that they were abnormal and almost sure

[22] Educational Policies Commission, *Education of the Gifted*, p. 37, National Education Association, 1950.
[23] *Ibid.,* p. 43.

to burn themselves out quickly or develop post-adolescent stupidity." His painstaking research and that of Paul Witty and others, however, dispelled these notions and made direct attacks on the prevailing psychology and pedagogy of gifted children. Furthermore, Terman states that "no race or nationality has a monopoly on brains." [24]

Among the characteristics of superior children, as listed in the *Baltimore Bulletin of Education,* are these: *physical*—usually healthier, stronger, larger, and heavier per unit of height than children in unselected group; *mental*—great intellectual curiosity, wide range of interests and information in divergent fields, copious vocabulary, rapid absorption of knowledge, high ability in making generalizations, ready interpretation of meanings, capacity to recognize relationships, and superior methods of work; *social*—enthusiasm for play, leadership in teams and clubs, desire for self-government and possible inclination toward domination; *emotional*—preference to work out their own methods of study, and relatively free from nervous disorders; *ethical*—high level of character development and generally courteous, careful, and kind. Terman warns, however, against the limitations of composite portraiture.

Subjective methods of identifying the bright have given way to scientific and objective measurement by means of intelligence tests and quantitative gauges derived from them, such as intelligence quotient (I.Q.) and mental age (M.A.). Specific knowledge about gifted children dates back to the publication of the Binet-Simon "Measuring Scale of Intelligence" in 1908, which was later revised and improved. Individual tests, such as revisions of the Binet, administered by trained testers, are more reliable than mass methods of identification, although group intelligence tests may serve as a screening device. Daily schoolwork and previous academic record may also form a semiobjective way of identifying bright students, although many average pupils may be overestimated and bright ones overlooked. A child with limited abilities who uses them to the maximum may outrank a brighter one who fails to employ his marked talents. Educational clinics manned by a staff of experts are valuable in the identification of gifted pupils.

Provisions for the Gifted. James Bryant Conant, who served as chairman of the Educational Policies Commission's study of gifted pupils, wrote: "To the extent that we now fail to educate the potential talent of each generation, we are wasting one of the country's greatest assets." [25]

It is indeed a social crime to neglect bright children, for they may be the greatest social asset. From the days of Plato's ideal republic to the

[24] L. M. Terman and M. H. Oden, *The Gifted Child Grows Up*, p. 141, Stanford University Press, 1947.

[25] James Bryant Conant, *Education in a Divided World*, p. 168, Harvard University Press, 1948.

present many proposals and programs have been advanced for the education of youth in terms of their ability. Good teachers of bygone days tried to challenge the bright pupils in their classes, since there was no separate administrative organization for them.

Educational provisions for gifted pupils include: acceleration or grade skipping, groupings in special classes or schools, enrichment of experiences by use of workshops, clubs or library, adaptations in regular classes,

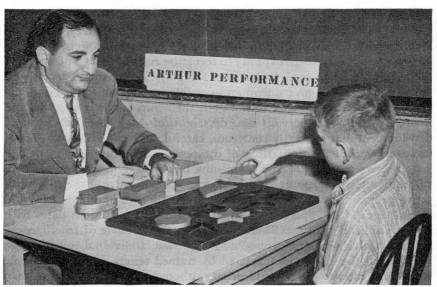

FIG. 10-11. Psychologist administers the Arthur Performance Test at Lincoln State Colony, Lincoln, Illinois. (*Courtesy of Illinois Welfare Bulletin.*)

guidance and use of community resources, and elective courses, especially in high school and college.[26] Among the earlier methods were W. T. Harris's promotion plans at St. Louis, the Cambridge system of varying the years required for completion of certain grades, and the Winnetka plan of meeting individual differences. Probably the first special school for gifted children in the United States was organized in 1905 at Worcester, Massachusetts.

Today provisions for mentally superior children vary all the way from mild adaptations in teaching methods and curriculums for individual students to special schools dedicated to the development of leadership through cultivation of special talents. Of course, bright children must be trained to serve as well as to lead. Just as society has a special responsibility to educate pupils who are gifted, so too these pupils should feel

[26] Educational Policies Commission, *Education of the Gifted,* pp. 49–70.

their unique obligation to render outstanding service to society. In life too frequently it has been assumed that "bright students take care of themselves." This is true in that they seldom become financially dependent upon others; but they do not and cannot take care of themselves in the sense that they make the fullest use of their capabilities. The late Leta S. Hollingworth contended an injustice is done the bright child by not realizing his full potentialities, and that American philanthropy needs a philosophy that pities less the follies of the moron and pities more the deprivations of the gifted girl or boy. Today schools and society are concerned with developing latent giftedness and the unending array of individual assets in human resources.

Recent curriculum studies stress the need of more satisfactory provisions for superior children since traditional curriculums are ill adapted to their needs. Often these provisions are within the scope of typical classroom procedure without special class groupings. It has been shown that enrichment of superior children can be supplied successfully through self-administered work units in the typical classroom. Many school systems have not followed the trend to separate bright pupils into special classes or schools. Instead they have operated on the theory that the capacity for leadership and social service of such pupils is best developed by keeping them with others of the same age and grade. This plan obviously puts upon each classroom teacher the responsibility of adapting instruction to the varying abilities of her pupils and necessitates many interesting and significant adjustments.

Another way of dealing with gifted children is by grouping them in special classes. Pennsylvania was the first state to make such classes mandatory. A common objection to this method is that the pupils may overrate their own importance. It has been shown, however, that when a child is placed with his mental equals, he has less opportunity to excel and consequently works harder. When superior children are held back because others in the class cannot travel at a rapid rate, the effect is apt to be doubly unfortunate—the former may become lazy and the latter may feel inferior. Many bright pupils need not walk the treadmill of exercise in learning; flashes of insight enable them to skip most of the drill. Enrichment classes in some schools allow the advanced pupils, in addition to the regular classwork, to carry on self-initiated projects and activities under the supervision of the teacher. Since much reading is done in these groups, an ample library is necessary. The amazing ability of a group of superior children, known as the Quiz Kids, to answer questions on a wide variety of subjects in a popular radio program has been attributed largely to their extensive reading.

The Los Angeles public schools and others have experimented for several years with special rooms for gifted children. The Buffalo public schools provide a work-study plan. An experiment geared to meet special needs was developed in New York City at the Speyer School, with the late Dr. Leta S. Hollingworth as educational adviser. Only half the school day was required for giving the gifted pupil the necessary training in the specific subjects; the other half was spent in enrichment work which permitted the children under direction to develop their cultural and literary abilities. The series of enrichment units in this elementary school included such everyday subjects as clothing, health, food, and shelter.

Efforts have been made to establish separate classes or high schools for mentally superior or talented students. De Witt Clinton High School in New York City has organized an "honor school" within the school; boys chosen from the school on the basis of tests and previous school records are given special challenges to learn, commensurate with their greater abilities. New York City has also established a high school devoted to development of talent in the fine arts. Numerous curriculums challenge the bright with special electives such as foreign languages, advanced mathematics, and "tough" science courses. Many schools, both elementary and secondary, unleash creativeness and self-reliance. Genius and talent must be developed at all ages; hence the need for scholarships for the bright and talented. The Ford Foundation for the Advancement of Education through its scholarships for the early admission to college of high-school students of high ability, the annual talent search of the Science Clubs of America, and hundreds of other private and public scholarships are bringing more bright youth into college and graduate work. The University of Florida is one of several institutions of higher education which has developed a comprehensive program for superior students. The American Association for the Gifted Child has helped to encourage talent. The National Manpower Council has warned the nation of "the acute shortages among high skilled professional, scientific, and technical workers needed in defense and essential civilian activities." The gifted student is an asset and a responsibility. Many foreign countries excel the United States in seeking, educating, and using youth of varying types and degrees of talents.

SLOW LEARNERS

Identification of the Slow Learner. Equality of opportunity to learn in a democracy demands adequate attention to the slow learner. This term includes the entire range of mental subnormality in pupils: Some, with I.Q.'s around 90, are very near the lower border line of intellectual normality and educability from 90 to 110 I.Q. According to Christine P. Ingram, those in the dull-normal group range from 75 to 90 I.Q., and the mentally retarded from approximately 50 to 75 I.Q.[27] The extremely

[27] Christine P. Ingram, *Education of the Slow-learning Child*, p. 4, Ronald Press, 1953.

mentally retarded, such as imbeciles and idiots, fall in the 20 to below 50 I.Q. group. This classification, of course, does not imply rigid demarcation between the various groups. I.Q. limits are debatable and indeterminate. The answer to the problem of classification stems not from the I.Q., but from countless other factors, such as past history, maturity, family, and educational climate. Some state laws specify that the eligibility of pupils for slow-learning classes must be determined by a qualified psychologist.

Among the characteristics of the mentally slow are these: *physical*—they closely resemble normal children of corresponding chronological ages; *mental*—their mental age and I.Q. suggest the limitations of the retarded child's abilities of association, comparison, comprehension, generalization, and symbolization as compared with the normal child; and *social*—because the mentally retarded pupil has less ability to learn from experience, to take in all the elements in a complex situation, to foresee the consequences, and to form judgments than has the normal child, he is less capable of making adequate social adjustments.[28] Some of the characteristics may be detected through age-grade progress reports, close observation by the teacher, and case studies. Any rule-of-thumb judgment must not be final. The American Association on Mental Deficiency recommends a mental examination for all backward children. This involves the use of standardized tests as mentioned for the identification of the gifted. Both physical and mental examinations should be given in many cases. Traveling clinics help to identify pupils who should be in state residential schools or in special classes or who should receive special school consideration because of mental deficiencies.

Provisions for the Slow Learner. Ever since Itard's efforts at the beginning of the nineteenth century to educate the feeble-minded boy whom he found wandering in a French forest, there has been interest in the mentally deficient child. Seguin, a pupil of Itard, aroused comment here in America and abroad by his lectures in behalf of special classes. Massachusetts, under the leadership of Samuel Howe, established a school for indigent feeble-minded youths in 1848; Providence, Rhode Island, provided a special class for children of low intelligence in 1896. Today many school systems have special classes for slow learners, owing to the stimulation of L. M. Terman and others.

Most mentally retarded pupils are placed in public-school ungraded classes or opportunity rooms where they are encouraged to work on their own level and at their own rate of achievement. Besides these special classes in the local schools there are also private schools and residential schools for the mentally deficient. Of such institutions in the United

[28] *Ibid.*, pp. 11–16.

States, some are predominately custodial in character with emphasis on physical care of and physical work by the inmates, whereas others are remedial with stress on the educational program.

These residential schools have a marked advantage over the day schools in that the former can work "with the whole child the whole day for the whole year." Unfortunately, however, a stigma is often associated with a slow learner in a residential school. This is no doubt due to the fact that many residents in state institutions for the feeble-minded are idiots and imbeciles, incapable of acquiring an adequate education which would permit their release from an institution except under very unusual circumstances. Some are incapable of even partial self-sufficiency and will be harbored in a state institution all their days, because their condition is that of simple and continuous mental inferiority. There are some idiots who lead a vegetative existence, but, as Elise H. Martens pointed out, all feeble-minded persons are not hopelessly uneducable. No sudden and unpredictable movement or spurt of growth can be expected, but they can and do learn. For "trainables" of this type some states have launched positive programs that go beyond mere custodial care.

The psychology of special education for subnormals emphasizes success rather than failure. It centers around the processes that they are best able to master. It takes into consideration their capacities, limitations, interests, and ultimate social destinies. The subject matter and activities for the mentally retarded should not only contribute to happy childhood but also to their probable needs in adult life. For example, their reading will include only the words that are frequently used; their arithmetic will generally involve the use of money and making change; and their chief goal in handwriting will be legibility. Usually the trainable mental defectives can learn to work with concrete materials better than with abstract ideas. Nevertheless they share the entire gamut of human feelings; they grow hungry and thirsty, they become sad and glad, discouraged and encouraged, and they love and hate. Dull pupils need more than drilling and repetition; they need an enriched and explained program and an opportunity to do interesting things. If they are given drill work, it must not be above their ability. They should be allowed a wide range of experiences to build up a background. The slow learners may be aided by smaller classes, promotion on the basis of effort linked with attainable achievement, and by remedial teaching, particularly in reading.

Unit organization of experiences and centers of interest are very effective ways of meeting the individual and group needs of the mentally handicapped pupils. Visual aids have also been a tremendous asset in helping them to grasp material, particularly ideas that are usually presented in abstract manner. For slow learners there is too much verbalism in most teaching methods. Activity programs have likewise been instrumental in developing the retarded child into a self-respecting, self-reliant adult.

Wetzel in his *Biography of a High School* pointed out that a term common years ago has been lost, and that this riddance is indicative of great changes in education. The word is "dumb." Nobody is stigmatized today as "too dumb to learn." Even the most severe cases of mental deficiency, such as idiot, imbecile, and Mongoloid, can master some tasks. The National Association for Retarded Children encourages parents to take a positive view toward their child. This is also the philosophy of the Pollocks in *New Hope for the Retarded*.[29]

The problem of educating students of low mentality will be of increasing concern to secondary-school teachers, since great masses of unselected students are entering and remaining in high schools. Intelligence quotients ranging from 75 to 90 are frequent. One of the most important phases of the education for the mentally handicapped is vocational and occupational training. Many of them can be trained for semi-skilled or unskilled occupations. Certainly the world would be a much less comfortable place without these citizens who often hold jobs in which normal persons would quickly lose interest.

MENTALLY MALADJUSTED

Identification of the Mentally Maladjusted. It is often difficult to discover those children and adults who are mentally and emotionally unadjusted. Their number is legion; hence their early identification is extremely desirable. Since many symptoms and causes can be traced to early childhood, every teacher is challenged to be a mental hygienist, alerted to danger signals.

The teacher should study the personal problems of all pupils. There are basic causes for all frustrations and conflicts. We must study to discover these causes. No pupil becomes mentally upset without a background of causations. Conflicts with parents, with older brothers or sisters, with associates; rifts between parents; aversions toward certain teachers, inner desires left unfulfilled, and dozens of other reasons fan the spark of discontent.[30]

The parents, and even his own peers, have often discovered the mentally maladjusted child before he reaches school. The observing teacher may see symptoms and find causes through personal interviews or case histories, and in the daily life of the child. The family physician and pediatrician-psychiatrist can lend a discerning eye and ear in early identi-

[29] Morris P. Pollock and Miriam Pollock, *New Hope for the Retarded*, pp. 3–13, Porter Sargent, 1953.

[30] W. W. Ludeman, "Every Teacher a Mental Hygienist," *Phi Delta Kappan*, May, 1953, p. 331.

fication. School psychologists and trained personnel in community clinics can help locate behavioral cases.

Provisions for the Mentally Maladjusted. The first task is prevention. The prevention of emotional ill health is a "must" in the program of the World Health Organization and in the local school system. The chief therapeutic resource, after the child starts school, is the classroom teacher.

Often the school contributes to poor mental health through its obsolete methods of teaching, its rigid standards for grade promotions with the consequent huge numbers of failures, and its inflexible curriculum. The curriculum should help build security in the minds and hearts of children. Socially useful work is one way to meet the need for self-respect, which is related to personal security. Mental hygiene should be an operational principle of the total school program, including cocurricular activities.

Furthermore, the exterior and interior of school buildings affect the overt behavior and inner thoughts of pupils. In its yearbook, *Creating a Good Environment for Learning*, the Association for Supervision and Curriculum Development states:

> Teachers who complain bitterly about conduct and lack of manners of pupils may do well to ask whether the drabness and institutional aspect of the entrance or of the lunchroom are designed to promote the niceties of social conduct. Even more important than the general physical characteristics of the school are the characteristics of the individual classroom.[31]

Marginally adjusted children—those on the border line of sound mental health—usually respond to group therapy in a wholesome building in a democratic environment.

Individual therapy in the treatment of psychotic and neurotic children calls for specialized services of the psychiatrist and the physician. Regarding these technical services and facilities, the *U.S. News & World Report* recorded these findings from official Congressional hearings:

> The number of mentally ill patients in the United States exceeds the number of patients suffering from any other types of illness. Approximately 50 per cent of all hospital beds in the United States are used for this group of illnesses. . . . The personnel shortage of physicians in this field of medicine is acute. . . .[32]

The National Mental Health Act passed by Congress in 1946 has helped states, counties, and cities through subsidizing psychiatric services and establishing a National Institute of Mental Health. The National Society for the Study of Education accented the problems and suggested solutions in one of its 1955 yearbooks, *Mental Hygiene in Modern Edu-*

---

[31] Association for Supervision and Curriculum Development, *Creating a Good Environment for Learning*, pp. 204–205, National Education Association, 1954.

[32] *U.S. News & World Report*, Nov. 6, 1953, pp. 78–80.

cation. The work of national, state, county, and local groups can be summarized in the catchword, "We can save the mentally sick."

SOCIALLY HANDICAPPED PUPILS

SOCIAL VARIANTS AS A GROUP [33]

Every child is at times socially atypical. Some pupils are oversocial, seeking constantly to be in a crowd; some are nonsocial, striving to avoid people; and others are antisocial, working against human beings and social institutions. These deviates may be termed "socially handicapped."

No one knows how many pupils are socially maladjusted. A White House Conference conservatively estimated that 3 per cent of the elementary-school children in the United States were socially handicapped or potentially so. The socially handicapped are found in every grade from the nursery school through the university and in adult life. Problem behavior has been defined as "that which is objectionable to others or which makes the individual himself unhappy." Behavior problems range all the way from temporary minor infractions of social etiquette to severe problems of delinquency, such as theft, adultery, or murder.

Identification of Socially Handicapped. As with pupils who are physically and mentally handicapped, the classroom teacher who is alert, sympathetic, and understanding can identify many cases of maladjustment. Behavior problem children are not merely disciplinary cases for the teacher to handle. Many have physical disabilities. Some should be institutional charges. All, however, are not severe cases. Some youngsters are merely petulant, plaintive, or overassertive. Often the home conditions are responsible: there is a high correlation between broken homes and child delinquency. Incorrigibility often has been associated with low intelligence, but studies show that delinquent minors in criminal institutions do not differ markedly in intelligence from typical minors on the street, although they are lower in the amount of educational achievement.

Teachers usually are impressed with behavior difficulties that interrupt the work of the class or the smooth functioning of the school, but are not so concerned with social traits that are symptomatic of serious maladjustments of life in general. Wickman's study and similar investigations reveal that teachers label as most serious such behavior problems as untruthfulness, bullying and cruelty, cheating, talking to other pupils in class, impertinence, and truancy. On the other hand mental hygienists note as highly undesirable such traits as depression and unhappiness, unsocial attitudes, withdrawal, suggestibility, resentfulness, fearfulness, overcritical attitude, suspiciousness, and restlessness. The latter traits

[33] See also Prevention and Reduction of Juvenile Delinquency in Unit IX.

are the most serious for the general adjustment of pupils to life. Children behave as they do because of the conditions existing at the time. Hence behavior is a symptom of underlying maladjustment and not a disease. Furthermore delinquency is no longer regarded as the result of a single factor; it is explained in terms of the effects from many unfavorable factors in multiple causation.

Classroom teachers need to know more about the significance of certain traits, to have experience in the observation of behavior so that they may recognize undesirable traits, to have training in the treatment of specific problems, and to know where to go for technical help in difficult cases. Asking children to fill out a rating scale on broad general behavior traits, such as loyalty and cooperation, without specific detailed definition is not a very reliable device for locating problem cases. Better results are obtained when the traits listed are carefully defined on objective evaluation and diagnostic instruments, such as behavior scales, inventories of attitudes, individual histories, diagnostic child-study records, and sociograms. Many of these incorporate data on the pupil's home life and related factors. A reliable way of studying a child intensively is the case-study method, which gathers systematically all types of information from all possible sources and then coordinates these many items in such a manner that the case worker or teacher sees the child as a real, living individual reacting to many stimuli in a surveyed environment. The autobiographical letter containing a straightforward self-portrait is a valuable tool in the hands of a qualified diagnostician. Clinics are the best means of identifying behavior problem children and starting them on the right road to better adjustments.

Provisions for the Socially Handicapped. One of the main provisions for the socially handicapped is a constructive attitude on the part of all. The change in attitude toward youth and delinquency has been characterized by successive slogans: punish *him,* reform *him,* deter *him,* and guide *him* and eliminate *it* (delinquency). Genuine help and prevention are directed toward deep-seated causes.

According to *Mental Hygiene for Classroom Teachers:* "Basic causes of maladjustment are such experiences as feelings of insecurity, of inferiority, of hostility, of guilt and conflicts of ideals and actions. . . . Representative examples include such manifestations as seclusiveness, extreme aggressiveness, truancy and tattling." [34] This list can be multiplied many times.

A threefold program consists of drying up sources of infection in the community (preventive), helping the child in trouble (remedial), and

[34] Harold W. Bernard, *Mental Hygiene for Classroom Teachers,* pp. 67–70, McGraw-Hill, 1952.

producing continuously wholesome living (developmental). All efforts must help to cut down the rate of production on the delinquency assembly line and speed up the development of personalities who live happily and constructively.

The specific treatment varies with the problem in such a marked degree that no single rule can be offered. Physical and mental examinations are very desirable for pupils who are extreme disciplinary problems. Psychiatric services are valuable. Group therapy serves to break down antisocial feeling and stultifying inhibitions. Many nonsocial children need assistance in making adjustments to their surroundings and associates. The Citizenship Education Project and other programs have revealed the extreme importance of group dynamics in interpersonal and intragroup relations.

In a literal sense a pupil may often learn as much from his classmates as he does from his teacher. Since this is true, his contribution to the productivity of the class is a leading element in a learning situation. . . . A collateral point is the fact that a class is more than an aggregate of individuals. In a sense, it is a sub-community with attractions, hostilities, identifications and systems of influence like those of any other community.[35]

The triple approach of preventive, remedial, and developmental work requires diversified activities and many types of institutions including the day school, parental school, and residential institutions.

Among the first cities that established public-school classes for delinquents during the last quarter of the nineteenth century were Cleveland, Chicago, Providence, New York, Indianapolis, and Newark, New Jersey. Some cities make definite provision for the segregation in special schools of those pupils who are socially maladjusted. Examples in Chicago are the Montefiore and Moseley Schools. An interesting experiment was the special class at the Little Red School House in New York City. Most special schools have a longer day and term, with a very flexible program adapted to individual needs.

At the close of the nineteenth century and the beginning of the next came the establishment of parental schools, which stand *in loco parentis*. In addition to supplying home needs, such as boarding and lodging, these schools serve to educate delinquents or potential delinquents, whose out-of-school status demands special treatment. A typical parental school is the boys' farm established by the city of Cleveland near Hudson, Ohio. Many youth find adjustments very difficult to make if they remain in their old home environment. In restructuralization through habit formation

---

[35] Howard Y. McClusky, "Speculations on the Future in Education," *School of Education Bulletin*, January, 1954, p. 51.

it is often necessary to substitute a new environment, new associates, and vital new goals for undesirable old ones. A child's effort to improve may be neutralized by other factors. The actions of problem children may often be traced to parents and teachers. Social workers and visiting teachers with superior personalities and a rich socioeducational background can supply valuable contacts between the school and the homes of delinquent or truant children.

The first state institution for the socially handicapped was organized at Westborough, Massachusetts, toward the middle of the nineteenth century. Today residential schools for the socially maladjusted are found throughout the United States. Unfortunately in most cases their administration is separated from that of the public schools. Furthermore the traditional idea persists that the residents are offenders who must be punished and that the institution is correctional rather than reeducative and redirective in social living. Fortunately the objectives and procedures of many of these institutions are being altered. Incarceration gives way to education; the negative is replaced by a positive force. The return of the individual to the community as a fairly well adjusted person, capable of entering into normal life, is the recognized objective of all these schools. Today many states are removing a large number of delinquent girls and boys from residential schools, allowing them to attend a regular day school, and paying for their board, room, clothing, and other essentials in foster homes, where they return to a more normal form of living. The interest and understanding of the foster parents and the continued cooperation of the state in placement and follow-up are factors conditioning the success of such care.

In Berkeley, California, a coordinating council consists of representatives from the police department, the welfare society, the health department, and other agencies interested in the prevention and treatment of juvenile delinquency. Philadelphia has a case-review committee for potential juvenile delinquents. Many counties and cities have children's courts. The late Father Flanagan, who in 1917 founded Boys' Town in Nebraska, claimed that there never had been a bad boy. His remarkable success in his haven for homeless and abandoned boys helped to stimulate nation-wide interest in a positive program for combating juvenile delinquency. J. Edgar Hoover, Director of the Federal Bureau of Investigation, has said: "We have youth in crime because we have failed to provide youth with proper outlets and upbringing. . . . Children are driven to crime because of deep-laid faults in society such as poverty, degeneracy, and because their elders neglect them." These problems involve a cooperative attack. The need for constant cooperation between school authorities and all public social service agencies is convincingly presented in the NEA Research Bulletin, *Schools Help Prevent Delinquency*.

Through local, state, national, and international agencies, such as city councils, the State Departments of Education, the United States Office of Education, the International Council for Exceptional Children, and the Personnel and Guidance Association, better services can be developed for socially maladjusted as well as other pupils.

OTHER EXCEPTIONAL PUPILS

To the many types of exceptional pupils already mentioned may be added an endless array of pupils with special problems, such as those living on federal reservations, those in rural or sparsely settled areas, those in congested city neighborhoods, the overly ambitious pupils, the lazy, the irregular in attendance, the homebound, the timid and passive, the overprivileged, the allergic, the diabetic, the adopted, the foster, the orphaned children, the left-handed pupils, the emotionally unstable, the impaired in mental health, the children of minority groups, the members of low-income families, the children from migrant families, and the refugee children. In connection with English refugees, the story is told of one little guest who was worried about starting school in America. He wanted very much to go to school, but was worried, he said, "because, you see, I've never learned American!" Transportation, housing, and schooling have been provided here in recent years for many children fleeing from other shores. Unlike the totalitarian or so-called "ism" countries, which aim to regiment children and their thinking, the public schools in America seek to cultivate a profound respect for individual*ism* in society. A democracy believes that every child, youth, or adult—normal or handicapped—is important.

SUGGESTED ACTIVITIES

1. Explain what is meant by a "pupil-centered" school. Evaluate this concept.
2. Defend or refute the statement that the organization of a typical school respects the individuality of the child.
3. Describe the normal physical, mental, spiritual, and social development of typical pupils in the elementary school, secondary school, and college.
4. Give a brief life sketch of some distinguished physically handicapped person, such as Helen Keller and Franklin Delano Roosevelt.
5. Explain provisions your state laws contain relative to the care and education of handicapped children.
6. Prepare a list of local organizations that cooperate with the schools in educating exceptional children.
7. List specific contributions that the medical profession makes to the welfare of handicapped children.
8. Describe a mechanical device that is a great aid in educating exceptional children.
9. Observe a class dedicated to the education of exceptional children, such as in a sight-saving room or a room for crippled children.
10. Study carefully one exceptional pupil, keeping a careful record of all pertinent data; also, one normal child.

11. List specific ways of helping a bright or a slow learner in school.

12. Explain how the teacher helps to discover the latent interests of children.

13. Describe what is meant by the "mental health" of the school pupil.

14. Examine police records to determine the type of school children who are brought before the court.

15. Visit a child-guidance clinic and observe the children and procedures.

16. Describe the particular problems presented by pupils who come from homes of the foreign-born or migrant parents.

DESCRIPTIVE BIBLIOGRAPHY AND AIDS

BOOKS

AMERICAN ASSOCIATION OF SCHOOL ADMINISTRATORS: *Education for American Citizenship,* Chap. VII, National Education Association, 1954.

The basic emotional needs of pupils.

ANDERSON, VIRGIL: *Improving the Child's Speech,* Chap. X, Oxford, 1953.

The child who stutters.

ARBUCKLE, DUGALD S.: *Student Personnel Services in Higher Education,* Chap. II, McGraw-Hill, 1953.

Organization and administration of student personnel services in higher education.

BAKER, HENRY J.: *An Introduction to Exceptional Children,* Part IV, Macmillan, 1953.

Children with epilepsy, psychotic difficulties, and miscellaneous neurological conditions.

BOSSARD, JAMES H. S.: *The Sociology of Child Development,* Chap. II, Harper, 1954.

The sociological approach to child behavior.

COOK, LLOYD, and ELAINE COOK: *Intergroup Education,* Chap. II, McGraw-Hill, 1954.

Minorities in the light of history.

EDUCATIONAL POLICIES COMMISSION: *Education of the Gifted,* Chaps. III, IV, National Education Association, 1950.

Identification and education of the gifted.

———: *Moral and Spiritual Values in the Public Schools,* Chap. IV, National Education Association, 1951.

A suggested program for accenting moral and spiritual values in the public schools.

FEATHERSTONE, W. B.: *Teaching the Slow Learner,* Chaps. II, IV, Teachers College, 1951.

Identification of the slow learners and guidance of their activities.

HAVIGHURST, ROBERT J.: *Human Development and Education,* Chaps. II, IV, Longmans, 1953.

Developmental tasks of infancy and early childhood, and of middle childhood.

HECK, ARCH O.: *The Education of Exceptional Children,* 2d ed., Chap. XXII, McGraw-Hill, 1953.

Education of delicate children.

INGRAM, CHRISTINE P.: *Education of the Slow-learning Child,* Chap. VI, Ronald, 1953.

Organization of special classes for slow learners.

IRWIN, RUTH BECKEY: *Speech and Hearing Therapy,* Chaps. III, IV, Prentice-Hall, 1953.

Identification of children who need therapy and organization of a speech and hearing program.

JERSILD, ARTHUR T.: *Child Psychology,* Chap. XIX, Prentice-Hall, 1954.

Personality problems and the search for self.

KILLILEA, MARIE: *Karen,* Prentice-Hall, 1952, 314 pp.

A moving story of the childhood of a handicapped girl, Karen, who suffers from the spastic form of cerebral palsy.

LENDE, HILGA: *Books about the Blind,* Chap. II, American Foundation for the Blind, 1953.

Education of the young blind.

PECK, LEIGH: *Child Psychology,* Chaps. XI–XIV, Heath, 1953.

Emotional and social development of children and their adjustments.

RAUBICHECK, LETITIA: *Speech Improvement,* Part IV, Prentice-Hall, 1952.

Tests and procedures for helping those with foreign accent.

STRANG, RUTH: *An Introduction to Child Study,* Part I, Macmillan, 1951.

The roots of behavior—the baby at birth.

WHEATLEY, GEORGE M., and GRACE T. HALLOCK, *Health Observation of School Children,* Chap. VIII, McGraw-Hill, 1951.

Helps for teachers in recognizing eye and ear defects in children.

WITTY, PAUL: *The Gifted Child,* Chaps. II, IX, Heath, 1951.

Suggestions for the identification of the gifted and for the educating process.

YOUNG, PAULINE V.: *Social Treatment in Probation and Delinquency,* 2d ed., Chap. XXIV, McGraw-Hill, 1952.

The role of the school and vocational guidance in the adjustment of delinquent youth.

ZUBECK, JOHN P., and PATRICIA ANNE SOLBERG: *Human Development,* Chaps. III–XII, McGraw-Hill, 1954.

Neural, glandular, physical, motor, sensory, learning, intellectual, emotional, social development.

CURRENT PERTINENT PERIODICALS AND PUBLICATIONS

American Annals of the Deaf
The American Child
American Journal of Mental Deficiency
American Journal of Sociology
Child Development Abstracts and Bibliography, Monographs
Children
Crippled Child
Exceptional Children
Hearing News
Journal of Abnormal and Social Psychology
Journal of Dentistry of Children
Journal of Exceptional Children
Journal of Negro History
Journal of School Health
Journal of Speech and Hearing Disorders

Mental Hygiene
Negro Digest
Nervous Child
Personnel and Guidance
Psychological Abstracts
Psychological Review
Quarterly Journal of Speech
Religious Education
Sight-saving Review
Sociological Abstracts
Special Education Review
Teachers' Forum for Blind Children
Understanding the Child
Volta Review
Yearbooks of educational organizations

AUDIO-VISUAL AIDS

BABY KNOWS BEST   5 min., sound

This film depicts the natural reactions of a baby to the tender loving care of a mother. Available on free loan from WNYC, Municipal Building, New York 17.

CHILD DEVELOPMENT AND A SCIENCE OF MAN   Phonograph record, 20 min.

A recorded lecture on child development by Dr. A. Gesell, noted author of books and experiments in child growth and development. Considers the broader implications of child development. Available from Sound Seminars, University of Cincinnati, Cincinnati, Ohio.

CHILDREN'S EMOTIONS — Two reels, sound

Correlated with Hurlock's book *Child Development*. Other films and filmstrips in the series are: *Principles of Development, Heredity and Pre-natal Development, Child Care and Development*, and *Social Development*. Produced by McGraw-Hill Book Company, 330 West 42nd Street, New York 36.

EXAMINING THE WELL CHILD — 18 min., sound, color

Sponsored by the Oklahoma State Department of Health, and intended primarily for medical personnel, this colored film accents the importance of periodic medical examinations of the child who has no apparent illness. Available from Samuel P. Orleans, 211 W. Cumberland Ave., Knoxville 15, Tenn.

GROWING UP WITH MIKE — Three filmstrips, color

These filmstrips, intended for elementary-school children, demonstrate how teachers can use audio-visual aids in helping pupils understand their own growth. Available from Encyclopaedia Britannica Films, Wilmette, Ill.

HEALTH FOR TOMORROW'S CITIZENS — 5 min., sound

This is the story of how the New York Department of Health safeguards the health of children in school. Available on free loan from WNYC, Municipal Building, New York 17.

THE HUMAN BODY SKELETON — 10 min., b&w or color

Shows the general skeletal portions of the human body and their functions. By photographing the inner workings of bones and muscles through fluoroscopes, the function of each set of bones becomes meaningful. Available from Coronet Films, Chicago.

LEARNING TO UNDERSTAND CHILDREN — Films and filmstrips

PART I. A DIAGNOSTIC APPROACH — 21 min., sound
PART II. A REMEDIAL PROGRAM — 23 min., sound

An understanding teacher makes the most of school opportunities to improve the social and scholastic achievements of a maladjusted girl of fifteen. Based upon Raleigh Schorling's *Student Teaching*. Available with text from McGraw-Hill, New York 36.

PASSING OF THE HICKORY STICK — Phonograph record, 13 min.

This radio transcription stimulates interest and discussion in methods of handling children. Compares the old-style discipline with modern classroom techniques. Available from the National Education Association, Washington, D.C.

PRINCIPLES OF CHILD DEVELOPMENT — Phonograph record, 20 min.

Dr. Ruth Strang of Teachers College, Columbia University, discusses the principles of child development upon which there is generally agreement among child psychologists. Available from Sound Seminars, University of Cincinnati, Cincinnati, Ohio.

SHYNESS — 23 min., sound

Produced by the National Film Board of Canada, this film shows how to deal with the problem of abnormal shyness. Teacher, psychologist, and parents bring about a change. Available from McGraw-Hill, New York 36.

TESTING INTELLIGENCE WITH THE STANFORD-BINET 18 min., sound

An overview of the types of items in the Stanford-Binet Intelligence Test. The test is administered to four children. The film also gives the meaning of such terms as intelligence quotient, mental age. It further demonstrates how the test results can be used. Available from Audi-visual Center, University of Indiana, Bloomington, Ind.

YOUR CHILDREN WALKING 20 min., sound

Produced by the British Information Services, this film emphasizes the importance of teaching a child to walk, to carry himself properly, and the need for appropriate footwear. Available from McGraw-Hill, New York 36.

TEACHERS

Teaching, the largest of all professions, permits the practice of idealism such as expressed by Henry Van Dyke in his tribute to the unknown teacher.

Teaching has undergone three stages of development, epitomized as training, preparation, and education.

Teacher education may be divided into two phases. The first, preservice education, involves the selection of students, in-college education, and certification and placement of teachers.

The second phase, in-service education, is concerned with internship in teaching, supervision, and other means of stimulating teacher growth.

The teaching profession collectively is interested in the welfare of its members, in professional ethics, and in professional organizations.

The teaching personnel includes classroom teachers, special teachers, those in federal jurisdictions and foreign countries, and teachers of teachers. A student may well ask: "Shall I become a teacher?"

OUTLINE OF CONTENTS

TEACHERS

Wholesome pupil-teacher relationships are portrayed effectively thus:

> Mark Hopkins sat on one end of a log,
> And a farm boy sat on the other;
> Mark Hopkins came as a pedagogue
> And taught as an elder brother.[1]

Many a successful pedagogue has taught as an elder brother or elder sister. The humanness in the teacher causes the boy on the other end of the log to resolve:

> The kind of a man I mean to be
> Is the kind of a man Mark Hopkins is.

This desire of the pupil to imitate his teacher-friend is a genuine tribute. Unfortunately, as the late Kenneth C. M. Sills of Bowdoin College once said, "We Americans have put too much emphasis on the log and not enough on Mark Hopkins. Excellent teaching in wooden halls is much better than wooden teaching in marble halls." One of the grandest, oldest, and most universal professions, teaching has this claim over all other professions: it permits one with broad human qualities to live creatively with youth.

The Role of the Teacher. Numerically, teaching is the largest of all professions. Approximately a million persons in the United States are engaged in this field. Teachers play an important role in the drama of life, not merely because of their large numbers but also because they work with pupils of all ages. They are found in all the areas considered in Part II, namely, pre-elementary, ele-

FIG. 11-1. Mark Hopkins memorial stamp. This stamp honors one of America's greatest teachers. Hopkins, who for many years was professor of moral philosophy and president at Williams College, was elected to the Hall of Fame in 1915. He possessed the unusual ability of inspiring and developing the latent powers of the individual student. (*Courtesy of Nation's Schools.*)

mentary, secondary, and higher learning, and education for out-of-school youth and adults. Furthermore, between the ages of five to eighteen or

[1] Arthur Guiterman, *Death and General Putnam*, p. 74, Dutton, 1935.

twenty-one youth spends more time with teachers than with parents. But the number of teachers, the number of years a pupil is in school, and the number of clock-hours he spends weekly with teachers do not make teaching a great profession. In the chapel at Wellesley College, Alice Freeman Palmer, professor of history and Wellesley's "incomparable president," is sculptured by Daniel Chester French as pointing her pupils to the heights. Hope and idealism make the teacher a great force in American life, despite the old barb: "Those who can, do; and those who can't, teach." In answer to this caustic comment, Oliver C. Carmichael of the Carnegie Foundation for the Advancement of Teaching says:

> The idealism of the leadership in all phases of American life is more largely affected by the teacher than by anyone else. Hence the potential influence of those who *teach* is greater than that of those who *do* since the outlook, competence, skill, and motivation of the latter are derived in large part from the former.[2]

In other words, the doer could not do if the teacher did not teach.

The Unknown Teacher. It is fitting that Henry Van Dyke should have sung the praises of the Unknown Teacher.

THE UNKNOWN TEACHER

I sing the praise of the Unknown Teacher.

Great generals win campaigns, but it is the Unknown Soldier who wins the war.

Famous educators plan new systems of pedagogy, but it is the Unknown Teacher who delivers and guides the young. He lives in obscurity and contends with hardship. For him no trumpets blare, no chariots wait, no golden decorations are decreed. He keeps the watch along the borders of darkness and leads the attack on the trenches of ignorance and folly. Patient in his daily duty, he strives to conquer the evil powers which are the enemies of youth. He awakens sleeping spirits. He quickens the indolent, encourages the eager, and steadies the unstable. He communicates his own joy in learning and shares with boys and girls the best treasures of his mind. He lights many candles which in later years will shine back to cheer him. This is his reward.

Knowledge may be gained from books; but the love of knowledge is transmitted only by personal contact. No one has deserved better of the Republic than the Unknown Teacher. No one is more worthy to be enrolled in a democratic aristocracy, "king of himself and servant of mankind."

—Henry Van Dyke

---

[2] Oliver C. Carmichael, *The Changing Role of Higher Education*, p. 52, Macmillan, 1949.

DEVELOPMENT OF TEACHING IN THE UNITED STATES

Historical Calendar—Teacher Education and Contemporaneous Events

The chronological table on the next pages juxtaposes events in the history of teacher education and other contemporaneous happenings.

Major Stages of Development

Teaching has undergone three not too well marked stages of development which have been epitomized by the terms: (1) teacher *training,* (2) teacher *preparation,* and (3) teacher *education.*

Teacher Training. The earliest teachers were not even trained: they taught or rather "kept" school by "rule of the thumb" or "with a heavy hand," without any specific practice or pedagogy. Gradually the need for definite training became articulate through the words and deeds of such men as Reverend Samuel R. Hall, who in 1823 established a private academy at Concord, Vermont, for the preparation of teachers; and Horace Mann, Edmund Dwight, and Reverend Cyrus Pierce—all real pioneers. Pierce became the first principal of the first state-supported normal in the United States, located at Lexington, Massachusetts. In 1939 the nation commemorated the centennial of public teacher education, for it was on July 3, 1839, that three young ladies commenced training.

FIG. 11-2. In the olden days untrained or trained schoolmasters ruled the classroom, often with a heavy hand. (*Courtesy of Culver.*)

Historical Calendar

TEACHER EDUCATION	CONTEMPORANEOUS EVENTS
1823—First private normal school started by Samuel R. Hall (Concord, Vermont)	1823—Monroe Doctrine initiated by President Monroe
1839—First state normal school established (Lexington, Massachusetts)	1839—Vulcanized rubber patented by Goodyear
1845—First state education associations organized in New York and Rhode Island	1845—Florida and Texas admitted to the Union
1848—City normal school established (Philadelphia, Pennsylvania)	1848—Peace pact signed between United States and Mexico declaring Rio Grande as boundary
1857—National Teachers Association formed (later the National Education Association)	1857—Dred Scott decision handed down by United States Supreme Court
1873—First part-time chair in professional education created at University of Iowa. First permanent exclusively professional chair founded at Michigan in 1879	1873—Credit mobilier—one of the greatest political scandals—investigated by Congress
1887—Teachers College, Columbia University, established (New York City)	1886—Statue of Liberty, a gift from France, unveiled on Bedloe's Island, New York
1893—Normal school at Albany, New York, made Albany State Teachers College and given power to grant degrees	1893—Grover Cleveland inaugurated as President of United States for second term
1896—First state-wide teacher-retirement system adopted (New Jersey)	1896—Gold discovered in Klondike, Alaska
1899—Colonel F. Parker chosen principal of Chicago Institute (later School of Education at University of Chicago)	1899—More than two thousand lives lost in Johnstown flood in Pennsylvania
1909—First state teacher tenure law passed (New Jersey)	1909—William Howard Taft inaugurated President of the United States
1916—American Federation of Teachers organized as affiliate of American Federation of Labor	1916—Panama Canal Treaty with Nicaragua ratified
1917—American Association of Teachers Colleges formed	1917—First World War entered upon by the United States

Historical Calendar—(*Continued*)

TEACHER EDUCATION (*Continued*)	CONTEMPORANEOUS EVENTS (*Continued*)
1919—First meeting of Progressive Education Association held	1919—Membership in League of Nations rejected by United States
1920—Association for Student Teaching organized	1920—Woman-suffrage amendment ratified by the states
1930—National Survey of Teacher Education authorized by Congress	1930—United States represented at London Disarmament Conference
1938—Future Teachers of America organized	1938—Fair Labor Standards Act with 44-hour week made effective
1938—Commission on Teacher Education organized by American Council on Education	1938—Flight made by Howard Hughes and associates around the top of the world in less than four days
1946—British-American exchange of teachers inaugurated	1946—Commission to study control of atomic energy created by U.N.
1946—World Organization of the Teaching Profession started at Endicott, New York	1946—Meat price controls ended, and other wartime controls except rent relaxed in the U.S.
1948—Three teacher-educating groups merged into American Association of Colleges for Teacher Education	1948—Religious instruction on released time declared unconstitutional by U.S. Supreme Court
1950—First issue of *Journal of Teacher Education* published	1950—Vienna, Austria, art collection shown in four major U.S. cities
1953—First meeting held by World Confederation of Organizations of the Teaching Profession (formerly WOTP)	1953—Department of Health, Education, and Welfare created by Congress with Secretary in the President's Cabinet
1953—Organization meeting held by International Council on Education for Teaching	1953—Dwight D. Eisenhower inaugurated as 34th President of the United States
1954—Two million persons employed by local, state, and federal school and college systems and educational services	1954—National debt limit increased by Congress from 275 to 281 billion dollars
1954—National Council for Accreditation of Teacher Education made operative	1954—Element 100 created in Argonne Laboratory and at University of California
1955—Retired teachers, whose pensions are tax financed, permitted to exclude up to $1200 annually from federal taxation	1955—Ten million more workers covered under provisions of revised Social Security program

Entrance examinations were required at the new normal school in Lexington. The enlightenment that came from this fire kindled in Massachusetts spread gradually to and down the Mississippi Valley and to the Pacific Coast. City school systems followed the lead of the states. In 1848 the city of Philadelphia, which as early as 1818 had been given the legal right to train teachers, established the first city normal school.

Teacher Preparation. The course of study at the Lexington Normal School was only 1 year in length; not until 1860 was the period doubled to 2 years. Many of the early students at normal schools attended only one term. Gradually it became apparent to educational leaders that teachers had to be *prepared* over a period of years rather than *trained* in a term of 11 weeks or a summer session or two. The quality as well as the quantity of instruction had to be altered. Instead of equipping the prospective teachers with a bag of tricks, it was necessary to prepare them for teaching and living with children.

For this purpose an institution with a higher rank than a 2-year normal training school was needed. The establishment of Illinois State Normal *University* in 1857 is symbolical of this upward reach in teacher preparation:

> It was set up as the unquestioned head of the state's educational system since there was at the time no state university. It was to prepare teachers for all branches of the common schools, including high schools. Its graduates were supposed to become educational leaders as well as elementary teachers. It was undoubtedly established as a *college for teachers* and to indicate its collegiate status it was called "The Illinois State Normal University." To the New Englander the term "Normal University" was an incongruous jumble of words, but in Illinois a "Normal University" meant a teacher-preparation institution elevated to the collegiate rank.[3]

The interest of higher education in the preparation of teachers was evidenced in the creation of education departments in colleges and universities. The first part-time chair devoted to professional training was established at the University of Iowa in 1873, and the first permanent chair at the University of Michigan in 1879. An institution that has markedly affected teacher education in America and abroad is Teachers College, established at Columbia University in 1887 by Nicholas Murray Butler, then professor of philosophy. A few years later the state normal school at Albany was given power to grant degrees. Toward the end of the century Colonel Francis Parker accepted the principalship of Chicago Institute which later became the School of Education, now the Department of Education, at the University of Chicago.

[3] Charles A. Harper, *A Century of Public Teacher Education*, p. 80, National Education Association, 1939.

Fig. 11-3. Then came the control of the prim schoolmistress. (*Courtesy of Brown Brothers.*)

Fig. 11-4. Today the teacher, as a leader and friend, directs the pupils in an informal atmosphere. (*Courtesy of Public Schools, New York City.*)

Teacher Education. Teacher preparation stresses vocational training, whereas teacher education is professional education at its best. William Heard Kilpatrick stated that one *trains* circus performers, buffoons, and animals, but one *educates* teachers. A modicum of training is necessary, but the real outcome desired is teacher education, which is broader, longer, and deeper than teacher training. It affects all areas of living, it requires many years of learning, and it has its roots in a vital philosophy of daily living with children.

The current emphasis on teacher education has no definite starting point; it was latent in the minds of the early educators. With the beginning of this century the name National *Education* Association came into use as the official title of the national organization of teachers. A 3-year survey, authorized by Congress and conducted under the leadership of E. S. Evenden of Teachers College, Columbia University, was designated "National Survey of Teacher Education." Among its published reports are *Teacher Education Curricula* and *Education of Negro Teachers.* The special committee organized by the American Council on Education in 1938 was entitled "Commission on Teacher Education." The names and content of courses for teachers, and current titles of professional periodicals, such as *Teacher Education, Journal of Teacher Education,* and *Teacher Education Journal,* indicate this shift in emphasis from training to education. The latter may be divided into two major phases: (1) preservice and (2) in-service education.

PRESERVICE TEACHER EDUCATION

Preservice education includes such factors as the recruitment and selection of students for the teaching profession, the in-college education of these candidates, their certification as teachers upon meeting the necessary standards, and their placement in teaching positions.

RECRUITMENT AND SELECTION OF STUDENTS FOR THE TEACHING PROFESSION

Recruitment. Driftwood is not the best educational timber. In order to secure better personnel many states have established scholarships for prospective teachers and legislated minimum salary schedules. The best human resources available must be attracted into the teaching profession through an "up-grading" of student personnel. In his 1953 State of the Union message, President Eisenhower called attention to the shortage of teachers, saying, "The nation as a whole is not preparing teachers or buildings fast enough to keep up with the increase in population."

In order to enlist in the teaching profession young people of high caliber, a national movement entitled Future Teachers of America was launched in 1938. The National Education Association, sponsor of this organization, has established a Future Teachers *Club* in each junior or senior high school where there is sufficient interest and leadership, and a Future Teachers *Chapter* in each college or teachers college interested in the improvement of the teaching profession.

Need for Selection. There is a marked trend toward continuous selection and elimination, which extends even into the period of in-service education. Medicine, law, and other professions have long been on the selective basis whereby the students must meet certain requirements before being admitted to training. Increasingly teacher-educating institutions are adopting policies of selective admission and retention.

Bases for Selection. The selection of students for the teaching profession is made usually on several of the following bases: the scholastic record of the applicant, participation in extracurricular activities, recommendation from the high-school principal, physical examination, quality of voice, use of English, personal interviews, personality ratings, and scores in a series of entrance examinations and aptitude tests.

The general characteristics essential to superior teaching ability are not revealed by a single measurement. Among the various devices for the prediction of teaching success are the Knight Teaching Aptitude Test and the Torgenson Test of Professional Information. Intelligence tests and psychological examinations are also used together with personality scales. A cumulative record covering the whole previous life of the candidate is also valuable. Selection should be viewed not as a single event but as a continuous process. The idea that any "good" young man or woman will make a good teacher must disappear.

TYPES OF TEACHER-EDUCATING INSTITUTIONS

The main institutions for educating teachers are (1) normal schools, (2) teachers colleges, (3) departments of education, and (4) schools or colleges of education.

Normal Schools. The first normal schools were established in order to prepare teachers for the elementary schools. Students were admitted on the basis of their elementary-school record. The curriculum was usually a year in length and contained very little of what is now considered professional education. Today a normal school usually offers a teacher's course of less than 4 years. It may be a state, county, municipal, or high-school normal, all of which are part of the public educational system. Several private normals prepare teachers for such fields as primary and physical education. Although there are still several normal schools in the United States, they are gradually disappearing in name and function, giving way to the nomenclature, philosophy, and organization of a teachers college.

Teachers Colleges. The teachers college is usually a degree-granting institution for teacher education which has replaced many of the old normal schools. The emphasis is shifting from teaching to learning, from teaching how and what and when to teach, to providing copious opportunities for prospective directors of learning to learn how pupils learn. Because there are so many skills and knowledges to be mastered by the prospective teacher, the period of preservice work is being lengthened from 2 to 4 and 5 years of work. The short period of teacher training becomes a longer span of teacher education. The old normal school has developed into a modern teachers college. Several interesting histories have been written of public teachers colleges. Among the outstanding private schools is Teachers College, Columbia University, concerning which the former dean, James E. Russell, has written his reminiscences. The largest private institution of this type with a wholly independent organization is George Peabody College for Teachers at Nashville, Tennessee. Nearly all states of the Union have established teachers colleges or state colleges with teacher education as one of their functions. Several of these grant masters' degrees, and a few award doctors' degrees. Whereas the old normal school trained teachers for elementary service only, the modern teachers college has spread its offerings to include the education of secondary and special teachers. Some educate teachers for colleges and universities.

Departments of Education. The liberal arts college usually includes a division known as the education department, with a professor as head and one or more teachers. The requirement in terms of hours of education is usually less than the minimum in teachers colleges. Student teaching usually is coupled with this program.

In some universities also the work in education is organized as a department, for example, the department of education at the University of Chicago. In some instances teacher education is a function of a department within a larger division such as social sciences or liberal arts.

Schools or College of Education. Professional work in the universities is usually centralized in a separate entity, the school or college of education. It may accept students at the beginning of the freshman year, at the end of a period of general education in the sophomore or junior year, or for graduate work. An illustration of the evolution of schools of education is shown in the history of the University of Michigan, one of the first American institutions to offer education courses. Its first permanent chair in this field, established in 1879, was called "The Science and Art of Teaching"; in 1921 it gave way to a "School of Education." The latter has rank coordinate with other professional schools of the University of Michigan with its own dean and faculty, a separate budget, and its own degrees. In graduate work, however, the unit serves as a department of the graduate school. The matter of graduate study is treated further in Unit VIII.

IN-COLLEGE EDUCATION FOR TEACHERS

The teacher is an interpreter of the general culture; hence his preparation must include general education. He teaches some specialized subject or generalized field; hence he needs subject-matter or field preparation. He teaches learning pupils; hence he takes professional work in education and psychology, including student teaching. These three areas—general education, specialization, and professional education—are considered briefly here.

General Education. Teaching is a broad profession and not a narrow trade. Teachers are, therefore, expected to have a rich cultural background as a common denominator. The importance of general education for the teacher is stressed in the following quotation from the American Association of Colleges for Teacher Education:

> A broad education program to equip the student with a wide range of competencies is needed by him both as a person and as a professional worker. Many aspects of such general education are also part of the teacher's professional equipment. Students must be helped to see the interrelatedness between this general education and professional education.[4]

Furthermore, the teacher is responsible for the general education of young Americans—the workers and citizens of tomorrow.

Specialization in Subjects, Fields, or Levels. Prospective teachers should complement a broad cultural and general education with specialization in terms of the subjects, fields, or levels in which they expect to teach. For the elementary school the preparation is usually in terms of grade levels and the subject and fields taught therein, whereas in the secondary schools the preparation is in subjects and fields. For teachers in the smaller high schools it is recommended that preparation be in terms of fields rather than specialized narrow subjects and that at least two fields be selected for possible work. In addition to specialization in academic work there must be concentration in child study and the methodology of learning and teaching, usually termed "professional" education.

Professional Education. The requirements in specific professional education are usually stated in terms of semester hours. A minimum in most states is 15 semester hours for certification; however, most teacher-educating institutions go beyond the legal minimum. A sample program of a

---

[4] Subcommittee of the Standards and Surveys Committee, *School and Laboratory Experiences in Teacher Education,* p. 61, American Association of Colleges for Teacher Education, 1948.

teachers college that requires 28 semester hours in education and psychology for secondary-school teaching is as follows:

Courses	Hours
Observation and reading	2
Educational psychology	3
American public education	3
Methods of teaching	3
Schools and community relations	2
Introduction to philosophy of education	3
Student teaching and special methods	10
Electives in education and psychology	2–4
Total hours in education and psychology	28–30

In some colleges this professional work is concentrated in the last year or two, but in the majority it is spread over the upper 3 years.

An essential phase of professional education is actual experience with children. As has been repeatedly stated, the verb "to teach" has two accusatives—the pupil and the subject. Some knowledge of pupils can be acquired through observation, participation, and direct student teaching.

An important aspect of preservice education is experience as a student teacher. Student or cadet or practice teaching, as it is variously termed, gradually inducts the prospective teacher into full responsibility of the teaching-learning activities under the skillful guidance of a supervising or critic teacher. This may well be the summation of all the student's work and the climax to a long period of steady initiation, including directed and undirected observation in the training schools and typical public schools.

Almost every teacher-educating institution provides facilities for students to experience actual teaching either in the campus laboratory school or in the regular public schools. The training school and student teaching will play increasingly dynamic roles. The national organization in this field is the Association for Student Teaching, organized in 1920.

Curricular Patterns in Teacher Education. These three areas are not organized into the same pattern. The American Association of Colleges for Teacher Education, in its report on laboratory schools, lifted out for illustration three types of curricular organization on the undergraduate level, to which a fourth has been added:

1. Four-year general and professional program, in which both general and professional education are spread through all 4 years

2. Two-two program, in which the professional education is offered only in the last 2 years, the first 2 years being given to general education

3. Professional sequence, in which professional education is concentrated in

the third and fourth years with one or more professional courses in the first 2 years

4. Five-year program, in which a student who has completed his bachelor's degree in liberal arts or other fields adds a year of intensive professional work

Obviously other patterns exist, including experimental approaches with small groups. Upon completion of a recognized course the student is usually ready for limited certification as a beginning teacher.

CERTIFICATION OF TEACHERS

A teacher's certificate serves to give status; to protect its holder against unfair competition with unqualified teachers; to control the granting of licenses; to protect children against incompetent teachers; to provide a means for the improvement of instruction; to yield information on which a continuous inventory of teachers and their qualifications may be based; and to authorize the payment of salaries.

All states require a license, certificate, or permit to teach in the public schools. Most states request a statement that the applicant for a teaching position is in good health. The minimum age requirement for teaching in some states is eighteen years. This is too low if teaching is to be a profession rather than a mere job. In general, standards for and procedures in certifying teachers ought to be improved. The late Edgar W. Knight stated that "any real reform is likely to be delayed in the education and certification of teachers until we have had an end of adding machine and clerical bookkeeping devices both in teacher-educational institutions and the state agencies that license teachers."

The better current practices include elimination of substandard or emergency certificates, 4 years of approved teacher preparation with a bachelor's degree as a minimum and with a fifth year as soon as possible, a minimum of 15 semester hours of professional work including student teaching, a probationary period of not less than 3 years under professional guidance, the discontinuance of permanent or life certificates, the centralization of certification in a state agency, reciprocity between states in certifying qualified teachers, and greater accent on qualitative competencies and professional growth.

PLACEMENT OF TEACHERS

The educated teacher, properly certified or able to meet legal certification requirements, is ready for work. Will she or he receive a position? The answer depends upon several contingencies, not the least of which is the candidate's ability in self-salesmanship.

Placement Agencies. Positions in education are usually obtained through: (1) noncommercial agencies and (2) commercial or private placement bureaus.

The most important noncommercial agencies are those maintained by normal schools, teachers colleges, and universities for placing their graduates and alumni. The services are gratuitous, although a small fee may be charged to cover incidentals of registration. A member of the faculty is in charge and serves as a liaison officer between the employer and future employee. The National Institutional Placement Association is seeking to promote greater economy and efficiency in the placement of teachers by educational institutions. Other noncommercial bureaus are maintained by state departments of education, state education associations, and state employment services.

The commercial agencies, several of which are banded together in the National Association of Teachers' Agencies, are those private bureaus which locate positions for teachers at a fixed percentage of their first year's salary. Fees vary with the nature of the services rendered. Usually a registration fee is required in addition to a percentage charge.

Studies of teacher supply and demand are made periodically. At present the information available for estimating the demand is limited and spasmodic; furthermore, little is being done toward controlling the supply of teachers. Of course not all persons who prepare for teaching desire or secure employment. The outstanding reasons for failures in placement are as follows:

Inadequate preparation	Low grades in practice teaching
Preparation in overcrowded fields	Poor personality
Too narrow specialization	Untidiness in dress
No extracurricular experiences	Physical defects
Low grades in teaching subjects	Religious and racial discrimination

Most of these obstacles to placement can be surmounted through programs of selective admission and retention, limited enrollment, and guidance. Although affected by cycles of unemployment, the teaching profession has increased steadily. Including teachers in private elementary and secondary schools, and instructional staff members in all institutions of higher education, the teaching profession in the United States now numbers much more than a million.

Appointment to Position. The prospective teacher must remember that in order to be placed he must be appointed or selected. The appointment of teachers—a power that should be sacredly exercised—is usually made upon the bases of credentials, record in college, participation in extracurricular activities, personality, personal interview, and experience. Then, too, there is a growing reliance upon examinations. The American Council on Education, through its National Committee on Teacher Examinations, and with the aid of a grant from the Carnegie Foundation, launched a series of tests as part of a nation-wide objective basis for testing candidates for teaching positions. The best practice in employing teachers is that whereby the board of education appoints persons recommended by the superintendent. Where there is no school executive, as in the thousands of one-teacher schools, the appointment is made by the board or by the county superintendent of schools. A teacher seeking a position in a village or city school system should apply directly to the superintendent of schools, but he should not apply unless there is a vacancy. After the candidate has obtained a position, he continues his growth through planned orientation and other phases of in-service education, a requirement that many other professions do not have.

IN-SERVICE TEACHER EDUCATION

INTERNSHIP IN TEACHING

In addition to the fact that it very vitally integrates the theoretical and practical aspects of the student's education, internship has many other significant values. It gives the beginning teacher a chance to spend the first year in a superior school under conditions conducive to growth, it provides guidance and supervision at the time when most needed, it makes possible a gradual transition from student to teacher, and it serves as a period of testing and probation. These values and others are derived from internship plans now conducted jointly by many institutions of teacher education and cooperating public schools.

SUPERVISION OF TEACHING AND LEARNING

Too brief preservice education necessitates much in-service learning. In contradistinction to preteaching, the in-service growth is more a result of doing than of listening. The essential bases for effective in-service teacher education are a continuing zeal for learning, a broad outlook on the role of the school in modern society, an understanding of learning procedures, the improvement of teaching skill, an appreciation of the role of administration, and, finally, the scientific use of evaluation procedures.

One means of achieving multiple in-service growth for all teachers is through supervision. At first supervision was limited to matters directly associated with classroom teaching, but now it is extended to the entire field of learning and teaching. This guidance is provided by the superintendent of schools, the principal, the department head, the supervisor, or the teachers themselves. There is a marked trend on the part of supervisors to encourage self-direction for teachers. The helping teacher cannot assume the entire responsibility for the improvement of instruction; all professionally minded teachers are very desirous of self-guidance and development. To this end the supervisor is not content with a laissez-faire policy, but, with complete faith in their ability to advance, she stimulates the teachers to progress. She visits their classrooms less and less as they grow in self-supervision. Just as the modern instructor seeks to teach through pupil effort, so the modern supervisor strives to improve instruction through teacher effort. The endeavors of teachers to reduce pupil failures are likewise being matched by genuine attempts of administrators to decrease the number of teacher failures.

OTHER MEANS OF STIMULATING TEACHER GROWTH

Over the main entrance to the New Jersey State Teachers College at Newark is the quotation: "Who dares to teach must never cease to learn."

FIG. 11-5. Teachers observe in one of Saginaw's industrial plants during visitation day, which is a part of induction week. Industry, business, and schools cooperate to make the visitations successful. (*Courtesy of Public Schools, Saginaw, Mich.*)

No person should decide to teach unless he is resolved to *learn,* for the real teacher is a part-time student all his life in a continuation school from which he does not graduate. Chaucer's description of the clerk of Oxenford applies to many an educator:

> Souninge in moral vertu was his speche,
> And gladly wolde he lerne, and gladly teche.

Learning to teach and teaching to learn are the goals of the artist teacher. The more one teaches the more educated he becomes. As Tennyson wrote:

> Yet all experience is an arch where-thro'
> Gleams that untravell'd world, whose margin fades
> Forever and forever when I move.

An old Arab proverb pithily poses this paradox, "The greater the diameter of light, the greater the circumference of darkness." A teacher must grow if his pupils are to develop. Teaching as a profession will advance as long as the individual teachers continue to progress.

The teaching profession, as no other, provides a challenge to continued growth. Yet too many teachers are bound by self-satisfaction and calloused complacency—they do not stretch forward in the pursuit of perfection. On the other hand many of them work too hard, endangering their health. They neglect recreation possibly because they do not know how to relax or to enjoy wholesome avocations or helpful hobbies. Some teachers need a change of environment or rest. The granting of periodic fellowships to teachers has been recommended in addition to paying their salaries. These scholarships would permit a year of travel, further study, or rest for outstanding teachers. It has been suggested that schools employ a "sabbatical stagger plan" whereby teachers who have been in service to the state for a period of six years or more be given a year's or half year's leave of absence with half pay, while substitutes are employed at reduced salaries.

Among the types of in-service educational growth are these:

Curriculum building
Constructive supervision
Demonstration and school visits
Consultative service in school
Summer study
Extension and home study
Professional and cultural reading
Travel
Sabbatical leave
Exchange teaching
Workshops and clinics
Institutes
Professional organization and meetings
Panel method of discussion
Research investigations and surveys
Salary increments and scholarships
Retirement plans
Tenure legislation
Fall planning conferences
Teachers' meetings
Visitations

With adequate preservice preparation, continuous in-service education can be designed to cover limitless possibilities.

TEACHING PROFESSION

Teacher Welfare

It is natural that teachers as a professional group and as individuals should look out for their own welfare as well as that of the children.

Among the welfare factors in which teachers are usually interested are (1) salaries, (2) tenure, and (3) retirement.

Salaries. Although salaries have increased steadily over a long stretch of time, teachers still earn far less on the average than do skilled tradesmen. Costs of living have mounted appreciably, and the educational qualifications for teachers have risen, necessitating a greater investment in preparation. The National Education Association has prepared the following principles of salary scheduling:

1. Minimum salaries should be high enough to attract well educated, promising young people into teaching.

2. Maximum salaries should be high enough to retain highly competent and professionally ambitious men and women in classroom teaching.

3. Equity of treatment to classroom teachers of like qualifications and experience is essential.

4. Annual increments should provide an orderly progress to the maximum salary.

5. The salary schedule should offer professional stimulation through incentives in recognition of professional qualifications.

6. Salary schedules should be adjusted periodically, with due consideration for trends in earnings in other professions and for changes in the cost of living.

7. Salaries of professional school personnel other than classroom teachers should be scheduled in accordance with the principles that apply to classroom teachers, with suitable recognition of responsibilities and preparation for leadership.

8. There should be professional participation by classroom teachers in the development and administration of salary policies.[5]

Robert M. Hutchins has said that society cannot get good schools without good teachers, and that by paying them like coolies society shows no respect for the teaching profession.

The minimum amount of salary varies widely from state to state.[6] The fact that teacher salaries in some states are very low has given rise to agitation for minimum-salary laws—a floor under wages.

Most school systems adopt a salary schedule. This is a plan for the payment of school employees formally accepted by the school committee or board of education. To a large degree it automatically determines the initial salary, the amount and number of yearly increments, and the maximum salary received by the various employees with specified qualifications. Among the factors determining the place of the teachers on the regular salary schedule are amount of professional education, number of years of service, ratings on an efficiency scale, and position held. A salary

[5] *NEA News,* Mar. 26, 1954, p. 3.

[6] Current statistics on teachers' salaries are published periodically by the Research Division, National Education Association.

schedule obviates the perennial question among teachers: "How m. money do you get?"

Teacher Tenure. Another ever-asked question is: "How long have you been teaching here?" Because of the large turnover, teaching has been called a procession rather than a profession. As to length, a teacher's contractual relationships are usually annual agreement, permissive contract for more than a year, continuing contract, or permanent tenure. Insecurity of tenure or uncertainty of holding one's position has always been a handicap to effective teaching. The basic principles that should control the framing and operation of tenure legislation have been prepared by the National Education Association.

Although legislation should protect teachers from discharge for political, religious, personal, and other unjust reasons, the laws should not prevent the dismissal of teachers for incompetence, immorality, or any unprofessional conduct. A too-rigorous tenure law may be a boomerang. The best tenure for teachers is that unsolicited security which is bestowed by an appreciative public for services sacrificially rendered beyond the call of daily duties.

Teacher Retirement. Another moot question among teachers and other professional people is: "When do you expect to retire?" or "What do you expect to do when you retire?"

In bygone years retirement was associated with physical or mental infirmities. Retirement provisions for aged and disabled employees originated as private or local enterprises on a charity basis. Today a different idea prevails: there is a growing sense of social and public responsibility for old-age protection. A newer trend is "phased retirement," whereby a teacher moves from full-time teaching, through successive stages of part-time work, to ultimate full-time retirement. Readiness for retirement is important.

Public responsibility for the retirement of teachers began in cities and local districts. Establishment of these systems reached the peak about 1915. Since that time many local plans have become inoperative or have been absorbed by state-wide retirement or pension systems. New Jersey was the first state to enact provisions for a state-wide retirement system for teachers in 1896. The majority of states have since followed suit, also Alaska, Hawaii, Puerto Rico, and the District of Columbia. Figure 11-6 depicts the operation of a state system. Retirement systems are supplemented by many varied and interesting forms of teacher welfare evolved by individual states and cities. In 1927, the Council of the California Teachers Association, Southern Section, authorized the establishment of a home for retired teachers who could not finance themselves. The first home was a five-room bungalow; larger quarters are now in use. A few associations and cities have similar arrangements. The National Education Association has cooperated with local, state, and national groups in promoting the social security of teachers. Many public- and private-school and college teachers benefit from the retirement provisions of the Social

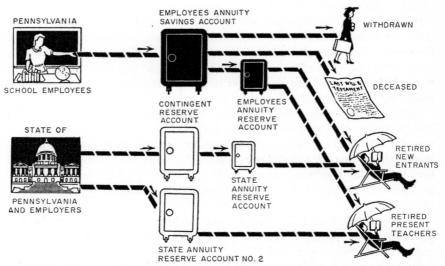

FIG. 11-6. Pennsylvania's teacher-retirement system. Pennsylvania has one fund called the School Employees' Retirement Fund, consisting of the accounts shown in the chart. The transfers are merely bookkeeping matters.

A percentage of the school employee's salary, determined by actuarial investigations, is deducted from each pay roll, and accredited to the Employees' Annuity Savings Account. The retirement board certifies annually the amount the state of Pennsylvania should contribute. The state pays semiannually into the Contingent Reserve Account for each new entrant, and into the State Annuity Reserve Account No. 2 for each "present employee." When a new entrant retires, an amount is transferred from the Contingent Reserve Account to the State Annuity Reserve Account.

The right-hand side of the diagram indicates that money is paid out when the teacher withdraws from the system, dies, or retires, either as a new entrant or as a teacher who was employed when the system went into effect. (*Courtesy of Research Division, National Education Association.*)

Security Act. A National Association of Retired Teachers has been organized.

PROFESSIONAL ETHICS FOR TEACHERS

The groups with whom teachers come in contact in their work are the board of education, the administrators, the supervisors, the teachers, the nonteaching staff, the pupils, the parents, and the community. A profession can rise no higher than the code of ethics it adopts and uses daily. As guides in the relationships of teachers with other groups, such codes have been evolved by state associations and the National Education Association.

PROFESSIONAL ORGANIZATIONS

Among the various ways in which educational organizations may be classified are these: by primary objective, such as the promotion of childhood education (Association for Childhood Education); by major function, such as the accrediting of schools (accrediting associations); by the significance of leaders in education (Horace Mann League or John Dewey Society); by type of membership, such as elementary teachers (Los Angeles Elementary Teachers Club); by religious affiliation (National Catholic Education Association); and by scope, such as geographical areas (Memphis Education Association or National Education Association). Because of their simplicity the geographical classifications, (1) local, (2) state, (3) national, and (4) international, are utilized here as a framework for outlining the professional educational associations.

Local Organizations. In some communities teachers are not organized at all, but nearly all public- and private-school teachers do belong "to a whole or a part of a whole." This banding together serves many purposes. The Department of Classroom Teachers states that it is the peculiar function of local teachers' organizations to provide teachers with an opportunity to understand the problems of their respective communities and to acquaint the public in each community with the needs of its teachers and its schools. As stated by Willard E. Givens, former executive secretary of the National Education Association, "In the local education association is found the growing edge of the organized teaching profession."

There is marked variation in types of groupings. Some organizations restrict membership to instructors in a certain field; others are open to all members of an educational staff of a particular school. No one type seems to predominate, although a single organization to include all teachers is growing in favor. Cities with more than one association often have a council, composed of representatives of each group, to look after common interests. Recent years have increased interest in and debate about the affiliation of local teachers' organizations with labor groups. This issue is presented later in Unit XVII. Suffice it here to state that teachers are becoming more sensitized to the problems of labor and that enrollments in teachers' unions have increased markedly in recent years.

State Organizations. The local unit may be organized as part of some larger whole, such as the county or state associations. Many of these are determined by fields, as social studies; by grade levels, as elementary teachers; or by function of personnel, as city superintendents. The main core of organized professional activity within the state, however, is the state-wide all-inclusive society, which is usually known as the "state education association" or "state teachers' association." The usual purposes of these organizations, as indicated in their state journals and as reflected in their activities, are to perform on a state-wide basis what the local groups seek to do. There is a major emphasis on professional improvement of the members, the advancement of teacher and pupil welfare, service to the schools and communities in the state, particularly through legislation, and active cooperation with the associations of other states and national associations.

In recent years many state associations or state departments of education have set up long-term planning commissions, which seek to view education within the state with a telescopic vision rather than with a microscopic dissection of minute current problems. This movement is one of the bright spots on the educational horizon, especially since it is being matched by long-term planning on a national scale.

National Organizations—General. The *Educational Directory* prepared periodically by the United States Office of Education lists numerous educational organizations whose names begin with the word "National" or "American." All these and many others are nation-wide in scope. Although most of them represent some special field, they are permeated with large elements of common interest. In recent years many national agencies have made critical analyses of particular aspects of American public education. *The Directory of Deliberative National Committees* lists over 250 such groups which prepare reports on various school problems. The American Council on Education, composed of representatives from various national associations and educational institutions, is a significant coordinating body. This council, organized in 1918, has sponsored such important projects as the Commission on Teacher Education and the American Youth Commission. One of its important member organizations is the National Education Association.

National Education Association. This all-inclusive educative organization is also the largest teachers' association in the world. It was organized in 1857 when 43 educators gathered in Philadelphia and formed the National Teachers Association. The name was changed to the National Education Association in 1907, when it was incorporated under a special act of Congress. Its membership is now far beyond the half-million mark. Its membership goal is expressed in the ideal: 100 per cent enrollment in local, state, and national associations, with every teacher at work on the problems of the profession.

In brief its purposes are these:

The National Education Association is dedicated to the upbuilding of democratic civilization and is supported by the loyal cooperation of the leaders of the United States to advance the interests of the teaching profession, promote the welfare of children, and foster the education of all the people.

It renders two kinds of services. First come those services that reach the members directly, such as the *NEA Journal,* issued nine times a year, and other publications, as well as conventions of the association in July, and of the American Association of School Administrators and allied organizations in February. These help to promote personal growth and educational research and to build up the common mind of the profession. The second type of service is indirect. Like the values which the citizen receives from his taxes, these benefits are often overlooked. An important function of the association is its campaign to create a public opinion that

Fig. 11-7. New headquarters of the National Education Association, Washington, D.C.

demands good public schools. It aims to elevate the character and advance the interests of the teaching profession and to promote the cause of education in the United States. It is not, however, an agency of the federal government.

The National Education Association, as an all-inclusive voluntary organization of teachers and administrators in pre-elementary, elementary, secondary, higher, and adult education, is a democratic institution. Its policies are determined by the representative assembly coming from all over the United States each summer in connection with the annual convention. This body consists of delegates elected by state and local organizations of teachers. The administration of the affairs of the association is handled by this representative assembly, a board of trustees, an executive committee, and a board of directors. The professional and clerical staff, working under the direction of the executive secretary, is housed in the association's own building at 1201 Sixteenth Street, N.W., Washington, D.C. This comprehensive association has 29 departments.[7] The following list prepared by the NEA omits the organizational names (association, conference, council, department), and gives only the field of professional activity:

Administrative women in education
Adult education
Art education
Audio-visual instruction
Business education
Classroom teachers
Deans of women
Educational research
Educational secretaries
Elementary-school principals
Exceptional children
Health, physical education, and recreation
Higher education
Home economics
Journalism directors of secondary schools
Kindergarten-primary education
Mathematics teachers
Music education
Retired teachers
Rural education
School administrators
School public relations
Science teachers
Secondary-school principals
Social studies
Speech education
Supervision and curriculum development
Teacher education
Vocational education

It has served the profession through such national commissions as the following: Legislation, Educational Policies, the Defense of Democracy, Safety Education, and Teacher Education and Professional Standards. It has allied organizations, such as the National Congress of Parents and Teachers, and it cooperates with many agencies, such as the American Council on Education and the Council on Cooperation in Teacher Education. It is not connected with labor unions.

American Federation of Teachers. This national organization of teachers is affiliated with the American Federation of Labor in order to gain allies in its fight against what it believes to be social, economic, and political injustices to the profession of education. Since 1927 it has been experiencing a steady growth. The Federation has two main objectives:

(1) It purposes to consolidate the teachers of the country into a strong group which would be able to protect its own interests. (2) It aims to raise the standard of the teaching class by a direct attack on the conditions which, according to the belief of the Federation, prevent teaching from enjoying the status of a profession. These conditions are: lack of academic freedom and of civil liberty, the absence of the opportunity for self-determination of policies and for democratic control.

[7] A short history of each department is published annually in the *Proceedings.*

Its official organ is *The American Teacher,* published nine times a year. Among its standing committees are: academic freedom, democratic human relations, pensions and retirement, protection of teachers' rights, state federations, taxation and school finance, vocational education, working conditions, adult and workers' education, child care, and educational trends and policies. An international organization made up of free teachers' unions outside the Iron Curtain has been established.

International Organizations. Several organizations listed in the *Educational Directory* contain in their titles the words "world" or "international"; only a few can be mentioned here. The International Council for Exceptional Children holds annual sessions. The National Education Association has an active Committee on International Relations, which aided in the preparation of *Education for International Understanding in American Schools.* The World Federation of Education Associations was a pioneering organization in the field of world-wide general education. Many countries were represented in the World Organization of the Teaching Profession, which was organized in Glasgow, Scotland, in 1947 and reorganized as the World Confederation of Organizations of the Teaching Profession in 1953 at Oxford, England. This organization has

FIG. 11-8. Four-square education associations—local, state, national, and world. Professional leadership upholds the torch of knowledge.

been recognized by the United Nations as an official consultative body. As previously indicated, the United States has a National Commission for UNESCO—United Nations Educational, Scientific, and Cultural Organization—and is actively working with the United Nations in world-wide education. W. G. Carr states that WCOTP is to UNESCO as the NEA is to the United States Office of Education.

The New Education Fellowship, which was founded in Heidelberg in 1918 with the main purpose of making education a "force for improving the world order," is another world-wide organization. Still another is the International Association of Professors and Lecturers, constituted in Brussels in 1947. Six years later was organized at Oxford, England, the International Council on Education for Teaching—a world-wide association for teachers of teachers.

Through educational organizations and publications, the teaching profession is constantly being improved and advanced. According to Mark A. May of the Institute of Human Relations at Yale University, "it is an open secret that in the hierarchy of respectability of professions in American society, the teaching profession ranks rather low." Through continuous and all-inclusive membership in strong, active organizations—local, state, national, and international—teachers can achieve the ethical, economic, and professional respectability toward which they are striving. Although the immediate purpose may sometimes be tinged with the minor motives of personal and professional profit and protection, nevertheless teachers' organizations at their best serve honorable means toward the worthy end of providing better educational opportunities for children through improving teaching personnel.

TEACHING PERSONNEL

Obviously most school positions are for teachers. The major types of teaching personnel described here are (1) classroom teachers, (2) special classroom teachers, (3) teachers in federal jurisdictions and foreign countries, and (4) teachers of teachers. Other persons engaged in educational work are treated in Unit XII.

CLASSROOM TEACHERS

Opportunities for the largest number of persons are in what might be called straight teaching or classroom teaching positions. Although there are numerous private and parochial schools, the public-school system affords the largest number of these teaching positions. Classroom teachers are found in nearly all the institutions mentioned in Units I through IV, *viz.,* national, state, county, and local systems. They work in all the academic levels considered in Units V through IX, *viz.,* pre-elementary, elementary, secondary, higher institutions, and education for out-of-school youth and adults.

SPECIAL CLASSROOM TEACHERS

Among the so-called "special teachers" are those who deal with (1) particular types of pupils, as the exceptional; (2) special methods or materials, as audio-visual education; (3) specialized subjects or fields, as vocational education; and (4) special institutions, as hospital schools.

Teachers of Special Pupils. Unit X centers around the two major types of pupils, *viz.,* the normal and the atypical. The former, because of their natural resourcefulness, ability, and ambition, may succeed in school and life despite their teachers, but the disadvantaged pupils may be further handicapped in a marked degree because their teachers are inefficient or not specially educated for their particular tasks. The atypical pupils, especially those severely handicapped, need teachers expert in the special areas appertaining to the major types of exceptional pupil described in Unit X. The laws of most states stipulate that teachers of exceptional children must have specialized preparation and possess particularized certificates.

Many educational institutions offer this special preparation. A number of residential schools offer preparation for teachers of exceptional children, particularly of the mentally handicapped.

In addition to special education for the individualized work, the teacher of handicapped children should have patience, a sympathetic and thorough understanding of the principles and facts of physical growth, buoyant optimism, and a healthy social philosophy. Several thousand more teachers are needed for the large number of handicapped pupils in the public schools. In view of the specialized preparation, the exacting nature of the task, and the special state aid for such children, the salaries of these special instructors are usually higher than those of the regular classroom teachers. The monetary rewards, however, are insignificant in comparison to the heartful thanks of those who profit most— the pupils, many of whom have ears but hear not, eyes but see not, tongues but talk not, and feet but walk not.[8]

Teachers with Special Methods or Materials. Among the teachers who devote full or part time to instructional procedures or materials of a special nature are those engaged in audio-visual or multisensory education. Schools of the air, made possible by radio, facsimile broadcasting, and television, will need many experienced teachers. Many schools have set up departments with directors of audio-visual instruction. Because of the close relationships between audio-visual education and the school curriculum, the directors and others engaged in this special work ought to understand thoroughly the curriculum and child growth in order to coordinate their efforts with those of the regular classroom teachers.

Teachers of Special Subjects or Fields. In a sense nearly every teacher works in a special subject or field. Each general subject or field offers many specific phases; for example, several different kinds of English are taught. There is always plenty of room at the top for persons who possess the uncommon blend of artistic sense and teaching skill. A shortage of superlatively good teachers exists in almost every area of learning.

A particular field that is increasing its number of workers is vocational education in all its phases—agriculture, home economics, trades, commerce, distributive occupations, and prevocational and vocational guidance. Much of the vocational teaching today is being done "on the job."

Teachers in Special Schools. Many teachers are employed in special schools, like church and Bible schools, technical schools, correctional institutions, experimental centers, and hospital schools. The last are briefly described here.

[8] See *Careers in Service to the Handicapped*, distributed by the National Society for Crippled Children and Adults, 1952, 53 pp.

Some hospital schools are in private institutions, whereas others are in municipal or state hospitals. The services rendered in this type of teaching are threefold: therapeutic, vocational, and general educational. It seems reasonable to expect that states will give increased financial and moral support to this type of teaching and that many positions will have to be filled in the years to come.

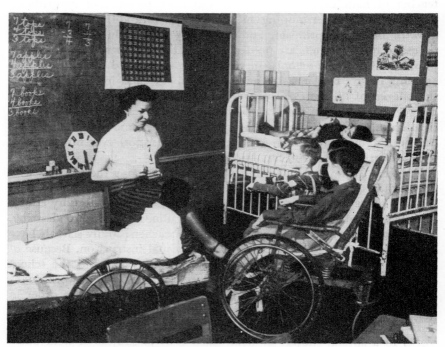

FIG. 11-9. Teacher in hospital school conducts an arithmetic lesson for pupils in bed, on cot, and in wheel chairs. (*Courtesy of Toledo Society for Crippled Children and National Foundation for Infantile Paralysis.*)

As to qualifications, the hospital teacher needs the same background of training and experience required for teaching normal children, plus some clinical work. His "personality quotient" needs to be high. In many states the regular requirements for teachers in general apply to hospital-school instructors, although usually the latter are specially qualified or certified by the state superintendent.

The hospital schools are not merely for children but for adults as well. This type of work promises to increase owing to the individual and nation-wide interest in adult education, the circumstance that patients in hospitals have leisure time to devote to study, and in some cases the fact that the patients have to be rehabilitated in new occupations.

Teachers in Federal Jurisdictions and Foreign Countries

A large number of teachers are employed or supervised by the federal government. Aside from the instructors in the nation-wide federally aided programs of emergency and vocational education, many persons teach in the federal reservations, in the territories, dependencies, and special areas in and outside the United States. In some of the dependencies, only natives or resident white people are employed as teachers.

Exchange Teachers. Another opportunity to teach away from home is provided by exchange teaching. Exchanges in teaching personnel are made between cities and between countries, usually for a 1-year period. The purposes of these temporary transfers are to trade educational and social ideas; to dissolve provincialism; to foster better feeling between sections of the United States and between various countries; to understand better the countries of the world; and to promote a broader outlook on the part of students, faculties, and communities. Teaching experience is usually a prerequisite for appointment as an exchange teacher.

Teachers of Teachers

Thousands of persons are engaged in teaching teachers, including work in public and private schools, normal schools, teachers colleges, and departments and schools of education in colleges and universities. Among the positions are those held by critics or supervisors of cadets in teacher-educating institutions or in affiliated schools, and by members of the various departments in colleges and universities, especially education and psychology departments. Opportunities for this work are thus available on all academic levels, from preservice education of prospective teachers for the nursery schools to the in-service education of faculty members in graduate schools.

The minimum academic requirement is a master's degree, with some courses in education and psychology, and practical experience in public schools. Increasingly, actual school experience is required of supervising teachers and regular collegiate staff members in order that they may be familiar with the needs of prospective teachers in these schools. The supply of new capable supervisors of student teachers is very limited. The supreme challenge to engage in teacher education lies in the unsurpassed opportunities to multiply oneself, since an instructor of prospective or regular teachers potentially reaches thousands of pupils. A teacher of teachers is also an indirect teacher of pupils.

Shall I Become a Teacher?

This unit on teachers concludes with the significant question, "Shall I become a teacher?" On this subject Joy Elmer Morgan wrote: "Your answer concerns not only you but in a most vital way the lives of hundreds and even thousands who for better or for worse will sit at your feet if you choose to devote yourself to the teaching profession, which both in numbers and influence is one of the major occupations of modern times."

Any person conscientiously seeking an answer to the query, "Shall I become a teacher?" should ask himself many other questions, since teaching is a complicated process involving numerous variables.

Personal. Among other queries the prospective teacher asks:

Have I a sound body, physical vigor, and good posture?
Have I good mental health and emotional maturity?
Can I cultivate a sound philosophy of life?
Do I have a constructive and positive outlook on life?
Have I sense of humor?
Have I a balanced ration in hobbies: mental, physical, social, and aesthetic?
Do I like books and other instruments of culture, such as art and music?
Have I a broad background of helpful information and useful skills?
Have I intellectual curiosity and a zeal for scholarship?
Do I or can I cultivate the habitual use of effective English?
Is my voice pleasant and audible?
Is my personal appearance attractive?
Is my pattern of thinking, speaking, and living such as to justify emulation?

Social. Realizing that the the teacher deals primarily with human beings, the candidate for teaching asks:

Do I cultivate a friendly, interested, and courteous manner?
Is my "personality quotient" adequate for dealing daily with human beings?
Am I able to get along with people in an interdependent society?
Can I lead or follow as the occasion demands?
Can I work cooperatively with my colleagues?
Do I enjoy working with children and young people?
Am I interested in and capable of directing some cocurricular activity?
Have I sufficient training in the social graces and niceties of group living?
Do I possess or can I develop a talent for friendship?
Have I a capacity for sympathetic understanding?
Am I sufficiently sensitized to human needs?
Do I believe in the improvability of the human race?
Am I vitally interested in promoting democracy through education?
Am I interested in community, state, national, and international welfare?
Do I see and feel the interdependence of school and society?

Professional. As a prospective member of a great profession, the candidate for admission asks:

Have I adequate physical vitality to meet the strenuous demands of teaching?
Have I the high moral and ethical standards demanded by this profession?
Have I a basic understanding of children and of teaching techniques?

Can I organize materials and activities so that pupils will learn economically?
Can I teach others how to learn for themselves?
Am I unafraid of hard work that brings few monetary rewards?
Can I dedicate myself to a profession that is devoted to service and sacrifice?
Would I rather earn my living by teaching than in any other way?
Am I willing and able to prepare for and grow in my profession?
Can I enter an old profession such as teaching with a pioneering spirit?

All these questions need not be answered in the affirmative instanter, but the prospective teacher who looks forward toward a *career* in his profession must constantly be alert to the present and future implications of these and other queries of a personal, social, and professional nature.

SUGGESTED ACTIVITIES

1. Give a brief history of the life of some great teacher or describe a teacher who helped you greatly.
2. Prepare a history of some institution engaged in teacher education.
3. Explain the purpose and program of the Future Teachers of America.
4. Debate selective admission for institutions engaged in teacher education.
5. Prepare a list of some commercial agencies that place teachers, and investigate their agreements.
6. Write a letter of application for a teaching position.
7. Examine the certification requirements for teaching in your state.
8. Describe some organized means for in-service education of teachers.
9. Make an annotated list of the best professional magazines available in your teaching field or area.
10. Defend your answer to the question, "Is teaching a profession?"
11. Debate the topic: "Resolved that teachers should join organizations affiliated with labor unions."
12. Prepare a history of the National Education Association or the American Council on Education.
13. Make a list of educational organizations in your state.
14. Visit the headquarters of your state educational association.
15. Study the laws of your state which deal with tenure, salaries, and retirement.
16. Describe the best elementary- or secondary-school teacher you know.
17. Interview an experienced teacher as to the handicaps and rewards of teaching. List in two parallel columns the disadvantages and the advantages of teaching.
18. Visit a teacher of special pupils.
19. Investigate the opportunities and rewards in teaching in a federal jurisdiction, such as the District of Columbia.
20. Investigate the types of positions available for teachers of teachers.
21. Make a critical self-evaluation to determine whether you should enter or remain in the teaching profession.

DESCRIPTIVE BIBLIOGRAPHY AND AIDS

BOOKS

AMERICAN ASSOCIATION OF SCHOOL ADMINISTRATORS: *Education for American Citizenship,* Chap. IX, National Education Association, 1954.
    The role of teachers in building citizenship.

AMERICAN ASSOCIATION OF SCHOOL ADMINISTRATORS: *Staff Relations in School Administration,* Chap. II, National Education Association, 1955.
 Personnel procedures in school administration.

ARBUCKLE, DUGALD S.: *Student Personnel Services in Higher Education,* Chap. II, McGraw-Hill, 1953.
 Teaching in institutions of higher learning.

ELSBREE, WILLARD S., and E. EDMUND REUTTER, JR.; *Staff Personnel in the Public Schools,* Chap. V, Prentice-Hall, 1954.
 Orientation for the newly appointed teacher.

GRAVES, ALBERT D.: *American Secondary Education,* Chap. XV, Heath, 1951.
 The teacher in secondary education.

GRUHN, WILLIAM T.: *Student Teaching in the Secondary School,* Part I, Ronald, 1954.
 Looking ahead to student teaching—getting started.

MURSELL, JAMES L.: *Successful Teaching,* 2d ed., Chap. XI, McGraw-Hill, 1954.
 Orientation to successful teaching.

MYERS, ALONZO F., and CLARENCE O. WILLIAMS: *Education in a Democracy,* Chap. VII, Prentice-Hall, 1954.
 Asking the question: "Shall I become a teacher?"

SPEAR, HAROLD: *Principles of Teaching,* Chap. XIV, Prentice-Hall, 1951.
 The teacher's welfare—tenure, sick leave.

WOODRING, PAUL: *Let's Talk Sense about Our Schools,* Chaps. VI, VII, McGraw-Hill, 1953.
 The teachers college in American education and the American teacher.

YEAGER, WILLIAM A.: *Administration and the Teacher,* Chap. XXIII, Harper, 1954.
 Ethics in the teaching profession.

CURRENT PERTINENT PERIODICALS AND PUBLICATIONS

Alumni bulletins
American Teacher
Catholic Education Review
Delta Kappa Gamma Bulletin
Educational Forum
Education for Teaching
Education Today
Harvard Educational Review
Journal of Negro Education
Journal of Teacher Education
Local association journals
Lutheran Education
NEA Journal
NEA News
News Bulletin
Newsletter of Council on Cooperation in Teacher Education

Novels dealing with teachers:
 Blackboard Jungle
 Silver Pencil
 Fair Is the Morning
 How We Fought for Our Schools
 Separate Star
 Hi Teacher
 Good Morning, Miss Dove
 A Song for Julie
 The End of the Week
Peabody Journal of Education
Phi Delta Kappan
Pi Lambda Theta Journal
Research Bulletin
State education association journals
Teacher Education
Teachers College Record
Yearbook of Education

AUDIO-VISUAL AIDS

ASSIGNMENT: TOMORROW   25 min., sound
 Deals with tomorrow's most exciting assignment—that of teaching children. The cast of characters consists of typical American children and their teachers. Produced by the National Education Association. If not available from the state education

association, it can be obtained from the National Education Association, Washington, D.C.

THE ELEMENTARY TEACHER 10 min., sound

Shows how elementary-school teachers grow and develop professionally. The first in a series of four films produced by the Audio-visual Center at University of Indiana, Bloomington, Ind.

PREPARATION OF TEACHERS 16 min., sound

How Jack and Elaine, two student teachers, live with children. Helpful for case studies. Made at Ball State Teachers College, Muncie, Ind.; produced in cooperation with the U.S. Office of Information for overseas use.

TOMORROW WON'T WAIT Transcribed radio program, 14 min., sound

Emphasizes the responsibility of every citizen to school children and teachers. Available from the National Education Association, Washington, D.C.

WHAT GREATER GIFT 28 min., sound, b&w or color

Dramatizes the classroom teacher as a professional person. Informational and inspirational. Available from the National Education Association.

OTHER PERSONNEL

In addition to classroom teaching, described in Unit XI, many other opportunities for service are available in American education.

Among the semiteaching personnel are part-time teachers, such as substitutes; off-campus leaders, as extension workers; personnel workers, as guidance and placement officials; and other specialists, including curriculum and research directors.

Many positions in the higher salaried group are of an administrative and supervisory nature. These positions are found in elementary, secondary, and higher education.

From professions other than teaching come many educational workers, such as librarians, doctors, nurses, accountants, architects, lawyers, and social workers.

Among the other nonteachers employed in public education are clerks, cafeteria workers, school custodians, bus drivers, publishers, salesmen, and day laborers.

OUTLINE OF CONTENTS

Introduction
    Varied opportunities in education
Part-time and Semiteaching Personnel
    Part-time teachers
    Off-campus workers
    Personnel workers
    Other specialists
Administrative and Supervisory Positions in Education
    Superintendents of schools
    Principals of schools
    Supervisors of instruction
    Department heads and college deans
    Presidents of educational institutions
    Other administrative officers
Educational Personnel from Other Professions
    Librarians
    Health personnel
    Business and building personnel
    School lawyers
    Other professional or semiprofessional groups
Other Nonteaching Personnel in Education
    School clerks and secretaries
    Cafeteria and lunchroom workers
    Building service personnel
    School transportation personnel
    Educational editors, publishers, and sales personnel
    Others employed in education

OTHER PERSONNEL

The following story is taken from a bulletin of the U.S. Office of Education:

Set in the wall of the main corridor of a public school in a small city of Iowa is a bronze tablet bearing, in low relief, the heroic likeness of a man and the inscription—"He gave thirty-two years of faithful service to the youth of this community." From the dedicatory program we learn that the tablet was placed "by its hundreds of donors with the belief that all those who shall frequent these halls in the years to come will be inspired, as we who present it were inspired, by him."

This superior personage, so memorialized, was not a member of the board of education; he was not a superintendent; not a principal; nor an exceptional teacher, but the school janitor or custodian.

The janitor or custodian is usually one of the many forgotten men and women who daily serve the youth in school.

Varied Opportunities in Education. In the average mind those adults who are associated rather exclusively with the learning of children are the classroom teachers. For many nonclassroom positions of significance in education, classroom teaching is a prerequisite, but many persons in education work are not directly engaged in teaching. No one can overestimate the importance of teachers, but neither should he ignore or forget the hundreds of other educational workers. Unfortunately the emphasis in recruitment of personnel for public education has been unbalanced—it has been delimited to the customary and established positions such as classroom teaching and has not revealed the wide range of educational activities in which careers have been established or are now emerging. This has tended to inhibit social progress and to drive away from educational service many talented persons.

There are now several hundred different positions in education. Approximately fifty types of educational work are described briefly in Units XI and XII. No rigid groupings can be made, since duties overlap, but the educational employees are listed under the following major types:

1. Teaching personnel—especially classroom teachers (see Unit XI)
2. Part-time and semiteaching personnel
3. Administrative and supervisory officers
4. Educational personnel from other professions
5. Other nonteaching personnel in education

Teaching personnel, especially classroom teachers, are described in Unit XI. The pages that follow are concerned primarily with those persons engaged in educational work other than full-time classroom teaching, as listed in the four remaining divisions.

PART-TIME AND SEMITEACHING PERSONNEL

Many educational workers do not devote a full school year or their entire time to teaching. Those who are not administrators may be grouped in four categories, *viz.*, (1) part-time teachers, (2) off-campus workers, (3) personnel workers, and (4) other specialists. Various persons within these groups are described briefly.

PART-TIME TEACHERS

Substitute Teachers. Opportunities for many persons, particularly married women, are afforded by part-time instruction in the form of substitute teaching. Occasional teachers should be carefully chosen according to definite standards. The fact that an unemployed person who taught 20 years ago needs a few dollars should not be the sole basis for selection. The candidate for substitute teaching is usually required to fill out and file with the superintendent of schools an application blank giving data as to education, ability, past experience, and certification. The applicant is also subject to an oral interview before being placed on the eligibility list. Adequate preparation is essential, since a poor substitute in one day may undo a week's work of the regular teacher.

Other Part-time Teachers. Among others who give a portion of their time to instruction are those special teachers employed for only a part of a day or week on a regular schedule. For example, a special music teacher may work a few hours daily; in college a specialist from the business world may teach an economics class or an expert surgeon may serve part-time as a special lecturer in certain aspects of surgery. Teaching provides part-time employment for many persons. With the great increase in pupils and the resultant shortage of teachers, many married women are entering or returning to full-time or part-time educational service.

OFF-CAMPUS WORKERS

Extension Workers. Many college and university instructors devote part of their time to teaching extension work. One important type of off-campus activity is the Cooperative Extension Service which involves the federal government through the United States Department of Agriculture, the federal government and the states through their land-grant colleges, the counties through their governing boards, and the local communities through their cooperating organizations and committees (see Fig. 12-1). All workers must be approved by the state and federal officials. This approval makes them employees of the agricultural college, which acts for the state, and of the United States Department of Agriculture.

Several members of the federal Extension Service devote themselves to extension administration, research studies, and teaching; an additional number are engaged in visual instruction and editorial activities. Foremost in the Cooperative Extension Service are the resident agents in the

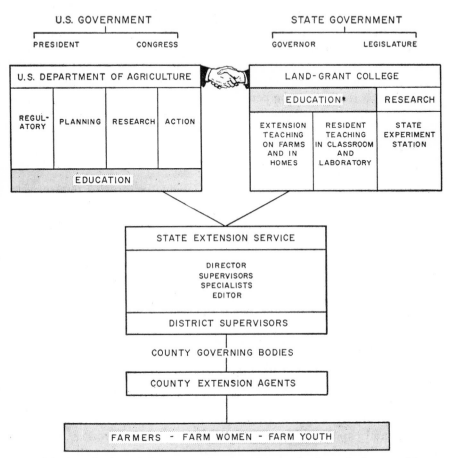

Fig. 12-1. Organization of the cooperative extension service in agriculture and home economics. (*Courtesy of U.S. Department of Agriculture.*)

counties and their assistants, *viz.*, the agricultural adviser, usually called the county agent; the home demonstration agent; and the boys' and girls' club agents or counselors. The National Association of County Agricultural Agents has recommended that county agents pursue systematic graduate study as a part of their activities. It is significant that the Advisory Committee on Education stated: "Everywhere in the Extension Service the work is considered as teaching."

Other Off-school-ground Workers. Today many others of the educational personnel spend much of their time away from the school grounds. For example, the coordinators in the federally aided vocational plan are constantly making contacts with employers and workers. Some of the personnel workers mentioned later spend much of their time in homes, fields, and factories.

PERSONNEL WORKERS

This unit and the preceding two deal with the personnel of American public education, including pupils, teachers, and other workers. Obviously many employees are especially delegated to tasks that deal almost entirely with the human or personal agents in education. This very important group, segregated here as personnel workers, includes (1) visiting teachers, (2) attendance officials, (3) guidance personnel, (4) placement officials, (5) deans of boys and men, (6) deans of girls and women, and (7) recreational leaders. These are singled out from a larger number for special emphasis in the succeeding pages.

Visiting Teachers or Counselors. A challenging form of service with dual duties is that performed by a visiting teacher or counselor, who acts as educator and social worker. Since she works with the two groups of adults who have the greatest influence on the child, *viz.,* parents and teachers, the visitor with her dual contacts is able to study the child as a product of both home and school. As a member of the teaching staff, she works closely with the school, and, as a social worker, she cooperates with existing social agencies. In many instances the visiting teacher is the home teacher or counselor. She is the representative of the classroom teacher in dealing with the pupil who must for physical or other reasons remain at home. As a social worker, she knows the organized social agencies upon which she can call for assistance in the material needs of the underprivileged pupil and his family. The visiting teacher also calls in the homes of well-adjusted, successful pupils.

The role of the visiting or home teacher requires insight, skill, conversational ability, a high degree of personal fitness, and the twofold basic training and experience of a teacher and a social case worker. Through a well-qualified visiting teacher the school looks *out* as well as *in* and stresses preventive as well as remedial procedures for normal and problem pupils. Visiting teacher work has its hardships, like any profession. The hours are irregular, including calls in the evening and often on Saturday and Sunday. Furthermore, tackling one serious problem after another brings a certain discouragement, and the constant handling of children's difficulties means a drain on the emotions. Despite these hardships, visiting teachers all over the United States are finding and losing themselves in this new educational profession.

Attendance Personnel. Among the employees of the school district are full-time or part-time census enumerators and attendance officials. Sometimes these two functionaries are combined in the same person, who may also be engaged in teaching. Although the trend is toward the establishment of a continuous school census, the enumeration of pupils of school age usually is a periodic task, especially in the small cities. The National League to Promote School Attendance is working toward a broader acceptance of the ideal of attendance work as an integral and continuing part of the total educational program.

The enforcement of attendance is a continuous obligation assigned to full-time workers in the larger school administrative units. These personnel workers are relatively recent in certain areas, for only since 1918 have all the 48 states had compulsory attendance laws. In the early days these employees were called "truant officers." Current practice favors a title such as "attendance worker," since it emphasizes the positive philosophy of improving the attendance of all pupils rather than the negative and often temporary remedy whereby a burly policeman caught a truant and dragged him back to school. The old practice aimed at making the pupil conform to the school laws, whereas the modern objective implies the willingness of school authorities to adjust the program to the pupil's peculiar needs, interests, and abilities. Home and school cooperation is sought.

Whereas an officer's badge and knowledge of school laws were formerly the prerequisites for an attendance worker, now the qualifications demand an understanding of child welfare problems and social case work. A national organization of attendance officers as well as state and local agencies are trying to raise the present level of school attendance service so that it will attract a competent personnel. The attendance supervisor should be a well-balanced, dynamic person, broadly experienced and adequately trained.

Guidance Personnel. Marked improvement in school attendance results from the adoption of guidance programs. Many persons are employed in this work which has been defined previously as "seeing through John and then helping John to see himself through." It involves studying an individual, learning his capacities, needs, and interests, guiding his efforts, and then seeing him through until he obtains a position and succeeds in it. Guidance ought to be systematic and functional so that students will not make important educational decisions, vocational choices, and life adjustments on mere guesses, false assumptions, or meager information. It is desirable for the counselor to have had experience as a classroom teacher.

The American Psychological Association has recognized three different levels at which counselors function. The first level they call "part-time counselor." It consists of persons who are carrying on some counseling in connection with their other duties in schools, industries, churches, or social agencies. The second level they designate "psychological counselor."

It requires the equivalent of 2 years of graduate training and would probably carry some sort of master's degree label. The third level they call "counselor-psychologist." It calls for a longer period of graduate work leading to a doctor's degree. Workers at all levels are direly needed today.

One type of specialized counseling is vocational, which has been defined as the process of assisting the individual to choose an occupation, prepare for it, enter it, progress in it, and retire from it. The work of the vocational counselor is outlined by the National Vocational Guidance Association, which lists the following specialized activities: study of the individual through interviews, school records, questionnaires, examination and tests, and employment records; study of the occupations, through surveys and compilations of literature; interviews with groups and individuals; employment certification and placement; follow-up services; and related activities, such as club work.

Placement Officials. Junior placement or employment for youth is becoming an increasing responsibility of the schools. In many cities the junior consultation service for out-of-school youth is also sponsored by the public schools. All placement workers have certain basic duties, whether they perform them in a school, social-service agency, or state employment service. The duties include: analyzing jobs, registering applicants, interviewing them, classifying registrants, receiving employers' orders, selecting and referring applicants to prospective employers, verifying placement, following up the employees, doing field work to contact employers, keeping records, preparing reports and statistical data, and continuously evaluating.

The placement worker's stock in trade is information about the world of work. Furthermore, he has to establish numerous contacts with school staff members, parents, school psychologists, employers, and community agencies. He must have as varied an occupational experience as possible, with prolonged training and education in the same disciplines as are required of other professional personnel who are dealing with human beings in their individual and social adjustment. This task is being increasingly recognized as a career that requires professional standards, certification, and supervised internship.

Many public and private agencies cooperate with the schools in solving the problems of youth placement. Some junior placement services are affiliated with state and federal employment bureaus.

Deans of Boys and Men. Many counselors for male students are called deans of boys in the high schools and deans of men in the colleges. In the secondary school some titles are dean of boys, vice-principal, assistant principal, administrative assistant, boys' adviser, boys' counselor, director of guidance, coordinator, class adviser, and guidance teacher.

The outstanding qualifications for deans in secondary schools are:

special training in guidance; a knowledge of adolescent physiology and psychology; a liking for and sympathetic understanding of teen-age boys, their problems and possibilities; the ability to aid in the solution of individual problems; the art of inspiring confidence and respect; and plenty of patience. Usually a master's degree is required. Among the responsibilities are attendance problems, vocational guidance, curriculum development, discipline, food and clothing for needy students, interviews with parents and prospective employers, supervision of leisure-time activities, and individual counseling.

Deans of men are found in most colleges and universities. Paramount among their many duties is that of counseling. The National Association of Student Personnel Administrators is one of the many professional organizations.

Deans of Girls and Women. The guidance of pupils is usually assigned to a person of their own sex. Obviously the administrative and supervisory responsibilities of the position vary with the size and type of school. The qualifications for deans of girls and women are similar to those for the deans of boys and men. The former have a national association which is a department of the National Education Association.

Recreational Leaders. The inextricable relationship of recreation and education is evidenced in the similarity of their objectives. In many communities, school authorities have incorporated play and leisure-time activities into the program at preschool, in-school, and post-school levels. The practice of providing for community recreation as part of a broad educational program is growing. Many communities have recreation in conjunction with school services. Although most communities do not supply the recreational-educational workers, the joint programs are steadily increasing.

The persons selected for the recreational leadership in school or community or joint programs should be carefully chosen for their personal and professional qualifications. Many directors are college graduates who have specialized in teaching and in group activities. Courses for developing leaders cover a broad range of subjects and activities, since recreation, which was once delimited to play or sports, now includes all activities involving the free use of leisure time. The most popular are swimming, picnicking, softball, and skating.

OTHER SPECIALISTS WITH SEMITEACHING DUTIES

Among the many specialists engaged in semiteaching in American education the following are mentioned here: (1) curriculum personnel and (2) research workers.

Curriculum Personnel. Several state departments, institutions of higher learning, and many city school systems employ persons especially trained in curriculum procedures. Such a worker is usually designated as director of the curriculum bureau, assistant superintendent in charge of the curriculum, curriculum supervisor, or director of surveys. The effort to adjust curriculums to the pupils and to societal needs, as indicated in Unit XIII, is a challenging task.

Research Workers. Early school administrators were guided primarily by guess, intuition, and practical experience earned by dint of trial and error. Today local, state, and federal educational divisions ferret out pressing problems and subject them to research.

A broad program of research operates as a steadying force in locating superior practices, in justifying expansion of programs, in facilitating scientific evaluations, in improving the quality of the program, in advancing the teaching profession, and in furnishing a common method of approach for all members of the staff. The classroom teacher may be a research worker. There are indeed many types of studies and experimentation that classroom teachers can and should make.

Usually the formal research of a school system is conducted or summarized by an administrator or a semiteaching worker known as the director of research. Such directors are usually located in large school systems that employ also one or more full-time workers, clerks and statisticians. Many of the latter are members of such national associations as the American Educational Research Association and the American Statistical Association. Directors of research are among the best trained workers in the educational system; several possess doctor's degrees. Many are women.

Despite the rather limited number of positions available at present as directors of research in various schools, opportunities in this field are multiplying. Furthermore, assistants are required in the various bureaus of research already established to conduct needed studies. Then, too, most state departments of education and many state educational associations employ a director of research and assistants. Many persons have been engaged in research conducted through the cooperative efforts of the Office of Education and various universities. In addition to the agencies already mentioned, educational foundations require annually a large number of skilled, well-trained persons who have the technical precision and professional background for educational research.

Audio-visual Coordinators. A growing field of service in schools and colleges is that of audio-visual education with its multisensory aids—slides, filmstrips, motion pictures, charts, radio, television, and allied materials and equipment. The coordinator of audio-visual education must be a specialist in the instructional materials of the curriculum, must see equipment and materials as tools—means for the achievement of the ends of education—and must understand learning.[1]

---

[1] Edgar Dale, *Audio-Visual Methods in Teaching,* p. 515, Dryden, 1954.

Fig. 12-2. Audio-visual specialists help facilitate the educational processes. (*Courtesy of Fulton County Board of Education, Atlanta, Ga.*)

ADMINISTRATIVE AND SUPERVISORY POSITIONS IN EDUCATION

Several thousand positions of an administrative or supervisory nature are available in American public education, particularly for persons with experience, leadership, and initiative. Contrary to general belief, these positions do not exclude women. Many county superintendencies are held by women; grade-school principalships and supervisory work are shared by women and men; the field of city superintendencies alone offers few opportunities for women.

Among the persons engaged in an executive capacity are (1) superintendents, (2) principals, (3) supervisors of instruction, (4) department heads and deans, (5) presidents, and (6) other administrators, including business and building officials.

SUPERINTENDENTS OF SCHOOLS

On the basis of the main geographical divisions, the superintendents of schools are (1) local, (2) county, and (3) state, whereas the chief school superintendent for the United States is known as the Commissioner of Education. American education also employs many assistant superintendents.

Local Superintendents.[2] The multiple duties of the city superintendent of schools are listed in Unit IV. His main function is to serve as the chief administrative officer of the board of education. He is usually called the city superintendent of schools, but in some instances he is designated as the community high-school principal or the supervising principal. Technically a local superintendent is the professional leader who works directly with the board of education as its chief educational officer. His is the best paid position in the public schools and also the most difficult. But the local superintendent finds many rewards other than monetary. Although a village may engage as superintendent a person just graduated from college, most accredited schools, especially in cities, require the superintendent to have graduate work, plus experience either in the classroom or as a principal or assistant superintendent. In addition to these professional qualifications the highest personal attributes are expected in the local superintendent of schools.

County Superintendents.[3] Nearly all the 3000 counties in the United States have a chief educational officer, usually designated as the county superintendent of schools. The duties and qualifications of these superintendents are enumerated in Unit III. The legal eligibility requirements in most states are low. Unfortunately most counties in the United States, instead of appointing their superintendents or commissioners from the best candidates available, elect them on a partisan ticket. A man or woman (many women are county superintendents in the United States) of demonstrated ability may lose an election because of wrong political affiliations. The situation is improving, however, and today in many states the county board of education or a similar body selects the superintendent from a list of thoroughly qualified persons. Low standards, popular election, and small salaries deter many promising candidates from an office which should call for educational statesmanship, rather than political strategy.

State Superintendents.[4] The usual tasks of the chief state educational officer are mentioned in Unit II. As in the case of the county superintendents, political affiliation is often a determining factor in the selection of a state superintendent or commissioner of education.

Many states have no minimum professional qualifications for the chief state school officer, and only a few states make any requirement as to graduate preparation. The opportunities for securing state superintendencies

---

[2] See also American Association of School Administrators, *The American School Superintendency*, Chap. XI, National Education Association, 1952.

[3] See also Shirley Cooper and Charles O. Fitzwater, *County School Administration*, Chap. V, Harper, 1954.

[4] See also Fred F. Beach, *The Functions of State Departments of Education*, Chap. II, GPO, 1950.

obviously are restricted by the number of states and dependencies, but unfortunately the vicissitudes of the office occasion frequent turnovers.

Assistant Superintendents. Since good administration involves both the centralization of authority and the delegation of responsibility, a school system employs not only an executive but also a staff of assistants. The increasing demands laid upon the chief educational officers have led to the development of many well-paid positions for assistant superintendents in charge of educational supervision, business management, and buildings and grounds. Many persons in the business side of education are known as business managers, secretaries, or clerks of the board.

To assistant county superintendents are usually delegated special activities, such as supervision or clerical work. Likewise the assistant state superintendents, directly under the chief official, head a special form of work in the state department of education. In many instances, local, county, and state assistants bear the brunt of the work. Assistant superintendencies are excellent training grounds for other educational positions; in and by themselves they also constitute an enviable opportunity for continuity in selfless service for others.

PRINCIPALS OF SCHOOLS

The unit of education that means the most to children, parents, and community is the individual school of which the principal is the head. Upon him rests a great responsibility. Many of these principalships are open to well-qualified men and women with teaching experience; for example, they may become elementary, secondary, assistant, or supervising principals. Usually a master's degree is the minimum requirement.

SUPERVISORS OF INSTRUCTION

Many educators are engaged in instructional supervision, a work that has been broadened to involve the entire field of teaching and learning, deepened to reach down into a functional philosophy of education, and elevated to higher altitudes through the better attitudes of teachers toward supervision. Six major functions of this work, according to an analysis of duties performed by supervisors, include study of the pupil, in-service education of teachers, conduct of curriculum investigations, preparation and installation of courses of study, selection of textbooks and preparation of materials of instruction, and conduct of public relations program. Most of these duties call for teaching experience and special preparation. The typical supervisory positions are those in elementary schools, secondary schools, and other educational institutions. Many counties and all state departments of education also employ supervisors. Supervision on all educational levels helps to implement the objectives of education through improving both teaching and learning.

DEPARTMENT HEADS AND COLLEGE DEANS

Heads of Departments. The large secondary schools and the colleges have semiadministrative officials known as heads or chairmen of departments. To them are delegated details of administration and supervision within their fields of instruction. Department heads in high schools were known as early as 1858 when Malden, Massachusetts, established commercial and Latin departments. At the present time some high schools with only a few hundred students designate heads for the larger departments, usually English, social science, and commerce. These persons are appointed frequently on the basis of seniority or desire to increase salaries, rather than on professional qualifications. In the secondary school the department head should hold a master's degree, whereas in colleges and universities he is usually expected to have a doctor's degree. His main task in all educational institutions is to improve instruction through aiding members of his department and cooperating with others on the staff.

College Deans. The liaison officer between departments and between them and the president of the institution of higher learning is usually the dean. Some universities have several: a dean of instruction, an administrative dean, and deans of women and men. These officers must possess at least a master's degree, several years of teaching experience, and administrative ability. In very few institutions is the position of dean a highly centralized administrative office. The dean's office almost universally combines teaching with administrative duties. With the recent rapid development of graduate work many colleges and universities have added a graduate division under the direction of a graduate dean or a chairman, who has a doctor's degree.

PRESIDENTS OF EDUCATIONAL INSTITUTIONS

Almost 1900 presidents direct the colleges and universities of the United States. Many of them have charge of private or parochial institutions, but a large number are directly engaged in public education, particularly the presidents of community junior colleges, state teachers colleges and universities, and land-grant colleges.

Presidents of Junior Colleges. The executive officer of the community or junior college, especially if it is linked with the high school, is usually known as the principal or superintendent. His duties are similar to those of a local superintendent of schools, although technically he is president of the institution.

Presidents of Colleges and Universities. Among the coveted and well-paid positions in American education are college and university presidencies, several of which are held by women. A presidency is not, however, a bed of roses devoid of thorns. Says one president in a caustic vein:

"A college president is so harassed by the time-consuming minutiae of administration and finance that he cannot be an educator." William A. Neilson, former president of Smith College, once urged a "Be-kind-to-college-presidents Week." The administrator of higher education has a difficult task but also unexcelled opportunities for educational leadership and for a permanent influence upon many phases of American life. The late Nicholas Murray Butler, in his autobiography, reveals the multiplicity of activities—social, economic, political, and educational—in which he engaged during his presidency of Columbia University for over fifty years. Busy years await anyone who ascends to the leadership of an American institution of higher learning.[5]

OTHER ADMINISTRATIVE OFFICERS

Long and varied is the list of administrative officers in schools, colleges, universities, and other educational work. Two of the many remaining officials engaged in administrative or supervisory activities are (1) business and (2) building officials.

Business Officials in Educational Institutions. Since education is a big business involving an annual expenditure of several billion dollars and an invested capital of many billions more, obviously schools and colleges must be run on a businesslike basis. The business official in the small town is usually the superintendent of schools, who works with the board of education in solving the financial problems of the district. In the large schools a business manager, an assistant superintendent in charge of business, or a board secretary or clerk carries the major financial responsibilities.

The ideal business manager has a practical background and teaching experience—a sharp business outlook and an educational point of view. There is a dearth of well-educated persons with teaching and business experience plus personal assets to qualify them for the office of assistant superintendent of schools in charge of business. A similar lack of well-educated business officers is evident in colleges and universities. Nationwide organizations are seeking to improve business personnel and procedures in schools and colleges.

Building and Grounds Superintendents. The business aspects of public education embrace the care and maintenance of buildings and grounds. Usually in the large city systems and in the colleges a separate administrative officer, such as the superintendent of buildings and grounds, is in charge. His duties are to supervise repairs, make inventories, direct the maintenance and operation of the plant, improve the grounds, and assist in the planning of new structures. Practical experience as a building con-

[5] For further information on the administration of institutions of higher learning, see Unit VIII.

tractor or in the building trades aids in the successful execution of these duties. As considered in Unit XV, the erection, operation, and maintenance of educational buildings call for a well-trained personnel.

EDUCATIONAL PERSONNEL FROM OTHER PROFESSIONS

Obviously most educational workers are teachers and administrators, but doctors and lawyers may also perform school duties. Among the other professions mentioned in the succeeding pages are (1) librarians, (2) health personnel, (3) business and building personnel, (4) lawyers, and (5) other professional or semiprofessional groups such as sociologists and social workers.

LIBRARIANS

The library is indeed an indispensable educational and social institution in a democracy. The role of libraries and books is treated further in Unit XV; attention is here directed to librarians. Among the staff members are librarians of public, school, college, university, government, and special libraries; reference librarians; readers' advisers; children's and young people's librarians; circulation, periodical, and special collection librarians; librarians in health and penal institutions; and librarians assigned to special subjects and to political units such as the city, county, and state. Several states have created the position of field visitor for school libraries. Every state has a library association.

The fields of employment for librarians are in (1) schools and colleges, (2) public libraries, (3) combined school and public libraries, and (4) others.

School and College Librarians. Broad culture, enthusiasm, approachability, tact, poise, and understanding are indispensable traits for school librarians, who are slowly being recognized as important members of the faculty.

Many institutions in the United States now provide thorough library education. The first school of library training was opened in 1887 at Columbia University. Today a school librarian should have a college education and at least one year of library-school training. In several states she must also possess a teacher's certificate or special state certificate.

Unfortunately elementary-school libraries are the last to be recognized for their importance in lifelong learning. Most elementary schools today are sorely in need of libraries and librarians. Many junior-high-school and high-school libraries are unorganized and inadequately staffed. College libraries, too, offer many opportunities for employment in this educational service.

Public Librarians. The status of the public library as an educational institution has long been established in America. Unfortunately more than a third of the United States—mostly rural territory—is without any kind of library service. Additional library personnel and equipment, especially for bookmobile services for rural areas, are urgently needed. If the successful librarian could be described in general terms, scholarship, professionalism, social consciousness, imagination, sense of humor, and acceptable personality would be requisite. The librarian is no longer a mere keeper of books but a scholarly administrator who uses scientific methods in making available library materials. This challenge to work in public libraries will be met by thousands of young people who yearn to live with people and recorded communications.

Combined School and Public Librarians. Some persons work in public libraries controlled by boards of education. The Educational Policies Commission envisioned the ultimate unification of all public educational activities, in communities or areas of appropriate size, under the leadership of a public education authority.

Other Librarians. Many public and private agencies other than schools, colleges, and cities employ librarians. Among these are: foundations, research associations, private firms, educational associations, settlement houses, hotels, and other agencies that promote reading and research.

HEALTH PERSONNEL

The school health program is composed of the following services, in whole or in part: health instruction, health examinations, medical attention, communicable disease control, promotion of mental health, provision of healthful environment and regimen, and health supervision of teachers and employees. To perform these services well, a large and varied personnel is needed, including the school (1) physician, (2) dentist, (3) nurse, (4) health educator, and (5) psychiatrist and psychologist.

School Physicians and Dentists. Ever since the city of Boston, faced with an epidemic of dreaded diphtheria, initiated in 1894 a program of school health inspection, the physician has assumed an important role in education. School dentists, too, have an important role in the health program of the school.

The health of the pupils is not the responsibility of the school physician alone; all doctors may promote this cause through participation in campaigns for immunization against contagious diseases, and in their daily duties as family physician. In their private practice the physicians, especially the pediatricians and psychiatric workers, have numerous heavy educational responsibilities devolving upon them.

The school physician or dentist, whether a full-time or part-time employee of the board of education or the city, has educational obligations, such as emphasizing to the pupils and parents the importance of proper care of the body. He should have a thorough understanding of the school health program. Inspections by the school dentist or doctor do not take the place of a careful and thorough examination by the family dentist or physician. Furthermore, medical care is not a public-school function.

School Nurses. The school nurses usually devote part of their time to the preparation of instructional materials, to giving individual health instruction and examinations, and to interpreting the results of the examinations to parent, child, and teacher. Success in this field requires certain natural qualifications, such as a genuine liking for children. In addition to natural accomplishments the school nurses must have high professional and educational qualifications. It is significant that the field of nursing, which was formerly almost 100 per cent for women, is now being entered by a number of men.

Health Educators. A position that is increasing in number and significance is that of health educator or coordinator. Many state departments, county boards, and local school systems employ personnel experienced in health and education to work with nonschool children, pupils, parents, teachers, nurses, doctors, and dentists. The professional preparation usually required is training and experience in health and teaching, with the technical degree of Master of Public Health. Some are Doctors of Public Health.

School Psychiatrists and Psychologists. A broad health program includes mental and emotional as well as physical health. Many schools and colleges are employing psychiatrists and psychologists in an effort to treat causes rather than symptoms of unusual pupil behavior, and to prevent mental illness and maladjustments. Only in the large school systems is a full-time psychiatrist or psychologist needed; part-time psychiatric services are obtained from hospitals, universities, foundations, or other agencies, such as clinics.

Clinical psychologists are increasing in demand. Groups such as the Association of Consulting Psychologists and the Division of School Psychologists of the American Psychological Association have helped to establish and elevate standards for clinical psychologists and for their training programs. The National Committee for Mental Hygiene has also made recommendations. Students contemplating a career in clinical psychology will find helpful these published recommendations. Obviously, since these specialists are to work with school pupils, they should have teaching experience.

BUSINESS AND BUILDING PERSONNEL

In addition to the business manager and the building and grounds superintendent previously mentioned as administrators, schools and colleges employ other members of the business and building professions on a part-time or full-time basis. These who belong to groups considered as professions are (1) accountants and auditors, (2) architects, and (3) engineers.

School Accountants and Auditors.[6] Many accountants are employed in educational work periodically or full time. They should be trained not only in accountancy but also in education. The accountant needs to know something about the educational program of the school, so that he may

FIG. 12-3. School architects are busy planning buildings for the great influx of pupils in the second largest city—Chicago. (*Courtesy of Public Schools, Chicago, Ill.*)

make interpolations and comments of an educational nature. There is a dire need for educational auditors—men and women seasoned by experience as school administrators, who are as thoroughly grounded in accountancy as is a C.P.A. Schools of commerce and education should assume aggressive leadership in preparing these experts. Improvement of current accountancy practices can be hastened by the appointment of educational auditors in the state departments of education. With the increased tendency toward uniform accounting systems in schools and colleges, and for compulsory audits of educational and extracurricular funds, the demand for school accountants and auditors will rise to new levels.

[6] See also Unit XVI and Chris A. De Young, *Budgeting in Public Schools*, pp. 450–451, Swift, 1951.

School Architects. Large city systems and some state departments employ full-time school architects. Some architectural firms specialize in school buildings, and others have a department of school architecture. The definite relationship of buildings to the curriculum makes school architecture extremely important. The school architect must have a thorough knowledge of modern education so that the building he designs will facilitate the education of the pupils. (See Unit XV.)

School Engineers. Most school buildings are in charge of engineer custodians. In the small systems the persons who direct the maintenance, operation, and care of school plant and properties are often called "janitors." In the large systems engineers are assigned to definite tasks in terms of their specialties, such as mechanical or electrical work, usually after having passed civil service examinations.

School Lawyers

Law is the basis for all school transactions, hence the significance of the legal profession in education. Among those engaged in school law work are (1) lawyers and (2) other legal advisers.

Lawyers. Most positions in this service, full time or part time, are available only to persons who hold a bachelor of laws (LL.B.) degree and membership in the bar. The Association of American Law Schools and the Council on Legal Education of the American Bar Association maintain certain standards for approving law schools. The typical law curriculum has had marked leanings toward the needs of private practice and has not given much emphasis to the needs of the schools. Only a limited number of law schools and teacher-educating institutions offer courses in school law. There is some demand in large school systems for well-qualified lawyers who have taught and have specialized in school law.

Other Legal Advisers. Many state departments have legal advisers who may or may not hold a legal degree although they have studied both school and general law. Their business is to help interpret the school laws. Occasionally lawyers who specialize in certain phases of law are called upon for school service.

Other Professional or Semiprofessional Groups

Among the many other professions or semiprofessions having representatives engaged in educational work are (1) school sociologists, (2) social workers, and (3) educational consultants.

School Sociologists. At present the public schools employ few sociologists. Courses in sociology, particularly in the secondary schools, would be far more functional if a sociologist were engaged to make actual community contact through social surveys and other means. The school has too long tried to insulate itself against direct community service. Administrators have been likely to think in terms of education but not of society. A crying need exists, therefore, for educational sociologists who seek the improvement of society as a whole rather than merely that of the schools. In addition to excellent personal qualifications the educational sociologist should possess at least a master's degree.

Social Workers. Social responsibility is the keynote of twentieth century legislation. In its publication *Social Services and the Schools,* the Educational Policies Commission states that "the schools, in particular, are obligated not only to see and provide for their educational responsibilities to the community but also to cooperate in providing welfare services that are closely related to education." Many writers have shown the need for this cooperation as they picture the migrant who teaches his children to pick fruit or cotton as long and as fast as their aching backs will permit, with never any thought of school. The task of social workers is economic and educational as well as social.

The social worker of today in contrast with the lady bountiful of yesterday is a trained member of a profession, usually holding one or more college degrees. Employees in some public agencies must have civil service status. Among the many forms of individual and group social services are child welfare, family welfare, community organization, institutional work, parole, probation, psychiatric social work, public assistance, unemployment relief, social group work, social research, visiting teacher, and the teaching of social service. Organizations such as the National Association of School Social Workers and the Russell Sage Foundation are seeking to make social service an attractive career. The schools need not only specially trained teachers, nurses, and counselors but also social workers who have the desire and ability to interpret democracy in terms of human betterment, as did Jane Addams, Julia Lathrop, and Florence Kelly.

Educational Consultants. Many school systems and universities employ various educational consultants or specialists to serve on a part-time basis. Usually they work on problems relating to buildings and finance. Most of them come from colleges and universities or private firms that specialize in advisory services.[7]

OTHER NONTEACHING PERSONNEL IN EDUCATION

Amid the vast array of nonteaching workers not definitely ranked as a professional group are the following: (1) school clerks and secretaries, (2) cafeteria and lunchroom workers, (3) building service personnel, (4) those engaged in school transportation, (5) school publications and sales personnel, and (6) others employed in education. Each of these groups is described briefly.

[7] See also Max R. Goodson and A. W. Foshay, "The Consultant—Your Partner in School Improvement," p. 4, *The Educational Trend* No. 1053, Arthur C. Croft, 1953.

SCHOOL CLERKS AND SECRETARIES

Many opportunities for educational work are available in the field
of clerical and office service, which includes typists, stenographers, secretaries, bookkeepers, and similar employees. These persons can and do
perform many tasks of an educational nature, thus releasing administrators and teachers for purely professional duties. So important to the

FIG. 12-4. Educational workers in the pupil-personnel department check the records.
(*Courtesy of Better Schools and of Public Schools, Cincinnati, Ohio.*)

schools and colleges is the office personnel that many an executive would
rather accept the resignation of two teachers than that of one clerk or
secretary. An important school business official, especially in the East, is
the school board secretary. Secretaries should be provided for every administrator, especially the county superintendent, in the number needed
to relieve him and his professional assistants from clerical duties. Many
attendance clerks are needed in public schools. Obviously secretaries, as
well as all school employees, should be appointed upon strict professional
bases rather than because of political influence or nepotism.

Many opportunities are available in the school offices for young people
who do not care for classroom teaching but who like the school atmosphere. It is not to be inferred that clerical help is of inferior quality; in

fact some of the best secretaries are those who have an academic degree and who have had some teaching experience. In order to secure and maintain a stable, efficient, and loyal group of office workers, it is necessary to have careful selection and training of new clerks, an adequate salary schedule, and justly planned provisions for tenure, working hours, leaves of absence, and retirement. The National Association of Educational Secretaries is developing a service program that seeks to make the secretarial positions in school systems a profession requiring specialized training and experience.

CAFETERIA AND LUNCHROOM WORKERS

The school cafeteria and lunchroom are powerful factors in the educative process of growing physically and socially. Their functional relation-

FIG. 12-5. Lunchroom workers play a vital role in the educational program. (*Courtesy of Public Schools, Chicago, Ill.*)

ship to the health program is evidenced in that a trained dietitian or home economics worker, often paid in part from federal funds, is usually a member of the cafeteria staff. Too much care cannot be exercised in the selection of a manager for the cafeteria or lunchroom.

Since cleanliness is essential to health, all the workers in the cafeteria must be immaculately clean. Periodic inspections should be made by the city health officers, the school nurse, or the cafeteria committee. The lunchroom can be a real asset to the school if it emphasizes the educational rather than the financial, and if it seeks to train children in health habits, in food standards, in business sense, in self-control, and in social niceties.

BUILDING SERVICE PERSONNEL

In the early colonial days most teachers performed the housekeeping duties in the schools, a practice that still exists in many rural communities. Today the large schools employ numerous caretakers and assistants with

FIG. 12-6. School custodians and engineers go to school. "Keep the school yard, shrubs, and trees in good shape," the landscape-gardening expert advises men attending the summer school for custodians. (*Courtesy of Illinois State Normal University, Normal, Ill.*)

specific titles and definite responsibilities, such as engineer, fireman, cleaner, carpenter, mower, electrician, and playground caretaker. In most systems, however, these duties devolve upon one person, who in the past has usually been called the "janitor." The more acceptable nomenclature today is school custodian (man) and school maid (woman). Whatever the term, the modern school requires from its custodian less manual labor but more knowledge and skill than were formerly required.

The custodian must be trained in the installation and care of delicately adjusted equipment and various machinery. The pioneer work of the late George F. Womrath of Minneapolis and others in providing this practical training is being expanded by colleges, universities, state departments, and other agencies. Eventually preservice and in-service training will be required of all custodians. Some systems have a civil service examination for the purpose of selecting desirable custodians. Among the great hindrances to the improvement of the school maintenance and operation personnel are too frequent political interference in their appointment, insecurity of tenure, no retirement allowance, low pay, and inadequate recognition.

SCHOOL TRANSPORTATION PERSONNEL [8]

Transportation has developed into a major educational enterprise, particularly in states that have adopted larger units of school administration. Several states are now paying part of the costs of conveying pupils, and many local districts have added the school-bus driver to their pay roll. In some instances the school-bus driver is accompanied by an assistant who flags the bus over unprotected railroad crossings and other hazards. The large systems employ various mechanics in their garages and repair shops. School transportation has developed to such significance that specific qualifications and training have been set for those engaged in this all-important work of bringing pupils in safety to the teachers.

EDUCATIONAL EDITORS, PUBLISHERS, AND SALES PERSONNEL

Thousands of persons who render educational services are employed in the publication of textbooks, in the manufacture of educational supplies and equipment, and in sales work. Contrary to general belief, those who enter the publishing and editorial field do not lose their educational status.

Educational Editors and Publishers. One aspect of textbook publication is editorial work. In addition to the editors, numerous persons are employed as directors of educational research service with publishers of textbooks. The work of field consultant for a textbook company is largely professional and includes such activities as lecturing or making informal talks to groups, training of teachers in service, and conferences with various kinds of committees and individuals. Opportunities for women, especially teachers, are multiplying in the textbook field. A challenging task for all educators, especially for classroom teachers, is that of writing articles and books for publication. More teacher-authors are needed.

Sales Personnel. Many persons are engaged in selling schoolbooks, supplies, and educational equipment. Undoubtedly the best textbooks, educational supplies, and school equipment in the world are made in America. These are available as teaching tools for American schools, but unfortunately the best is not generally used. Restricted budgets and the apathy of the general public account in part for this situation. Then, too, many classroom and laboratory teachers are not acquainted with the

[8] See also Unit III.

wide variety and high quality of modern educational materials. Promotional and sales personnel, traveling from schools to colleges, from educational exhibits to state and national conventions, serve as so-called "educational missionaries" and spread the news of improvements. The best preparation for this salesmanship is teaching and business experience.

OTHERS EMPLOYED IN EDUCATION

Workers in Educational Organizations. Organizations of an educational, recreational, and professional nature employ thousands of trained workers. For example, the National Congress of Parents and Teachers, the Boy Scouts and Girl Scouts of America, the 4-H Clubs of America, educational fraternities, sororities, foundations, national educational associations, and countless other groups, some of which are enumerated in Unit XIV, draw heavily upon the teaching profession for their personnel. Among professional groups in education is the national organization known as the National Association of Secretaries of State Teachers Associations.

Career Service in Education. The three largest groups in the employed personnel of the typical city school system have been mentioned, *viz.,* teachers, custodians, and clerks. Among the many others not yet listed are day laborers, laundresses, electricans, plumbers, and messengers. Some of these have detailed, pigeonhole jobs, but most of them perform tasks that permit initiative and growth.

The improvement of many nonteaching positions requires more than higher standards of recruitment. These positions, especially for clerks and stenographers, must become a "career" service if they are to enlist an adequately trained personnel. By a career is meant a lifework in an honorable occupation, which one normally takes up in youth with the expectation of advancement and pursues with happiness and profit until retirement. School service should be a public service so organized and conducted as to encourage careers.

Though the role of some employees in education may appear insignificant, yet each professional or nonprofessional worker, from the chief executive officer of the educational institution down to the lowest paid day laborer, can make a direct and significant contribution to American education.

SUGGESTED ACTIVITIES

1. Explain the type of educational work other than teaching that might interest you. Why?

2. Compare the salaries, other rewards, and opportunities for personal and professional growth in several different positions in education.

3. Enumerate some of the obstacles faced by substitute teachers.

4. Investigate the nature of extension work.

5. Discuss the type of personnel work in education that appeals to you. Why?

6. Investigate the opportunities for training as a school librarian.

7. Find out what qualifications your state requires for city, county, and state superintendents of schools.

8. List some of the advantages and disadvantages in being a school principal, supervisor, or head of a department.

9. List types of positions available in higher education.

10. Describe the ideal qualifications for a college president.

11. List the duties of a school or college business manager.

12. Find out what positions in health work are offered in the large schools.

13. Evaluate the role of the school architect.

14. Tell why accountants and auditors are needed in public education.

15. Give the duties of school attorneys.

16. Explain some of the functions of a school psychologist.

17. Describe the role publishing firms play in education.

18. Interview a salesman for a textbook company and learn about his work.

19. List what you consider the ideal qualifications for a school custodian.

20. Discuss the importance of transportation services in education.

21. Prepare a list of national professional organizations of educational personnel other than teachers.

DESCRIPTIVE BIBLIOGRAPHY AND AIDS

BOOKS

AMERICAN ASSOCIATION OF SCHOOL ADMINISTRATORS: *The American School Superintendency*, Chap. XI, National Education Association, 1952.
> The city superintendent of schools today.

ASHEIM, LESTER: *The Core of Education for Librarianship*, Appendix D, American Library Association, 1954.
> The characteristics of professional librarianship.

BARTKY, JOHN A.: *Supervision and Human Relations*, Chaps. XIII, XIV, Heath, 1953.
> The supervisor in the elementary and secondary school.

BENSON, R. A., and J. A. GOLDBERG: *The Camp Counselor*, Chap. III, McGraw-Hill, 1951.
> Preparation and general responsibilities of the camp counselor.

COOPER, SHIRLEY, and CHARLES O. FITZWATER: *County School Administration*, Chap. XV, Harper, 1954.
> Personnel accounting in education.

DEMING, DOROTHY: *Careers for Nurses*, 2d ed., Chaps. I, II, McGraw-Hill, 1952.
> Choosing a career and hospital nursing.

ELSBREE, WILLIARD S., and E. EDMUND REUTTER, JR.: *Staff Personnel in the Public Schools*, Chap. XVI, Prentice-Hall, 1954.
> The legal status of the staff personnel.

INGHAM, HARRINGTON V., and LEONORE R. LOVE: *The Process of Psychotherapy*, Chap. II, McGraw-Hill, 1954.
> The role and qualifications of the psychotherapist.

JACOBSON, PAUL B., WILLIAM C. REAVIS, and JAMES D. LOGSDON: *Duties of School Principals*, Chap. XXIII, Prentice-Hall, 1950.
> The future of the school principalship.

LINN, HENRY H., LESLIE C. HELM, and K. P. GRABARKIEWICZ: *The School Custodian's Housekeeping Handbook*, Chap. I, Teachers College, 1948.
> Responsibilities of school-building service employees.

SWANSON, MARIE: *School Nursing in the Community Program*, Chap. IV, Macmillan, 1953.
> Selection of the nurse: personality, education, and professional preparation.

TAYLOR, HAROLD: *On Education and Freedom,* Chap. II, Abelard-Schuman, 1954.
>The college president and his role.

TYLER, LEONA E.: *The Work of the Counselor,* Chap. XI, Appleton-Century-Crofts, 1953.
>The selection and training of counselors.

CURRENT PERTINENT PERIODICALS AND PUBLICATIONS

American Journal of Psychiatry
American Journal of Psychotherapy
American Library Association Bulletin
Bulletin of National Association of Secondary-school Principals
Chicago Principals' Club Reporter
Journal of Consulting Psychology
Journal of Educational Research
Journal of National Association of Deans of Women
Journal of School Health

National Elementary Principal
National Secretary
Personnel and Guidance Journal
Personnel Journal
Social Security Bulletin
Social Service Review
Today's Secretary
Vocational Guidance Quarterly
Wilson Library Bulletin
Yearbooks of educational organizations

AUDIO-VISUAL AIDS

THE BUS DRIVER   One reel, sound
>This film, designed for pupils, shows the work of a bus driver, the role of busses in transportation, the operation of motor vehicles, and problems of traffic safety. Available from Encyclopaedia Britannica Films, Wilmette, Ill.

COUNSELING—ITS TOOLS AND TECHNIQUES   16 min., sound
>Indicates the important guideposts in counseling and demonstrates good counseling procedures. Available from Carl F. Mahnke Productions, Des Moines, Iowa.

DUTIES OF A SECRETARY   30 min., sound
>Depicts the first day's work of a new secretary, revealing good and bad office practice and her successful adjustment to an office. Available from Business Education Films, New York.

THE EVOLUTION OF A CLINICAL PSYCHOLOGIST   Records or tape
>A recorded address by a clinical psychologist on the meaning of that work. Problems of training, interprofessional relationships, and personal philosophy are discussed. Available from Sound Seminars, Cincinnati, Ohio.

THE LIBRARIAN   11 min., sound
>Shows that the first requisite for librarians is a liking for people, since they bring people and books together. Depicts five general types of librarians in action, as well as specialized workers in adult education, films, recordings, music, etc. Available from Carl F. Mahnke Productions, Des Moines, Iowa.

OFFICE ETIQUETTE   15 min., sound
>A refresher for experienced office workers and a helper for students. Illustrates the lessons learned in a first-year typing class. Demonstrates three comprehensive rules of office courtesy. Available from Encyclopaedia Britannica Films, Wilmette, Ill.

YOUR FRIEND, THE PUBLIC HEALTH NURSE   Filmstrip with record, 15 min.
>Depicts the public health nurse in action: the kinds of people she serves, the variety of problems she meets, and some of the results in protecting family and community health. Available on free loan from Metropolitan Life Insurance Company, New York.

Part IV

PROVISIONS FOR EDUCATIONAL MATERIALS AND ENVIRONMENT

Preview of Part IV

PROVISIONS FOR EDUCATIONAL MATERIALS AND ENVIRONMENT

The pupils and teachers need plans, tools, and a place in which to live creatively. The program, facilities, and environment markedly affect teaching, learning, and living.

The design for education is found in the curriculum, which consists of all the experiences that pupils have under the guidance of the schools. It is life material used in building soul structure. The modern curriculum is developed cooperatively by administrators, teachers, pupils, and laymen. Most schools are engaged in the continuous task of curriculum revision (Unit XIII).

Related to the curriculum as a dynamic part of pupil's education are the extracurricular or cocurricular activities of the school. The cocurricular programs have accumulated great importance at all levels of American education. They help the youth of America to conserve and develop a democratic way of living (Unit XIV).

In order to work effectively, the teacher and pupils need supplies and tools. They must also have a place to use these tools. The school grounds and buildings constitute the workshop or laboratory of American education. The modern school building is intimately fitted to human needs—physical, educational, psychological, and aesthetic. The students and teachers breathe into the architect's creation the breath of wholesome life. The building is not merely located in the community; the school is a part of the community. Modern schoolhouses are needed in many communities (Unit XV).

The curricular and the cocurricular activities, the supplies and the equipment, and the grounds and buildings are made available through public expenditures for education. Equalization of educational opportunity and burden is the golden rule of educational finance—"Thou shalt educate thy neighbor's children as thine own. . . ." Expenditures for education are not a cost—they represent a long-term investment for which the public should be willing and able to pay (Unit XVI).

Part IV

PROVISIONS FOR EDUCATIONAL
MATERIALS AND ENVIRONMENT

Curricular activities. One of the most important curricular activities on all educational levels is that of global relationships and world understanding. (*Courtesy of Public Schools, Bloomington, Ill.*)

Cocurricular activities. The work of safety patrols or junior officers is a cocurricular activity that contributes to safety education. (*Courtesy of Public Schools, Chicago, Ill.*)

Educational buildings. Buildings like this Canal Zone Junior College at Balboa are sorely needed in the 48 states and dependencies because of obsolescence and increased demands. (*Courtesy of Panama Canal Zone.*)

School finance. Men reconciling school checks before they are filed in the Department of Finance, Chicago Public Schools. (*Courtesy of Public Schools, Chicago, Ill.*)

Fig. 13-1. Educational materials and environment provided through financing.

CURRICULUM

In the educational glossary prefacing this unit the curriculum is defined as consisting of all the experiences which pupils have under the direction of the school. Among the related elements are the program of studies, the course of study, and schedules.

The curriculum is the tangible expression of educational objectives wrought by dint of individual and collective thinking and working. It is a means toward the end of better teaching, learning, and living.

Numerous principles underlie curriculum development: the curriculum is rooted in a philosophy of education; it is developed cooperatively; it is constantly modified; it must provide for individual differences; it must encourage the creative; it must link itself with guidance; and it should accent constant evaluation.

Diversity characterizes the manner in which curriculums develop in the various educational areas and geographical sections of the American scene. The most common technique is that of democratization through committee production of curricular materials.

Many of the patterns for curricular materials employ unitary procedures in some vital reorganization of experiences. Several accent common learnings or core curriculums.

From a limited offering the curriculum of American education—both public and private—has steadily evolved through the cross-fertilization of educational theory and practice.

Outline of Contents

CURRICULUM

Stuart Chase in *The Tyranny of Words* wrote negatively about the current babel of tongues, the gobbledygook of educators, and professional pedaguese. In his later book, *Power of Words,* he deals with the positive role of speech power. "Students must communicate about communication, and use it in order to learn it. . . . If the teacher has a good map of the verbal jungle, he or she is less likely to lose the youngsters." [1] Particularly bewildering is the jungle of terminology used in curriculum work. Hence at the outset an effort is made to map out the more common curricular terms in a brief glossary.

Curriculum Glossary [2]

action research. Careful, unbiased investigation of a problem through observation or demonstrated performance. It may involve the active participation of many persons. It usually is associated with or followed by movement or progress toward a goal.

activity curriculum—movement—program. A curriculum, movement, or program in which emphasis is placed on active participation of the pupil, as distinguished from one in which the pupil is relatively passive and the teacher active. Activity involves goal-seeking with purpose as its conscious manifestation. Care should be taken to avoid the common error of conceiving of activity in its overt physical aspects only.

articulation. The fitting together of parts. The term is most used with reference to the provision of continuity in the educational offerings of the various levels of the school organization, such as between the junior high school and the senior high school.

assignment. A term becoming obsolete with the spread of modern philosophies of education accenting pupil initiative, pupil activity, and problem situations. The role of the teacher is that of guide and counsel. Thus, the term "assignment," with its connotation of formality and teacher domination, is not appropriate for this type of school situation. Activities imposed by the group, including those suggested by the teacher as a group member, and those imposed by the individual upon himself, constitute the modern version of the traditional assignment.

class period. Class period or conference period used in preference to the outmoded term "recitation period," except where reference is actually made to the traditional recitation.

common learnings or core curriculum. The basic curriculum, consisting of experiences considered desirable for all. It comprises the persistent problems of living. It is preferred to "common subjects."

[1] Stuart Chase, *Power of Words,* pp. 273, 277, Harcourt, Brace, 1953.

[2] Adapted from Superintendent of Public Instruction, *The Language of Modern Education,* Department of Public Instruction, Commonwealth of Pennsylvania, 1939, 46 pp., and Carter V. Good, *Dictionary of Education,* McGraw-Hill, 1945, 495 pp.

correlation. Relation of materials from different subject fields. The term represents a transition from the subject organization of the curriculum to the new organizations, which abandon subject lines.

course of study. An element of the curriculum consisting in the activities or experiences designed to achieve the objectives of the field, arranged in sequence. The course of study embraces the objectives, materials of instruction, method, outcomes, and means of evaluation for the curricular segment covered. It constitutes, therefore, a guide to the teacher and is usually set up in written form. The course of study is beginning to give way to a teacher's guide.

curriculum. The organized experiences of an individual under the guidance of the school. Accurately, it can be defined only in retrospect, since each individual has a different set of experiences and thus a different curriculum. The original meaning, from the Latin derivation, is race course, thus, the track or route followed under the school's guidance. For practical purposes, the term is applied to the series of experiences in which pupils are expected to engage. In the elementary school there is but one curriculum, disregarding special classes. In the secondary school, where groups of pupils have different objectives, there are commonly two or more curriculums, such as the college preparatory, scientific, general, and homemaking curriculums.

developmental tasks. (Defined later in this unit.)

education. (Defined later in this unit.)

examination. A device used to discover the extent to which an individual or class has achieved a given level of accomplishment or has mastered certain knowledge. Its connotation is formal, teacher-imposed; hence it is not best suited to the uses of modern education. "Evaluation" is suggested as a more effective term. It implies the interpretation of the testing results.

experience. A term used frequently with reference to the curriculum, since the learner's experiences are understood to be the means by which learnings are developed and therefore are the significant elements of the curriculum. Care should be taken not to limit its meaning to overt activities, since many significant experiences are largely mental or emotional, even though the situations that stimulate them are external to the learner.

general education. The common denominator of the education of all. It is designed to equip a student with a wide range of competencies needed by him both as a person and as a professional worker. It accents the "general art of the free man and the citizen."

grade. The school-year level of a pupil or class, as grade 6 or eighth grade. This is to be distinguished from "mark."

group dynamics. Working together in such a way that each member of the group contributes to the maximum of his ability in reaching decisions and in implementing them. The group and individual become dynamic in the application of democratic principles to all areas of living, including education.

guidance. Help given to aid an individual in making a choice or in changing his behavior. Guidance as an activity of the school is concerned with needed adjustment. In its best form, it occurs before the need arises, thus enabling the individual to make his own choice at a time of crisis. True guidance does not indicate the choice to be made but provides the data necessary for intelligent choice. The term has become so closely associated with vocational guidance, in connection with which it was first used, that to avoid confusion, it is advisable to indicate the phases of guidance intended, as health guidance, emotional guidance, or educational guidance.

instruction. Since Roman times, the concept of teaching has been associated with the term "instruction," literally, to build into. The modern concept involves more than teaching. As now understood, instruction is the process that gives form and direction to educative experience. Thus museums, libraries, textbooks, school journeys, curriculum planning are all instructional, having as their direct purpose the furtherance of education.

integration. A process of unifying, or making whole, characteristic of living organisms. Personality may be described as integrated, being an attribute of a living organism. A curriculum, on the other hand, cannot rightly be said to be integrated, since it is not biological. It is suggested that the term "fused" be used in curriculum work. The word is also used to denote racial desegregation.

learning. Growing or changing, as a result of experience. The term is essentially synonymous with education, its product being a modification of personality resulting from experience as opposed to maturation.

lesson. This term is fast becoming obsolete, for its implication of the acquisition of a small segment of information during a brief period is not in accord with modern methods of studying subject fields organized into relatively broad areas of activity for considerable periods. Especially is the related term "lesson-plan" in disfavor, implying a rigid procedure rather than the flexible planning characteristic of the best modern practice.

materials of instruction. All materials used to further pupil activities. These include books, pictures, films, notes, exhibits, and construction materials. Broadly conceived materials of instruction comprise the whole body of content and experiencing with which the child is concerned in school—recognizing also out-of-school experiencing which may be directly related to and which conditions in-school experiencing.

need. A gap between an existing condition and the normal or desired. The general pupil needs—physical, mental, social, and spiritual—must be met, as well as the specific requirements for keeping the individual in desirable equilibrium.

objective. That which is set up as a goal, to give direction to procedures. "Aim" and "goal" are widely used terms which may be regarded as synonymous, though attempts are sometimes made to differentiate between them. Of the three, objective is preferred. The term "objective" may be broken down and classified. An ultimate objective is an objective that was set up for the pupil to attain at some remote time, possibly during the school year, possibly in a later grade, and even possibly later in life. An immediate objective, on the other hand, is one that could be attained in a very short time, possibly during a particular school period or possibly during the study of a unit. Immediate objectives are used as steppingstones in attaining ultimate objectives.

personality. Generally considered to be the total of an individual's characteristics, distinguishing him from other individuals. It is also commonly used to indicate the emotional aspects of the individual as distinguished from physical and mental qualities.

philosophy of education. A basic attitude in the light of which educational practices are interpreted, evaluated, and criticized. There are many philosophies of education; for example, the philosophy of Dewey or a teacher's philosophy of education.

problem. A situation calling for solution and requiring a choice among several alternatives. Exploration of all possible alternatives and a weighing of their values is implied. Such a situation has special value as a stimulus to learning if it involves issues closely related to the interest of the learner.

program of studies. The outline of curricular offerings of a school; the complete array of courses of study comprising all the curriculums. (See also curriculum and course of study.)

project. In its essential features a problematic situation and its solution in a natural setting. A project comprises four essential steps: purposing, planning, executing, and judging. It is essentially self-motivating.

recitation. In the traditional sense, class time devoted to a particular subject, in which pupils reply to questions covering the content of the textbook. It is replaced by such terms as "conference," "work period," "meeting," and "discussion," which carry the connotations of modern philosophies of education.

resources—community. Material and personal assets available locally in teaching and learning. These are exemplified respectively by a museum and a person versed in Indian lore.

schooling. Attendance at school. This is to be distinguished from education.

semester hour. A credit unit of one class-hour per week for one semester. It is preferred to "credit" or "unit" as a more definite term.

subjects. Usually applied to areas of human knowledge that are so arranged because of the similarity of knowledge involved rather than because of their relatedness in life experiences. Because of its logical, rather than psychological, nature, and because of its implication of subject matter mastery for its own sake, the term is misleading when used in relation to modern educational viewpoints. "Area of experience" is suggested as a substitute.

teaching. Basically an activity on the part of a person more mature with respect to learning experience, designed to further the education of another. Thus it is possible for a child to teach an adult. In the school situation, teaching may be defined as the provision for experiences and guidance of activities designed to promote learning on the part of those engaging in the activities. The essential element of guidance is deemed so important by the so-called "progressive education" that some of its proponents altogether reject the term "teaching," for which they substitute "guidance."

unit of learning. A group of coordinated activities resulting in the adjustment of the individual to a life situation. The unifying element is not, as frequently conceived, the subject matter or pupil interest, but the learning product. This outcome is a definite adaptation of personality representing the ability to meet a whole life situation.

OBJECTIVES OF EDUCATION

Since the curriculum is a direct outgrowth of the aims and purposes of education, attention is here centered upon some definitions and the major goals of education.

WHAT IS EDUCATION?

This common but difficult question may be attacked from both the negative and the positive sides.[3]

What Education Is Not. Education is not a mere preparation for life—getting ready to do things, rather than doing them. Education is not synonymous with schooling; it begins with the parents before the child's birth, whereas schooling usually starts about the fifth year of life. Education is not simply the acquisition of knowledge or the accumulation of grades, credits, and degrees. Education is not book learning; much wisdom comes from activities other than reading a textbook. Education is not something apart from life; it does not thrive in a cloistered atmosphere. Education is not a summation of discrete parts; it is a whole that is greater than its components.

What Education Is. On the positive side education has been defined literally and figuratively. Here are some of the old and new concepts:

A good education consists in giving to the body and to the soul all the beauty and all the perfection of which they are capable. —Plato

What sculpture is to a block of marble, education is to the soul. —Addison

'Tis education forms the common mind;
Just as the twig is bent the tree's inclined. —Pope

Education is the instruction of the intellect in the laws of Nature, under which name I include not merely things and their forces, but men and their ways; and the fashioning of the affections and of the will into an earnest and loving desire to move in harmony with these laws. —Thomas Henry Huxley

Education has for its object the formation of character. —Herbert Spencer

Education is what is left after you have forgotten what you have learned from books. —Anonymous

Education alone can conduct us to that enjoyment which is, at once, best in quality and infinite in quantity. —Horace Mann

Knowledge does not comprise all which is contained in the large term of education. The feelings are to be disciplined, the passions are to be restrained; true

[3] Another approach is to define education in terms of biology, psychology, sociology, etc.

and worthy motives are to be inspired; a profound religious feeling is to be instilled, and pure morality inculcated under all circumstances. All this is comprised in education.   —Noah Webster

Education is a social process; our schools and colleges neither operate in empty space nor serve identical communities.   —James Bryant Conant

Education is that reconstruction or reorganization of experience which adds to the meaning of experience, and which increases ability to direct the course of subsequent experience.   —John Dewey

The popular concept today is that of Dewey, *viz.,* that education is growth resulting from experiences. This education may be good, bad, or indifferent, although common usage refers to socially desirable development. If education is conceived in terms of growth, then it is as difficult to "educate" children as it is to "grow" plants. The teacher as a gardener of human growth seeks to provide conditions conducive to development through learning. Basically education is a lifelong learning process involving all-round development accompanied by adjustments within oneself to things, circumstances, and people. Intrinsic self-adjustment and extrinsic social adjustment are both concomitants of healthy growth. Educators must be concerned with the direction in which such development should be kept moving, and the ultimate goals toward which it should be directed. In the final analysis, the objectives of education are determined by the very nature of man himself.

The depth, length, breadth, and height of education are revealed more pointedly in its objectives, aims, or purposes than in terse definitions. These objectives when implemented by a functioning curriculum become a program of social action.

Objectives Defined by Individuals

Just as education is a process of growth, so too the objectives of education slowly evolve. Every statement of purposes develops from the judgment or scale of values held by some person or group. Educational leaders and professional groups have listed the objectives in various ways. A few illustrative statements by individuals and groups are included here.

Herbert Spencer's Classification of Objectives. Herbert Spencer, who has never been accorded his just place in the field of education, as early as 1861 revealed his social insight through his published classification of human activities as a basis for grouping educational objectives. His five major areas of human conduct were as follows:

1. Self-preservation
2. Securing the necessities of life
3. Rearing and discipline of offspring
4. Maintenance of proper social and political relations

5. Activities which make up the leisure part of life, devoted to the gratification of the tastes and feelings [4]

This list helped to popularize the practice of classifying human activities.

James Bryant Conant's Objectives for Public Education. In answer to his own question, "Why should one be taxed to provide schools for other people's children?" Harvard's former president James Bryant Conant gives these reasons:

1. Education for citizenship
2. Education for the good life
3. Vocational education, of which professional education is a special case [5]

This threefold division of education, Conant states, may serve as a rough guide to a layman seeking to penetrate the tangle of verbosities that surrounds many academic discussions.

Robert J. Havighurst's Developmental Tasks. Robert J. Havighurst, chairman of the Committee on Human Development at the University of Chicago, defines this term as follows:

A developmental task is a task which arises at or about a certain period in the life of the individual, successful achievement of which leads to his happiness and to success with later tasks, while failure leads to unhappiness in the individual, disapproval by the society, and difficulty with later tasks. The prototype of the developmental task is the purely biological formation of organs in the embryo. [6]

He lists sequential activities for the various periods in life:

Developmental Tasks of Early Childhood

Learning to walk
Learning to take solid foods
Learning to talk
Learning to control the elimination of body wastes
Learning sex differences and sexual modesty
Learning physiological stability
Forming simple concepts of social and physical reality
Learning to relate oneself emotionally with siblings and parents
Learning to distinguish right from wrong and developing a conscience

Developmental Tasks of Middle Childhood

Learning physical skills necessary for ordinary games
Building wholesome attitudes toward oneself as a growing organism
Learning to get along with age-mates

[4] Herbert Spencer, *Education,* p. 32, Appleton-Century-Crofts, 1861.
[5] James Bryant Conant, *Education in a Divided World,* p. 69, Harvard University Press, 1948.
[6] Robert J. Havighurst, *Human Development and Education,* p. 2, Longmans, 1953.

Learning an appropriate masculine or feminine social role
Developing fundamental skills in reading, writing, and calculating
Developing concepts necessary for everyday living
Developing conscience, morality, and a scale of values
Achieving personal independence
Developing attitudes toward social groups and institutions

Developmental Tasks of Adolescence

Achieving new and more mature relations with age-mates of both sexes
Achieving a masculine or feminine role
Accepting one's physique and using the body effectively
Achieving emotional independence of parents and other adults
Achieving assurance of economic independence
Selecting and preparing for an occupation
Preparing for marriage and family life
Developing intellectual skills and concepts necessary for civic competence
Desiring and achieving socially responsible behavior
Acquiring a set of values and an ethical system as a guide to behavior

Developmental Tasks of Early Adulthood

Selecting a mate
Learning to live with a marriage partner
Starting a family
Rearing children
Managing a home
Getting started in an occupation
Taking on civic responsibility
Finding a congenial social group

Developmental Tasks of Middle Age

Achieving adult civic and social responsibilities
Establishing and maintaining an economic standard of living
Assisting teen-age children to become responsible and happy adults
Developing adult leisure-time activities
Relating oneself to one's spouse as a person
Accepting and adjusting to the physiological changes of middle age
Adjusting to ageing parents

Developmental Tasks of Later Maturity

Adjusting to decreasing physical strength and health
Adjusting to reduced income
Adjusting to death of a spouse
Establishing an explicit affiliation with one's age group
Meeting social and civic obligations
Establishing satisfactory physical living arrangements [7]

[7] *Ibid.*, pp. 9–283.

These developmental tasks need to be met with graduated curricular materials and significant life experiences.

OBJECTIVES PREPARED BY PROFESSIONAL GROUPS

Collective professional opinion as to what constitutes the goals of education has been crystallized periodically in statements prepared in connection with local, state, regional, and national programs, such as those described later in this unit. Illustrative group statements on the purposes of education are the North Central Association objectives and the Life Adjustment Principles, as formulated respectively by a regional and a national committee. The latter are in Unit VII. Here are summarized general objectives or the purposes of education in American democracy, prepared by the Educational Policies Commission.

Purposes of Education in American Democracy. These are both general and specific. Some of them undoubtedly possess the important quality of universality and eternal validity. The commission identified four aspects of educational purpose, centering around (1) the person himself, (2) his relationship to others in home and community, (3) the creation and use of material wealth, and (4) socio-civic activities. The first area calls for a description of the educated *person;* the second, for a description of the educated *member of the family and community group;* the third, of the educated *producer or consumer;* the fourth, of the educated *citizen.* The four great groups of objectives are stated as those of:

1. Self-realization
2. Human relationship
3. Economic efficiency
4. Civic responsibility

Each of these, related to the others in a whole, is capable of further subdivision. A summary of each major objective is presented in *Policies for Education in American Democracy.*[8] As pointed out by the Educational Policies Commission, the applications of values vary from place to place and from hour to hour; hence it is impossible in a dynamic, changing world to develop detailed purposes that are universally applicable and perpetually enduring. Therefore both the philosophic fundamentals of education and the curriculums must be subject to constant revision if they are to be meaningful to the people and effective in schools, colleges, and life. Furthermore, realistic objectives should stimulate goal-directed activity and develop into desirable outcomes. Too often objectives exist merely for historical purposes and are as ineffective as New Year's resolutions.

[8] Educational Policies Commission, *Policies for Education in American Democracy,* National Education Association, 1946, pp. 185–252. In this volume a chapter is devoted to each major objective. See also the Commission's *Public Education and the Future of America,* Chap. I, "Public Education and Some Great American Principles," National Education Association, 1955.

PRINCIPLES UNDERLYING CURRICULUM DEVELOPMENT

A common practice in the initiation of programs for curriculum development is to prepare a list of basic principles or guiding assumptions. This initial attack provides a unified point of view and a basis for consistency of action among the educational workers as they develop curriculums.

GENERAL PRINCIPLES BASIC TO CURRICULUM DEVELOPMENT

The Curriculum Is Broad and Comprehensive. As defined previously, the curriculum consists of the "organized experiences of an individual under the guidance of the school." Some authorities go to the extreme in stating that the curriculum consists of all the experiences a person has, irrespective of what, when, and where. Obviously there must be some delimitation. Generally, however, the term "curriculum" is interpreted broadly.

The curriculum is not simply a series of printed pages written in some central office for the information and guidance of the teachers in the classroom. Such published materials are often extremely helpful to the teachers in their work, but the curriculum itself is not what is written but what is done. Today's program for youth accents the kind of experiences he ought to have rather than the names of the subjects he should take. These experiences are facilitated and directed through the development of curricular materials. The activities and materials are as broad as life itself. The curriculum is life material used in building body, mind, and soul structure.

The Curriculum Has Its Roots in a Philosophy of Education. A broad well-grounded curriculum reaches down into the bedrock of the school's educational principles. Since educational philosophy is primarily concerned with a criticism of experience, it is obvious that its formulation follows prolonged study. As William James once stated, philosophy is a particularly obstinate effort to think closely. A deep, sustaining philosophy is more likely to result from the leisure meditation of the Indian oriental who spends hours in contemplative thought than from the mile-a-minute dash of the occidental who does much of his thinking while he talks. There is imminent danger that teachers will seek to "Simonize" their curriculums by applying hastily a thin top coat of diluted educational philosophy. A frame of reference cannot be formulated in one teachers' meeting—it is evolved from life through continual reflection. Furthermore, caution must be expressed against the current practice of parroting the trite phrases of educational theorists instead of building a strong philosophy upon the inner convictions and firsthand knowledges of those who work daily with pupils and who have digested the thoughts of yesterday's and today's scholars.[9]

Curriculum Building Is a Democratic, Cooperative Enterprise. Whether it be a local, state-wide, or national program, cooperative effort is essential in curriculum work. One postulate of democracy is that persons enjoy those things in the building of which they have shared. This is doubly true in regard to the curriculum of the school. The course of study is not

Fig. 13-2. Panel discussion for the high-school divisions. Parents, teachers, and businessmen participate in the discussions of curriculum and related topics. (*Courtesy of Public Schools, Saginaw, Mich.*)

a dictator's manifesto or an executive fiat. The modern curriculum is based upon the democratic tradition that the purposes and programs of education should be developed cooperatively through the "interactive processes of living." Furthermore, participation is not limited to teachers and administrators. Pupils, parents, interested patrons, and specialists, as active agents in the educative process, can contribute to the broadened offerings of the community school. Hence of extreme importance in curriculum building are "group dynamics"—the productive processes of collective actions and interactions in furthering school and society.

The Administrative Organization Should be Simple and Flexible. An individual teacher, zealous for curriculum reform, need not wait for com-

[9] Chris A. De Young, "Thinking and Writing on Education Today," *Educational Trend*, No. 452, Arthur C. Croft, 1952, 4 pp.

plex administrative machinery to be installed locally or for a slow-moving state-wide program to be launched. The organization for curriculum production, especially in the typical school, may be very simple, with equipment and personnel added as needed and as funds become available. The committee system can be employed with a wide degree of fluidity and a high degree of effectiveness.

The Housing of the School Should Conform to the Curricular Needs. A principle hard to apply in many schools is that of adjusting the building to the educational program rather than that of developing a curriculum that will conform to the brick and mortar limitations imposed by existing structures. Many school buildings are obstacles to educational progress. A typical illustration is a high school erected before the course in auto mechanics was introduced so that today it is impossible to bring an automobile into or near the building. The housing as well as the educational supplies and equipment should function in the service of educational goals.

The Curriculum Must Provide for Individual Differences. A basic principle is that the curriculum should recognize the pupil as an individual who has a right to his own characteristic type of personality development under such guidance as is needed. Figuratively, some puny pupils are required to struggle with a 20-pound load when all they can carry is 10 pounds, whereas mentally husky individuals who can shoulder 50 pounds with ease are permitted to play with ounces. The former practice results in retardation, and the latter produces lazy workmen. A difficulty with the old order of curriculums was that the child was divided: the teacher demanded one thing and the pupil's nature and interest dictated another loyalty. Individual differences must be considered if the pupil is to develop his "personality quotient," to use his own leisure time wisely, to select a suitable vocation for himself, and to be a dynamic part of a larger whole. Meeting these individual requirements does not necessitate a contest between individual and societal needs, and between specifics and generalities. Education has general principles applicable to the whole of its citizenry, but it must be individualized even in social application.

The Creative Must Be Encouraged. Since education tends to become too wooden and mechanical, much emphasis today is placed upon developing creativeness in the pupil and teacher. The school, which often stifled genius, now encourages deviations from a fixed pattern. Gone is the day when all pupils in an art class drew a flower in identical patterns and with the same color. Creative self-expression is the antithesis of moronic imitation. Intrinsic interests rather than extraneous assignments goad pupils to action. *Memoriter* learning except in basic essentials is being dethroned. Skills are taught through functional use in meaningful situations. Curriculums are built out of knowledge about the individual pupil. The modern curriculum functions best under an eclectic procedure, which necessitates that teachers think creatively and ingeniously of many learning-teaching possibilities.

Guidance Is Inextricably Linked with the Curriculum. One cannot isolate a guidance program from the curriculum; their synthesis is inevi-

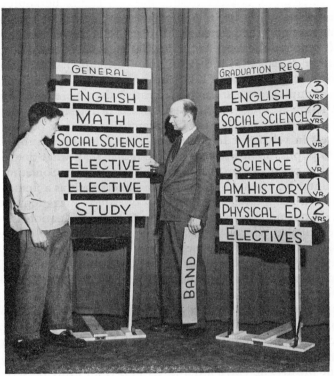

Fig. 13-3. Preregistration coupled with curricular guidance in the junior high school. This junior high school has four curriculums: college preparatory, vocational, commercial, and general. As pictured above, the general curriculum calls for all ninth-graders' taking English, some type of mathematics, social science, two electives, and "study." (*Courtesy of Public Schools, Idaho Falls, Idaho.*)

table. A growing practice is to map out in advance a tentative curriculum for all four years of the student's proposed stay in the high school. This tends to make the student feel that each course is a part of a larger plan for rounding out his education. This long-term curricular outlook is also being provided for college students in an increasing number of institutions. Guidance is not a disparate service to be performed only by specialists. The classroom instructor, through the curriculum, makes many adaptations to allow the pupil a maximum of self-direction. The course of study is in itself a mere guide for the teacher. Modern school administration is designed to provide curricular help for both students and teachers through person-to-person guidance and individual therapy as well as group advisement.

The Curriculum Should Be Life-centered. Although the individual pupil must be recognized, the modern school is not restricted to a child-centered curriculum. Neither should the curriculum be adult-centered. The focal point is life itself. A life-centered curriculum recognizes the past of the race plus the present and future life of the learner and society. To be life-centered the modern curriculum must function 24 hours a day.

Evaluation Is Essential for Pupil and Curriculum. Evaluation in its broad scope is replacing tests. Many instruments of diagnosis and reliable measures of pupil growth are employed rather than mere pencil-and-paper tests and lesson reciting, which often consists of repeating to the teacher stereotyped phrases and clauses. The atomistic character of appraisal revealed itself in yesteryear in the extreme emphasis upon subjects rather than upon pupils, upon what they wrote rather than what they did.

Evaluation of curricular materials is also inevitable. Sometimes this is made voluntarily; often, however, circumstances such as a financial stringency force a reappraisal of a school's offerings. Accretions in course offerings do not necessarily mean improvement; elimination is unavoidable in curricular reform. This involves a related principle expressed many years ago by Herbert Spencer in the query, "What knowledge is of most worth?" A pupil receives his formal education in a relatively short span; hence evaluation must result in the elimination as well as the addition of curricular materials.

Constant Curriculum Revision Is Imperative. It is law of growth that things must change; hence constant curricular modifications are inevitable. Teachers are likely to work feverishly on curriculum reform for a few years and then write an indelible "finis" to materials committed to permanent print. The curriculum at its best is an evolving series of experiences; hence it does not need to be copyrighted for 28 years or registered in the United States Patent Office. Constant revisions, which should be made in such a manner as to avoid educational chaos, will lead to intellectual emancipation for the schools and will enable educators to meet the challenges of contemporary life. A changeless curriculum postulates a static society, and, vice versa, an unchanging society demands no curricular innovations. Education must recover what is valuable in the residue of the past, but it must also break away from the authority of outworn tradition.

PROCEDURES IN CURRICULUM DEVELOPMENT

Intertwined with the principles just enumerated are the procedures or techniques in curriculum development. Several major approaches and steps are listed, and then a few detailed techniques are described.

Approaches to Curriculum Work

Three major methods of *organization* for curriculum improvement are: centralized, decentralized, and centrally coordinated approaches.[10] The last, a partnership program of administrators and teachers, is widely used.

The usual approaches to curriculum *activity* are: the cooperative development of basic principles that underlie the evolution of curriculums; a study of the characteristics and needs of pupils, adults, and society; or the immediate direct attack upon subject matter and content, as through a production committee for mathematics. Often these approaches are combined, or each is lifted up for periodic emphasis as curriculum building progresses.

Major Steps in Curriculum Development

Curricular procedures are influenced so markedly by the community, school, and personnel engaged in the work that it is impossible to set up a uniform series of sequential steps. Some of the major procedures followed in a local school system are as follows:

Inviting cooperation and support for curriculum reorganization
Organizing personnel for curriculum development
Formulating tentative statement of guiding curricular principles
Selecting procedures for developing curriculums
Educating teachers in techniques of revision
Consulting outside specialists for assistance
Formulating general aims, objectives, or functions of education
Studying needs, interests, and abilities of pupils
Surveying legal prescriptions affecting the curriculum
Making historical surveys of curriculum development
Getting parental opinion on the curriculum
Investigating community and societal characteristics and resources
Making detailed activity or job analyses
Collecting and analyzing curriculum materials and research studies
Selecting and organizing content
Suggesting teaching-learning procedures
Correlating work in various areas and levels
Determining approximate time allotments
Establishing minimum standards of achievement and growth
Organizing experimental groups and conducting extensive tryouts
Checking content for unnecessary duplication or omission of essentials
Editing material for expression and form
Selecting textbooks and library materials
Recommending other supplies and equipment
Educating teachers in the use of reorganized curriculum
Preparing materials for evaluating pupil growth

[10] Ronald C. Doll, A. Harry Parsons, and Stephen M. Corey, *Organization for Curriculum Development*, pp. 1–9, Teachers College, 1953.

Appraising results of curricular reconstruction
Providing for continuous development of the curriculum
Interpreting the program continuously to the public

A few of the detailed techniques employed by curriculum workers will be described briefly.

SPECIFIC TECHNIQUES IN BUILDING CURRICULUMS

Organization of Personnel. Curriculum work is best promoted under a simple but effective coordination of workers. An illustration of how a school system is organized for curriculum building is depicted in Fig. 13-4. One notes the use of an educational council which works closely with the curriculum department in the development of materials.

Survey of Legal Prescriptions. No group engaged in curriculum work can afford to ignore the mandates of the lawgivers. To the courses of study the lawmakers have added many requirements, from the general order in the first grade that basic instruction must be in the English language to the federal stipulation that land-grant colleges must teach military science. The most frequent legal accretions to the curriculum concern the teaching of United States history, civics, safety education, and the evil effects of narcotics and alcohol, plus the obligatory observance of special days.

Investigation and Use of Community Resources. The community school as an agency for achieving social ideals seeks to draw upon curriculum resources in the local setting as well as in larger spheres. Periodic inventories of the community resources made by pupils, teachers, and others will help to locate potential sources of curriculum enrichment and of work experiences for pupils.

Activity or Job Analysis. In this technique the surveyor makes a detailed study of the various duties entailed in a particular job, such as office secretaryship. After the minute tasks have been located and defined, the school can better prepare a student for this position by giving him much specific information and many direct experiences. One of the chief proponents of these analytical procedures has been W. W. Charters, who has applied this technique to teaching. The curriculum at Stephens College, Columbia, Missouri, has been built primarily upon an analysis of activities performed by women.

Research and Experimentation in Curriculum Development. With the twentieth century began that emphasis in education which is called the "scientific movement," although from the days of Benjamin Franklin a small group of educators have been interested in objectivity and the scientific spirit. Gradually educators in larger numbers turned to experimentation and research instead of to opinion, tradition, and the pastepot-and-scissors method of making courses of study.

SUPERINTENDENT OF SCHOOLS

|
|---|

DIRECTOR OF INSTRUCTION

EDUCATIONAL COUNCIL

Membership

(Chairman, elected)

Director of Instruction

Director, Elementary Education

Director, Secondary Education

Director, Vocational Education

Director, Extended Services

Director, Child Development and Guidance

Members rotating biennially:
  1 Supervisor
  1 Department Chairman
  1 each senior high, junior high, and elementary principal.
  4 classroom teachers:
    2 elementary, 1 junior high, and 1 senior high.
Lay citizens

Rotating members elected at large by the groups with which associated.

EDUCATIONAL COUNCIL

Responsibility: The educational council is directly responsible to the director of instruction and reports only to him.

Function: Formulation of the philosophy, principles, and objectives essential to a sound educational program in a democratic society.

Duties:

1. Analyze critically the educational interests and needs of the City of Wilmington.

2. Work closely with the curriculum development department in the development of curriculums to be followed at all levels.

3. Prepare recommendations to the director of instruction and the administrative cabinet suggesting procedure designed to implement the program required.

4. Plan procedures for the integration and coordination of the program from kindergarten through adult education.

5. Recommend procedures for the examination and evaluation of the program now in effect in each division of the school system to determine its effectiveness in achieving its purposes.

6. Suggest ways and means of improving the educational program.

7. Recommend to the committee on professional growth desirable steps in the development of greater professional competence among the entire staff.

8. Suggest ways and means of demonstrating the power of education to develop competent American citizens, thus gaining public understanding, cooperation, and support.

FIG. 13-4. Organization of educational council. The council works closely with the curriculum-development department in promoting curricular activity on all levels. (*Courtesy of Public Schools, Wilmington, Del.*)

Some research, however, does not merit the name, since it is mere busy work. Not only is much research of inferior quality, but significant findings obtained scientifically have been interpreted and applied in an unscientific manner. Teachers must become educated consumers as well as indefatigable producers of research. Among the genuine research investigations that have had a marked influence on the curriculum are controlled studies of how human beings learn, as Gesell's investigations of the early years of childhood; experimentation with learning in animals, particularly white rats and monkeys, as Kofka's work with the insight in monkeys; research to find the most needed subject matter, as Hocking's early study of place geography; investigations of maturation and grade placement, as the work of the Committee of Seven in Arithmetic; construction of intelligence tests, as the new revision of the Binet test; the development of various types of achievement tests, as the well-known Stanford achievement tests for elementary schools; and the perfecting of the newer types of evaluation, as the measures prepared by Tyler and his associates. Pioneers who gave much thought and effort to research in building curriculums are E. L. Thorndike, W. W. Charters, and Charles Judd. Today research and experimentation have numerous implications for the classroom teachers as well as for the builder of a more scientifically prepared mental diet for the pupils.

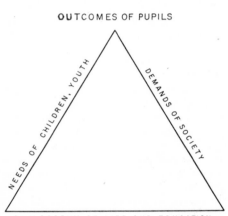

Fig. 13-5. Factors in curriculum development. The base of the triangle is a philosophy of life and education. (*Courtesy of Ivol Spafford, Vergil Herrick, and Paul R. Pierce.*)

Illustrative Diagram. Some of the techniques and principles in curriculum development are illustrated by the equilateral triangle shown in Fig. 13-5. The three factors to be given paramount consideration are indicated by the sides of the triangle:

1. A factor basic to the modern curriculum is the philosophy of life and education possessed by those who are making the curriculum. Here the question of values, understandings, and procedures essential to the democratic society arises.

2. There are the needs of society. Social changes are occurring rapidly and new issues are constantly emerging. Among the areas of social change are population movement, technological development, and home living. The curriculum must take into account the need for dealing with such developments.

3. But in a democratic society the interests and needs of the individual pupils are as important as the needs of society. Changes in psychological principles, enunciation of new laws of learning, and data from pupils' physical, mental, and emotional development profoundly affect the building of an educational program.

The relationship of the three factors is shown in the diagram, in which the philosophy of life and education of those responsible for the educational program forms the baseline of the chart, the needs of the pupils and the needs of society the sides, and the apex the outcomes for the pupils.[11]

The outcomes for the pupils are affected by the way in which curricular materials are organized.

ORGANIZATION OF CURRICULAR MATERIALS

TYPES OF CURRICULUM ORGANIZATION

Curricular patterns range from the traditional type to extreme experimentation. Five of the curricular patterns with alternate designations are (1) subject or traditional, (2) correlated or fused, (3) broad fields or areas, (4) core or common learnings, and (5) experience or functional curriculums. These types, which are not mutually exclusive and have numerous variations, are described as follows.[12]

Subject Curriculum. This is characterized by a large number of subjects taught independently of each other. Most of the time of the pupil is spent in learning from books and other written and printed materials in various subjects in which the accumulated wisdom of experts in that field has been recorded. The emphasis is upon the learning of subject matter selected long before the children appear in the classroom.

In such a curriculum, history, geography, and civics usually are isolated subjects (see Fig. 13-6).

Correlated Curriculum. Here the underlying ideas are those described for the subject curriculum. The starting point is subject-matter-set-out-to-be-learned. The correlated curriculum can be carried out in numerous ways which can be conveniently arranged on a scale. At the bottom would be located the casual and incidental efforts to make relationships between or among subjects. At the top of the scale would be located those conscious and definitely planned efforts to see that relationships among subjects were made and carried out effectively.

Among the correlations may be those between subjects within a field, as social science, or between subjects within two or more fields, as English and history. Subjects may be fused so that boundaries disappear.

The Broad Fields Curriculum. This is composed of a few fields rather than a large number of small subjects. In broad fields under the subject philosophy the learning area is restricted, although definitely broader than what would be

[11] Adapted from Paul R. Pierce, "The Curriculum Council of the Chicago Public Schools," *Chicago Schools Journal*, March–April, 1949, p. 177. See also Vergil E. Herrick, "Developing a Curriculum for a Democratic Social Order," *Significant Aspects of American Life and Postwar Education*, pp. 28–29, University of Chicago Press, 1944.

[12] Adapted from L. Thomas Hopkins, *Integration: Its Meaning and Application*, pp. 197–275, Appleton-Century-Crofts, 1937, Good, *op. cit.*, pp. 113–114, and American Association of School Administrators, *American School Curriculum*, pp. 57–70, National Education Association, 1953.

expected as a summation of various subjects. In broad fields under the experience philosophy the learning area is greatly increased.

Examples of these broad fields or areas are social science and the language arts.

The Core Curriculum. This includes subjects or a common body of experiences required of everyone but with variability of content and activities to meet

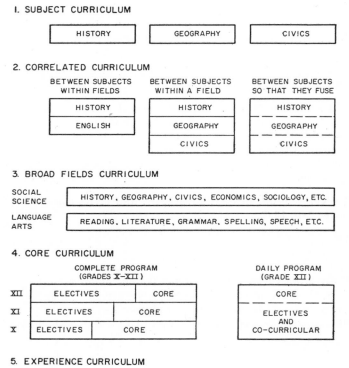

FIG. 13-6. Major types of curriculums.

the varying needs of individuals. The term core is used to cover a wide range of types of curriculum practice.

Part of the work in the senior high may be a basic core running through grades 10, 11, and 12 with variable time allotments. A certain portion of each day may be devoted to the core, or common learnings.

The Experience Curriculum. This is a series of purposeful experiences growing out of pupil interests and moving toward an ever more adequate understanding of and intelligent participation in the surrounding culture and group life. The experience curriculum has its beginnings in the situations which confront children in their immediate living.

Fig. 13-7. A plan for the emerging curriculum. Lester Dix suggests for the four major areas the study of self-development, social environment, natural environment, and human expression and communications as represented in the arts. The disciplines named in the outer parts of the three circles do not form an exhaustive list. In the pure science area, for instance, there might be twenty-five or thirty. Moreover, the appropriate emphasis in this plan would be upon the most lately developed and currently functional aspects of these disciplines, for instance, biochemistry or biophysics. A similar emphasis is proposed for the social sciences. (*Lester Dix, 1 Charter for Progressive Education, p.* 62, *Teachers College,* 1939.)

A comprehensive example is the directly functional curriculum suggested by Lester Dix. Dix proposes for the general divisions of his functional curriculum the following, illustrated in Fig. 13-7:

1. The Study of Oneself—embracing the functions of guidance, of health development and emotional adjustment, of the provision of basic necessities, of play, recreation, club, and hobby interests, and all social activities.

2. The Study of the Social Environment—the evolution, functions, and structures of cultures, particularly American society.

3. The Study of the Natural Environment—the relationship of man and nature; his sciences of control, adaptation, and utilization.

4. The Study of the Arts—the evolution, materials, skills, and attitudes of the arts of human expression, communication, and imagination.[13]

These areas are overlapping fields. The directly functional type is a variety of experience curriculum. Two kinds of curricular organization currently stressed in many schools are the core curriculum previously described and the organization of subject matter and activities in teaching-learning units. Because of the significant role of units in current curriculums, this organization of materials and activities is described further.

UNITARY PROCEDURES IN TEACHING AND LEARNING

Much confusion exists in regard to the term "unit," which is applied to many aspects of American public education.

An *administrative unit* is a school district—a geographical area which constitutes usually the territory legally under the direction of a board of education. It may be a small rural district or a large county unit of school administration.

The *attendance unit* may be identical in area with the administrative unit where there is but one school building to which all pupils go. In most cities the one administrative unit consists of several attendance units—schools that pupils in designated parts of the city attend.

The term is also applied to a level or *unit of school organization* such as the elementary school, or the secondary unit.

Sometimes the term designates a *unit of school construction,* as a school building, or a part of a building, as the home economics unit.

Toward the close of the nineteenth century the New York State Board of Regents started to measure a pupil's work in the high school in terms of "counts." The currently accepted method of calculating a high-school pupil's work quantitatively is the *Carnegie unit,* which was defined by the Carnegie Foundation for the Advancement of Teaching as "a course of five periods a week throughout the academic year." More recently suggestions have been made that this count be altered to semester hours or some other measure.

The term is now widely applied to *teaching-learning units*—organized instructional materials and experiences that emphasize the organismic point of view that the individual functions as an organic whole.

In its broadest sense, a teaching-learning unit is a teacher-pupil designed series of significant experiences so related as to function in the all-round development of an integrating person in a dynamic world. This concept stresses the fact that the unit embraces both learning and teaching, involves both pupil and teacher activity, calls for planning, includes significant experiences, aims at many-sided development through a totality of learnings, and seeks to develop not an integrat*ed* but an integrat*ing*

[13] Lester Dix, *A Charter for Progressive Education,* p. 57, Teachers College, 1939.

person who can adjust to ever-changing situations in a kaleidoscopic world. Furthermore, unit procedures are not designed exclusively for children but are used extensively and effectively for any learner—be he child, youth, or adult.

Historical Evolution of Teaching-Learning Unit. The forerunner of the unit method was probably Johann Friedrich Herbart (1776–1841). The five Herbartian steps were: preparation, presentation, comparison, generalization, and application. One center of the Herbartian movement in the United States was Illinois State Normal University at Normal, Illinois, where Charles De Garmo, the brothers Charles and Frank McMurray, and other great teachers, several of whom studied in Germany, helped spread Herbart's ideas and started the Herbartian Society, now the National Society for the Study of Education. The Herbartian method was especially well adapted to the logically organized materials of instruction.

The current emphasis on the unit method of instruction was stimulated by Professor Henry C. Morrison of the University of Chicago. Through his classroom instruction and his writings, Professor Morrison's interpretation of the unit became widely accepted throughout the United States and abroad. The five Herbartian steps have their modern counterpart in the Morrisonian operative technique of exploration, presentation, assimilation, organization, and recitation. This is coupled with the mastery formula which is to pretest, teach, test the result, adapt procedure, teach and test again to the point of actual learning.[14] Others have modified and interpreted the Morrisonian technique. Many state curricular groups and local school systems have adopted and adapted the unitary procedures in teaching and learning.

Organization of a Teaching-Learning Unit. The order and number of elements included in a teaching-learning unit vary with the pupils, teacher, supervisor, school, and community, but the following list covers most factors in its organization:

1. A meaningful title—relationship with other units
2. Objectives—teacher and pupil; general and specific; minimum essentials
3. Grade placement—academic level
4. Approximate time elements—hours per day; number of weeks
5. Orientation—setting the stage; preparing pupils, teacher, and community; gathering data on pupils and local situation; pupil-teacher planning
6. Initiation of unit—pretest; suggested leads or approaches, exploratory questions; problem raising; presentation; lecture
7. Guidance of pupils—oral and written directions; developmental discussion; plans for work; unit guide sheets

[14] Henry C. Morrison, *The Practice of Teaching in the Secondary School*, p. 81, University of Chicago Press, 1936.

8. Organization of teaching-learning materials—outline of content

9. Suggested activities—individual and group; curricular and cocurricular; initiating, developing, and culminating

10. Proposed teaching-learning procedure—directed study; assimilation of materials; recitation; organization of responses; provisions for correlation

11. Suggested materials and equipment—basal text or texts; elements of the environment; articles of achievement; audio-visual aids

12. Adaptations—provisions for flexibility and individual differences

13. Descriptive bibliography—pupil and teacher

14. Evaluation—actual outcomes in terms of objectives achieved, as measured by tests, reviews, reports (oral and written), anecdotal records, and other measures of personal growth and social living; evaluation of the unit

15. Report and historical record of the unit—illustrative teacher and pupil materials; diary of progress

16. Provision for continuous revision—perfecting the unit

The mechanical make-up or format of the unit should give consideration to such elements as initial page, table of contents, numbering of pages, title headings, binding, and other physical features.

As previously indicated, the eclectic method of teaching and learning employs many techniques and curricular patterns, including the teaching-learning unit just described. The unit does not have any rigidly fixed content but is flexible to meet times, places, and circumstances. One of its chief assets is that it involves more than a mere reorganization of traditional subject matter. A realistic unit of work is a designed program of dynamic living.

CURRICULUM DEVELOPMENT IN THE UNITED STATES

HISTORICAL DEVELOPMENT OF CURRICULUMS

In the early days of American public education the curriculum was very simple in pattern although its content was heavy—too substantial for many. The pre-elementary program did not exist. The elementary school stressed four R's—reading, 'riting, 'rithmetic, and religion. In the high school the emphasis was on college preparation, whereas in the college there were no electives. The curriculums for out-of-school youth and adults were unknown. Today offers a marked contrast. Some of the curricular changes that have taken place are mentioned in Part II, Units V–IX, where historical overviews are presented for pre-elementary, elementary, secondary, and higher education, and for education for out-of-school youth and adults.

Various Committees. Important factors in the historical development of curriculums have been and still are the efforts of various national committees. The *Report of the Committee of Ten,* published in 1893, was a significant document in the history of American education. Associated in this work with Charles W. Eliot, then president of Harvard University, were such eminent leaders as William T. Harris, James B. Angell, and Henry Churchill King. Their report marked the beginning of the emancipation of secondary schools from the domination of college entrance requirements interpreted largely in terms of mathematics and language requirements; it included the findings of nine national conferences made up of leading educators in as many subject matter fields.

The *Report of the Committee of Fifteen,* published in 1895, was another pioneer document in the fields which it covered, *viz.,* the training of teachers, the correlation of studies in elementary education, and the organization of city school systems. This committee included in its membership William T. Harris, William H. Maxwell, and Andrew S. Draper.

A Committee of Nine on "The Articulation of the High Schools and Colleges," which, like the two preceding committees, was named by the National Education Association, recommended in 1911 that the completion of practically any broad, well-planned, high-school curriculum should be accepted as preparation for college. A year later this committee recommended that a "Commission on the Reorganization of Secondary Education" be appointed with 12 subcommittees to study the reorganization of high-school subjects. Among those who served on this commission and its subcommittees were: Thomas H. Briggs, Alexander Inglis, Henry Turner Bailey, James F. Hosic, Philander P. Claxton, and William H. Kilpatrick. This commission formulated in 1918 the Cardinal Principles of Secondary Education, previously mentioned.

A dynamic influence in curriculum development, through establishing goals and policies, has been the National Education Association. Its Educational Policies Commission, in collaboration with the American Association of School Administrators, has published several monumental works affecting curriculum development. Various departments of this association have issued and will continue to disseminate publications in the field of curriculum.

Among the other national societies that have stimulated curriculum reform are the National Society for the Study of Education through its yearbooks, the Progressive Education Association through its Eight-year Study, the Commission on Life Adjustment through its efforts to meet the imperative needs of youth, and the American Council on Education through its various commissions, such as the American Youth Commission and the Commission on Implications of Armed Services Educational Programs. The United States Office of Education has also been active in promoting two programs, "Zeal for American Democracy" and the aforementioned "Life Adjustment."

Despite the possible setbacks now and then, the years to come will find pupils and teachers gaining strength in learning, teaching, and adjusting democratically through their curricular and cocurricular activities.

CURRENT STATUS OF CURRICULUM DEVELOPMENT

As just indicated, the curriculum of today is the result of a slow but steady development. Through the combined efforts of local, county, state,

FIG. 13-8. Curriculum conference in service center. (*Courtesy of Public Schools, San Diego County, Calif.*)

regional, and national agencies the curriculum is becoming functional and elastic. In no area of public education has so much improvement been effected in the last decade as in curriculum.

Some General Curricular Trends.[15] Among the trends discernible today in the development of curriculums are the following general indications:

1. A broadened concept of the curriculum to embrace all the experiences which pupils have under the guidance of the teacher
2. An understanding of the philosophy that undergirds society, education in general, and the local school system
3. An application of the best developments of the psychology of learning and physical growth, particularly maturation
4. A consideration of sequential developmental tasks in meeting the life needs of pupils and students

[15] For specific trends in pre-elementary, elementary, secondary, higher, out-of-school youth, and adult education, see the concluding portions of Units V–IX, respectively.

5. A functional concept of correlation—an integrat*ing* child

6. An extension of the classroom through utilization of community resources

7. A reorganization of the program of studies on the bases of great central concepts, understandings, themes, fields or units, but with protection for pupils against the neglect of necessary skills, informations, and attitudes

8. A supplementing of measurement through pencil-paper tests by a many-sided program of qualitative evaluation

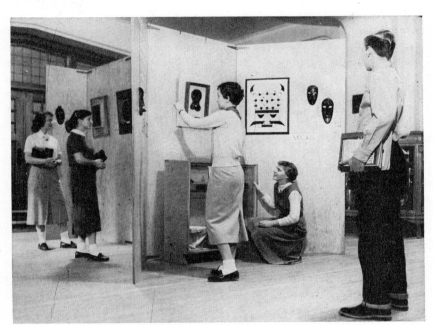

FIG. 13-9. A curricular trend—unleashing the creative talents of students and teachers. This art gallery in Hughes High School, Cincinnati, was created as a joint project of students and teachers in a teamwork to bring the enjoyment of art to the whole school. Here art students benefit as they see their own work exhibited with that of others, and their schoolmates view new displays each week. (*Courtesy of Better Schools and of Public Schools, Cincinnati, Ohio.*)

9. An elimination of some of the "deadwood" in the curriculum and the substitution of validated content

10. A development of a cooperative program of continuous curriculum revision by all pupils, teachers, administrators, and laymen

11. An unleashing of individual creative efforts by pupils and teachers

12. A specific remedial program based upon careful individual diagnosis

13. An incorporation of cocurricular activities in the school program

14. A utilization of a wide variety of materials and equipment, including multisensory aids, and the establishment of an instructional materials center

15. A designing of school buildings to meet the requirements of a flexible program

16. A development of curricular guides containing "rich sources of raw materials" and curriculum laboratories for materials

17. A functional program of curricular services to meet fundamental human needs—mental, physical, social, and emotional

Lester Dix describes four patterns of curricular emphasis as trends proceeding in the order named: the *traditional,* which addresses itself to the maintenance of the present status, with little planned relationship to the needs of young people who have been required to accept it; the *society-centered,* which is the chief type of current modification, with its social emphasis induced by the recently developed social consciousness in American thought; the *personality-centered,* which is hardly yet discernible in actual existence, with its efforts to utilize the mounting knowledge of individual growth and development; and the *directly functional* curriculum, which remains largely in the form of theory and verbal description, with its emphasis upon the study of the great fundamental areas of life activity.[16]

Although the curriculums of today are more functional than those of yesteryear, the future demands a critical evaluation of both current offerings and future accretions in order that present gains may be consolidated and dynamic growth guaranteed to the pupils of today and tomorrow.

In conclusion, perhaps the most conspicuous current trend in the development and organization of curricular materials on all educational levels, and particularly in the elementary and secondary school, is the emphasis on democratic living. Democratic ideals and practices have been receiving mere lip service in many schools. Too many pupils do not even know what democracy is, and too many teachers are hazy on the subject.

To counteract this serious shortcoming various groups are striving to implement the great goals of democracy through citizenship-laden content in curriculums.[17] In this age, aptly called "an upset in the metabolism of human history," the danger is great, but the need for democratic living is greater, and the opportunity is the greatest in the history of American education.

SUGGESTED ACTIVITIES

1. Differentiate clearly between curriculum, course of study, program of study, and syllabus.

2. Collect definitions of education. Write in one paragraph your definition.

3. Analyze critically several sets of objectives of education.

4. Prepare a list of principles that underlie curriculum development.

[16] Dix, *op. cit.,* pp. 51–56.

[17] American Association of School Administrators, *Educating for American Citizenship,* Chap. XI, "Practicing Effective Citizenship," National Education Association, 1954.

5. What is meant by "developmental tasks"?

6. Discuss the part the classroom teacher plays in curriculum development.

7. If possible, attend a meeting of teachers working on curricular problems.

8. Draw a diagram of the organization of school personnel engaged in curriculum work in some school system with which you are familiar.

9. Make a visit to a curriculum laboratory and analyze the materials there.

10. Examine courses of study in your major field of interest.

11. Investigate the legal prescriptions set up by your state legislature for the curriculum in elementary and high schools.

12. Make an investigation of the resources in your community with a view to discovering teaching-learning materials.

13. Gather a few illustrations of scientific findings established by research and applicable to a school curriculum.

14. Give a life sketch of a pioneer in curriculum like E. L. Thorndike.

15. Discuss the function of educational measurement and evaluation.

16. Describe ways of organizing curricular materials, such as core curriculum.

17. Examine several teaching-learning units.

18. Visit a class in which the teacher and pupils are working on a unit.

19. Describe a state program of curriculum building.

20. Prepare a report on the curriculum recommendations of national groups, such as the Commission on Implications of Armed Services Educational Programs.

DESCRIPTIVE BIBLIOGRAPHY AND AIDS

BOOKS

AMERICAN ASSOCIATION OF SCHOOL ADMINISTRATORS: *American School Curriculum,* Chaps. V, VI, National Education Association, 1953.

> Curriculum developments in elementary and secondary schools.

———: *Education for American Citizenship,* Chap. XIII, National Education Association, 1954.

> Evaluating education for citizenship.

ASSOCIATION FOR SUPERVISION AND CURRICULUM DEVELOPMENT: *Action for Curriculum Improvement,* Chap. VII, National Education Association, 1951.

> Frontiers of curriculum development.

BRIGGS, THOMAS H.: *The Secondary School Curriculum: Yesterday, Today, and Tomorrow,* Teachers College, 1951, 89 pp.

> A series of lectures accenting the need for vision in curriculum constructing, and proposing wider participation of laymen.

CUNNINGHAM, WILLIAM F.: *General Education and the Liberal College,* Part II, Herder, 1953.

> Curriculum of the liberal college.

DRAKE, WILLIAM E.: *The American School in Transition,* Chap. IV, Prentice-Hall, 1955.

> Modern tendencies in education.

FEATHERSTONE, WILLIAM B.: *A Functional Curriculum for Youth,* Chap. II, American Book, 1950.

> The school's distinctive role in solving the youth problem.

GWYNN, J. MINOR: *Curriculum Principles and Social Trends,* Chap. IV, Macmillan, 1950.

> Economic factors in curriculum building.

HARAP, HENRY: *Curriculum Trends at Mid-century,* Chap. I, South-Western, 1953.

> Emergence of the contemporary curriculum movement.

HAVIGHURST, ROBERT J.: *Human Development and Education,* Chap. XII, Longmans, 1953.

Developmental tasks and the school curriculum.

HUTCHINS, ROBERT M.: *The Conflict in Education in a Democratic Society,* Chap. V, Harper, 1953.

Liberal education in a democracy.

KEARNEY, NOLAN C.: *Elementary School Objectives,* Part III, Russell Sage, 1953.

Implications of objectives for educational practice, research, and measurement.

MCNERNEY, CHESTER T.: *The Curriculum,* Chap. XIV, McGraw-Hill, 1953.

The curriculum for tomorrow.

NATIONAL SOCIETY FOR THE STUDY OF EDUCATION: *Adapting the Secondary-school Program to the Needs of Youth,* Chaps. VII, VIII, University of Chicago Press, 1953.

Designing programs to meet the common and special needs of youth.

ROMINE, STEPHEN A.: *Building the High School Curriculum,* Part III, Ronald, 1954.

Structuring the curriculum.

SAYLOR, J. GALEN, and WILLIAM M. ALEXANDER: *Curriculum Planning for Better Teaching and Learning,* Chap. X, Rinehart, 1954.

Core curriculum plan.

SHEATS, PAUL H., CLARENCE D. JAYNE, and RALPH B. SPENCE: *Adult Education—The Community Approach,* Chap. XIII, Dryden, 1953.

Community resources, program planning, and coordination in adult education.

ZERAN, FRANKLIN B. (ed.): *Life Adjustment Education in Action,* Chap. XXIV, Chartwell House, 1954.

Putting the program in action for secondary-school youth.

CURRENT PERTINENT PERIODICALS AND PUBLICATIONS

Courses of study

Curriculum Bulletin

Curriculum and Materials

Educational Leadership

Educational Theory

Periodicals in specific fields:

  Arithmetic Teacher

  School Arts Magazine

  Journal of Business Education

Philosophical Review

Progressive Education

Research Bulletin

Review of Educational Research

School Life

State curriculum journals:

  Washington State Curriculum Journal

Yearbooks:

  American School Curriculum

AUDIO-VISUAL AIDS

BUILDING AN OUTLINE   One reel, sound

Shows the process of a pupil reducing material to an organized list of ideas— one of the curricular tasks. Available from Coronet Films, Chicago.

A CORE-CURRICULUM CLASS IN ACTION   Filmstrip

Presents the work of a ninth-grade class organized on a core-curriculum basis. Follows the class from its first meeting through various pupil-teacher planned activities and evaluation. Available from Audio-visual Materials Consultants Bureau, College of Education, Wayne University, Detroit.

IMPORTANCE OF GOALS   19 min., sound

A case study of a thirteen-year-old girl. Illustrates the kinds of goals not often met in the classroom. One of the films in the series correlated with Herbert Sorenson's *Psychology in Education,* McGraw-Hill, 1948, 535 pp. Available from McGraw-Hill, New York 36.

INDIVIDUAL DIFFERENCES   23 min., sound

A shy, deliberate learner, different from his classmates and from his older, socially adept brother, has a series of failures. After a conference with his parents and learning more about his individual differences, the teacher uses his musical talents and makes him feel his own importance as a person. Available from McGraw-Hill Book Company, New York 36.

THE WHY AND HOW OF GUIDANCE   Two filmstrips, 49 frames, silent

These filmstrips show that effective guidance is the shared responsibility of home and school. This responsibility can be developed through tasks that are in accordance with one's maturity. Available from Popular Science, 353 Fourth Avenue, New York.

COCURRICULAR ACTIVITIES

In modern education many of the old *extra*curricular activities are becoming less *anti*curricular and more *co*curricular. These activities play an important role on all educational levels. The validity of the democratic faith is demonstrated daily in numerous cocurricular activities.

Among the objectives of cocurricular activities are educating for democracy, promoting good citizenship, developing leadership, building sound character, promoting social living, and using leisure time wisely.

The major types of cocurricular work are guidance activities, student participation in democratic government, journalism, music, speech, clubs, athletics, and auxiliary organizations and activities.

Among the essential elements in a cocurricular program are a functional organization of the local program, capable sponsors for the activities, stimulation and restriction of student participation, adequate financing of the program, and cooperation with state and national organizations. A well-balanced program of cocurricular activities offers to every student some organization of which he can be a member, to which he can render service, and by which he in turn can be helped.

OUTLINE OF CONTENTS

COCURRICULAR ACTIVITIES

Edna Ferber, in her interesting autobiography, *A Peculiar Treasure,* devotes more space to the extracurricular or cocurricular aspects of her school life at Ryan High School of Appleton, Wisconsin, than to the curricular side of her formal education there. Thus she reminisces:

The ancient ramshackle firetrap was not merely the place in which I and my classmates had spent four years grubbing away at algebra, geometry, economics, English and physics. We had had four miraculous years of the most exhilarating and heartening fun. I have never seen a public school like it. It was for us, a clubhouse, a forum, a social center, playground, a second home. We danced, flirted, played tennis there; learned to think and speak on our feet, learned a sense of humor and fair play, learned, in the best sense of the word, freedom of thought and conduct.[1]

The permeating influence of character-building activities in schools is generally acknowledged. The most classic tribute is the oft-quoted phrase of the Duke of Wellington that the battle of Waterloo was won on the playing fields of Eton. James Bryant Conant predicts, "It may be that the ideological struggle with Communism in the next fifty years will be won on the playing fields of the public high schools of the United States."[2]

Relationship of Curricular and Cocurricular Activities. Today the various *extra*curricular activities of the school are becoming less and less *anti*curricular and more and more *co*curricular. Formerly the curriculum was so formal, academic, and teacher-dominated that any informal, semi-academic, and pupil-initiated undertaking was labeled as "extracurricular." The latter included all those pupil enterprises that were not a part of regular classroom subjects. They were usually under the direction of the school but were conducted at the close of the school day. Their phenomenal growth was due largely to the dullness and monotony of the regular curriculum. Fortunately, the term "extracurricular" is disappearing.

In many schools the old extracurricular activities are assuming a prominence and function parallel with the curricular undertakings. Wherever possible, extracurricular activities should grow out of the curriculum and return to it.[3] They are so closely related to the curriculum that they are properly called "cocurricular." They may also be called "extracurricular," "extraclass," "collateral," "semicurricular," "incurricular," or "nonclass."

[1] Edna Ferber, *A Peculiar Treasure,* p. 84, Doubleday, 1939.

[2] James Bryant Conant, *Education and Liberty,* p. 62, Harvard University Press, 1953.

[3] E. K. Fretwell, *Extra-curricular Activities in Secondary Schools,* p. 2, Houghton Mifflin, 1931.

These activities do not exist by or for themselves—they contribute to the whole program of the school. This broad accent makes it desirable that the active sponsors of the organizations be regular staff members of the school.

Role of Cocurricular Programs. These programs have accumulated importance on all levels of American public education. In the pre-elementary and elementary school the cocurricular enterprises are so closely allied to the curricular program that there is often no distinction between the two. On the secondary level, particularly in the junior and senior high schools, many cocurricular meetings are scheduled during the school day but are not arranged as classes. In the junior and senior colleges the student activities revert to being almost extracurricular. Usually graduate students in universities are so busily concerned with study, research, and other problems that they neglect nonacademic activities, ofttimes to the detriment of their physical, social, and mental health. Harry L. Wells, former vice-president of Northwestern University, states that universities treat their extracurricular activities "too lightly." [4]

PRINCIPLES THAT UNDERLIE COCURRICULAR ACTIVITIES

In the preceding unit are listed several basic principles that underlie the development of the curriculum. Here some prime tenets of the program of cocurricular activities are enumerated.

FRETWELL'S SEVEN SIGNPOSTS

E. K. Fretwell, a pioneer in promoting knowledge of and practice in extracurricular activities as an important phase of teacher education, has erected seven signposts as guides along the extracurricular way. They are paraphrased thus:

1. The school shall develop a constructive program of extracurricular activities.
2. This constructive plan of extracurricular activities shall grow out of the life of the school.
3. This constructive plan shall recognize the pupil as a citizen of the school.
4. Teachers shall accept wholeheartedly the responsibility of developing the school's extracurricular activities.
5. Extracurricular activities shall be supervised.
6. Intelligent public opinion shall be developed concerning extracurricular activities.
7. The principal is responsible for the school's extracurricular activities. [5]

In elaboration and supplementation of these helpful directions, some additional principles are cited.

[4] Harry L. Wells, *Higher Education Is Serious Business*, Chap. IX, Harper, 1953.
[5] Fretwell, *op. cit.*, pp. 1–18.

SUPPLEMENTARY PRINCIPLES AFFECTING COCURRICULAR ACTIVITIES

Educating for Democratic Living. A cardinal tenet governing the school program is that America must educate for a progressing democracy. Cocurricular activities can help the school youth of America to conserve and develop the cultural pattern of a democratic way of living. Educational leaders have urged greater opportunity for pupil participation in the government of the public schools, so that by the time the students have reached the senior year in high school they are able to take over a major part of the responsibility for their own education and for their life together within the institution. The validity of the democratic faith is demonstrated daily in numerous cocurricular activities.

Promoting Good Citizenship. The school promotes good citizenship within its walls and out in life. The cocurricular activities provide excellent opportunities for pupils to study citizenship and "to put their creed into deed." Students may acquire civic intelligence and loyal citizenship through having membership in a democratic group, drawing up a constitution and bylaws for the organization, becoming eligible for holding school offices through the filing of petitions, registering for elections, voting intelligently in an election, taking the oath of office, demanding integrity and efficiency in officeholders, and submitting to a rigorous daily examination of conduct as citizens in the school and in society. These activities help to bridge the gap between the formal knowledge of the structure of government as gleaned from books and the informal but functional daily practice of citizenship in the complex arena of life.

Of specific interest in this connection, especially to out-of-school youth and those of college age, is the growth in Citizenship Recognition Day, which is designed to receive annually into citizenship with suitable ceremonies all those young men and women who have reached voting age.

Developing Leadership. The principle that school activities should develop leadership is compatible with promoting good citizenship and democratic living. As former congressman T. V. Smith has pointed out, each person should lead his fellows where his knowledge justifies and follow where his ignorance compels. Both leading and following are essential in conserving human resources. Cocurricular activities are potential producers of leadership qualities in students. Unfortunately some sponsors inhibit rather than inspire leadership. This is true of the athletic coach who gathered the boys around him before the game and said: "Now, boys, the purpose of this game is to develop character and leadership; now go in there and do just what I tell you to do." The old practice whereby the coach appoints the captain is replaced by the democratic election of the captain by the team. The debate coach who writes the speeches for his team does not stimulate independent thinking thereby.

By and large the sponsors and students sense the leadership training possibilities in cocurricular activities, for they know that the future leaders of the nation are now in the classroom and on the playgrounds.

Promoting Social Living. Although cocurricular activities seek to develop the individual, their larger emphasis is upon group living. The fraternal rather than the differential marks these organizations, which provide many opportunities for teachers and pupils to meet as friends, to foster the sharing mood, and to cultivate the art of companioning. These groups stress the fact that the school is society and that social life is a part of the racial heritage.

Utilizing Effective Motivation. The individual as a dynamic organism living in a social environment releases his energies and talents under personal and social motivation. The cocurricular acts are psychologically sound and are in greater consonance with human nature than are many curricular activities. The former are builded upon inner urges and intrinsic drives of pupils. They are concerned in a large degree with the release of potential energy under internal and environmental stimuli. They epitomize learning by doing. The cocurricular program, through such means as eligibility lists for athletes and membership in honor societies, may motivate lagging students to improve their curricular work. Many situations outside the classroom unlock powers of genius and unleash the highest development of human personalities.

Using Leisure Time Wisely. As work time decreases, leisure time increases. Unfortunately many leisure activities of youths and adults are merely time-killing amusements. Too often recreation wrecks rather than builds. As the late Dean Inge wrote, "Our minds are dyed the color of our leisure thoughts, and the inner man makes the outer." Therefore, as John Dewey stated, "A new conception of the uses of leisure has to be created; boys and girls need to be instructed so that they can discriminate between the enjoyments that enrich and enlarge their lives and those which degrade and dissipate." The quality of life and one's success in it are often determined by the degree of intelligence with which one uses his leisure time. Youth cannot solve this problem alone; the cocurricular program of the school should help him to develop the ability and inclination to spend his spare time wisely. Clubs, especially those of a recreational and hobby nature, make distinctive contributions to the present and possible future needs of the pupils. The school's educational-recreational program is a positive means for promoting the worthy use of leisure time, through what Thomas Briggs called teaching pupils to do better those desirable activities that they will do anyway. Many life-long avocational interests that pay generous social annuities are started in the school's cocurricular program. The carry-over power of school activities can be raised even higher through better and wider selection of activities and greater individual mastery of the skills involved.

Exploring Vocational Possibilities. Vocational as well as vacational possibilities are explored in a broad program of school activities. Often a student's abilities are inventoried and developed during the presentation of a class play, the production of a school annual, the editing of a school paper, or the business managership of a school event. Therefore every school should have a club or organization to meet the needs, interests, and abilities of each pupil. Then the cocurricular program can supplement the curricular offerings by promoting vocational interests and special aptitudes.

Building Sound Character. The cocurricular activities are not designed with the negative purpose of killing time but with the positive intent of building sterling character. If a youth has warped ideals, low standards of conduct, or improper attitudes, the school program of activities seeks to modify them. This is not accomplished through sermonizing, for character is caught rather than taught. Through the impact of group mores, ideals of sportsmanship, and a perennial program of character-in-action, the organizations of the school strive ceaselessly to elevate individual as well as group standards. To this end the sponsors must themselves seek to raise their "personality quotient" and to lead lives that are positively above reproach and impeccably honest. The sacred principles of careful custodianship and honest stewardship of funds must be maintained by sponsors and students alike. Time-honored civic and moral values must be stressed if the varied and extensive program is to justify the time and money expended upon it.

MAJOR TYPES OF COCURRICULAR ACTIVITIES

The complex interrelation of the numerous cocurricular activities makes it difficult to group them, since many may be classified properly under several headings. The following eight classifications are arbitrarily established here for the purposes of organized arrangement:

Guidance activities
Student participation in democratic government
Journalistic activities
Musical organizations and activities
Speech activities
School clubs
Athletic activities
Auxiliary organizations and activities

These various undertakings might have several subdivisions.

Fig. 14-1. Many of the sound principles in and major types of cocurricular activities are revealed in the composite picture from one Midwestern high school. (*Courtesy of Don Smith and New Trier Township High School, Winnetka, Ill.*)

GUIDANCE ACTIVITIES

Although all cocurricular activities contribute to personal, social, educational, avocational, vocational, or other phases of life guidance, some organizations are directly characterized by their guidance function. Chief among these are (1) the class organziations, and (2) the home rooms.

Class Organizations. An old and prevalent cocurricular activity is that of class or grade organizations. These groupings may be found all the way from the kindergarten through higher education. The classes usually elect a president, vice-president, secretary, treasurer, representatives to the student council and other organizations, and a class sponsor or sponsors from the faculty. Preferably all classes, except the incoming freshman class, choose their officers and sponsors in the spring before the close of the school year. This permits more careful planning, more mature selection of plays to be given in the fall, and enables other organizations dependent upon class elections, such as the student council, to function early in the fall.

The main function of the class organization, particularly in the freshman year, is that of orientation and guidance. This orientation may well begin before the freshmen arrive on the grounds. A spring visitation day when the whole school plays host to the visiting eighth graders is a growing practice. In many institutions of higher learning a freshman week is an effective phase of a larger program of adjustment. Special assemblies for freshmen and the utilization of class meetings are common methods of orientation. The guidance function is particularly effective again in the senior year when in class meetings and home-room organizations particular emphasis is given to the student's adjustment to his future college or out-of-school activities. Although this aspect of guidance is stressed usually in the later years of the student's schooling, it should be a part of a pyramidal program which has its broad base laid early in his school career.

Home Room. The class organization is affected by the existence of a home-room program. Most elementary pupils are assigned to a room which is their home during the school day. This plan is continued in the secondary school and helps to bridge the gap between grades. Under the guidance of an older person, the teacher, the pupil finds in his school home the common bonds of understanding and allied interests that characterize family life.

This integration center serves many purposes, such as helping the pupil feel at home, developing desirable pupil-teacher relationships, guiding the pupil, building desirable ideals and habits of citizenship, and expediting the handling of administrative routine. Thus the home room is not merely an administrative arrangement; it is a learning environment

rich in opportunities for cultivating citizenship and democracy through
well-organized procedures. The group and personal contacts stimulate
friendships and make the student feel that he has a place even in a large
high school. The Detroit house plan, employed in a modified form in
Evanston (Illinois) Township High School, is an example of this individualized administration, which encourages students to share in the
task of ruling themselves and to develop poise and assurance.

The membership of the room is arranged on any one of several bases
such as by alphabet, by intelligence or ability ratings, by horizontal

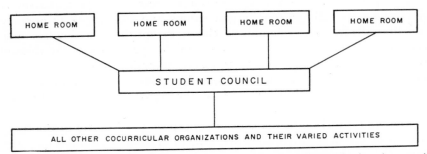

Fig. 14-2. Organization of cocurricular activities. In this type of organization the genesis
is the home room, from which representatives are elected to the student council designed as the controlling and centralizing agency for all cocurricular organizations and
activities. In several schools the classes elect representatives to the council. Often representatives from various clubs and organizations send delegates to the council meetings.

sectioning (as by grades), by vertical arrangement cutting across all years,
by first-period class, by chronological age, by sex, by previous school, by
major interest, or by curriculum. Each school should select the organizational pattern that best fits its peculiar needs.

The predominating activity of the home room is guidance. Therefore
the teacher in charge must be genuinely interested in pupils and their
welfare. Some sponsors visit the homes of their counselees in order to
learn more about them and their background. Through arrangements
made by parent-teacher organizations a home-room father or mother
often cooperates with pupils and teachers.

To be educationally effective, the home room needs a well-balanced
program of activities planned by a special room committee or all-school
committee on programs and activities. An important feature is the daily
meeting arranged as a part of the regular school schedule. Appropriate
programs are often exchanged between rooms or presented in assembly.
All school members should participate in some home-room activity—this
is the essence of democratic participation in home life. The home room
may well be the starting point in the organization of the cocurricular

activities, as shown in Fig. 14-2, which indicates that representatives from it serve on the student council.

STUDENT PARTICIPATION IN DEMOCRATIC GOVERNMENT

The decades of the 1940's and the 1950's in American public education will undoubtedly be known for the emphasis upon democracy. The American Council on Education, the Educational Policies Commission, the Citizenship Project with headquarters at Columbia University, the United States Office of Education, the National Association of Student Councils, the American Legion, and many state and local organizations have directed attention to the current problem of making democracy work, especially in education. As John Dewey has said, "If there is one conclusion to which human experience unmistakably points it is that democratic ends demand democratic methods for realization." [6] A cocurricular group that fosters the practice of democratic procedures is the student or school council. Also designed to help students share in some or all phases of self-government are school service organizations, such as the safety and citizens' clubs; boards of control; student-faculty committees; home rooms; interclub and interfraternity organizations; and informal student-faculty-community partnerships. The student council is the most prevailing type of formal organization. It is discussed here under the headings: What the Student Council Is Not, and What the Student Council Is.

What Student Council Is Not. The following statements are intended to correct a few misconceptions regarding the student council:

1. It is not a substitute for school administrators. The public pays the school executives to manage the school, thus centering responsibility in trained educational leaders.

2. A student council is not a supreme court. It is not a substitute for the board of education, which is the highest legally established authority for the conduct of the affairs of the school district.

3. It is not a robot of the administration or faculty. The council president and secretary are not just radio announcers making announcements, often in the preordained words of the principal.

4. It is not a secret society. Its business is not conducted behind closed doors.

5. It is not a spy system. It is not instituted as a "snooper council" to ferret out violations of school regulations.

6. The council is not a group of do-nothings. Seldom do the members refuse to work at challenging tasks.

7. It is not merely extracurricular—it is cocurricular and often curricular. It is not apart from but a part of the educational program.

[6] John Dewey, *Freedom and Culture*, p. 173, Putnam, 1939.

8. It is not confined to secondary schools and colleges. Many elementary schools have superior pupil-participation programs.

9. The student council is not a spasmodic organization that is here this year and gone the next. It provides a long-term program for improving the school.

Fig. 14-3. Student-council-sponsored school election. (*Courtesy of Heley and of Public Schools, Deland, Fla.*)

What the Student Council Is. On the positive side, the student council is all-important:

1. It is a body of school citizens dedicated to cooperative living in a democratic society. The school council promotes a community way of living through providing an apprenticeship in the practical processes of genuine democracy.[7]

2. The student council is a training ground. The development of continuous constructive citizenship among its members and the student body is its chief challenge.

3. It is a parliamentary body. A concomitant learning from student council work is the opportunity for the members to practice parliamentary procedure. They draw up their constitution, bylaws, rules, and regulations and abide thereby. It is a formal forum for freedom.

4. The council is an organization for building school morale at all times.

[7] Lester A. Kirkendal and Franklin R. Zeran, *Student Councils in Action*, p. 1, Chartwell House, 1953.

A vigorous council is a dynamo which daily generates energy, enthusiasm, and loyalty to the faculty and school.

5. The student council is a challenge to a high sense of honor and honesty. Its task is to make the ethical health of the entire student body so wholesome that cheating and stealing will be condemned.

6. The student council is a stimulant to scholarship. The members should be intelligent representatives of the school community.

FIG. 14-4. Student-council-sponsored drive for clothing, supplies, and toys for Korea. This "lift for Korea" was integrated with the community-wide campaign. (*Courtesy of Public Schools, Quakertown, Penna.*)

7. The student council is for the development of satisfactory leadership in school and society. Although followers are needed to cooperate with leaders, student council membership provides opportunity for leadership.

8. The council is supposed to stimulate and regulate cocurricular activities. In many schools all organizations are chartered by the council.

9. To develop intelligent voters is one goal of student council activities. Voting in student council elections should be such an interesting and stimulating experience that the student looks forward to the time when he can vote as a citizen of his community, state, and nation.

10. Finally, the student council through its numerous activities is a personalized instrument for unifying the school. The story is told of a piccolo player who stopped in the midst of a selection because he felt he was not making a

contribution. The orchestra leader, whose ears detected the inactivity, stopped the entire orchestra to remind the piccolo player that his efforts counted. So too a student council seeks to make each person in school feel that he has a part to play in the harmonious symphony of the socialized school in a democratic society.

JOURNALISTIC ACTIVITIES

The benefits of journalistic activities in schools are manifold to the pupil. Here is his environment clarified and interpreted for him. While

FIG. 14-5. Sixth-grade pupils mimeograph their school newspaper, the *Oak Orchard Owl.* (*Courtesy of Oak Orchard School, Medina, N.Y.*)

he reads his school paper, he is informed of his world; guided personally, vocationally, and educationally; and influenced toward desired attitudes and habits—good taste, tolerance, sound thinking, citizenship, and school spirit.[8] These are the objectives toward which journalistic efforts are directed in elementary, secondary, and collegiate institutions. The major types of student publications are (1) newspapers, (2) annuals, (3) handbooks, and (4) magazines and other publications.

School Newspaper. The most common form of student publication is the newspaper. These papers may be daily, biweekly, weekly, bimonthly,

[8] Regis Louise Boyle, "Student Publications," *Bulletin of National Association of Secondary-school Principals,* February, 1952, p. 57.

or monthly. Many elementary-school papers are mimeographed, whereas in the larger high schools and colleges the papers are printed. Often in elementary and small secondary schools the pupils and teachers cooperate with the local newspaper in producing a school page.

At least half of the public high schools have some form of news organ. Paralleling the growth in scholastic journalism has been the increase in state, regional, and national press associations for schools, among these being the National and the Columbia Scholastic Press Associations. Annually the Educational Press Association publishes a helpful yearbook. The cumulative efforts of these associations, the courses in school journalism, and the enriched training of the sponsors of publications have all contributed to making the school newspaper today an important agent in the transmission of ideas and school spirit. Furthermore, through this medium many young people first learn the privileges and responsibilities involved in the freedom of the press in a democracy. Significantly, the principals of the schools usually ranked the newspaper as the most important extracurricular activity.

School Annual. The yearbook, which may be traced as far back as the collegiate booklet, "Profiles of Part of the Class Graduated at Yale College, September, 1806," is usually an expensive publication. In many quarters justification for its costly existence is seriously questioned. Numerous schools now print a less expensive brochure dedicated especially to the senior class; others have their annuals mimeographed or typewritten. Many benefits that might accrue to the students from creating an annual are sacrificed when the make-up of the book is planned solely by the sponsor and executed by paid commercial talent. The yearbook, once the only publication in most schools, is now being subordinated to the school newspaper, although its archival function will always give it a place in the program.

Handbook. A publication of growing popularity is the freshman or institutional handbook. This manual is a far more effective aid in freshman orientation than the old-fashioned hazing. Inexpensive handbooks packed with useful information and published in concise and attractive form are welcomed by newcomers to the complex life of the modern high school or college, whether they be new students, teachers, or board members. These small books also provide an inexpensive vehicle for interpreting the schools to the parents and general public.

Magazines and Other Publications. The current emphasis upon unleashing creative efforts and developing literary interests of pupils has focused attention upon school magazines and similar avenues for expression. The number of magazines submitted to the National Scholastic Press Association is steadily increasing. These periodicals, issued in duplicated or printed format, constitute outlets not only for literary creativeness and insight, but also for expression through drawings, cartoons, and photographs. A unique publication is a carefully designed and cleverly edited student-faculty magazine, which presents, chiefly through photographs, a story of the students and faculty members at home, at school, and in their cocurricular activities. Several schools and colleges issue alumni bulletins.

Many school organizations issue their own publications. For example, the Future Farmers of America may prepare its local program for the year in a printed form. The student council often publishes a bulletin in connection with its activities. School publications of all types and the numerous allied journalistic clubs, such as the Quill and Scroll, are vitalizing agencies in the education of the consumer and the producer—the reader and the writer.

MUSICAL ORGANIZATIONS AND ACTIVITIES

Many curricular and cocurricular activities center around music, which is classified here as (1) vocal and (2) instrumental. Singing is often com-

FIG. 14-6. One of the popular cocurricular activities is the high-school band. The curricular and extracurricular programs in music call for good building facilities, such as this acoustically treated band room with stationary risers. (*Courtesy of Public Schools, Grand Haven, Mich.*)

bined with acting, as in operettas, and with instrumental accompaniment, as in a cantata. The music groups are naturally interested in both performing and listening. A separate music appreciation club may be organized for nonperformers who are unable or unwilling to produce music but who as consumers are desirous of raising their level of music appreciation. "Music for everyone and everyone for music" is fast becoming a school realization.

Vocal Organizations and Activities. The chief vocal organizations, either curricular or cocurricular, are glee clubs—boys', girls', or mixed. Their chief objectives are recreation, entertainment, and appreciation. Their origin may be traced to the old "singing schools." Today a typical secondary school or college has several glee clubs, such as a first, second, and freshman group for either or both sexes. The *a cappella* choir is increasing in popularity. The operetta, allowing opportunity for solos, duets, quartets, and other combinations, is a pleasing musical entertainment, especially in the elementary and junior high schools.

Instrumental Organizations and Activities. The instrumental groups most frequently formed in secondary schools are bands and orchestras. Smaller groupings such as string ensembles present chamber music, whereas harmonica and other instrumental clubs meet the music hobby interests. The various musical organizations may contribute jointly to a public program or festival, the latter usually being given outdoors. In some cities skilled musicians from the various schools are selected for an all-city glee club, orchestra, or band. Many states stage an annual program of high-school talent.

SPEECH ACTIVITIES

The drama is one of the oldest mediums of organized human speech, extending from the Greek plays down through the French and Elizabethan plays to the present period of drama, which includes legitimate, motion-picture, and television acting. The greatest forensic activity in American life was during the revolutionary period when oratory flourished. Today the emphasis is upon informal techniques, such as panel discussions and forums.

Dramatic Activities. Generally school dramatics are handled either in regular classes or through cocurricular activities. The major productions or one-act plays may be promoted by a local drama club or a chapter of National Thespians, or by the junior or senior class. Usually the work is divided among various committees for costuming, lighting, scenery, and advertising. The drama coach may encourage the more backward students to self-expression through acting; he may even contribute to the legitimate stage through the development of latent histrionic talent in his pupils. Many by-products accrue from drama whether it be a farce, comedy, melodrama, tragedy, or socio-drama. Among these concomitants are the extensive reading of many plays and the acquiring of clear enunciation. In fine, the school drama helps students to see, to read, to hear, to act, to construct, and to write their own plays.

Forensic Activities. The chief forensic activities are declamations, orations, debates, poetry reading, extempore speaking, choral reading, tele-

Fig. 14-7. Students "concentrate" in dramatizations. (*Courtesy of New Trier Township High School, Winnetka, Ill.*)

casting, radio speaking, panel discussions, and forums. Several speech activities, for example, decision or nondecision debates, are conducted on an interschool basis. Original oratory appeals especially to students who possess creative literary talents and who hope thereby to inform, impress, or persuade the audience to thought or action. Debates constitute the chief activity in the field of public speaking and are the most criticized. If properly conducted, however, debates may help pupils to think logically, to organize materials carefully, to cultivate mental alertness, to analyze an argument critically, to promote reliance upon facts and research rather than prejudice, and to develop a lifelong interest in socioeconomic and governmental problems. Debate and discussion are the breath of democracy. Poetry reading, extempore speeches, choral reading, broadcasting, forums, junior town meetings, classrooms organized as national congresses, model United Nations assemblies, and panel discussions are among the popular forms of speech activities, all of which can contribute markedly to wholesome character development. A major objective in contests in speech and other competitions should be "not to win a decision or to secure a prize but to pace each other on the road to excellence."

School Clubs

Nearly all cocurricular activities may be classified as clubs. Nowhere in the school life is more freedom and variety displayed than in the names

Fig. 14-8. High-school students combine curricular and extracurricular activities. These students used the "flying classroom" in a flight to New York City for a sightseeing tour. The trip was part of the students' preflight aeronautics course. Each student earned his own fare by doing odd jobs here and there. (*Courtesy of Public Schools, Elkhart, Ind.*)

of the clubs. Their amazing variety testifies to the individualistic interests of youth as well as to its gregariousness. Because it is impossible to classify all clubs on a single basis, the National Survey of Secondary Education established the following seven categories on the basis of an analysis of their constitutions and programs: (1) student government, school service, and honorary; (2) social, moral, leadership, and guidance; (3) departmental; (4) publications and journalistic; (5) dramatic, literary, and forensic; (6) musical; and (7) special-interest clubs. To these should be added (8) the athletic clubs, which are a part of the sports activities considered later.

Louis Adamic has said, "People without a firm sense of 'belonging' cannot properly develop, cannot play their full parts in the American scene." Through a wide variety of organizations, the school seeks to interest each student in at least one meaningful cocurricular activity in which the desideratum is not mere membership but active and voluntary participation on the part of the boy or girl. Unless there is some surveillance the clubs are likely to grow up like mushrooms and then die; hence all charters should be granted by the student council or a similar organization and adequate sponsorship provided. Any club that fails to function or to live up to the tradition of the school should be warned and then disbanded if no improvement results. Emerson once said, "We send our children to the master but the boys educate them." School clubs, an outlet for the urge to gregariousness, should have definite educational and recreational values.

ATHLETIC ACTIVITIES

Often the extracurricular activities of schools and colleges that receive the major share of financial support and the largest amount of publicity are of an athletic nature. A well-balanced physical education program in secondary schools and colleges includes athletics, in addition to the regular programs for guidance and instruction in health and physical activities. Athletics include two major phases: (1) intramural sports and (2) interscholastic. These are not disparate elements but parts of a larger whole.

Intramural Sports. The term "intramural," derived from the Latin words meaning "within the walls," refers to the activities conducted within the walls of a particular school. The intramural sports program may also include several schools within a city.

Intramurals, as distinguished from interscholastic sports, encourage participation by local boys and girls with a minimum of the competitive spirit. Based upon the theory of athletics for all, the intramural program seeks to maintain many sports for the sake of all students rather than for the sake of a few athletic teams. It is directed toward developing lasting recreational interests and sport skills in people who must live in a highly industralized civilization.

Many intramural sports have been transferred from the open lot or street to the school grounds; many of them carry over during the vacation

FIG. 14-9. Youth of all ages enjoy physical activity. Upper view—two kindergarten boys in the foreground are ready to toss the small ball during play period (Zeeland, Michigan). Center view—high-school boys toss the 6-foot ball in the air during intramural competition (Erie, Pennsylvania). Lower view—De Paul plays the University of Illinois in intercollegiate basketball competition (Champaign-Urbana, Illinois).

periods. Initiative is maintained through a system of student managers. Units of competition vary: in one school it may be by classes and in another on the basis of physical aptitude tests. In addition to the activities listed later under interscholastic athletics, the following are among the favorite intramural sports: swimming, hockey, touch and flag football, softball, badminton, ping-pong, volleyball, shuffleboard, horse shoes, archery, hiking, camping, and various winter sports. In recent years intramural programs, sports days, and physical activity clubs have enlisted many students under the direction of well-trained instructors and coaches.

Interscholastic Athletics. This is the most maligned part of the entire cocurricular program in schools and colleges, particularly the latter. The Educational Policies Commission commences its publication *School Athletics* with several positive affirmations, including these:

> We believe in athletics as an important part of the school physical education program. We believe that the experience of playing athletic games should be a part of the education of all children and youth who attend schools in the United States.
>
> Participation in sound athletic programs, we believe, contributes to health and happiness, physical skill and emotional maturity, social competence and moral values.
>
> We believe that cooperation and competition are both important components of American life. Athletic participation can help teach the values of cooperation as well as the spirit of competition. Playing hard and playing to win can help build character.[9]

Critics find fault with huge football stadiums, large gate receipts, larger expenditures, postseason games, salaried athletes, athletic scholarships, lax scholastic requirements for athletes, long practice sessions, game schedules that take athletes away from their studies, and high-salaried and overzealous coaches whose tenure depends upon the production of winning teams. Despite these accusations, interscholastic athletics continue to grow. Conscientious efforts are being made to elminate or reduce the evils in the system, including "athlete's head." [10]

Most schools have developed a system of major and minor sports. The former usually include football, basketball, track, and baseball; the latter embrace tennis, swimming, wrestling, golf, fencing, and boxing.

Many changes occur in athletic competition through progressive modifications of the rules. For example, several innovations have been made in football since it first started, as witnessed by a bronze tablet on the wall surrounding the football field at Rugby school in England:

---

[9] Educational Policies Commission, *School Athletics,* p. 3, National Education Association, 1954.

[10] Interscholastic athletics are discussed further in Unit XVII.

> This stone commemorates the exploit of William Webb Ellis, who with a fine disregard for the rules of football as played in his time first took the ball in his arms and ran with it, thus originating the distinctive feature of the Rugby game. —A.D. 1823

This "shocking" change was followed years later by the introduction of the forward pass. Many small high schools have turned to six-man football teams. Modifications like these are constantly being made for the benefit of either the players or the spectators or both groups.

AUXILIARY ORGANIZATIONS AND ACTIVITIES

Ancillary to the curricular or extracurricular programs are the following: (1) assemblies and programs, (2) commencements, (3) parliamentary procedures, (4) social, and (5) miscellaneous activities.

Assemblies and Programs. In the early days the assembly was a period of devotional exercises, perhaps an outgrowth of the college chapel. These "morning exercises" are found even in the small rural school where a few minutes each day are devoted to announcements and other activities.

The purposes of the assembly, which Fretwell calls "the town meeting of the school," are numerous, but conspicuous among its modern uses are the following: orientation into school life, cultivation of school spirit, unification of the entire school, dissemination of general information, inspirational help, spiritual aid, opportunity for pupils and faculty to appear before an audience, all-school special convocations, installation of student council, and cultivation of effective listening and courteous audience habits.

The programs are planned by an assembly committee and usually given once a week. Something is lost in the school or college where assemblies or convocations are held only once or twice a year. The growing practice of increased student and audience participation in assemblies is a wholesome trend. These convocations may be held outdoors.

Many programs are presented by students and faculty sponsors for community organizations like the parent-teacher association, noonday luncheon clubs, and women's clubs. These performances help to interpret the school to the community; therefore the participants and the type of program should be carefully chosen. Usually a large number of pupil performers increases not only the benefits to the participants but also the number of interested spectators.

Commencement. The old-style graduation program has been replaced by the modern vitalized commencement, often held outdoors. Even the old-fashioned mottoes, banners, and streamers have given way to a simpler and more effective decoration. The present commencement means more than the mere handing out of diplomas to graduates after they have listened to a long-winded orator. It means a pupil-planned program in which the activities are a culmination of the year's work. Elaborate graduation exercises for eighth graders have been superseded by promotion exercises designed to shift the emphasis from graduation to continuation. Such a program centers attention on the students and helps

FIG. 14-10. Bicentennial commencement exercises held at Columbia University. Only a fraction of the spectators are shown. Many high schools and colleges use an outdoor setting for such events. (*Courtesy of Columbia University, New York City.*)

to enlist community interest in the school and the results of its work. The important parts of the older graduation programs, as class history, will, poem, and prophecy, are scheduled on class night during commencement week. The senior vesper service in the high schools and the baccalaureate service in the colleges and universities sound a spiritual note in the commencement week activities. Each year the National Education Association publishes a very useful *Commencement Manual*, which contains numerous suggestions for improving commencement programs.

Parliamentary Procedures. Nearly all cocurricular organizations employ parliamentary procedures in the conduct of their meetings. As the name indicates, parliamentary law and practice have been derived from the traditions and rules for transacting business in the British Parliament. Later the terminology was applied to the routine usages of any deliberative assemblage. In America, which as a young nation has not had the time or inclination to develop respect for moldy traditions, a unique system of written and unwritten laws has evolved for the conduct of legislative assemblies and organized bodies. The person responsible for the plan most widely used in the United States is General Henry M. Roberts of the United States Army. His *Rules of Order* is usually the

Fig. 14-11. Elementary-school pupils participate in the maypole dance on "Friendship Day." (*Courtesy of Public Schools, Highland Park, Ill.*)

final dictum regarding actions taken or to be taken by deliberate bodies. Some organizations select a member as parliamentarian whose chief function is to rule on questions relating to the proper conduct of meetings.

A functioning knowledge of these procedures gives grace, poise, and dignity to the presiding officer and helps to ensure the rights of the members. In a democracy these rules for the conduct of meetings protect the rights of the minority and restrain the majority from undue privileges. Naturally parliamentary law is designed as a facilitating tool and should not be used as an end in itself so that it obstructs rather than abets efficiency.

Social Activities. An individual must learn to live not only with himself but also with others. Nearly all cocurricular activities encourage companionship between the individual and his associates and provide social functions that "rub down the rough spots." These may be parties, teas, banquets, homecoming celebrations, or dances. Participation in these festivities, particularly in the preadolescent and adolescent ages, helps a student to feel at home in a social environment and gives him a lifelong appreciation for the little niceties, the social techniques, and pleasurable amenities so necessary in a human world. School parties, properly supervised, promote simple pleasures and platonic relationships between boys and girls, and counteract in a measure the present undue emphasis upon commercialized amusements.

Unfortunately, for some students the socializing process is carried to excess through too many social affairs. Furthermore, the school environment alone does not ensure fraternizing on the part of the participants. Overstreet, in his *Guide to Civilized Loafing*, caustically pictures the couples who attend a dance in perfect isolation from every other couple. A modern social dance is often a most unsocial phenomenon. Under reasonable guidance, periodic school-sponsored social affairs can be associational activities for social therapy and character development.

School Lunch Program. Most schools today have a lunch program. At its best the lunch period involves not only the serving of food, but also definite physical, social, emotional, and educational values. It becomes a broad curricular and cocurricular activity.

The financial support of school lunch programs has traveled the long road from the national emergency aid of the 1930's, through the federal surplus program of the 1940's, to the local, state, and federal-subsidized aid of the 1950's.

Camping and Outdoor Education. Ranking high in character-building potentialities are camping and other forms of outdoor learning, teaching, and living. Historically it was only yesterday that most of the education for the original Americans—the Indians—took place in the freedom and reality of God's great out-of-doors. Today, too much education is limited to windowed walls, firm floors, and ceilinged classrooms.

Various educational organizations have long recognized the value of outdoor education, especially camping. Charitable associations sponsor camps for the underprivileged and private ones often cater to the well-to-do, but millions of youth do not enjoy continuous out-of-door living. Hence many school systems seek to provide outdoor education and camping as curricular and cocurricular activities. Of increasing popularity are the various types of outdoor camps—the permanent, the summer, the week-end, the overnight, and the travel camp or youth hostel. The camp is becoming one of the school's best laboratories.

Miscellaneous Activities. Many auxiliary organizations are found in schools and colleges. Of a military nature are military training camps, schools, and special units, as the Reserve Officers' Training Corps (ROTC). Among the organizations meeting the religious needs of students are the Young Men's Christian Association, which was formed in 1844, the Young Women's Christian Association, the Hi-Y, and the Girl

Reserves. Secret societies, as a rule, are not permitted in public elementary and high schools, though numerous in most colleges and universities.

Growing in favor are the school-sponsored educational trips. These afford students the opportunity to visit local, county, state, and national sites. A favorite destination for senior classes is Washington, D.C. The National Capital School Visitors Council, a daughter organization of the Bureau of University Travel, has been organized to assist groups visiting the nation's capital.

Among the hundreds of other cocurricular activities found in American public educational institutions are alumni organizations, student speakers' service bureau, correspondence and personnel exchange with students in foreign countries, visitation of other schools by students, and social service work, particularly at Thanksgiving and Christmas. The organization and administration of these activities constitute a major task in American education.

ORGANIZATION AND ADMINISTRATION OF COCURRICULAR PROGRAMS

The remaining phases of cocurricular activities to be considered here are (1) development of the local program, (2) sponsorship, (3) participation, (4) financing, and (5) cooperation with state and national organizations.

DEVELOPMENT OF THE LOCAL PROGRAM

Many teachers and administrators who formerly tolerated extracurricular activities as necessary evils are now aggressively promoting the program that pays increasing dividends on society's investment.

Initiating the Activities. Most cocurricular programs have their genesis in the home rooms and in class organizations from which come the student council representatives. All proposed organizations should be evaluated carefully before they are started. Furthermore, they should be begun on a modest scale. For example, if a school does not have home rooms, such a system is best introduced gradually, preferably after a close study and visitation of other schools by both teachers and pupils. The plan can then be presented by student leaders. Unless there is a demand for it, an organization should not be launched. The formulation of objectives for the entire cocurricular program may well constitute an important element in its organization and administration. Furthermore, the program must be consonant with the peculiar needs of the community.

Administering the Program. Since the principal of the school is responsible to the board of education, he should have the right of veto power over any and all actions of extracurricular groups. Of course, he will seldom exercise this direct control, and then with discretion. Greater diplomacy on the part of principals, superintendents, teachers, and boards of education will prevent many a "school strike."

Scheduling the Activities. School organization for extraclass activities generally follows one of these three patterns:

1. The *activity period,* which is intended to provide for most extraclass activities *within* the daily time schedule,
2. The *core program,* which consolidates much of the extraclass activities with the class activities,
3. The *before-school and after-school activities program,* which provides for most of the extraclass activities *outside* the regular school session.[11]

A growing practice is to schedule the cocurricular activities in the daily program. This increases the participation of pupils, especially of those who, because of bus transportation or early home-going, cannot remain after school. A special portion of the day is allotted in the regular schedule, usually a set time, as the first or last hour in the morning, or a floating period. If there have been seven regular periods, an eighth period is added during which all organizations meet. Such arrangements reduce the sponsor's afterschool work and obviate parental criticism that pupils spend most of their afterschool hours at school.

The scheduling of the activities as a whole is not sufficient; the programs for each organization must also be carefully planned. A complicated problem is that of avoiding conflicts between groups, particularly in a high school where the gymnasium and auditorium are combined. Wherever possible, it is very desirable to make school activities a part of a community calendar.

Evaluating the Activities. The activities must constantly be evaluated. Ofttimes a club starts with much gusto and then disintegrates. An annual report, plus periodic checkups by a student-faculty committee, will aid in determining whether the charter should be regranted the next year. If a group is guilty of misconduct of a serious nature, a warning may be issued and the charter revoked if the abuse continues. Every organization should seek a worth-while project for its year's work. A stepping-up program, like that of the Scouts with their tenderfoot, second-class, and first-class stages, aids in evaluating individual and group progress. It has been found in field work that those institutions with strong, balanced, graduated extracurricular programs make outstanding contributions in promoting an active, intelligent loyalty to democratic ideals.

SPONSORSHIP OF COCURRICULAR ACTIVITIES

Qualifications of Advisers. The success of many an extraclass organization may be traced to the sponsor. Although the latter does not assume

[11] Ellsworth Tompkins, "The Relation of Activities to the Curriculum," *Bulletin of the National Association of Secondary-school Principals,* February, 1952, p. 15.

the dominant role that she does in the classroom as a teacher, nevertheless she can exert a real influence. Some general qualifications for sponsors are sympathy with boys and girls, their temptations, and problems; ability to win the confidence of both youth and parents; capacity to lead and to follow; willingness to be identified wholeheartedly with the organization and to put in extra hours of work in its interest; high standards of personal conduct and morals; sense of humor; alertness to what is going on outside as well as inside school; and good sense of values in the expenditure of time, money, and talents. Besides these general requirements, the directors of certain groups need specialized training, for example, the sponsors of journalistic, athletic, and music events. There is no set pattern for sponsors. On the whole they must possess the quality of "teaching as though they taught not," while bearing constantly in mind the purposes for which the activity is designed.

Selection of Advisers. How shall the sponsors be chosen? Usually the procedure involves selection by the principal, election by the pupils, or a combination or compromise. For example, pupils may choose a sponsor from a recommended list. Often the advisers for activities that call for technical training are appointed to that task when employed by the board of education and superintendent of schools. Both sponsors and pupils should be happy and congenial in their cocurricular relations.

Training of Advisers. The typical secondary-school teacher is called upon to supervise at least one extraclass activity. A good preparation for this assignment or choice is to have participated in this activity in high school and college and to have taken a course in extrainstructional duties, such as offered in many colleges and universities. These courses are designed to give prospective or experienced teachers a knowledge of the entire cocurricular program and an opportunity to assist in sponsoring a specific group. Furthermore, many books and periodicals aid the sponsors of school activities. A popular periodical is *School Activities.* A magazine helpful to both students and sponsors of student councils and chapters of the National Honor Society is *Student Life,* issued under the aegis of the National Association of Secondary-school Principals. Many secondary and college teachers secure positions because of special qualifications for sponsorships of extracurricular activities.

Coordination of Efforts. In recent years, particularly in large schools, concentrated efforts have been made to coordinate the entire extracurricular program. To this end a director supervises all the activities or a committee of sponsors may meet periodically to plan the coordination of efforts. An example of the recognition given to extraclass life in general education is the extracurriculum division at Stephens College, Columbia, Missouri, one of the coordinate educational divisions of the college. It is administered by a director, who, with the aid of teachers, advisers, and residence-hall counselors, encourages students to utilize out-of-class life as a means of attaining individual objectives.

Participation in Activities

Stimulation of Participation. A goal in extraclass work is that of universality—all pupils in the school participating in at least one cocurricular activity. This necessitates promotion and stimulation, preferably by the student body. Many schools and colleges now require a certain number of extracurricular units toward graduation. Most activities, except those overemphasizing interscholastic competition, are based upon the slogan, "The more the merrier."

Restriction of Participation. A corollary is the principle that participation must be restricted. These are two parts of the same basic idea that cocurricular activites must be regulated in order to avert the danger that the pendulum for some pupils will swing to the extreme of nonparticipation and for others to that of overparticipation. In the latter case the cocurricular becomes anticurricular. Two methods of curtailing the ambitions of the overzealous or talented individual are a point system and a program of majors and minors. The former assigns to each activity a specified number of points and stipulates the maximum permitted each student. The latter divides activities or offices into majors and minors, each student being restricted to a specified number. Sometimes an effective control is a sliding scale whereby the aggregate number of points or majors that a student may carry is determined by his scholastic and health records and his years in school. A system of checks and balances tends to distribute more evenly the opportunities for both participation and leadership. Any method of encouraging, limiting, or redirecting participation necessitates an accurate record of the membership and officers of the various organizations.

Participation in Contests. Many school people are contest minded—they accept numerous invitations to compete for prizes and honors. Several boards of education have been forced to pass rulings against the abuse of contests; many state educational organizations are aligned against competition. Some state-wide high-school activities associations decide which contests shall be held. The Contest Committee of the National Association of Secondary-school Principals periodically issues lists of approved national school contests in which the educational values outweigh the direct or implied commercial or propaganda aspects. The tendency is to replace highly competitive events by festivals, play days, nondecision debates, and other forms of talent matching which are not dominated by the slogan "anything to win."

Financing the Activities

Budgeting. Too often, extracurricular organizations "go into the red" because of poor initial planning of finances. Each group ought to prepare a budget consisting of its proposed program of activities, estimated expenditures, and proposed receipts. Furthermore, a central committee should draw up one consolidated budget for all the school activities. Aside from its function as a control, the budget has a definite educational value if the students participate in planning and executing it.

Sources of Receipts. Among the usual sources of revenue for the cocurricular program are the following: student fees, funds from the board of education, sales, donations, and gate receipts. A common procedure is an activity fee whereby each student pays a fixed amount that covers all activities. An allotment board composed of students and teachers allocates the funds to specific organizations and activities.

Expenditures. All expenditures for extracurricular activities must be carefully accounted for. Usually both receipts and expenditures are administered through a central treasurer who may be a clerk in the principal's office or an instructor in the commerce department. He is usually assisted by student treasurers who work under his immediate surveillance.

Auditing and Protection. All extracurricular accounts should be carefully checked. This includes the preaudit of bills before they are paid, the monthly audit, and the annual audit. The audits should be of two types: the administrative check usually made by students, faculty, or a fiscal officer within the employ of the school; and the independent examination of accounts conducted by a person not connected with the school system. Some states require that all extracurricular school funds be audited by a bonded person employed by the school district. Everything should be done to ensure protection of both money and persons who handle it, particularly since many schools use public funds to finance part of the cocurricular activities.

Cooperation with State and National Organizations

State Organizations. Many local cocurricular groups are chapters of state organizations or are banded informally in state groupings. Interscholastic high-school athletic groups are often affiliated in a state high-school athletic association, which divides the state into districts. Some states have a high-school activities association that encompasses a large number of varied cocurricular undertakings. The principals, sponsors, and students meet in conferences and conventions. A noticeable trend is the development of a formal state-wide organization with a competent executive staff to direct and coordinate all interscholastic activities.

National and International Organizations. Some local and state associations are affiliated with national and international organizations.

Fig. 14-12. Five Washington-area girl scouts show Mrs. Dwight D. Eisenhower at the White House some of the "kits for Korea," consisting of drawstring bags filled with necessities for Korean children. (*Courtesy of United Press.*)

Among the projects of the American Youth Commission of the American Council on Education was that of gathering information about national agencies that serve youth. Many are primarily membership organizations. Several groups listed here in tabular form have local and state chapters

Girls	*Boys*	*Mixed Groups*
Camp Fire Girls	Boys' Clubs	Allied Youth
Future Homemakers	Boy Scouts	Catholic Youth
Girl Reserves	Fraternities	4-H
Girl Scouts	Future Farmers	Future Teachers of America
Thespian Society	Hi-Y	Quill and Scroll
New Homemakers	New Farmers	Junior Red Cross
Sororities	ROTC	National Forensic League
Y.W.C.A.	Y.M.C.A.	National Honor Society
		Protestant Youth
		Student Councils
		Student Editors

in schools and elsewhere. Among the many national organizations in which secondary-school youth hold memberships are those shown in the accompanying table. Then, too, many national meetings are held for students, as for example the National Conference on Student Participation in School Administration. America does not have "a" youth movement—it has many movements, since its youth belongs to many organizations and has many allegiances. A well-balanced program of cocurricular activities includes not only independent organizations developed locally but also chapters of such state, national, and international organizations as are demanded and approved.

SUGGESTED ACTIVITIES

1. Develop principles that you think should govern cocurricular activities.
2. Define the qualities required of student leaders.
3. Investigate why many class and home-room organizations are ineffective.
4. List the main criticisms against student councils. Enumerate some of their accomplishments.
5. Collect samples of school publications and evaluate them.
6. List the musical organizations in the elementary or high school in your home town.
7. Tell in what typical speech activities students engage outside of classwork.
8. Enumerate all the clubs found in your high school or college. Evaluate their programs.
9. Describe a good intramural physical-education program in a high school.
10. List in two parallel columns the advantages and disadvantages of interscholastic competition in high-school athletics.
11. Attend a meeting of an elementary- or secondary-school club.
12. Outline an assembly program for some high-school club.
13. Describe a "new-type" vitalized high-school commencement.
14. Evaluate one or more social affairs held in high schools and colleges.
15. Describe a military organization found in high schools or colleges.
16. Diagram a plan for coordinating the extracurricular activities of a school.
17. List the desirable qualities of a sponsor for a specific extracurricular activity.
18. Indicate how an activity program is financed in a high school.
19. List some national organizations that have chapters in secondary schools. Describe one in detail.

DESCRIPTIVE BIBLIOGRAPHY AND AIDS

BOOKS

BENNETT, M. E.: *College and Life,* 4th ed., Chap. V, McGraw-Hill, 1952.
    Values in college campus activities.
CHISHOLM, LESLIE L.: *The Work of the Modern High School,* Chap. XV, Macmillan, 1953.
    Extracurricular activities in the high school.
EDUCATIONAL POLICIES COMMISSION: *School Athletics,* Chap. XI, National Education Association, 1954.
    Summary of recommendations regarding athletics.

FALVEY, FRANCES E.: *Student Participation in College Administration,* Chap. XII, Teachers College, 1952.

Current trends in student participation in the college community government.

GRUBER, FREDERICK C., and T. BAYARD BEATTY: *The Activities Program in the Secondary School,* Chap. IX, McGraw-Hill, 1954.

Club programs in high schools.

GRUHN, WILLIAM T.:*Student Teaching in the Secondary School,* Part III, Ronald, 1954.

At work with guidance and extraclass activities.

KIRKENDALL, LESLIE A., and FRANKLIN R. ZERAN: *Student Councils in Action,* Chap. X, Chartwell House, 1953.

Duties of the faculty sponsor.

LAI, WILLIAM T.: *Championship Baseball,* Chap. I, Prentice-Hall, 1954.

How to make a big leaguer, as presented by Buck Lai, scout and instructor for the Dodgers.

LITTLE, WILSON, and A. L. CHAPMAN: *Developmental Guidance in Secondary Schools,* Chap. IX, McGraw-Hill, 1953.

The home room and its possibilities.

SHEPARD, GEORGE E., and RICHARD E. JAMERSON: *Interscholastic Athletics,* Chap. XII, McGraw-Hill, 1953.

Intramural sports in the athletic program.

SMITH, JOE: *Student Councils for Our Times,* Chap. III, Teachers College, 1951.

Foundation principles for effective student councils.

THOMPSON, NELLIE ZELTA: *Vitalized Assemblies,* Chap. II, Dutton, 1952.

Planning the year's program.

WELLS, HARRY L.: *Higher Education Is Serious Business,* Chap. IX, Harper, 1953.

Higher education and its light treatment of extracurricular activities.

WEYAND, ALEXANDER M.: *The Olympic Pageant,* Chap. II, Macmillan, 1952.

The first revival of the Olympic games in Athens, Greece.

CURRENT PERTINENT PERIODICALS AND PUBLICATIONS

Allied Youth
American Farm Youth
American Junior Red Cross Journal
Boys' Club Bulletin
Bulletin of National Association of
  Secondary-school Principals
Camping Magazine
Children's Activities
Club publications:
  The Rostrum
Commencement Manual
Extending Education
Girl Scout Leader
Handbooks:
  AYH Handbook and Hostelers Manual

Hobbies
National Sports Weekly
Plays
Recreation
School Activities
School Press Review
Scouting
Seventeen
State publications:
  Illinois Interscholastic
  Minnesota Youth
Student Life
Yearbooks of educational organizations
Youth Leaders' Digest

AUDIO-VISUAL AIDS

FACILITIES FOR LEISURE   Radio transcription, 15 min

Radio script written by W. K. Streit, a leader in health and physical education. Available from the National Education Association, Washington, D.C.

FILMSTRIPS IN SPORTS   Seven sets, color

A series of seven filmstrips on baseball, tennis, golf, bowling, archery, tumbling, and badminton. Accents fundamental skills. Available from Society for Visual Education, 1345 W. Diversey Parkway, Chicago 14.

FIRE IN THEIR LEARNING   19 min., sound, color

Shows ways of teaching and learning fire safety as part of the ongoing program of a fourth-grade teacher and her pupils. Available from the Safety Commission, National Education Association, Washington, D.C.

HOW TO MAKE A PUPPET   12 min., sound, b&w or color

Details all the steps in the making of the hand puppets so popular in art, drama, and handicraft classes. Available from Bailey Films, 6509 De Longpre Avenue, Hollywood 28, Calif.

ON THE ROAD TO TOMORROW   10 min., sound

Portrays the 4-H clubs and the significance of their work. Available from Castle Films, New York.

SILVER ANNIVERSARY OF FFA   35 min., sound, color

The story of a Future Farmer of America attending the twenty-fifth anniversary convention of this national organization. Available from the U.S. Office of Education.

STUDENT GOVERNMENT AT WORK   10 min., sound, b&w or color

Demonstrates the actual work of a student council on particular problems. Available from Coronet Films, Chicago.

YOUR CHILDREN'S PLAY   20 min., sound

Shows children of various ages enjoying themselves in their own games in their own way, and parental reaction. Available from British Information Service, 30 Rockefeller Plaza, New York 20.

EDUCATIONAL SUPPLIES, EQUIPMENT, AND BUILDINGS

In the learning-teaching process, pupils and teachers need educational tools and a place in which to work. These constitute the educational environment that stimulates learning.

Books are the tools most frequently used. Extensive reading requires many books. In their selection the educational interests of the pupil should be the basic criterion. The library is the heart of the school, with arteries running into each room.

Other instructional supplies and equipment include ancillary reference material such as the dictionary, and audio-visual aids such as the sound film. All these materials ought to be selected in terms of the educational purposes and program of the school.

The supplies and equipment are housed in school buildings located on suitable sites. The school site conditions the development of an adequate building program. The building should be a functional creation so artistically designed and equipped that its beauty charms the student. The school of tomorrow will be a community workshop designed to meet the daily needs of all learners in the community. The ideal expressed in "we, the people," should permeate the planning of school buildings in community, state, and nation.

OUTLINE OF CONTENTS

Introduction
    Role of materials in education
    Supplies and equipment defined
Schoolbooks
    Historical development of textbooks
    Selection, adoption, and purchase of schoolbooks
    School libraries
Other Instructional Supplies and Equipment
    Ancillary reading materials
    Multisensory aids in learning
    Miscellaneous supplies and equipment
    Selection, purchase, and use of materials
School Sites, Buildings, and Equipment
    Building programs
    School sites
    Educational buildings
    Equipment for buildings and sites
    Community schools

EDUCATIONAL SUPPLIES, EQUIPMENT, AND BUILDINGS

"What is the greatest invention in human history?" To this question there are many answers but for education there is only one: "The greatest invention is printing." The first press in the territory now included in the United States was set up at Harvard College, Cambridge, Massachusetts, by Stephen Daye in 1639. In the three hundred and more years that have elapsed since that time the relationship between the printing press and institutions of learning has been vital. The publishing of educational books today constitutes a big business. Linked with printed publications is the manufacture of educational supplies and equipment.

FIG. 15-1. Thirteen-month-old Judy looks puzzled by these stacks of books—enough to fill an 18-foot shelf—she will have to read from first grade through high school. Many books, school-lighting engineers have found, have excessively low visibility characteristics. (*Courtesy of General Electric, Cleveland, Ohio.*)

Role of Materials in Education.[1] No farmer would send his hired help to work in the fields without providing suitable supplies, tools, and equipment. Many school board members, however, ask their teachers "to make bricks without straw"—to teach without the necessary learning materials. Paradoxically, in America, which leads the world in the publication and manufacture of school supplies, thousands of school pupils are empty-handed or poorly supplied with educational materials.

The American Association of School Administrators in *American School Curriculum* suggests certain general criteria which instructional materials should meet. They should be:

1. In harmony with a stated philosophy of education as developed by educators, laymen, and students.
2. In keeping with the specific, desired learnings.
3. In accord with the latest research on efficient methods of learning and the ways in which human beings grow and develop.
4. Accurate in factual content.[2]

Many materials in machine-making America fail to meet these criteria.

Much school equipment is archaic. Although many teachers drive to school in this year's model of automobile, they use constantly in the classroom much equipment and many supplies of Model T vintage. The quality of school supplies is as important as the quantity. For example, an inferior grade of penmanship paper may be a decided handicap to neatness in handwriting. Restricted budgets and the apathy of the general public account in part for the failure to provide the best. Then, too, many classroom and laboratory teachers are unfamiliar with the wide variety and quality of modern educational materials. Even after being supplied with the latest tools of learning, teachers and pupils often do not use them effectively. For a proper learning-teaching environment, supplies and tools are essential; they are, however, merely physical means for facilitating the educational process. All aids to teaching may prove sterile unless they are applied intelligently.

Supplies and Equipment Defined. A supply item is usually distinguished from a piece of equipment in that the former has a shorter service life than the latter. An illustration of the first is school chalk, which is used up in a short period of time; an example of equipment is a school desk, which may last for several years. Textbooks are technically considered as equipment, whereas workbooks may be either equipment or supply items. Supplies and equipment may also be classified on the basis of whether

[1] Association for Supervision and Curriculum Development, *Creating a Good Environment for Learning,* Chap. VIII, "Physical Resources Are Important," National Education Association, 1954.

[2] American Association of School Administrators, *American School Curriculum,* p. 191, National Education Association, 1953.

they are primarily instructional or building items. Instructional supplies and equipment are exemplified respectively by chalk and books, whereas two building items are illustrated by sweeping compound and drinking fountains. Building supplies and equipment are given special emphasis in the last part of this unit. Here the educational supplies and equipment are grouped as (1) schoolbooks, and (2) other instructional supplies and equipment.

SCHOOLBOOKS

HISTORICAL DEVELOPMENT OF TEXTBOOKS

Early American Textbooks. The change in schoolbooks forms a fascinating chapter in the history of American education. The hornbook, a paddle-shaped contrivance which hung from the pupil's neck, usually contained the Lord's Prayer and the alphabet. *The New England Primer,* an example of the small morally.compact textbook used in the colonial days, is said to have taught millions to read and not one to sin. *McGuffey's Readers* emphasized the Bible and morals by means of interesting stories. America's textbook best seller—over 100,000,000 copies—was the *Elementary Spelling Book,* the "blue-back" speller of Noah Webster, about which it has been written: "No other secular book has reached so many minds in America as Webster's Spelling Book, and none has played so shaping a part in our destiny." [3] In this speller one finds a list such as the following "words of seven syllables having the accent on the fifth":

im ma te ri al' i ty	im pen e tra bil' i ty
in com pat i bil' i ty	per pen dic u lar' i ty
im per cep ti bil' i ty	in de fen si bil' i ty
ir re sist i bil' i ty	val e tu di na' ri an
in com bus ti bil' i ty	an ti trin i ta' ri an

Another speller bore the ambitious title, *New England's Perfect Schoolmaster.* The titles of books reveal marked changes between yesteryear and now.

In early American education, memory was a cardinal virtue. For the schoolmaster there was a book entitled *Mnemonics Applied to the Acquisition of Knowledge,* whose authors, Pike and Pike, challenged any six men to learn as much as the Messrs. Pike could in any given length of time. For pupils there was Grimshaw's huge volume devoted to "tables and explanation necessary to be learned by heart by every pupil studying arithmetic." Often the textbooks, which contained valuable materials in small-type footnotes, failed to challenge the interest of the reader.

In the development of modern schoolbooks the four main influences were: child psychology, textbook publication as a specialized industry,

[3] Harry R. Warfel, *Noah Webster: School Master to America,* p. 53, Macmillan, 1936.

the improvement in printing and binding, and research by authors and publishers.

The Textbook in Modern Education. Over a century ago Emerson, in his memorable address, "The American Scholar," distinguished clearly between the use and the abuse of books. Although books contain the inheritance of past thinking and as such are invaluable to the scholar, they should not be a substitute for his own thinking. On the other hand, some things can be learned better and more economically from books than from other sources.

Selection, Adoption, and Purchase of Schoolbooks

Procedures in Selecting Textbooks. In contrast to the old practice, whereby one person, usually the administrator, selected the textbooks used by the teachers and pupils, is the more democratic procedure by which an appointed or elected committee of teachers recommends the texts. In this way teacher and pupil interests, needs, and likes are known and given consideration. Obviously the educational interests and needs of pupils must have priority in the writing, publishing, and selecting of textbooks.

The two general techniques in evaluating textbooks prior to their adoption are subjective judgment and objective appraisal. Usually both are employed. The one is a casual examination of the book or books, often preceded by a sales talk by a representative of a book company or the receipt of a letter or descriptive folder. The other technique is a painstaking scrutiny by means of a check list, score card, or guide for textbook analysis. Some of these are intended for all books in general, whereas others are for a specific field or an area, as first-grade reading. Guides for textbook analysis usually contain the following major items: authorship, date of publication, suitability of content, organization, vocabulary burden, readability, methods of teaching and learning, teaching aids, pupil helps, mechanical make-up or format, and miscellaneous details, such as illustrations and physical attractiveness. Content, format, and suitability are the "big three."

The content of American textbooks has been criticized as being too radical or too conservative.[4] Certain groups have launched periodic attacks on textbooks, especially those in social science. They claim that, although few can be classified as subversive, many of the books tend to instill in the reader's mind a discontent with American democracy and the workings of private enterprise. Certain members of the Congress of the United States have questioned the content of textbooks as "un-American." In answer to the question, "In your opinion, how satisfactorily do school textbooks help pupils to attain the American ideal of 'equal op-

---

[4] This issue is further discussed in Unit XVII.

portunity for all'?" a professor in the teaching of social studies expressed the following opinion: "No book that attempts to deal with any vital issue or problem in a vital way can be published at the present time without balanced sentences in which one pressure group is played off against another, or without the usual dodges of a so-called judicious character." Several book surveys stress the need for using objectivity and coming to grips with basic issues. As Howard E. Wilson has pointed out, the fault lies often in the courses of study for which the textbooks are prepared. Discretion must of course be used in selection of materials for schoolbooks, but there is too much timidity in the writing and publishing of materials not only on American democracy but on many controversial issues. Some textbooks in American history are published in two editions, one to be used north of Mason and Dixon's line and the other south of it. Frequently books have to be written for particular states because of legislation that prohibits the inclusion of certain materials. Schools should furnish enough books on a particular subject to present different points of view, particularly for older pupils. The texts should be chosen not only for content but also for eye appeal.

The format or mechanical construction of the book is a very important factor. The physical appearance is affected by size of page and book, binding, cover, paper, illustrations, type, spacing, and margins. Many schoolbooks have been too "textbooky." Today better paper, types, colored illustrations, and binding materials, plus stronger binding processes, make textbooks attractive, appealing, and durable. The modern textbook is an invitation to learning, silently saying, "Look, and read me." Most of the changes in format that have been effected through the joint efforts of teachers, administrators, librarians, authors, and publishers are improvements. A few of the modern tendencies, such as freakish page make-up that presents broken lines of varying lengths and placements, present difficulties, especially to young readers. The American Institute of Graphic Arts, through leading book designers and printers, has launched a nation-wide campaign for better looking books—books that please the eye as well as the mind. Several awards are issued annually, including the Newberry medal to the author of the outstanding book for children, and the Caldecott award to the illustrator of the most distinguished picture book for children.

Adoption of Textbooks. Textbooks, supplementary readers, and workbooks usually are adopted by (1) local authority, (2) the county superintendent or county board of education, or (3) a state textbook commission.

The most usual procedure in the choice of basal textbooks is that of local selection upon the recommendations of teachers. This permits adaptability to conditions such as the length of the school year and the nature of the community. A major handicap in this method is that students moving from one district to another, even within the same county, do not find uniform textbooks.

Many times the selection of textbooks is made by either the county superintendent or the county board of education. The county superintendent is frequently assisted by a committee of teachers in the adoption of textbooks.

Another method is that of state-wide adoption, usually by a state schoolbook commission. Approximately half the states have statutes requiring uniform textbooks. The largest single purchaser of textbooks in the United States is Texas, which buys books for all elementary-school children in the state.

Purchase and Distribution of Textbooks. After the textbooks have been selected and adopted, they are purchased and distributed for use. The distribution of books to pupils is usually accomplished through three major purchasing procedures: (1) pupil purchase, (2) school ownership, and (3) other methods.

The common practice whereby pupils purchase their own books may be argued pro and con. It stimulates a learner to begin the acquisition of his own library and relieves school board finances. On the other hand it retards the introduction of up-to-date textbooks. The basic objection to this procedure is that it is not fully in accord with the democratic concept of supplying free education and free instructional materials. To furnish free instruction but to require the purchase of educational tools is an anomaly.

Frequently a caste system prevails in American public education, since the pupils who live on one side of the railroad tracks are able to purchase textbooks while those on the other side are denied equal opportunity to learn because their parents cannot afford to buy adequate learning material. The supplying of free textbooks by the board of education is far more common on the elementary than on the secondary level. There are many pertinent obstacles, especially that of defraying the cost. The pupil purchase of basal textbooks remains one of the hidden costs of so-called free education.

The rental of textbooks has been called "a child of the depression." The books, purchased by the board of education or other agencies, are rented to the pupils on a per capita or per subject basis. The fee system is similar to the rental plan: the school or pupil may purchase the basal text for a course such as high-school English, and then upon payment of a fee the pupil is supplied with the classics and other required supplementary materials. There are numerous other deviations and combinations of systems. No matter what procedure is used in supplying children with textbooks and materials, it is necessary to keep these tools up to date and to increase in most schools the amount of money thus expended.

SCHOOL LIBRARIES

Their Role in Education. The library ought to be the heart of the school, with arteries running into each room. The plan of extensive reading requires much supplementary material. This means that administrators and teachers should be familiar with library work and competent to guide pupils in the use of library and supplementary materials.

FIG. 15-2. Pupils should be surrounded by books in a good library. (*Courtesy of Marsh Studio and of Public Schools, Cincinnati, Ohio.*)

Schools and libraries should have a close and cooperative relationship. In a few large cities and in many small districts the school library is operated as a branch of the city or county public library and draws freely on the larger library collection. "Rolling libraries" and "bookmobiles" are increasing in number and in services to rural areas. Tennessee is one of several states where the county circulating library system has proved very successful. Several school districts cooperate in the establishment of a central library system whereby the books obtained are made available by a well-planned system of circulation.

Evaluation of School Library. In measuring the adequacy of school libraries, a publication of the Cooperative Study of Secondary School Standards states that a satisfactory book collection for a secondary-school library should have a fairly high rating in number of titles, balanced distribution, appropriateness for secondary-school purposes, and recency of publication.

A rough index of balance is the number of volumes in the various areas of the Dewey Decimal System whereby nonfiction books are arranged according to numbers and decimals. The major classifications in this system are as follows:

000	General works	500	Natural science
100	Philosophy	600	Useful arts
200	Religion and mythology	700	Fine arts
300	Sociology	800	Literature
400	Language	900	History

Subdivisions of these major classes are used. Fiction books are listed alphabetically by author. Modern education requires a well-balanced library in every building as a central opportunity for extended reading experience. Furthermore, in a pupil-centered library the emphasis is on the reader rather than the book.

Equipment for the Library. Among the items of equipment other than books, are suitable lights, clock, lounging chairs, reading tables and chairs, charging desk for librarian, cabinet and stand for card catalogue, magazine rack, vertical files, bulletin boards, newspaper holders, display racks, dictionary stand, book truck, an atlas case, a display case, and a regulation executive's desk for the librarian. These articles should come from dependable firms, harmonize with the other school furnishings, and reduce eyestrain.

OTHER INSTRUCTIONAL SUPPLIES AND EQUIPMENT

Space does not permit a detailed list of all the supply and equipment items other than books that are found in a modern school. The two types singled out for emphasis are (1) ancillary reading materials, and (2) multisensory aids to learning.

ANCILLARY READING MATERIALS

The Dictionary. An important book, which should receive special attention in all educational institutions, is the dictionary. A large dictionary placed on a bookshelf or desk in the front or rear of the room is not adequate. Each pupil ought to have an attractive dictionary gauged to his level and at hand for steady use. This may be supplemented by larger lexicons available for the group. Extensive reading and frequent reference to a dictionary help to develop a copious vocabulary and fine discrimination in meanings.

The Workbook. Recent years have witnessed a growing demand for workbooks and kindred materials. Valuable as workbooks may be, an intelligent teacher will not rely implicitly upon anything mechanical; she will vary the mediums of work as well as the methodolgy.

Newspapers. Students are interested in newspapers. Today thousands of classrooms contain newspapers. Many teachers employ the news, magazine, financial, and sport sections as means of general knowledge enrichment; they depend upon the book review, magazine, theater, movie, art, music, radio, science, travel, and hobby sections for cultural guidance and enrichment. Yale's famous professor of English, William Lyon Phelps, once said the newspaper is one of the greatest aids to vitality Americans have. The emphasis on newspaper reading in schools has been primarily for keeping up with current events. The habit of reading current news is, of course, a first step, and the human-interest story is probably a natural starting point. The ultimate aim is to develop an intelligently critical attitude.

Magazines. Allied with the use of newspapers is that of magazines and periodicals. Many schools subscribe to publications such as *Our Times, Reader's Digest, My Weekly Reader,* and *Scholastic.* The current emphasis on candid photography and pictorial sections in popular magazines introduced these aids in the public school. It is obvious that the school must give attention to the selection and use of periodicals.

Tests. An important function of the school is that of comprehensive evaluation, which includes testing. Many good standard tests are available for schools; these are helpful for grading and promoting pupils, for evaluating the efficiency of instruction, and especially for diagnostic purposes. Each school should include in its budget an allowance for the purchase of such materials. Obviously the choice of a test will depend upon the purpose for which it is to be used. Standard tests are usually accompanied by a manual giving data on their validity and reliability, and containing instructions for giving, scoring, and interpreting the tests. The weakness in most testing programs is that the papers accumulate dust in an office and that teachers and administrators do not translate the implications into action. Many educational supplies and pieces of equipment deteriorate from disuse or abuse.

Multisensory Aids in Learning

Multisensory aids, usually delimited to audio-visual, include many facets of learning. Utilizing the five senses of seeing, hearing, smelling, tasting, and feeling, the multisensory materials run the gamut of the alphabet from the touch-and-see ABC block in the nursery to the smell-and-taste of zymurgy in the college chemistry laboratory. In the "cone of experience," Edgar Dale lists the various types of audio-visual aids, as well as their relative position in a scale from the apex of verbal symbols to the broad base of direct, purposeful experiences:

1. Verbal symbols
2. Visual symbols
3. Recordings, radio, still pictures
4. Motion pictures
5. Television
6. Exhibits

7. Field trips
8. Demonstrations
9. Dramatized experiences
10. Contrived experiences
11. Direct, purposeful experiences [5]

These divisions obviously overlap and include many specific mediums such as bulletin boards, books, and films of all types.

FIG. 15-3. Audio-visual aids center. (*Courtesy of Public Schools, San Diego, Calif.*)

Films. Of the motion picture, George F. Zook, when president of the American Council on Education, said, "It is the most revolutionary instrument introduced in education since the printing press." Another significant development is the text-film which is correlated with a textbook and followed by a tailor-made filmstrip to capitalize on pertinent, meaningful discussion and evaluation.

Radio. The action of the Federal Communications Commission in allotting several channels on the ultrahigh radio waves to nonprofit educational broadcasting is of extreme importance to schools. The United States Office of Education, through its Federal Radio Committee, promoted a much-needed educational emphasis in radio. H. V. Kaltenborn,

[5] Edgar Dale. *Audio-visual Methods in Teaching*, p. 43, Dryden, 1954.

news commentator, speaking of the radio as the "fifth estate," has said that the radio, wrongly exploited, is capable of creating confusion, discontent, ignorance, incompatibility, intemperance, and moral and social disintegration; but just as easily it may concentrate on public enlightenment, intellectual stimulus, social awareness, diplomatic cooperation, greater understanding, and economic recovery. The Federal Communications Commission allocated numerous channels for the noncommercial

FIG. 15-4. High-school students in radio broadcasting over WDTR, Detroit's own FM station. (*Courtesy of Public Schools, Detroit, Mich.*)

educational FM (frequency modulation) service, with its static-free, high-fidelity bands. Increasing in use is the audiocorrespondence course, the lesson material for which is broadcast. Through the addition of the so-called "fourth R" (radio) many rural schools are losing their one-teacher status. Many large schools have installed central sound systems in order to multiply speech and learning.

Television. The latest and potentially the most powerful educational tool is television, linked with facsimile broadcasting. A lesson received through the eye and ear gates has a double chance of retention by the learner. Like radio, television has its limitations, but it also has great potentialities as a teaching device. The television screen may become the electronic blackboard of the future. The campus "closed circuit" can be an open sesame.

Educational television, still in its infancy, is an expansion of America's frontier of mechanical ingenuity and creative thinking. It may affect teaching-learning procedures, class size, classroom layout, and school buildings. In *Television in School, College, and Community*, the author states:

Those who are thinking creatively on the subject of television in American schools and colleges are finding that their investigations of this new medium

Fig. 15-5. Elementary-school pupils have their flute program telecast over WICU, TV. (*Courtesy of Public Schools, Erie, Penna.*)

involve a thorough reexamination of the full picture of education today. Television is the trigger that is setting off this reexamination.[6]

One of the biggest television "networks" is the cheapest—the United States mail—whereby stations equipped with kinescope facilities can ship programs to other stations for retelecasting at later, convenient hours. This new medium and methodology in teaching—television—has a clear challenge not only to the teacher of regular in-school pupils but also to leaders in pre-elementary and adult education.

[6] Jennie Waugh Callahan, *Television in School, College, and Community*. p. 5, McGraw-Hill, 1953.

MISCELLANEOUS SUPPLIES AND EQUIPMENT

A study of current school budgets or of supply catalogues reveals an endless array of educational supplies and school equipment, from a small piece of chalk to a microscope, and up to a large expensive grand piano or bus. All special types of rooms, such as household arts, industrial arts, fine arts, laboratories, cafeterias, gymnasiums, and auditoriums contain special supplies and equipment.

FIG. 15-6. Thousands of school busses costing millions of dollars transport millions of pupils daily. (*Courtesy of Public Schools, Bakersfield, Calif.*)

SELECTION, PURCHASE, AND USE OF MATERIALS

Many principles and procedures are involved in the selection, purchase, and management of materials. Supplies and equipment should be selected in terms of the educational program of the school. For that reason teachers should be consulted as to the need.

Ethics in Handling School Supplies and Equipment. In order to improve the selection of school supplies and equipment and to maintain a high professional standard of conduct, a code of ethics has been developed by the Associated Exhibitors of the National Education Association. This code should be supplemented by a nation-wide code for schoolteachers and administrators relative to the handling of textbooks, supplies, and equipment. For example, some administrators, teachers, and professors have a penchant for collecting free textbooks by asking publishers for samples, under the pretext of possible adoptions. Another unethical procedure often followed by teachers is that of duplicating or mimeographing portions from textbooks. Portions of a copyrighted book should not be duplicated unless the permission of the publisher has been obtained. The present standard of ethics in the selection, sale, and use of textbooks and school materials is a challenge to the teaching profession and to those engaged in schoolbook and supply business to improve current practices.

Fig. 15-7. College students studying vertebrate histology with the aid of microscopes. Equipment used at all levels of education and in all types of institutions represents a necessary investment of several billions of dollars. (*Courtesy of Macalaster College, St. Paul, Minn.*)

Use of Supplies and Equipment. Despite this so-called machine age, schools do not use enough mechanical aids in making their work more scientific, interesting, and accurate. Administrators and teachers should take advantage of technically accurate and professionally useful devices, like the audiometer, which is the best known way of testing the hearing of pupils, and the lightmeter, which is an accurate measure of the foot-candles of light in any part of a room.

Modern classrooms are equipped with steel file cases. The teacher should know how to file personnel records and other materials for present and future use. Records and reports are becoming more numerous as activity increases in the field of child and teacher accounting. The classroom furniture—desk, files, and cupboards—should be arranged economically, for many useless steps can be eliminated through an alert analysis of arrangements within the room.

Consumer education in the purchase and use of educational supplies and equipment is on the increase. Information in regard to analyses of products is available from federal agencies, like the United States Bureau of Standards, and from organizations, like the National School Supply Association. Additional literature and corroborating research are needed in connection with the manufacture, purchase, and use of school supplies and equipment. In order to make teaching-learning aids more readily accessible to teachers, many schools have established special rooms as instructional service centers. Pupils and teachers need instruction in the wise and economical use of school materials. Unfortunately many pupils willfully destroy property and some unwittingly damage materials through improper use, as in the careless handling of a textbook or of playground apparatus.

SCHOOL SITES, BUILDINGS, AND EQUIPMENT

The influence of environment in the life of a child is appropriately expressed in the following lines from Walt Whitman:

There was a child went forth every day,
And the first object he look'd upon, that object he became,
And that object became part of him for the day or a certain part of the day,
Or for many years or stretching cycles of years.[7]

School sites, buildings, and equipment are a material part of the daily scenes of the child. The building should be intimately fitted to human needs—practical, psychological, and aesthetic. The building ought to be planned as a unified collection of functional relationships, erected in such close sympathy with its surroundings, and so fittingly furnished that its beauty charms the students who breathe into the architect's creation the breath of life.

BUILDING PROGRAMS

School Building Needs. As indicated by President Eisenhower in a State of the Union message, one of the most critical problems in American education is that of providing adequate and satisfactory school housing. Various factors have contributed to the acute shortage in school-housing facilities. From its survey of the nation's educational structures, the

[7] Walt Whitman, *Leaves of Grass,* p. 306, Doubleday, 1931.

United States Office of Education concluded that the more important of these factors are: enrollment increases, mobility of population, reorganization of school districts, extension of the school program, school construction backlog, and financial problems.[8] The problem is more acute now than at any time in the nation's history, and the crisis will continue to worsen. For example, as to the first of the enumerated factors,

FIG. 15-8. One of the oldest wooden schoolhouses in the United States, if not the oldest. This schoolhouse at St. Augustine, Florida, is a competitor for historical honors with the still-standing Nathan Hale school in Connecticut and the one erected at York Village, Maine, in 1745. (*Courtesy of Ewing Galloway, New York.*)

it is predicted that the enrollment in elementary and secondary schools will increase 40 per cent in the decade from 1950 to 1960. School-housing shortages may seriously impair the quantity and quality of learning.

Long-term Master Plans. The erection of educational buildings is a long-span proposition. Inasmuch as a new structure usually involves bonded indebtedness, it is necessary to project the estimated cost 15 to 20 years in the future. This is not unwarranted, since the building may be used for 50 years or more.

The master plan is a complete, comprehensive, and long-range plan made by a school district to meet the anticipated growth of a school system over a period of

[8] U.S. Office of Education, *Report of the Status Phase of the School Facilities Survey,* p. 8, GPO, December, 1953.

years. It must be flexible enough to allow for unforeseen contingencies. It must be regarded as a document of considerable authority and yet it is not so sacred but that it can be revised if changed conditions seem to warrant it.[9]

Each individual building is a part of the ultimate master program, which should embrace three essential and integrated phases, *viz.:* (1) the educational, (2) the expenditure, and (3) the financing plan.

Educational Plan. School buildings and sites are merely facilitating mediums for the instructional process. Functional planning demands that the educational aims of the school be translated into an actual workable program for the architect, and then that his drawings and specifications be checked with it.

One of the first prerequisites to an improved school plant is a clear-cut statement of the community's beliefs regarding public education. . . . Since the schools belong to the public, the school's aims should be also the public's aims. A joint enterprise, such as the public schools, requires joint participation in crystallizing beliefs. . . .[10]

Expenditure Program. Costs fluctuate with the price of materials and labor, and the purchasing power of the dollar. It is not improbable that building costs will increase, especially if beauty as well as utility is to be considered. Certainly there should be a difference in the appearance of a manufacturing plant and a school building. On the other hand too much money has frequently been spent. New schoolhouses have not always been based upon real necessity; sometimes they have been erected because of local pride, competition with a neighboring district, or selfishness. School board members and administrators seeking to perpetuate their names on a brass plate in the entrance to a new school may saddle the community with a debt that outlasts the building. Some building programs halt educational progress. Teachers and pupils are better off in a less pretentious structure that can be financed than in one that has so taxed the fiscal resources of the district as to drastically curtail funds for educational purposes.

Financing Plan. The erection of new school buildings or the rehabilitation of old structures is usually financed by the community through the pay-as-you-go plan or some means of borrowing. Since the former method calls for payment out of the current school budget, it is used sparingly and only in large cities. The second plan calls for either long-term or short-term bonds or loans. It is recommended that bonds should not extend over a period longer than 20 years. Usually the erection of a build-

[9] Charles Wesley Bursch and John Lyon Reid, *You Want to Build a School?* p. 45, Reinhold, 1947.

[10] American Association of School Administrators, *American School Buildings,* pp. 45–46, National Education Association, 1949.

ing is preceded by a school election that authorizes the board of education to bond the district. A marked trend is that of paying some of the building costs from the state treasury as part of the minimum foundation program. Typical state grants are: stimulation aids, flat grants, emergency aids, continuing grants, equalization grants, loan funds, and money from state building authorities or commissions. Several bills in Congress have included the provision of federal funds for the planning and/or construction of local school buildings. Congress has allocated funds for the nation-wide survey of school facilities and for the construction of school buildings in federally affected areas.

School Sites

The school site—its size, dimensions, character of the ground, location of the building, and space for play—is of fundamental importance since it conditions not only the development of an adequate recreation program but also possible additions to the existing school plant. In the early days plots of ground unfavorable for other purposes were chosen for schoolhouses. Conditions were so deplorable that Horace Mann, in a supplement to his first annual report in 1838, pleaded for the improvement of school sites and buildings. Much advance has been effected in the last hundred years.

Development of the Site. The school site, which is as important to the complete educational program as classrooms, must be planned to serve its many uses effectively. Among the factors in site selection and development are: (1) its location, (2) nature of the soil, (3) size and shape, (4) location and orientation of the building, (5) outdoor activity spaces, (6) service areas and facilities, and (7) planted areas. Two of the factors—size and landscaping—are here lifted out for brief emphasis.

Size of Sites. Most school sites are too small. Even in rural communities where farm land can be purchased rather inexpensively, many elementary schools have a fenced-in area so small as to prohibit a game of baseball. The grounds around many secondary schools are hopelessly inadequate, especially in parking facilities. Furthermore, the modern program of health and physical education requires several additional acres. The National Council of Schoolhouse Construction recommends, as minimum site areas for elementary schools, five acres, plus an additional acre for every 100 pupils of ultimate enrollment; and for secondary schools, 10 acres, plus an additional acre for every 100 students of peak enrollment.

Landscaping and School Gardens. Much importance must be placed upon the aesthetic influence of the school site. Its beautification and upkeep may depend upon a standing committee on school grounds and buildings from the board of education, a teacher-pupil committee, or a special group from the parent-teacher association. Landscaping helps to soften the building and to hide some of the ugliness of foundations. The daily picture of a beautful school in a natural setting is uplifting and beneficial to all. The wonders of nature upon the school premises, as trees, shrubs, grass, and flowers silently unfold their splendors, may initiate a program for beautifying the entire community.

Fig. 15-9. Tall trees towering over the one-story elementary-school building enhance its beauty and utility. (*Courtesy of Warren S. Holmes and of Public Schools, Whitehall, Mich.*)

EDUCATIONAL BUILDINGS

Types of Construction. After the site has been selected, the next major step is to erect the carefully planned structure. Aside from classifications as to style of architecture, buildings are also grouped in terms of the degree of fire safety: A, B, C, D, and E. Type A buildings represent the greatest protection in materials of construction, since the gross structure and interior are of fire-resistive materials. The term "fire-resistive," which is preferred to "fireproof," means that the parts of the building so labeled are made of nonburning or fire-resisting materials such as steel, stone, brick, tile, and metal lath. Types B, C, D, and E make increasing use of more inflammable materials, the last being constructed chiefly of wood. Records of the National Fire Protection Association reveal an average of seven or eight school fires a day, very few of which originate in Type A buildings.

One development in architecture is dimensional coordination of building materials and equipment, popularly known as modular or unit construction.

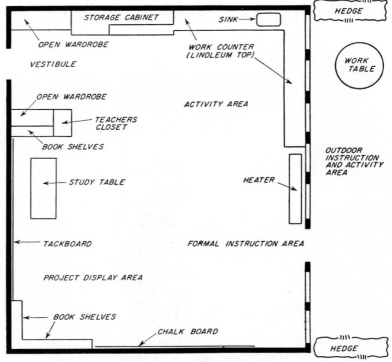

FIG. 15-10. Modern elementary classroom, Franklin Elementary School, Bakersfield, California. Points to note, beginning at the upper left-hand corner: Open wardrobe at either side of entrance door. Storage cabinet, which has shelves with doors and drawer units. Work table with linoleum top, tackboard above, and cabinets below. Sink near the corner. Work counter continued under windows, making two sides of the activity area. Heater under windows. Door to outside activity area, which is two-thirds paved and one-third left clear for planting. Chalkboard at one end of formal instruction area. Tackboard continued around corner above low shelves. Alcove for project display and study center formed by study table, bookshelves, and teacher's closet. A self-contained classroom would also include toilet facilities. (*Courtesy of Public Schools, Bakersfield, Calif., and American Association of School Administrators.*)

The basis of dimensional coordination is a continuous three-dimensional grid with lines 4 inches apart to which all building dimensions and details are referred. Four inches were determined as the optimum size for the standard module. As the program develops, more products will be so designed that their dimensions, plus the required joint, will fit the 4-inch dimension (or multiples thereof) in the modular grid.[11]

[11] *Ibid.*, p. 211.

When all building materials and equipment are designed in 4-inch multiples, large savings in construction may be expected.

The types of construction materials defy classification. Technical mediums are extremely varied, including directional glass blocks, pressed wood, colored plastics, hard and spongy rubber, and many metallurgical

Fɪɢ. 15-11. The tallest public school building in the world—Lindsey Hopkins Vocational School, Miami, Florida. This 15-story structure, equipped with modern elevators and teaching-learning equipment, enables the school personnel to offer a rich, diversified program of vocational education to secondary-school youth. (*Courtesy of McKay Aerial Photos and Maude G. Woods.*)

miracles. Factory-fabricated materials are used in increasing quantities. Many schools employ structural materials and architectural designs indigenous to the particular region.

School buildings are also classified on the basis of temporary and permanent structures. Among the temporary types is the so-called "portable building," usually found in large cities or in areas of rapid growth in school population. Today thousands of pupils are housed in these temporary or war-surplus structures rather than in permanent fire-resistive buildings.

As to shape, school buildings are usually erected in the form of the letters T, I, U, N, B, E, H, X, or O, or combinations or modifications thereof. Each shape possesses distinctive advantages and limitations. Buildings may have three degrees of enclosure: the closed, the semiopen with porch or patio effect, and the enclosed but unroofed play space.

The height varies from a one-story structure, the prevalent type, to "skyscraper" schools in large cities, as, for example, the 15-floor Lindsey Hopkins Vocational School in Miami, Florida. In California the one-floor type has become increasingly prevalent, owing in part to the safety factor in times of earthquakes. Among the many interesting and functional school buildings today are the homemaking cottages, like that in Hatfield, Pennsylvania. The building of superior schoolhouses is of course a highly technical task requiring the cooperative efforts of school superintendents, school consultants, engineers, building architects, landscape architects, health specialists, contractors, lawyers, and experts in air conditioning, lighting, and sanitation.

Characteristics of a Good School Building. Buildings can have a personality. The essential qualities of a good school structure include:

1. Educational adequacy	6. Expansibility and contractibility
2. Safety	7. Flexibility
3. Healthfulness	8. Durability
4. Efficiency	9. Utility
5. Economy	10. Beauty

Many buildings actually mar the beauty of the landscape and make a sad contrast with surrounding structures. The architect must be allowed the reasonable luxury of artistic creativeness if school buildings are to be satisfyingly beautiful and functionally useful.

Steps in Planning and Constructing a School Building. Many steps are involved in the erection of a new school building. The major sequences are (1) preliminary steps, (2) the preparation of educational plans, (3) financing plans, (4) spending plans, and (5) evaluation. These processes are detailed in various publications, like *American School Buildings.* Here three substeps—operation, maintenance, and evaluation—are treated briefly.

Operation. The daily operation of the school plant should be so efficient as to facilitate instruction and to house healthfully the pupils and teachers. For this reason, custodial service is an outstanding factor. (See Unit XII as to the role of the janitor-custodian.)

Maintenance. By maintenance of the school plant is meant the care and upkeep of the structure, which involve necessary repairs and frequent painting of the rooms and buildings. In addition to resistance to the "wear and tear" of its human occupants, a building must wage a perpetual battle against the elements of water, wind, sun, and extremes of temperature. A school-painting renaissance is needed in many communities. Paint, usually regarded as a mere protection, is an integral part of a structure. The use of bright color, an essential phase of Egyptian architecture, has been revived. Large school systems have specially trained maintenance men for carrying on needed renovations. Teachers and

Fig. 15-12. Classroom building on the main campus of the University of Miami, Coral Gables, Florida. This building contains 56 classrooms and a lecture hall. Of contemporary style of architecture, it is designed to take full advantage of daylight, yet to exclude direct sunlight. Each room is, therefore, evenly lighted by daylight. Also, on cloudy days and at night, the electric lighting is automatically and rheostatically controlled to keep the light standard uniform. The building is so situated as to take full advantage of prevailing breezes. Overhanging walkways and roof permit open doors and windows at all times, excepting in driving rains.

pupils, through cooperation with the administration and the custodial force, can make decided contributions to effective and economical operation and maintenance of the school equipment, plant, and grounds, as well as to their beautification.

Evaluation of School Buildings, Sites, and Equipment. Two general criteria in the evaluation of school facilities are: "How effectively do they promote the instructional process?" and "How do they protect the health of the pupils and teachers?" In many school districts an independent survey of buildings is made to determine strengths and weaknesses. Usually a score card or check list is employed in evaluating physical facilities. The *Strayer-Engelhardt Score Card for Elementary School Buildings* is an example. The score card is based upon a total of 1000 points, with ratings from 600 to 1000, superior; 500 to 599, good; 400 to 499, fair; 300 to 399, poor; and less than 300, inferior. This card gives a general overview of a school building and its content.

An important test in evaluating a school building program is the utilization of the plant. The percentage of utilization usually is calculated by taking the number of class periods when each room might be utilized and then checking that against the periods it is actually in use.

EQUIPMENT FOR BUILDINGS AND SITES

Building Equipment. The various service systems enumerated on the Strayer-Engelhardt score card indicate the types of equipment found in most schools. The one discussed here is lighting.

Gradually organizations like the National Society for the Prevention of Blindness, the Illuminating Engineering Society, and the American Institute of Architects are making the public conscious of eye health. Few classrooms have adequate and appropriate lighting, either natural or artificial. "Better light for better sight" means basically the admission of abundant natural light through careful, efficient window planning, and the controlled use of artificial lighting when needed.

Among the many trends reported in *American School Buildings* and elsewhere are these: [12]

Emphasis in school lighting now is less than formerly on quantity and more upon quality of light, which is determined by the location and intensity of the source of light and its surroundings or environment.

Light intensities of from 20 to 40 foot-candles are desirable for classrooms.

The brightness of any light source or other surface in the schoolroom environment should not exceed 500 foot-lamberts. (The foot-lambert is a measure of surface brightness. Foot-candles times reflection factor equals foot-lamberts.)

Bilateral lighting, clerestory lighting (windows on the wall opposite or above the main windows), and directional glassblock in properly designated installations increase the quantity and aid the distribution of natural light in a room.

Natural lighting should be controlled, and children should be seated so that no excessive glare is within the normal visual field.

Properly chosen colors help to provide desirable brightness-balance in schoolrooms. . . .

Many modern buildings include an instructional-materials center, which contains anything a teacher may find helpful in classroom teaching. This service center facilitates instruction.

An increasing number of school buildings are equipped with photographic aids, electric typewriters, tape recorders, radio, television, and various types of modern electronic equipment.

Multipurpose rooms, such as cafetoriums, for cafeteria and auditorium, reduce costs of construction.

[12] *Ibid.,* pp. 242–243.

Many school buildings, especially in coastal, large cities, are including bomb shelters in this atomic age.

School sites are larger, permitting more "campus school" planning.

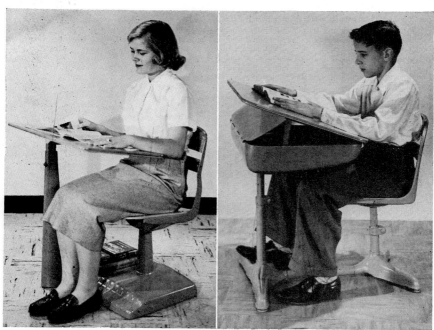

FIG. 15-13. Seating is extremely important. The high-school girl on the left is using a single-unit desk and chair which is readily movable. Easy-to-use and visible book storage is provided on the steel base. It has a nylon swivel-bearing adjustable seat. It is variable in height for use in the seventh through twelfth grades. On the right the elementary-school boy is using a one-piece desk-and-chair combination with the desk top at a 20-degree slope, which can be readily adjusted also to the conventional 10-degree or level position. Most new desks today are available in natural birch finish which has 30 to 50 per cent reflectance in conformity with the accepted brightness ratios. (*Courtesy of American Seating Company.*)

Site Equipment. The establishment and maintenance of school playgrounds are so important that most states have provided for them in their school laws. The immediate vicinity of a school building is often used for kindergarten playground and for apparatus for small children. Older children also need play space and equipment. They look forward to the recess period because they can go out to play. The major criteria for selecting equipment should be benefits to and interests of pupils, initial cost and upkeep, and safety. In this era of cycling, simple stands for parking bicycles should be provided on school property.

On the secondary-school level the athletic fields and areas for intramural sports should be well supplied with suitable equipment and storage spaces. Bleachers are an important part of the grounds equipment where a staduim is not provided with seats. In addition to the regular athletic program of the public schools, playground work and recreation in general have spread out into many new situations. The demand for winter-sports facilities is increasing.

Fig. 15-14. Free form for fun. The free form in sculpture has been adapted to playground use in this surrealisticlike equipment. At the left boys play on a stone and concrete slide, cave, and climbing apparatus. On the right, the multicolored sphere becomes a climbing labyrinth when entered. (*Courtesy of United Press.*)

COMMUNITY SCHOOLS

Community Playgrounds. The school's program for leisure should be integrated with the community's needs. The facilities in and out of school must be available to persons in and out of school. School grounds should be planned with an eye not only to future generations but also to the adult life of the community.[13]

One neglected phase of school and community life is the summer program. Too many schools are closed for two, three, or four long months, the very time when they might be directing play activities. Articulation of all community efforts in the development of a 12-month program of education includes a flexible, unregimented vacation plan for children.

[13] National Society for the Study of Education, *The Community School,* pp. 92–95, University of Chicago Press, 1953.

The grounds of the public schools are a part of the community's recreational resources.

Community School Buildings. The school is not merely located in a community; it is part of the community. Paid for by the people, it pays back dividends through helping to raise ideals and practices. The isolationist policy is disappearing, and school buildings are becoming community structures. In some territories and dependencies of the United States, particularly Alaska, the school buildings are centers of economic, social, and recreational life for the natives. School buildings ought to be designed not merely for children but for all learners. The community reaches into the school, and vice versa.

The Educational Policies Commission recommends that school boards become public education authorities charged with full powers and full responsibility for the conduct of all public educational activities within the community and that the educational plant be planned for use by the whole population according to a definite program for meeting neighborhood social needs.

School Planning and Community Coordination. Cooperation and coordination between the town and the school are essential if the community is to be school-centered. The erection of a building is facilitated through a coalition between the school district and the city government. In New England this coordination is easily effected since the building of a school is primarily a function of the city government. The same cooperation is possible in cities where the entire school budget is under the direction of a board of education.

In many localities schools have been constructed without regard for adult and community requirements. Cooperation between schools and other youth-serving or adult education agencies depends in a large measure on the degree to which those responsible for schoolhouse design are building the schools for community use. For example, too frequently there is insufficient space, or none at all, for museum collections. It is the exception rather than the rule to find adequate provisions for such important phases of modern educational offerings as conferences, community activities, recreation, adult education, medical and dental clinics, student activities, vocational subjects, music, and community as well as school libraries.

The first three words of the Constitution of the United States, "we, the people," express the thought of cooperation. This ideal should permeate the planning of school buildings and educational programs in the community, state, and nation.

SUGGESTED ACTIVITIES

1. Discuss the role of materials in American education.
2. Prepare a short history of schoolbooks in American education.

3. Contrast an old schoolbook with a modern one in the same field.

4. List some titles of schoolbooks published prior to 1900 and of recent books.

5. How are textbooks adopted in your district or county?

6. Arrange a debate on the subject of state-wide adoption of textbooks.

7. Examine or prepare a score card for evaluating a textbook in your major field.

8. Prepare a list of the books given the Newberry or the Caldecott award.

9. Investigate the methods by which textbooks are furnished to pupils in the schools of your community.

10. Explain the statement, "The library is the heart of the school."

11. Prepare an assembly program for national book week.

12. Investigate thoroughly the Dewey decimal system for classifying books.

13. Visit a public-school library. Report on the books, equipment, and librarian.

14. List the advantages and disadvantages in the use of a workbook.

15. Make a scrapbook for the contents of one issue of a daily newspaper, showing how the clippings might be used in various school subjects or areas.

16. Examine two standardized tests in your major field of interest.

17. Investigate equipment used in audio-visual education.

18. List the radio and television programs that have an educational emphasis.

19. Suggest how teachers can promote effective use of supplies and equipment.

20. List the steps necessary in securing a new school building.

21. Examine a score card for evaluating school buildings.

22. Arrange a discussion on the school as a community center.

DESCRIPTIVE BIBLIOGRAPHY AND AIDS

BOOKS

AMERICAN ASSOCIATION OF SCHOOL ADMINISTRATORS: *American School Buildings,* Chap. XIV, National Education Association, 1949.
> Instructional furniture and equipment for schools.

———: *American School Curriculum,* Chap. VII, National Education Association, 1953.
> Better aids to instruction.

ASSOCIATION FOR SUPERVISION AND CURRICULUM DEVELOPMENT: *Creating a Good Environment for Learning,* Chap. VIII, National Education Association, 1954.
> The importance of physical resources in learning.

BUTTERWORTH, JULIAN E., and HOWARD A. DAWSON: *The Modern Rural School,* Chap. VIII, McGraw-Hill, 1952.
> The school plant in the rural community.

CALLAHAN, JENNIE WAUGH: *Television in School, College, and Community,* Chap. II, McGraw-Hill, 1953.
> Equipment for educational telecasting.

DALE, EDGAR: *Audio-visual Methods in Teaching,* Chap. XX, Dryden, 1954.
> Color as an aid in teaching.

MACOMBER, FREEMAN GLENN: *Teaching in the Modern Secondary School,* Chap. VIII, McGraw-Hill, 1952.
> Materials of instruction in secondary education.

MILLARD, C. V., and ALBERT J. HUGGETT: *An Introduction to Elementary Education,* Chap. I, McGraw-Hill, 1953.
> Present-day buildings, equipment, and materials in elementary schools.

NATIONAL SOCIETY FOR THE STUDY OF EDUCATION: *Mass Media and Education,* Chap. X, University of Chicago Press, 1954.
> The classroom and the newspaper.

NEWSOM, CARROLL V. (ed.): *A Television Policy for Education,* Part II, American Council on Education, 1952.

The significance of television for education and basic planning, as accented at an Educational Television Program Institute.

RESEARCH COMMITTEE ON SCHOOL BUSINESS LITERATURE AND BIBLIOGRAPHY: *A Selected Bibliography of Business and Plant References for the School Administrator,* Association of School Business Officials, 1953, 169 pp.

A helpful annotated list of references.

U.S. OFFICE OF EDUCATION: *Report of the Status Phase of the School Facilities Survey,* Section II, GPO, 1953.

Report of nation-wide survey of school-plant problems.

CURRENT PERTINENT PERIODICALS AND PUBLICATIONS

American Library Association Bulletin
American School Board Journal
American School and University
Architectural Forum
Audio-visual Communication Review
Booklist
Consumers Research Bulletin
Educational Screen
Educational Television Newsletter
Film News
Institutions Catalog Directory
Journal of Association for Education by Radio and Television
Library Trends

Listenables and Lookables
Magazine of Art
Nation's Schools
Progressive Architecture
Review of Educational Research
School Arts Magazine
School Executive
School Life
School Management
See and Hear
Television Forecast
TV Today
Yearbooks of educational organizations

AUDIO-VISUAL AIDS

Blueprints

A collection of blueprints of school and college buildings will prove interesting and instructive. A print of a single room can be used as a starting point.

Exhibits

An exhibit of old and new textbooks and equipment and pictures of buildings can be prepared by the class. Exhibits held in connection with educational conferences are helpful.

INCREASING TEACHING EFFECTIVENESS WITH TAPE RECORDINGS   Slide film, 15 min., sound

Helpful hints on how a teacher can enhance his teaching with the use of tape recordings. Available from Minnesota Mining Company, Minneapolis.

INTRODUCTION TO THE GLOBE   Five filmstrips, color

Deal with *Continents and Oceans; Up and Down; North, South, East and West; Night and Day;* and *Hot and Cold Places.* Available from Jam Handy Organization, 2821 East Grand Boulevard, Detroit 11.

THE LIBRARY   Six filmstrips

Filmstrips designed to promote better study habits and greater use of the library and its facilities. Available from Young America Films, 18 E. 41st Street, New York 17, N.Y.

FINANCING OF PUBLIC EDUCATION

Educational materials and other elements in the teaching-learning environment are made possible through public financing. Bitter battles have been fought on behalf of public support for education. Complete support is not yet won.

Among the principles that underlie the financing of public education are these: public-school finance must be related to public finance; educational opportunities and burdens should be equalized; and fiscal planning is necessary for education.

The principal instrument in fiscal planning for public education is the school budget, which is a complete financial forecast consisting of (1) the educational program, (2) the estimated expenditures, and (3) the probable receipts. The first of these has been treated previously.

School expenditures are classified in various ways. A constant question is: "Where does the school dollar go?"

School receipts are likewise grouped under various classifications. "Where does the school dollar come from?"

Public-school finance embraces all educational institutions and undertakings supported in part or whole by taxation. Many schools and colleges are financed privately.

OUTLINE OF CONTENTS

FINANCING OF PUBLIC EDUCATION

Chance, charity, churches, courts, chattel, commodities, credit, and cash were common sources of fiscal support in the early days of American public education.

Lotteries and similar games of chance were legitimate means of raising money for schools and colleges in colonial America. These indirect and painless ways of obtaining funds took the place of direct taxation. Then too, much education was financed through charity. Direct gifts by individuals and groups to semipublic or charity schools enabled many poor children to obtain some "pauper schooling." Churches through their denominational schools have always financed the education of many children. Barter, the exchange of commodities and services, has been frequent even in the present century. One commodity was wood. In lieu of money a parent furnished the equivalent in wood to keep the schoolroom warm in winter. The teacher often "boarded around," receiving his board and room in exchange for part of his services. The practice of barter was revived during the depression of the 1930's when many school employees received gasoline coupons, grocery purchase orders, and I.O.U.'s in return for part or all of their services. Many novel methods have been resorted to in the long effort to finance the public schools through the use of credit.

The best means of support, viz., cold cash, was gradually made available for the operation of schools. Tuition was charged at an early date. A unique form of cash support was provided in the "rate tax," which was assessed pupils on a per capita basis to cover the costs of schooling above the funds provided locally.

Taxation for school support was at first on a permissive basis. The little word "or" in early legislation proved a mighty obstacle in the development of mandatory public support. It was not until about 1825 that direct taxation of all property for the support of schools was generally recognized.

The Battle for Publicly Supported Education. Cubberley uses the term "battle" to describe the efforts to win public funds for education. It was indeed a prolonged war in which the major victories may be recorded as follows:

1. Permission to communities to organize a school district and to levy a local tax for schools on the property of those consenting

2. Local taxation extended to all property, regardless of consent

3. The organization of school districts made easy, and mandatory on proper petition

4. Small state aid to all organized school districts to help support a school

5. Compulsory local taxation to supplement the state aid

6. Permissive, and later compulsory, township or county taxation to supplement the district taxation

7. Larger and larger state support, and assumption of public education as a state function

8. Extension of the taxation idea to include high schools as well as elementary schools [1]

The present era is marked by three additional struggles in financing schools:

1. Extension of the taxation idea to include pre-elementary education, college education, and education for out-of-school youth and adults

2. Equalization of educational opportunity and burden through state and national equalization funds

3. Procurement of sufficient funds to meet the critical shortages in school and college buildings and in teaching personnel

The extension of public education from the pre-elementary age through adult life has been considered previously; the equalization principle is presented later as one of the basic tenets in modern educational finance; and the battle for more fiscal support is discussed in Unit XVII.

Today public educational finance includes: such local educational provisions for the public as are supported solely by local funds; community and state financing of pre-elementary, elementary, secondary, and, in certain sections, higher and adult education; state financing of the educational institutions, especially schools of higher learning and residential schools for handicapped children; state and federal support of certain joint efforts, as the land-grant colleges; federal financing of several projects, as veterans' education; and local, state, and federal support of certain special fields, as Smith-Hughes vocational education. In addition millions of dollars are spent annually for the support of private and parochial educational institutions and of numerous foundations.

PRINCIPLES UNDERLYING THE FINANCING OF PUBLIC EDUCATION

The basic assumptions underlying American public education should and do have a profound effect upon the expenditures for the public schools. The financing of American public education today is based upon numerous political, economic, and social postulates, several of which have been incorporated in The School Finance Charter. Several desirable objectives are found in "School Finance Goals" published by the National Education Association.

---

[1] E. P. Cubberley and Walter C. Eells, *An Introduction to the Study of Education,* p. 478, Houghton Mifflin, 1933.

THIRTEEN BASIC PRINCIPLES

Thirteen related principles basic to the financing of American public education are presented here. These principles are neither automatic nor all-inclusive.

1. *Public-school Finance Must Be Related to Public Finance.* Public-school finance is only a part of the larger whole, *viz.*, public finance. The fact that public-school finance is a part of public finance is illustrated in the distribution of the tax dollar in any community. The implications of this fact are far reaching:

> Since the school is only one of the many enterprises supported by the public taxation, schoolmen may well approach their own isolated interest from the broad view of *public* rather than *school* financing. Other general activities, such as those of fire and police departments, aim at goals similar to those of education—they seek to protect the individual, his property, and his right. Education, in the long run, serves as a form of local, state, and national insurance for which the public ought to be both willing and able to pay.[2]

School teachers and administrators must see the financing of schools in relationship to the problem of support for all public functions, just as public officials must see the correlation of school and public finance. This first tenet, therefore, may be termed the principle of economic interdependence. It calls for economic and social vision.

2. *School Finance Should Be the Servant of Education and Society.* Finance should function as the servant, not as the master of education and society. The child is more important than the dollar. In many school systems, however, money is the dictator, and education is the slave. The opposite condition is likewise unfortunate, whereby lavish spending brings financial disaster to the school district and the allied taxing units. School finance helps to give a child the best education possible within practical limits.

Educational finance serves not only schools but also society. It is a social as well as economic factor. The social motive, thus far subordinated, now bids fair to assume a larger control in public education. Educational finance is indeed the servant of society as well as the handmaiden of education. Money spent for public education is an investment for the defense of the American faith in democracy.

3. *Public Education Should Be Fiscally Free for All Pupils.* Basic to the financing of public education is the democratic concept of free education. How long education should be provided at public expense is a debatable question. Practices vary markedly between states, but there is general agreement that children should be educated through high

[2] Chris A. De Young, *Budgeting in Public Schools*, pp. 4–5, Swift, 1951.

school at public expense. Some authorities would extend tuition-free schooling through the junior-college years. This does not mean that everything is free. Many costs are hidden. There is disagreement as to the number of elements that should be provided without cost to pupils. For example, in the education of rural high-school pupils, some states furnish only tuition, whereas others include free transportation, textbooks, or board of pupils in lieu of transportation. Many states have set up what is called a defensible minimum program to be furnished tuition-free to all pupils. Along with the American bill of rights, including guarantees for freedom of speech, of religion, of the press, and of assembly, is the dictum that American public education shall be free to all pupils. The emancipation proclamation in school finance precludes dependence upon charity, fees, and tuition. Free public education is the American's birthright.

4. *The State Should Be Primarily Responsible for Public Education.* The Tenth Amendment to the Constitution of the United States made education the primary responsibility of the individual states (see Unit II). Hence the support of public education became mainly a matter of state concern. Today every state makes some contribution from its revenues for the support of public schools through many types of funds, some of which are described later. An inconsistency exists, however, between the legal intention to provide state support and the many cases of neglect and inadequacy. For the nation as a whole, state governments supply only about 40 per cent of the cost of schools. Furthermore, the method of distributing such aid is an important factor. Despite favorable argument for federal support of public education, the fact remains that the individual states will have to give more assistance to schools, particularly through the application of the next principle.

5. *Educational Opportunity and Burden Should Be Equalized.* Strayer and Haig in 1923 were the first to give a clear-cut picture of the equalization principle. Their analysis interpreted this principle as the complete equalization of the burden of a satisfactory minimum educational program below which no locality could be allowed to go, but above which any locality would be allowed to rise by means of local support. In contradistinction to the payment-for-effort or matching principle, the operation of the equalization plan tends to shift to more able communities some of the undue burden carried by the less wealthy localities (see Fig. 16-1). Most states today have a state-local "partnership foundation program" in which the commonwealth bestows more on those schools which have less in fiscal resources.

In brief, the equalization principle means that governmental agencies collect educational funds where the money is and spend the money where the pupils are. Every man's property and income must be taxed to educate every man's child. Even though a man chooses to send his own children to a parochial or private school he is not exempt from contributing his support to the education of all children. The golden rule in educational finance is: "Thou shalt educate thy neighbor's children as thine own."

At first this idea of equalization was applied to small areas, as the county and state. Now the old slogan "the wealth of the state must edu-

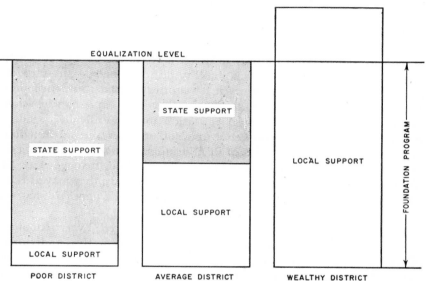

FIG. 16-1. How state equalization works in three types of districts. In the poor district local effort to support schools produces only a small fraction of the cost of a state-guaranteed minimum or foundation program. In the district of average wealth, the same effort produces about half the needed fiscal support. The wealthy district receives no state equalization aid because the local wealth back of each child is great enough to more than finance the minimum program. This district serves as a lighthouse to indicate better practices. Obviously there are state funds in addition to those for equalization.

cate the children of the state" is being supplemented with the clause "and the wealth of the United States must be used to equalize the education of all the children in the nation." Furthermore, the phrase "all the children in the nation" implies that more adequate educational opportunities and greater financial support be provided for exceptional or atypical children, since their learning opportunities, as in the case of the blind, are below par, and the costs of their instruction are above average. American public education will not be genuinely democratic until there is nation-wide application of the principle that opportunity and burden shall be equalized for all learners.

6. *Lighthouse Schools Can Indicate Better Practices through Their Richer Resources*. Related to the promotion of equalization of opportunity and burden is the principle of adaptability. According to this rule, "the state tries to keep schools progressive by preserving local initiative and utilizing other devices." Its early application consisted in a program of fiscal rewards to a community for supporting its schools. This "reward for effort" device is being modified because in practice it gave most help to the rich district. The modern interpretation of this principle makes for the continuous adaptation of the local schools to changing needs and demands. It enables many districts to stand out as lighthouses to warn of dangers and to point the way to better lanes to travel. The successful operation of the efficiency or adaptability principle necessitates state aid but not 100 per cent state support. It requires an underburdened property tax which can respond to local initiative. This explains why school people generally want boards of education to be fiscally independent, that is, free from fiscal dependence upon other governmental functions.

7. *Efficiency Must Be Practiced in Educational Finance*. The efficiency principle is aimed at promoting expertness in school management. Despite the fact that most school people are conscientious, they may at times be inefficient. A cardinal principle of public-school finance is that efficiency shall always be promoted.

8. *Education Should Be Economically Administered*. Every school system must practice economy at all times. Groups as well as individuals should heed the advice of Ralph Waldo Emerson "to make money spend well." The term economy is often misunderstood, since there are false and true economies. Educators and laymen must distinguish between retrenchment and economy. Retrenchment is merely a reduction in expenditures. Genuine economy is effected through intelligent spending and vigilant administration. Benjamin Franklin wrote: "Human felicity is produced not so much by great pieces of good fortune that seldom happen, as by little advantages that occur each day."

9. *Increased Responsibilities Must Mean Increased Costs*. Those who are prone to cut the educational budget with one hand and to give the school increased responsibilities with the other should realize that the two acts are incompatible. Among the major causes for rise in school expenditures are (1) decline in purchasing value of the dollar, (2) increase in enrollments, (3) increase in the size of the educational tasks, especially in the relatively expensive junior-college years, and (4) higher standards of educating, akin to the higher standards of living in vogue today. The first causal factor is primarily monetary. The last three are educational in nature and account for a large share of the enlarged costs. The exten-

sion and enrichment of educational services call for expansion in school revenue.

10. *Fiscal Management of Schools Cannot Be Identical with That of Private Business.* A common fallacy is to liken the fiscal management of public schools to that of private business. Although both strive after economy and efficiency, they differ decidedly. In the first place the former is a public matter, and the latter is mainly private. Then too, one is education and the other is business. Furthermore, although money is invested in both public education and private business, the major objective of the latter is quarterly cash dividends, whereas the former seeks long-time returns in character, personality, skills, and the changes wrought in the child through growth and development. A business, although employing many people, is run for the special benefit of a few stockholders; public education is conducted cooperatively for the benefit of all members of society. Of course, the public schools can profit much from observing private business even though they are dissimilar in philosophy and function.

11. *Personnel in Fiscal Management Should Be Well Trained and Honest.* Both business and school officials advocate that those engaged in fiscal management be well trained. The persons handling school finances should have specific training for their jobs. The school treasurer, the superintendent, the business manager, or whoever is in direct charge of school finances should be versed in the theory and practice of business accounting. Increasingly, superintendents of schools and other staff members are taking courses in school finance and business management.

The personnel should be not only efficient but also impeccably honest. As a precautionary and custodial measure, all persons who handle school money should be bonded. The staff is usually trustworthy, but unfortunately the schools are tempting objects for despoliation by greedy politicians and racketeers.

12. *Expenditures for Public Education Should Be Recorded and Reported.* A person may be careless about recording his personal receipts and expenditures, but he cannot be so with public money, which must be accounted for meticulously and honestly. The receipt of money and its expenditure should be registered promptly and accurately. Records ought to be kept in a fire-resistive vault and subjected to scientific scrutiny through periodic audits, preferably by independent auditors.

Not only must school money be accounted for, but its receipts and expenditure should be reported to the board of education, the teachers, the taxpayer, and the public. The old cry was "taxation without representation," but the new complaint is "taxation without explanation." Fiscal reports are improved by numerous explanations and attractive illustrations. The concept of stewardship, also termed the fiduciary or prudential principle, calls for a perennial procession of publicity. A periodic channel for publicity is provided through the nation-wide annual American Education Week.[3] One objective of such organizations as the National Congress of Parents and Teachers and the National Citizens' Commission for the Public Schools is to interpret and improve public education continuously through grass-roots programs.

in their interest...

VISIT YOUR SCHOOLS

AMERICAN EDUCATION WEEK

FIG. 16-2. American Education Week. This is a joint effort to interpret public education as an investment. Parents are urged to visit schools and check on their investment.

13. *Fiscal Planning Is Necessary for Public Education.* Educational welfare necessitates fiscal planning. Many administrators build their curriculums carefully but estimate their finances hurriedly. Many school boards spend months going over blueprints for buildings but devote a half hour to the fiscal framework for the education of children.

Education is a long-term investment by the public, which reaps dividends in the enriched lives of its citizens. A long-term fiscal program is

[3] Helpful information on the observance of this week may be obtained from the National Education Association, Washington, D.C.

essential, since schooling extends forward not backward; the education of a child calls for a long-period plan not only because he requires eight to fifteen years of schooling, but also because the entire cost is often borne by one school district. Long-period budgeting for education is an attempt to substitute intelligent forecasts for the opportunism of a laissez-faire philosophy. Effective long-range forecasting must rest upon improvement in the short-term fiscal plan; that is, the annual school budget.

BUDGETING IN PUBLIC EDUCATION [4]

The budget is an important instrument in education. Through it, many of the basic principles of public-school finance, if not all, are applied to actual situations.

FUNCTION OF THE BUDGET IN PUBLIC EDUCATION

Evolution of the Modern School Budget. Years ago the school budget consisted of one major item, *viz.*, expenditures. One director probably

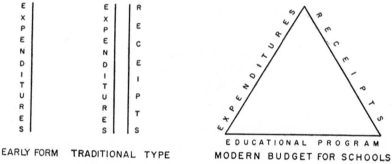

EARLY FORM   TRADITIONAL TYPE   MODERN BUDGET FOR SCHOOLS

FIG. 16-3. Evolution of the school budget.

met another in the country store and asked, "How much money shall we spend for the school next year?" "We spent $1200 last year—" So the budget for that district became $1200, which indicated the limit on expenditures. Later, school officials, imitating the business world, drew up a budget not only of estimated expenditures but also of probable receipts, with the latter presumably greater than expenditures. The modern school budget, as indicated in Fig. 16-3, differs visibly from a commercial or a traditional budget in that the first is represented by an equilateral triangle. In this balanced triangle, the educational program is the base, which represents the working plan of the school, the qualifications of the teachers, and other educational specifications including supplies, textbooks, and program of supervision. The estimated expenditures necessary to conduct this educational program form the spending plan. The pro-

[4] Additional material may be found in De Young, *op. cit.*

posed receipts to pay for putting the plan into operation constitute the financing plan. The school budget, then, is a detailed professional forecast, consisting of both (1) estimated expenditures and (2) receipts, based upon (3) the proposed educational program.

Function of the School Budget. Despite its numerous shortcomings the public-school budget serves many practical purposes, some of which are as follows:

1. The budget is a servant of education.
2. It gives an overview of the entire school system.
3. It aids in analysis of new and old school activities.
4. It develops cooperation within the school.
5. It stimulates confidence among the taxpapers.
6. It estimates the receipts.
7. It determines the tax levy.
8. It authorizes expenditures.
9. It aids in administering the school economically.
10. It improves accounting procedures.
11. It aids in extracurricular activities.
12. It projects the school into the future.[5]

The entire period of time covered by the budget is designated as the fiscal year, which usually extends from July 1 through June 30. An increasing number of schools, however, prepare long-term as well as annual budgets.

PROGRESS OF THE ANNUAL SCHOOL BUDGET

Budgeting in public education may be divided into four major steps: (1) preparation, (2) presentation and adoption, (3) administration, and (4) appraisal.

Preparation of the Budget. Budget building is a continuous job. The starting point is the development of an educational program that helps to make the school budget a professional document rather than a statistical report. This educational emphasis in school accounting is made possible through the cooperation of all staff members and the board of education. The preparation of the educational specifications is inextricably linked with the development of the spending and financing plans for the budget.

Presentation and Adoption. After the budget has been prepared in tentative form it is usually presented to the board of education and to other legal and extralegal groups. Fiscal publicity plays an important part in the broader program of public relations. Various techniques aid in interpreting the budget to the boards of education, the school personnel, and the general public. After the budget has been presented with

[5] *Ibid.,* pp. 9–14.

interpolations, it is legally ratified by the proper body or bodies, such as the board of education and the city council.

Administration of the Budget. After the estimated figures have been transferred to the school accounting books as initial entries, the budget is ready to be administered. It functions not as a dictator but as a definite guide for the economical and efficient conduct of the schools.

Appraisal of Budgets and Budgetary Procedures. One means of appraising budgets and budgetary procedures is the school audit. Then there is also the objective appraisal of the format and content of the document itself. The annual document can best be appraised in relation to a long-term budget of two or more years. In the final analysis the role of budgeting in public education must be evaluated in terms of the service it renders to the learner and society.

SCHOOL EXPENDITURES

The school budget, as previously mentioned, consists of three parts, *viz.,* the educational plan, the expenditure program, and the financing plan. The educational plan is treated throughout this volume and particularly in Unit XIII. The remainder of this unit is devoted to the two other programs, *viz.,* those for expenditures and receipts.

CLASSIFICATION OF SCHOOL EXPENDITURES

School expenditures may be classified in at least five different ways, *viz.,* by (1) character, (2) organization units, (3) objects, (4) functions, and (5) funds.

Character Classification. This arrangement of school expenditures is a uniform system usable in schools of all sizes. The eight major headings in the character classification, with typical disbursements, are as follows:

Expenditures by Character	*Illustrative Expenditures*
General control (administration)	Superintendent's salary
Instruction	Teachers' salaries, school supplies
Auxiliary services	School services, transportation
Operation of plant	Janitors' salaries, water, fuel, light
Maintenance of plant	Upkeep on ground and buildings
Fixed charges	Fire insurance, taxes, rents
Debt service	Principal and interest on loans, bonds
Capital outlay	Purchase of sites, buildings, equipment

The first six of these major headings are often grouped under current expenditures. Supplementary classifications, such as "stores," "revolving funds," and "advancements," are also used.

Organization Units. In many schools the expenditures are classified according to organization units, for example:

Kindergarten	Senior high	Buildings
Elementary grades	Junior college	Departments
Junior high	Adult education	Subjects

The number of units depends upon the size and administrative organization of the district.

Object Classification. Expenditures may be grouped according to the object or thing purchased, such as, equipment, supplies, sites, buildings,

FIG. 16-4. Large city school systems microfilm their financial accounts. (*Courtesy of Public Schools, Chicago, Ill.*)

and subdivisions within these categories. This plan of grouping as tables, chairs, maps, and globes facilitates the obtaining of bids from vendors.

Functional Classification. Basic activities or functions may be utilized in tabulating expenditures. Examples are:

Administration	Health	Library
Attendance	Instruction	Supervision
Cocurriculum	Maintenance	Transportation

Because of overlapping and other difficulties encountered in functional classification this system is not widely used in public schools.

Fund Accounting. Many states stipulate that expenditures must be segregated according to special allotments, such as educational or building funds. There is a marked trend, however, away from earmarking school money by creating special funds.

Combination of Classifications Recommended. The basic method of grouping expenditures is the character classification already mentioned. A combination of several systems may be used. The classroom teacher, as well as the administrator, increases his effectiveness through his ability to identify expenditures and to interpret school costs.

COSTS OF PUBLIC EDUCATION

Where the School Dollar Goes. The school tax dollar does not go into hiding; it is seen in circulation. But teachers and administrators are fre-

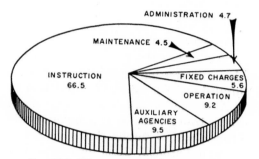

FIG. 16-5. Where the school dollar goes.

quently asked: "Where does the school dollar go?" "How is the money spent?" The classroom teacher as an agent in the public relations program should be fortified with facts so as to give an intelligent answer to such inquiries. Naturally the dollar is not spent in the same way in every school system. Two extremely variable items listed under character classification are debt service and capital outlay.

For the entire United States, the percentage distribution of the school dollar for current expenditures is revealed in Fig. 16-5.

Annual Cost per Pupil in Average Daily Attendance. The percentage distribution of the school dollar is not the only way of calculating school costs. Another method is that of figuring the cost per capita for an area as large as the United States or as small as a local school district. The basis in determining these unit costs is usually the average daily attendance (a.d.a.), the number enrolled in school, or the total population of the United States.

Annual Cost per Pupil Enrolled and per Capita of Population. The cost of education in the public elementary and secondary schools can be calculated also on the basis of the number of pupils enrolled. This total unit cost is less than the cost per pupil in average daily attendance (see the fourth column in the accompanying table). Another unit, less reliable than per pupil average daily attendance, is the cost per person in the United States (see the third column).

Year	Total expenditures for elementary and secondary education	Cost per capita of population	Cost per pupil enrolled
1876	$ 83,082,578	$ 1.88	$ 9.37
1886	113,322,545	1.96	9.72
1896	183,498,965	2.59	12.66
1906	307,765,659	3.59	18.49
1916	640,717,053	6.36	31.48
1926	2,026,308,190	17.39	81.90
1936	1,961,103,765	15.27	74.38
1946	3,124,550,348	22.06	134.10
1956	7,000,000,000 (est.)	43.21 (est.)	225.80 (est.)

The tabulation shows interesting trends in public-school expenditures both per pupil enrolled and per capita of population by 10-year periods from 1876 to 1956. As the nation develops a program of lifelong learning for all individuals, the cost per capita of population will be increasingly indicative of the rough cost of public education per consumer.

Daily Costs per Pupil Enrolled. Costs for education may also be calculated on the basis of the daily rather than the annual expenditures indicated thus far. In a typical school the costs for current expenditures average approximately a dollar a day for each pupil enrolled. The cost-per-day unit for calculating school expenditures is advantageous, since it is small, easily handled, and readily understood by the man in the street.

These data on school expenditures, either for a state or for the nation as a whole, refer only to the direct expenditures for public schools. The complete cost of education in America embraces expenditures by a large number of private and parochial schools, by institutions of higher learning, by libraries, by children for school supplies, and by parents who pay indirect costs such as the loss of possible earnings by older students.

The total expenditures are inadequate measures of either the cost or the worth of education. Increasingly the public is learning to evaluate this service not in terms of dollar aggregates but by means of standards and results achieved. The quality and quantity of educational returns must be considered as well as the nature and amount of expenditures. Furthermore, expenditures are made possible only through the receipt of adequate revenue.

SCHOOL RECEIPTS

CLASSIFICATION OF SCHOOL RECEIPTS

There is less uniformity in classifying school receipts than in classifying expenditures. Receipts are usually grouped by: (1) taxing or political unit, (2) method of production, (3) accounting classification, and/or (4) specific funds. Each of these methods is briefly described here.

FIG. 16-6. Many schools use machine accounting. Here the assistant brings to the accountant some school money to be recorded immediately by machine. (*Courtesy of Public Schools, Rochester, Minn.*)

Taxing or Political Unit. A convenient way to group estimated or actual school receipts is according to the taxing unit that provides the revenue. These main political units are local, township, county (parish), state, and federal. Patently these geographical categories overlap somewhat. For example, property taxes may come from more than one political unit.

Method of Production. The more common forms of financing public education are listed alphabetically here:

Endowments	Inheritance tax	Rentals
Gas tax	Interest	Sales tax
Grants	Personal-property tax	Subventions
Income tax	Real-estate tax	Tuition

It is difficult to determine the exact methods by which all school revenue is obtained.

Accounting Classification. School accountants usually label receipts as: (1) revenue or actual receipts, (2) nonrevenue or future obligations, and (3) advancements or revolving funds.

Examples in the three main categories are as follows:

Revenue Receipts	*Nonrevenue Receipts*	*Revolving Funds*
Tuition	Sale of school land	Textbooks resold
Real-estate tax	Sale of school bonds	Cafeteria funds

This accounting classification is endorsed by several national and state organizations.

Specific Funds. It has been suggested that legal stipulations separating school money into special distinct funds be abolished. Many of these regulations, however, have long histories that fortify them against change. Rigidity in accounting is exemplified in Illinois where school money must be separated into educational and building funds. Numerous special school funds have been created by state legislatures.

State and National Uniformity Recommended. Many other systems of revenue classification are employed. The most common practice is that of listing receipts by local, state, and federal sources. As in the case of expenditures, a combination of systems is recommended, with due regard to state laws and national uniformity, as advocated by the United States Office of Education.

SOURCES OF SCHOOL REVENUE

Where the School Dollar Comes from. People are usually more interested in the answers to the question, "Where does the school dollar go?"

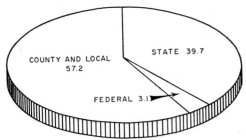

FIG. 16-7. Where the school dollar comes from.

than in those to the query, "Where does the school dollar come from?" The latter, however, is more important, for it goes to the root of the American economic system. Since school finance is a segment of public finance, the teacher and administrator are drawn into broad problems of public financing when they seek the deep sources of the dollar that the school receives. As in expenditures, there is little uniformity in receipts throughout the United States.

Decrease in Revenue from Local Sources. In continental United States the county contributes a small part of school revenue. The consolidation of schools and the enlargement of the taxing unit to embrace entire counties cause county and local sources to coalesce. The proportion of school revenue derived from local districts in the United States as a whole has decreased markedly in the past two decades from 80 to less than 60 per cent, including county support.

RECEIPT OF SCHOOL REVENUE

Although all school revenues are derived from federal, state, county, township, and local units, the types of receipts and the methods of financing public education vary widely. Two main sources, *viz.,* taxation and nonrevenue receipts, are presented here elliptically and briefly. A third source, apportionments, is treated later under the caption Distribution of School Funds.

Taxation. Edwin A. Seligman defines a tax as "a compulsory contribution from the person to the government to defray the expense incurred in the common interest of all without reference to special benefits conferred." In other words, through taxes people contribute to the cost of different services and common social purposes. Since most of the support for American public education comes from taxation in its myriad forms, laymen, teachers, and administrators desire a good tax system, which is not too dependent upon a single tax, such as that on property. The general property tax is becoming increasingly unsatisfactory because of the difficulty in assessing all kinds and classes of property at the same rate. Many European nations have to a large degree abandoned this method, but in America some modified plan of taxing property for schools will exist for a long time.

A tax bill is rarely welcome. The first school-tax notice may seem to a new homeowner like a request from the school: "Let us place your name on our wailing list." But the late Justice Oliver Wendell Holmes, who willed his estate to his country, said: "I like to pay taxes. It is buying civilization." Certainly when the American citizen pays his taxes for public education he is helping to buy civilization.

Among the numerous plans for making the property tax less painful are classification of property; equalization of assessments; more economical, efficient, and honest administration in assessing, levying, and collecting taxes; and the inclusion of the property tax as a part of a broader tax base. It is the abuse rather than the use of the property tax that constitutes a menace to the schools. As Emerson wrote in his essay on "Compensation," "If you tax too high, the revenue will yield nothing."

A promising revenue is the income tax, on which England depends in a far greater degree than America. In seeking new springs of revenue, however, school people must remember the statement: "What is left to the taxpayer is as important to the country's economy as what is taken from him." Linked intimately with the problems of broadening the tax base for school support are the issues of increasing efficiency through the consolidation of small weak units and of reducing costs through carefully planned economies. Archaic taxing systems are not the only cause of trouble, for even where tax systems have been revised, revenues are often inadequate. Some of the difficulty lies not so much in the failure of taxation as in increased expenditures. Many schools may well give less emphasis to raising more funds to spend and may well devote more thought to spending with less money.

Nonrevenue Receipts. As previously defined, nonrevenue receipts do not constitute a genuine source of income, since they incur an obligation that must be met at some future date. These receipts include mainly the revenue either from selling property and bonds or from obtaining loans. Since property is not frequently sold by the school district, attention is directed here to the common practice of borrowing money.

The prevalent ways of financing schools when cash is not available are (1) long-term and (2) short-term obligations, and (3) refinancing. Illustrative of the first are the straight-term bond, which is used for a stated number of years, to be repaid or refunded at the date of maturity; the sinking-fund bond, which is made for a definite period of years, to be paid from a fund which is collected and invested during the term of the bond; and the serial bond, which is paid in installments during the period of the total bond issue. Among the numerous types of temporary school finance are short-term bonds, short-term loans, tax-anticipation warrants, scrip, and other forms of paper money. Refinancing or refunding involves the legal procedure of reestablishing an old debt as a fresh obligation, perhaps at a lower rate of interest. Often this merely postpones the evil day of accounting for past debts.

Many schools have erred in borrowing too much money. Practices such as erecting school buildings beyond the ability of the community to pay within a reasonable length of time, funding debts for annual expenditures, legislating state-wide tax limitations that are inadequate, collecting only a meager portion of the tax levy, and creating sinking funds that disappear are costly procedures that work the greatest hardships upon

Is their education
worth 3ᶜ a day to you?

the Citizens Committee urges you . . .

VOTE ⊗ YES
for the Leyden Community High School
BOND ISSUE
Saturday, March 7

. . . because

FIG. 16-8. In thousands of communities the citizens are being asked to vote "yes" on bond issues to permit boards of education to raise funds for new school buildings and sites.

the generation now in school, for later as adults they will have to pay the costs of their own schooling.

DISTRIBUTION OF SCHOOL REVENUE

The development of a sound system of raising money for public schools is a major problem. A sequential task of prime import is the distribution of the money thus obtained. School money may be collected by reliable methods but distributed through unsatisfactory channels.

As the word "distribution" indicates, school funds are allocated to the states, counties, or local districts by a higher organization. The federal government allots its Smith-Hughes fund to the states, and the latter give it to the local districts. In West Virginia, the state treasury apportions certain school funds to the county units.

Bases for Distribution of Funds. The bases upon which school monies are distributed are very important. Among the criteria for the apportionment of funds for education are: the number of children of school age who reside in the district or county as revealed by the school census; the number of children enrolled in the schools; the number of children in average daily attendance (a.d.a.); the "weighted" pupil with special consideration given to the rural or atypical pupil; the number of teachers employed; the number of instruction units (usually one teacher for each stated number of pupils); the partial or complete support of a state-prescribed minimum educational program; and other forms of flat grants and equalization programs. Combinations of these apportionment methods are employed in several states.

State Equalization Fund. As the term connotes, an equalization fund is intended to equalize educational opportunity and burden. Too often the type and amount of a child's schooling are the result of chance or geography. The child who through the felicity of circumstances lives in a school district that can tax a railroad line or a uranium company enjoys enhanced opportunities for an all-round education. The accidental meanderings of a river several hundred years ago often determine the boundaries that demarcate superior and inferior educational opportunities. Unfortunately, even when the highest permissible tax rate has been applied to the areas of low valuation, the funds secured are insufficient to run the schools in many districts throughout the United States. Even if a model tax plan were put into effect, the poorer districts and states would still be unable to support their schools adequately.

No state provides complete support for its public-school program, but some pay either the entire state-approved cost of all public schools or the principal items of necessary expense. The funds for these equalization plans have been derived from state-wide sources. Approximately three fourths of the states distribute all or part of their state school funds upon an equalization plan. Every state needs a program, built upon research and individually patterned, which provides for local initiative and state equalization. This forms the groundwork upon which a federal equalization program may be based.

Federal Equalization Fund. Education is not primarily a personal benefaction, such as the sidewalk leading to one's home. Nor is it merely a community benefit, like a street light. Rather it is a boon to all. In many ways it is comparable to a city street which is also a state highway and a national route. Both the building and the maintenance of that local-state-national highway are the obligation of all people, not just of those who happen to live near or travel that route. Likewise in the building and maintenance of schools, the local, state, and national interests are merging.

Yet the very schools designed for promoting common local, state, and national welfare may fail in their task. As an illustration, witness the inability of the depressed economic areas and groups to provide proper education for their children from generation to generation. Any federal funds that are or may be made available for public education should be so distributed as to guarantee equity and to correct the present glaring inequalities in the use of school funds for children of the different races. According to many fiscal experts, no sound program of local or state taxation can be devised and established which will support in every community a school system that meets minimum acceptable standards. Time can never efface the inequalities in natural resources that exist between states. Therefore, unless the federal government participates in the financial support of the schools and the related services in the less able areas, several million children in the United States and the outlying territories and possessions will continue to be denied the educational opportunities that should be regarded as their birthright. Most recommendations and recent proposals for federal aid stipulate positively that such grants shall not entail federal control over education. They also specify that the money shall be apportioned to the states, except that for cooperative educational research, which shall be administered by the United States Office of Education.

Several decades ago Rutherford B. Hayes, then President of the United States, sent to Congress a message in which he said: "No more fundamental responsibility rests upon Congress than that of devising appropriate measures of financial aid to education, supplemental to local action in the states and territories and in the District of Columbia." This challenge has not yet been adequately met. Federal aid to public education is one of the moral "musts" of America.

FINANCING OTHER PHASES OF EDUCATION

As previously stated, American public education is broader than schooling. Accordingly public-school finance is not exactly synonymous with public educational finance. The former is usually restricted to public elementary and secondary schools, whereas the latter embraces expenditures and receipts for all educational institutions and undertakings supported in part or whole by public taxation. This distinction, however, is hard to follow since in some places these areas overlap or fuse. One of the remaining forms of American public education not yet treated from the fiscal viewpoint in this volume is that of publicly supported higher education.

PUBLICLY SUPPORTED HIGHER EDUCATION

Public elementary and secondary schools receive more tax dollars than do public institutions of higher learning. The operating or current educational expenditures for *all* institutions of higher education total approximately two billion dollars a year.

The President's Commission on Higher Education grouped the sources of income available for the financing of current educational expenditures under four main headings: (1) philanthropy or private sources, (2) student fees, (3) public sources or government appropriations, and (4) miscellaneous, including receipts from sales and services of organized institutional activities. Obviously, publicly controlled institutions of higher learning receive less from philanthropy, less from student fees, and more from public sources than do the private colleges and universities.

The state is the chief provider of income both for teacher-educating institutions and for other public higher education. The next source of income is institutional, such as tuition, fees, and sales. The state leads in the support of teacher education and other higher education; the local districts rank first in the support of elementary and secondary education. The branch of higher learning receiving the largest share of county assistance is the gradually disappearing county normal school, whereas the junior college and the municipal university are the usual recipients of local tax support on the higher level. Local, state, and federal support of public higher education will undoubtedly increase as a result of larger enrollments, the prolongation of secondary education, and the development of various phases of public adult education.

In its forward look, the President's Commission on Higher Education optimistically overestimated the enrollment of students in colleges and universities. To help meet the proposed expenditures the Commission recommended three types of federal aid to higher education: (1) for current educational expenditures by publicly controlled institutions, (2) for capital outlay by publicly controlled colleges and universities, and (3) for a national program of scholarships to be administered by the states in accordance with general standards established by the federal government.

The later Commission on Financing Higher Education reached the unanimous conclusion that the "nation should call a halt at this time to the introduction of new programs of direct federal aid to colleges and universities," and deemed it "undesirable for the government to expand the scope of its scholarship aid to individual students." [6]

---

[6] Commission on Financing Higher Education, *Nature and Needs of Higher Education*, pp. 157–158, Columbia University Press, 1952.

OTHER PUBLICLY SUPPORTED EDUCATION

Federal Projects. Other publicly supported educational projects of nation-wide and world-wide significance are the various national surveys authorized by Congress and the promotion of democratic educational systems in Germany, Austria, and Japan. Congressional grants have financed such outstanding surveys as those of secondary education, teacher education, school finance, higher education, and Negro education. Through such agencies as the War and State Departments, many educational experts from the United States have served as consultants in occupied areas, and many teachers, students, and other educational personnel from foreign countries have visited and studied in the United States.

In addition the federal government has continued and expanded its regular activities to assist education. The most significant project has been the federal fiscal support of the G.I. bills, which have aided directly and indirectly many institutions of secondary and higher education. (See Unit I for further details on federal financing of public education.)

State Support. In the state of Wisconsin, for example, public educational finance embraces the following agencies which expend the indicated number of pennies and mills of each dollar received:

Purpose of expenditure	*Pennies and mills of each dollar for state education*
Public schools	72.4
University of Wisconsin	17.2
Stout Institute	0.4
State teachers colleges	2.9
Wisconsin Institute of Technology	0.05
Vocational and adult education	5.6
Department of Public Instruction	0.3
County rural normal schools	0.3
County school of agriculture and domestic economy	0.05
County superintendent and supervising teachers	0.5
State schools for deaf and blind	0.3
Total	100.00

This list of educational institutions and functions reveals that public-school expenditures constitute but one aspect of state disbursements for education. Every commonwealth provides funds from its treasury for one or more special projects in connection with the public schools, or as separate undertakings, such as the library (see Unit II).

Local Support. Local and intermediate school units, such as the county, township, and city school districts, sponsor many educational projects. The county pays most of the bills for the office of the county superintendent of schools, the county normal schools, county libraries, agricultural agents, and certain club activities like the 4-H (see Unit III).

Local and intermediate school units promote types of public education in addition to schooling for children. Among these activities are recreation and other phases of adult education, library and museum facilities, and special projects predicated on local needs, interests, and fiscal abilities (see Unit IV).

PRIVATELY FINANCED EDUCATION

In the early days of the United States most education was privately supported; even today a large share of the funds comes from private sources. American freedom involves the precious privilege of choice.

Choice presupposes diversity of things from which to choose. What most protects freedom of choice in America is the great diversity of its institutions, none of which possesses overriding power. This multiplicity of competing units prevents any single political party, institution of government, corporation, labor union, church, or university from dictating what all men shall do or think. Human beings and their institutions being what they are, total power is not safe in the hands of any single group no matter how well-intentioned.[7]

Liberty in learning is buttressed by a variety of educational institutions.

PRIVATELY SUPPORTED HIGHER EDUCATION

This diversity in structure, control, and support is especially prevalent in higher education. Private sponsorship often is religious in character. According to the findings of the Commission on Financing Higher Education, which published a series of reports in 1952, private institutions obtain their largest single source of income from student fees, the proportion being lower at the universities and professional schools because of the sizable amounts received from the federal government for research services. Private benefactions include gifts from alumni, friends, foundations, corporations, and others. Interest from endowments accounts for more than 10 per cent of the income for institutions of higher learning other than junior colleges.[8] A few private colleges receive aid from state and local governments.

OTHER PRIVATELY FINANCED EDUCATION

Secondary, elementary, and pre-elementary education is widely supported by private and church-related agencies. For example, denominational high schools enroll one of every 10 secondary students. More than three million children are in Roman Catholic elementary schools, and

7 *Ibid.*, p. 31.
8 *Ibid.*, pp. 120–121.

the number and proportion are increasing. The schools for these children are supported in large measure by tuition and the sponsoring church or private corporation. These independent institutions are largely dependent upon voluntary giving. Much adult education is financed privately. The Ford Foundation has channeled through the Fund for Adult Education substantial sums for research and pilot projects. Privately financed education is a *sine qua non* in the United States.

Conclusion. A national inventory of school expenditures was appropriately captioned *Unfinished Business in American Education.* "Still Unfinished Educational Obligations" can be the title and challenge of many supplementary reports. Another survey has been captioned caustically and realistically *Our Children Are Cheated.* Some of the failings of American schools can be remedied only by spending more money: "The soil in which education grows in one half of the communities of America is too poor." It is therefore advocated that more fiscal fertilizer be added to enrich the educational soil, especially in barren areas.

SUGGESTED ACTIVITIES

1. Define and illustrate the terms: equalization fund, foundation program, tax delinquency, public hearing, school bonds, unit costs, school audit, tax rate limitations, personal property tax, fiscal year, and fiscal independence.

2. Make a list of some educational inequalities in your state.

3. Defend or criticize the proposition: "Collect the money where it is and spend it where the pupils are."

4. Examine a school budget and evaluate its format and content.

5. Analyze an annual financial report of a school district.

6. Attend a public hearing on a school budget.

7. Find out how much it costs per year for current expenses to educate a pupil in the public schools of your state.

8. Find out the costs per student for current expenses in the institution that you are now attending.

9. Draw a large circle to represent a dollar. Divide it in segments to show where the school dollar goes in your district or state.

10. Draw a large circle to represent a dollar. Divide it in segments to show where the school dollar comes from in your district or state.

11. If the assessed valuation of a school district is $2,000,000, and the local board of education decides upon a tax rate of $1 per hundred, how much tax money can be levied from this source? If the percentage of tax delinquency is 20 per cent, how much tax money can be collected from this source?

12. Change the following tax rates into mills per dollar:
   $1.00 per $100 assessed valuation
   $23.10 per $1,000 assessed valuation
   $0.012 per $1.00 assessed valuation

13. Trace the history of school support in your state.

14. Analyze the program of state aid to schools in your state. Evaluate its strong and weak points.

15. Learn how your state institutions of higher learning are supported.

16. Trace the history of federal grants to education.

DESCRIPTIVE BIBLIOGRAPHY AND AIDS

BOOKS

ALLEN, H. K., and RICHARD G. AXT: *State Public Finance and State Institutions of Higher Education in the United States,* Chap. II, Columbia University Press, 1952.
Educational and general income of state institutions, as reported by the Commission on Financing Higher Education.

AMERICAN ASSOCIATION OF SCHOOL ADMINISTRATORS: *Public Relations for American Schools,* Chap. X, National Education Association, 1950.
School finance in public relations.

BURKE, ARVID J.: *Financing Public Schools in the United States,* Chap. XX, Harper, 1951.
Accounts, audits, and reports in financial management.

BUTTERWORTH, JULIAN E., and HOWARD A. DAWSON: *The Modern Rural School,* Chap. XXV, McGraw-Hill, 1952.
Financing rural schools.

COOPER, SHIRLEY, and CHARLES O. FITZWATER: *County School Administration,* Chap. XVI, Harper, 1954.
School business management in county and rural systems.

DE YOUNG, CHRIS A.: *Budgeting in Public Schools,* Chap. I, Swift, 1951.
The balanced budget—education, expenditures, receipts.

HECK, ARCH O.: *The Education of Exceptional Children,* 2d ed., Chap. XXX, McGraw-Hill, 1953.
Financing of special education.

HUTCHINS, CLAYTON D., and ALBERT R. MUNSE: *Expenditures for Education at Midcentury,* GPO, 1953, 134 pp.
Mid-century report prepared by the U.S. Office of Education in cooperation with the National Council of Chief State School Officers.

JOHNS, R. L., and E. L. MORPHET (ed.): *Problems and Issues in School Finance,* Chap. VIII, Teachers College, 1952.
Federal participation in education, as reported by John K. Norton and E. Edmund Reutter, Jr.

KATONA, GEORGE: *Psychological Analysis of Economic Behavior,* Chap. I, McGraw-Hill, 1951.
The need for psychology in economics.

KIRKENDALL, LESTER A., and FRANKLIN R. ZERAN: *Student Councils in Action,* Chap. VIII, Chartwell House, 1953.
Financing and evaluating problems in student-council work.

KNIGHT, EDGAR W., and CLIFTON L. HALL: *Readings in American Educational History,* Chap. V, Appleton-Century-Crofts, 1951.
Source readings on gaining public support and control for education.

MILLETT, JOHN D.: *Financing Higher Education in the United States,* Chap. XII, Columbia University Press, 1952.
College building needs and financing.

MORPHET, EDGAR L., and ERICK L. LINDMAN: *Public School Finance Programs of the Forty-eight States,* Chap. VI, GPO, 1950.
Working toward a better finance program—report of a cooperative study.

MORT, PAUL R., and WALTER C. REUSSER: *Public School Finance,* 2d ed., Chap. I, McGraw-Hill, 1951.
Development of educational finance and its principles.

NATIONAL COMMITTEE ON THE PREPARATION OF A MANUAL ON COLLEGE AND UNIVERSITY
BUSINESS ADMINISTRATION: *College and University Business Administration,* Chap. I,
American Council on Education, 1952.
Principles of college and university business administration.

REEDER, WARD G.: *School Boards and Superintendents,* Chap. IV, Macmillan, 1954.
Financial support of the schools.

SHEATS, PAUL H., CLARENCE D. JAYNE, and RALPH B. SPENCE: *Adult Education,* Chap.
XVIII, 1953.
Financing adult education.

SHEPARD, GEORGE E., and RICHARD E. JAMERSON: *Interscholastic Athletics,* Chap. IX,
McGraw-Hill, 1953.
Budgeting and financing athletic programs.

WELLS, HARRY L.: *Higher Education Is Serious Business,* Chap. XVI, Harper, 1953.
Budget preparation and control of finances in higher education.

CURRENT PERTINENT PERIODICALS AND PUBLICATIONS

American School Board Journal
Budgets of local schools
College Public Relations
Educational Research Service Circulars
Financial reports of local schools
Journal of Accounting
Nation's Schools
Office Executive
Office Management
Proceedings of educational organizations
Public Relations Ideas

Research Bulletin
Review of Educational Research
School Business Affairs
School Executive
School Life
School Management
State publications
Statistical Abstracts
Surveys, local and state educational
Taxes
Yearbooks of educational organizations

AUDIO-VISUAL AIDS

ACTION FOR YOUR PUBLIC SCHOOLS   20 min., sound
Excerpts from speeches made at a dinner sponsored by the National Citizens
Commission for the Public Schools. Among the speakers were James Bryant Conant,
General Omar Bradley, and Roy E. Larsen. Available from the Commission, 2 West
45th Street, New York 36.

EDUCATION IS GOOD BUSINESS   One reel, sound
Shows that more shoppers, more magazine readers, and better quality of living
are produced by better schools—the foundation of business. Produced by the U.S.
Chamber of Commerce, the National Education Association, and the Iowa State
Education Association.

Exhibit of Annual Fiscal Reports
Make a collection of annual fiscal reports from local and state school systems
for display and study. These reports include budgets, annual financial reports,
and school audits.

Exhibit of Financial Accounting Forms
Collect from the state department of education and from county and local
superintendents of schools various financial accounting forms, including those
for cocurricular activities.

FEDERAL AID   Filmstrip, 57 frames

The case for federal aid is graphically presented in this filmstrip, which is available with 32-page lecture notes from the National Education Association, Washington, D.C.

THE FIGHT FOR BETTER SCHOOLS   18 min., 16 and 35 mm., sound

This film is based on the premise that, because public schools are the heart of democracy, people must work—and fight, if need be—for better schools. The story of how a county (Arlington, Va.), a state (Arkansas), and an organization (the National Citizens Commission for the Public Schools) work for better financial support for public education. Available from March of Time, New York.

Filmstrips

Several state departments and state educational associations have prepared filmstrips that reveal problems in the financing of public education.

Movie Trailers   35 mm.

Each year the National Education Association prepares for use in local theaters a short movie trailer dealing with education and American Education Week. Available from National Education Association, Washington, D.C.

Scrapbook of Newspaper Clippings

The students and instructor can prepare a scrapbook of newspaper clippings dealing with various aspects of public taxation and school support in their community or state.

Part V

INTERPRETATION OF EDUCATION

Preview of Part V

INTERPRETATION OF EDUCATION

Public School Segregation Illegal, High Court Decides

Taxpayers Group Opposes Federal Aid to Education

EDUCATIONAL TV IS A HIT ON COAST

Pioneer Los Angeles Station Has a Growing Audience After First Six Months

Public Apathy Is Greatest Enemy To U. S. Schools

Supreme Court Follows Up Ruling On Segregation

WASHINGTON, D. C. —(P)—

Teaching Facts About 'Isms' In Schools Favored

Majority Favor Lowering Voting Age to 18 Years

SUMMER FOR PLAY, EDUCATOR INSISTS

Dr. Gans Would Jail Teachers or Parents Who Make Junior Study in Vacation Time

Says Teachers Haven't Right To Strike

Forestall Attacks

What's Ahead for Educational Television?

TEXTBOOK CENSORS ALARM EDUCATORS

Groups Charging Subversion Put Pressure on Schools and

U. S. LOSING WAR ON TEEN CRIME, SAYS KEFAUVER

Educator Raps Subsidization of Athletes

Are Schools Too Expensive?

National Board Pro and Con

Help Public Decide Critical Needs

Jersey Supreme Court Bars King James Bible in Schools

The Fight Over "Common Learnings"

IN DEFENSE OF THE CRITICS OF AMERICAN PUBLIC EDUCATION

Academic Freedom and Academic Responsibility

Teacher Shortage

The Tug of War For Money for Schools

Educators Weigh Public School Critics; Provide "Ammunition" Against Attacks

Have We Failed To Educate For Democracy?

FIG. 17-1. Some of the many controversial issues. These clippings from newspapers and periodicals indicate the wide range of debatable issues in American education. They give printed evidence that education is not a mysterious cloak under which perplexing problems are hidden from the public. These headings and subcaptions, which in themselves constitute challenges to critical thinking, are positive proof of the freedom of the press—a feature of American democracy that is not found in press-curbing, mind-closing dictatorships.

Part V

INTERPRETATION OF EDUCATION

Fig. 17-2. Forum discussions on controversial issues. There are many controversial issues that need to be discussed, especially by young people who contemplate entering the teaching profession. Forums and panel discussions promote freedom of speech. (*Courtesy of School Life.*)

ISSUES AND TRENDS IN AMERICAN PUBLIC EDUCATION

This concluding unit deals with some of the issues and trends in American public education. They are organized under the four major topics used in this volume: (1) organization and administration, (2) areas of public education, (3) personnel, and (4) provisions for educational materials and environment. The issues presented are challenges to thoughtful study. A discussion of them, either in the classroom or elsewhere, invokes that fundamental principle of civil liberties which Voltaire expressed succinctly in the words: "I disapprove of what you say, but I will defend to the death your right to say it."

Coupled with a discussion of issues is a presentation of some educational trends. One of course sees and hears readily the visible and noisy surface movements; he must dip deep below to find and feel the silent and basic undercurrents.

This unit serves as a review or overview of the 16 phases of education discussed in the preceding units. This synthesis helps to bind the significant components into a dynamic whole—American public education.

OUTLINE OF CONTENTS

Introduction
  Issues in public education
  Trends in public education
  Role of discussion in education
Organization and Administration of Public Education
  National program of education
  State systems of education
  County and intermediate school units
  Local school districts
Areas of Public Education
  Pre-elementary education
  Elementary education
  Secondary education
  Higher education
  Education for out-of-school youth and adults
Personnel in Public Education
  Pupils
  Teachers
  Other personnel
Provisions for Educational Materials and Environment
  Curriculum
  Cocurricular activities
  Educational supplies, equipment, and buildings
  Financing of public education
Conclusion

ISSUES AND TRENDS IN AMERICAN PUBLIC EDUCATION

A teacher had given her pupils the assignment of writing an example of a complete sentence. After the work had progressed for a while she looked over the shoulder of one of the boys and said, "Jimmie, that's a good sentence, but where is the period?" Jimmie replied, "Oh, that's still in the pencil." Many trends in American public education are still in the pencil—they cannot be written with a period as "finis." As long as education is an evolving, growing organism, it will have a future tense. This means it will be characterized by uncertainty, constant flux, and innumerable controversial issues. As stated by Paul Woodring in *Let's Talk Sense about Our Schools,* "Never before in our history has there been such widespread discussion of public education as today." The bicentennial keynote of Columbia University was aptly chosen, "Man's right to knowledge and the free use thereof."

Issues in Public Education. In this concluding unit, almost a hundred debatable issues are stated briefly; a few are examined in detail. Some of the questions are persistent and hackneyed, whereas others are temporary and recent. Some are circular in that they return to their starting point. Many of the issues are linked with collateral problems of daily living. Some are residues of a hoary past, some are born of the present, and some are "embryonic of the future." Fortunately public education is anchored in the history of American civilization and at any given moment operates within the accumulated heritage of that civilization. Much of this volume has been devoted to the historical background and gradual evolution of American public education. This concluding unit enumerates many issues that have existed, but it especially stresses current problems.

Obviously, owing to limitations of space, only a few pertinent issues can be presented in some detail. Consequently this unit leaves many fundamental questions in education wholly or partially unanswered. In a period of national and international flux, it is suicidal to develop a positive sense of finality in educational matters. For some problems there is no hope of ultimate solution. For many issues there are no uniform answers. Furthermore, the solution to a problem is likely to produce a further need—for example, the development of the junior high school settled many problems but also created others. The task of education is unending; hence there can be no surcease in the striving for perfection. The process of public education can be interrupted but not terminated.

Trends in Public Education. Many issues are associated with forward movements and educational trends. Since it is difficult to separate issues

and trends, both are presented here in close juxtaposition for each of the
16 phases of education. Each issue is followed by an abbreviated summary
of a current trend appertaining to the stated problem. Many trends appear distinctly near at hand; others are only vaguely discernible on the
horizon, like distant frontiers, unknown and unexplored. Some are like
near-by weather vanes, indicating the direction the wind is blowing at a
particular time. Some are like uncertain soil upon which one would pitch
a movable tent but not erect a permanent educational structure. Some are
like tested rock, which a nation might well use in building its educational
edifice. Some trends are like insidious termites, seemingly insignificant,
but destructive to the foundations of American democracy. Some of the
desirable trends are like weak children who must be nursed to strength
if they are to be powerful factors in American education and democracy.
Some are like healthy working citizens who symbolize strength and reveal
the higher characteristics of American idealism.

Role of Discussion in Education.[1] Before presenting some basic issues
and trends in education, it is pertinent to explore briefly the role of discussion, especially in education.

> Discussion should be one of the most important things in the world, for it is
> almost our only arena of thinking. It is here that all the jumble of ideas and im-
> pressions that we get from reading and watching are dramatically placed in con-
> flict. Here only is there a genuine challenge to put them into some sort of order.
> Without discussion intellectual experience is only an exercise in a private
> gymnasium.[2]

The group adventure of planned mental exploration can cover a wide
spectrum of ideas in education.

Every issue has at least two sides. Many problems are like the two-
edged sword. For example, the beam from a cyclotron can make pluto-
nium for the destructive atom bomb, as well as isotopes for cancer treatment. Many issues have more than two sides—they are multifaceted.
Often the consideration of a problem is comparable to tossing a cube up
into the air and letting it fall at random with this or that facet visible for
review. And then it is tossed up again and another phase is exposed.
Many problems have a fulcrum on which the issues seesaw back and forth.
A shift of emphasis or a changed position may continue the alternating
seesaw of thoughts. One must discuss controversial issues with what Cole-
ridge called "that willing suspension of disbelief." An open mind of
course is not synonymous with an empty mind. The ultimate aim in a

[1] Also see later in this unit, under Curriculum, the issue "Shall Controversial Subjects
Be Discussed in the Schools?"

[2] Randolph Bourne, "Arena of Thinking," *Adult Education Journal*, April, 1945,
p. 62.

discussion of educational problems is to elevate the participants to finer and higher planes of thinking, decision, and living.

ORGANIZATION AND ADMINISTRATION OF PUBLIC EDUCATION

NATIONAL PROGRAM OF EDUCATION

1. *Shall Federal Aid Be Granted to Education?* That is, shall the central government give money for general education?

Pro. For years the need for and advantages of federal aid to education have been weighed against the dangers and disadvantages. Marshaled for federal support are many politically prominent men and professionally eminent educators. Terse summaries of their arguments are these:

Many millions of school children in educational slum areas of the United States are not receiving a good education. A minimum level or fiscal floor under education is essential for all people, if the federal government is to operate for the greatest good of the greatest number. The mobility of population in an auto and air age seriously affects the education of at least one million migrant children. Teachers' salaries are low, and hence the shortage of teachers is great. The increased rate of pupil population far exceeds the building rate for schoolhouses. Many children attend substandard school buildings. Huge differences exist between communities and states in their ability to support adequate educational programs. Many areas with the greatest need have made the greatest effort, or at least a reasonable one, to provide suitable education. As indicated by the United States Chamber of Commerce in its historic study, *Education, An Investment in People,* education tends to expand and upgrade consumer demands. In fact, education, income, and volume of business tend to spiral up or down together. In fine, fiscal malnutrition in education affects the health of the national economy. Education is the most important business in the United States.

Con. Typical of opposing opinions held by many distinguished men and women are the following:

Past experience with such funds, as Smith-Hughes aid to agriculture and home economics, have demonstrated that a measurable degree of policy-making and program-planning responsibility has been surrendered to federal officials. Federal aid to education means federal control. The United States Constitution does not mention "schools" or "education," hence the support of education is a state and local responsibility. The federal government, which engaged in deficit spending for at least two decades, does not have the funds. States, with balanced budgets, are better able to finance education than is the federal government. States and local communities are closer to the need. Also, they are better watchdogs of the treasury than is faraway Washington, D.C. Looking to the nation's capitol for federal handouts is weakening the initiative and integrity of the people. Federal aid will accelerate the centralization of education. Education must remain "grass roots" in program and support.

Related Issues. This broad question, however, must be subdivided into several related issues, only three of which are discussed here, *viz.,* (1) Will federal control accompany federal aid? (2) Shall federal aid be granted to all states? (3) Shall such aid be given to all schools?

(1) *Will federal control accompany federal aid?* Will such aid result in a federal school system? Will it mean prescription from Washington and a leveling conformity to national standards?

Of course, there must be some federal control of expenditures. If the money is spent for a particular purpose, such as equalizing educational opportunity, then the United States will see that the provisions of the law are met. The central government has a definite obligation to specify accounting classifications and to audit accounts. Since most people believe in at least the minimum requirements and safeguards, this form of control need not be objectionable. However, the Hoover Commission on the Organization of the Executive Branch of the Government stated: "Grants-in-aid programs have removed large areas of discretionary power from the hands of state officials and have transferred a measurable degree of policy-making and ultimate responsibility and control for public services to the national government." Such federal interference with the control of state and local education need not necessarily accompany national aid. Most proposals for federal aid to education are based on the theory of contributing to the states in order to enable them to improve and more efficiently operate their educational systems.

(2) *Shall federal aid be granted to all states?* Here again there are two schools of thought. One, which carries with it a measure of political expediency, advocates flat grants for every state. The other point of view is represented by President Dwight D. Eisenhower, who favors help for poorer sections but opposes a general over-all program of assistance to all the states. In view of the mounting federal expenditures and the danger of growth in federal paternalism, giving aid only to the needy states that make a commendable effort of their own is in line with the minimum effort of placing a federal floor under education. Too often federal aid is merely a process of redistributing taxes that the central government has collected from local sources. This problem is related to the ones involved in separating sources of revenue for local, state, and national governments.

(3) *Shall federal aid be granted to all schools?* Shall colleges receive aid? Shall private and sectarian schools and colleges benefit from federal funds? The President's Commission on Higher Education recommended aid to higher institutions, but the later Commission on Financing Higher Education opposed unanimously the expansion of federal aid to colleges and universities at this time.

Illustrative of the thinking on aid to sectarian schools are three types of bills proposed in Congress. One expressly forbids federal funds to be expended for private or parochial schools. Another seeks to straddle the state-church controversy by granting funds for such general purposes as improving the health of all children. Still another passes the responsibility to the state governments. In approximately half the states, some of the state or local school funds are being used to provide transportation, books, or tuition for children attending private or parochial schools. If such federal legislation were passed, it would temporarily transfer a difficult decision to the states, for the issue would return to Washington to the bench of the United States Sureme Court. In the past the Supreme Court has held that state and local aid is for the *child* and not the *school*. The issue of federal funds for private and sectarian schools has not as yet been settled by Congress. What the ultimate answer will be is a matter of speculation. It has been suggested that the matter might be handled by means of an amendment to the federal Constitution.

Conclusion. The majority of people, as shown in various studies and polls, approve of the "principle" of federal aid to education. The difficulties, as usual, come in the application of this principle. Countless proposals and counterpropositions have been made for implementation. The following are a few concluding statements:

Federal funds are now being given for so many different forms of education, and on so many different bases, and so many new requests are constantly being made that a Presidential Commission on Educational Finance on a permanent basis is desirable. In other words, government funds should be available for a continuing study of finances for education. Any and all such programs should be projected on the triangular bases of (1) educational purposes, (2) estimated expenditures, and (3) proposals for revenue. This calls for broad-gauge and long-range planning. Federal grants ought to be made to public elementary and secondary schools, especially in needy areas which make a real effort to provide education.

The President's Commission on Higher Education has recommended a program of scholarships and fellowships to be administered by the states and to be made available for undergraduate, graduate, and professional students. Scholarships, somewhat similar to the old NYA aid, have been suggested also for secondary youth. These grants would be made directly to individuals who would be free to attend either privately or publicly controlled institutions that meet acceptable standards. These funds would help educational institutions indirectly and avoid the questionable policy of granting public funds to private schools and colleges. The Commission on Financing Higher Education deemed it "undesirable for the government to expand the scope of its scholarship aid to individual students."

Federal support may well be granted for adult education. The funds, if assigned to the states and counties for over-all planning, would not violate the principle of separation of church and state on a federal level.

Another purpose for which federal funds could be granted is the improvement of teacher education and the reduction of the shortage of teachers. The United States Office of Education and state departments may well strengthen their work in this field.

In view of the great need for educational buildings, federal funds have been granted outright to state and local governments for making surveys of needs, and planning public works, including school buildings. Many school districts, federally affected with increased enrollments, are receiving federal grants for current and capital expenditures. The President's Commission on Higher Education proposed that capital outlay expenditures be approved for public institutions of higher learning.

Educational experimentation needs federal financing. Pilot experiments with curriculums can produce educational energy and cause chain reactions in local schools.

Direct aid in material rather than cash can continue to be given through army–navy–air force donations of surplus property to educational institutions. The Department of Agriculture has donated many supplies to the school lunch program.

Federal funds are provided to educational institutions indirectly through the general practice of tax exemption, which, within reasonable limits, is just and wise.

When and if federal aid is granted to the schools, the formula by which it is distributed should not be so complicated that only the financial experts and God understand it!

2. *Shall There Be a Minimum, Basic Program of Education for the Nation as a Whole?* Just as several states have prepared a foundation program for the schools within their boundaries, so too the United States as a unit should set up minimum standards to be met by all schools of the nation. The Educational Policies Commission has outlined the kind and amount of education that would increase the positive economic effects of education. This program calls for lifting the poorest schools to a minimum of efficiency.

3. *Shall There Be a National Board of Education Comparable to a Local Board of Education?* That is, shall there be a national board of education, which shall determine nation-wide policies and evaluate practices in education?

At present no such national board really functions for all education. It has been argued that a competent commission, selecting the United States Commissioner of Education as its own executive without reference to party politics, would follow the American tradition of acknowledging the function of education in American democracy and of separating its leadership and administration from other governmental functions. There are some educational organizations which have officially recommended the establishment of the United States Office of Education as an independent, adequately financed agency, directed by a national board of education, appointed by the President with the consent of the Senate. Mrs. Oveta Culp Hobby recommended and Congress approved the appointment of nine persons to a National Advisory Committee on Education. The function of this small committee is to counsel the Secretary of Health, Education, and Welfare. This is not the equivalent of a national board of education, which the NEA and many others have consistently recommended for years (see Fig. 1-1). The creation of a national board of outstanding citizens could do much to provide lay leadership in education. A small board of education serving on the national basis seems as desirable as the state, county, and local boards.

4. *What Is the Role of Private Institutions in the National Program of Education?* In this volume extreme caution has been used in avoiding the term "federal system." The first unit is entitled "National Program of Education." In this nation-wide program in the United States, private schools do and should play a conspicuous role, although the public schools predominate on the elementary and secondary levels. The public schools have helped to accent the homogeneity of American education. The private schools stress this too, but they contribute especially a wholesome heterogeneity.

Especially important is the role of independent institutions in higher education:

There are weighty reasons why higher education should not follow the example of primary and secondary education which is predominately under public control. By its very nature higher education cannot be universal. . . . The vigor of higher education depends upon its being free. Higher education is exploratory in nature. . . . Monopoly of control is incompatible with the free market of ideas. . . . The two systems of control, public and private, are a challenge to each other. Our society would be impoverished by the decline in vigor of either kind.[3]

The United States is the only nation in the world which has this dual system of higher education. It is indeed a heritage to be preserved.

STATE SYSTEMS OF EDUCATION

1. *Shall the Individual States, Rather than the Federal Government, Be Primarily Responsible for Public Education?*

Pro. That the states are in their own areas the legitimate units of educational control seems to be manifest for several reasons, as reported in

[3] Commission on Financing Higher Education, *Nature and Needs of Higher Education*, pp. 41–42, Columbia University Press, 1952.

such studies as *Responsibility of the States in Education—the Fourth R*, by the Chamber of Commerce of the United States, and *The Forty-eight State School Systems*, a research project of the Council of State Governments. According to the latter:

> State responsibility for education is firmly embedded in the constitutions of the several states and buttressed by tradition and court decisions. This responsibility of the governments of the several states for the education of their citizens is much more than a theory or a tradition or a legal convention. An examination of the efforts of the states to strengthen their public school systems indicates that it is a living principle guiding the recommendations and actions of governors and legislatures in each of the forty-eight states.[4]

The debates of the constitutional conventions in the various states reveal that a great majority of the delegates felt that it was the duty of the state to establish and maintain a system of public education for the purpose of educating its citizens. The states are the generally accepted legislative units for public education, whereas the contained areas—district, town, city, township, community, and county—are the units to which much administration has been delegated.

Con. In this general issue of federal power vs. decentralization, numerous arguments are advanced for the extension of federal control. Some authorities state that federal expansion is inescapable. The load of taxation has tended to shift to the federal government, indicating federal responsibility. In the report *Federal-State Relations in Education*, issued by the American Council on Education and the Educational Policies Commission, the writers frankly stated:

> The factor which above all others has pushed us toward federal control of education in recent times is the fact that present facilities for the financial support of education in a considerable number of states and localities are so meager that the basic job of providing educational opportunity for all has not been performed. Educational shortages revealed in illiteracy, in physical deficiency, and failure adequately to provide for children and youth in many ways, rise to plague us in times of crisis. Congress responds with hasty, indirect, and expensive educational legislation in futile attempts to make up for past shortcomings. This process has resulted in a rising tide of federal controls over education. It can continue to do so in the future until education becomes largely federalized.[5]

Advocates of more federal control cite the tremendous advance in vocational education as evidence that nationally financed and sponsored projects mean advancement. Many persons are of the opinion that education in America is too decentralized and that a strong central system such as is

[4] Council of State Governments, *The Forty-eight State School Systems*, p. 4, 1949.

[5] Educational Policies Commission, and Problems and Policies Commission, *Federal-State Relations in Education*, p. 46, National Education Association, 1945.

found in some foreign countries would help to accelerate progress, especially in educational slum areas. Furthermore, the federal government could enforce uniform accounting for all schools and stipulate other minimal standards.

Trend. Despite the temporary drift toward federal centralization during and following the Second World War, the long-term trend is toward continuance in the path of states' rights as begun by the Tenth Amendment to the Constitution of the United States. The federal government, however, under the preamble of the Constitution, has the right to direct and stimulate education as a means of promoting the general welfare. President Eisenhower has aptly said: "The control and direction of public education is a state and local responsibility. However, the federal government should stand ready to assist states which demonstrably cannot provide sufficient school buildings." During the early years of grants to education there was little or no attempt on the part of the United States to control or administer the schools. Starting with the First Morrill Act in 1862, the national government commenced to exercise some degree of control through the allocation of funds for certain phases of education. An excessive amount of federal authority has been exercised over many aspects of vocational education. Bills for providing federal aid have definitely stipulated that education shall not be controlled by the United States government.

2. *Shall the States, Rather than the Local Communities, Be Primarily Responsible for the Ultimate Control of Public Education?* In colonial days the local communities held the primary responsibility for and control over the schools. Later the states regained some of the powers that had been delegated to the local school districts. This reversal of policy indicates a trend toward state centralization, which may soon reach a limit.

School districts, more than any other form of government, are of direct interest to the local community; therefore the administration of the schools should be kept close to the people. Too much authority over education is being centralized in the governor as the state's supreme executive officer. In certain essentials the state board of education should be in control. For example, the state may well prescribe a uniform budgeting and accounting system for schools. A state may well recommend a foundation program, but the specifics should be applied by the local school district. The major problem confronting the American people is not to decide at which level of government the major responsibility shall be fixed, but to study educational needs and determine which level of government, local, county, state, or national, can best carry on particular functions. Differentiated responsibility need not cause competition; it should make for integration of the component parts.

3. Shall the State Assume Greater Responsibility in the Support of Public Education? Shall the state as a central agency increase its appropriations for public education? The trend, as evidenced by statistics, is toward decreasing the amount of local support and increasing state support. This, of course, is linked with equitable distribution, discussed later.

4. Shall a State Board of Education Exercise Some Control and Supervision over the Elementary and Secondary Schools of the State? A state board of education is needed to act as the chief authority in school matters. Nearly all the states have established such a board. It is hoped that the remaining few will soon do likewise.

5. Shall the State Superintendent of Public Instruction Be Elected Rather than Appointed? Shall he "run" for office or shall the office seek him? The trend is toward appointing state superintendents. The choice may be made by the governor or preferably by the state board of education. This method is slowly gaining acceptance. Just as the popular election of city school superintendents has become obsolete, so too the election of county and state superintendents will give way to appointment.

County and Intermediate School Units

1. What Are the Major Differences between County and Intermediate Units? The essential differences between these two major types of organization for educational administration are succinctly summarized by Julian E. Butterworth and Howard A. Dawson in *The Modern Rural School.* Excerpts follow:

County-unit Organization

1. Within the county unit there are no subordinate districts. There may, however, be local district committees or local trustees. . . .

2. The area included is usually the political county, but it may include two or more counties. . . .

3. There is one superintendent for the entire district, but most local schools have a principal or head teacher responsible to the county board of education through the county superintendent. . . .

4. The county superintendent has such assistant superintendents, directors, supervisors, and special teachers attached to his office as his board allows him. . . .

Intermediate-unit Organization

1. The intermediate unit is composed of a number of smaller districts, each with its own board of education or trustee. . . .

2. The present types are usually coterminous with the political county but need not be. . . .

3. Each local district, except one-teacher and other small districts, has a superintendent (or principal) who is the executive officer of the board and responsible to it. . . .

4. The superintendent of the district has such assistants as may be allowed him. . . . Except as the law or agreements among local boards give them authority, they act cooperatively with local officials.

County-unit Organization	*Intermediate-unit Organization*
5. The county is the local taxing authority for schools. It receives state aid and uses all its funds for maintaining all the schools of the county.	5. In many states . . . the intermediate district may levy taxes to assist the constituent districts. State aid for the constituent districts may be given directly to them, or to the intermediate district for allocation. . . .
6. Because the county unit constitutes a single system of schools, there should, theoretically at least, be no significant differences among the several attendance areas in the scope and quality of education. . . .	6. Since each constituent district levies its own taxes, some districts are likely to maintain a better program than others in the same intermediate districts. This may be a stimulating influence on all constitutent districts.[6]

Between these two patterns is a continuing conflict in theory and practice. Each has its advantages and disadvantages. Each can thrive in a propitious place and cordial climate of cooperation. History and research will be the judge and jury to decide the individual cases.

2. *Whose Responsibility Is It to Transport Pupils to School?* Specifically, in consolidated school districts who shall pay the costs for bringing pupils to school daily?

The magnitude of the school transportation problem is revealed in the fact that several million students are carried daily. The cost of transporting these pupils, once borne by parents, is now paid in whole or in part by the local school district or state. An increasing portion is being defrayed by the state. Eventually federal aid may be given for equalizing educational opportunity through paying part of the cost of bringing pupils to school.

3. *How Can Adequate Professional Supervision Be Obtained for Developing Satisfactory Programs of Instruction in Rural Schools?* State departments of education are expending more money than they did formerly to provide better supervision of rural schools. Furthermore, there is a trend toward a more creative type of self-supervision which permits greater participation of teachers in supervisory programs, curriculum building, and studies of child development.

4. *Shall the County Superintendent of Schools Be Appointed by a County Board of Education Rather than Elected by the People?* He ought to be given every opportunity to be a professional educator rather than a professional politician. Unfortunately, the states that do not have appointive county educational officers are very slow to accept this preferable method of obtaining educational leadership in the county.

[6] Julian E. Butterworth and Howard A. Dawson, *The Modern Rural School*, pp. 350–353, McGraw-Hill, 1952.

LOCAL SCHOOL DISTRICTS

1. *Shall the Controlling Educational Agency Be a Board of Public Education Rather than a School Board?* That is, shall the function of public education be expanded and coordinated under a board that shall have the oversight and direction of all education financed by and for the public, or shall the supervision of the local public-school system be the only task of the controlling board?

Pro. The liberal point of view in terms of philosophy of education and money is that the local body should be a board of public education, which embraces all aspects of learning for all individuals—children, youth, and adults. The pros say that schooling and education are not synonymous or coterminous. Hence a board of public education is to be charged with the conduct of all forms of education where this activity is not in direct conflict with statutes or laws to the contrary. If this philosophy were implemented with a program of action, it would call for additional thousands of educational workers and for increased expenditures for public education.

Con. The idea of a board of public education is opposed by many educators and laymen. The conservative point of view, particularly of the taxpayer who has to foot the bill for the expansion of public education, is that the local district is responsible for the minimal schooling of youth of elementary- and high-school age, from approximately six to sixteen years. It builds a high fence or wall around the schoolyard and makes the schools exist solely for young pupils. It means that collateral forms of education and recreation are a responsibility of the individual or city rather than a public cost chargeable to education.

Trend. The functions of American public education have expanded so that the local educational agency is becoming a board of public education in legal control not only of the local public schools but also of related public functions like social service. The preface for the yearbook *The Expanding Role of Education* states:

As we cross the threshold into a new world, there is more to do in education than any nation has yet seriously attempted. Education must reach more people; it must regularly include many areas of experience and types of services that now are found only "in the twilight zone" of accepted practice. Because the schools are social institutions, however, substantial progress toward these goals must rest on the sure foundation of public endorsement.[7]

Of course, practical limits are imposed by the fiscal resources available for financing all educational projects and by the community's willingness to centralize these projects under the board of public education. It is recom-

[7] American Association of School Administrators, *The Expanding Role of Education*, p. 6, National Education Association, 1948.

mended that the state legislatures pave the way for this expanded concept by legally designating the local governing body as the "board of public education." The abbreviated term "school board" is not in harmony with the enlarged horizons of American public education.

2. *How Shall the Board of Education Select the Superintendent of Schools?* The following are some of the recommended procedures in choosing the superintendent of schools: (1) Public announcement of a vacancy assures prospective candidates, as well as professional sources which may be asked for recommendations, that they act within the scope of professional ethics. (2) Personal standards and professional qualifications, tailor-made to fit the needs of the local school system and the local community, should be clearly listed. (3) After a preliminary list of candidates has been prepared, a few are selected for interview. (4) Sometimes the board or a group of representatives visits the home communities of the leading prospects. (5) Final responsibility for electing the superintendent resides in the full board alone. (6) Favorable and timely public announcement of the election smooths the way for the new appointee and makes for continued public confidence in the board.[8]

3. *Shall the Board of Education Establish Single Rather than Dual or Multiple Control of the Internal Organization of the Schools?* Shall the superintendent be the sole executive, or shall a business manager or attorney be appointed by the board with a status equal to that of the superintendent?

The single executive type of school administration is the desirable form, although the increased responsibilities of the city superintendent of schools demand that some duties be delegated to an assistant who may be in charge of instruction or of business affairs under the direction of the superintendent.

4. *Is the Administration of the Local Schools Democratic?* The administration of schools is becoming more democratic. In theory and practice the trend is toward a "declaration of interdependence" between members of the board of education, administrators, teachers, pupils, and laymen. Education for democratic living is a current watchword of the school.

AREAS OF PUBLIC EDUCATION

PRE-ELEMENTARY EDUCATION

1. *Shall Public Education Be Delimited to Schooling in Certain Areas, as Elementary and Secondary Levels, or Shall It Be Broadened and Lengthened to Embrace Lifelong Learning?* The three r's—reading, 'riting, and 'rithmetic—once served as a formula to designate the extent of

---

[8] American Association of School Administrators, *Choosing the Superintendent of Schools,* National Education Association, 1949, 12 pp. See also the National Education Association yearbook, *The American School Superintendency,* pp. 112–114, 1952.

one's schooling. Today the scope of one's education is more appropriately epitomized by the three l's—life-long learning. It has been said that man is a learning animal. It must be added that he learns as long as he lives, from the time he enters this world until he reaches the end of what Shakespeare called the "seventh age," that is, senescence. Recent investigations prove that learning is lifelong: it registers a child as he creeps upon the stage of life and graduates him as the curtain falls on the last act. In this continuous educational drama, one may play and work in at least five acts: pre-elementary, elementary, secondary, collegiate, and adult.

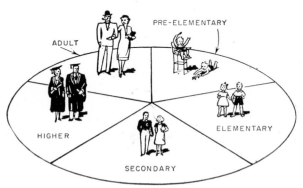

FIG. 17-3. Lifelong learning.

2. Shall the Various Organizational Levels of Education Be Articulated More Effectively? In 1899 John Dewey pointed out the waste in education due to the lack of coordination between the various periods or units that make up the public-school system of the United States. The main reason for this lack of articulation is that each unit of the school system originated under different conditions. The university started as a group of professional schools during the medieval period. The grammar school, which later became the academy and high school, was imported from England during the seventeenth century. The elementary or primary school arose in Europe out of a popular movement in the sixteenth century when it became necessary to know reading, writing, and arithmetic. The kindergarten came to America in the nineteenth century as an importation from Germany. Despite this dissimilarity in origin, the consecutive levels of education ought to be articulated closely into a unified whole.

3. At What Age Shall Free Public Education Begin? Specifically, shall early education be incorporated as part of the public-school system?

It is difficult to answer the question as to when American public education should begin. Very few public schools offer both a nursery school and a kindergarten. Many persons oppose early education for all children at public expense because of the additional taxes involved. Despite this objection, the American people are gradually accepting the theory that at least kindergartens may be included as a part of the public-school system. The American Federation of Labor, the National Congress of Parents and Teachers, the American Association of University Women, and other civic and professional organizations have lent their support to the movement for nursery and kindergarten schools. Most states have taken a generous attitude toward kindergarten support, but by and large few states and local communities have furnished nursery education.

ELEMENTARY EDUCATION

1. *Shall the Elementary School Be Characterized by So-called Progressive Education?* Shall it be child-centered or subject-centered?

Pro. Benjamin Fine of the *New York Times* has succinctly summarized the pro and con arguments on the issue of progressive education. Its proponents say:

1. Progressive education develops a richer curriculum than does the traditional school, and attracts a higher caliber of teacher.
2. Progressive education graduates have a high record of entrance to college and successful work after they have entered.
3. Progressive schools develop better relations among the children, teachers, and parents than do other schools.

Con. Three major arguments against progressive schools are:

1. The discipline of the child is neglected. Progressive schools turn out children who are rude and undisciplined, with little respect for authority.
2. The fundamental skills—reading, writing, and arithmetic—are slighted. Children in these schools are unable to read or write properly.
3. The curriculum is vague, indefinite, and flexible. Pupils don't get a course in history or geography, but something called "social studies." [9]

Trend. These arguments pro and con, plus many more, bring into rather sharp focus several important issues, particularly as they affect elementary education. The elementary school is and will be more progressive than the secondary school or the college. Elementary education has moved steadily toward an activity school. The main activity, of course, should be learning. Its aim is the "perfectibilian goal of the ideal man," who works at doing good, not merely being good. Progressivism is a characteristic that does not readily lend itself to statistical treatment, unless it be an enumeration of its millions of satisfied pupils. It has, of course, reaped

[9] Benjamin Fine, "Influence of the Progressive Schools Is Now Found throughout the Country," *The New York Times*, Mar. 14, 1954, p. E11.

many benefits from the helpful and pointed observations of its perennial critics, especially the so-called "essentialists."

In answer to the question, "Is progressive education obsolete?" Emeritus Professor Boyd H. Bode of Ohio State University has aptly written:

> If democracy is here to stay, then the spirit of progressive education can never become obsolete. We may discard the name and we may discontinue it as a separate organization, but we can never surrender the vision which it has tried to bring us of a new basis for peace on earth and good will among men.[10]

It is this progressive spirit of education which will continue to characterize much modern education, especially in the elementary school.[11]

2. *Shall the Elementary School Be Reorganized?* Today most elementary schools are reorganized rather than grades 1 through 8. The trend continues toward a rearrangement of the traditional eight elementary grades. At the lower end there is a dipping down into pre-elementary education. The upper grades are gradually being recast into some type of secondary unit, such as the junior high school. Unfortunately many so-called "junior high schools" are too dominated by the philosophy and program of elementary education.

3. *Shall Pupils Be Graduated from the Elementary School with Formal Exercises?* Or shall the emphasis be shifted to promotion to the next higher unit?

In theory the desirability of eliminating eighth-grade graduation exercises is being widely accepted. In practice, however, many communities still magnify the completion of eight grades of schooling. The trend is to eliminate formal *graduation* exercises and to substitute a *promotion* day when the emphasis is placed upon encouraging the pupils to enter the high school.

4. *Shall More Men Be Engaged as Teachers in the Elementary School?* Although women obviously make better teachers in the primary grades, additional men are needed in the intermediate and upper grades or junior high school. Too many youngsters attain adolescence without having had a male teacher. Except for emergency situations, such as a national defense program that draws upon the man power of the nation, the trend is to encourage more men to take the elementary education courses and to urge their employment by elementary-school systems.

SECONDARY EDUCATION

Although many issues and trends in the elementary field apply also to secondary education, the latter has its unique and distinctive problems.

[10] Boyd H. Bode, "Is Progressive Education Obsolete?" *School and Society,* November, 1947, p. 414.

[11] See also Carleton Washburne, *What Is Progressive Education?* Chap. X, Longmans, 1952.

Some issues in secondary education in turn extend into colleges and universities.

1. *How Can the Holding Power of Secondary Schools Be Increased?* Or conversely, how can dropouts be reduced?

Status. According to the late Frederick Lewis Allen in *The Big Change,* an important factor in changes in America from 1900 to 1950 has been the immense spread of secondary education. In 1900 less than one American boy or girl out of ten of high-school age was actually in high school; now over eight out of ten are.[12] Attendance in secondary schools has improved markedly in the first half of the twentieth century, but the second half of this century should see added achievements in attendance. Too many youth, especially boys, drop out of high school. National surveys indicate that out of every 1000 children in the fifth grade, only about 500 graduate from high school.

Shortcomings. If the philosophy is accepted that all youth who can benefit from secondary education should go to high school, then the shortcomings causing dropouts should be examined. National surveys such as those of the United States Office of Education, state surveys like that in Illinois, and countless local researches indicate many reasons why students leave high school voluntarily and involuntarily. Among them are these:

Lack of student motivation; parental indifference; teachers' insensitivity to basic needs of youth; red tape imposed by administrators; community callousness toward secondary education; illness of the student and/or relatives; competing opportunities for full-time employment; lure of car and cash; early marriage; voluntary or compulsory military service; inadequate mental ability to cope with existing curriculums; inability to adjust to high school; inadequate transportation facilities and long distances from home to school; limited fiscal resources of student, parent, or school district; poor school buildings; crowded conditions in schools; high hidden costs in so-called free education; unwillingness of some parents to sacrifice for their children; and unsatisfactory conditions of underprivileged youth and those in minority groups.

Suggestions. Gleaned from experience and from various sources are these suggestions for increasing the holding power of high schools:

Improvement of student motivation—the will to learn; sensitization of all—especially parents, teachers, and administrators—to the imperative needs of preadolescent, adolescent, and postadolescent youth; special education facilities for the physically handicapped; increase in part-time and summer employment opportunities; more liberal income-tax laws as to exemptions for students; postponement of military service until after graduation; more money for schools; improved bus and building facilities; scholarships for those in need and for superior students; better vocational and educational guidance; more vocational

---

[12] Frederick Lewis Allen, *The Big Change,* p. 222, Harper, 1952.

education; work programs; challenging extracurricular activities; involvement of students and parents in the school program; reduction of hidden costs; and adaptation of the secondary school to the needs of youth.

2. *What Is the Role of General Education in Secondary Education?* Specifically, how shall general education be organized and presented in high school?

Numerous proposals for general education on the secondary level have been made. One is tersely referred to here, *viz.*, the Harvard report *General Education in a Free Society.* At the center of their scheme for general education, both in high school and college, the Harvard committee placed three inevitable areas of man's life and knowledge: "the physical world, man's corporate life, his inner visions and standards." These three areas may be expressed as (1) natural science with mathematics, (2) social studies, and (3) humanities, respectively. Justification for this threefold division is found not only in the *content* of the areas but also in terms of their respective *methods* of knowledge. For example, the natural sciences "describe, analyze, and explain," while the humanities, consisting chiefly of English and the arts of music, drawing, painting, and modeling, "appraise, judge, and criticize." [13]

Other proposals have been made for the general education of youth, as for example, the plan of the Educational Policies Commission in *Education for All American Youth—A Further Look,* previously mentioned in Unit VII. I. L. Kandel compares and contrasts these two plans, and concludes: "As far as the function of secondary education is concerned, an examination of the facts revealed during the war justifies the conclusion that they point to the type of education advocated in the Harvard report rather than to that proposed by the Educational Policies Commission." [14] General education remains the most important area of learning in the secondary field. Patently it will ever be supplemented in the comprehensive high school by prevocational, vocational, and preprofessional work. Much experimentation is needed with many types of programs, and one or more may evolve that are superior to any yet proposed. The success of any plan "depends finally on the teacher's quality of mind and spirit."

3. *Is the Junior College Secondary or Higher Education?* Leonard V. Koos thus summarized a few of the many pros and cons of this issue:

Higher Education. The belief that the junior college is higher education finds its chief support in an important fact in the history of American education which is not common knowledge. Everyone knows that the preparatory offering of the

[13] Harvard Committee, *General Education in a Free Society,* Chap. IV, Harvard University Press, 1945.

[14] I. L. Kandel, *The Impact of the War upon American Education,* p. 122, University of North Carolina Press, 1948.

2-year junior college corresponds with the courses given in the first 2 years of colleges and universities, but too few are aware that this *content* was, in the main, inherited from the *upper* years of the college of a century ago. Even more to the point are the facts that the 4-year *junior college* now emerging on our educational scene coincides in age span of students with that of the *college* of a century or more ago. The curriculum of the modern 4-year junior college, like that of

FIG. 17-4. Shall more youth follow secondary or higher education via the junior-college route? (*Courtesy of Illinois School Board Journal.*)

the old college, consists in a composite of what we think of as high-school and college education. In those earlier days this limited college comprehended higher education in the United States. . . .

Secondary Education. Advocacy of the attitude of regarding the junior college as secondary education had its origin in comparisons of the American system, inclusive of the junior college, with the organization of continental European education. In Europe the secondary schools—for example, the *Gymnasium* in Germany and the *lycée* and *collège* in France—carry through the equivalent of our second college year. There higher education proper, as represented by the university, begins where the secondary school ends. . . .

The most cogent consideration in behalf of regarding the junior college as secondary education emerges from its expansion from a merely preparatory institution to one in which the educational level it represents becomes universalized. Something of this expansion is suggested in the wide scope of service urged for the junior college by the Educational Policies Commission of the National Education Association in its report, *Education for All American Youth*. . . . The full expansion of the junior college promises to be on a par with a prior universalization of the high-school level.

Conclusions. The gist of this review seems to be that both parties to the controversy are right. The advocates of regarding the junior college as higher education are right as to the *statics* of the junior college as an institution, which in its preparatory service reproduces the courses traditionally given in collegiate years. Whereas the advocates of regarding it as secondary education are right in respect to the *dynamics* of the institution, in some degree in a preparatory service to a rapidly expanding higher educational program but mainly in its progress toward a comprehensive democratic service.[15]

The author joins Koos in preferring the dynamic view of the junior college rising upward from the democratized lower school rather than the static view of one stemming from selective higher education downward.

HIGHER EDUCATION

1. *Shall Higher Education Be Characterized by More Intellectualism?* Shall higher education be dominated by the conservatists' emphasis upon "intellectualism" rather than by a progressive reliance upon an experimentalist theory of knowledge?

Pro. The outstanding exponent of intellectualism today is undoubtedly Robert M. Hutchins, former chancellor of the University of Chicago. In his lectures at Yale University, Hutchins deplored an "anti-intellectualism which denies, in effect, that man is a rational animal." More recently he attacked the elective system thus:

A university student in America may be able to elect almost any course he chooses; he takes examinations in each of these courses given by the teacher who taught it. . . . This means the wise student will study the professor rather than the subject. He will elect those courses which are the easiest, or which are offered at the most convenient times and places.[16]

I deplore the multiplication of trivial courses, in cosmetology, fishing and tap dancing, which swell the catalogues of great American universities and which have no purpose except to help the student while away four years without using his mind.[17]

---

[15] Leonard V. Koos, "Is the Junior College Secondary or Higher Education?" *Junior College Journal*, November, 1947, pp. 113–114.

[16] Robert M. Hutchins, *The Conflict in Education in a Democratic Society*, p. 60, Harper, 1953.

[17] *Ibid.*, p. 12.

Hutchins derides "the concept of the educational system as a gigantic play-pen in which the young are to amuse themselves. . . ." [18] He advocates discussion of the greatest books of the greatest writers.

Aligned with Hutchins are many mental giants of yesteryear like Plato, Aristotle, Saint Thomas Aquinas, and John Locke, as well as well-known educators of today like Mortimer Adler, Stringfellow Barr, and Arthur E. Bestor.

Con. Diametrically opposed to the conservative point of view of rationalism, as exemplified by the brief quotations from Dr. Hutchins, is the progressive philosophy of experimentalism as stated by the late John Dewey and interpreted by William Heard Kilpatrick. In his Kappa Delta Pi lectures Dewey reasserted his faith in education that is grounded upon a well-developed philosophy of experience:

> I assume that amid all uncertainties there is one permanent frame of reference: namely, the organic connection between education and personal experience, or, the new philosophy of education is committed to some kind of empirical and experimental philosophy. . . . The educational system must move one way or another, either backward to the intellectual and moral standards of prescientific age or forward to ever greater utilization of scientific method in the development of the possibilities of growing, expanding experience.[19]

Kilpatrick labels the type of education espoused by Hutchins as the old "Alexandrian" type:

> [The Hutchins-Adler school of thought disregarded the fact] that man is a behaving organism and that ideas are the basis of behavior, and if you want to build character you have to emphasize action and behavior.[20]

> The idea of taking Newton's *Principia,* which is about the first book of modern science, and using that as a text for learning modern science is ludicrous.[21]

To Kilpatrick such an education represents a "rejection of the intellectual advance of the last three hundred years." This progressive philosophy of experimentalism is preached by many educators as an antidote to Hutchins's Alexandrianism.

Trend. This conflict in pedagogy is age-old. It is a battle in theory more than in practice. The conflict will continue. On the battle scene now and then appear new protagonists with old and new word weapons, such as Arthur E. Bestor with his incisive *Educational Wastelands,* and Paul Woodring with his counterattack *Let's Talk Sense about Our*

---

[18] *Ibid.,* p. 93.

[19] John Dewey, *Experience and Education,* pp. 12–13, 113–114, Macmillan, 1938.

[20] William Heard Kilpatrick, *Philosophy of Education,* p. 224, Macmillan, 1951.

[21] Samuel Tenenbaum, *William Heard Kilpatrick, Trail Blazer in Education,* p. 282, Harper, 1951.

Schools. There will always be an unstable equilibrium, especially in higher education, caused by such recurrent questions as that regarding intellectualism. To education belongs the perennial task of preserving some degree of stability and yet admitting constant change. As is often the case, going too far in one direction causes a reaction of equal extent in the other. The Hutchins-Dewey controversy is a natural and necessary contention in theories, a bitter battle of books, and weary war with words. An armistice is unlikely. Skirmishes may be won now and then by either side but the war goes on. At present the experimentalists seem to be winning over the intellectualists.

2. *Who Should Go to College?* Should college and university doors be open to all who wish to enter? This question is closely related to the preceding issue on the role of intellectualism in higher education.

The Commission on Financing Higher Education devoted an entire volume to this problem—*Who Should Go to College?* Byron S. Hollinshead, writing for the Commission, outlined three chief points of view concerning the problem:

1. Let us continue to enlarge the number who go to college, say its exponents, and let us expand the facilities in higher education by doubling them during the next ten years. . . . This position applies the philosophy of primary and secondary education to higher education, and it indicates a strong belief in the perfectability of man by increasing the amount of time he spends in schools and colleges.

2. The opposite position . . . is that higher education should provide the facilities necessary to meet the needs of those who present themselves at the colleges, providing the students can meet the entrance requirements and providing the colleges can finance their programs from student fees and other income. This would mean that higher education would function as it has in the past. . . .

3. There is a third position which is somewhat of a compromise. Proponents of this position would agree that a higher percentage of students should go to college, but they would say that the percentage of young people with ability to do creditable four-year college work is closer to 25 percent than to 32 percent and that the percentage of those who would benefit from two years of college training is closer to 35 percent than to 50 percent. They assume that some of these young people will need assistance in the form of scholarships if they are to go to college. However, they would insist upon good standards of performance from the students who are to get the aid.[22]

These three major positions may be modified by details and by variations or combinations. Undoubtedly the lower percentage figures used by the Commission on Financing Higher Education in its 1952 report are closer to the desideratum for the admission of college students than were the

[22] Byron S. Hollinshead, *Who Should Go to College?* pp. 39–40, Columbia University Press, 1952.

overly optimistic higher estimates proclaimed by the President's Commission on Higher Education in 1948. As Arthur E. Bestor comments critically in *Educational Wastelands,* "A college needs students who are not merely apt but well trained, if it is to be an institution of *higher* learning." [23]

The discussion of this issue terminates with a disquieting quotation from James Bryant Conant, former president of Harvard:

> In the United States we have come perilously close to endorsing the view that a college education is a "good thing" for everyone; the only limitation has been expense, and working one's way through college has, for many, removed this hurdle. Having a multitude of colleges with no method of insuring any conformity to educational standards and emphasizing the nonintellectual side of college life, America could hardly claim that their colleges were selective.[24]

Institutions of higher learning must practice not merely rigid selective admission but also higher standards in the selective retention of students.

3. *Is the Admission of Students to College on Democratic Bases?* Telltale data and observations on this issue have been accumulated in numerous studies. Among the questionable practices followed by some colleges and universities in admission procedures are these: admitting veterans on the basis of General Educational Development (GED) tests and denying the privilege to other mature persons; giving preference to applicants from the state in which the institution is located; legislating against those who are foreign visitors because they are not citizens of the United States; setting up rigid subject-matter patterns for entrance; demanding extremely high tuition charges; favoring children of alumni; and discriminating against students on the basis of race and/or religion. Much progress has been made in recent years, however, in opening higher educational opportunities to all qualified persons, without discrimination as to race or religion. College admission is not on a democratic basis as long as students who could benefit therefrom are denied the privilege because of economic difficulties. To aid these deserving students many types of scholarships have been established or proposed, including the National Science Foundation, state, and national fellowships.

EDUCATION FOR OUT-OF-SCHOOL YOUTH AND ADULTS

1. *Shall Youth Be Given the Vote at the Age of Eighteen?* In his 1953 State of the Union message, President Eisenhower stated:

> For years our citizens between the ages of 18 and 21 have, in time of peril, been summoned to fight for America. They should participate in the political

[23] Arthur E. Bestor, *Educational Wastelands,* p. 149, University of Illinois Press, 1953.

[24] James Bryant Conant, *Education and Liberty,* pp. 46–47, Harvard University Press, 1953.

process that produces this fateful summons. I urge Congress to propose to the States a constitutional amendment permitting citizens to vote when they reach the age of 18.

Pro. Some arguments on this issue, which holds so many implications for education, are selected from the *Congressional Digest:*

Extending the suffrage to 18-year-olds will broaden the base of democracy not only for the number of young people which it immediately adds to our voting population but also by encouraging the participation of these people at an age when they are enthusiastic and interested in government and politics. This will enable us to make real inroads on voter apathy in the United States. . . . There is no better civic training than the exercise of the vote. . . . Youth ought to have a voice in determining its own future.

—Senator Hubert Humphrey, Minnesota

I think our failure to give 18-year-olds the right to vote amounts to a criticism of our 150 years of free education in the United States. It seems to me to be a sad reflection on the American school system, and one which is not deserved. On questions involving affairs of state, political issues, and problems of statesmanship, I will put the judgment of the average 18-year-old alongside the judgment of the average older citizen any time.   —Senator Wayne Morse, Oregon

The minimum age for employment under our civil service laws is 18 years of age. . . . Under our Penal Code the federal courts at the discretion of the Attorney General may and do commit 18-year-olds to a federal prison. . . . At 18 a young man may volunteer his service in our country's armed forces, without his parents' consent. At 18 a young man is required by law to register for selective service, and be inducted voluntarily, or involuntarily, without his parents' consent.

—Colonel W. R. Watson, retired, United States Air Force [25]

Con. Typical arguments against giving the vote to 18-year-olds are:

Youth is usually emotional and expresses his passionate convictions more than does the adult. The youth is like a white paper; it will take any impression. We have glaring examples of evils of youthful voting or teenage voting in Germany, in Spain, and in Italy, as well as Russia. . . . Youth cannot evaluate as can its elders, and for that reason, I think it would be baneful to have teenage voting. . . . The age of 21 has been time-tested through the centuries, as the age of maturity for voting. We only get our wisdom teeth after 20. . . . To my mind, the draft age and the voting age are as different as chalk is from cheese. The thing called for in a soldier is uncritical obedience, and that is not what you want in a voter. . . . We will do a grave injustice to democracy if we grant the vote to those under 21.   —Representative Emanuel Celler, New York

Callow youth is to be accorded the same privilege as grownups, at a time when we already have a mass of ignorance in the voting area. The above is not to

[25] "The Question of Lowering the Voting Age to 18," *Congressional Digest,* March, 1954, pp. 74, 78, 80, 88.

say that there are some who are well qualified to vote, but it is to say that the great mass of the youth of this country is absolutely unfitted to participate in government. . . . Do we not now have enough X quantities participating in government already, without adding to them?

—George W. Williams, former United States District Judge, Virgin Islands

If we are going to have a democracy, if we are going to fulfill our purpose of government, we must have intelligent and wise voters. Since voting is a right conferred by the State, the States can take away the vote from those persons whom they think are not capable or wise enough to participate in the function of government. . . . The young people under 21 years of age today do not have the experience and wisdom to exercise the vote. . . . While it is true that the 18-year-old today has more education, generally, than the average voter of 50 years and up, our adult population also has more education than the adult population of several years ago. It is a relative matter.

—Kenneth W. Colegrove, Professor of Political Science [26]

Trend. Georgia is currently the only state in which eighteen-year-olds have the right to vote, even for President of the United States. A poll of superintendents of schools in Georgia, as reported by *Nation's Schools,* indicated that 93 per cent approved the action. A nation-wide Gallup poll asked this question of samples: "Would you favor or oppose lowering the voting age limit so that persons 18, 19, and 20 years old could vote in elections?" The responses are tabulated thus:

Answer	Per cent of adult vote	Per cent of vote by young people
Favor	58	64
Oppose	34	31
No opinion	8	5
	—	—
Total	100	100

From a 5-to-1 ratio opposed to the measure 15 years earlier, opinion has shifted to a 5-to-3 ratio in favor. This is one of the greatest changes in opinion ever recorded by a Gallup poll. The possibility of individual action by states or a nation-wide constitutional amendment will provide educators, students, and public with a challenge to improve citizenship education and to reinforce it with direct voting experience.

2. *What Are Desirable Standards for Services for Delinquent Youth?* The Federal Bureau of Investigation (FBI) reports that crime is outstripping population rate of growth 4 to 1. Many of these offenses are committed by youth. In addition to a preventive and development program, what standards can be applied to the agencies serving those who do get into trouble?

[26] *Ibid.,* pp. 81, 83, 85, 87.

The U.S. Children's Bureau has prepared *Recommended Standards for Services for Delinquent Children.* One criterion for each of the five divisions is sampled here:

Police. All police officers should receive instruction in the handling of juveniles in their basic course.

Juvenile Court. Every community, rural or urban, should be served by a juvenile court, whose protection and services are available to all children who need them.

Detention Home. A delinquent child who must be kept in secure custody should be held in a specialized detention facility, and not in a jail or police lockup.

Training School. The training school should receive only those young people who are in need of and who can profit by its services.

Services at the State Level. In every state a single department or agency should have authority and responsibility for serving delinquent children. . . .[27]

There is common agreement that these agencies must be improved.

3. *When Should Public Education End?* Specifically, shall adult education be made a legitimate part of public education? Since subjects requiring maturity can be learned only by the experienced, the education of adults is extremely important. Adult learning is not merely remedial, to correct mislearning or to substitute for education missed previously; it is a sequential and essential stage in lifelong learning. It is difficult to establish terminal facilities for education at public expense. For persons physically or mentally handicapped, free education should never cease. There is a growing conviction also that adult education, along with the education of out-of-school youth, should be a legitimate charge against public funds. In the years to come, adult learning will assume a more conspicuous and effective role than in the past.

4. *How Shall Adult Education Be Financed, When Funds Are Insufficient for the Preceding Phases of Learning?* Finance studies reveal that adult education does not cost much—it equals approximately 2 per cent of the day-school expenditures. Since it is largely part-time instruction, the cost is only a fraction as much per person as full-time elementary, secondary, or higher education. In most cases regular taxes, plus small fees, furnish most of the receipts.[28] But as adult education grows in scope, in enriched services, and in numbers involved, much more money will be needed.

[27] Children's Bureau, *Recommended Standards for Services for Delinquent Children,* pp. 1–18, GPO, 1953.

[28] Homer Kempfer and William R. Wood, *Financing Adult Education in Selected Schools and Community Colleges,* pp. 26–27, GPO, 1952.

Educationally the first twenty years are well provided for through public financial support. But what about the next fifty years? . . . It is the adults themselves who pay the cost of government. It is the adults themselves who pay for the educational system that we now have. When will these same adults order and pay for a continuous education for themselves—educational opportunity for all for the first twenty years plus the next fifty? [29]

Support for adult education will have to come from public and private funds. The main source for the former obviously is taxes. The latter includes many resources: personal fees, private donations, parochial funds, and contributions from industry and labor. Adult education must clarify its purposes, organize its program, and launch an aggressive battle for ample budgets.

PERSONNEL IN PUBLIC EDUCATION

PUPILS

1. *Shall School Pupils Be Segregated?* Specifically, shall Negro students be educated in separate schools? Or shall education seek integration rather than segregation?

History of the Problem. The history of America's No. 1 dilemma in education is a long one. Ambrose Caliver, Negro, assistant to the United States Commissioner of Education, and Emery M. Foster, white, head of Reports and Analysis in the same office, have thus summarized this story:

During the early days of slavery in America, Christian missionaries were influential in starting the custom of teaching the slaves to read and write. . . . They also extended their concept of education to include preparation for citizenship as well as Christianity. . . . Another force which was gathering strength and momentum . . . was the spirit of freedom which resulted in the American Revolution and finally in the emancipation of the slaves. . . . In spite of laws making the education of Negroes a crime, punishable by the severest penalties, many of them succeeded in securing the rudiments of knowledge. . . . So, by the time of Emancipation, it is estimated that about 5 per cent of the Negroes were literate. . . . The beginning of the Civil War was the signal for unleashing the pent-up desire of Negroes for education. . . . The Freedman's Bureau, established by Congress in 1866, considered education to be one of its major functions. . . . Public education at that time was not popular even for the whites. Reconstruction legislatures had established the principle of equal distribution of school funds between the two races. . . . By 1900 the pattern had been firmly set. School statistics show that the pattern of discrimination continued for nearly a half century. In 1896, the Supreme Court handed down its historic decision in the *Plessy v. Ferguson* railroad accommodation case. The theory underlying

[29] Hugh W. Norman, "Twenty–Plus Fifty," *Community Teamwork*, December, 1953, p. 2.

this decision that separate but equal facilities did not violate the Constitution gave the highest government sanction to the pattern of segregation, which is now challenged before the Court.[30]

Status of Problem at Mid-century. Up to the historic decision of 1954, the courts recognized the authority of the various states to permit or require segregation in public schools. In 17 states and the District of Columbia school segregation of Negroes and white pupils was required by law. In some states permissive legislation protected partial segregation practices.

A clearly discernible trend was the change in attitude of the courts toward the "separate but equal" doctrine. In the case of *Corbin v. County School Board* in 1949, the Court stated, "The question cannot be decided by averaging the facilities provided for the two classes of pupils . . . and comparing one with the other, since the rights created by the Fourteenth Amendment are individual and personal. . . ." The U.S. Department of Justice, in its supplemental brief in 1953, stated: "The judicial inquiry . . . is not simply to determine whether there is equality as between schools: the Constitution requires that there be equality as between *persons.* The Fourteenth Amendment compels a state to grant the benefits of public education to all its people equally, without regard to differences of race or color."

Thus, prior to the historic decision of the United States Supreme Court in 1954, discussed in Unit X, the courts approached a definition of equality that at least implied the concept of identity.

Transition toward Integration. Prior to the Supreme Court decision outlawing segregation, many steps had been taken toward solving this problem locally, statewise, and nationally.

Suits were filed in many local communities against segregated schools. In the meantime many boards of education permitted the transfer of Negro students upon application. Gradually desegregation spread.

From out-of-state scholarships and state professional schools for Negroes some commonwealths have moved to the admission of Negro graduate and professional students to state universities. Prior to 1954 New Jersey, Illinois, Indiana, and some other states that observed segregation in the public elementary and secondary schools legislated against the practice.

On a nation-wide basis the military forces preceded the public schools in the integration of personnel. In 1948 President Harry S Truman issued an executive order which provided among other things "that there shall be equality of treatment and opportunity for all persons in the armed services without regard to race, color, religion or national origin."

Antisegregation policies and procedures of many parochial schools

[30] Ambrose Caliver and Emery M. Foster, "Education of Negroes: Progress and Present Status in the Segregated Pattern," *School Life,* March 1954, p. 87.

precipitated progress. For example, the Roman Catholic Church has been desegregating its schools for some time. Mixed athletic competition has helped to advance the status of Negroes.

Racial integration in education is a long-time process. As indicated in Unit X, evolutionary rather than revolutionary measures should be employed, especially in Southern states which have long practiced segregation in schools and in other areas of living.

The legal aspects of desegregation, including the initial Supreme Court decision and the follow-up decrees, must be considered in the crucial context of long-established traditions, and current social, political, psychological, and economic factors. As indicated by W. W. Brinkman, editor of *School and Society,* integration will have "to proceed at varying rates in different localities." In some areas complete desegregation, including Negro and white teachers working with mixed classes, will not be accomplished in this generation.

The Supreme Court decision did not end segregation. As stated by Charles H. Thompson, editor of the *Journal of Negro Education,* "When the law no longer obtains, the real work of developing racial integration can begin with some probability of a favorable result." Integration, a word long used in schools, is on the agenda of educational history in the United States.

2. *Shall Special Classes Be Organized for Exceptional Pupils?* The number of special *classes* for exceptional pupils, including the gifted, is increasing. Segregation of handicapped children in special *schools* is not gaining in favor. Several types of exceptional children may be found in certain state residential schools, like the Virginia School for the Deaf and Blind, and in local institutions, such as the Smouse Opportunity School of Des Moines, Iowa. In the Illinois plan for special education of the handicapped is this statement indicative of the current trend:

An essential objective in the education of handicapped children is to prepare them to take their places in the social and economic life of their community. It is a corollary of this principle that no child should be served in a special class if he is able to take his place in the regular classroom. Most classes for special education should be so located that the contacts with normal children in school and on the playground will naturally develop.

It follows that children in special classes should be transferred back to the regular class as soon as the need for special attention ceases. The needs of some handicapped children can be best met by the provision of special or supplementary services such as transportation, speech correction, lip reading, etc., without recourse to special classes.

The grouping of pupils and the methodology of instruction depend in a practical school situation upon the specific needs of the exceptional child, the training of the teacher, and the available facilities and finances.

3. *Is School Discipline Out of Date?* [31] Is discipline a minor function in the training of children? Shall teacher-educating institutions give less attention to equipping teachers to meet problems of discipline?

' Some would banish from educational vocabulary and practice the word "discipline." The concept of discipline in its highest sense of discipleship should not be discarded if education is to build genuine character. Many years ago Edmund Burke said: "Society cannot exist unless a controlling power upon will and appetite be placed somewhere; and the less of it there is within, the more there must be without." Self-discipline is, of course, better than external pin-drop discipline. Former President A. G. Ruthven of the University of Michigan in a baccalaureate address, "Discipline as a Factor in Social Integration," stated that the development of self-control is, or should be, the main objective of education. Since no teacher can be a success until he or she has learned the art of classroom discipline, teacher-educating institutions and writers of educational textbooks must not neglect this aspect of education. It is significant that when administrators or boards of education seek new teachers, many times their first question is: "Can she maintain discipline?" Too much softness, and not enough preventive and remedial measures, may prove the undoing of many beginners in the teaching-learning art.

TEACHERS

1. *How Can a Larger Number of Able Teachers Be Recruited and Retained for the Profession?* Among the numerous suggestions for alleviating the shortage of well-qualified teaching personnel are these, arranged by the mnemonic letter R:

Recognition. Teaching itself must be recognized as a profession. In India, for example, the teacher is a respected "guru." Instructors too can be heralded for their continuing contributions to civilization.

Research. This includes comprehensive long-term studies of teacher demand and supply on local, state, regional, and national bases. More investigations are needed to find out why teachers enter and leave the profession. These data can be utilized in student-guidance programs.

Recruitment. Nation-wide campaigns, supplemented by "grass-roots" publicity programs, can help recruit the best human resources into the profession. Enlisted recruits can be organized in elementary, secondary, and higher-education institutions, as "Future Teachers of America." Scholarships give realism to recruitment.

Reorganization. Programs for the preservice and in-service education of teachers must be drastically reorganized.

Reciprocity. Greater reciprocity in teacher preparation and certification between colleges, cities, states, and nations will facilitate transfer.

[31] See also Arthur T. Jersild, "Discipline," *Baltimore Journal of Education,* April, 1954, pp. 27–32.

Registration. Voluntary registration of persons not teaching but qualified to do so, and a census of former teachers, as well as the compulsory registration of employed teachers, make a valuable inventory of available human resources.

Reemployment. Many former teachers, some retired, can be brought back into teaching service on a full-time or part-time basis.

Reeducation. Many former and current teachers need to retool their minds and methods through programs of reeducation.

FIG. 17-5. They're waiting for the teacher. Maybe it's you! (*Courtesy of Public Service Advertising Council and Citizens Commission for Public Schools.*)

Reconversion. As demands in various teaching fields and areas shift, many surplus teachers can be reeducated and redirected into areas of critical shortages.

Retention. Many young teachers are lost to the profession because they are not given sympathetic, adequate help in their early work. Many experienced and capable teachers are driven from the profession for various reasons.

Retrenchment. Some of the current demands for personnel can be alleviated by elimination of small classes and the reorganization of small school districts.

Reductions. Conversely some overworked teachers can be retained through decreases in class size, elimination of extra duties, and reduction in red tape. Most teachers would welcome a curtailment of restrictions regulating their personal lives.

Recreation. Many teachers fail to cultivate hobbies and recreational activities. This failure is also a challenge to communities that employ them.

Relaxation. Related is the re-creation of the body, mind, and soul through relaxation in an atomic age of supersonic speeds.

Rest. Schools can provide more opportunities and facilities for the teacher to rest during the day. Remuneration should be adequate to provide vacation periods.

Residences. Since apartments and homes are difficult to obtain and expensive to buy, many more school districts should provide housing for teachers.

Resources. Good physical resources, such as up-to-date and available teaching equipment and modern school buildings, improve the efficiency, and hence the morale of the teacher.

Rotation. Some teachers can climb out of a rut through rotation of duties and rooms. Exchanges between classes, schools, communities, and countries produce new ideas and challenges.

Representation. Increased representation by teachers and others in policy making adds zest to teaching. Obviously, they need membership and representation in professional and other groups.

Rapport. Such tangible intangibles as rapport and esprit de corps give "pep" to the profession.

Retirement. More adequate provisions for security in old age will reduce worries. Gradual or phased retirement will enable teachers to adjust more easily to their change in status.

Remuneration. Salaries generally must be increased to attract, retain, and reward those who make teaching a career.

Rewards. Money is secondary or tertiary to the real teacher. Other intangibles, such as cooperation of parents, respect and gratitude of the learner, and status in the community, are the intangible rewards that can make teaching one of the greatest professions.

Rededication. The constant rededication of teachers to their high calling, and their daily example, will attract many more of their pupils into the teaching profession.

2. *Should Communists Teach in American Schools and Universities?* The Educational Policies Commission in *American Education and International Tensions* clearly enunciated what may become the general policy for the schools and colleges of America:

> Members of the Communist Party of the United States should not be employed as teachers. Such membership, in the opinion of the Educational Policies Commission, involves adherence to doctrines and discipline completely inconsistent with the principles of freedom on which American education depends. Such membership, and the accompanying surrender of intellectual integrity, render an individual unfit to discharge the duties of a teacher in this country.[32]

The Commission condemned the careless, incorrect, and unjust use of such words as "Red" and "Communist" to attack teachers and other persons who in point of fact are not Communists but merely have views different from those of their accusers. The whole spirit of free American education will be subverted unless teachers are free to think for themselves.

[32] Educational Policies Commission, *American Education and International Tensions,* pp. 39–40, National Education Association, 1949.

The great difficulty comes, of course, in determining who shall decide whether a teacher is a Communist.

The American Federation of Teachers, AFL, in its thirty-fifth national convention voted overwhelmingly not to defend any teacher proved to be a Communist party member. But the resolution declared it the duty of any federation local "to see that a teacher accused of being a member of the Communist party or any other totalitarian organization has every opportunity to clear himself of the charge." The Federation condemned attempts to impose loyalty through restrictive legislation: "Such discriminatory and restrictive actions can only be considered unworthy of our American ideals of freedom of inquiry and discussion."

The Association of American Universities has issued a statement, signed by the heads of 37 institutions, insisting on loyalty as well as freedom. The statement reads in part:

Above all, a scholar must have integrity and independence. This renders impossible adherence to such a regime as that of Russia and its satellites. No person who accepts or advocates such principles and methods has any place in a university.

Condemnation of communism and its proponents is not to be interpreted as readiness to curb investigation and research.

3. *Shall Teachers Have Academic Freedom?* This is related to the preceding issues. Thinking about academic freedom must not become too narrow:

Only when we widen the focus can we hope to get a true picture of academic freedom, and this broadening must be sufficient to include the entire social pattern. It must bring into focus not only the teacher and the administration, but also the pupil who sits in the classroom, the parents who send their children to school and pay the taxes, and the *fundamental values of the social pattern.*[33]

Two justices of the United States Supreme Court, Minton and Douglas, are quoted briefly as majority and minority opinions in the 6-to-3 decision on the celebrated Feinberg Case which upheld the New York State law disqualifying persons of communistic affiliations from teaching in the public schools.

A teacher works in a sensitive area in a schoolroom. There he shapes the attitude of young minds toward the society in which they live. In this, the state has a vital concern. It must preserve the integrity of the schools.

—Minton

The Constitution guarantees freedom of thought and expression to everyone in society. All are entitled to it; and none needs it more than the teacher.

—Douglas

[33] S. E. Frost, Jr., "Academic Freedom: A New Perspective," *Educational Forum,* March, 1949, p. 347.

Chief Justice Earl Warren has called upon American institutions of higher education to demonstrate new vigor for "free investigation and faithful research by the unfettered minds of free American scholars." A teacher with good taste and sound scholarship who does not go to the extreme limits in pursuit of academic freedom should encounter few difficulties. No one should take too literally the avowed guarantee of academic freedom, since practical limits always seem to be considerably narrowed. A national study indicates that, while few teachers are dismissed, demoted, or otherwise disciplined for exercising free speech, the majority of them deal cautiously and speak guardedly on controversial subjects because of fear of punishment. This indicates that there are some limits to academic freedom but that most teachers evidently do not transgress. The subjects that are most dangerous to teach include communism, religion, sex, politics, economics, and international relations. The emphasis should be on freedom for the learner to learn rather than on license for the teacher to say any thing any time. The higher the academic level of the learner the greater should be the academic freedom of the teacher. As Harvard's President Nathan Pusey stated to the National Press Club, "A scholar or scientist has an obligation to investigate and report new ideas in his field, even when his conclusions may be unpopular among the general public."

4. *Shall Teachers Join Labor Unions?* The answer of the National Education Association is emphatically "No." In a classic editorial, Joy Elmer Morgan of the *NEA Journal* wrote "A Declaration of Professional Independence," in which he penned these poignant phrases:

> Teachers' unions are born of desperation and thrive on catastrophe. As conditions improve they will diminish, as they did after World War I. Even at their peak they have grown less rapidly than our professional associations. Our National Education Association, with its affiliated state and local associations, is the only organization that unites or has the possibility of uniting the great body of teachers in this country.

Teacher membership in unions varies widely, depending partly on whether labor unions are strong or weak in the community. In many schools the board of education has expressed its policy in this matter. For example, the Board of Education in Detroit, Michigan, stated its practice concerning employee memberships in organizations as follows:

> Employees of the board of education are assured, as far as the board is concerned, and pursuant to its established policy, continuance of employment will not be affected in any way by membership or nonmembership in any craft, technical, professional, fraternal, or employee organization not subversive in character; further that employees are free to join or to refrain from joining any such organization without jeopardizing their employment by so doing; also that whether they be members or nonmembers of such organization, employees may

continue to bring to the board and its committee for consideration and adjustment any matter concerning their employment or relationship to the board.

It is desirable to make membership or nonmembership in unions a matter of personal choice, without coercion either way. The American Federation of Teachers, the only teachers' organization affiliated with the American Federation of Labor, was organized in Chicago in 1916. Its membership increased greatly in the past decade. The trend is toward affiliation with labor groups, although only a very small percentage of all teachers are now members of a union.

5. *Should Teachers Strike?* The typical reaction of professional workers is found in the resolution adopted by the American Association of School Administrators in convention assembled: "We disapprove the use of the strike as a means of securing the rights of professional workers. This type of conduct will react ultimately to the detriment of teaching as a profession." The American Federation of Teachers (AFL) pledged itself to a "no strike" policy. The organization, however, also pledged itself to support local unions in efforts to obtain adequate salaries and satisfactory working conditions and redress for legitimate grievances.

In nearly all communities there will be no need for teacher strikes if interested committees representing the public, the board of education, and the teachers work together on problems of teacher salaries, working conditions, living arrangements, and other matters of teacher welfare. Informed and alert citizens will see that justice is done to the teaching profession and to the children of America.

OTHER PERSONNEL

1. *Shall Federal Social Security Include Teachers and Nonteaching Personnel?* When social security legislation was enacted into law in 1935, it did not include those employed in educational institutions operated on a nonprofit basis or employees of federal, state, and local governments. Since then many teachers, professors, and nonteaching personnel have evinced interest in retirement and survivorship protection under the federal plan. Thousands of educational workers have come under the umbrella provided by their contributions, those of their employers, and those of the Social Security Administration. Many teachers are under retirement programs that combine state systems with federal social security. Obviously, educational employees are reluctant to accept social-security coverage unless it provides benefits equal to or better than existing retirement systems. The trend is toward wider acceptance of the benefits of federal social security solely or in combination with other retirement systems.

2. *Shall Nonteaching Employees Be Selected on the Merit Basis?* Obviously the answer is "Yes," but unfortunately much current practice does

not harmonize with the best in theory. Improved methods of selecting the nonteaching personnel of the schools are urgently needed. Many of the nonteaching positions mentioned in Unit XII are available through civil service. Since the smooth administration of all institutions of learning is strengthened by the efficiency of the nonteaching personnel, well-defined principles of selection, high standards in appointments, and adequate provisions for social security must be established.

3. *Shall School Employees Be Required to Take an Oath of Allegiance?* Specifically, shall teachers be obligated to take such an oath?

Much intangible pressure has been brought to bear upon outspoken teachers and school employees. The usual effort at legal control takes the overt form of an oath of allegiance. In some states teachers in private as well as public schools must submit to this requirement. The trend is to require teachers to swear allegiance to state and country. Waves of patriotism and the danger of subversive foreign influence cause periodic crests of compulsion.

A disloyal teacher cannot be sworn into allegiance to democracy. No one can be made loyal by administering an oath to him. Enjoying the full rights guaranteed him by the Constitution and Bill of Rights, a teacher can interpret their benefits with greater insight and deeper zeal. It goes without saying that the ideals, traditions, and Constitution of the United States must be upheld by Americans of all ages and classes. But education that inculcates an innate love of country is a more potent means to this end than is legislation that involves external compulsion.

PROVISIONS FOR EDUCATIONAL MATERIALS AND ENVIRONMENT

CURRICULUM

1. *Are the Curriculums "Tough Enough"?* Do they represent a "retreat from learning"?

Attacks. Arthur E. Bestor, whose volume *Educational Wastelands* bears the subtitle "The Retreat from Learning in Our Public Schools," attacks the curriculums of schools and colleges as being "watered down."

When Americans, a century or so ago, committed themselves to the ideal of universal democratic education, they were not thinking in terms of the trivia that fascinate many present-day educationists. They did not intend, by making education universal, to debase and destroy it. They were not seeking to water down the great tradition of disciplined and liberal study. . . . The issue is drawn between those who believe that good teaching should be directed to sound intellectual ends, and those who are content to dethrone intellectual values and cultivate the techniques of teaching for their own sake, in an intellectual and cultural vacuum.[34]

[34] Arthur E. Bestor, *Educational Wastelands*, pp. 38, 11, University of Illinois Press, 1953.

Bestor devotes an entire chapter to criticism of "life-adjustment education."

In *The Conflict in Education in a Democratic Society,* Robert M. Hutchins also disapproves of current curriculums:

> The principal reason for the popularity in the United States of what is called Progressive Education, in which Mr. Dewey also had a hand, is that the children have a good time in school. In a child-centered society, like that of the United States, any effort to insist on painful work in school naturally encounters resistance.[35]

Counterattacks. A colleague of Mr. Bestor at the University of Illinois counterattacks thus:

> Bestor is objecting to any and all attempts to modify the modern equivalent of the medieval *trivium* and *quadrivium.* . . . If the colleges' success in this enterprise can be questioned, given the relatively homogeneous population they enroll, may not the high schools be permitted to try different methods than the disciplines, when such methods appear to be rewarding and when the stakes are so high? Must they be charged with culpability when they so try? [36]

A professor at the University of Michigan answers Bestor's charge that "the school makes itself ridiculous whenever it undertakes to deal *directly* with 'real-life' problems, instead of *indirectly* through the development of generalized intellectual powers":

> Professor Bestor's explication and defense of the disciplines is largely based on the now discredited faculty psychology. . . . For the better pupils, the ones for whom the schools were originally established, the process described is probably fairly effective. But for the slower growing and less intelligent (whether rich or poor) it may not be so effective as other ways in attaining our educational objectives, or more specifically, in developing the ability to meet problems intelligently (ie., training to think).[37]

Renewed Warfare. The attacks, such as made in Bestor's *Educational Wastelands,* Lynd's *Quackery in the Public Schools,* Hutchins' *The Conflict in Education in a Democratic Society,* and in current periodicals and newspapers, renew an age-old war which may continue forever. Rather than taking sides, it is better to go down deeper and seek the causes of the conflicts in education, and then to search for solutions. A basic cause for current conflicts in curriculums is the confusion in concepts. The goals of education in the United States need to be carefully defined for the various groups and levels of American schools. Constructive criticism

[35] Hutchins, *op. cit.,* p. 86.

[36] R. Will Burnett, "Mr. Bestor in the Land of the Philistines," *Progressive Education,* January, 1954, pp. 65, 85.

[37] William Clark Trow, "Academic Utopia?" *Educational Theory,* January, 1954, pp. 460, 502.

and specific suggestions can come from the nation, the state, and especially local areas. A national board of education and state, county, and local boards can well address themselves to the task of defining goals.

What is the role of criticism in the process of seeking goals?

. . . . the history and tradition of our country make it plain that the essence of the American way of life is its hospitality to criticism, protest, unpopular opinions, and independent thought. . . . America has grown strong on criticism.[38]

If the critics are sincere, their attacks will spur improvement in curriculums. But, as indicated in Paul Woodring's *Let's Talk Sense about Our Schools:*

The fundamental issue in education today is not whether something called "progressive education" is better than some other kind of education. Nor is the issue between the education of today and the education of one generation or a hundred generations ago. The question facing us is this: What is good education for American children? [39]

As Ralph Waldo Emerson once said, "The enemy of the best is not the poorest, but the good." Calloused complacency and satisfaction with good curriculums will war against their becoming the best. In their quest for the best, curriculum builders may well seek the shibboleth, "Our utmost for the highest."

2. *What Shall Be the Relation of Religion to Public Education?* This is not a new issue. Horace Mann, as secretary of the state board of education in Massachusetts over a hundred years ago, fought to exclude from the schools any narrow sectarian religious teaching. He nevertheless entertained the hope that schools would find a way to foster nonsectarian religious faith. This dream has not been realized. Sectarianism has been replaced by secularism; narrow denominationalism has been followed by irreligious worldiness.

The United States Supreme Court has rendered two decisions with respect to religious education in the public schools. The first, given in 1948 in the McCollum Case, ruled against released-time instruction as practiced in Champaign, Illinois. The second ruling in 1952 dealt with the Zorach Case in New York City; it declared this practice constitutional. These apparently contradictory opinions are explained as follows:

In the McCollum case the classrooms were used for religious instruction and the force of the public school was used to promote that instruction. Here [in the Zorach case], the public schools do no more than accommodate their schedules to a program of outside religious instruction.

38 Hutchins, *op. cit.*, pp. 24–25.
39 Paul Woodring, *Let's Talk Sense about Our Schools*, p. 200, McGraw-Hill, 1953.

We are a religious people whose institutions presuppose a Supreme Being. We guarantee the freedom to worship as one chooses. . . . We find no constitutional requirement which makes it necessary for government to be hostile to religion and to throw its weight against efforts to widen the effective scope of religious influence. The government must be neutral when it comes to competition between sects.

Thus religious instruction on released time is legal under certain conditions. The proposal of the New York Board of Regents that all the state's public schools open the day with a nondenominational prayer has met with mixed response.

As indicated by the American Council on Education in *The Function of the Public Schools in Dealing with Religion,* the public school is limited, as the private institution is not, in its treatment of religion. It is illegal for the public schools to teach religion in the sense of attempting to inculcate sectarian religious beliefs.

Even if agreement could be reached among the religious minded on a "common core" or set of basic propositions common to and acceptable to Roman Catholics, Protestants, and Jews, there would remain the non-religious groups in the community who would maintain that their rights were violated by any attempt to inculcate general propositions embodying religious beliefs.

On the other hand to be silent about religion may be, in effect, to make the public schools an anti-religious factor in the community.[40]

The tax-supported institutions of learning in the God-fearing United States should not overtly or tacitly be on the side of paganism. On the other hand, the testimony of the ages is that church and state should be separated.

The Educational Policies Commission believes that moral and spiritual values can be actively promoted in the public schools by:

1. Defining as goals the accepted moral and spiritual values in our society
2. Encouraging and helping the individual teacher
3. Giving attention to moral and spiritual values in teacher education
4. Teaching these moral and spiritual values at every opportunity
5. Utilizing all of the school's resources
6. Devoting sufficient time and staff to wholesome personal relationships
7. Assuming an attitude of friendly sympathy toward the religious beliefs and practices of students
8. Promoting religious tolerance actively
9. Teaching about religion as an important fact in our culture [41]

[40] Committee on Religion and Education, *The Function of the Public Schools in Dealing with Religion,* p. 6, American Council on Education, 1953.

[41] Educational Policies Commission, *Moral and Spiritual Values in the Public Schools,* p. 80, National Education Association, 1951.

Whether public schools generally can teach *about* religion without explicitly or implicitly teaching religion is a moot question that will probably be unsolved for many years to come.

3. *Shall Sex Education Be Taught in the Schools?* This issue raises many questions.

What is sex education? It is more than the story of flowers, bees, and birds, and the sex life of animals and humans. It is more than teaching the biological facts of life. It is more than such narrow topics as venereal diseases. It is a broad approach to the personal guidance and social adjustment of children, youth, and adults. In its wider aspects it may be called personal and social adjustment, orientation to life, wholesome living, or family relations.

Where shall it be taught or learned? Too much sex education is gleaned at the so-called "gutter level," in the back streets, poolrooms, and isolated retreats, and through direct illicit experience. Worthy family relations should be started in the home, extended in the school and college, and elevated in church and synagogue. Since the issue is here delimited to schools, the accent is placed there.

When shall sex education be taught? As a part of family relations it can be learned implicitly in the early grades, building upon the groundwork of the family in the home, as suggested in such pamphlets as *How to Tell Your Child about Sex*. Subject to parental understanding and cooperation and guarded limitations, the major stress upon sex education can be placed in the secondary school as a phase of the larger problems of personal and social adjustment. In college and classes for out-of-school youth and adults the accent shifts to courtship and marriage, care of the child, home life, and family relationships, thus completing the cycle.

Who should be taught? First of all, suggestions for teaching sex education should be given to parents and to teachers. A community institute on family living can serve as an adult preparation for a cooperative home-school program for children and youth.

Who should teach? Bringing in outside specialists often calls too much attention to the subject. The potential teachers are school nurses, school doctors, and teachers in related fields such as home economics, biology, health and physical education, psychology, social sciences, and others. Teacher-educating institutions and state certification agencies need to direct attention to the needs for well-qualified teachers in this growing field.

How shall learners be taught? First of all, the method should bring about a wholesome attitude toward the human body and human society. Sex education, if taught, must be presented on a high moral plane. Group instruction must be supplemented by personal guidance. Much factual material can be presented through audio-visual aids, which should be carefully prepared and previewed by various groups. Obviously not everything should be taught. Human decency, group heterogeneity, and the proprieties of society demand sacred silences and planned omissions.

4. *Can the Gap between General and Vocational Education Be Bridged?* Unfortunately a misunderstanding has arisen in the minds of many people in regard to the relationship of general and vocational education. The issue is often one of academic vs. vocational, general vs. specific, theoretical vs. practical. This issue becomes increasingly important as secondary schools admit all young people of high-school age.

It is helpful to dip below the surface ripples and ask, "What is the major purpose of education in a democratic society?" The chief aim is to promote the optimal development of all individuals in American society. Both general and vocational education contribute to this unified purpose.

General education should concern itself with the development of common ideals, understandings, and abilities, and with the cultivation of special capacities, abilities, and interests *up to the point of developing technical competence.* Special (or vocational) education should concern itself with the development of technical proficiency in a context of common ideals, understandings, and abilities.[42]

Teachers of academic and vocational subjects need to sign a declaration of interdependence. Federal aid for vocational education should be consolidated with general aid for elementary and secondary education. Particularly in an unstratified society is it necessary to maintain unity in education and to provide funds and opportunities for vocational education without sharply isolating it.

5. *Shall Controversial Subjects Be Discussed in the Schools?* That is, shall debatable issues be discussed in elementary, secondary, and higher educational institutions by the students, teachers, or both, backed by such facts as can be marshaled to support their opinions?

Well-guided discussion of controversial problems of interest to the students and appropriate to their respective levels is an aid in teaching and learning. Certain questions cannot be discussed intelligently by children in the lower grades. Furthermore some subjects, such as religious controversies, are taboo in any public school. Of course, what may be controversial in one school or community may not be so in another. Disputable issues are bound to arise in democratic America. But since these questions may often be freighted with dynamite, they must be handled with care. The crucial problem is how to select issues and relate them to the curriculum design of the school. Discussion of debatable issues should

[42] Harold Alberty, "Bridging the Gap between General and Vocational Education in High School," *Educational Forum,* January, 1949, p. 214.

provide an opportunity for the pupil to learn rather than for the teacher to preach or propagandize.

6. *Shall the Curriculums of the Schools of the United States Seek to Promote International Understanding?* Yes, that is a positive trend. From kindergarten through graduate school, by means of countless curricular subjects (especially languages and social science), by cocurricular activities, and by exchange of scholarships, the schools can help to develop a spirit of interdependence based upon mutual understanding. The pupils now in the schools ought to be intelligent world citizens. "If our children are to make a contribution to the attainment and maintenance of peace and to the development of a stable world order, they will be called upon constantly to interpret events in the light of these factors." [43]

A specific issue in international education is whether or not communism should be taught. Dwight D. Eisenhower, when president of Columbia University, stated: "Ignorance of communism, fascism, or any other police-state philosophy is far more dangerous than ignorance of the most virulent disease." The Educational Policies Commission advised that members of the Communist Party of the United States should not be employed as teachers, but proposed that:

Young citizens should have an opportunity to learn about the principles and practices of totalitarianism, including those represented by the Soviet Union and by the Communist Party in the United States.

Teaching about communism or any other form of dictatorship does not mean advocacy of these doctrines. Such advocacy should not be permitted in American schools.

The schools should continue with vigor their program for giving young citizens a clear understanding of the principles of the American way of life and a desire to make these principles prevail in their own lives and in the life of their country.[44]

This approach enables the teacher to stress American citizenship but to place it significantly in the larger context of world relationships.

COCURRICULAR ACTIVITIES

1. *What Shall Be the Role of Athletics in American Education?* Can educators reduce the evils, improve the good, and proclaim a program of athletics for all?

False Values and Bad Practices. The Educational Policies Commission indicates some of the false values that mar athletics in many schools:

[43] The Committee on International Relations, *Education for International Understanding in American Schools,* p. 9, National Education Association, 1948.

[44] Educational Policies Commission, *American Education and International Tensions,* pp. 37–40.

1. Overemphasis on winning
2. Glorifying star athletes
3. Disparaging the non-athlete
4. School games as public spectacles

The Commission lists eight types of bad athletic practices:

1. Overemphasis on varsity
2. Distortions in the program
3. Coaches under pressure
4. Financial woes
5. Recruiting by colleges
6. Involving younger children
7. Neglecting the girls
8. Distorting school organization [45]

The identification of false values and bad practices should lead to a broad attack against them. This remedial program involves pupils, teachers, administrators, boards of education, other local citizens, and state and national athletic associations.

Affirmations of the Good. The Commission lists several affirmations, including these:

> We believe in athletics as an important part of the school physical education program. We believe that the experience of playing athletic games should be a part of the education of all children and youth who attend school in the United States. We believe that participation in sound athletic program contributes to health and happiness, physical skills and emotional maturity, social competence and moral values. We believe that cooperation and competition are both important components of American life. Athletic participation can help teach the values of cooperation as well as the spirit of competition.[46]

Certainly educators, students, and the public must capitalize more effectively on the positive and potential values in school athletics.

Positive Programs. Athletic affirmations have been and can be implemented by positive programs. A few elements in recommended programs are:

Elementary school. For children in grades 1 through 6, developmental needs will be met most adequately if physical activities are largely informal and noncompetitive. In the upper grades the activity program must plan for some differentiation of interests between boys and girls. Informal activities such as play days, sports days, and occasional invitational games which involve children of two or more schools should be encouraged.

Junior high school. Boys and girls in junior high school need a program of athletics different from that provided for either elementary school children or senior high youth. Junior high school pupils are not yet physically ready for sports that call for much endurance and strength or for a viogorus body contact. Boxing, ice hockey, and tackle football are not recommended. . . . The intramural program should offer many options. Junior high school pupils can profit from informal games with children of other schools.

---

[45] Educational Policies Commission, *School Athletics*, pp. 6–10, National Education Association, 1954.

[46] *Ibid.*, p. 3.

Senior high school. All students, boys and girls, should have opportunity to take part in occasional informal extramural competition. Each sex needs some sports in separate groups. Each sex needs frequent periods when appropriate sports can be enjoyed together. Post season championship contests should be abolished. Coaches should be teachers of physical education.[47]

Many evils in grade- and high-school athletics stem from collegiate practices. One of the many groups interested in these problems is the American Council on Education. Their Committee on Athletic Policy has made several recommendations, including these:

College and university. The remedies proposed by this Committee have four chief objectives: to relieve external pressures, to insure institutional control, to suggest general standards of acceptable practice, and to invoke measures of enforcement. . . .[48]

Space does not permit a listing or discussion of their specific recommendations. One extreme point of view on collegiate athletics is that of former chancellor Hutchins, who wrote: "I like intercollegiate football, but I recommended its abolition at Chicago, because the game in this industrial, big-time form has nothing to do with education, and yet has the effect of diverting everybody's attention from the educational problems with which universities should be wrestling." [49] On the contrary, Army's football coach Earl ("Red") Blaik, irritated by persistent de-emphasizers of intercollegiate sports, has taken a flying tackle at them and their "theory of mediocrity." Said he, "They've made it so you feel there's something shameful about having a good team." [50] Between the extremes of those who would eliminate and those who would glorify are the many who would retain but improve the programs, and capitalize on the countless assets in athletics.

2. *Shall Secret Societies Be Permitted in Public Elementary and High Schools?* The high-school fraternity and sorority are not without their defenders, who say that such organizations satisfy the natural urge for close friendship engendered by membership in closed groups, and that they prepare for the pattern of college and adult life. But on the elementary- and high-school levels these organizations are objectionable on at least three counts: they are inconsistent with the democratic way of life, they may be harmful to the boy or girl who joins them, and they are often detrimental to the school that has to contend with them. With so many varied clubs and activities available, it seems unnecessary to

[47] *Ibid.,* pp. 27, 28, 30, 33, 35, 41, 44, 46, 60, 62.

[48] Special Committee on Athletic Policy, *Report,* American Council on Education, 1952, 8 pp.

[49] Hutchins, *op. cit.,* p. 12.

[50] *Time,* Mar. 1, 1954, p. 36.

implant secret organizations in educational institutions below the collegiate level. It is significant that many college sororities and fraternities have substituted "help week" for "hell week."

3. *Shall School Services, Such as Recreational and Camping Programs, Be Made Available on a Year-round Basis?* Shall pupils have directed educational experience for 12 months and the teachers have employment the year round? In its look into the future, the Educational Policies Commission furnished educational services of a cocurricular nature to pupils on a 12-month basis in the hypothetical Farmville elementary schools. An actual example of such a program is the Glencoe, Illinois, elementary district. One of the significant developments for summer activities is camping experience.

4. *Shall American Youth Who Reach Voting Age Be Given Formal Recognition?* Shall citizenship day be a national project?

Many young men and women reach voting age each year, without receiving any public recognition and without realizing the significance of citizenship in a self-governing republic. To remedy this deficiency, a formal type of recognition may well be a cardinal part of a nation-wide program for all new voters.

EDUCATIONAL SUPPLIES, EQUIPMENT, AND BUILDINGS

1. *What Can Be Done to Relieve the Serious Shortage in School Housing?*

Status Surveyed. Like the old woman who lived in a shoe, the teachers of America have so many children they don't know what to do. As indicated in Unit XV, the predicted increase in enrollment for the elementary and secondary schools will greatly aggravate the problem of shortages in school housing in this decade and the next. The Bureau of Labor Statistics foresees a college enrollment of almost four million by 1970. Candidates for seating space in pre-elementary and adult education programs will also increase markedly if *Fortune*'s prediction of population comes to pass:

Year	Population
1960	175,000,000
1965	185,000,000
1970	195,000,000
1975	206,000,000

Local, state, and national surveys reveal the school-housing needs. The *Report of the Status Phase of the School Facilities Survey,* prepared by the United States Office of Education, pointed out that a half million more classrooms are required in public elementary and secondary schools. Over a half billion square feet of floor space are necessary in these schools to replace obsolete buildings, relieve overcrowding, provide needed additions other than classrooms, and house enrollment increases. The total costs of the nation's school plant needs are estimated conservatively at more than ten billion dollars. This may double soon.

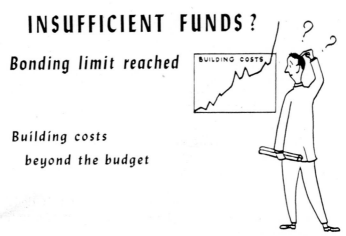

INSUFFICIENT FUNDS?

Bonding limit reached

Building costs
beyond the budget

F<small>IG</small>. 17-6. What can be done to help relieve the serious shortages in school buildings? (*Courtesy of Armco Drainage, Metal Products.*)

Solutions Suggested. Among the numerous suggestions for meeting the shortage are the following, all of which are not equally significant or sound:

1. Increase class size. The standard recommendation, however, for elementary-school pupils is 25, with a maximum of 30.

2. Schedule half-day sessions. Too many pupils are now being cheated with half-day rations.

3. Reorganize small districts and attendance units. This may increase transportation costs but reduce maintenance and construction costs.

4. Make surveys. Often an impartial evaluation of room utilization will reveal extra classroom space.

5. Modify the curriculum. Alternating subjects with small enrollments often saves space as well as salaries.

6. Conduct school on the four-quarter basis. Use of classrooms in summer school can help reduce class size or the number of sections needed during the regular year in high school.

7. Rent other buildings in the community. In emergency situations many school districts have moved to available places including churches.

8. Erect or purchase temporary structures. Many war-surplus buildings have been put to classroom use.

9. Plan new buildings carefully. Changes from blueprints often add extra costs.

10. Economize in building new structures. Countless savings such as using

modular materials and reducing ceiling heights can be effected without resultant cheap construction.

    11. Select capable consultants, architects, and contractors.

    12. Erect identical buildings. However, this is seldom feasible.

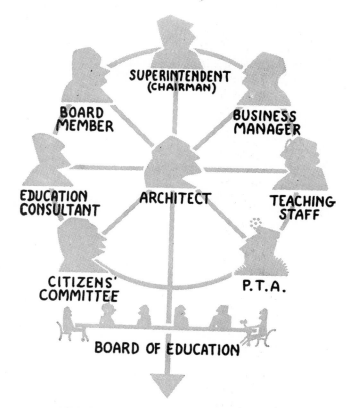

FIG. 17-7. How can people cooperate in securing necessary school buildings? An answer, presented pictorially here by an architect, is the formation of a planning council. (*Courtesy of Guenther of Outcalt, Guenther and Associates.*)

    13. Reduce vandalism of school property.

    14. Rehabilitate existing structures.

    15. Reduce interest rates or amounts paid in interest.

    16. Sell school bonds "across the counter" or popularize the purchasing of school bonds.

    17. Reduce, eliminate, or modify some of the tax limitations imposed on school districts.

    18. Increase the bonding power of many local districts.

19. Increase the resources for taxing by getting full, fair assessment of properties—real and intangible.

20. Create reserve funds and protect them.

21. Utilize idle funds—local and state.

22. Secure technical assistance from state-department experts in school buildings.

23. Modify existing building codes if they are too restrictive.

24. Use the "pay-as-you-build" procedure in a large district.

25. Increase state aid through stimulation grants, flat grants, emergency and continuing grants, equalization grants for school plants, through school-building authorities that borrow money for local districts, and through combinations of these aids.

26. Establish state foundation programs that provide for capital needs.

27. Seek federal aid for capital outlays. Except in federally affected school districts and in emergency areas, and as "pump-priming" funds, this source of money is to be eschewed.[51]

These suggestions must be supplemented by the ability and willingness of the taxpayer to foot the bill for necessary school housing for the children of today and tomorrow.

2. *Shall Public-school Buildings Become Community Centers?* Today public schools are erected as community buildings. The two-way movement—the school moving outward from its four walls, and the community coming into the school—is a vital means of mutual enrichment. This reciprocity enables the community to utilize school facilities for adult learning and recreation and allows the schools to tap community resources. This local teamwork accents the sociological as well as educational aspects of public partnership.[52] In the words of the yearbook of the National Society for the Study of Education, "the community school program, in a very real sense, represents the essence of democracy." [53]

3. *What Shall Be the Role of Educational Television?* A perennial critic of education and American anti-intellectualism excoriates television thus:

The prospect that television opens before us in America, with nobody speaking and nobody reading, suggests that a bleak and torpid epoch may be ahead

---

[51] Many other suggestions and elucidations of these practices are found in such books as H. H. Linn's *Practical School Economies*, Teachers College, 1934, or articles like A. J. Burke's "Some Proposals for Better Financing of Schoolhouses," *Nation's Schools*, February, 1954, pp. 48–51.

[52] The disappearance of the wall that traditionally separated the school from the community is depicted in color in the motion picture *School and Community*, available from the publishers of this text.

[53] National Society for the Study of Education, *The Community School*, p. 286, University of Chicago Press, 1953.

in which the populations will eventually sink in accordance with the principles of evolution to the level of the lowest form of vegetable life.[54]

Dr. John C. Neill of Pennsylvania State College of Optometry has concluded that TV enthusiasts may suffer loss in night vision and may experience an increase in eye trouble.

Obviously, educational television is in its infancy, but this period will markedly affect its future. A television policy for education is sorely needed.[55] Illustrative of the thinking of a land-grant college is the following statement from the "Television Broadcasting Policy" of Michigan State College:

> Education may be defined as the process by which society preserves and transmits its intellectual heritage. Television, as a new medium of communication, holds tremendous potentiality for the realization of the educational purpose and the fulfillment of this process.

Television is a two-edged sword. Just as atomic energy can be used to cure cancer or destroy people, so too television can assist education or impair the vision of pupils, teachers, and parents. It can be the electronic blackboard or colored bulletin board of the educative processes. Fortunately the Federal Communications Commission has allocated several television assignments for noncommercial, educational use.

4. *Shall Each State Establish a Uniform System of Textbooks through State-wide Adoption?* In all states of the Union, school textbooks are adopted in compliance with statutory regulations. At least one state legislature wanted to require an anticommunist certificate from the publisher of each textbook used in the state. About half the states require the use of uniform textbooks either for the state as a whole or within schools of specified grades, whereas the remainder permit choice by the local board of education. Most authorities recommend that the responsibility be delegated to the local boards, but as usual practice limps far behind theory. Today the teachers are consulted in the selection of textbooks much more than formerly. Parents and pupils should also have the opportunity to express opinions as to the books used in school. Objective evaluations are helpful. Impartial groups, like the National Conference of Christians and Jews, have published helpful studies—for example, *Prejudice in Textbooks.*

5. *Shall Textbooks Be Supplied to Pupils at Public or at Personal Expense?* Thousands of indigent children are allowed the free use of textbooks. Elementary and secondary schools should furnish all pupils with

[54] Hutchins, *op. cit.*, pp. 18–19.

[55] For a discussion of this topic see the report of the Educational Television Program Institute, as found in *A Television Policy for Education,* American Council on Education, 1952, 266 pp.

the basal textbooks at public expense. To provide free instruction and then to require the purchase or rental of learning tools is an anomaly in American democratic education.

Financing of Public Education

1. *Shall the Board of Education Be Fiscally Independent Rather than Dependent?* Shall the local board of education be autonomous rather than a part of the city government? Shall the board of education or some other agency, such as the city council, determine the school budget and/or educational tax levy?

Pro. In general, schoolmen, convinced of the importance of education, want complete fiscal independence. Among the many arguments in favor of this freedom are these:

Schools should be kept independent of political control.
Fiscal control leads to *de facto* control of educational policies.
Fiscal dependence complicates school administration.
Fiscal independence is the only sure way to protect school funds from diversion to non-school purposes.[56]

Con. Political scientists, with an overview of the entire government, favor fiscal dependence for boards of education. Among their reasons are these:

There is need for a unified and coordinated local financial structure.
Determination of expenditures for all purposes should permit the weighing of the relative merits of each service. This requires a single legislative authority.
Coordination of services in which the schools and municipality are mutually interested are facilitated.
Those elements left [by the state] to local control and responsibility are in reality legitimate aspects of municipal government in the same way as police protection, public health, and similar services of general social significance.[57]

Trend. In theory the trend of educational administration continues toward fiscal independence, but in practice it is toward a greater degree of voluntary and legal cooperation between school management and city government. The question seems to be not one of legal independence or dependence but one of the degree of voluntary interdependence. Progressive search should continue for that basic pattern of monetary relationships which will provide the public with the best possible educational services and, at the same time, will be defensible in terms of the essential principles of good public administration.[58]

[56] National Conference of Professors of Educational Administration, *Problems and Issues in Public School Finance*, p. 302, Teachers College, 1952.
[57] *Ibid.*, p. 303.
[58] Research Bulletin, *Fiscal Authority of City School Boards*, p. 78, National Education Association, April, 1950.

2. *Shall Federal Aid Be Granted to Education?* (This controversial issue is the first one discussed in this unit.)

3. *What Should Be Done about Hidden Costs in Education?* Free education is an anomaly in America. In both public and private schooling many so-called incidental expenses must be borne by pupils or parents. Common examples are textbooks, workbooks, gym suits and shoes, extracurricular dues, and countless other required, semivoluntary, and voluntary fees. In large families these hidden items, heaped on top of taxes, school clothing, and lunch money make education almost prohibitive, especially in high school and college. They accelerate dropouts, stimulate overemployment by pupils, and cause extra sacrifices by parents.

Many school districts, therefore, are adding these extras to their regular current budgets in order to reduce the many monetary irritations. This practice throws more of the burden of costs on nonparents and those whose children are not in school. Practical educational administrators and the cooperating student councils strive to reduce hidden costs to a minimum.

4. *Shall More Money Be Expended for Schools?* In a Gallup poll, 3000 representative voters throughout the country were asked, "Would you be willing to pay higher taxes for school aid?" In response, 15 per cent had no opinion, 30 per cent were opposed, but 55 per cent were willing to pay more for education.

Can the United States spend more for education? The Brookings Institution, nationally known for its intensive and extensive research studies, has concluded that the United States can safely expend thirty times as much for education during the next 100 years as at present. Currently, less than 2 per cent of the total national income is used for education. This nation still spends more for luxuries or alcoholic drinks than for education.

The National Association of Manufacturers, in its statement *This We Believe about Education,* challenged all groups and individuals to provide support for education:

Through contributions by private individuals, organizations, clubs, and associations, through the growing practice of corporate giving, and through a sufficient allocation of tax funds at local and state levels, adequate financial support must be provided to keep public and private schools—elementary, secondary, and collegiate—improving in quality and expanding in size at least as fast as the population they serve.[59]

The Committee on Education of the United States Chamber of Commerce stated the conclusions of one of its studies in its title, *Education—an Investment in People.* Furthermore, its investigation, *Education Steps*

[59] Educational Advisory Committee and Council, *This We Believe about Education,* National Association of Manufacturers, p. 22, February, 1954.

Up Living Standards, pointed out that a direct relationship exists between the level of education and income in the ten countries studied.
"The more the education increases, the higher the income rises." Furthermore, more money spent on the right kind of education will add to personal knowledge, subtract from mass ignorance, multiply human happiness, and increase the cultural dividend. In fine, expenditures for education are an investment rather than a cost. Ignorance is expensive.

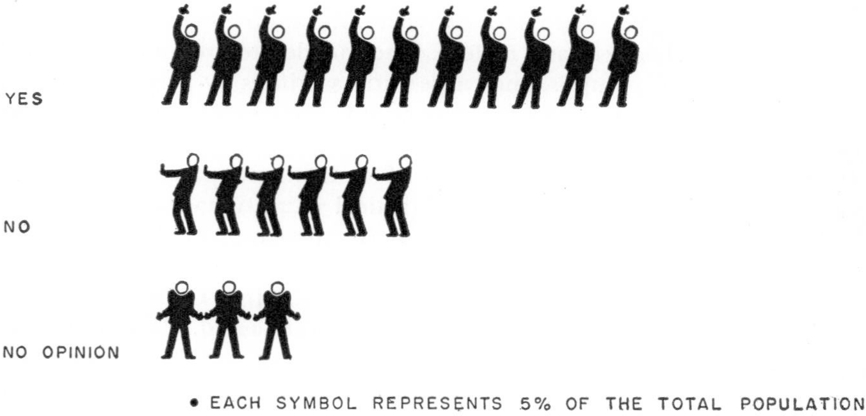

YES

NO

NO OPINION

• EACH SYMBOL REPRESENTS 5% OF THE TOTAL POPULATION

Fig. 17-8. Poll regarding educational expenditures. In one of the Gallup polls the question was asked, "Would you be willing to pay higher taxes for school aid?" In interviews with 3000 representative voters throughout the country were obtained the pictured responses, *viz.*: willing to pay higher taxes for school aid, 55 per cent; not willing,
30 per cent; and no opinion, 15 per cent. Thus over half the people sampled would be
willing to pay more for education.

5. *What Are the Basic Surpluses and Shortages in American Education?*

Surpluses. The main areas in which American education—both public
and private—has accumulated surpluses are:

Children. Never before have so many youngsters sought to enter schools and
colleges of this land. This surplus can be made the nation's richest resource.

Criticism. American education is currently surfeited with criticism. The at-
tackers range all the way from fierce foes to fond friends.

Courses. Piecemeal additions to the curriculums, especially in high school and
college, have led to a superfluity of subjects. Too many minor subjects cause
teachers to lose sight of the major objects of education.

Shortages. The major deficits in American education are well known:

Materiel. As previously indicated, public elementary and secondary education
require a half million more classrooms. These shortages for private institutions
are great too. Satisfactory sites, efficient equipment, and more modern materials
are sorely needed.

Manpower. The shortage of well-qualified teachers—men and women—is threatening to undermine the foundations of America's free educational system. Teaching should have a reservoir of human resources.

Money. As previously indicated, more money must be found for education in all the levels discussed in Units IV to IX, namely, pre-elementary, elementary, secondary, higher, and adult education. The main sources are the geographical areas presented in Units I to IV, namely, national, state, county, and local.

Morale. The shortages in buildings, teachers, and dollars have inflicted much damage upon the morale of the personnel—teachers, pupils, and parents. Unfortunately, a lowered *esprit de corps* encourages the caustic critics of education.

Balance Sheet. The balance in educational finance is still on the positive side of the ledger. The deficits are more than counterbalanced by the assets and dividends accumulated over the years by teachers and parents devoted to youth.

CONCLUSION

Many of these crucial issues in education are born of deeper problems in society. In their solution the teacher is aided by ripened experience in the classroom and by the seasoning processes of living, which also help in the identification of trends as wholesome, neutral, or undesirable. In the solution of these practical and many-sided problems, however, no unilateral explanation will suffice. John Dewey, in his *Experience and Education,* cautions against aligning oneself too positively with a single point of view:

> It is the business of an intelligent theory of education to ascertain the causes for the conflicts which exist and then, instead of taking one side or the other, to indicate a plan of operations proceeding from a level deeper and more inclusive than is represented by the practices and ideas of contending parties.[60]

For this plan of operations the teacher needs a personal philosophy of education and living, rooted in the best of the past and nourished by the conditions of modern society. The development of this personal philosophy will help the teacher not merely to teach school, but to define values and to establish goals for the betterment of education. The best *ideas* for improving education, and thereby life itself, must be projected upward and onward as *ideals.* Thus will American public education help to bring to pass the great American dream of perpetuating democracy.

SUGGESTED ACTIVITIES

The major activity for this unit is to arrange a series of panel discussions, forums, debates, and oral or written reports on some salient issues and trends in American public education. In order to serve as a review of all the units in this volume, the topics might be spread over the 16 major areas.

[60] Dewey, *op. cit.,* p. v.

DESCRIPTIVE BIBLIOGRAPHY AND AIDS

Books

Numerous references listed at the close of each of the preceding sixteen units may be consulted. The footnote references in the units also indicate additional sources for material on issues and trends in American public education.

Current Periodicials and Publications

For current periodicals pertinent to the several issues discussed in this unit, and to problems not presented, the student should consult the list of Current Pertinent Periodicals and Publications found at the close of each of the preceding sixteen units. Especially helpful in connection with this unit is the publication issued periodically by the Research Division of the National Education Association and the American Association of School Administrators under the caption, "Education in Lay Magazines." Furthermore, current nonprofessional periodicals, such as *Harper's Magazine, The Atlantic, The Saturday Evening Post,* and *Time,* and countless newspapers contain articles on educational issues and trends.

Audio-visual Aids

For audio-visual aids useful in considering the various issues in American public education, the reader will refer to the list of such aids at the close of the related unit. Especially helpful for this unit is the 28-min. color motion picture film *Freedom to Learn,* which deals with the teaching of controversial issues in the classroom. Prints are available from state education associations or the National Education Association, Washington, D.C.

The bulletin board can be used very effectively with this unit. On a particular issue, one part of the bulletin board may be reserved for the arguments "pro" and another section for the "con."

Student-made and commercially purchased posters such as those published by the Educational Policies Commission can direct attention to some pertinent issues and trends in education.

By means of an opaque projector various cartoons, photographs, and clippings may be projected upon a screen for discussion purposes.

Slides and photographs made by students will help to sharpen some of the issues and to portray effectively many of the trends.

INDEX OF PERSONS

INDEX OF TOPICS

Buildings and grounds personnel, 388–390
service, 394–395
superintendents of, 385–386
Business officials, 385
Business personnel, 388–389
Busses, school, 78, 481

C

Cafeteria workers, 393–394
Camping and outdoor education, 458
Canada–United States Committee on Education, 34
Career service in education, 373–374, 396
Carnegie Foundation, 352
Catholic schools (*see* Parochial schools)
Certification of teachers, 351
Character education, 298–299
through cocurricular activities, 439
Chautauquas, 267, 272–273
Child Study Association of America, 122
Children (*see* Pupils)
Church nights, 274
Citizenship, promoting, 437
Citizenship day, 575
Citizenship Education Project, 331, 443
City colleges, 226–227
City school systems, 89, 159, 189
Civil Aeronautics Authority, 19–20
Class organizations, 441
Class period defined, 403
Classification, of school expenditures, 509–511
of school receipts, 513–514
Classroom teachers, 364
(*See also* Teacher education; Teachers)
Clerks, school, 392–393
Clubs, adult, 274–275
school, 451–452
Coast Guard Academy, 234
Cocurricular activities, 434–467
cooperation with state and national organizations, 463–465
financing of, 463
issues in, 572–575
local program of, 459–460
organization and administration of, 459–465
participation in, 462
principles of, 436–439
relationship with curriculum, 435–436
role of, 436
sponsorship of, 460–462
trends in, 572–575
types of, 439–459
Coeducation, history of, 179, 217

Colleges and universities, 206–245
athletics in, 574
bases for admission to, 552–553
deans of, 384
of education, 348–349
education of teachers in, 349–351
extension courses, 270–271
family-life education and, 122
land-grant, 17–18, 229–232
presidents of, 384–385
(*See also* Higher education)
Commencement activities, 455–456
Commission on Financing Higher Education, 208–210, 223, 228, 241, 534, 535
Commission on Junior College Terminal Education, 194
Commission on Life Adjustment Education for Youth, 188, 427
Commission on Reorganization of Secondary Education, 185, 427
Commissioner of Education (*see* County superintendents; State superintendents and commissioners; United States Commissioners of Education)
Common learnings (*see* Core curriculum)
Communists as teachers, 562–563, 572
Community centers, schools as, 578
Community colleges, 192–196, 224–225
(*See also* Junior colleges)
Community resources, use of, 418
Community school, 76–77, 163, 495
buildings of, 495, 578–579
community coordination with, 495
playgrounds of, 494–495
Compulsory education, 150
Conference of Allied Ministers of Education, 35
Congressional Library, 33, 277–278
Consolidation of districts, 76–79
Constitution of United States, no mention of education in, 4, 10–12
Tenth Amendment and education, 11, 43–44, 502, 539
Constitutions, state, provisions for education in, 44–45
Consultants, 391
Continuation and part-time schools, 257
Contrasts, in elementary education, 168–169
in higher education, 218
Control, single, dual, and multiple, 99
Controversial issues in education, 528–584
Controversial subjects, discussion of, in schools, 532–533, 571–572
in textbooks, 472–473
Cooperation, in cocurricular activities, 463–465